INSTRUCTIONAL ASSESSMENT

An Integrative Approach to Evaluating Student Performance

INSTRUCTIONAL ASSESSMENT

An Integrative Approach to Evaluating Student Performance

SANDRA HOMLAR FRADD
University of Miami, Bilingual, ESOL and Multicultural Programs

PATRIA LARRINAGA MCGEE
Orange County, Florida Public Schools

WITH
DIANE K. WILEN
Broward County, Florida Public Schools

 ADDISON-WESLEY PUBLISHING COMPANY

Reading, Massachusetts • Menlo Park, California • New York
Don Mills, Ontario • Wokingham, England • Amsterdam • Bonn
Sydney • Singapore • Tokyo • Madrid • San Juan • Paris • Seoul
Milan • Mexico City • Taipei

Library of Congress Cataloging-in-Publication Data

Fradd, Sandra H., 1941-
    Instructional assessment: an integrative approach to evaluating
student performance / Sandra Homlar Fradd, Patria Larrinaga McGee
with Diane K. Wilen.
      p. cm.
    Includes bibliographical references and index.
    ISBN 0-201-53964-0 : $28.95
    1. English language—Studying and teaching—Foreign speakers—
Evaluation. 2. English language—Ability testing. I. Larrinaga
McGee, Patria. II. Wilen, Diane Kriger, 1949- . III. Title.
PE1128.A2F66 1994
428' .0076—dc20   93-41934
                                                           CIP

ISBN: 0-201-53964-0

2 3 4 5 6 7 8 9 10 - CRS - 98 97 96 95

Contents

Dedication

This book is dedicated to our husbands and families who have been put on hold for the past year so that we could "write one more chapter," "finish one more paragraph," or "proofread one more section." John Fradd, Terry McGee, and Barry Wilen have all, in their own ways, contributed to the conceptualization, development and preparation of this book. In addition, our families deserve an important note of recognition and appreciation for their patience and support in making this book possible.

About the Authors

The book began almost ten years ago when a multilingual school psychologist, Patria Nicholas Larringa McGee, in a school district with a growing population of non-English language background students, identified a group of students who manifested learning disabilities as well as limited English proficiency. She wanted assistance in assessing these students and developing a program that would meet their needs. One of the psychologist's many letters of request found its way to a nearby university where a program for training school personnel to assess and instruct students in the process of learning English was just beginning to be developed. The response was immediate. "Yes! We will work with you." The initial interactions between the school district and the university personnel, and in particular, Sandra Homlar Fradd, produced several federally funded training projects and a long-term professional friendship between the psychologist and the director of the project.

During the past decade the psychologist and the educator have collaborated in the development of effective assessment and instructional practices at local, state, and national levels. This book is the outgrowth of these activities. Training projects continued to be implemented to extend the information and services developed in earlier projects. One of the projects funded to promote collaboration among school personnel brought Diane Kriger Wilen into the training development process.

This collaboration has also brought us a clearer understanding of both the needs of the students we seek to help and the concerns of other educators who are also engaged in working with these students. The purpose of the book is to integrate current information on the assessment and instruction of non-English language background students in a practical approach that encourages problem-solving and fosters collaboration among educators, both instructional and support personnel.

Sandra Homlar Fradd was one of the first bilingual special education teachers in the country. In Dade County, Florida, where she began teaching LEP students in 1970, she initiated the development of a program for handicapped students who were limited in English proficiency. Since that time she has continued to develop assessment procedures and instructional programs for students, and training programs for the school personnel who work with them. During the past decade she has directed eleven different training and research projects designed to assist school districts to meet the needs of diverse linguistic and cultural groups. In this capacity she has collaborated with educators from all over the United States and other countries to develop training programs and materials to address the needs of non-English language background students. Sandra holds a Ph.D. from the University of Florida, where she is the Associate Director of the Institute for Advanced Study of the Communication Processes. She is also associate professor and program coordinator for Bilingual, ESOL, and Multicultural Programs at the University of Miami.

Patria Larrinaga McGee is a bilingual school psychologist in a large urban school district in central Florida. During the past ten years Patria has worked not only with Spanish-speaking students, but has also developed procedures for assessing students whose first language is Haitian Creole. She has experience as well in assessing students from many other language backgrounds. Because she realized the limitations of current standardized tests and procedures is assessing these students, she has developed alternative procedures and materials for determining students' strengths and needs. In addition to her responsibilities at the school district level, Patria has assisted in developing training programs for handicapped non-English language background students at the district, state, and national levels. Our experiences using procedures and materials she developed in this capacity form the basis for this book.

Diane Kriger Wilen also has extensive experience as a bilingual school psychologist. Currently she provides training and technical assistance to bilingual and monolingual school psychologists in a large urban school district in south Florida serving over 40 language groups. In addition to her responsibilities as a school psychologist, Diane has developed training procedures for preparing school personnel to effectively use interpreters and translators in assessing students.

Introduction

Appropriate assessment and educational planning are essential in order to provide meaningful services for students for whom English is not the only language. Sometimes these students are referred to as limited English proficient (LEP); sometimes they are considered to be bilingual. Many times they are treated as if they were monolingual learners. However these students are classified, school districts frequently are puzzled about what to do with them when they are unsuccessful in regular programs. Much has been written about the need to minimize bias in assessing students, but little has been done to assist school psychologists, speech-language pathologists, and other educational personnel to actually conduct meaningful assessments or to use assessment information to develop effective instructional programs.

In most states, students who are determined to be limited in English proficiency receive less than equitable special education services. Few data are available on the numbers of non-English language background students who are actually given such services. It may be that students are not identified for special education until they are determined to be proficient in English. However, the issue is not really one of language. It is a matter of evaluating students whose prior experiences are different from those of the mainstream population and of developing programs that are responsive to these students' strengths and needs. It is clear that without appropriate instruction, many students who could be successful fail because their learning difficulties and requirements are seldom identified or addressed.

This book meets a critical assessment need: the need to develop legally and educationally defensible assessment procedures for use with non-English language background (NELB) students, students who are still in the process of learning English, even though they may have been certified as being English proficient. It explains in detail how to select and utilize a variety of procedures, to generate appropriate information on which to base educational decisions, and to use this information for programming and monitoring students. The book has been written by colleagues who have collaborated for nearly a decade on both the assessment of culturally and linguistically diverse students and the preparation of personnel to work effectively with NELB students. This extended period of planning and developing ideas has enabled the authors to learn what works and how to assist other educators.

Because the book is not an edited collection, it presents a unified voice from beginning to end. Initially, the book shows how the assessment process can be improved using integrative measures referred to as instructional assessment. Case studies in each chapter provide insight and specific detailed information on how to conduct meaningful assessments and implement programs. Data provided within the case studies are not always complete. The information included has been selected to illustrate specific points, not to provide a representative sample of all the potential information that could be collected about an individual student.

The purpose in this text is to provide educators with both the information on which to make effective educational decisions, and the knowledge and insight to enable them to apply this information in both theoretical and practical contexts. To achieve this outcome, a variety of suggestions, activities, and case studies are presented, through which educators can gain experience and insight in developing their own effective practices.

When issues of language difference and cultural diversity are considered within the context of assessment and instruction, collaboration and the involvement of multiple contributors is essential. Early school effectiveness research illustrates the importance of a common vision of the educational process. Within the current process of educational reform, the importance of a common vision cannot be underestimated. It is essential whenever there are multiple contributors and anticipated long-term changes. The value of a common vision is promoted within the instructional practices undertaken to meet the needs of NELB students. This approach seeks commonalities and the understanding and valuing of differences.

Ground is being broken in the development of effective and innovative responses to personnel preparation, and in the discovery of new and effective ways to assist students who have typically been at risk for educational failure because quality educational programs have not traditionally been available. We invite you to join us in making new discoveries and sharing them with others. A vision of equity and educational excellence is essential for developing effective instructional programs. Equally important is the vision of the importance of dynamic collaboration in promoting student growth. The educational changes needed to meet the needs of students in the 21st century involve collaboration and personal skill development and commitment. We invite you to share in collaborative efforts to promote effective educational change by sharing your visions and your innovations in making education appropriate and meaningful.

Chapter Overviews

The first chapter, "Concepts of Instructional Assessment," introduces and defines many of the terms used throughout the book. The concept of instructional assessment is introduced and developed within the chapter. The chapter also sets the stage for understanding the changes that are currently occurring in the assessment process by identifying and discussing the forces of change currently at work at all levels of the educational system. Change in the way that education is conceptualized and provided is both fostered and challenged by these forces. The result is a struggle for educational reform. Seldom are the needs and concerns of students who are not yet proficient in English articulated within discussions of educational reform. As the nation's school-age population becomes increasingly diverse, the needs of this growing portion of learners are central to discussions of educational reform. The importance of identifying and including this group of learners is emphasized in Chapter One. The chapter initiates a discussion on assessment that continues throughout the book. Concepts of performance and instructional assessment are considered within the context of the changing assessment paradigm and changing perceptions of educational needs. Terms used within the assessment process are also introduced within this chapter. Characteristics of formal and informal assessment procedures are identified and notions of performance assessment are introduced as sources of information for identifying and addressing students' instructional needs.

Chapter Two, "Understanding Language Performance," sets the stage for assessing students' educational performance. This chapter provides background information on language development and differentiates between academic and social language skills. The chapter also emphasizes the importance of professional development in obtaining and using information on students' performance in determining their needs. Collection of student data for developing and testing hypotheses about their needs is also discussed within this chapter.

"Assessing Oral Language Development," Chapter Three, provides a comprehensive overview of the process of oral language assessment. Aspects of literacy development are introduced initially through oral contexts. Specific suggestions for observing, assessing, and monitoring students' oral language performance are offered within the chapter. Chapter Three serves as a companion to Chapter Four, "Differentiating Language Disorders from the Effects of Limited Opportunities for Language Learning," by providing the background information with which case studies of students with differenct types of language learning difficulties can be considered. Information provided in Chapter Three is used in the concrete contexts of the cases studied in Chapter Four to discuss and demonstrate the language development process.

The focus of the assessment process shifts from oral language to written language and academic achievement in Chapter Five, "Towards an Integrative Academic Performance Assessment." This chapter provides the rationale for change in the ways that achievement testing is conducted. It provides an overview of an integrative, curriculum-based approach to assessing academic performance and suggests steps for developing a viable assessment framework. The development of literacy and mathematics skills among new learners of English is reviewed to highlight the learning processes that become the focus of assessment.

Chapter Six, "Assessing Academic Performance Through Contextualized Measures," is a companion to the previous chapter. Specific techniques and evaluation methods for observing, assessing, and monitoring students' academic performance and progress are presented as congruent with trends in instructional practices and educational measurement. Alternative assessment procedures, such as curriculum-based assessment, are discussed and illustrated through mini-case studies.

Assessment is not only a process of collecting and interpreting student data, it is also a process of advocating for students through the judicious selection and use of meaningful and relevant data sources. Chapter Seven, "Advocacy in the Assessment Process," emphasizes the critical roles that educators play in assisting students by advocating for their needs in working with the students' families and communities as well as within the educational system. In this chapter suggestions are offered for interviewing family members, and for training and using interpreters and translators to assist in the assessment process.

Reasons for assessing students' performance vary. One possible use for assessment data is to determine whether or not students require more specialized intervention than can be provided in typical classrooms. Historically, the exclusive use of standardized tests to identify special needs NELB students has led to problems of overinclusion in special education programs. Chapter Eight, "Identifying Special Needs," offers mini-case studies and exemplifies the use of alternative methods to assist decision-making for special education purposes.

Consideration is given to the social, academic, and cognitive development of the students within the case studies.

Chapter Nine, the final chapter, "Using Assessment Information to Promote Instructional Effectiveness," provides several important functions. Initially, it provides a means for synthesizing and summarizing the information provided throughout the previous chapters. Case studies are provided so that the information can be organized and synthesized. However, the chapter also serves to move the assessment process away from a single focus on the student as an individual with unique needs and toward a more comprehensive perspective of students' needs within the context of the total instructional process.

The authors would like to acknowledge the contributions of a number of persons who have assisted in the conceptualization and development of this book. For conceptualizing, writing, and editing: Elia Vazquez-Montilla, Jannette Klingner, Maria Acosta, Sandra Southmayd, Joanne Schvandez, Ana-Maria Bradley-Hess, Tery Medina, Rosalia Fernandez-Gallo, Joan Pomerantz, Nancy Terrel, and the students who reviewed and commented on early drafts of the manuscripts, Alberto Ejes, Pauls Glassmoyer, Sonya Rodriguez, MarcArthur JeanLouis, Mariana DeFrancisco Laney, and Carol Dieudonne. And for secretarial assistance and support, appreciation goes to Beverly Mayo, Carol Fogel, and Mary Ann Potter. Over the years we have seen and interacted with thousands of students and their parents. Such service in the public schools system is possible only with the opportunity to consult with other educators, and obtain the feedback and emotional and professional support provided by such colleagues as Lissette Villanueva and Rose Irizarry.

Theories and conceptualizations in education remain just that if their worth is not proven in the classroom setting. Implementation of new ideas can only take place in classrooms where teachers are flexible and open to change. Most special thanks go to those teachers, especially Zahira De Jesus, who are willing to experiment with and implement new or different ideas and to cross the line between theory and practice.

INSTRUCTIONAL ASSESSMENT

An Integrative Approach to Evaluating Student Performance

Chapter 1

Concepts of Instructional Assessment

In the world of schools and educators, there are many diverse ideas and practices related to the concept of assessment. The process of assessing students, that is, the process of determining students' instructional needs and providing them with instruction corresponding to those identified needs, is a concept that has become a part of the general tradition of U.S. public education. Yet the notion of providing students with instruction according to their needs has also been a myth, especially if the students come from home backgrounds where languages other than English are spoken. Educators have not really been trained to assess students. In the general preparation that educators receive, little attention has been given to preparing school personnel to work with students who communicate in languages other than English (Office of Bilingual Education and Minority Languages Affairs 1990; U.S. General Accounting Office 1987b). Educators have learned to quantify students' performance. But quantification is not the same as a process of assessment attuned to determining and meeting student needs. This book is about the type of assessment that leads to instruction which in turn promotes learning and successful achievement.

Throughout the United States the ways that the assessment process has been conceptualized is changing. These changes are occurring within the context of national educational reform. We realize that there has to be a better way to educate our national population of young learners. The whole process of conceptualizing what assessment means, how it should be done, and how to utilize the information is moving from a static process of recording what students did toward a dynamic process that promotes success for students and educators alike.

Within the educational reform movement many voices have articulated the issues and concerns facing our nation. Few have clearly voiced these concerns as they relate to the educational needs of non-English language background (NELB) students. Nevertheless, these students, more than any other group, have the potential either to make major contributions to our national economy or to become an economic liability greater than any that we have previously faced (National Commission on Testing and Public Policy 1990; Pallas, Natriello, & McDill 1989). We cannot continue to overlook the educational needs of NELB students; we must prepare ourselves to provide effective instruction and educational opportunities to all students.

The purpose of this book is to assist educators in developing meaningful assessment procedures and instructional programs for NELB students. This chapter provides background information important to the conceptualization of meaningful assessment and relevant instruction programs. The chapter is divided into three main sections containing information on concepts and terminology, an overview of issues in assessment related to policy and program implementation, and an overview of current and emerging practices. We refer to the process of assessment described in this book as *instructional assessment* to indicate the types of assessment procedures that we find helpful in understanding the instructional needs of students. We also use this term to link assessment with instruction. We have chosen the term as an indicator of the type of information needed to effectively work with students from non-traditional linguistic and cultural backgrounds. Many students have not been exposed to the knowledge and the skills they are expected to know and on which they are tested. While standardized formal assessment procedures are integrated into the assessment process, the focus is on measuring student development through the assessment of the skills and information students have been taught. Throughout the book the terms *meaningful assessment* or *meaningful information* are used. The emphasis throughout is the implementation of procedures that provide information that can be useful in lesson planning, material selection, observation, and classroom management. Instructional assessment refers to the evaluation and monitoring of students' progress in a variety of instructional contexts.

As one group of educators observed, "Oh, yes, we all know how to test students. We do collaborate in the assessment process. We just don't know how to explain what we do to other people." Many educators have a great deal of information and insight about students. But it is not until they have to share this information with other groups of professionals that they realize they may not fully understand the assessment process or that they lack a comprehensive framework and the terminology for conveying this information to others (Fradd, in press). If information remains in an esoteric state, a state where it is understood only by those who produce it, the value of the information is diminished. The value of the producers to provide meaningful information may also be questioned. In this era of instant communication, it is essential that we not only understand how to identify students' needs but that we are able to articulate these needs to others.

Within the field of education, each group of professionals has developed a set of terminology and relevant concepts. Each group has its own ways of problem-solving and its own ways of reporting information (Fradd 1989; 1991). If educators are unable to explain their ideas, procedures, and results to each other, how can they develop a shared understanding of what they are doing?

No one individual or group of professionals has all the skills or all the information required to effectively work with diverse groups of students. Only through interaction and sharing of resources and information, can we come to really understand our students and their instructional needs. Our purpose is to build upon the current knowledge base so that all the individuals who work with non-English language background students can provide insight into the students' needs and instructional progress. The intent is to promote communication and understanding across professions so that the knowledge base, the skills, and the resources available within each profession can become part of a larger knowledge base to benefit both the students and the professionals who teach them. While focus of attention may appear to be on classroom teachers who play a central role in assessment, other school personnel, such as speech/language pathologists, school psychologists, social workers, guidance counsellors, and administrators are also key school personnel involved in determining and meeting students' needs. It is for all these audiences that the book is developed.

This chapter is designed to assist educators in creating an information base from which you can, in turn, promote effective instructional practices within the system. The subsections within this chapter are organized to promote active participation. Where appropriate, we encourage you to pause and carry out some of the suggested activities. If you are participating in a collaborative training project, you may want to divide up activities and share the results. Most importantly, you may find the information more useful to you if you pause from time to time and try to explain your ideas to colleagues and receive feedback from them.

Before presenting information on assessment, we want to discuss some of the reasons why this information is needed and how it may be used. Little is known about the target populations of students who come from diverse cultural and linguistic backgrounds. Because in the past the numbers of students from diverse backgrounds have been small, little attention has been given to their specific needs. However the numbers have grown disproportionately to the student population as a whole. With this growth comes the need for more information and greater consideration of the instructional requirements for all students. As a result, educators across the nation are concerned with effective practical assessment procedures. Although the focus of this book is on assessment, the rationale for its development grows from the need for information that enables educators to effectively organize programs to determine and meet students' needs. In order to do this educators need to understand the terminology and concepts currently used to identify students within the mainstream, and to realize how these terms and concepts may be different for students who are in the process of learning English as a new language. An additional set of terms has developed within the field to identify and define the target students. This lexicon continues to be defined and refined to reflect current thinking about the learning process. There are many implications for the applications of the various specialized terms. Educators need to understand these implications in order to effectively work with students. Educators are realizing that the assessment process for identifying the instructional requirements of mainstream, typical students is complex and under revision to reflect current research on learning (Aaron 1991; Stanovich 1991). If the process is complex for students who are considered to be typical, the process is even more difficult for students about whose cultures, languages, and learning styles only limited information is available. In this first section of the first chapter, we discuss some of the terms that are used to identify and describe the populations of students for whom the book is intended. Next we summarize information on the changing demographics and the process of educational reform. The third section presents an overview of concepts of assessment as they relate to culturally and linguistically diverse learners.

SECTION ONE

DEMOGRAPHIC SHIFTS REQUIRE A NEW CONCEPTUALIZATION OF THE TERMS IDENTIFYING STUDENTS FROM DIVERSE LANGUAGE BACKGROUNDS

Within this section, information is presented on two separate yet interrelated topics: (a) demographic shifts, or population changes; and (b) the terms used to identify students in the process of learning English as a new language. You may want to consider this information within the context of demographic and social changes occurring within your state and school district. Local, state, and national trends may impact directly or indirectly on your worksite.

GROWTH AND DIVERSITY OF THE NATION'S SCHOOL-AGED POPULATION

The United States is a multiethnic country, a nation of immigrants. Major influxes of immigrants are not new. In the 19th and 20th centuries, during peak periods of immigration, the nation had to accommodate many newly arrived groups of persons from diverse linguistic and cultural backgrounds. In comparison with previous times of high immigration, however, even greater population changes are occurring today. Never before in our history has the nation faced greater ethnic and linguistic diversity (U.S. Government Accounting Office 1987 a, b).

Ethnic diversity is especially noticeable within the nation's schools (U.S. Department of Justice, Immigration and Naturalization Service 1987; Waggoner 1987). It is not uncommon, for example, for large school districts to report student membership representing more than 150 different countries and territories (Dade County Public Schools, Management Information Services 1989; U.S. Government Accounting Office 1987a). More than 100 different languages may be spoken within the schools. In these districts it is not unusual to find 10 or more languages spoken in one classroom (Armstrong 1991; Bradley 1991; Lucas & Katz 1991).

Not only is there diversity among the recently arrived immigrant populations (Fradd 1987a), but there are also large ethnic clusters of persons born in the United States who have maintained their home language and culture (U.S. Department of Commerce, Bureau of the Census 1987a; 1987b). Becoming integrated into the mainstream is not necessarily a goal, or even a feasible reality for many of these persons (Bernal, Saenz & Knight 1991; Hayes 1989; Paulston 1980). A widening disparity is occurring between the culturally and linguistically diverse populations and the mainstream population of the nation (Stern & Chandler 1987). Differences in educational levels and experiences of many of the ethnically diverse students and the expectations and requirements of the schools they must attend become sources of disparity between the mainstream and ethnically diverse groups (Erickson 1985: Plisko 1984). Differences between the culture and expectations of the schools and the performance and achievement of ethnically and linguistically different students occur in part because of a general lack of preparation of school personnel to address issues of cultural and linguistic diversity (Bradley 1991; Gilmore & Glatthorn 1982; Montalvo 1984; Roos 1984).

The contemporary incorporation of new populations of students into the mainstream is different from the process that occurred with earlier generations (Paulston 1980). Differences occur not only as a result of the diversity of linguistic and cultural groups represented within current immigrant populations, but also as a result of increasing demands of a technologically oriented economic system (Fradd 1987a). During earlier periods of immigration, a strong back and a willing pair of hands were considered major assets for earning a living. A willingness to work was sufficient to enter the work force (Berrel 1978). In earlier eras acculturation into the mainstream occurred across several generations as immigrants moved into ethnic ghettos or enclaves in order to learn to participate in the mainstream of society (Weatherford 1986). Today, with the automation of many previously labor intensive jobs, manual labor is no longer a valuable resource. Technical literacy is becoming an essential for mainstream employment (National Center on Education and the Economy 1990). In order to effectively participate in the mainstream economy, today's workers must not only be literate in English, but they must be able to apply higher order thinking skills. Those learners who fail to master technical skills remain marginalized within the smaller, less profitable ethnic economies (National Commission on Secondary Schooling for Hispanics 1984). Or worse, they fail to find meaningful employment of any type (W.T. Grant Foundation 1988). To effectively participate today, students must learn in one generation what typically took two to three generations in the past.

Until recently immigrant families tended to settle in urban and rural areas where previous groups had already established communities. Often urban centers tended to be favorite locations for initial settlement because of the availability of employment, public transportation, and low cost housing. Within the urban centers, newly arrived groups became socialized to the new culture and language, and to the expectations for participating within the larger society

(Robey 1989). However, recent data indicate that persons of non-English language background are settling across the nation, in the suburbs as well as within the inner cities and rural areas. The suburbs were previously considered primarily centers of middle class populations which, although they might have been racially and ethnically diverse, had similar educational experiences and cultural expectations. Such is no longer the case. The population shifts currently occurring have made the population composition of the suburban schools similar to that of the urban schools.

Along with the increasing diversity of student populations comes an increase in complexity of the educational requirements of the students. The instructional changes experienced by the urban systems are now being experienced throughout the nation. Few school districts in the nation are excluded from this process of change (Bradley 1991; Penfield 1987).

Differences in English language proficiency and cultural expectations for performance between the school and the diverse ethnic communities present well documented educational challenges for the last decade of the 20th century (Armstrong 1991; Bouvier & Davis 1982; Waggoner 1987). These challenges are expected to continue and to increase throughout the beginning of the 21st century as the birthrates of the newly arrived and already established language minority communities continue to surpass the growth rate of the middle class mainstream (Armstrong 1991; Waggoner 1987).

Because the population changes taking place in highly impacted school districts are occurring at a rapid rate, it is important to be aware of the changes and to provide proactive services and programs. Proactive educational efforts anticipate changes and prepare for them in advance rather than waiting until after the changes occur and responding to them from a reactive posture (Braden 1989; Braden & Fradd 1987; Fradd, Weismantel & Braden 1987).

RESEARCH IN PRACTICE:
Growth and Diversity of the Nation's School-Age Population

1. **How many different language groups are represented in your school? In your school district?** Estimate first, then try to locate reliable statistical information. What are the best sources of information?

2. **How many different countries and territories are represented by the students enrolled in your school?**

3. **How have the demographics of your school and your school district changed during the past 5, 10, 20 years?** Are the majority of the educators in your school aware of these demographic changes? Consider making a chart

illustrating changes in ethnicity and language use within your school or community.

4. In some communities students from non-English language backgrounds have high socioeconomic status. In other communities they are low. In terms of socioeconomic status, some districts have a mixed distribution of students from diverse language backgrounds. What is the socioeconomic status of non-English language background students in your school? Is there a relationship between socioeconomic status and referral for special education services? Determine the percentage of NELB and LEP students on free/reduced lunch. How does that percentage compare with the percentage of the school as a whole? Can you explain these results?

5. What is the ethnic and linguistic composition of your school faculty? Are there faculty members with whom the students can interact and use their home language? What are the school and district doing to promote positive interaction?

TERMS FOR STUDENTS FROM DIVERSE LANGUAGE BACKGROUNDS

Assessment of Whom?

The terms used to discuss the students from non-English language backgrounds vary by region and profession. In order to have a meaningful discussion, a set of agreed upon terms is an essential first step. Throughout the book, we continue to develop concepts and the terms used to discuss them. Within this section we address only the terminology applied to the target population.

While the population of students who use languages other than English for communication within their homes and communities is growing (Armstrong 1991), there are, as yet, no agreed upon terms to identify these students. Changes in terminology illustrate changes in the ways that people perceive a given topic. Observation of these changes in social dialogue is referred to as social semiotics. This subsection examines some of the changes in terms applied to linguistically diverse students.

Language Minority

The term *language minority* has consistently been applied during the past several decades to students from diverse language groups. This term is used in two different contexts. It can refer to students who come to school from homes and communities where the language of communication is not English. Initially when the term was first used, these students represented a small portion of the total national population of school-aged students. The term also refers to students from non-dominant cultural groups, students who come to school with experiences and perceptions that are not only viewed as different from those of the mainstream, but are less valued than the mainstream experiences (Cummins 1989). Although the term *language minority* has been widely used, it is conceptually misleading. In many areas, especially in urban centers, students from diverse language and cultural groups have become the majority population (U.S. Department of Education, Office for Civil Rights 1986). To continue to refer to this group as a minority is not only inappropriate, it is inaccurate.

If the intent is to indicate a difference in the power or status of a group, then a new term, *non-dominant language* or *non-dominant culture* may be more appropriate. However, both of these new terms also have limitations, if the intent is to refer to all students whose first language is not English. The term non-dominant reinforces the concept of being a minority or not belonging to the larger society. These terms may be semantically more appropriate to describe current demographic changes than the widely used *language minority* or *minority language* terminology (Bradley 1991; Taylor 1991).

Limited English Proficient

Within the population of students who come from non-English language backgrounds, many are so proficient in English that no one would know they spoke a language other than English, unless they were heard speaking the other language. There is, in fact, a range of proficiencies from native English speaker to non-English speaker. Within this group, students who lack English proficiency are referred to as *limited English proficient*. The term *limited English proficient* or *LEP* is used by the U.S. Department of Education, Office of Bilingual Education and Minority Languages Affairs, to designate populations of students who encounter instructional difficulties because they lack language skills in English. Federal funding to school districts, states, and university training and research programs with a focus on this population must show a focus on the development of effective programs to enable students to develop English language proficiency. The major focus of all federal funding under the category of *bilingual education* is the acquisition of English, not the maintenance or development of another language (See for example, P.L. 100-297). The term *English proficiency* was introduced in the mid 1970s. Its introduction illustrates a change in the conceptualization of the needs of these students over the past 20 years (Fradd & Vega 1987). When programs were first initiated for these students, the students were referred to as *limited English speaking ability* (LESA). The focus of instruction was on enabling the students to literally speak English better. Perceptions of instructional efforts have increased from merely being able to speak the language to having language proficient skills in listening, speaking, reading, and writing. This change also signals a shift from focusing attention on students' social language use to their effective participation in academic instruction, including math, science, social studies, and language arts (Fradd 1987b).

Some school districts and state agencies have not yet made the complete shift. Although few districts continue to use the LESA terminology, many fail to assess students' academic progress and to monitor special English language instruction and support when students begin to sound proficient in English. Sounding like a native speaker in a social conversation is not the same as performing academic tasks at a rate commensurate with mainstream students (Cummins 1984).

Potentially English Proficient

Some school districts and professionals have begun to use the term *potentially English proficient* or *PEP* to refer to the students learning English as a new language (Fradd 1991). This term emphasizes the students' potential rather than their limitation. It represents another shift in the perceptions of educators toward students in the process of learning English. It is an important innovation, especially in an era when limitations in language proficiency may be confused with handicapping conditions (Vazquez-Montilla 1991). Being limited in the ways that one can communicate in a given language is not a handicapping condition, and should not be viewed as such. The use of the acronym PEP may not have the desired consequences because its use has the potential effect of making students' needs seem possibly trivial, especially when used in combination with other words such as the *PEP Committee* to study the needs of *PEP students* and *PEP families*.

Other Alternative Terms

Recently, efforts have been made to refer in positive terminology to students in the process of learning English as a new language. Some of the more interesting terms include SOL (speakers of other languages) (Diaz Soto 1991) and EL SOL (exceptional learners who are speakers of other languages) (Dade Country Public Schools 1991). The search for positive terms is an important indication of the dissatisfaction with current perceptions of the target students as limited instead of enabled by their capacity to perform in other typically not valued ways. If the target students are to be referred to as "limited," then students who can use only one language should be referred to as EOs (English only students) (Diaz Soto 1991). Until an official alternative term is designated, however, it may be necessary to continue to use the federal term *limited English proficient*. One of the more interesting aspects of the developing fields of bilingual/ESOL education is the changing terminology used to refer to both programs and participants.

Bilingual

The term *bilingual* is one of the most widely used terms for referring to the target students. Some educators refer to students who are placed in bilingual or English for speakers of other languages (ESOL) programs as bilingual students or *bilinguals*. Sometimes the ESOL programs in which these students are enrolled are also called *bilingual programs*. The term *bilingual* means use of two languages. The term implies a degree of proficiency in two languages. When used to designate students in the process of learning English as a new language, this term can also be misleading, if students have proficiency only in one language, or if they attend programs where English is the only language of instruction (Castellana 1991).

If such students are perceived to be bilingual, then they may be expected to perform tasks they are unable to accomplish (Hakuta 1986). Failure to perform may be inferred as a disability on the part of the student rather than a limitation of the learning opportunities in which the student is being instructed. If instruction occurs in what are referred to as *bilingual programs*, then one would expect to find the use of two languages for both academic and social communication. When English is the only language of instruction, the program cannot realistically be titled a bilingual program. Most instruction of the target students in the United States is in an English rather than a bilingual context (U.S. General Accounting Office 1987a).

Politically, bilingual education is perceived as a controversial topic (Porter 1990; Rodriguez 1982; Schmidt 1991). Political forces have lined up on both sides of the English-only versus the use of native language instruction to argue for funding, educational opportunities, and educational rights. Educators can become embroiled in the politicalization of instruction, rather than its effective implementation. When politicalization occurs, the goals of instruction can be overlooked. Rather than continuing the debate that has raged for more than twenty years, efforts must be made to identify goals and objectives that can produce a common ground on which to build mutual understanding for promoting student achievement (Wong Fillmore 1991; Porter 1990).

L1 and L2

The literature on bilingual education frequently contains references to L1 and L2, or the acquisition of the first language and the second language. The use of the terms *first and second language* is appropriate if we are discussing issues related to the first and second language acquisition process of people who learned two separate languages at two different times. In the past, students often had one language more or less developed before they began to learn a new language. Often the new language was introduced as a part of entering school. However, today in the United States readily available media, such as television, and the dominance of English within the mainstream community, provide exposure to English from birth. For children born here or entering the U.S. as toddlers, English is a first language, even if they are from a non-English language background. For these students, when they enter school there is no first and second language acquisition process. Exposure to both languages simultaneously results in children entering with two first or native languages. Little research is available on the phenomenon of dual language acquisition. Research on age of acquisition does indicate that children with two or more first languages may be vulnerable to learning difficulties (Collier 1987; 1989). Being exposed to two languages simultaneously may also predispose these bilingual learners to types of behaviors that are different from those of monolingual learners. For students who are exposed to two or more languages from birth, it may be more accurate to use the terms *English and non-English languages*, rather than first and second languages, to refer to their languages. The use of this terminology may also promote the avoidance of over-generalization of re-search information from other language settings, such as Canada and Europe, where the term first and second language acquisition originated and where the instructional programs tend to be quite different from those in the United States (Cummins 1984).

The stated philosophy of the United States as represented in the educational goals established in federal legislation (see the Bilingual Act, P.L. 100-297 for examples) with respect to limited English proficient students is rapid mastery of the English language, mastery of appropriate academic and vocational skills, and integration within the economic and social system of the nation. In this context, the mastery of English is the primary consideration and the rationale for specific funding. In this instructional context, the terms English and non-English may be more appropriate as well as more accurate.

Non-English Language Background

The term *Non-English language background* or *NELB* is used in describing the target population of students addressed within this text. This term also has advantages and disadvantages. It does not currently convey a sense of status or limitation. It correctly identifies students as having origins other than the mainstream English-speaking population without penalizing them for their origins. It is a broad category that includes all students from other countries or territories or homes within the United States where English is not the dominant or only language. The term can be a useful demographic descriptor for data collection and for monitoring student progress.

In communicating information about language proficiency, the term does have a limitation. Both students who are English proficient and those who have not yet developed proficiency in English are members of the NELB group. As a measure of language skills, the term *limited English proficient* is more appropriate. The purpose of using the more inclusive term NELB is to focus on the needs of the larger group of learners who may have educational needs that go undetected, unmet, and little understood. LEP students receive special English instruction; NELB students who are not LEP do not receive this type of assistance. When students have been certified to be able to participate in regular English instruction, little consideration is given to their continued need for language development. If these students experience frustration or failure, they may be perceived to have learning disabilities or other limitations rather than continued language learning needs (Garcia & Ortiz 1988). Many of the students in the NELB category continue to need English language skill development and support in order to successfully participate in academic instruction. Limited English proficient students are a subset of non-English language background students.

Limited data are available on the numbers of non-English language background students who actually receive special education services (Baca & Cervantes 1991). This limitation exists, in part, because students may not be identified for special education until they are determined to be proficient in English. At that time information on language or ethnic backgrounds may not be collected or may be disregarded. The issue, however, is not only one of language. It is also a matter of comprehending that students from ethnically and linguistically different backgrounds may have had prior experiences that are different from the mainstream population. They may not have developed the learning styles or the same instructional orientation as their mainstream peers (Westby in press b). Because their learning responses are based on their prior experiences, their lack of experience within the mainstream context may make them vulnerable to many learning difficulties. Without appropriate instruction, many students who could be successful fail because their learning difficulties and requirements are seldom identified or addressed in a developmental supportive manner. Formalized collaborative structures which support effective instruction are essential in reaching students and integrating instruction into a unified school-wide effort (Stedman 1987; West & Idol 1987). The development of effective programs for these students, NELB students in general, and LEP students in particular, is the focus of this book.

RESEARCH IN PRACTICE:
Terms for students from diverse language backgrounds

1. What are the terms used in your school and school district to identify the target students? How do the terms you use compare with the terms presented here? Are there any discrepancies in meanings? Are there additional terms that should be added to this list?

2. What are your instructional goals? How do you plan to achieve these goals with students who may not understand what you are communicating to them? Does the selection of a set of terms to refer to these students make a difference in the way educators think about how to plan and provide for these students?

3. What role does politics play in education? Consider the controversy over bilingual education in the United States. If you are not familiar with that debate, you may want to consult the following references: Cummins 1984, 1989; Fradd 1982, 1985; Fradd & Tikunoff 1987; Porter 1990; Rodriguez 1982; Schmidt 1991. Do you feel that it is important to take a personal stand on these issues? How does this debate impact on the ways you address the needs of the students within your school?

SUMMARIZING SECTION ONE

Demographic shifts require a new conceptualization of the terms identifying students from diverse language backgrounds

This section presented information on the terms currently being applied to students who compose a unique subset of the total population of school-aged children. Some of these terms can be misleading when inappropriately applied. The information has been presented here to encourage educators to reflect on the terms used at their worksites to relate to students from homes where languages other than English are used to communicate. Students who come from these home backgrounds bring diverse learning styles and experiences that impact on the learning process. In order to be effective, educators need to be aware of difficulties imposed by the use of inappropriate terminology as a first step toward addressing the needs of the target students.

WHAT CAN YOU DO?

1. Why is it important to develop a common set of terms for referring to a specific group of students? Do these terms promote a positive, accurate understanding of these students' needs?

2. What can you do to promote the use of accurate terms in categorizing and describing the students in your school?

SECTION TWO

FORCES OF CHANGE IN EDUCATION AND EDUCATIONAL REFORM

The decade of the 1990s was predicted to be an era of educational reform. Many educational innovations were under way when a series of financial disasters created a national financial crisis. The financial crisis triggered a national recession which in turn affected funding for education. Reduced financial allocations and budget cuts impacted on educational reform at all levels. Trends toward reduced student-teacher ratios, improved inservice programs and other advances were halted as administrators faced budget deficits. As you work through this section, consider the interplay between national, state, and local trends, and educational outcomes for non-English language background students. Consider too the impact of these trends for all students and for the school personnel who serve them.

THE CHALLENGE OF EDUCATIONAL REFORM

A great deal has been written during the past decade about educational reform, yet little has been accomplished in effectively promoting academic success with students considered to be at risk of educational failure (Cuban 1990; Passow 1991; Polonia & Williams 1991). Little has been done throughout the reform movement to seriously address the instructional needs of students from non-English language backgrounds, especially those who have been identified as difficult to reach (Andrews & Morefield 1991). In all of the reform movement, little attention has been given to ensuring effective instruction of students from diverse language backgrounds, especially when those students may be handicapped (Fradd, Weismantel, Correa, & Algozzine 1990). In spite of the fact that researchers and policy makers have pointed out that non-English language background learners are the fastest growing group and the one placing the greatest impact on national resources, little has been done to prepare school personnel to effectively work with these students (Armstrong 1991; Levin 1989; Pallas, Natriello & McDill 1989). The importance of education for these students has been established by the National Commission on Testing and Public Policy (1990) which emphasizes the growing proportion of the labor force composed of NELB workers.

Effective instructional practices have been identified for all students, even those at risk (Murphy 1989; Slavin & Madden 1989). Research shows that an integrated approach to serving at-risk students promotes equity of instructional opportunity (O'Neil 1991; Willis 1991). What is needed is a process for providing school personnel with the knowledge of how to use effective practices with all students. Changing the assessment process is a key factor in implementing effective instruction. The process of increasing the capacity of educators to make decisions about students is an active, results-oriented process that impacts educational policy as well as instruction at many levels (Kean 1991; Neil 1991).

RESEARCH IN PRACTICE:
The Challenge of Educational Reform

1. What reform activities have occurred in your school or school district within the past five years? What impact did these reform measures have on students? Interview colleagues and ask them what they think about the current educational reform movement in your district. How many specific reforms can your colleagues name? What impact have they observed? Were any reform efforts directed at students considered to be at risk of educational failure?

2. What types of educational reforms are still needed? What additional changes are required to meet the needs of at-risk students? For example, is there an established policy and procedure for identifying students who are limited in English proficiency (LEP) when they arrive at school? Is this practice applied consistently? What happens to these students once they are identified? Is this information being tabulated so that the school and school district have accurate records of the newly arrived students? Is there a system for reporting demographic changes across time? Do educators have easy access to this information? Are they aware of these changes? What changes do they suggest as a result of their awareness of these changes?

3. Consider the reform movement in funding school programs. How will funding changes impact your school and your district?

4. Differentiate proactive and reactive responses to the increasing ethnic diversity within the schools.

THE HISTORICAL FOUNDATIONS OF CHANGING ASSESSMENT PRACTICES

Educational systems across the nation are engaged in a process of cultural and instructional change such as they have never before faced. The national need for educational change has been characterized as the foundering of the public educational system at epidemic proportions, a concern comparable to the AIDS epidemic in its potential for severe consequences if change is not effective in educational sectors for all of the nation's students (Fuchs & Fuchs 1990).

The forces currently fomenting the need for change have been gathering energy throughout the century. Legal rights, funding formulas, and resource allocations are being challenged in the courts, the legislatures, and a variety of other forums throughout the nation (Baker 1991; Brandt 1991; Futrell 1989; LeTendre 1991; Sizer 1991; Timar 1989). Local and state governing agencies are seeking to make schools and school districts more accountable for the resources expended and are promoting the measurement of academic achievement of students within their jurisdiction (Glickman 1990; O'Neil 1990). Parent and community leaders want more direct involvement in and control over both inputs and outcomes of the educational process (Ayers 1991). Professional groups, too, have indicated that they desire and expect to have more participation in the decision-making process than they have previously experienced (Brandt 1990; Joyce 1991; Murphy 1991; Timar 1989). National and local student advocate groups are promoting equitable educational outcomes and improvement in the quality of educational opportunities for students who have traditionally not achieved well within the present system (National Coalition of Advocates for Students 1988; Willshire Carrera 1989).

The efforts of interest groups to bring about educational change can be categorized into two major concerns: the need for *equity in educational opportunities*, and the drive for *educational excellence*. Forces focussing on equity have demanded inclusion and effective participation of all students within the educational system at every level (Sizer 1991). The forces for academic excellence are more diverse. Efforts for academic excellence have promoted two different types of programs: (a) programs to develop basic literacy skills; and (b) programs to promote quality education. Quality educational efforts include such diverse areas as the development of higher order thinking skills, the recognition of the whole child within the educational process, and the importance of the participation of a technologically literate work force within a global, international economy. While these forces are not mutually exclusive, their goals are not synonymous nor mutually supported. The achievement of the goals of these diverse advocacy groups, should they be realized, would have profound effects on the nation. To understand the potential impact of the potential implementation of the changes, it is helpful to observe the current movements within the context of previous reform efforts.

The forces striving for equity and educational excellence have initiated a variety of reforms. These include diverse efforts, such as the *restructuring* movement to promote greater participation of educators within the educational decision-making process (see, for example the *Phi Delta Kappan* April 1991, and *Educational Leadership* April 1990, May 1991); the *regular education initiative* to promote greater responsibility for educational outcomes of all but the most disabled students within the regular education setting (Stainback & Stainback 1984; Wang & Reynolds 1985; Wang & Reynolds 1986; Wang, Reynolds & Walberg 1988; Wang, Reynolds & Walberg 1989); and the development of *alternative assessment procedures* for determining students' educational needs and measuring their achievements (Ascher 1990, Berry 1991, California Department of Education 1990). All of these movements are interrelated in their focus on the needs of culturally and linguistically diverse students. All are outgrowths of reform movements initiated in the 1950s to establish equal educational opportunities for students. They also represent examples of ways that the national system is being pushed politically and economically to respond to the pressing need for a more technically oriented, highly trained work force.

Educational changes initiated in the 1950s were the most revolutionary of the century. The Supreme Court declared that school districts must consolidate their resources and their pupils into a unitary system (Alexander 1985). This decision overturned the status quo that had existed for almost 200 years and generated an unprecedented movement for individual rights (Berdine & Blackhurst 1985). Resistance to federal interference in states rights created opportunities for educational innovation, such as federal subsidies to impoverished school districts and regions with large populations of low-achieving students. Along with the educational subsidies came a process of federal monitoring and the threat of withdrawal of support for school districts failing to comply with integration requirements (Fradd & Vega 1987). To avoid states rights conflicts and complaints of interference, federal funding initiatives were promoted as a process for *supplementing* but not *supplanting* state and local educational efforts. Funding for the first bilingual programs was included in this supplemental process because many students who were limited in English proficiency were also identified as among the nation's most needy. In supplementing the regular instruction provided by the local school district, the new federal funding created a new model of instruction, *the resource center*, which initiated a series of long-term consequences. Initially, to avoid the appearance of interfering with the established program provided by the local school district, the supplemental services available through federal funds were provided in resource rooms outside the regular classroom setting. The pull-out or resource model of instruction has tended to promote fragmentation rather than consolidation of educational resources. In supplementing regular education, the federally funded programs undercut the educational autonomy of the regular program by establishing a process of teaching, testing, and monitoring students. The resource room concept also contributed to several beliefs about the teaching and learning process, especially as it relates to the needs of diverse learners. It promoted the belief that many students could be more effectively served outside the regular classroom, and conversely, that teachers in regular classrooms were not prepared to effectively address the needs of diverse learners (Fradd 1987b). Recently, resource room instruction has been questioned because of the debilitating effects such programs tend to have on participating students. Instead of providing students with the type of instruction they need to function successfully within the mainstream, the resource programs remove students from the sources of typical language, behavior and learning. It also removes the expectation that the students can and will learn to function within the mainstream if they are removed from it (Gartner & Lipsky 1987; Jenkins, Pious & Jewell 1990; Skrtic 1991).

During the past several decades legislation and litigation have established the expectation that all students should receive an appropriate, effective education (Fradd & Vega 1987). Despite the realization that limited English proficient students should be included within this expectation, states and school districts have been slow to respond in ways that promote effective educational outcomes (Baez, Fernandez, Navarro, & Rice 1985; Hakuta 1986; Paulston 1980; Staff 1986). The debate continues. District federal courts have found in favor of litigation requiring school districts to: (a) assess the needs of all students and base instruction on well-grounded theoretical and pedagogical principles to meet those needs; (b) ensure that programs are well-implemented, including texts, support materials, trained and credentialed personnel, and an integrated instructional plan that provides for articulation across instructional settings and monitors students' progress in mastering English and developing academic skills; and (c) prove effective in meeting the needs of limited English proficient students (Baez et al. 1985; Fradd & Vega 1987). These requirements have been upheld in several district courts and appear to be an operational procedure for litigants seeking to obtain educational equity for NELB students (Perez 1991).

New federal support can be found for programs addressing the needs of NELB students receiving special education services. This support comes in the form of the Individuals with Disabilities Education Act (20 U.S.C., Education of the Handicapped Act Amendments of 1990) or IDEA. The Act calls attention to the changing demographics within the United States and highlights the increasing numbers of NELB and other minority children. It specifies that educational agencies seeking federal funds for special education more comprehensively consider ways to improve services to culturally diverse students, including improved personnel preparation, procedures for ensuring that assessment procedures and materials are not biased or discriminatory and that instruction leads to effective educational outcomes (Staff 1991).

The decade of the 1980s has been a period in which educational leaders and policymakers have sought to determine how best student needs might be met. Early in the decade a significant body of research was generated on effective school programs (Edmonds 1979; Madaus, Airasian & Kelleghan 1980; Purkey & Smith 1983). Initially the research addressed general classroom populations, but grew to include bilingual and multicultural populations as well (Stedman 1987; Tikunoff 1985; Tikunoff & Vazquez 1982). This research produced enlightening results. Commissions were formed to promote educational reform (National Commission on Excellence in Education 1983). One of the primary effectiveness issues of research emphasized by these commissions was the need for a shared vision of educational expectations.

As the movement continues, the importance of a clear shared vision has become operationalized within many states as a set of educational goals used to promote standardized achievement testing and increased high school graduation requirements (Carnegie Foundation for the Advancement of Teaching 1988). State and local school districts have implemented comprehensive assessment programs to monitor student progress and to ensure that students master required basic skills at various points within the educational process (Ascher 1990). The impact of these policies has implications for the success of students who are considered at risk of educational failure, students who may typically be from non-English language backgrounds (Pallas, Natriello & McGill 1989). The question of how to raise standards through the establishment of a series of tests and additional requirements, without increasing the potential that many students will leave school without completing their education has not yet been answered (McDill, Natriello & Pallas 1985). This quesiton is only beginning to be considered (Damico, Roth, Fradd, & Hankins 1990; De Avila 1991).

The movement toward standardization and accountability in the 1980s reinforced and expanded the use of uniform measures of student behavior and performance and uniform guidelines for placing students in special programs (Toch 1991). As efforts toward enforcing uniformity have gained power, other counterarguments have been offered about the effects of standardization on teachers and students. Standardized assessment, it is argued, removes teachers from the role of decision-maker and places them in the role of technocrat or follower of decisions made by others. Overuse of standardization information has the effect of encouraging teachers to teach to the test rather than promoting effective learning. Teaching to the test promotes a measurement driven curriculum, reduces teachers' instructional creativity, and encourages minimum standards and performance (Ascher 1990; Damico et al. 1990).

Clearly issues of educational restructuring, including the involvement of regular, ESOL, and special education teachers in collecting data and making decisions about the performance of their students, are intrinsically interwoven with the process of promoting educational equity and excellence. Educators have also argued that shared responsibility for the education of all students requires collaboration and consultation across settings in determining students' needs, not dictation by one group to another (Heron & Harris 1987). The rigid application of assessment and placement criteria has been perceived as the creation of a set of artificial barriers to educational equity and excellence for both students and teachers (Skrtic 1991). Efforts have recently been initiated to remove these artificial barriers by reconceptualizing the process of assessment and instruction.

New as well as continuing forces are shaping this change in assessment. Among these forces one of the most influential is the drastic budget reduction in many areas of state and local spending, and changing economic priorities (Cage 1991; Harp 1991; Toch 1991). However, the force and the focus of educational reform are not going away. Recent innovations have created alternatives to the standardized measurement driven assessment. For example, the use of curriculum-based assessment provides teachers and students with feedback to promote effective instruction and sustained academic growth. Computer technology has created many new opportunities for student instruction as well as data collection. The innovations in assessment go hand in hand with modifications in the instructional process. Innovative instructional approaches such as cooperative learning, learning strategies, use of advanced organizers, and process learning have also lead to more productive and meaningful instruction. Most importantly, these changes reveal a strong indication of the shift in conceptualizing the whole assessment and instructional process. These approaches also reveal a perception of the need to support learning by maximizing opportunities to learn and evaluating individual growth and development. Assessment is beginning to be seen as a set of opportunities to enable students to reflect on what they are doing and to synthesize what they know about a topic, a process, or an idea. Assessment is also being conceptualized within the larger context of enabling groups of learners to organize, synthesize, and evaluate their performance together. This approach is more consistent with interactive societal behavior in general. Responsibility for assessment outcomes is shared by the group rather than the individual, and thus reflects the instructional and decision-making process as a microcosm of society (National Science Foundation 1991).

Emphasis on the appropriate use of assessment results shifts the focus from a *sorting process* that separates students into discrete categories and toward a *synthesizing and evaluating process* where students and teachers come together to determine the results of their performance and to determine ways in which performance can be improved, when necessary, and celebrated whenever appropriate. By reconceptualizing the roles of both teachers and students, the shift in perceptions has the potential for promoting real educational restructuring. Where the period of the 1980s was a time of shifting toward teaching to the test in order to ensure the attainment of basic skills, instruction in the 1990s is moving toward the use of meaningful learning and assessment outcomes (Shavelson, Carey & Webb 1990).

Technological advances have also created the mechanisms for determining the attainment of national educational goals by comparing student achievement within individual classrooms, and within and across schools, districts, and states (Kean 1991). The outgrowth of these technological innovations has also produced a new view of the usefulness of psychometric measures in the assessment process. The focus of this new view is on performance testing, or new ways of examining what students can actually do (Ascher 1990; Berry 1991; California Department of Education 1990; National Science Foundation 1991). Plans are under way for the development of *performance based assessment* as a vehicle to be used in combination with other forms of standardized tests in evaluating student outcomes (Berry 1991). The paradigm shift toward inclusion of alternatives to traditional assessment means that school personnel, both those in direct instructional roles and those in support roles, will be expected to become familiar with these new tests and procedures. The potential for positive changes in policy and practice toward a more equitable education of all students is considerable (Rothberg 1990).

As we examine the process of educational reform in the 1990s, we find many limitations as well as much encouragement. Few leaders within government and within the nation's universities have indicated a willingness themselves to understand the issues of equity or excellence (Bracey 1989; Carey 1989). Some of the same arguments voiced so clearly in the past will be rephrased and recommunicated in this decade (Lewis 1991). It is incumbent upon all of us who believe that it is not only possible but important to have both a unitary vision and effective instructional programs for all our students to continue to develop and share our ideas. Learning through doing, learning through sharing, and learning through refining can promote the type of educational system that enables students to participate and to be successful.

RESEARCH IN PRACTICE:
The Historical Foundations of Changing Assessment Practices

1. Differentiate between the results of efforts to promote educational equity and efforts to promote educational excellence.

2. The decade of the 1990s was initially thought to be the decade of educational reform; characterize the major innovations to date.

3. List and describe the forces continuing to promote educational reform in the last decade of the 20th century.

4. How do efforts at educational reform influence conceptualization of the assessment process?

DEVELOPING THE CONCEPT OF INSTRUCTIONAL ASSESSMENT

The term *assessment* refers to all the information that may be obtained about students to promote effective instruction. For this reason the term *instructional assessment* is used to describe the process for collecting information on students' performance and using it to make decisions that produce successful academic outcomes. The instructional assessment process is results based and student oriented. It encompasses not only information collected on specific standardized tests, but also information collected across a period of time within a continuum of instructional interactions. Not only must these assessment procedures fulfill the policy and legal requirements for minimizing bias (Fradd & Vega 1987; Kretschmer 1991), but they must also generate meaningful information on which to base educational decisions.

Appropriate assessment and educational planning are essential in providing meaningful services to students for whom English is not the first or only language. Criteria for developing appropriate assessment of NELB students include:

- **legally defensible assessment procedures** (procedures that respond to current state and federal legislation and litigation decisions)
- **positive procedures that lead to effective instructional outcomes** (procedures that can be monitored and evaluated in terms of effective outcomes)
- **instructionally relevant procedures** (procedures that are responsive to the constraints and requirements of classroom settings)
- **collaborative procedures** (procedures that promote information and resource sharing).

RESEARCH IN PRACTICE:
Developing the Concept of Instructional Assessment

In your own words write down what the term instructional assessment means. Ask three other educators to tell you what the term means to them. Save these responses and refer back to them as you work through the book and again six months after you complete these activities. Think about differences and similarities in the ways that professionals consider the assessment process. Does the use of this term provide insight into the process of collecting and using practical information? Think about how this process applies to specific students with whom you work.

ASSESSMENT FOR WHAT?

There are several perennial questions school personnel want to answer when initiating the assessment of non-English language background students. A primary consideration in assessing NELB students is their placement within an instructional program. Special instructional programs for students in the process of learning English as a new language are sometimes available for students with limited English proficiency. These programs generally have entry criteria for participation and exit criteria for moving the students into successful performance in English-only instruction. The past several decades have been marked by legislation, litigation, and executive orders emphasizing the school districts' responsibilities in meeting LEP students' instructional needs. As a result of these actions a national policy of sorts has gradually evolved with respect to these students (Fradd 1987a). The development of this policy has been documented and summarized in a memorandum from the Assistant Secretary for Civil Rights to the Office of Civil Rights Senior Staff (Williams 1991). This memorandum emphasizes the importance of providing students with instruction that enables them to successfully participate in the regular education programs. Factors to be considered in deciding if programs are meeting students' needs in moving toward successful regular grade participation include: (a) students' ability to maintain academic progress on a level equal to that of their age and grade peers; (b) students' ability to participate successfully in all aspects of the school curriculum without special accommodations that result from limited English language skills; and (c) the grade-retention and drop-out rates of formally LEP students in comparison with their non-LEP peers.

If students' behavior and academic progress do not meet with district expectations, often one of the first questions asked is some version of "Is this student handicapped?" or "Should this student be in a special education program?" A great deal has been written about the process of assessing non-English language background students to determine eligibility for special education programs (Figueroa 1989; Hamayan & Damico 1991; Langdon 1989; Rueda 1989). The question of establishing eligibility criteria for placement in special education is both a legal and a policy consideration, in addition to an instructional concern. With current funding requirements, it is a valid concern, but rarely one that addresses students' needs.

Once the question of possible special education eligibility is posed, the means for arriving at an answer is essentially prescribed. The student must undergo evaluation of some kind to verify the presence of a handicapping condition. The questions of "What test or tests should be used?" is then asked by school personnel searching for standardized instruments. To date there is no such test. Neither is there a magic formula for collecting the most relevant or meaningful information. Many times we make our best guesses about what would be appropriate, and then observe and monitor the students' progress to fine tune and modify instruction as changes seem warranted. With appropriate instruction as the focus, assessment becomes a process, not a means to an end. Questions about special education placement derive from a dual educational system that mandates funding categories rather than effective practices.

The case studies contained within this book provide information and suggestions for assessing students' progress in regular and special English language or bilingual programs. Emphasis is placed on assisting students to effectively participate within the mainstream. Consideration is also given to determining students' eligibility for special education services. The focus of the book is on meeting students' needs, not determining their instructional placement. Throughout the book the emphasis is on moving toward success in developing effective language skills. At the same time we recognize the importance of providing appropriate and defensible legal responses to educational concerns. We show how, by combining standardized and informal assessment information, we can provide both legally and instructionally responsive information focussed on meeting students' needs.

RESEARCH IN PRACTICE:
Assessment for What?

1. Find out why students are assessed in your school. Create an assessment information chart. Make two columns on a sheet of paper. In the first column, list the reasons why you assess students. In the second, list reasons you believe students in general are assessed at your school. Ask three colleagues the same questions: why they assess students and why students in general are assessed. List the colleagues' personal reasons in the first column and their general reasons for assessment in the second. Is there a match or a mismatch between the personal and the general reasons for testing students?

2. What do you think about the assessment process? Write down what you personally think.

3. What do other people think about assessment? Keep a running list of reasons, rationale, reactions and general information about what other people think about assessment. You can develop the information for this list by tuning into conversations you have or that you listen to during the school day. Think about the accuracy and appropriateness of this information. React to these reasons in writing. We encourage you to keep these observations private, at least for a while.

4. Do the reasons for assessing students differ if the students are considered to be proficient in English or limited in English proficiency? You may want to write a brief observation paper on the similarities and differences in the assessment of English proficient and limited English proficient students.

CHANGES IN THE ASSESSMENT PARADIGM

A system change is needed in terms of the perceptions of personnel who serve typical and handicapped learners. This change is currently taking place. The change is really a paradigm shift in the ways that educational leaders, policy makers, and practitioners think about the learning process. This shift, or change in perspective, encompasses a global perception of students as learners and considers their education the responsibility of all those who provide instruction and support (Will 1986). Currently there are two systems: one for students who are in regular programs and another for students in special education programs. The legal requirements, funding categories and allocations, program services, and perceptions of what constitutes an appropriate education are different for each of the systems (Wang & Reynolds 1985; Wang & Reynolds 1986; Wang, Reynolds & Walberg 1988; Wang, Reynolds & Walberg 1989). Administrative structures governing the two programs contribute to a lack of coordination and cooperation (Stainback & Stainback 1984). Even the language used to communicate among professionals about students differs by professional training and position (Fradd 1991).

The movement toward unifying the two systems and making them into one results, in part, from budget reductions and deficits. Educational systems can not really afford to maintain two separate structures. The move toward a unitary program also results from the growing awareness that there is no real educational justification for separating students into programs based on special fund-ing categories. In addition to questions about whether a student qualifies for special education services, educators are beginning to ask about the types of ser-vices that would be appropriate and how these can be provided to enable stu-dents to be effective learners. Consideration is also being given to procedures for monitoring the effectiveness of special and regular education placements (Sem-mel, Abernathy, Butera & Lesar 1991; Wang & Reynolds 1985; Wang & Reynolds 1986; Wang, Reynolds & Walberg 1988; Wang, Reynolds & Walberg 1989).

As the paradigm changes, long term efforts at providing appropriate instruction for all students are beginning to be considered along with short term qualification and placement decisions for special needs students (Jenkins & Pious 1991; Miller 1991; Thousand 1991). Practices in effective instructional assessment for non-English language background students can also be used effectively with mainstream students. Proactive organization of instruction to define and meet students' needs is being seen as one of the real purposes of assessment (Braden & Fradd 1987). This proactive process involves the whole school community, not just a select group of personnel who have been trained to administer tests.

RESEARCH IN PRACTICE:
Changes in the Assessment Paradigm

---

1. **Describe assessment as it relates to students in regular education classrooms. Describe assessment as it relates to students being considered for placement in special education programs.** Do you have any difficulties discussing either area of assessment? Ask colleagues what they think and find out if they agree with you.

2. **What are the differences in practice and perspective between regular and special education?** Ask two other colleagues who teach in regular and special education programs to describe assessment as it relates to special and regular education. Compare their responses. Are they similar or different? Do your colleagues have any difficulties with this activity? If you or your colleagues had difficulties with this activity, how did you feel about asking these questions? What can be done about obtaining clarifications so that everyone understands the process?

3. **How can information on regular education and special education assessment be used to promote understanding and collaboration within your school?** Make a list of suggestions and discuss them with your colleagues. Should this discussion be moved to a different arena?

EMPOWERMENT

With the exception of ESOL and bilingual specialists, classroom teachers[1] have not generally engaged in the assessment of their students' language

---

[1] The term *classroom teacher*, as it is used here, refers to personnel whose principal role is to provide direct instruction to students. For purposes of discussion such personnel could include typical regular education, special education, ESOL, bilingual, and other subject area specialists.

proficiency (Toohey 1984). Teachers are responsible for making significant educational decisions about students' instructional requirements. They are also responsible for initially identifying students' limitations. For that reason, they are the school personnel most likely to refer students for special educational services when the students do not make anticipated progress (Algozzine, Christenson & Ysseldyke 1982; Carter & Sugai 1989). Because they work with children on a daily basis, classroom teachers are familiar with students. Teachers' familiarity provides them with insights into students' needs and performance not available to other educators unfamiliar with the students. Familiarity with adults is a key factor influencing assessment outcomes for minority students. Minority students are more likely to perform well for teachers whom they know and with whom they identify, than with adults with whom they are unfamiliar. Because familiarity is less of an important factor with mainstream students than it is with minority students, it often has not been given consideration in planning for and interpreting test results (Fuchs & Fuchs 1989). Yet classroom teachers are in positions to collect reliable data on students' performance and are an essential group to promote meaningful assessment.

Apart from time constraints, there are several reasons why teachers usually have not conducted comprehensive assessments of their students. The first and greatest reason is that they have not been trained to collect and use assessment data beyond the information obtained from a typical spelling test (Diaz, Moll & Mehan 1986; Herbst 1989). Because of this lack of training, teachers who might collect data have had little incentive and few peers with whom to share this information. In addition, teachers have had no real reason to collect information on students' language proficiency when instructional programs have required the use of a preestablished curriculum that teachers must teach (Adelman 1989; Apple 1991; Fradd in press).

The change process in data collection promotes change in a variety of other arenas. As part of the restructuring process currently occurring within education, hierarchical relationships are being modified to become more collateral and cooperative. As teachers develop assessment expertise, they become effective producers of assessment information, and wise consumers of the assessment information provided by others. Developing the assessment skills necessary to make effective and accurate determinations about students' needs can result in a power shift from the hierarchical relationships to collateral relations where all personnel are viewed as having insight into students' capabilities and needs (West & Idol 1987). But reducing the boundary lines among educational roles and empowering personnel to collaborate and to share information also has the potential to create controversy and professional misunderstandings. Before embarking on a change program to increase personnel competencies, educational leaders need to be aware of the potential negative as well as positive consequences. Educators require training in communication and in collaboration, as well as in obtaining and using student information.

The change process is not simple and straightforward. Even when teachers are empowered to become skillful in collecting and using meaningful assessment information, modifications in assessment practices can have only a limited impact unless other school personnel are also provided with a similar understanding of assessment. While teachers have always collaborated on an informal basis, the process of developing effective assessment procedures requires that teachers also become empowered to share data with other personnel, both informally and formally. As a result of the need to exchange information, a new set of professional skills is being identified as part of effective instruction (Heron & Harris 1987). These skills are developed in a context of collegiality and shared insights. As these skills develop within the school setting collaborators discover the need for a shared language of common meaning. This language is composed of a set of terms and a way of thinking that is shared by all personnel responsible for meeting the educational needs of students. The result of this collaborative process is both the development of a network of collaborators within the school and school district, and the organization of teams of personnel capable of making effective educational decisions and sharing in the responsibility for their outcomes (Fradd 1991).

As teacher competence in conducting assessments increases, perception of what constitutes an effective assessment is also changing (Carter & Sugai 1989). Not only are there formal procedures traditionally considered to be important, but informal procedures are beginning to be viewed as contributing to the assessment process. The integration of informal procedures into the assessment process impacts directly and indirectly on what teachers learn and know about their students. The change process addresses ways in which students are perceived as learners and ways in which students' educational experiences can be evaluated as they learn new skills and knowledge. Changes occur in the ways educators view not only their students, but also themselves and their responsibilities (Hord, Rutherford, Huling-Austin & Hall 1987).

RESEARCH IN PRACTICE:
Empowerment

---

1. Are classroom teachers involved in making educational decisions? List the kinds of educational decisions in which you have been involved during the past two years. Is your role similar to or different from the roles of other educators in terms of educational decision making? Ask colleagues about their involvement. Does involvement change perceptions of students and schools, or perceptions of educational roles? Has it impacted your perceptions? How?

2. **How is information on student performance obtained from teachers in your school?** How is it shared? Is this process useful? Do teachers feel involved in the decision making process? Is the involvement similar for all students, or are some students treated differently? Are some teachers treated differently? If you found it difficult to answer these questions, think about the reasons.

3. **Why does the process of collaboration need to be considered in the development of assessment skills and instructional competencies?**

4. **Does your school have a process for promoting collaboration?** Is it effective? Would you improve it? How?

SUMMARIZING SECTION TWO
Forces of Change in Education in Educational Reform

This section presented information on demographic changes occurring within the nation's schools. These changes have heightened the need to provide effective instruction to all students. One of the groups of students most at risk of educational failure is students from non-English language backgrounds, especially students who are not proficient in English. Educational reform is occurring within educational programs across the nation. Educational assessment is a principal area of reform. The way that assessment information is collected, analyzed, and utilized is a major area of change. Instead of focussing on what students have not done, the focus is on promoting student performance. The term instructional assessment was introduced here as a concept of using assessment to promote academic achievement. As part of the change process, school personnel are learning to collaborate in collecting information and to communicate informally and formally about students' performance.

WHAT CAN YOU DO?

1. **What do you know about the student population within your school and school district?** Can you describe this population so that other educators understand the demographic composition and socioeconomic status of these students? What implications have you drawn from this information?

2. **Have you considered the similarities and differences between the students and the faculty in your school?** What instructional considerations can you make from this comparison?

3. **What educational challenges does your school face?** What aspects of educational reform have been successful? What is still needed?

4. **What is instructional assessment?** What does it mean to you?

5. **How are you involved in the process of improving educational opportunities for the students within your school?**

6. **What role does collaboration play in developing effective programs?**

SECTION THREE
THE DEVELOPMENT OF ASSESSMENT CONCEPTS

In the previous sections, you were asked to consider why schools assess students. In this section we consider the rationale for assessment practices by examining the concepts of standardization, validity, and reliability. Textbooks and other scholarly writings have devoted a great deal of time to these constructs. Educators who are interested in a more scholarly approach to the application and meaning of these terms are encouraged to refer to additional sources (See, for example, McLoughlin & Lewis 1986; Salvia & Ysseldyke 1988; Sattler 1988; Swanson & Watson 1989; Thomas & Grimes 1990).

Sometimes educators are intimidated by the terms of educational testing and measurement because, although these terms were studied in college courses, they were seldom applied in meaningful contexts. The purpose of this section is to provide a practical approach to applying technical assessment terminology. In order to make the assessment process uniform and the results applicable to all learners, the process must be standardized. In standardizing the process, we also want to know how to make information valid and reliable. A working knowledge of this information is important in guiding educators in the selection of assessment materials and procedures, and in making decisions about how and when to apply them. This information can also assist educators in accepting and using assessment information. In other words, we can become effective producers and consumers of assessment information if we have a working knowledge of basic assessment constructs from a practical, student oriented perspective.

Two types of assessment procedures are typically used with regular and limited English proficient students. These include: (a) academic and achievement tests; and (b) ability and intelligence tests. In addition, students suspected of having learning difficulties, especially language learning problems, are sometimes given tests to determine their level of language development. These are, of course, usually given in English.

Information on these different assessment procedures is discussed throughout the text. Specific information is presented here on general assessment concepts. In addition, information on performance assessment is highlighted within this section because this type of assessment presents a new assessment trend that enables educators to monitor students' progress in mastering new concepts and skills. This innovation is important in meeting the needs of LEP

TABLE 1-1. TYPES OF ASSESSMENT PROCEDURES

ACADEMIC/ACHIEVEMENT

Formal	Informal
Standardized / Norm-Referenced	Daily School Work
Criterion-Referenced	Observations
Performance Measures	

ABILITY/INTELLIGENCE

Formal	Informal
Standardized / Norm-Referenced	Observations
Group	
Individual	

LANGUAGE PROFICIENCY

Formal	Informal
Standardized / Norm-Referenced	Daily School Work and
Discrete Point	Performance
Holistic	Cloze Tests
	Language Sampling
	Written
	Oral
	Observations
	Interviews

students because these students enter with different experiences and knowledge bases. Since many of the current procedures may be biased against culturally and linguistically diverse students, it is up to educators and school systems to find the processes, materials and strategies that promote effective, fair, and equitable assessment practices.

USING THE CONCEPT OF STANDARDIZATION

Standardization refers to the process of establishing a uniform code of size, quantity, or quality. The need to standardize instruments or procedures arises out of the reality that each person who creates or administers a test might have a different method for using it. Each instrument or method could provide different information about a student's performance. Because of administration differences, we could have a file folder full of information about a student without really knowing what that information means because there was no standard way to compare data (Bennet-Kastor 1988).

The standardization process was first applied in commerce to weights and measurements. Inches, feet, and yards became standard units of measurement. Everyone who used the system had rulers with the same size inches. The standardization process for measuring students' academic performance is much more complicated than measuring their height or weight. There are no inches and no single ruler that can be applied to determine cognitive or linguistic growth.

Application of standardized norms.

In order to develop a standard format for measuring students' performance in comparison with a representative sample of similar students, exactly the same instrument must be used in the same way to collect the same information. This is referred to as norming. The sampling group must include a range of students from diverse ability groups; a range that goes from students who can perform all or almost all the tasks to students who can perform few, if any, of the tasks. These data then provide a range of responses that can be combined in order to make comparisons of the *normal population distribution* of a representative group. When a statistically large enough group of students participates in such an activity, the performance of the majority tends to fall within a middle range. This type of population distribution can be depicted on a normal population distribution curve. Means or averages, and standardized scores such as percentiles, stanines, and standard deviations can be calculated with this information. Such standardized scores are known as norms, and are used to compare students' performance with that of the population on which the instrument was standardized. This distribution is shown in Figure 1-1.

When a student's general background of experiences is different from those on whom the test was normed, the test is probably inappropriate for evaluating present performance or predicting future outcomes for this student. For a non-native English speaker and for a speaker of some dialects of English, every test

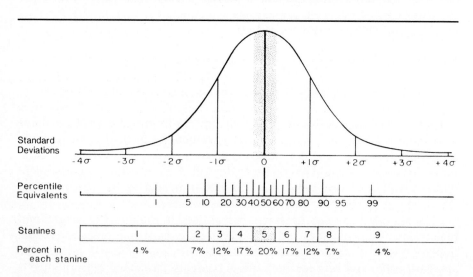

Figure 1-1. Normal population distribution.

given in English becomes, in part, a language or literacy test (American Education Research Association, 1985). Often assessment specialists recognize the discrepancy between the population for whom the test was developed and the population on whom it is being used, but they fail to take actions to avoid the inappropriate use of the information (Salvia & Ysseldyke 1988; Sattler 1988). Accurate measures of the academic performance of large groups of students are difficult and expensive to develop. In determining the appropriateness of using the norming sample to make comparisons with a new population, it is the similarities and differences in students' experiential background that must be considered, not the ethnicity or race of the students. Factors such as visual or auditory impairments, socioeconomic and geographical differences, and prior instruction and learning all influence students' experiential background. If the differences between the norming population and the target group are substantial, then it is inappropriate to generalize about the performance of the target group by using standardized data from the norming population.

What happens if the currently available tests are determined to be inappropriate for the target population? What other alternative measures can be used to assess the current progress of these students or make predictions of their future performance? Some leaders have suggested that all forms of standardized assessment be eliminated in testing culturally and linguistically diverse students. Others suggest that special standardized procedures be used with culturally and linguistically different students. Manipulation of statistical procedures to minimize the bias in errors and to increase the accuracy of the assessment has become a recent approach (Boyan 1985). Arguments about the use or elimination of standardized instruments have raged for the past several decades (Sattler 1988). These arguments have produced volumes of literature (Barona & Garcia 1990), but few substantive results (Figueroa 1989).

Interpreting standardized norms.

By definition, standardized achievement results ensure that approximately 50% of the students taking the test will be above the mean and 50% will be below. The largest portion of the students will score in the middle range between the fourth and sixth stanines. Students performing at either end of the range, at the first or ninth stanines, may have only missed or correctly answered a few more questions than students whose scores were centered more toward the middle of the group. These differences do not necessarily indicate the students' full ability or their limitations in participating in the school curriculum. Inferences are made about students' current performance, future achievement, and potential ability based on this information.

Precision in using and providing assessment information is important. The inches must be the same size if we are all using a 12 inch ruler to measure a foot. In order to be considered generalizable, standardized norms must be applied in the ways in which they were developed. When test data are obtained from

NELB students, caution must be used in interpreting the results. Appropriately applied standardized tests may tell us how discrepant the NELB students' performance is from the norm or the mainstream. This information can be helpful in planning an instructional program to ensure successful achievement for all students. In order to provide legally and pedagogically defensible information, it is recommended that assessment instruments not be used in a destandardized manner. More appropriate uses of such measures would include obtaining information regarding the student's base line of functioning and progress in acquiring language and the content being assessed (Loyola, McBride & Loyola 1991).

Interpreting risking conditions.

Students who achieve below the average of their class or school tend to have many learning difficulties and present a strong picture of being at risk of educational failure. Two groups of students tend to score below the 40th percentile, those who are handicapped and those who have not yet developed English language proficiency equal to that of their age peers. Standardized tests do not differentiate between lower levels of achievement that are the result of a disability and those that show a lack of English proficiency. Students who score in the lower range, at or below the 40th percentile or the 4th stanine, are at high risk of educational failure. Statistically, this represents approximately 40% of the population. These students tend to repeat grades, leave school before graduation, and participate in antisocial activities with negative consequences (Damico et al. 1990). Educators are beginning to conceptualize low performance as an indication of a need for specialized instruction and support and not necessarily as an innate characteristic of the student (Garcia & Ortiz 1988). In Figure 1-2 the shaded areas of the normal population distribution curve indicate the levels where students are at risk of educational failure.

Promoting standardized data collection procedures.

The standardization process requires uniform methods for collecting assessment information. Results can be influenced both negatively and positively. Interpersonal interactions within the testing situation, such as the way the tester looks or speaks, can influence students' perceptions and modify the results. Culturally and linguistically different students' perceptions may be different from those of mainstream students in terms of what is anticipated or considered appropriate (Gibbs & Huang 1989; Phinney & Rotheram 1987). One of the differ-ences that has been well identified is these students' responses to unknown and familiar adults. Culturally and linguistically different students are less likely to provide unknown adults with as complete versions of their performance as they do with familiar adults, such as teachers with whom they work on a daily basis.

One of the many methods professionals use to assist students in trying to obtain representative assessment information is to alter the norms. There are many ways to alter norms. One way is by accepting an answer from a bilingual student in either language and marking it as though it were given in English. If the norms were developed to include responses from other languages, then the responses could be accepted if they fit the norms. If the norms were developed using only English responses, then the acceptance of responses in other languages invalidates the norms.

Some professionals argue that to fail to give the student credit for correct responses in another language is punitive. If a student can provide a substantial amount of correct information in another language, these responses should be reported and included in the evaluation report. It is essential to obtain as much information about a student's performance as possible, especially if the student is experiencing learning difficulties. In a formal assessment, in order to maintain the standards established by the test instrument or process, students cannot be given credit for information provided in another language, if the test was normed only in English. Formal tests are not the only or even the best source for obtaining information on student performance.

Other concerns must be addressed when the assessment process moves away from the use of standardized instruments toward the use of methods and materials more reflective of the target students' prior background experiences. The materials and procedures may be more responsive to the students' needs, but they may not reflect the training and experiences of the school personnel who are to use them. This concern is the topic of the next subsection.

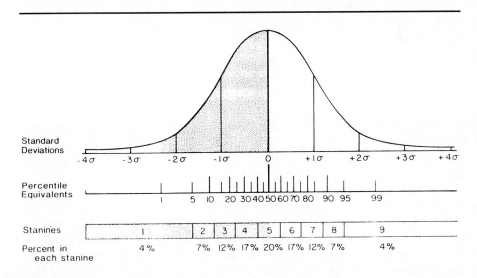

Figure 1-2

RESEARCH IN PRACTICE:
Using the Concept of Standardization

Summarize the concept of standardization. What does standardization mean in terms of the interpretation of test results? What does it mean in terms of collection of assessment information? How does this concept apply in the collection and use of assessment information in your school? How can educators learn to work together to observe students' performance?

ADDRESSING THE CONCEPT OF VALIDITY

From a practical standpoint, assessment *validity* refers to the appropriateness of the test or assessment procedure for a student or group of students. Does the test item or procedure measure what we want to know? Assessment validity is important because many times we are required to determine students' performance based on a specific measure, usually a norm referenced or criterion referenced test.

The term *norm-referenced tests* refers to instruments that have been administered to large groups of students according to specific guidelines so that the sample of people taking the tests is representative of the population in general who might be expected to perform the tasks assessed, such as for example, all fourth grade students. By following specific statistical procedures, if a sample of people taking the test is large enough and includes a broad range of academic abilities, then the results of the test can be generalized to indicate where, within the population range, the performance of a specific student falls. In terms of assessment, *criterion-referenced* refers to tests that require a student to demonstrate a specific performance level such as 80% or 90% of all the items correct in order to indicate mastery of a specific body of information or a specific skill.

When we review the results of a criterion-referenced or norm-referenced assessment for a particular student, we may disagree with the reported outcomes. We may determine from our personal observations that the student's performance is either higher or lower than the results reported by the test. When there is a discrepancy between what teachers observe and what tests report, teachers tend to discount the validity of the standardized tests or the information provided by them. The whole standardized process may appear to be a waste of time. It would be easy to dismiss the discrepancy between observed and documented results by believing that teachers really don't know what students can do anyway. That could be true. It could also be argued that the amount of funds expended to develop tests that would be representative of linguistically and culturally diverse students could be better expended in other areas since, by definition, the results will never fairly represent the performance of students who are a minority within the population.

Standardized assessment procedures do have a role in U.S. education. Arguments to the contrary, nationally normed tests do provide important data with respect to the performance of culturally and linguistically diverse students in comparison with other groups or with the total population. Using national, state, or district norming information, specific school and district norms can be generated for different discrete groups of students such as recently arrived immigrants, students from single parent homes, and students in free or reduced lunch programs. With respect to an individual student's performance, standardized tests can indicate the discrepancy between a student's performance and the performance of the mainstream group. But standardized test results do not indicate whether this discrepancy results from some innate difference or from differences between the experiences of the mainstream and the individual. Neither does this information reveal whether an individual or a group of students had the opportunity to learn the material being assessed.

Applying the concept of validity.

The concept of assessment validity can be applied in a number of circumstances. Consider, for example, some of the widely used language proficiency and dominance tests to determine entering students' proficiency in English. On the initial administration, the test appears to underrate the students' ability to communicate in English. They are able to do more in interpersonal interactions than the test says they can do. However, on successive administrations of the test, the results indicate that the students have greatly improved in their English proficiency. According to the test, these students may be exited from special English language programs because of performance in English. Yet when these same students are placed in regular English language instructional programs, they appear to be limited in their ability to participate successfully. Some educators refer to these students as *born again LEPs* because they appear to have regressed to a former, more limited, state of English proficiency.

With respect to test validity, there are a number of explanations for discrepancies between teacher observation and reported test results. The test may, for example, have underestimated the students' English proficiency because they were not accustomed to performing in this type of test taking situation. Or the test items may have required specific information with which the students were unfamiliar. Later, after the students had been enrolled in the program and had become acquainted with testing procedures, materials, and specific items, the test may have overestimated their proficiency with the larger context of the English-only classroom. A measure of English proficiency may not be valid for the purposes for which it is used.

A more accurate, or valid, measure of students' English proficiency could be the observation of their behavior in a number of situations where they are expected to perform in English. Observational settings would include both social and academic environments. Students could also be interviewed to obtain their perceptions of their performance and ability to perform in English. Such observations are time consuming and difficult to standardize so that all students receive equal opportunities to demonstrate their ability to perform.

RESEARCH IN PRACTICE:
Addressing the Concept of Validity

Summarize the concept of assessment validity. What does it mean in terms of non-English language students in your school? Is test validity ever discussed? What can you do to make the assessment process valid for your students? Are there procedures and instruments that seem to be more valid for your students? Why do you find them to be more valid?

APPLYING THE CONCEPT OF RELIABILITY

The term *reliability* refers to the capacity of the measurement process to consistently and accurately measure students' performance. In other words, the reports of results should be consistent across time. Of course issues of test exposure, learning, and maturation also must be considered in discussing a test's reliability. The above example of a language proficiency test under- and overestimating students' performance in English indicates that it was not a reliable means for determining students' English language proficiency. At the same time we must consider that no formal assessment instrument may be a reliable or valid measure of language proficiency over an extended period of time. Students are in the process of learning and growing intellectually as well as linguistically. No single instrument may be able to keep pace with this growth.

Correlations of different English language proficiency tests indicate that language proficiency tests are not accurate or reliable predictors of students' ability to perform academic reading and math tasks. Proficiency tests are not highly correlated with each other. Different tests measure different aspects of language performance. Trained teachers' ratings of students' English language proficiency have been found to be more reliable predictors of their performance on academic measures than proficiency tests (Ulibarri, Spencer, & Rivas 1981).

RESEARCH IN PRACTICE:
Applying the Concept of Reliability

Summarize the concept of assessment reliability. What does it mean in terms of non-English language students in your school? Is test reliability ever discussed in this context? What can you do to make the assessment process appropriate for your students? Consider giving students two tests that are purported to measure the same type of information in different ways and report on the outcomes of each test. Were there major differences? Can you explain the differences you observed?

EXAMINING FORMAL AND INFORMAL ASSESSMENT PROCEDURES

Both formal and informal procedures have strengths and limitations. The term *formal procedures* refers to standardized, norm-referenced tests. *Informal procedures* refers to procedures that have not been standardized. These include but are not limited to observations, interviews, organized tasks, elicited and natural language samples, and organized and randomly collected work samples. Typically most informal procedures are locally produced. With the movement toward performance assessment, some school districts and states are using informal assessment procedures as a vehicle for developing new and different types of standardized procedures to be used district and statewide (Berry 1991). This section presents a comparison of the features of current formal and informal assessment procedures typically used by school districts. This information is followed by a brief discussion of the types of procedures being developed under the category of performance assessment. Both informal and formal procedures provide information that can be useful in understanding the needs of non-English language background students. As school personnel become more proficient and judicious in the use of informal measures, the reliance that currently exists on formal measures will decrease.

Strengths of formal assessment procedures.

Standardized formal tests have many advantages as well as limitations. The advantages are presented first, followed by the limitations. Formal procedures can provide information on an individual's or a small group's standing within a larger group. Formal standardized achievement tests can tell a school district about the performance of the limited English proficient students on math computation in comparison with the students' age or grade peers within one school or throughout the district. Standardized information can also be helpful in planning a school curriculum, making a district-wide instructional change, or in promoting equity of educational opportunities. Districts are using such information to assist them in selecting instructional materials and in evaluating instructional approaches with specific language and culture groups, as well as the school population as a whole.

Standardized achievement tests can reveal general areas of deficiency, although they neither tell teachers specific skills in which individuals are deficient, nor reveal the type of information that is helpful in planning individualized instruction. Teachers tend to like certain aspects of the formal assessment process. Ease of administration is one of the teacher-favored aspects. By following specific instructions presented with the prepackaged materials, teachers can be certain they are fulfilling the requirements of the standardization process. Because of the relative ease of administration and scoring, school personnel can be trained in a brief period of time to administer most standardized tests. Because of the multiple choice or short answer format of most standardized tests, a relatively large number of questions can be answered within a brief period of time. In addition to ease of administration, most standardized tests are relatively easy to score. Many are constructed in a multiple choice format, and provide a score key for more complex responses. Most of the widely used achievement tests can be machine scored and reported. The results are returned in district, school, class and individual printouts that can be shared with parents and the community. Most results come with suggestions for interpretation.

Limitations of formal assessment procedures.

Formal testing procedures may fail to accurately assess students' academic progress for many reasons. Tests must be administered according to prescribed procedures with regard to seating, time allocations, and materials. Even after practice, many students fail to comprehend how to complete the test questions. Multiple choice tests are not typically motivating or interesting to complete. They can be extremely frustrating for low achieving students. Frustrated students may void answering the questions, for example, by randomly shading in the bubbles for the test items with patterns and pictures. Other students invalidate the machine scoring process by writing on the tests or the machine scored scan sheets instead of filling in the bubbles. While students may know the answers, they may also require more time than is allocated by the standardized timing requirements to complete their responses.

Some teachers also find the requirements of the standardized testing process restrictive and unmotivating, and the time required for testing excessive. Administration of a full battery of tests to a classroom size group of students may require the better part of several mornings or even a week.

Teachers may fail to respond to the requirements of the testing process due to their lack of motivation or their frustration with the tasks. Because teachers are often not directly involved in the production of standardized assessment information, they may fail to comprehend its utility or to apply the information. They may also fail to see how such information fits into their instructional plans. In order for test information to be relevant to teachers, they must comprehend its utility and know how to apply it. Sometimes the training and skill development necessary for effective use of standardized procedures does not occur.

In terms of expense, there is a broad range of costs depending on the type of test administered. In general the per person cost of tests is relatively low. However, when students are being considered for special education, the total cost, including salaries and benefits to assessment personnel, is estimated to be approximately half of the total cost of special education programs (Shepard & Smith 1983). Some educational leaders suggest that this level of expenditures could be better spent in instruction (Rueda 1989).

Strengths of informal assessment procedures.

Informal procedures have many advantages over formal standardized tests. Informal tests can be administered in multiple languages. Responses to test items can also be accepted in multiple languages or forms of communication. Items or tasks can be developed to reflect the culture and interests of specific groups of students. Since informal assessment procedures can embrace a large range of behaviors as well as specific subject matter, materials and activities can be developed for use in diverse settings. Teachers can informally assess students while walking through the corridors on the way to lunch, on the school bus, or in the park as well as in the classroom. From these interactions, teachers can learn not only about the students' ideas and interests, but also about the ways students organize and present information. Informal procedures can be administered by persons who are familiar with students, thus encouraging students to produce their most complete and representative performances (Fradd, Barona & Santos de Barona 1989). Similar procedures can also be conducted by persons unfamiliar to the students to determine performance discrepancies and to accustom students to interact with a variety of persons.

Limitations of informal assessment procedures.

Such diversity in assessment procedures has obvious limitations in terms of uniformity or reliability of the results produced. The results are dependent on the capacity of the persons who administer them to select and use reliable and valid procedures. Unless they are well trained, educators tend to overestimate their students' performance (Fuchs & Fuchs 1989). Many teachers recognize their limitations and are reluctant to develop or use informal assessment procedures if they have not been trained in using these assessment methods. Without training, teachers tend to find such procedures cumbersome and time-consuming. Fortunately, the movement toward the use of whole language instruction and evaluation is providing educators with the skills and knowledge to generate and use informal assessment information (Goodman, Goodman & Hood 1989). As teachers become more sophisticated in the ability to assess students, support personnel are increasingly turning to them for assistance in making judgments about appropriate placements and types of instruction for students with special needs (Heron & Harris 1987).

Comparisons of formal and informal procedures.

There are no simple solutions to the puzzle of how best to assess students' instructional needs or monitor their progress toward the development of academic and social skills. One of the ways that we can begin to complete the puzzle is through the development of a clear understanding of the strengths and limitations of formal and informal assessment measures. This information is summarized in Table 1-2.

TABLE 1-2. A COMPARISON OF THE STRENGTHS AND LIMITATIONS OF FORMAL AND INFORMAL ASSESSMENT MEASURES

FORMAL MEASURES	INFORMAL MEASURES
• Based on statistical procedures selecting representative norming populations and minimizing bias	• Based on professional judgement and the needs of participating students
• Designed to compare individuals and groups with populations designed to be representative of larger norms	• Designed to compare individuals with themselves and with other small local groups of students
• Administered according to specific, strict guidelines in terms of seating, time, and response mode	• Administered according to the needs of the students and the teachers
• Administered by trained teachers and support personnel, depending on their training and credentials	• Usually administered by teachers but may be administered by anyone interested in collecting the data
• Data collection oriented	• Student and teacher oriented
• Usually English language based	• Based on any language or combination of languages
• Composed of prepackaged, easily scored materials	• Composed of locally generated, not necessarily easily scored, materials
• Usually rely on short, often multiple choice responses	• No fixed length or type of response; responses tend to be lengthy

RESEARCH IN PRACTICE:
Examining Formal and Informal Assessment Procedures

1. Compare the strengths of formal and informal assessment procedures.

2. Compare the limitations of formal and informal assessment procedures.

3. In determining the needs of NELB students, why is it important to be aware of the similarities and differences in assessment procedures?

PERFORMANCE ASSESSMENT: A PROMISING PRACTICE

Researchers and practitioners have long been aware of the limitations as well as the advantages of formal and informal assessment procedures as they currently exist (Oller 1979). Efforts to integrate formal and informal procedures have produced a new approach to assessment, *performance assessment.* This innovation promises to provide the best of both the formal and informal procedures. The limitations inherent within either formal or informal procedures may continue within performance assessment, too. Performance assessment aims to directly measure the desired behavior. It provides a vehicle for assessing both what students can do and what they have achieved within a specific instructional program. Writing is assessed by asking students to write, and problem-solving is assessed by measuring students' real problem-solving skills. Other avenues of performance assessment include open-ended questions, demonstrations, experiments, and group as well as individual projects (Berry 1991).

Strengths of performance assessment.

On a small scale, applications of performance assessment promote the development of portfolios of student work that reveal progress across time. Teachers have traditionally been encouraged to collect, display, and analyze student work. However, the current innovations promote the use of specific activities to periodically elicit students' work as a type of focussed, behavior-based assessment procedure that integrates knowledge and skills. Students are also asked to evaluate and to reflect on their own work. An extension of this type of assessment is believed to access students' ability to take what they have learned in school and apply it in real world situations for which they are being educated. Such assessment practices clearly promote higher order thinking skills as well as the basic skills currently measured in multiple choice tests. Applications of performance assessment procedures are impacting the organization and implementation of the instructional process. Results indicate that this innovation has the potential for generating higher levels of interest and motivation than traditional instructional and assessment procedures (California Department of Education 1990).

Limitations of performance assessment.

While some advocates believe that performance assessment will replace paper and pencil multiple choice tests, to date large-scale applications of performance assessment procedures have not been developed or field-tested. Realizing the potential advantages of directly assessing students' performance, research initiatives are being made to create such assessment opportunities (National Science Foundation 1991). However, there are limitations. The evaluation of open-ended, short answer, essay, and portfolio products is as time-consuming and potentially biased as any other form of evaluation. To minimize subjective bias, teams of school personnel must be trained in instructing students, in working with students to create products to be evaluated, and in using uniform holistic scoring procedures for a variety of products. This time-consuming, labor-intensive evaluation process is far more expensive than standardized formal procedures. Current financial restrictions limit potential opportunities for large-scale research and implementation of this innovative assessment process (Cage 1991). However, school-based implementation of specific performance assessment strategies provides many opportunities for observing students, understanding how they grow cognitively and socially, and how they develop academic skills.

Features of performance assessment.

Performance assessment is an innovation that many educators are just beginning to explore. There are many different activities and tasks that fall within the general category of performance assessment. These promising practices permit teachers to gain a perception of students' process skills, thinking skills, attitudes, group behavior, and creativity. They also enable teachers to discover how to effectively involve students in the learning process. By developing profiles of students' strengths and limitations, these same measures can also be used to evaluate the instructional process within a classroom or within a school. It is recommended that several different methods be combined to provide the clearest picture of student achievement and program effectiveness (Malone 1991). Table 1-3 suggests factors to be considered in choosing assessment methods.

Each assessment procedure facilitates the collection of specific kinds of data. Each also has built-in limitations as to the data that can be collected, the amount of time required for data collection, the types of settings in which the data are collected, and the difficulty in scoring. The formats and languages in which the data are collected can be adapted depending on the students' needs

TABLE 1-3. FACTORS TO BE CONSIDERED IN SELECTING PERFORMANCE ASSESSMENT ACTIVITIES

- Can material that is relevant to the students be integrated into this procedure?
- Can the procedure, including the scoring and the benefits to students, be clearly explained to the students?
- Is the scoring of this procedure relatively easy?
- Does the scoring reflect the weight of various objectives?
- Can the procedure be used in grading students? If yes, is it relatively objective and reliable?
- How many students can be involved at one time?
- Will learning the results of this procedure enable students to improve their performance?
- How much class time does the procedure require?
- Does the procedure encourage learning during the performance of the activity?

TABLE 1-4. EXAMPLES OF PERFORMANCE ASSESSMENT MEASURES

- **Portfolios:** Exemplary illustrations of individual or group work collected from many different potential sources, such as homework samples, pages from student journals, quizzes, projects, class notes, and audio or video tapes.
- **Self-Reports:** Written or oral reports of problem-solving experiences requiring students to reflect on their performance of a task either collectively or individually.
- **Student Completed Checklists:** Task-focussed checklists that enable students to record, monitor, and report progress in accomplishing learning goals. Checklists can consist of pictorial as well as written items.
- **Structured Interviews:** Two types—(a) specific questions embedded at critical points within a task so that students must reflect and respond about what they have done, what they are doing, and what they plan to do; (b) general questions structured to encourage students to reflect on overall performance and to gain insight into their accomplishments, attitudes, and capabilities.
- **Content Essay Questions:** Questions on subject matter content typically responded to in written essay form, but which can also be adapted to oral responses. As opposed to the simple content essay items, questions may include concrete situations requiring action, analysis, or evaluation in reporting an important historical event, or in acting as the leader of a group about to make a critical decision.
- **Hands-on Performance-based Tasks:** Students are required to complete a task or demonstrate a skill. Performance measurement can include both the process of task completion as well as the final product.
- **Observation:** Specific focused examination of task performance. Peers as well as teachers can be involved in the observation process through the use of checklists during specified time segments.
- **Inventories:** Self-reports of preferences, accomplishments, and limitations. This type of assessment can be useful in determining students' interests, their perceptions of their performance, and their preferences in planning future activities.
- **Curriculum-based Assessment:** Frequently repeated, timed samples of students' performance in skill areas such as reading and math. Data can be graphed and monitored in terms of student progress and effectiveness of instructional techniques.

**TABLE 1-5. SALIENT FEATURES OF PERFORMANCE
ASSESSMENT MEASURES**

Method	Number of Students	Preparation Time	Scoring
Portfolios	large group	short	holistic, lengthy, complex
Self-Reports	large group	short	lengthy, complex
Student Completed Checklists	large group	long	short
Structured Interviews	individual or small group	long	lengthy, complex
Content Essay Questions	large group	short	holistic, lengthy, complex
Hands-on Performance-based Tasks	large group	varies	holistic, lengthy, complex
Observation	individual	short	holistic, short
Inventories	large group	varies	objective
Curriculum-based Assessment	individual or group	varies	objective

and the instructional resources of the programs. The measures described in Table 1-4 illustrate collection methods typically considered as examples of the process assessment (Council for Exceptional Children 1988, Malone 1991). Table 1-5 provides specific information on these data sources. Where group administration is indicated, the same measure can be administered to individuals or small groups and scored as if it were administered to a large group, once the holistic scoring criteria have been established.

RESEARCH IN PRACTICE:
Performance Assessment: A Promising Practice

1. Describe the strengths and limitations of performance assessment.

2. What specific skills will teachers need in order to successfully implement programs using performance assessment?

3. Select one performance measure, implement it in your worksite, and report the results.

SUMMARIZING SECTION THREE
The Development of Assessment Concepts

Standardized tests have the statistical properties of validity and reliability in measuring the performance of large groups of students on specific tasks or bodies of information. The information gained from the use of standardized tests can be applied to the performance of individuals on the same measures to determine individual standing within the assessment group. However, standardized assessment procedures may not be valid or reliable measures of NELB students' performance or ability, if the NELB students have not had adequate instruction and opportunities to master the material being assessed. The philosophy of assessment within our national culture applies the information gained through standardized assessment procedures more as a sorting process to determine achievement and ability levels than as a means for supporting student learning. If educators disagree with this approach, then it is up to us in concert with policy makers and assessment developers to determine and use more appropriate procedures. As schools become more diverse and formal standardized measures become less valid or reliable in assessing the academic or cognitive abilities of the students, the use of informal measures becomes more comprehensive and appropriate. Although standardized measures continue to remain strong indicators of the students' performance and continue to play an important role in the process of evaluating programs and materials, their use will be combined with a variety of other sources of information. As school personnel become more sophisticated in their own expertise in assessing students, formal tests will play a less important role in the direct evaluation and instruction of students (Kean 1991; Neill 1991; Reissman 1991). Suggestions have been offered here for alternative ways to examine student performance. Performance assessment examines not only the final products of student learning but the process of achieving final outcomes. These assessment innovations have the potential to impact not only the ways teachers collect data on students, but also the ways students are perceived and the ways instruction is provided.

WHAT CAN YOU DO?

1. **What does the standardization process mean to you?** Why is it important in assessing culturally and linguistically different students to ensure that standardization of the assessment be maintained? What aspects of the concept of standardization are especially important to monitor when collecting and interpreting data on non-English language background students? How can you promote the appropriate use of standardized assessment measures?

2. What do the concepts of validity and reliability mean? Are they considered in the assessment process with non-English language background students in your school? Can you comfortably use these terms to discuss the assessment process?

3. What are the basic differences betweeen formal and informal assessment procedures? Can you clearly explain to colleagues what these differences are and how these differences may impact on the assessment performance of students? Can you effectively participate in a discussion on this topic with school psychologists and speech/language pathologists? Are there differences in the ways that assessment data are discussed with different groups of professionals?

4. In what specific ways is performance assessment currently used in your school? How do teachers currently evaluate student performance? Are there other ways that student performance could be measured? How can this information be shared with other educators to encourage students' active participation and the successful development of academic skills?

SUMMARY OF CHAPTER ONE
Concepts of Instructional Assessment

This chapter has presented an overview of concepts related to instructional assessment. If you have participated in the activities as well as reviewed the contents, you should have a developed insight in the following areas:

• **Changing demographics within your school district and work site**

• **The importance of instructional and assessment procedures responsive to students' prior experiences**

• **Student assessment within your school**

• **The need for assessment procedures that reflect student learning**

In reflecting on the issues of equity of educational opportunity and educational excellence, how do you believe the students in your school are being instructed and assessed? Do you have some new insights about the assessment process in general and your specific role in meeting the educational needs of non-English language background in particular? For the moment you may want to continue to reflect on these insights and observations. After you have worked through the next two chapters, we will encourage you to share these insights with colleagues.

The next chapter, Chapter Two, provides an overview of information on instruction and assessment of limited English proficient students with a focus on data generated within the United States. You may find this information useful in placing the assessment practices used in your school, school district and state in the context of developments on the national level.

Chapter 2

Understanding Second Language Performance

This chapter sets the stage for assessing students' educational performance. Within this chapter concepts of academic and social language are introduced and discussed. Students from non-English language backgrounds may appear orally proficient in social language in English and be assessed as if they were English proficient. They may even be treated as if they were monolingual in English. Many factors influence the ways students develop communication skills and use language in academic and social settings. Before we can begin to assess students' language performance, we need to consider these influences. Treatment of students as if they were monolingually proficient in English occurs when school personnel have not been trained to understand and to differentiate between students for whom English is the only language and students for whom it is a new or additional language.

Our expectation is that, with effective instruction and support, students will become academically and socially proficient in English. In the process of learning English, students do require instruction and support. In order to provide the type of instruction and support that students require to become successful, educators need to be equipped with the assessment skills to observe, probe, and monitor students' progress. While English language tests can be used in this assessment process, in order to accurately interpret the results, professionals need a clear understanding of the differences between students who have developed language in an environment where English has not been the principal or only language of communication and students whose only language is English. These differences include attitudes and beliefs as well as aspects of culture and opportunities for learning. The need for professional development in understanding and using information relevant to the acquisition of English as an additional language is emphasized within this chapter.

SECTION ONE

INCREASING THE PROFESSIONAL KNOWLEDGE BASE

This section has three major purposes: (a) to highlight the relationship between language and cognitive development and to emphasize the importance of an understanding of that relationship in providing effective instructional practices for students in the process of developing English as a new language; (b) to point out the current limitations of the professional knowledge base in working with students for whom English is a new language and to suggest new directions in which the profession is moving to increase professional capacity to meet growing needs; and (c) to provide information on language development that can be used to expand the current professional knowledge base in meeting the needs of NELB students.

THE RELATIONSHIP OF LANGUAGE AND COGNITION

Language proficiency is closely related to intelligence and general ability. For children, the relationship between language and intellectual development is so close that the two developmental areas are difficult to separate (Oller 1983; Rice 1980). Because of the interrelatedness of language and cognition, tests of language performance can also be tests of intellectual ability. Stated in a different manner, developing students' language proficiency can also impact students' ability to think, to perceive, to structure ideas, and to generate meaning from language. Promoting students' language development promotes students' cognitive ability and intelligence (Fradd 1982; Harley 1986). The relationship of language and cognitive development is a potentially powerful, yet little-considered aspect of the learning process (Fradd 1985).

The global relationship.

Evidence of the global relationship between language, cognition, and the measurable changes brought about through language development lies in longitudinal studies of students who develop high levels of language proficiency in two languages in comparison with control groups of similar students who develop proficiency in only one language. After an extended period of instruction and language development, the students who become bilingual achieve higher levels of academic performance and intellectual ability than their monolingual peers as measured by standardized tests (Cummins & Swain 1986; Flores 1981; Harley 1986; Lindholm 1991). The concept of language proficiency is not just an abstract idea, it is central to the issue of the effective education of all students (Harley, Cummins, Swain & Allen 1990). While the focus of this text is on the education of NELB and specifically LEP students, it is important to underscore that the research on bilingual language acquisition is relevant to learners in general, not just a small but rapidly growing segment of the school-age population.

The need to educate students from diverse non-English language backgrounds has changed from a unique situation occurring within a few school districts to a pressing national need, resulting in changes in the measurement of the performance of these students over the past three decades. Changing the knowledge base from which educators operate can make a substantial change in the way that both instruction and assessment are provided. Increasing educators' awareness of the influence of culture and environment on students' performance and providing them with knowledge based on what students do, as opposed to what adults think they do, can significantly impact on the ways that instruction and assessment procedures are conceptualized (Berko-Gleason 1985). The target population of students discussed here is elementary and middle school learners whose learning styles and patterns differ greatly from both older teenagers and adults as well as younger pre-school-age children (Lindfors 1987). Increasing the knowledge base from which educators draw upon to address the needs of NELB students in general and LEP students in particular, requires that we differentiate between an understanding of the folk wisdom of learning and the empirical reality. In the Western Hemisphere where monolingualism predominates, bilingualism and efforts to empower, as well as educate NELB students remain controversial and misunderstood educational topics (Lambert 1990). The purpose of this chapter is to address the folk wisdom and the myths that have developed about second language learning from the body of empirical research that has developed over the past 30 years. This section provides an overview of research on second language acquisition as it relates to the assessment and development of English language proficiency among students for whom English is a new language.

Differentiating competence and performance.

Simply stated, performance cannot be equated with competence. What students do in one language context or learning environment may or may not be indicative of their overall language competence. Many factors influence students' performance. It is up to educators to observe students, determine motivating and inhibiting factors, and provide opportunities for students to use language in ways that promote overall competence (Chomsky 1972).

Although various factors involved in the second language learning process have been recognized, the inter-relationship among these factors has not been widely considered in the assessment and instruction process (Garcia & Ortiz 1988; Ortiz 1987; Russell & Ortiz 1988; Wilkinson & Ortiz 1986). When students' performance in their non-English language is considered, the information may be used as an indicator of limited cognitive ability or communication, rather than a strength or a source of potential cognitive strength (Ortiz & Maldonado-Colon 1986; Wilkinson & Ortiz 1986). Considered within the context of research on proficiency in language learning, it is essential that educators reconsider students' language proficiency from a whole language as well as a skills perspective (Goodman, Goodman & Hood 1989).

RESEARCH IN PRACTICE
The Relationship of Language and Cognition

1. **Explain the relationship between language and cognition. Why is an understanding of this relationship important?**

2. **What is the difference between competence and performance? How might an understanding of this difference affect the process of assessing a student for whom English is a new language?**

THE NEED FOR A COMPREHENSIVE KNOWLEDGE BASE

Limited English proficient students, like students with learning disabilities, are found in all of the states in the union (McGuire 1982). In terms of size, there are approximately the same number of school-age students who have been identified as having handicapping conditions as there are students who have been identified as limited in English proficiency. However, the opportunities for obtaining equitable educational treatments for the two groups of learners are not comparable in terms of personnel preparation and availability of programs and resources.

All fifty states, the District of Columbia and most U.S. territories have personnel preparation programs that provide training and credentialing in special education. Although all states have certification in meeting diverse types of special student learning needs, only 50% of the states have certification in ESOL (Garcia 1991). An additional 10% have endorsements or other types of credentialing in ESOL (Fradd, Gard & Weismantel 1988). Few states have training or credentialing programs in bilingual education. Differences in state requirements make it difficult to generalize about program requirements or learning opportunities for LEP students. (Emphasis here is on the opportunities for educating LEP students because once students have been determined to be proficient in English, they are included in the monolingual population without further consideration of linguistic or cultural differences.) Not all states have special language instruction for LEP students. Even in states where programs exist, services are not available to all the students who need them (Development Associates and Research Triangle Institute 1984; Fradd, Weismantel, & Gard 1988).

States with established standardized assessment criteria for LEP students generally exit students from special English language programs when they are able to achieve somewhere between the 30th and the 50th percentile on standardized tests. Since not all states have established standardized assessment exit criteria, some states limit participation in ESOL programs to two to three years.

Because of the limited opportunities for personnel training, there are limited numbers of educators who are prepared to address the needs of LEP students. Limitations in the number of trained personnel with insight into the needs of LEP students create a cycle of limitations that manifests itself in three areas: (a) few educators prepared to work directly with students and families; (b) few training programs funded and institutionalized to prepare educators to work with LEP students; and (c) limited policies and programs reflective of the needs of LEP students and the school personnel who work with them.

As a result of these limitations, myths or folk knowledge has developed about how children learn languages and the relationship of language to the learning process (Staff 1991). Addressing these limitations and these myths provides a starting point for increasing the knowledge base needed to meet the needs of LEP students.

Training and resource limitations.

While the number of books and materials available for assessing and instructing LEP students and for preparing personnel to work with LEP students has grown rapidly over the past 15 years, the pace of current production has not kept up with the demand. Limitations continue to exist in the available resources and in the preparation of the school personnel who use them, especially in meeting the needs of students who may be both limited in English proficiency and experiencing learning difficulties. Despite the increasing possibilities that teachers will have LEP students in their classrooms, few teachers have been prepared to effectively address the unique needs of these students. An example of the limitations of personnel preparation is found in a recent review of the most widely used current survey books for introductory level special education training. These texts contained a paucity of references to multicultural concepts or content with dealing with topics related to cultural diversity. Practically nothing was included on bilingual language assessment. Most important of all, preservice educators using these texts received insufficient information about the possibilities that they would be expected to teach handicapped and at-risk students who are not proficient in English (Foster & Iannaccone 1991). Without established expectations for professional competencies, the same myths and misunderstandings that currently exist will prevail with future generations of educators.

Limited awareness of what students do.

Educational literature published during the first part of this century up until the early 1960's presented a negative image of bilingualism. This image originated from inaccurate and inappropriate comparisons of bilingual students who were learning a new language with monolingual students who were already proficient in that language. These studies of bilingual students did not take into consideration factors such as socioeconomic level, opportunity to learn, and the fact that many of the students were losing proficiency in their home language in the process of becoming bilingual (Cummins 1984). Some school personnel function under mistaken notions about second language acquisition and bilingualism that continue to prevail because little information has been provided to alter these notions.

People learn languages for many reasons. As adults, people make conscious choices about whether or not to participate in an activity or learn a new language. These choices and alternatives are not always as available to children. When children are faced with the option of expressing themselves in a new language or remaining silent, some choose not to communicate at all. Many cases have been recorded of students who become selectively mute rather than speak a new language. This type of selective mutism is different from the type of silence popularly called the *silent period*, which occurs when students develop receptive language before they become expressive (Krashen 1987). An awareness of the difference between selective mutism and a silent period, when learners develop listening skills before expressing themselves, is just one example of kinds of information required to promote effective instructional practices. The need to differentiate between two similar, yet different, behaviors also illustrates the importance of becoming careful observers of what children do, rather than what adults think they do.

To continue on with this example, children who display a silent period when they first enter an environment where their language is not the medium of communication usually engage in private, inner-directed speech. To the casual observer these students may appear silent. This silent period is typically brief, lasting only a few weeks, until the students become adjusted to their new environment (Saville-Troike 1988). Selective mutism is different. It is more pervasive and long-lasting. It is one of the few options children have to learning and using a language that they do not want to speak. Assumptions have been made and materials developed that treat the silent period as if it were a phenomenon for all second language learners, when in reality it is not (Wong Fillmore 1976; Fradd 1984).

In the western hemisphere where monolingualism predominates, there are many misunderstandings and misconceptions about bilingualism and the acquisition of new languages. These misconceptions, such as the current notion of the silent period, stand in the way of progress in implementing programs that lead to both the equity of educational opportunity and real excellence in education. The authors' own personal experiences as well as the personal experiences of adults and children in the United States attest to these difficulties. Students in U.S. public schools are given instruction in English literacy skills through reading and language arts, as well as subject area instruction from kindergarten through high school. Most colleges and universities require several additional courses in English for graduation. There are few comparable programs for developing proficiency in other languages, even for students who arrive at school orally proficient in a non-English language.

Expectations.

Not all languages are learned peaceably or happily in many places around the world. In environments where bilingualism, even multilingualism, is expected, the development and use of two or more languages may be a fairly straightforward experience. Even so, multilingual people attest to the reality that different languages are learned and used in different conditions. These differences in opportunities and expectations for use yield different levels of oral proficiency and literacy (Spolsky 1986).

During the past several decades there has been a renewed interest in developing proficiency in other languages in the United States. This interest has grown, in part, as a result of information from Canada and other parts of the world on the advantages of bilingualism (Lambert & Tucker 1973). Increased international trade and global competition have also promoted interest in studying other languages and cultures (Lurie 1982; Jorge, Lipner, Moncarz & Salazar-Carillo 1983; Snowdon 1986). As a result of this growing interest, a number of programs have developed that provide second language instruction to English speakers. A review of research findings in the United States corroborate the positive Canadian results. High levels of second language proficiency can be developed without negative impact on the development of English language skills (Genesee 1985). However, the information developed on second language programs for students who are proficient in the dominant language of the school cannot be applied directly to programs for those students who are speakers of other languages and are developing proficiency in English. It is important to distinguish between these two types of second language learning opportunities in developing appropriate assessment strategies.

Changes in expectations and opportunities.

Nationally, educators view the availability of information on meeting the needs of LEP students as a priority in providing effective instruction. Information on language assessment and the development of effective instructional programs has been identified as essential in states that are highly impacted by LEP students (Baca, Fradd & Collier 1990). The need for improved training of school personnel in general to work with LEP students has been recognized by the U.S. Department of Education. The Office of Bilingual Education and Minority Language Affairs (OBEMLA) has established a priority for funding of all Bilingual Education Training Development and Improvement Programs to focus on preparing universities throughout the nation to develop graduate and undergraduate programs in bilingual and ESOL education (Staff 1991b). The Office of Special Education and Rehabilitative Services (OSERS) has established a funding priority to develop programs to prepare personnel to work with minority students in general. Included within this general group of culturally and linguistically diverse students are NELB students and particularly LEP students (Staff 1991a).

RESEARCH IN PRACTICE
The Need for a Comprehensive Knowledge Base

---

1. Why do myths about second language persist?

2. What is the silent period of language learning? How is it different from selective mutism?

3. Why is it important to observe and understand students' behavior in order to provide them with effective instructional services?

ADDITIVE AND SUBTRACTIVE ENVIRONMENTS

There are two types of programs that provide bilingual instruction in the United States: (a) programs for students who are already proficient in English and who want to learn a new language; and (b) programs for students who have a home language other than English and who must learn English in order to participate in the mainstream education process. The intent and the outcomes of these two types of programs are conceptually and programmatically different. Students who add a new language while maintaining and developing English experience *additive bilingualism,* a continued development of English while *adding* a new language (Lambert & Tucker 1972). Additive bilingual language acquisition encourages a learning process where children consistently have at least one language in which they can effectively think, feel, and communicate as illustrated in Figure 2-1a. Cumulative positive cognitive benefits accrue to students who develop native or near-native proficiency in two or more languages. In order to maintain these benefits, one language must be maintained while the other is added. Research with additively bilingual students reveals that in addition to being able to communicate with a larger world, children who become bilingual in an additive environment experience increased creativity, greater problem solving ability, and, in general higher levels of intelligence over time than matched monolingual age peers. This finding holds true even for students categorized as learning disabled (Cummins & Swain 1986).

Subtractive bilingualism occurs in environments where students' home language is not valued and maintained. In this learning environment students generally lose proficiency in their home language as they gain proficiency in the new language (Lambert & Tucker 1972). Students in subtractive environments are encouraged to learn the new language of the larger community as quickly as possible so that they can become like the other students. They, in effect, subtract one language to replace it with another. In contrast to additive bilingual language development, subtractive bilingualism produces powerful negative consequences in addition to the loss of proficiency in the non-English language. Typical bilingual programs in the United States are *transitional,* that is, they are designed to promote the learning of English and content so that students can transition to monolingual classrooms (Fradd & Vega 1987). When the transition to all English occurs, little consideration is given to the maintenance or continuation of the other language (Development Associates, Inc. & Research Triangle Institute 1984). Bilingual education for students who are not proficient in English in the United States is generally a subtractive process.

Approximately 10% of all LEP students in U.S. public schools receive transitional bilingual instruction through federally funded projects. Most LEP students in U.S. schools participate in English-only immersion programs (U.S. General Accounting Office 1987). Students who are enrolled in monolingual immersion programs tend to lose proficiency in their non-English language quickly as they slowly gain proficiency in English. This subtractive process of losing proficiency in one language while gaining it in another can create a zone of risk for LEP learners. Students who are learning English as a new language are aware of the linguistic and cognitive limitations imposed on them by their lack of proficiency in the new language (Cummins 1981; 1984).

The conceptualization of learning environments as factors in the learning process is important in understanding students' language performance. Students functioning within the zone of risk, those students who are losing proficiency in their home language while making limited progress in learning English, may produce similar results on standardized tests as students with bona fide learning disabilities. Using standard measures of language proficiency and ability, it is sometimes difficult to differentiate students who may be learning disabled or communicatively impaired from normal students functioning in subtractive bilingual environments. Figures 2-1a and 2-1b illustrate the additive and subtractive bilingual language learning processes.

RESEARCH IN PRACTICE:
Additive and Subtractive Environments

1. **Explain the concepts of additive and subtractive bilingualism.** Although the information was not presented in the text, what characteristics do you think would be found in an additive language learning environment in terms of (a) students; (b) teacher; (c) teacher training; (d) parents; and (e) community that would support the language learning process? How would those characteristics be different in a subtractive environment?

2. **Is the learning environment of your school additive or subtractive?** What features listed above are present in your environment for supporting communication, academic learning, student engagement, and positive self-concept?

3. **Why is an understanding of additive and subtractive bilingualism important to language assessment?**

Figure 2-1a. Additive bilingual language acquisition. There is continuous progress in the first language (top bar) while the new language (bottom bar) is added.

Figure 2-1b. Subtractive bilingual language acquisition. The first language declines as the new language increases.

THE MYTHS OF LEARNING AND AGE OF ACQUISITION

Many myths have been perpetuated in our society about the ease with which children become bilingual. When we reflect on the belief expressed by many people in the United States that "children can easily pick up a new language," it is curious that our nation has largely remained a population of monolinguals. If becoming bilingual is easy, why are there not more bilingual persons in the United States? Generally, it is monolingual individuals who hold the opinion that becoming bilingual is easy. In part, this perception comes from the observations of childhood bilingualism. Children who can communicate in several languages are fascinating to watch. Children can learn languages, but they are not as effective language learners as adults. Just because they can learn in several languages and the respective cultures does not mean that functioning in two languages is simple or easy. This subsection explores age differences as factors in the development of proficiency in English as a new language.

Age myths.

In order to establish effective instruction programs for students of all age levels and levels of language proficiency, a variety of factors including the types of skills and knowledge acquired most easily at different ages must be considered. Research on the relationship of age of language acquisition and academic skill development comes primarily from countries other than the United States with long-term instructional programs to promote the development of full bilingual proficiency (Genesee 1978; Harley 1986; Lambert 1990). It is up to us to draw upon this knowledge to develop instructional implications for students learning English as a new language in the United States.

Advantages of older learners.

Clear differences exist between the language skills of students who start learning a new language at an early age and students who are older when they start to learn a second language. As second language learners, teenagers and adults with already established literacy skills have clear initial advantages over young children. The greatest advantages displayed by older learners are found in the areas of general comprehension, grammar and vocabulary learning, and performance on abstract thinking tasks. These advantages occur because older learners who have developed literacy skills in one language begin the task of learning a new language with a fully developed system for carrying on the abstract thinking process of acquiring literacy skills in a new language. We all know persons who can read, write, and pass complex literacy tests in a foreign language, yet they cannot make the simplest request in social conversation in the same language. For this reason, learning a foreign language is often viewed as a task requiring a high level of intellectual ability. Such is not really the case. Only the development of literacy skills requires intellectual ability. Developmentally handicapped learners are also capable of becoming bilingual, even multilingual. For evidence of this type of language learning ability, visit any class for trainable or educable mentally handicapped learners in an urban center with larger numbers of NELB and LEP students. You will see students who are equally proficient in two or more languages and who are communicating to the best of their ability using all the languages in which they are proficient. Language learning is not so much a question of ability as it is of opportunity. Positive, effective opportunities do tend to impact in the long term on general ability in terms of the manipulation and integration of symbols, ideas, and concepts.

Advantages of young learners.

Children also have advantages. They tend to be playful and willing to experiment with sounds and symbols. They are generally less anxious about making errors than their older counterparts. They often imitate expressions and ways of interacting and doing things. Children tend to master the phonology, that is, the sounds of the language, and some of the non-verbal aspects of communication such as body movements, more easily than older learners. As a result of this tendency to learn the sounds and movements, children tend to appear as if they are speaking more proficiently than older learners. Children are not usually required to perform abstract tasks. They are not expected to know the names of many items. In comparison with older learners, children receive fewer sanctions for making grammatical errors. In general, the cognitive demands made on younger children to function effectively in the target language are not as great as they are on older learners (Cummins & Swain 1986; Harley 1986).

Age-related Differences.

Age-related language-learning differences appear in comparisons of academic performance on larger groups of NELB students on standardized tests.

Initial research indicates five to seven years are needed to achieve proficiency on standardized academic measures (Cummins 1984). In a comprehensive U.S. study of the length of time required to achieve at the 50th percentile on standardized tests, students were divided into three age groups: 5-7, 8-11, and 12-15. Several important findings came out of this study. The first was that in comparison with their monolingual age peers, the students who began learning English in the 8-11 year old group, not the younger group of learners, were the first to achieve at the average level. A second important finding was that different aspects of language development required different amounts of time to occur in the LEP students. The 8-11 year old cohort achieved the 50th percentile on language arts and math computation measures after only two years of academic instruction. However, four to six years were required for these same students to achieve similar results in social studies, science, and reading.

Students who started English instruction between the ages of 5 and 7 lagged one to three years behind the performance of the students who began at age 8-11 when they reached the same grade level. The younger students remained behind the middle group in overall academic gains. These findings support the hypothesis that older students are more capable academic language learners. It also illustrates the zone of risk that can develop when students begin the second language learning process in a subtractive environment without well-developed literacy skills in their first language.

Although older, the 12-15 year old group had an advantage over younger students; they had developed literacy skills in their first language. The presence of these skills did influence the amount of information they could master in a given period of time. Nevertheless, the older students had the greatest difficulty of all three groups for several reasons. First, they were expected to master a large amount of information in order to catch up to their monolingual age peers with whom they were being compared. Second, the older students had to learn all of the subject matter content as they learned the English language and culture. Third, as teenagers, they tended to be less playful, less willing to take risks, and more vulnerable to the perceptions and reactions of their peers. Over-all, in spite of the fact that these students had well developed cognitive skills at the time they participated in the study, they were vulnerable to the subtractive learning process because of affective aspects of the language learning process. Projections indicate that six to eight years would be required for the older students to achieve at a level comparable to their age peers. Many never reached this level while they were enrolled in high school. High dropout rates should not be surprising in areas where NELB students are expected to compete with monolingual age peers without instructional support (Damico et al. 1990).

The researchers who conducted this study indicated that they did not believe the use of multiple choice, standardized tests was the most appropriate or adequate measure of proficiency or performance. The data did provide a means of comparing the achievement of students from diverse non-English language backgrounds with similar measures of monolingual English proficient age peers. The data provided insight into the length of time required for NELB students to actually enter the mainstream of academic performance. Differences in performance on the subsections of the test distinguished the instructional areas most easily mastered by NELB from those instructional areas requiring additional time and instructional support.

The students in this study were advantaged in comparison with many other NELB students throughout the country. They were enrolled in a school district with a well-implemented ESOL program. This school district also provided home language support in most languages of the participants. The majority of the NELB students participating in this study were from middle-class families who held high expectations for their academic progress. Few students have more advantageous learning conditions in the U.S. than the participants of this study. The implication is that even greater amounts of time may be required for NELB students to achieve at an average level on standardized tests (Collier 1987; Collier 1988; Collier 1989; Collier & Thomas 1989). A summary of research on the length of time required to develop academic English proficiency in the U.S. includes the following findings (Collier 1989):

- There are differences in the length of time required to learn different aspects of the curriculum. These differences are based on the subject areas being tested. Language arts and mathematical computation skills appear to be learned most quickly. Attainment of the 50th percentile requires at least two years of instruction.

- For all students who are educated in two languages, that is to say students with literacy skills in two languages, a minimum of four and perhaps as many as seven years, is required to achieve national norms in the areas of reading, social studies, and science.

- Immigrants beginning to learn English between the ages of 8 and 11, *with age appropriate literacy skills in their native language,* appear to be at the optimum stage for developing academic skills in English. When instruction is provided only in English, they require five to seven years to achieve the 50th percentile on nationally normed standardized tests in reading, social studies, and science. This age group appears to master academic skills in English faster than older or younger students.

- Children under the age of 8 who arrive in the U.S. with little or no prior school experience may take as long as seven to ten years, or perhaps longer, to achieve average performance levels in reading, social studies, and science on standardized tests.

- Adolescent arrivals with little or no prior exposure to English and who are unable to continue to receive instruction in their native language while mastering English and academic skills do not have enough time in high school to develop these skills at an average level.
- In terms of enabling students to participate in the mainstream, consistent, uninterrupted academic instruction and language development are more important than the specific number of hours students are enrolled in a course or program of instruction.

Instructional myths.

The myth of ease of acquisition equates *early acquisition* with *ease of acquisition* (Cummins & Swain 1986). This perception leads educators and policymakers to tend to concentrate bilingual instruction for LEP students in the early grades (Development Associates and Research Triangle Institute 1984). Acceptance of this myth also tends to foster another myth: equation of the use of social language skills with language proficiency. If students sound proficient, then they must be proficient in all areas of language performance. Perpetuation of this myth also tends to diminish educators' awareness of the difficulties students have in developing academic skills and establishing a personal identity within the new language (Cummins 1981). The perpetuation of this myth prevents school personnel from becoming prepared to organize instructional environments to meet students' needs.

Several national studies have been conducted to determine the types of instructional support available in effective bilingual instructional programs (Tikunoff 1984; Tikunoff & Vazquez 1982) and in effective special alternative (English-only) instruction programs (Tikunoff & Ward 1991). The purpose of these studies was to determine the instruction and support required to enable LEP students to be successful in regular classrooms. Of all the significant instructional features found to be important for meeting the instructional needs of LEP students, only two were different from those found to be essential for successful instruction in general. These two were: (a) the use of the students' language and culture in instruction while providing them with instruction that enabled students to learn the culture and expectations of the school (Tikunoff 1984); and (b) student access to and use of the home language in instruction and in interactions with peers (Castenada 1991). Significant instructional practices for LEP students in special alternative programs include:

- Instruction designed to promote active participation;
- Communication that facilitates concept development;

- Lessons structured to promote whole group, cooperative group, and peer interactions;

- Communication that incorporates non-verbal signals as well as specific language to promote understanding, instructional transitions, a classroom structure;

- Communication that incorporates the use of students' non-English language in instruction and peer interaction (Castenada 1991).

Providing students with the instruction and support needed to enable them to be effective learners is not so much a matter of providing entirely new programs as it is a matter of reconceptualizing current programs to provide the flexibility to enable a broad range of students to participate successfully. Younger and older students both represent age groups that are highly vulnerable to the negative effects of subtractive bilingualism. In order for schools to promote effective instructional practices for NELB students who may be at risk of educational failure, educators must be informed about the conditions, the myths of language learning, and the effective strategies that can be implemented to promote successful learning.

RESEARCH IN PRACTICE
The Myths of Ease of Learning and Age of Acquisition

1. **Summarize information on age differences in learning a new language and in learning to perform academic tasks.**

2. **What does the term** *instructional support* **mean?** How might instructional support differ for students who are proficient in English and students who are limited in English proficiency?

3. **Why is it important for educators to understand age differences in the development of language proficiency?**

4. **Compare the ease of learning a first language with learning a new language.** What do these implications have for education in general?

THE COMMON UNDERLYING PROFICIENCY OF LANGUAGE

One of the most important discoveries to come out of the research on second language acquisition is the development of the theory of underlying common proficiency (Cummins 1979; Cummins & Swain 1986). The developing body of research in this area supports the idea that as students learn a language, they develop cognitive abilities, or thinking skills that can be transferred and applied in learning a new language. The cohort of students aged 8-11, cited in the Collier study above, had an advantage over the older and younger students. They had participated in academic instruction and developed literacy skills in their non-English language before they started to learn English. The younger cohort of children, ages 5-7, had received little or no formal literacy instruction prior to entering school in the United States and did not begin learning English with the same background of transferable skills as the older students. The literacy experiences and the resulting cognitive skills provided a background on which the older students could draw. These underlying cognitive skills are referred to as *common underlying language proficiency* (CUP). The CUP hypothesis holds that students who have learned to perform academic tasks in one language have underlying cognitive skills that are transferable across languages. In learning another language this underlying proficiency provides a clear advantage for students who have developed literacy skills (Cummins & Swain 1986).

Separate underlying proficiency (SUP) is an opposing hypothesis about language learning. The SUP hypothesis proposes that language learning consists of discrete units of information, each contained with separate languages within the mind. Neither hypothesis is easily tested. Language development is a lengthy, long-term process. As the Collier results indicate, comparisons of standardized measures cannot be made accurately until students have mastered both the language and the academic skills being tested. Sometimes as many as five to six years are required before noticeable differences appear between matched groups (Collier 1989, Cummins 1984; Cummins & Swain 1986; Harley 1986). However, long-term results do indicate the presence of an underlying proficiency. Students who have achieved literacy in one language achieve literacy skills more quickly and more completely in English than comparable students who have not developed literacy skills in their first language. Students who can apply the underlying proficiency skills can be considered advantaged in comparison with preliterate and non-literate learners. In some cases the advantage may not be observable until students have developed a high level of academic proficiency in English, a period of ten years after they began learning English as a new language (Flores 1981).

Most of the currently available data come from research with immigrant students who were learning a new language as the result of entry into a new country, or with immersion students who were receiving instruction in the new language for all or the greater part of the school day, while their home language skills continued to develop within the context of the home, the community, and the national media, outside the influences of the school. Little data are available on the length of time required by students who were born in the United States of NELB parents to develop academic language proficiency in English. However available data from studies with the U.S. born students provide us with insights. Studies examining the progress of students born in the United States or who arrived at an early age, whose families maintained the non-English language at home, indicate that these students were more successful in academic subjects than similar students whose parents used only English at home (Dolson 1985a; 1985b). In addition to supporting academic achievement in English, the maintenance of the language of the home is also essential for parent-child interactions, in promoting parent participation in the educational process, and supporting continuity among family generations (Wong Fillmore 1991).

The concept of the common underlying proficiency of language has been compared to an iceberg with its tip sticking out of the water. Most of the ice remains invisible under the water; only a small portion of the iceberg can be seen above the water. The visible part can be compared to the most obvious and easily observed aspects of language, the sound, the grammar, and the vocabulary. The aspects of learning most frequently tested in school include knowledge and comprehension. They are also aspects of the visible tip of the iceberg in terms of the development of the foundation of academic success. In both cases, the linguistic knowledge and the conceptual academic foundation, the tip of the iceberg areas, are most visible and easily tested, but are not necessarily the most important aspects of learning or language development. The most important areas of learning include the underlying proficiency of the language, such as the ability to apply information in a variety of contexts, the ability to synthesize information and to draw conclusions and inferences, the ability to analyze information and to determine its relevance and applicability, and the ability to evaluate outcomes and make judgments. These essential skills are less visible, less easily measured, and less observable. They remain, so to speak, under the water, less accessible but more essential to the whole learning process than the more easily measured language skills (Shuy 1981). In considering the development of bilingual language proficiency, the iceberg can provide a good analogy. The concept of the iceberg of common underlying bilingual proficiency is depicted in Figure 2-2.

RESEARCH IN PRACTICE
The Common Underlying Proficiency of Language

---

1. Explain CUP and SUP. What is meant by underlying proficiency of language? Does your school district develop the CUP aspects of students' learning experiences? How can we utilize CUP to promote learning?

2. Which aspects of language proficiency are most easily tested? Why?

3. How would you test the underlying aspects of language proficiency?

4. Is it possible to transfer cognitive skills across languages? The text did not explain how this transfer might occur. What do you think?

THE ROLE OF CULTURE IN LANGUAGE LEARNING

Culture is a mediating factor that influences perceptions, interactional styles, and ways of communicating in the development of language proficiency (Cummins & McNeely 1987; Cummins & Swain 1986; Cummins, Swain, Nakajima, Handscombe, Green, & Tran 1984; Shuy 1981). In referring to Figure 2-2, culture is a mediating variable that influences the ways that the world is perceived and understood. Culture influences the ways in which language proficiency develops and how language is used in communication and interaction (Westby in press b).

Culture is not easily defined or understood. As a concept, culture refers to the customs, beliefs, perceptions, and social institutions and values that characterize every society or group of people. It is the product and outgrowth of human learning. Culture guides people in determining how they feel and how they will act on their feelings. It is the sum of a group's learned behaviors,

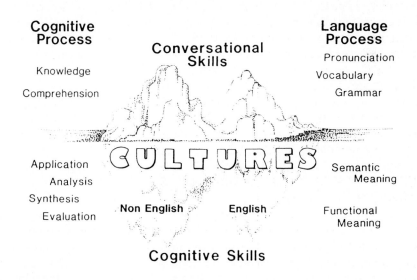

Figure 2-2. The iceberg is a symbol of the more visible and less visible aspects of language proficiency.

attitudes, and material possessions (Hall 1977; Geetz 1973; Goodenough 1981). As an agent of group continuity, culture influences the ways people think and perceive. As a product of people's learning, culture is modified by collective group behaviors and events. People who have similar cultural ties or common-alties may be defined as composing culture groups. Culture is the sum of group experience as expressed by individual members.

High and low context cultures.

The development of literacy and the application of literacy skills vary by culture group or cultural norms. Group behaviors have been classified in a number of different ways. The concepts of *high context* and *low context cultures* is one way of observing and understanding the behaviors of students from diverse cultural backgrounds (Hall 1973). High context cultures are character-ized by group behaviors oriented toward group rather than individual interac-tions and outcomes. People who learn to function within high context cultures live and interact within a group. Group life tends to be highly predictable and, as a result, group members learn to anticipate each other's actions. Information is so familiar that only a limited amount of verbal interaction is required for effective communication to occur. Communication tends to revolve around the resolution of daily life activities. In high context cultures time is not spent explaining information or events that are already well known. Children who grow up in high context cultures learn much of what they know through observation rather than specific verbal instruction. Time orientation is *polychronic*, multiple functions or events tend to occur simultaneously in no specific order or sequence. Children from high context cultures may have difficulty learning to verbalize according to mainstream expectations. They may be reticent to talk about already known topics, and may feel as if they are showing off when explaining something obvious. Activities that require sequencing, planning for the future, or structuring according to mainstream expectations may appear to be foreign to students from high context environments. However, because of differences in culture and in prior learning experiences, high context children may have strengths in understanding and relating to others and in using language as creative and playful forms of expression not generally observed in children from the mainstream culture (Westby & Rouse 1985).

The mainstream culture of the United States is classified as being low context (Hall 1976). Low context cultures tend to have an individualistic, rather than a group, orientation. Members of low context cultures tend to use lan-guage to achieve many functions such as specifying, clarifying, organizing, directing, predicting outcomes, and planning for the future. In low context cultures, children receive specific verbal instruction on how to perform tasks. Children are frequently told or verbally taught how to perform rather than being shown or encouraged to observe adults. They also receive explanations of

the reasons for activities and the consequences of actions. These explanations
focus on categorization, sequence, and cause and effect relations that tend to
structure the ways that children think and perceive. Time orientation is
monochronic, activities are planned, scheduled, and performed in a lineal sequence. This sequence is thought to have a logical progression from beginning
to end. The culture of the mainstream home is congruent with the culture of the
school. When students enroll in school, they generally come with what have
been termed *readiness skills,* skills believed to be essential for effective school
learning (Hall 1976; Westby & Rouse 1985).

Culture acts as an intervening variable in promoting or discouraging the
use of students' languages in various settings (Au 1980; Moll & Diaz 1987). For
example, in some cultures, children are expected to watch, but not express
themselves verbally in the presence of adults. Children in these cultures learn
to wait for an invitation to participate. In other cultures, children may be the
focus of attention. In these cultures, children may be repeatedly asked to
demonstrate knowledge that is well-known to the rest of the group. As a result
of these differences in performance expectations and rituals of participation,
culture must be considered in the context of developing and displaying language skills (Cummins & McNeely 1987; Cummins & Swain 1986; Harley 1986;
Shuy 1981). Because culture structures the ways people think and perceive,
cultural values and perceptions tend to encourage certain types of interactions
and to discourage others. Differences between the culture of the home and
school, the home-school mismatch, can influence the ways teachers and students perceive and relate to each other. Within the mainstream, students who
have been encouraged at home to volunteer information and to ask questions
are perceived as being bright and inquisitive by teachers who share the same
values. Students from cultures where asking questions is perceived as showing
off or revealing one's ignorance tend to watch and learn. These children may
appear uninterested, unwilling, or unable to learn when they interact with
teachers from low context mainstream cultures (Iglesias 1985). Specific differences that significantly affect the ways that students and teachers behave and
perceive include (Greenfield 1984; Westby & Rouse 1985):

- Group versus individualistic behaviors;

- Communication to meet immediate versus future needs;

- Language that obviates or requires elaboration;

- Polychronic versus monochronic use of time;

- Logical, sequential organization of thought versus other patterns of
  organization.

Perceptions and patterns of self-identification.

Students who learn to function in two or more languages and cultures develop diverse orientations toward the use of the language represented within each of the cultures. These orientations or patterns of self-identification can be categorized in at least four different ways (Cummins 1981a):

- **English monolingualism.** Identification with mainstream U.S. cultural values and the use of English, and rejection of the non-English language culture;

- **Positive bilingualism.** Positive identification with both the mainstream culture and the use of English and the non-English language and culture;

- **Limited bilingualism or monolingualism in the non-English language.** Rejection of the mainstream culture and the use of English, and positive identification with and use of the non-English language and culture;

- **Limited communication skills and language development.** Rejection of both the mainstream culture and the English language and the non-English language and culture, and identification with a small subculture separate from either the home or the mainstream identity.

Students may participate in different categories of self-identification as they participate within the educational and the acculturation processes. When students perceive either the home culture or the mainstream culture as making demands that they are unable to fulfill, the tendency is to move toward the culture identification with the language and culture in which success can be achieved (Szapocznik, Kurtines & Fernandez 1980).

School as agents of culture.

In terms of language learning, not only are NELB students expected to master the components of the new language system, the phonology, morphology, syntax, and semantics, but they also must learn the cultural aspect of language performance (Oller 1993). Schools act as agents of the mainstream culture. They instruct students in ways that will enable them to function within the mainstream. To function successfully within the mainstream, students are expected to learn to use language for many purposes, such as planning, predicting, ordering, and categorizing (Tough 1977). For many students the use of language to achieve these purposes or functions is new. Use of language to achieve these purposes may at times be uncomfortable, but with motivation, guidance, and opportunities for meaningful practice, students can learn to communicate in new ways (Vazquez-Montilla 1991; Westby & Rouse 1985).

Culture plays an important role in the development and use of language. The role of culture must be considered in the acquisition and use of language. For example, in some cultures the notion of talking about the process of learning, the observation of one's personal strategies for performing a task, or the monitoring of one's success or failure to comprehend does not occur. Students from cultures where metacognitive skills are not used may not demonstrate these skills in academic English without instruction and support. Once students become aware of the skills involved in producing and comprehending academic language, they may be able to apply the skills within their non-English language to promote achievement (Chamot & O'Malley 1984; Diaz, et al. 1986).

RESEARCH IN PRACTICE
The Role of Culture in Language Learning

---

1. Define culture. What specific aspects of students' behavior have you observed to be related to cultural similarities and differences? How can we discuss these cultural aspects of behavior without being stereotypical or pejorative to one group or another?

2. What information is conveyed by the concepts of high and low context cultures? Do you think you tend to be more high or low context in your cultural orientation? What about the students and the adults with whom you work? Are there interpersonal difficulties brought about by these cultural differences?

3. How does culture influence performance?

4. Why might an understanding of specific cultural similarities and differences be important in assessing students' language performance?

UNDERSTANDING CONTEXT AVAILABILITY AND COGNITIVE DEMAND

Language proficiency is inseparable from academic achievement. One of the most powerful breakthroughs in the development of an explanatory theory of students' academic performance is the framework of context embedded – context reduced, cognitively demanding – cognitively undemanding communication activities (Cummins 1981; Cummins & Swain 1986; Donaldson 1978)

Context availability.

Language skills are often perceived as a dichotomy between oral and literate styles of interaction. In addition to oral and literate language distinctions functioning as a dichotomy, or opposites, language functions can also be perceived as a continuum extending from *context embedded,* personalized interactions to a series of *decontexualized,* impersonal symbols. This contextualized/decontexualized continuum can be visualized as a horizontal plane. The far left represents communication that can be context embedded communication understood from information conveyed within the environment. The far right represents context-reduced language that is abstract, symbolic, and difficult to understand without specific knowledge of the system. Figure 2-3a presents the range of context embedded and context reduced communication.

Examples of contextualized and decontextualized communication abound in the classroom. A teacher holding two balls, a large and a small one, leans forward and asks Tran, "Would you like the large or the small ball?" Tran observes the teacher leaning toward him with a questioning expression on her face and a ball in each hand. He does not have to fully comprehend her words to guess that she is asking him to select a ball. Support for this guess could also come from previous observations of the teacher interacting with other students. Tran smiles at the teacher and reaches for the big ball. Teacher responds by saying, "Oh good! Tran wants to play kickball," and she asks another student,

Context ————————————————————————— **Context**
Embedded   **Reduced**

Figure 2-3a

the small ball to Jimmy. From this interaction it is not clear what Tran actually understood. The explicit feedback the teacher provided, however, enabled Tran and other students like him to associate word and meaning and to build oral comprehension (Wells 1986). It is clear that Tran comprehended the intent of the teacher's communication because it was accompanied by context embedded information.

An example of context reduced communication could be a baseball game broadcast over the radio. Radio communication is more context reduced than television. A baseball fan might be able to listen to the broadcast in an unknown language and, because she has enough prior knowledge about the game and the presentational form of the information, be able to follow along and enjoy the broadcast. A person who is fluent in the language of the broadcast, but unfamiliar with the game, might have difficulty understanding exactly what was happening and not enjoy the game. The person who enjoys the baseball broadcast brings the context of baseball games to the listening process while the native speaker of the broadcast language brings only the words. Additional examples of context embedded and context reduced language are presented in Table 2-1.

TABLE 2-1. CHARACTERISTICS OF CONTEXT EMBEDDED AND CONTEXT REDUCED LANGUAGE

Context Embedded	Context Reduced
Language Examples	
• Oral words and phrases associated with specific events such as greeting and leave-takings	• Communication and discourse such as lectures and written texts
• Ritualized familiar questions	• Science lesson questions
• Conversations with friends about a party they attended together	• Writing a letter to a company for a position
• Small group discussion of a simple hands-on science experiment	• Individual completion of written social studies test
Language Characteristics	
• Frequent turn-taking	• Lengthy paragraph or chapter length language
• Frequent use of slang, short phrases and sentences	• Emphasis on correct, formal language
• Limited word variety	• Emphasis on varied, comprehensive vocabulary
• Use of non-verbal support	• Little, if any, non-verbal support
• Shared, common knowledge of topics between communicators	• Communication on known and frequently unknown topics
• Use of voice intonation, stress and pauses	• Reliance on symbolic representations for support

Cognitive demand.

Not only can language be perceived on a horizontal range of increasing abstraction, but it can also be conceptualized on a vertical range of increasing difficulty. To be effective, instruction must be appropriate to students' levels of linguistic proficiency and development. Initially, all communication is cognitively demanding (difficult) and context reduced (abstract). As students gain an understanding of the interpersonal communication occurring around them, they are able to participate effectively in interpersonal interactions. In children, this interpersonal social language development provides the foundation for academic language development. For example, if students learn to function in a group, they can discuss a class assignment together before beginning the task. As they proceed with the task, they can check each other's work, and gain feedback and support. This type of group interaction is important in developing literacy skills, especially with high context students (Halsall 1985).

The concept of cognitively demanding or undemanding communication tasks is easy to understand. Language at the upper part of the vertical line represents communication activities that are easily carried out. For example, pointing at the sky and making a noise could be understood to mean, "Look, there goes an airplane." At the lower end of the horizontal line is cognitively demanding communication, such as the preparation of a term paper on linguistic symbology. This type of communication is abstract and cognitively demanding. It is dependent on the correct manipulation of symbols and concepts. Figure 2-3b illustrates the range of cognitively undemanding – demanding communication represented by the vertical plane.

Integrating these two continua produces the four quadrant conceptualization of language (Cummins 1984; Fradd 1987a) illustrating contextual support and cognitive demand in communication. To be understood as meaningful, the vertical and horizontal continua must be seen as moveable and changing according to the difficulty of the task and the support provided by the environment for understanding and participating within the communication (Cummins & Swain 1986).

Initially most, if not all, communication is cognitively demanding and context reduced. As students master interpersonal skills and learn to understand communication formats and styles, they are able to function successfully in a context embedded school environment where they observe and relate communication to real world happenings. The intersection point of what is context embedded and cognitively demanding varies by many factors such as an individual's experience with the communication tasks, prior knowledge of the topic, and the presentational format of the communication. The intersection point changes as individuals become proficient with the language and the experiences communicated within the language. Figure 2-3c presents the intersection of the horizontal line and vertical lines.

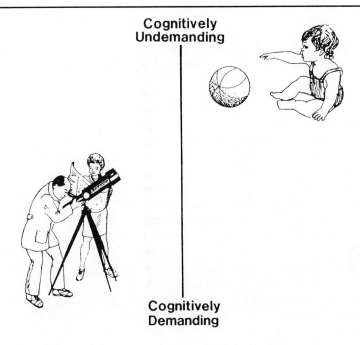

**Cognitively
Undemanding**

**Cognitively
Demanding**

Figure 2-3b

RESEARCH IN PRACTICE
Understanding Context Availability and Cognitive Demand

1. **What do the terms *context embedded* and *context reduced* language mean?**

2. **"The concept of context embedded and context reduced language is cognitively demanding."** Decode this statement and explain it to a colleague.

3. **What do the related concepts of *availability of contextual information* and *cognitive demand* of a task have to do with the information on *age of acquisition?*** Explain how language might be cognitively demanding at one stage in a student's life and undemanding at another. What role does maturity play in learning to use cognitively demanding language? What are the implications for instruction of students who have and have not been exposed to literacy concepts in the non-English language? Explain how the availability of contextual information might support or hinder learning.

4. **How do the concepts of context embedded and context reduced language influence the assessment process?** How do these concepts relate to the assessment of literate and non-literate students?

Range of Contextual Support and Cognitive Involvement in Communication

Cognitively Undemanding

Context Embedded

Context Reduced

Cognitively Demanding

Figure 2-3c

SUMMARIZING SECTION ONE
Increasing the Knowledge Base

This section presented information on the need to increase the professional knowledge base of educators working with NELB students. Current practices are based, at least in part, on myths that have evolved about how children learn rather than on research on childhood bilingualism and second language learning. There are many factors that influence students' performance in communicating and in using language in making meaning. A strong relationship exists between language and cognition. Initially, cognition promotes language development, but as the result of language development, cognition can be influenced either positively or negatively to promote or diminish general intellectual ability. Additive language learning environments promote the development of bilingual ability, creativity, problem solving, and higher order thinking skills. Subtractive language learning environments promote the learning of a new language at the expense of the first language. There is a common underlying language proficiency that exists across languages. The development of one or several languages can promote the development of children's general intellectual ability. As a result of this underlying proficiency, cognitive skills developed in one language can promote the development of similar higher order skills in another. This underlying proficiency is not as easily observed or tested as the more obvious language and academic skills such as grammar, pronunciation, and vocabulary, or knowledge and comprehension. However, underlying proficiency can be observed in longitudinal studies of bilingual and monolingual students. Longitudinal research reveals that major cognitive gains are found in favor of bilingual learners.

When children initially begin the process of learning a new language, everything is cognitive demanding and context reduced. After gaining experience in the language, students learn to observe the environment for clues about the meaning and intent of communication. Within the school setting, context reduced language refers to language that is dependent on the specific understanding and manipulation of symbols. Students who have had experience in developing literacy skills in one language can transfer this knowledge to the mastery of literacy skills in a new language. Factors such as age of arrival as well as prior literacy knowledge influence the learning process. Students between the ages of 8 and 11 appear to be at the optimal age for learning a new language if they have already developed literacy skills in one language. Those students require the least amount of time in developing academic skills in a new language.

Culture also influences language development and use. Students from low context cultures tend to use language for planning, organizing, sequencing and predicting. Students from high context cultures tend to use language for rapport building, for specifying and naming. Each culture brings specific expectations for how language is used and how children are to participate and interact with adults. Because the culture of the school represents the dominant culture of the nation, NELB students with cultural orientations that are congruent with the mainstream culture appear to learn English and to acquire the necessary cultural skills for effective participation, unlike some students from cultures that are different from the mainstream.

WHAT CAN YOU DO?

1. **Reflect on the information presented within this section.** Make a list of terms and ideas used to convey an understanding of the difficulties involved

in learning a second language on par with one's age peers. Explain the information to your colleagues.

2. How do the hypotheses of age of acquisition and context reduced language relate to the needs of LEP students in your school? What can you and your colleagues do to support effective language instruction? How does this support relate to instruction in social studies, science, and reading?

3. Plan an assessment process that addresses language proficiency development from the standpoint of the availability of contextual information and cognitive demand. How is your plan different from current practice?

SECTION TWO

THE NEED FOR RESEARCH AND HYPOTHESIS TESTING

During the past 30 years the amount of research available in the area of second language acquisition has grown substantially. However, much still remains to be discovered on how languages are learned. As was discussed in the first section of this chapter, educators have not been kept well informed about the process or variables that influence learning a new language, while at the same time mastering the content of subjects typically taught at school. There are many ways that the limitations of personnel preparation can be overcome. One important way is through the involvement of school-based personnel in the extension of research and development of new knowledge, as well as its applications.

Involvement of school-based educators in the research and development of new knowledge is important for several reasons. Through involvement and participation in research, school-based personnel increase their own personal repertoire of skills. They gain insight into the process of developing and refining questions, and seeking information to answer the questions being posed. They become clearer in their own thinking about the topics under consideration. And, more importantly they have the potential to make important contributions to the field.

School-based educators are often uncomfortable in discussions of theory and research. The idea of conducting research may be seen as something that other people do in other places, usually ivory towers, that has no real bearing on what happens in schools. Research may be seen as unrelated to the real work of schools. As a result of the activities proposed in this book and the ideas you generate, educators may develop their own research agendas and make discoveries about the process of language learning and the assessment of language skills. Information is presented in this section to encourage you to develop your own field studies and to become a part of the group of contributors to the area of second language learning.

THE VALUE OF THEORY AND HYPOTHESIS TESTING

Recently, during a week-long training in the area of bilingual special education with representatives from school districts in a state highly impacted by the presence of LEP students, representatives were to develop a plan for an 18 hour course they would provide for personnel in the districts they represented. As a requirement of the training, participants had to develop an agenda for the course. During the first two days of training there were many requests for developing a draft of a training agenda as a guide for the participants. Near the end of the week, one of the participants asked anxiously if everyone was required to follow the agenda. Reassured that she did not have to use the draft, she replied, "Great, because I could get through that theory part in about 15 minutes, but what I really need time for is the practical stuff." This example illustrates the frustrations that university and school-based personnel experience when collaborating with each other. School-based educators are faced with pressing, practical, real world needs, and often do not see the importance of foundational information on which to base educational programs, plans, and decisions. Because most researchers are based at universities and centers where they present information to students and colleagues, they must be able to discuss their work from a theoretical perspective. Even the most practical, applied researchers are often considered theoretical in the eyes of the school personnel whose practices they hope to influence. In order for the research in second language acquisition to be meaningful, researcher-type educators must become practical and cognizant of the constraints of time and resources within the school system. At the same time, school-based educators must become comfortable and knowledgeable in discussing issues from a theoretical as well as a practical perspective. Our intention is to encourage collaboration in promoting interactions that lead to new insights and understanding in this field.

There are other reasons, in addition to the reluctance of school-based personnel to enter into theoretical discussions, why research generated in the field of second language acquisition or bilingual education has not been considered applicable or relevant in school or district-based decision-making. In the past, policymakers and researchers have tended to ask simplistic, unanswerable questions such as, "Which program is best?" without clearly examining specific requirements, or design and implementation factors (Cummins & Swain 1986). Educational decisions are highly impacted by political philosophies and politics. Policymakers and educators have been reluctant to consider research results that did not agree with their own political philosophy or prevailing conventional wisdom about how children learn. Sometimes they chose to use the explanation that not enough research has been conducted as a means of avoiding the harder questions of how and when to apply what is already known to current settings (Schmidt 1991).

A substantial body of research currently exists on which we can draw to promote understanding about how students learn a new language. Some of the critical factors influencing educational outcomes in terms of learning English as a new language have been presented within this chapter (Cummins & Swain 1986; Harley 1986). Research findings have an important value.

Although the conclusions from these research findings cannot be applied directly across instructional situations, we can develop theories and test hypotheses. This theory generation and hypothesis testing process enables us to account for a variety of factors involved in the learning process. The process also enables us to make predictions about what students will do in different learning environments and to organize environments that we predict will produce the most effective results. The value of theoretical principles lies in their ability to account for research findings in a variety of contexts. If a theory cannot be used to account for a particular set of outcomes, then it is incomplete or inadequate and requires further development (Cummins & Swain 1986; Mishler 1990).

Developing and testing hypotheses.

Recent breakthroughs in the conceptualization of research have led to more coherent, collaborative approaches that bring teachers and researchers together (Chilcott 1987; Goswami & Stillman 1987). Traditionally, research posed questions and designed ways to answer them. However, this approach made suppositions about the research population that may not have been accurate or may not have been accounted for within a traditional research paradigm.

In contemporary schools, there are many variables that must be accounted for, such as the cultural and linguistic diversity of the students and the faculty. Even in a single classroom, students may have had a range of diverse experiences that lead them to think and perceive in ways that are different from each other and from their teachers. Meaningful observations, accurate descriptions, and representative interpretations of students' and teachers' behaviors and perspectives can provide understanding for both the interactions and learning outcomes. Case studies, oral histories, and narrative analyses are examples of applied research approaches that provide meaning and insight into the instructional process (Allendar 1986). These forms of research can be used to support and supplement each other in increasing educators' understanding of their students (Mishler 1990).

Where previous research paradigms attempted to create laboratory-like experimental designs with carefully controlled variables, the innovative, action- oriented approaches of the emerging paradigms function on the premise that research is done to illuminate and to develop understanding. This does not rule out experimental designs, but suggests that both large and small scale research agendas are important and contribute to a general understanding of the learning process. The difficulty with large scale experimental designs is that they fail to account for diversity or to address the learning processes of small, diverse groups of students (Solomon 1991). Researchers, like teachers, need to know and understand the participants as well as the data they are collecting (Goswami & Stillman 1987). As teachers' perspectives and students' voices are brought into the research agenda, the questions become modified to incorporate the insights and the understandings of these essential participants as well as the larger mainstream concerns (Gitlan 1990; Martin 1987).

Focussed observation permits meaningful description, which in turn provides insight, and leads to hypothesis development and testing. We describe situations and develop and test hypotheses as part of our everyday work. Consider that we are in the process of collecting data on a specific student who is experiencing learning difficulties in reading. As we collect this information, we naturally begin to think to ourselves, " I believe this student is responding in this way because .... " That belief statement is based on a focused observation that becomes the basis for developing a hypothesis about the student's performance. Following that thought we develop a hunch (or form a hypothesis) about what the student is doing. We follow up on our hunch (test the hypothesis) by making some changes in the room or in the instruction (intervention or alteration of variables) and we watch to see what happens (monitor and observe the related behavioral outcomes). Observation, hypothesis testing, variable alteration, and monitoring are all part of the instructional day. However, when we talk about them in research terminology, they tend to sound and appear different. These behaviors may, in fact, be different in the sense that in an empirical research agenda we would establish specific criteria for observing the students, we would create methods for monitoring and recording changes, and we would determine beforehand the criteria for evaluating the potential changes that might occur when variables were altered. The process remains the same.

Now let's translate this behavior into a real world situation. One day we notice that the student is having difficulty paying attention in a reading group. We ask a colleague to come in and watch the student with us. As we watch, we notice that the air conditioning vent is right over the reading table and the air frequently blows on the students as they are seated together at the table. The student in question has learned to be polite and respectful, but has a hard time paying attention when she is cold. The observer begins to wonder if the cold blast of air conditioning is influencing the student's attention and responses at the reading table. Our hypothesis is that the student in question is not behaving appropriately and does not appear to be learning because of the cold environment surrounding the reading table. In order to test the hypothesis, we change the location of the reading activities and observe for behavior changes. Soon we determine if the change in location makes a difference in performance. We continue to monitor and to collect other evidence. There is a constellation of factors that could influence this student's performance in reading. We may or may not have selected one of them. The air conditioning may be the most obvious and pressing difficulty, but it may not be the only one. As we continue to observe, we may consider the appropriateness of the instructional material in relation to the student's ability to understand and respond to instruction. We also continue to develop and to test new hypotheses about this student's prior experiences in relationship to current needs.

Once an hypotheses has been tested and found to be valid, it can be used to predict and modify future behavior. For example, if we observe that all the students who are recent arrivals from the Caribbean have difficulty sitting in areas where the air conditioning blows directly on them, we can predict that Juana, who recently arrived from the Dominican Republic, will have difficulties with the air conditioning. We may not always be able to change the seating or turn off the air, but we can reconsider the times specific students work in different parts of the room. The rest of the students may be enlisted to assist us in organizing the room. To facilitate their support, we may want to have a geography lesson on the similarities and differences among the climates of the countries and geographical regions represented by the students of the class-room. Just in case, we may also want to have a few extra sweaters available for tropical students.

The strategies used here are not really new. Effective teachers have always observed their students and modified instruction accordingly to meet observed needs (Saxon 1991). The difference between this type of individual effective instruction and the model proposed here is that with the press for time, teachers may not always gain or share these insights and observations. They may not have the time to observe students and reflect on their behavior. In addition, teachers, like many other educators, may not have had the individual experi-ences that make them sensitive to the variety of needs of students from diverse cultural and linguistic backgrounds. Educators cannot be expected to be sensi-tive or be aware of all the subtle differences that influence class participation and successful learning. By working together, they can observe and share insights. Current action research involves collaboration and problem-solving by bringing together a variety of people within an instructional context. Shared problem-solving encourages global, goal oriented thinking. It also provides a vehicle for modeling the use of higher order thinking skills with students by involving the students themselves in the process (Farrell, Peruero, Lindsey, & White 1988).

RESEARCH IN PRACTICE:
The Value of Theory and Hypothesis Testing

1. **What do teachers need to be involved in research?**

2. **What are some of the difficulties of collaboration in research between universities and classrooms? What are some of the benefits?**

3. Describe the process of generating a hypothesis and testing it.

4. Apply the process of generating and testing hypotheses to the following situation: A school is implementing a new whole language reading and language arts program. Students in a first grade class are being exposed to the process of learning to read through writing and exchanging materials such as stories, poems, letters, and other literacy forms. The students are all middle class; all attended kindergarten prior to entry into first grade. Many of the students are bilingual in English and Spanish. Even though many of the students are bilingual, none of the students who are proficient in Spanish are as proficient in English as they are in Spanish. The first grade teacher observes that the students who are Spanish proficient exhibit reading and writing behaviors that distinguish them from the monolingual English speakers. The Spanish proficient students seem to be less constrained by a need to conform to the conventions of orthography than the English proficient students. As a result, the Spanish proficient students are more willing to attempt to write many words that they do not know how to spell. Their letters and stories in English are longer and more complex than the writings of the English proficient students, even when the bilingual students appear to be less proficient in oral English than the English proficient students. The English proficient students appear to be more concerned with getting the correct form than with communicating their ideas in writing. The teacher has discussed the importance of writing and value of being able to put one's ideas down on paper, even when the words have different spellings. She remains at a loss to explain the behavioral differences she continues to observe between the two groups of students, and to organize instruction that will enable the English proficient students to become more expressive in their writings while also encouraging the Spanish proficient students to become more accurate in their use of form and spelling. Generate several hypotheses regarding the behavior differences of the English proficient and Spanish proficient students, and suggest specific procedures that can be used to test these hypotheses within the classroom.

SUMMARIZING SECTION TWO
The Need for Research and Hypothesis Testing

The second section of this chapter is brief. It contains a short overview of the value of educational research and theory development. The purpose of this section is twofold: (a) to promote collaboration between school and universities in developing the knowledge base needed to identify and meet the needs of NELB students; and (b) to encourage educators to become aware of generating and testing hypotheses as a means for determining students' needs.

WHAT CAN YOU DO?

1. What is educational theory?

2. Why is it important for school-based educators to become involved in research on second language acquisition?

3. What is an hypothesis? How do you develop and test hypotheses? Give examples of hypotheses that you have developed and tested.

4. What is action research? Describe an example of action research that you have conducted or that you would like to conduct.

5. How does research relate to the development of theory?

6. How is educational theory relevant to educational policymaking and to classroom instruction at the school level-based? Are there other ways educational theory influences educational services for LEP students?

SUMMARY OF CHAPTER TWO
Understanding Second Language Performance

In this chapter we have examined aspects of second language acquisition that impacts on the ways that educators conceptualize and comprehend the language acquisition process. We have discussed the need for collaboration between university-based and school-based educators in generating reality based information on how students learn. Topics of language acquisition and the variables that influence the acquisition and use of language are central to this necessary collaborative effort. Chapter Three builds on the information presented in this chapter by providing both theoretical knowledge of language proficiency and specific practical suggestions for assessing student performance using this information.

Chapter 3

Assessing Oral Language Development

The assessment of students' language performance is one of the first actions that schools take in identifying students' needs. For students learning English as a new language, this assessment process is vital to their appropriate placement and instruction. The language assessment process can provide educators with a great deal of information, not only about the ways students sound and communicate, but also about the ways they perform and think (Rice 1983). Much of the information that is obtained through assessing students' language is not used as effectively as it might be. Sometimes this information is even misunderstood and misused because educators have not been trained to collect or interpret the information effectively (Willig 1986).

Chapter Three addresses the topic of oral language performance in relationship to school achievement. The purpose of this chapter is to provide general information on important aspects of the language assessment process. The chapter reviews communicative aspects of language proficiency and discusses a variety of ways for observing and measuring academic language. Within this chapter specific elements contributing to the overall measurement of language proficiency are discussed. Suggestions are offered for conceptualizing the elements of oral language proficiency and for using informal assessment procedures in determining and monitoring students' language development. The chapter concludes with information contrasting limited language development with language impairments.

SECTION ONE

IDENTIFYING THE ELEMENTS OF ORAL PROFICIENCY

Within this section, information is provided about the general process of assessing students' oral language proficiency. A discussion of performance assessment procedures typically used in measuring students' progress and achievement was provided in Chapter One. In this chapter, the discussion focuses on a variety of informal measures of oral language performance. Differences between formal and informal assessment procedures were discussed in Chapter Two. While standardized procedures contribute to the assessment process, the use of more informal measures is also important. Informal performance measures enable educators to examine what students do to communicate meaning. A list of some of the language assessment procedures used to determine students' language performance is provided in Table 3-1. Suggestions for using these measures are offered throughout the chapter. The skills and competencies of the personnel involved are central to the effectiveness of the process.

Before an appropriate assessment process can be implemented, the purposes for conducting the assessment, such as the intended uses of the information obtained, need to be specified. If the purpose for determining a student's oral proficiency is to place the student in an instructional setting, such as a bilingual or ESOL program, then the process and the way the information is reported is much different from that for determining more specific needs, such as the development of an instructional plan or placement in a special education program. Determining a student's oral proficiency is a process typically carried out through the use of some type of standardized instrument[1] requiring only a brief amount of time, typically 10 to 15 minutes per language. Although this type of assessment is not comprehensive, and the data produced are not sufficient for preparing an instructional plan, it does fulfill minimum requirements for placing students within a general area or level of instruction. This type of assessment usually also provides information on language dominance.

---

[1]A listing and review of standardized assessment instruments is not provided within this text because such information is readily available elsewhere (See for example, Damico & Hamayan 1991, or Fradd & Weismantel 1989).

TABLE 3-1. LANGUAGE ASSESSMENT MEASURES

FORMAL	INFORMAL
Standardized	**School Performance**
Norm-Referenced	**Receptive/Expressive Language**
Criterion-Referenced	**Comprehension**
Discrete Point Measures of:	Oral cloze tests
Lexicon	Sentence verification
Syntax	Story retelling
Morphology	**Production**
Phonology	Retelling stories
Pragmatics	Generating stories with support
	Creating stories without support
	Interpreting stories
	Predicting outcomes of stories
	Language Sampling of:
	Social interactions
	Problem solving behaviors
	Imagination
	Questioning
	Predicting
	Directing
	Inferring
	Organizing and relating

LANGUAGE DOMINANCE AS IT RELATES TO LANGUAGE USE

In many school districts, the establishment of a student's *dominant language*, the language in which the student can best communicate, is an important part of the language assessment process. The outcome of the process is an important product, the determination of a student's most proficient language. Students are usually classified as dominant in one language or another. However, some students are balanced, equally proficient in both languages (Fradd 1987a). The determination of a student's dominant language may be made through formal tests using lists of single words, or through more complex measures. In using simple or complex measures, educators often fail to recognize that many variables influence the production and use of language. Language dominance may vary depending on the task and persons involved in the act of communicating (Mattes & Omark 1984).

Students' performance opportunities for social language skill development influence measures of language dominance. For example, students may be dominant in their non-English language in discussions involving topics about the home or community, and dominant in topics related to school and academic studies in English (Fishman 1976). Dominance tests that focus only on one or two topics provide different information from tests that focus on multiple topics and contexts. If only one topic, such as school-related activities, is selected for assessment in English, students who are new to the school environment may score low in English. After a year or two of instruction, if the same measures are used, these same students may score much higher in English. The second measurement may not be indicative of students' overall ability or growth, as much as indicative of newly acquired knowledge of specific activities and vocabulary. In order to accurately describe students' language skills, a variety of tasks or language functions must be sampled (Mattes & Omark 1984).

In establishing a student's dominant language, it is important to take into consideration not only the language in which the student communicates most effectively, but also the relative proficiency of both or all of the student's languages. For example, students with learning disabilities or developmental delays may be equally proficient in two languages. However, neither of those languages may be adequately developed to enable these students to participate in instruction in a regular classroom setting without support. Similarly, students who were born and raised in a non-English language environment in the United States may not have had the opportunities to develop a strong language base in their non-English language or in English. Without this fundamental language base, these students may be unable to participate effectively in regular classrooms without support. For all practical purposes, these students may be _balanced bilinguals,_ but they may also be ineffective learners. Balance in terms of language proficiency is important, but information on language dominance and balance must be combined with information on the levels of proficiency and the contexts or topics in which the information was obtained (Fradd 1987a).

Tests of language dominance alone may not be sufficient. Such tests may indicate that, for some balanced bilingual students, English proficiency may be on par with that of the other language, but may not serve the student well in academic settings. Although English may be the dominant language, students may not know how to use English language skills in context-reduced academic settings. The more important questions are "What are students able to do in English?" and "How do the students perform when presented with academic tasks?" Achievement of established levels of proficiency does not necessarily ensure the necessary skills to permit academic performance (Ascher 1990).

RESEARCH IN PRACTICE
Language Dominance as It Relates to Language Use

1. **What do the terms language _dominance_ and _proficiency_ mean?**

2. **Why do indicators of language dominance vary by task and context?** Relate this information to the definition of academic language.

3. Is language dominance considered in the assessment of students in your school? Do you think that dominance is an important measure? Does information on dominance influence perceptions about students?

DIFFERENTIATING PROCESSES FROM PRODUCTS

For most students, basic dominance and proficiency assessment may be all that is required for them to begin receiving instruction. However, if students are encountering learning difficulties, other instruments and processes provide different types of information. Before embarking on a process of assessment, educators need to determine what they want to know and how the information will be used. If all that is needed is a quick placement screening, then it would not be economical or logistically practical to use more lengthy or complex procedures.

Practicality is an essential requirement. Teachers often argue that they cannot be expected to test large groups of students on an individual basis if they are also expected to be responsible for instructing them. What this argument often does not take into consideration is the fact that there are many types of assessment. Teachers tend to think only of the formal type. They fail to recognize that they are constantly assessing their students' progress. What is needed is a process for enabling teachers to collect information on a consistent, on-going basis and to compare this information across time in monitoring individual students' growth and in making decisions about groups as well as individual students. Assessment procedures that promote observation and assessment simultaneously, as students are engaged in the processes of producing language, interacting, and learning in meaningful contexts, enhance teachers' understanding of their students and the learning process.

The limitations in using assessment procedures, such as those currently available for establishing dominance and proficiency, are that proficiency, like language dominance, often varies across settings and task demands (Tikunoff 1987). Since students are constantly learning and growing, language development is not a static process. A score obtained today will probably not be representative of that same student's proficiency in six months. However, performance testing can be conducted as an on-going process that reflects the growth and the changes occurring both in students' ability to think and to express themselves. For young learners, academic second language proficiency develops more slowly than social language proficiency because the structure of academic language is more context reduced and abstract than the language used to communicate in social settings. In addition to being more abstract and linguistically complex, the language used to communicate academic concepts occurs only in specific settings and contexts. In general, the opportunities for young language learners to observe and acquire specific aspects of academic language required for effective participation occur less frequently than opportunities to observe and participate in social interactions (Williams 1988).

In her seminal work on children's acquisition of English as a second language, entitled "The Second Time Around," Lilly Wong Fillmore (1976) observed that there were two kinds of learners: (a) those who observed other students and tried to use new words and phrases that they heard other students using in order to communicate and interact with their peers; and (b) those who shyly watched from the sidelines until they had developed a level of confidence and proficiency that enabled them to communicate in more complete language forms than the first group. Fillmore's research found that the first group became more successful language learners. She referred to them as "grabbing a phrase and holding on." She found that children who grabbed new phrases also exhibited behaviors that enabled them to participate and to be accepted, important skills in promoting initial language learning. As they tried new phrases, these students acted as if they understood what was happening and that they knew what they were saying, even when they did not. This semblance of understanding encouraged other students to interact with the new language learners and enabled them to continue to observe first-hand what their peers meant by their communications. Thus, simulating understanding and sustaining interactions with native speakers leads new language learners to more complete understandings of the language. Active participation promoted the development of social language skills that then formed the basis for academic language development. Since Fillmore's seminal work, further research confirmed that young learners acquire social language through interaction and observation (Fillmore 1982). Learning to grab a phrase and hold on is an important strategy that can be generalized and applied to academic as well as social language situations. While the strategy works in both social and academic settings, the explicit meaning of content area language is not necessarily as explicit as the meanings conveyed through social interactions. Unless teachers make language meaningful and explicit, and organize environments that promote observation and interaction, new language learners are often lost. If there are too many phrases to be grabbed, and if these phrases are not closely linked to observable meanings, academic language development may not occur, even for the most successful social language learners (Fillmore 1985). Providing students with varied opportunities to observe and imitate increases their opportunities for learning. Comparing the behaviors of students who are effective observers with the behavior of students who are less people or task oriented provides insight into both the process of learning a new language and the strategies of promoting effective academic performance (Chamot & O'Malley 1984).

RESEARCH IN PRACTICE
Differentiating Processes From Products

1. **What do the terms** *process* **and** *product* **mean in terms of language assessment?** Why is a differentiation between process and product important?

2. **How can process information be related to products?** Consider ways teachers make academic instruction explicit and meaningful. How are teaching behaviors different when teachers realize that they must make meaning explicit from when teachers proceed with instruction as though everyone understood? What are the student behaviors in each of these instructional settings?

NATURALNESS OF COMMUNICATION

Naturalness is one of the first elements identified by contemporary language researchers as influential in evaluating the overall form and content of communication. Within this context, *naturalness* refers to the authenticity or desire of the individuals engaging in the interaction to satisfy their own needs and goals. When communication occurs for the purpose of achieving personal goals, the focus is on meaning and outcome, not on form or appropriateness. Communication occurring to fulfill the request of a person in authority, such as a teacher within a school setting, is obligatory and often not real, natural, or authentic. The concept of naturalness is important because students, like all individuals, respond differently when fulfilling an obligation initiated by others than when initiating a personal intent of their own (Burt & Dulay 1978). Using this definition of naturalness, most of the language produced in school could be classified as obligatory rather than natural. In fact, this differentiation is accurate. Much of the language occurring in schools is unique to the school setting and does not occur in other environments such as the home or the community (Cazden 1988; Iglesias 1986).

The concept of natural communication occurring in schools may be illusory. Much has been written about the importance of establishing school environments in which language is produced naturally as an outgrowth of students' own desires to communicate. Assessment within school environments, it has been suggested, should occur in environments that resemble the home culture (Bennet-Kantor 1988). But how can such assessments occur in school contexts?

In many contemporary schools few opportunities may exist for students to produce language that is spontaneous or purposeful as they might at home (Gonzales & Hansen-Krening 1981). Application of the terms *natural* and *obligatory* must be carefully considered in assessing children's language. Researchers have developed many ways to describe the stages of child language production (Lindfors 1987). Within the changing research paradigms, however, little attention has been given to the relationship of the stages of social and academic language development through which children pass. An understanding of this relationship can be insightful in relating the production of language within natural and obligatory environments to overall academic progress. Determining the purpose of assessment is important in deciding whether observations and data collection should occur in a homelike, natural environment or in a school-like, obligatory environment. Differentiating between social and academic language contributes to the knowledge base on which such assessment decisions can be made.

To be effective communicators, students must learn to function in both natural and obligatory environments. Part of the role of the educational process is to promote effective communication across settings. However, until students have developed the competencies and capacity to participate effectively within the mainstream, consideration of the students' current level of functioning and communication styles is important in assessing their needs. Providing a natural environment in which students want to interact is an important first step in moving them toward effective communication in obligatory environments (Bennet-Kantor 1988).

Facilitative, natural environments are most important in evaluating the language of reluctant learners, students who may be waiting in the shadows until they develop the confidence and proficiency to communicate effectively. If the student is clearly not successful in the mainstream assessment process, then more naturalistic, context embedded procedures need to be used in an effort to determine in which contexts a student does communicate. For these students, it is essential to promote opportunities in which they want to communicate, and in which they identify with those persons with whom they are to communicate as accepting and acceptable interactors. In such cases, use of the home language, approximation of the home environment, and even the involvement of family members may be necessary to provide maximum opportunities for effective and meaningful interaction. Such environments may be inappropriate, however, in assessing students' academic language production since, by definition, this type of language is obligatory and context reduced. For students who are being tested to determine if they can successfully participate within the mainstream classroom, assessment modifications that promote naturalness would be inappropriate and could even be misleading in learning about the students' abilities to participate without major adaptations (Mattes & Omark 1984). In seeking the optimum language production environment, we are looking for aspects of the environment and of the communication process that promote language production, and we are looking at what the students can produce and comprehend in this optimal environment.

Evaluating the environments in which communication and instruction occur is important in establishing an effective and meaningful assessment process. Consideration should be given to selecting or establishing the environment that promotes the production of the type of information desired. In order to provide such an environment in a specific testing situation, it is necessary to observe students and determine how students participate in natural and obligatory settings (Saville-Troike 1985).

Language samples can reveal a great deal about how students interact and how they think. Observations of students' monologues and interactions with others provide insights into students' linguistic and cognitive development. Throughout this chapter suggestions are offered for collecting and analyzing students' language. In order to collect and use samples representative of students' development, educators need to be aware of many factors that influence language production. The discussion of natural and obligatory environments underscores the fact that settings, persons, and interactional styles can strongly influence students' communicative acts. If students are requested to produce language in settings or with persons with whom they are uncomfortable, the language may not be representative of students' real communicative ability. Here the notion of collecting representative language is developed further.

When settings and tasks are organized to promote the production of language for the purpose of observation and analysis, the act of collecting the language is referred to as *elicitation*. Elicitation can imply an explicit process where a student is placed in front of an audio or video recorder and requested to talk. Sometimes, when the recording process is made the focus of attention, students become so conscious of the process that they fail to produce representative language. The elicitation process does not have to interfere with communication. The process can be made less explicit by recording students interacting or communicating to achieve group or individual purposes. When students are recorded frequently and encouraged to review their own performance, they usually become quickly accustomed to the process and communicate in a similar fashion with or without recordings (Carrasco 1979).

RESEARCH IN PRACTICE
Naturalness of Communication

---

1. **What do the terms *natural communication* and *obligatory communication* mean?** Give examples of natural and obligatory communication. Why are these concepts important in language instruction and assessment?

2. **When would assessment occur in an obligatory environment? When in a natural environment?** Specify the reasons for your answer.

3. **Why is it important to give students experiences with recording**

equipment before actually recording language samples to be used in observing students' language development?

IDENTIFYING RECEPTIVE AND EXPRESSIVE LANGUAGE SKILLS

Observation and assessment of specific skills may be needed to determine students' unique learning needs. For example, bilingual students have developed disparate sets of skills in their two languages. Because of differences in the cultural expectations for language use and the opportunities for language learning, students may have learned to perform some skills in one language and different skills in the other. These separate sets of skills may not necessarily be overlapping or interactive, at least at surface level, in ways that promote effective academic performance in English.

Difference in receptive and expressive language development is one of the areas in which anecdotal data indicate significant discrepancies between language systems. Non-English language background students may be found to have highly developed receptive language skills and low levels of expressive language in their non-English language (Waggoner 1984). Students with little or no expressive language, other than English, may be categorized as limited English proficient because their receptive non-English language is more comprehensive than their expressive skills in English. Development of high levels of receptive language may be common in households where children are encouraged to watch and observe rather than verbalize and express (Westby & Rouse 1985). When students arrive at school, they are encouraged to express themselves in English. English then becomes their language of expression, but not necessarily their language of strength in terms of comprehension. Because separate sets of receptive and expressive skills may develop in each language, students may be limited in language proficiency in both languages in terms of the skills required for effective school participation (Wong Fillmore 1985). These disparities can result in lower levels of overall communicative competence. As a result, students may appear limited in their cognitive abilities in comparison with similar age peers who have had different opportunities to develop both receptive and expressive language skills. It is important to keep in mind that the limitations may exist in terms of skills the students have developed, but not necessarily the students' abilities to develop skills.

Determining the students' dominance and proficiency can influence the ways the students are treated. If identifying these students as English dominant places them in classrooms without assistance in developing both receptive and expressive language skills, what was at one point a lack of limited skill development can, over time, become a lack of cognitive development (Ortiz & Garcia 1986; Rice 1983; Waggoner 1984).

Because academic success is highly dependent on well-developed receptive language skills, educators must ensure that young learners have opportunities to acquire these skills. Observation and assessment of specific sets of literacy skills within each language and the comparison of receptive and expressive language skills in both languages are necessary in order to provide students with the support needed to achieve classroom success. Accessing students' expressive and receptive abilities in both languages and in several learning and social contexts promotes not only the determination of the students' current levels of functioning, but also promotes teachers' insight into the language development process for students learning to function with multiple language systems. When discrepancies occur between receptive and expressive language, strength within an area can be used to promote expressive proficiency.

Examples of ways to assess expressive language skills are found throughout this chapter. When assessing receptive skills, care must be taken to provide activities that students can accomplish easily. The level of difficulty of the tasks and the number of tasks to be accomplished in a series can influence students' performance. Giving students a series of commands is one of the simplest ways to learn about their receptive language abilities. Giving first a one step command, such as "Put your hand over your head," and observing the student's performance can reveal the student's ability to follow directions. Slowly increasing the number of words per command and the number of commands per turn can gradually reveal how much command-type language a student can process at one time. If a student is unable to follow directions or seems to falter, both hearing acuity and receptive language ability need to be considered as potential reasons for this limitation. Screening tests for hearing are always a good idea whenever there is any concern about a student's language development. Additional receptive tasks include listening games of all types. Younger students like to play games like "Simon says" and "Mother, may I?" For older and more mature students, games that involve following sequences of directions in marking or arranging pictures can provide the same type of information. If activities are presented in a game-like rather than test-like format, students not only learn to display receptive language skills but look forward to opportunities to develop them.

RESEARCH IN PRACTICE
Identifying Receptive and Expressive Language Skills

1. **Explain the terms** *receptive language* **and** *expressive language*. Why are these terms important in assessing students?

2. **Collaborate with a colleague in developing a series of receptive language**

tasks for younger and more mature learners. Consider gender in the development of the tasks. Field test your tasks from the perspective of process and product. Share the results with a group of educators.

QUESTIONING AS A VARIABLE

Many factors influence the ways students communicate. Both the tasks to which the students are requested to respond and the questions students are asked influence their performance (Lindfors 1987; Tikunoff 1987). The focus of this subsection is on the process of posing questions and analyzing ways to promote competence.

There are three general types of questions that teachers ask in the course of a day: (1) those requiring a yes/no answer; (b) those requiring an informational response; and (c) those requiring a choice (Lindfors 1987). Yes/no and choice questions usually generate brief amounts of language. Because of the brevity of the information generated, these types of questions are referred to as *closed questions*. Questions that generate discussion or which encourage students to produce large chunks of language are referred to as *open questions*. An awareness of the amount of potential openness that a question may present is an important factor in eliciting a representative sample. For example, in a closed measure, a student might be asked a question such as, "Do you have any brothers?" for which only a "yes" or a "no" answer would be appropriate. A slightly more open version of the question could be, "How many brothers do you have?" to which the student could answer, "I don't have any brothers," or "five," or "I have five brothers at home," or some other variation of the same type of answer. Because several answers are considered appropriate, the second question is considered more open. A third variation of the same question is even more open in the form of the request, "Tell me about your family," to which the student can respond by describing each of the brothers or providing some information about each family member. Closed questions are usually used to initiate a conversation and to select a topic of conversation. Open questions are used to provide students with opportunities to respond with their own information. In using questions as a vehicle for eliciting language samples, the initiation of the request for information occurs with someone other than the student providing the information, unless part of the task is to have the student ask questions. Questioning can be an effective and appropriate method for collecting language as long as educators are aware of the constraints being placed on the student. For example, a student who was asked primarily closed questions should not be evaluated as producing restricted or limited language.

There are other restrictions imposed by the question asking process. These deal with the process of moving from learning to function in a concrete setting toward the use of abstract language. Children first learn to respond to and ask questions about concrete objects. Initially they ask questions by producing intonation changes in their voices and then by using "what" and "where" words. A little later they become aware of questions related to "who." Further development occurs as children become aware that inverted word order can also indicate a request for information. At about the same time, they become aware of the value and importance of the word "why," even though they will not understand cause and effect relationships for some time. Later still, they begin to relate information to the steps and processes for completing tasks, and to understand the relationship of time to presence or absence of persons or events. At that point they begin to use question words such as "how" and "when." The process unfolds in several directions. Children learn to manipulate voice intonation and they learn to use question words and word order in making requests. Clearly, the development of language is a long-term process closely related to the development of cognitive abilities (Lindfors 1987; Rice 1980).

An awareness of this developmental process is important for two reasons: (a) students must have cognitive skills in place in order to be able to produce and respond to different types of questions; and (b) for children, second language acquisition occurs as a parallel process that mirrors the process of first language development but at a faster rate. Having these stages in mind enables educators to avoid asking questions to which students cannot effectively respond and to rephrase questions in ways that facilitate communication (Blank & White 1986). Table 3-2 illustrates the general development of questions as children learn a first language.

RESEARCH IN PRACTICE
Questioning as a Variable

1. **What do the terms** *open* **and** *closed* **mean in terms of language assessment?** Give examples of both open and closed requests.

2. **Explain the developmental process of questioning.**

3. **Why is an understanding of this process important for educators?**

4. **Is it essential that students be aware that they are being recorded? Why?**

TABLE 3.2. THE DEVELOPMENTAL PROCESS OF
LEARNING TO ASK QUESTIONS

- Voice Intonation
- Concrete Question Words such as "What," "Where," and then "Who"
- Inverted Word Order using Did, Does, Is, Are
- The Question Word "Why"
- "How" and "When" Question Words
- Complex Questions

DISCRETE POINT ASSESSMENT

The graphic of the iceberg presented in Chapter Two (Figure 2-2) illustrates the concept that within overall language proficiency, there are specific discrete, measurable aspects of language from which many assessment instruments have been constructed. Awareness of these discrete language functions has promoted the development of specific discrete measurable elements referred to as the *discrete point* elements of language. The concept of *form* is another term used to refer to discrete point measures. Form refers to the ways the discrete elements are presented, rather than the meanings communicated within the school context. The elements of form, or the discrete point aspects of language, are considered as essential to the effective production of language as the communication of meaning. However, the measurement of discrete elements does not provide a great deal of information about the student's overall ability to communicate meaning. The discrete elements, as the iceberg illustrates, are not the sum and total of language. They are only aspects of the surface structure that reveal how the student's production conforms to a general idealized model of language (Damico 1991; Oller 1983). A more comprehensive conceptualization of bilingual children's language is currently emerging. In the meantime, it is important to understand the measurement of discrete point elements and the ways these discrete elements may be assessed, as one step toward comprehensive language assessment (Ambert 1982). The measurement of discrete point elements continues today in most schools. Most typically it occurs in the assessment of written language that also tests students' reading and writing skills. A descriptive list of discrete point elements and suggestions for their assessment is presented in Table 3-3. Within this list, consideration is given to the ways that language can be assessed in terms of naturalness and openness. These activities provide suggestions for observing as well as measuring students' performance. To avoid difficulties with reading and writing skills, suggestions for assessing students' proficiency within the oral mode of communication are offered.

TABLE 3-3. SUGGESTIONS FOR DISCRETE POINT ASSESSMENT

- **Phonology (pronunciation and production of the sounds of language)**

  Less open: Provide a student with simple pictures that elicit specific sounds and ask them to name the item or items in the pictures.

  More open: Provide a student with pictures with many objects or activities to elicit phrases and descriptions of items or activities.

  More open and natural: Have a group of students discuss the same pictures together.

  Even more open and natural: Listen to students interact with each other and with other adults.

- **Morphology (the suffixes, prefixes, and tense aspects of grammar)**

  Less open: For *suffixes*, provide a student with simple pictures of single and multiple objects such as *a toy* and many *toys, an orange* and *oranges, a knife* and *knives* and have them name both the singular and plural items. Students may differentiate between singular and plural items by adding the appropriate sounds to make plurals. Students may differentiate between vowels and consonants by using the articles *a* and *an* before vowels and consonants.

  More open: For *verbs*, provide a student with pictures of children engaged in activities. Have them tell what the children are doing. Then ask, "Pretend it's yesterday. Tell me what this girl was doing." Students should provide both the present tense action and the past tense action. For *prefixes*, have multiple pictures of contrasting pictures such as *mother* and *grandmother, happy* and *unhappy,* and have students give the name of the first item and then produce another word with the same last part but with a new meaning by adding a new prefix.

  More open and natural: *For all aspects of morphology,* listen to students interact with each other and with other adults and observe how tenses, plurals, and other word endings are used.

- **Syntax (the organization patterns of grammar)**

  Less open: Say incomplete sentences with missing verbs to a student and have the student respond with the missing parts.

  More open: Provide a student with pictures of children engaged in activities and ask the student to produce descriptions of the items and activities and ask you questions about the pictures. Look for the ways the student expresses descriptive language including *word order,* such as *dog brown* and *go boy* and appropriate word usage.

  More open and natural: *For all aspects of syntax,* listen to students interact with each other and with other adults and observe how they use word order to convey meaning.

- **Semantics (vocabulary and meaning)**

  Less open: Have a student name items in pictures.

  Somewhat more open: Say incomplete sentences with missing naming words to a student and have the student respond with the missing words.

  More open: Provide a student with pictures of multiple items or of children engaged in activities and ask the student to produce a story about the pictures. Observe the different ways the student expresses ideas.

  More open and natural: *For all aspects of semantics,* listen to students interact with each other and with other adults and observe how they use words to convey meaning. Observe the differences in the ways students express themselves with adults and with peers to determine if they use different vocabulary to express the same or similar ideas with different groups.

Until recently, language assessment has focused almost exclusively on the discrete elements of language, the tip of the iceberg that is most easily observed and quantified. There are diverse ways language can be quantified. The results of the quantification are dependent, in part, on the activities in which students engage. Results of the measurement of student performance are not necessarily indicative of students' total linguistic repertoire or of their competence, especially if the assessment involves literacy forms or other forms with which the student is not familiar. Changes are beginning to occur within the assessment process resulting from research conceptualizing language as a whole system rather than as a compilation of discrete units and from the realization that by observing what students do with language it is possible to determine how they learn, as well as what they have learned. The elements considered within the discrete point measurements, combined with additional elements of academic language, provide a useful vocabulary or lexicon for describing what students do and their ability to demonstrate what they know (Ellis 1985).

RESEARCH IN PRACTICE
Discrete Point Assessment

1. Define the discrete point elements of language. Why are these elements measured?

2. How can the measurement of these elements be important if the field of language assessment is moving away from discrete point measures and toward the use of more holistic measures?

LANGUAGE PROFICIENCY AS COMMUNICATIVE COMPETENCE

Within the past decade researchers and educators have begun to conceptualize language as including both the overt behaviors (the discrete point elements) observed within the surface structure and the underlying thought and perception that promote thinking and cognition (Rice 1983). This new conceptualization has been defined as *communicative competence* (Canale & Swain 1980), a focus on the student's ability to convey meaning within a variety of situational contexts (Savignon 1983). Modifications in the way that language proficiency is defined and viewed have shifted the focus of assessment away from the measurement of discrete point elements in isolation toward the use of strategies that analyze language from a more comprehensive, holistic perspective (Goodman, Goodman & Hood 1989). Assessment of language from this perspective includes the measurement of a variety of academic skills and abilities applied in diverse contexts to organize, present, and comprehend thought and meaning (Harley, Allen, Cummins & Swain 1990). The conceptualization of language as interactive components promotes the observation of what students do in authentic communication settings. This focus does not diminish the importance of the sounds communicators make or the grammar they produce. Grammatical and phonological accuracy remain important, but this information is integrated within a larger picture that includes both discourse competence and sociolinguistic competence (Bachman 1990; Canale & Swain 1980; Harley, Cummins, Swain & Allen 1990). *Discourse competence* refers to the ways that communicators maintain or change topics, and the ways that they exchange ideas and information. *Sociolinguistic competence* refers to the communication styles used to communicate and exchange information. Communication styles include variations in tone, register, dialect, and non-verbal information. Consideration is given here only to the oral aspects of communicative competence that provide the foundation for academic performance. A description of these components and suggestions for their assessment is provided in Table 3-4. The relationship of communicative competence within the development of academic proficiency is discussed further within the next subsection.

As can be seen from the table, aspects of both social and academic language are involved within the concept of communicative competence. The development of academic language proficiency creates the greatest challenge for students learning English and for educators who must determine the progress

TABLE 3-4. ASSESSMENT OF COMMUNICATIVE COMPETENCE

DEFINITIONS OF COMPETENCY COMPONENTS:

Grammar	*Discourse*	*Sociolinguistics*
Grammatical accuracy	Comprehension and coherence of text	Socially appropriate language use

PRODUCTIVE COMPETENCE

Grammar	*Discourse*	*Sociolinguistics*
Structured elicitations	Story telling and retelling	Role-plays, interviews involving different social situations

RECEPTIVE COMPETENCE

Grammar	*Discourse*	*Sociolinguistics*
Sentence level: select the correct form	Paragraph level: select the correct sentence	Speech-act level: select the correct words or phrases

of these students in developing communicative skills. Since the introduction of the notion of communicative competence, researchers and educators have continued to consider additional new aspects of language use and language proficiency. New components of the overall concept of what students need to be able to do in order to participate effectively within academic settings have been studied during the past decade. Much of this research is based on written literacy (Stanovich 1990). However, since oral literacy skills form the basis for written literacy development, the application of this new information within oral contexts is important for students learning English along with academic knowledge (Westby in press b). Academic language proficiency is considered next.

RESEARCH IN PRACTICE
Language Proficiency as Communicative Competence

---

1. Describe the concept of *communicative competence*. What components of earlier language measures are included in this concept?

2. Describe how the assessment of communicative competence changes depending on the type of language and how the production modes change.

3. Why is the concept of communicative competence important in assessing language at school?

EXAMINING COMPONENTS OF ACADEMIC LANGUAGE PROFICIENCY

In the discussion of communicative competence, the measurement of discrete linguistic elements has been subsumed within the construct of the global ability to communicate. General information on communicative competence by itself, however, does not provide a clear understanding of the types of skills and strategies necessary for successful participation in academic environments.

Communicative competence within academic settings can be discussed from the perspective of a confluence of interactive skills, or as subcomponents of academic proficiency. Here the influence of the written presentation of language cannot easily be separated from the oral. The way that language is organized in formal academic written interactions influences the way that it is presented in formal oral contexts. For example, a lecture contains many of the same linguistic academic features as a written presentation of the same topic.

A lecture may even be more difficult for a new language learner to comprehend because the text is not visible and cannot be easily retrieved for review
(Cummins 1984).

The components of literacy development can be conceptualized within a
framework focusing on the measurement of communication moving from
context embedded toward context reduced environments, such as those found
within most school settings (Westby in press b). Here the term "text" refers not
only to written bodies of language, but also to oral language used to communicate a set of concepts or ideas, such as those presented in a lecture format. The
subskills or components of academic competence are listed and defined in
Table 3-5.

Each of these components interacts with the others to form a structure for
producing and understanding formal, literate language. All of these components can be drawn upon to comprehend and to make inferences and predictions about the intent and meaning of communication (Westby in press b). A
comprehensive assessment of a LEP student's academic language proficiency
would focus on the process that the student uses to make meaning from
language. This assessment would also examine the products, the expressive
production of the language, as well as the written forms. Information on the
development of these components could be included in a comprehensive
assessment in both English and non-English languages. Written and oral forms
can be used for comparisons, but the oral form cannot be separated from the
written. What students can talk about, they must also be able to express in
writing. What they read, they must also be able to discuss orally. The process of
academic language learning is interactive. Overemphasis on one area of language development delays the learning process as a whole.

Students with weaknesses in one area may compensate by using skills from
another area to achieve an equivalent result. Observation of these components
provides information about how students process information and how in-

TABLE 3-5. COMPONENTS OF ACADEMIC LANGUAGE PROFICIENCY

• **Knowledge of sociolinguistic styles** (appropriate use of language in
diverse social and academic contexts, use of specific instructional and
social registers)

• **Knowledge of text structure** (systematically organized patterns of
meaning)

• **Knowledge of content schema** (integrated units of meaning)

• **Metalinguistic knowledge** (awareness of the language system)

• **Metacognitive knowledge** (awareness of one's processing language to
understand and use information)

struction can be organized to assist them in developing the competencies necessary to perform literacy tasks. Figure 3-1 illustrates the literacy components and emphasizes the interconnectedness of each element within the process. Examples of activities for assessing academic language development are also included.

Knowledge of sociolinguistic styles.

A knowledge of sociolinguistic styles enables students and teachers to modify their communication to respond to the needs of the audience (Dore 1986). The term *sociolinguistics* is often used to refer to the ability to produce and appropriately respond to language in context (Harley 1990). Culture influences

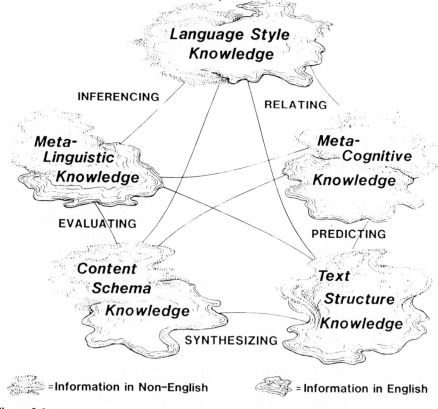

Figure 3-1

Adapted with permission from: Westby, C.E. (in press b). "Communicative refinement in school age and adolescence." In W.O. Haynes & B.B. Shulman (eds.) *Communicative development: Foundations, processes and clinical applications.* Englewood Cliffs, NJ: Prentice-Hall.

communication styles. Within the general category of cultural influences, there are many variables that influence the comprehensibility and appropriateness of a communication (Hall 1973). Gender, religion, and age all contribute to differences among seemingly congruent groups of individuals from similar socioeconomic and geographic regions (Spradley & McCurdy 1972). Instances of miscommunication occur not only among groups from similar sociocultural backgrounds, but from different geographic regions within the same country as well as between diverse ethnic groups (Lieven 1984). Narrative styles provide excellent examples of cultural differences. Oral narrative styles, for example, are associated with specific socioeconomic groups. Stylistic differences can also be observed in many different types of narratives. Highly group specific interactional styles can be observed in people who are well - acquainted with each other (Brice Heath 1983; Rice 1986; Tannen 1990).

Gestures, paralinguistic features, and rates of speech all influence the ways that people are understood or misunderstood. Just as the use of different languages in communicating provides a sense of bonding for the people involved, so too does congruence of communication styles within the same language influence the ways communicators are perceived as well as understood. A knowledge of sociolinguistic communication styles is important for both producing and interpreting the communication (Abbeduto & Nuccio 1989). This knowledge enables communicators to differentiate intents, such as differences in the ways that anger, teasing, and humor are expressed (Lieven 1984; Van Kleeck & Schuele 1987). Students from non-mainstream backgrounds may be aware of some of the aspects of communication that make their language more or less comprehensible to others, but they may not be aware of all of the important features. Nor may they understand how to modify their communication sufficiently to provide the level of comprehensibility required for persons unfamiliar with the speech of non-native speakers (Saville-Troike 1985).

Application of the knowledge of sociolinguistic features involves the evaluation of the communication processes. Research analyzing oral narratives of ethnically diverse students reveals that more competent students demonstrate an ability to adapt their communication when interacting with adults and peers that is not observed in the less competent students. Differences occur in the types of information conveyed, the ways feelings and emotions are expressed, the ways that information is linked together, and the use of gestures and sound effects to communicate meaning. Some students are highly dependent on gestures and sound effects to carry the meaning of their communication. The use of gestures, sound effects, and other paralinguistic actions does not necessarily indicate a learning problem, but these actions are rich sources for observing the ways in which exchanges of meaning are facilitated or impeded. When these behaviors call attention to the student, detract from the meaning being communicated, or are used in place of words to convey meaning, they signal the need for supportive and comprehensive observation. These behaviors may not necessarily be indicators of an innate student limitation, but they present a data-set of information from which to prepare and provide instruction (Fradd, Barona & Santos de Barons 1989; Saville-Troike 1985). An understanding of communicative differences between age, gender, and cultural groups enables educators to observe students to determine if there may be a lack of age-appropriate communicative skills (Westby, Van Dongen & Maggart 1989).

Knowledge of narrative text structure.

Knowledge of text structure refers to an understanding of the ways that texts are organized and used to represent ideas and to communicate meaning. Narratives and expository language are the two major types of academic text structures. Understanding the organization and purposes of texts enables students to successfully engage in context reduced communication (Piccolo 1987; Williams 1988). This understanding is also important in developing higher order thinking skills (Benderson 1984).

Developmentally, narratives are important because they are the first language forms that require speakers to produce extended monologues rather than interactive dialogues. The actions and materials from which narratives develop are initially based on real world happenings (Westby 1985). As a result, narratives are the texts most closely linked to oral language, and are the academic texts most easily understood by young second language learners. Because narratives or stories are usually based on real world experiences, they can serve as a bridge between context embedded and context reduced language. Narratives are frequently used to develop students' awareness and understanding of academic language. The study of narrative structures has received a great deal of attention from researchers because they represent a vehicle for analyzing how students develop an understanding of language (Feldman 1985; Williams 1988). As producers and participants in sharing narratives, children learn to compare and reflect on their personal experiences and the experiences of others. They learn to sequence and structure text in ways that lead to the development of more abstract language forms. Narratives are found in all cultures, although not all cultures use them for the same purposes (Damen 1987; Silliman & Wilkinson 1991).

Story grammars are a type of narrative used in reading instruction based on the developmental patterns of children's language. This type of narrative is a simple form found to facilitate recall and comprehension of the events and of the meaning of a story. In comparison with basal readers, story grammars have been found to promote higher levels of comprehension, because children are better able to comprehend information presented in familiar contexts (Feldman 1985; Witrock, Marks & Doctorow 1975). The advantage of story grammars over basal texts is the familiarity that learners have with the textual information.

Story grammars are composed of two structural units, *settings* and *episodes*. Setting information introduces the characters and provides information on the location of the story. Episodes are composed of a set of categories of information: (a) beginnings that establish reasons for the characters' actions or reactions; (b) the characters' reactions to initial actions; (c) problem-solving attempts; (d) outcomes to these attempts; and (e) endings that bring the story to a conclusion (Feldman 1985).

[handwritten margin note: Exp. of story grammar]

Narratives are an elaboration of basic story grammars. An understanding of the use of story grammars and narratives provides insight into the ways children produce and comprehend language. This understanding enables teachers to provide the type of academic instruction that facilitates language development, information retention, and the acquisition of the structural features of academic language (Silliman & Wilkinson 1991).

Narratives that children produce can be classified according to developmental sequences (Fradd, Barona & Santos de Barona 1989; Hedburg & Stoel-Gammon 1986). Initially narratives appear as "heaps" or groups of words that appear unrelated. A close observer or a teacher who has experience in working with children who are learning to relate their ideas see these piles of words as related to a topic (Applebee 1978). Eventually, as children gain experience with the ways that stories are told and information is communicated, these groupings take shape in sequence and form. The development of the ability to relate narratives can be evaluated in terms of the relatedness of the statements, the temporal sequence, causal relationships, goals, plans, complications, and interactions. The overall organization of the narrative also provides an understanding of the child's level of development. For example, the narratives of beginning story tellers may have clear beginnings and endings, but may have little substantial information within the middle. Gradually, children become aware of the importance of the information provided by the organization of the central theme of the story, and the middle emerges as the structuring and relating of an event.

Samples of students' narratives can be obtained by having students produce their own stories, retell stories told to them by adults or other children, reorder and sequence scrambled stories, or complete stories given to them with no ending (Koshinen, Gambrell, Kapinus, & Heathington 1988; Westby et al. 1989). These developmental levels of narratives are presented in Table 3-6.

Recently the idea of using children's own language in reading instruction and literacy development, referred to as whole language instruction, has gained popularity. The popularity of the whole language movement has resulted in debates between proponents of basal and of whole language instruction (Goodman 1986; Sawyer 1991). The debate over basal and whole language instruction has polarized the conceptualization of learning to read into two camps, one that is described as defining the reading process as learning to recognize series of letters, sounds, and symbols, and the other as promoting the

TABLE 3-6. DEVELOPMENTAL LEVELS OF NARRATIVES

Levels	Properties
Descriptive Sequence	Descriptions of characters, environment, and actions without causal relationships
Action Sequence	Series of chronologically but not causally ordered actions
Reactive Sequence	Action sequence where one action causes another without planning or consideration of relationships.
Abbreviated Sequence	Action sequence where character's goals are presented without explanation of a plan for achieving them
Complete Episode	Goals and plans are described
Complex Episode	Elaboration on the complete episode with multiple plans, attempts, and sequences
Interactive Episode	Narrative with more than one episode

Adapted with permission from Hedburg, N.L. & Stoel-Gammon, C. (1986). Narrative analysis: Clinical procedures. *Topics in Language Disorders, 7,* 58-70.

communication of meaning. These may be extreme definitions. Both approaches to reading have merit. However, for students who do not bring to the reading process the perspectives and prior experiences of the mainstream reader, the process of extracting meaning from print can be a complex and often confusing one. Basal reader instruction, for these students, has been described as piecing together meaning from language fragments (Weaver 1991). If this process appears labor intensive, confusing, and time consuming for monolingual students who are proficient in English (Garnett 1986), how much more difficult can it be for students who are learning the sounds, symbols, meanings, and the culture of a new language simultaneously?

As a result of the abstraction and decontextualization of the language, many children experience learning difficulties when they first enter school. The observation and assessment of students' production and comprehension of narratives provide a starting place for understanding their ability to put together phrases and sentences in a meaningful, orderly manner to communicate about a personal experience (Lindfors 1987; Westby 1985). This personalization of instruction, combined with experiences that enable students to move from concrete to more abstract ways of communicating, assists students to build on their prior experiences in developing literacy (Westby 1985).

Knowledge of expository text structures.

Learning to organize and present ideas in a narrative format appears to facilitate the transition to more abstract, context reduced expository language.

Students with knowledge of expository language structures perform significantly better on measures of reading comprehension than students who are unfamiliar with these formats (Westby in press b). Expository formats include six basic types of structures: (a) description; (b) enumeration; (c) sequence; (d) cause/effect; (e) comparison/contrast and (f) problem/solution. Each of these types of text offers a different format for presenting information (Englert & Hiebert 1984). Students can be taught to select and use the various formats according to the requirements of the information to be presented. They can also be made aware that authors use predictable text patterns to present their ideas. Understanding these patterns enables students to predict the format and the semantic organization used within each pattern. Relating pictorial information to the texts can also promote text comprehension and text memory (Abel & Kulhavy 1986). Table 3-7 presents key words used to signal presentational formats. It offers suggestions for observing and enabling students to identify and use different types of expository text structures in oral and written discourse (Picolo 1987).

Each of the different types of expository text structures can be organized into a graphic or a semantic map illustrating the specific properties and linguistic structures that support it (Picolo 1987). As students gain control in producing expository language, they learn how to structure texts to access and control meaning (Bergenske 1987). Typically students receive less instruction in expository test organization than they do in narrative development, yet they are expected to successfully use expository text information in all content areas, including science, social studies and math problem solving. Observing students' production of narrative and expository texts provides a vehicle for understanding the development of academic language.

Both older and younger learners can be assisted to develop an understanding of academic language through the use of reading guides, or guiding activities and questions that enable students to work through a text. Reading guides can be used as a substitute for one of the most common teaching practices, the study questions at the end of a chapter text. In order to use academic language meaningfully, students require not only an understanding of the factual information presented within the text, but they also require an understanding of the implied content, such as perspective, voice, and underlying themes. By working together using a study guide, students can access text format relating the smaller pieces of information to the larger context. Reading guides can be developed to assist students in working together to construct this information. This constructive process differs from the more traditional question-answering process because it encourages students to share their perspectives, to consider alternative explanations, to locate the sources of their beliefs and knowledge within the text or the underlying structures, and to organize ways to access and integrate information meaningfully (Lovitt & Horton 1987; Woods 1988). Working interactively provides opportunities for oral as well as

TABLE 3-7. KEY WORDS, PURPOSES, AND SUGGESTIONS
FOR IDENTIFYING DIFFERENT TYPES OF EXPOSITORY TEXT
ORGANIZATION IN ORAL AND WRITTEN DISCOURSE

Text Structure	Key Words	Purpose	Identification
Descriptive Language	None; attributes of specific topics such as appearance, sensation, performance	Presentation of information to create a visual image	Telling how something looks, feels, acts
Enumerative Language	Sequences with number terms such as *first, next, finally*	Provide main topic and supportive information	Lists relating main idea and supporting topics
Sequencing Language	Sequences with linking words such as *then, before, after*	Link main topic with correct order of sequential information	Directions presented for doing, or making something
Cause/Effect	Topic sentence + supporting detail *so, so that, because, in order to, since*	Explain reasons	Tell why something happens or exists
Comparison/ Contrast	Paragraphs on likeness and differences, *alike, resembles, same as, unlike, compared to*	Make comparisons	Show similarities and differences
Problem/ Solution	Topic sentence and paragraph description of problem and solutions *a problem is, a solution is, the answer*	Illustrate need and importance, persuade, enlist support	Show reasons, use persuasive language, describe consequences

written language development. Observation of students' interactions as well as the resulting products enables teachers to assess students' progress in the development of content schema within an oral context (Pehrsson & Denner 1988).

Knowledge of content schema.

The ability to analyze language into meaningful linguistic units is an essential part of learning to use and produce academic language. In learning to read, students who continue to focus on the decoding of language sound by sound and word by word fail to grasp the meaning being communicated by the sounds and words. Moving from discrete point to whole language assessment means conceptualizing language in larger and more diverse components than those provided by the word, phrase, or sentence. Comparisons of the content found within phrases, sentences, paragraphs, and larger bodies of text provide insight into the differences that children experience in understanding and producing meaning. This is done most easily and efficiently initially through the presentation of language in written formats. But these lessons can be extended through oral presentations of stories and expository information.

The organization of content schema influences comprehension and comprehensibility of language. Understanding text schema requires more than an understanding of the words and sentences from which texts are composed (Pehrsson & Denner 1988; Westby in press a). It requires that learners understand the ways language is sequenced and presented. This understanding is influenced by students' prior experiences with oral language as well as their experiences with academic language.

Proficient language users apply their knowledge of text and culture to construct meaning from text. Less proficient learners can be assisted in this constructive process through explanations, group discussions, and practice in making inferences. Discussion of cultural variables in the presentation of oral and written academic language can be insightful for older learners.

For younger children, assessment can involve the telling of a story from a wordless picture book. Children who are unfamiliar with the episodic aspects of a story may fail to realize that each page moves the story forward. They may present a simple description of the contents of the page without linking it to the next pictorial event. If students are hesitant or have difficulty in providing a story, they can be asked guiding questions that assist them in focusing on the relationship of events and inferring outcomes (Westby in press b).

Metalinguistic knowledge.

The term *metalinguistics* refers to the conscious and unconscious awareness of language use and organization. It refers to the ability to talk about language in terms of forms and processes, as well as meaning and content. The development of metalinguistic knowledge occurs in six different areas: (a) repairing communicative breakdowns; (b) adjusting language to listener requirements; (c) evaluating content and form; (d) analyzing language into linguistic units; (e) understanding and producing rhymes, puns, and riddles; and (f) using figurative language (Kamhi 1987). Difficulties with metalinguistic tasks appear to stem from encoding information into the system rather than retrieving information that is already in the system (Kamhi 1987).

All areas of metalinguistic knowledge are important in the development of academic proficiency. An awareness of word boundaries, or the knowledge of how to separate sounds into meaningful units, is a significant predictor of reading comprehension. Closely related to the awareness of word boundaries, in terms of reading ability, is the ability to relate sounds to written symbols and to produce written versions of oral texts (Westby in press b). Children from environments where literacy skills are introduced before they enter school arrive at the process of learning to read and of using academic language with many of the precursors of successful reading already in place (Sulzby 1985). Students who have not developed these skills will find talking about the noun or locating the verb in a sentence a difficult and probably meaningless task.

Metalinguistic awareness can be developed through games and play activities where a knowledge of the language system is called into use and illustrated with concrete examples (Duchan 1986; Schuele & Van Kleeck 1987). The development of bilingual literacy skills also appears to promote metalinguistic awareness. As students become aware of the arbitrary nature of language and the relationship of words and meaning, they realize that aspects of language can be separated from the properties of meaning. Learning to function in two languages appears to provide young learners with more insight into ways that language is organized than functioning in only one language. Thus, bilingualism tends to promote metalinguistic development (Cummins & Swain 1986). Researchers have also observed metalinguistic development in mainstream children's language. Information from monolingual and bilingual students provides insight into the potential development of metalinguistic skills in NELB students. While this information is insightful, it should not be used to infer developmental expectations. Many factors influence the development of metalinguistic awareness (Van Kleeck & Schuele 1987). Students who do not conform to predictable developmental milestones observed in children from mainstream families, and students from home environments with limited literacy experiences, are not necessarily developmentally delayed, even when their behavior, as measured by standardized tests, indicates a delay or disability. Slower than expected development of metalinguistic skills may be an indicator of students' limited experiences in learning to observe and talk about language and their limited awareness of language as a system. These are teachable and learnable skills. Only after extensive exposure to meaningful literacy experiences can we infer with some degree of assurance that a student is demonstrating a disability.

Informal assessment of school-age students' metalinguistic knowledge can be done through observing the ways they handle books, pencils, and crayons. If they take a book, orient the book so the pictures and text appear right side up to them, and turn the pages from right to left, it can be inferred that they have

[handwritten margin note: Bilingualism promotes metalinguistic development]

some awareness of printed language. In contrast, students who may hold the book upside down or use it as a projectile may have had little experience with books and probably do not have an understanding of their purposes. Similar observations can provide information on ways that students have learned to handle other school materials needed for effective literacy participation. Commercial tests are available for assessing metalinguistic development (Schuele & Van Kleeck 1987). As with all assessments, discretion must be used in applying test information to NELB students. A lack of metalinguistic skills does not necessarily indicate the presence of a disorder, but does provide information on where to begin instruction. Suggestions for informal assessment are offered in Table 3-8 as examples of ways that metalinguistic knowledge may be observed.

Metacognitive knowledge.

Metacognition refers to the understanding that learners have about their own efforts in achieving effective outcomes and their ability to regulate their behavior in order to be successful. It means knowing how to organize and monitor one's own efforts, and being aware of one's knowledge about something. Application of metacognitive knowledge requires conscious awareness of one's own behavior, evaluation of one's personal behavior, reflection on this behavior, and regulation and control of one's behavior in a variety of settings (Chamot & O'Malley 1984; Westby in press b). Metacognitive knowledge can be useful in enabling students to develop and use strategies for executing and monitoring their performance on social and academic tasks (Hudson & Fradd 1987). It influences the monitoring and execution of communication activities. Metacognitive knowledge interacts with sociolinguistic skills in monitoring and determining whether a message was provided appropriately and whether it was comprehended as intended. If the message was not produced or comprehended, the speaker has a number of choices regarding the results. He or she may decide to discontinue efforts to be understood, search for new information to promote understanding, locate alternative communication modes, or devise alternative ways to engage the listener. These alternatives range from requesting information on what was not understood to changing the topic (Dollaghan 1988; Ellis 1985). Other examples of the use of metacognitive knowledge include ways that students organize information, such as note-taking skills; rehearse information, such as reviewing for a test or practicing a speech; or apply study skills, such as setting up a study area in order to complete homework. Metacognitive knowledge is the foundation for the application of learning strategies and study skills.

Researchers in both special and ESOL education have developed strategies to enable students experiencing learning problems to develop effective metacognitive strategies in order to become successful learners (Chamot & O'Malley 1984, 1986; Deshler & Schumaker 1986; Deshler, Schumaker & Lenz

TABLE 3-8. SUGGESTIONS FOR INFORMAL ASSESSMENT OF METALINGUISTIC KNOWLEDGE

WORD CONSCIOUSNESS
- Substituting names and referents
  - Can the student use a nonsense word for the real name of a friend or a play item?
  - Will the student allow the teacher to change referent names and continue to understand the context of communication?

- Using multiple names for the same item
  - Does the student realize that items have different names depending on the language of communication? Can the student demonstrate this knowledge?

- Substituting parts of words or sounds
  - Can the student add or subtract words or sounds and change meaning? Is the student aware that the meaning is changed when part of the word is different?
  - Can the student differentiate meaningful words from nonsense words when sounds are changed?

CONSCIOUSNESS OF SENTENCES AND WORDS
- Substituting words within sentences
  - Can the student substitute different words in a sentence and realize that the meaning may have changed?

- Showing an awareness of word boundaries
  - Can the student separate each word in a sentence from the other words?

- Showing an awareness of the contexts of language
  - Does the student show an awareness of sounds, such as voice tone, and pauses that convey meanings such as anger, surprise, happiness, concern?
  - Does the student show an awareness that by changing language, both the sounds and meanings may change?
  - Can the student guess at the locations of the communications by listening to the background sounds?
  - Can the student predict outcomes and relationships by listening to brief conversations?

1984). Strategies in both ESOL and special education make valuable contributions to student learning. Both types of strategies, however, also have limitations. Special education strategies are highly structured, explicitly taught, and easily observed and monitored. They are limited in their applicability with LEP students, since they assume that students have English language skills and are functioning at a minimum of a fourth grade reading level. The ESOL strategies are less explicit and focused and are not as easily taught or monitored. They are relevant to the needs of LEP learners since they make no assumptions about students' language proficiency or their level of literacy development. ESOL strategies can be adapted to the needs of both literate and non-literate learners (Hudson & Fradd 1987). In using ESOL strategies, students are encouraged, not only to apply the strategies, but to discuss applications in monitoring their performance. The process of reflecting on and discussing performance promotes the development of metacognitive skills. Reflection also increases students' success in executing strategies (Chamot & O'Malley 1984). Discussion provides students with a means of learning about what others do and how they organize for success. Observations of such discussions provide educators with insights into students' perceptions of their own skills and of their strategies in developing and applying skills (Chamot & O'Malley 1986). Informal interviews can also provide insight into students' perceptions of their effectiveness in academic tasks and in the process of developing the skills to become successful (Chamot & O'Malley 1984).

RESEARCH IN PRACTICE
Examining Components of Academic Language

1. **Relate the concept of context reduced language to the concept of academic language.** How do the components of academic language presented in this subsection relate to the concept of context reduced language? Why is this relationship important in comprehending the concept of academic language? Is this information considered in assessing students in your school?

2. **Define the components of the academic language and then provide examples of how you would assess students' performance in each area.** How are these components discrete skills and how are they interactive? Why is it important to be aware of these components?

3. **How is language defined in your school setting?** How does this definition influence the way that language is measured?

ASSESSING COMPREHENSION

One of the most important reasons for assessing students' language is to determine what they understand as well as what they are able to produce. Frequently the focus of assessment is on production rather than comprehension (Ellis 1985b; Krashen 1987). Recent research indicates that assessment of comprehension may be an effective way to determine students' instructional needs (Aaron 1991; Stanovich 1991). Measuring students' ability to comprehend and interpret language can provide educators with information that enables them to predict not only students' instructional needs, but also to anticipate the potential types of reading difficulties that students may encounter. Measurement of students' language comprehension is actually a means of measuring their experience with literacy concepts (Miller 1990). Assessment of students' language comprehension appears to be a trend of the future that, when combined with other practical measures, may replace current measures of intelligence or ability in determining students' needs and instructional placement for academic instruction. Anticipating instructional difficulties and meeting them proactively is also an innovative trend of school districts seeking effective means for assisting typically difficult to reach students, students often referred to as "educationally disadvantaged" or "at-risk of educational failure" (Braden & Fradd 1987; Rothman 1991). Such assessment serves as a means for accelerating instruction rather than remediating it. These trends are consonant with the philosophy of promoting students' effective initial instruction, rather than placing unsuccessful students in remedial programs. Predictive validity obtained through the assessment of students' language comprehension is still under development, but bears further attention from educators seeking to provide comprehensive and meaningful assessments for their students (Aaron 1991; Mestre & Royer 1988).

Several measures can be used to determine students' language comprehension. These include: (a) cloze tests; (b) sentence verification tests; and (c) story retelling measures. Each of these measures provides similar types of data in terms of students' ability to comprehend and recall information. Each also provides insight into different aspects of students' ability to understand and respond. These measures can be developed informally and can also be standardized to monitor students' progress across time or to determine individual development in comparison with other students. Each is discussed next.

Cloze tests.

Cloze tests consist of passages from which words are omitted at regular intervals. The students' task is to provide appropriate substitutes for the missing words (Oller 1979). Cloze assessment procedures can be used in measuring students' listening or reading ability. The ability to complete passages by filling in the gaps is a measure of students' capacity to use contextual clues to infer meaning (Pérez & Torres-Guzmán 1992). Cloze measures can be developed by selecting complete stories of between 250 and 350 words. Sources for stories include commercial literature, basal readers, stories produced within the language communities of the school, or student-developed stories. Passages with different levels of difficulty can be selected to assess a range of comprehension levels. Fifty words are removed from the selected passages, by removing every fifth, sixth, or seventh word depending on the length of the passage. No words are removed from the first or last sentence. No prepositions or proper nouns are removed. Before being given a cloze test, students need to practice completing cloze activities, such as filling in the blank (Mattes & Omark 1984).

A qualitative analysis of students' responses can provide insight into their ability to participate in specific instructional activities. If students are able to provide appropriate words that fit the context of the communication, then they are able to understand the language of the text. If they substitute words that do not fit grammatically or semantically, these substitutions may be indicators, not only of students' level of language development, but also of aspects of their instructional requirements. Comparable passages can be created in two languages to determine students' ability to comprehend in both languages. Discrepancies in students' performances in the two languages can be used to determine their general ability to focus on language as a system of meaning. The process enables teachers to gain insight into students' ability to use different types of texts, to understand diverse communication styles, and to use syntactic and semantic rather than graphophonemic or phonemic clues for interpreting meaning (Mattes & Omark 1984; Pérez & Torres-Guzmán 1992).

Sentence verification tests.

Sentence verification procedures require students to analyze selected passages and compare them to other passages that are similar to and different from a designated text (Mestre & Royer 1988). The sentence verification process is similar to the cloze procedure in that it requires students to examine units of language from the syntactic and semantic level rather than the graphophonemic or phonemic level. Rather than supplying specific words, the verification tasks ask students to compare the sentence meanings. Younger students and students with limited metalinguistic and metacognitive skills, students who have not learned to objectively examine language, may have difficulty with this assessment process (Mestre & Royer 1988).

Like the cloze procedures, comparable sentence verification tasks can be developed in multiple languages from commercial or local sources. They can be used bilingually to determine the language in which students are more proficient and more capable of functioning academically. Computer software is under development to enable educators to construct sentence verification passages and to administer and score these procedures electronically (Mestre & Royer 1988).

Story retelling measures.

Of the three measures presented here as procedures for determining students' language comprehension, story retelling activities are the most open, the most facilitative of students' personal performance. Short age-appropriate stories are selected for students to listen to and retell. Story passages containing between 100 and 150 words are recommended for students between five and eight years of age. Longer stories may be appropriate for older students. As with the other comparable measures, stories can be selected from commercial or local sources and developed for use in multiple languages. Since it is not possible to observe and analyze all of the aspects of the stories as the students produce them, responses can be recorded for further analysis. Recordings can also be used to determine performance in describing events, organizing information in sequence, and communicating the salient aspects of the story (Mattes & Omark 1984).

Researchers analyzing students' narratives from the aspect of sequential development have developed a framework for identifying the level of story production (Hedburg & Stoel-Gammon 1986; Van Dongen & Westby 1986). This framework is useful in understanding the sequential narrative development (Fradd et. al. 1989). The developmental sequence for analyzing the properties of narratives is presented in Figure 3-2.

Using the framework presented in Figure 3-2, narratives can be analyzed in terms of predictable developmental sequences. Initially, students talk of events by relating words, phrases, and sentences to specific actions. At this level, children's communication may appear to be disconnected and unrelated to the

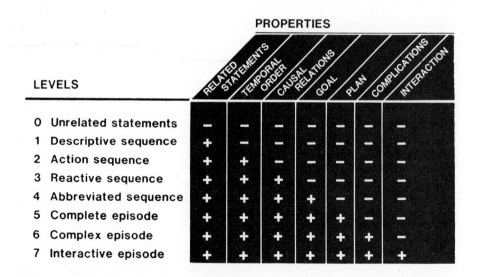

PROPERTIES

LEVELS	RELATED STATEMENTS	TEMPORAL ORDER	CAUSAL RELATIONS	GOAL	PLAN	COMPLICATIONS	INTERACTION
0 Unrelated statements	−	−	−	−	−	−	−
1 Descriptive sequence	+	−	−	−	−	−	−
2 Action sequence	+	+	−	−	−	−	−
3 Reactive sequence	+	+	+	−	−	−	−
4 Abbreviated sequence	+	+	+	+	−	−	−
5 Complete episode	+	+	+	+	+	−	−
6 Complex episode	+	+	+	+	+	+	−
7 Interactive episode	+	+	+	+	+	+	+

Figure 3-2. Structural Properties of Story Grammars

event being described (Wallach 1990). As students gain experience in telling stories, they produce more complex narratives. Following the mainstream framework, students in the process of learning to tell stories usually produce descriptive lists of words and phrases, level one narratives. Next they move toward producing language that includes actions and temporal order, a level two sequence. The next stage of development, level three, includes not only actions but reactions that show an understanding of cause and effect relationships. As language develops, students at level four include an understanding of a goal to be attained through these actions. More complex episodes, such as those produced at level five, include not only goal oriented actions, but also a clear plan of action. Level six and seven narratives result in stories that include complications and then interactive episodes with several sequences of actions, goals, and plans. Typically, mainstream students can tell and retell level seven stories by the time they are seven years old. However, non-mainstream students may require several years of exposure and development before they are able to retell stories at this level.

Videotaped observations of students retelling their stories can be an important part of the assessment process. Videotape recordings of students telling or retelling a story provide insight into the students' general orientation toward the communication process, as well as their ability to relate the specific story in question. Students from culturally and linguistically diverse backgrounds may have developed communication styles that differ from the mainstream style. Recordings permit review of specific aspects of the story teller that may differ from expectations. Students who appear hesitant or restricted may be trying to accommodate their narrative production to their perceptions of the model they have been provided. Recordings also permit review of the story telling process as a whole event, as well as an observation of discrete segments. As students gain experience telling and retelling stories in the ways that stories are told in the mainstream, their language usually begins to conform to the typical mainstream narrative patterns. Students should be encouraged to continue to develop and use the patterns expressed within their homes and communities as well as the mainstream patterns of the school.

It goes without saying that teachers need to be sure the model they present for story telling and retelling reflects the type of language they want students to produce. Students are usually good imitators of what they hear and see. The original narrative presented to the students for retelling must contain all the features students are expected to include in retelling their narrative. If, for example, the students are provided with a narrative that contains only a descriptive sequence, a level one-type narrative, it is improbable that they will retell a story at a higher level. If students are presented with a story in halting, sing-song voice, they will probably produce an equivalent type of story. When students produce strange stories, comparisons with the original or an equivalent story can provide insight into the source of difficulty.

Students may react not only to the language but the ethnicity of the story teller (Fuchs & Fuchs 1989). If students are experiencing difficulties in retelling a story, the teacher may want to consider having diverse role or language models provide the same or an equivalent story. Teachers may also want to invite observers who are familiar with students' language and culture to monitor the ways stories are being presented to students. Cultural and linguistic informants may be able to assist teachers in developing strategies for producing narratives that are congruent with students' cultural experiences and linguistic expectations.

Teachers can use videotaped models as well as live models for promoting story retelling. The use of videotaped stories can promote the standardization of the assessment process. The objective of this assessment process is to determine students' strengths as well as their limitations, so that instruction can be provided at a level that will enable students to experience success.

Students who are proficient in more than one language should be encouraged to continue to develop and use both English and their non-English language. Although bilingual students may be able to retell their stories in either language, there are potential differences that may occur in the retelling process in English and in the non-English language. In terms of quantitative measures, such as the overall length of the retold story, bilingual students may be on a par with their monolingual age peers. However, in terms of qualitative measures, bilingual students may not be as competent as their monolingual counterparts. Specific differences may be observed in stories involving emotional reactions. Differences in the quality of retold stories may result from differences in students' prior experiences and opportunities to retell equivalent stories in two languages. Differences could also occur when students' exposure to diverse texts and literature forms are limited (Mace-Matluck & Koike 1991).

RESEARCH IN PRACTICE
Assessing Comprehension

---

1. Language comprehension has been identified as one of the most important and productive measures of students' ability to use language effectively. Why? Explain how this could be and provide examples to support your answer.

2. What does it mean that in tasks assessing comprehension, students are expected to focus on the syntactic and semantic aspects of language rather than the phonemic and graphophonemic aspects? How does this focus fit with the current emphasis on whole language instruction?

3. Why might it be productive or insightful to develop equivalent measures of students' comprehension skills in two languages?

4. Explain the implications of the following findings: (a) a student is found to have a significantly higher level of comprehension in English than in her non-English language; (b) a student is found to have a higher level of comprehension in his non-English language than in English, but this difference is not significant; (c) a student is found to have limited comprehension skills in both languages?

5. Three examples have been offered for assessing students' comprehension. Collaborate with a colleague to develop specific measures that could be used to assess the comprehension of students with whom you work. Encourage colleagues to develop other comparable comprehension measures. Share your experiences with other educators in your school. Do these activities assist you and the educators with whom you work to understand the needs and the instructional levels of your students in ways that you were not able to obtain through traditional measures?

SUMMARIZING SECTION ONE:
Identifying the Elements of Oral Proficiency

This section has presented an overview of information on ways that language proficiency is defined and assessed. Factors that influence performance were identified and described. Strategies for addressing these factors were presented. Typically, academic language proficiency is assessed through written format. However, oral academic language development is usually a precursor for written language development in young language learners. Examining students' oral language development in social as well as academic contexts is important in providing them with appropriate learning opportunities. In determining students' proficiency, the process of communicating and of providing meaning is differentiated from the products of communication. For new language learners, attempts at creating and grasping meaning are initially as important as the resulting products. Through supporting new learners' efforts at accessing and developing meaning, teachers provide the scaffolding for both cognitive and linguistic language development.

In assessing academic language development, it is important to differentiate between discrete point and holistic communication. Discrete point assessment examines products from a purely linguistic perspective. Holistic communicative assessment subsumes linguistic knowledge within a communicative framework. Examples were offered in this section for assessing students' performances on a range of oral tasks. This range included a variety of specific activities that produce insights into the ways that students organize information as well as produce it. Dynamic, interactive assessment of both social and academic language provides starting points as well as strategies for continuing the development of meaningful language and the cognitive academic language development required for success in school. Here receptive skills usually exceed productive skills so that both listening and speaking activities are necessary for monitoring students' growth. An understanding of students' receptive and expressive skills in both social and academic contexts is important in meeting the needs of all students who are learning English as a new language; it is essential for students who may be experiencing learning difficulties.

WHAT CAN YOU DO?

1. List and describe the type of information that might be collected to determine the academic and social language proficiency of LEP students. How might this process be different for non-LEP NELB students? For students in general? Would every student require this type of assessment? What criteria might be used to differentiate students needing a comprehensive assessment from students who do not?

2. What is the important information that needs to be assessed about the proficiency of students learning English as a new language? What are the constraints to assessment that the attainment of this information presents?

SECTION TWO

ASSESSING ORAL LANGUAGE PERFORMANCE

S ection Two addresses the measurement of oral language performance within school settings. The first part of the section is devoted to the operationalization of the concept and process of measuring linguistic proficiency. Suggestions are offered for eliciting, observing, and analyzing performance. Next, proficiency information is combined with information on students' performance on academic tasks involving language and communication skills to develop an integrated assessment of language performance.

MEASURING LANGUAGE PROFICIENCY

Language development occurs in predictable sequences from initial sound production to the relationship of sound and symbol creating and interpreting meaning. While some aspects of the process of learning a new language are similar to the strategies and the procedures of first language learning, some aspects are different. Second language learners bring a sense of maturity, cognitive development, and a knowledge base of the task of making meaning out of unknown sounds and symbols that they did not have when they began learning their first language. When students' backgrounds contain successful experiences in literacy development, they can apply these experiences in the transition toward academic as well as social language development in the new language (Collier 1987). In order to understand students' developmental second language proficiency, it is important to assess language skills in both English and the non-English language. If a student is experiencing learning difficulties and is being considered for special education placement, federal law requires assessment in the student's native language. How this assessment process is to occur has not been specified. States and school districts have addressed this requirement through a variety of guidelines and approaches (Baca & Cervantes 1989). Given that few training programs are available for preparing school psychologists, speech pathologists, or special educators for this task (Fradd et al. 1990; Wilen, Fradd & Vázquez-Montilla 1991), the approaches as well as the results of the assessment process have the potential for as much diversity as the students being assessed. The information presented here is not designed to be used to differentiate students with learning disabilities from students with naturally occurring second language learning needs. It is a beginning step in the process of identifying students' performance in the process of learning English as a new language and for providing meaningful input relevant to students' instructional needs. If students are not successful in regular instructional settings, this information can be used for determining how their needs can best be met.

DEFINING LANGUAGE PROFICIENCY

For purposes of discussion within this subsection, language proficiency is defined as the elements of form, content, and sociolinguistic competence found within the act of communicating, in either oral or written modes. The components, such as metalinguistic and metacognitive knowledge, discussed in the first section of this chapter, are also relevant to successful communication, and are considered within this section as components of the process of observing and integrating the measurement of proficiency and performance.

Language development has been visualized as a triangle with the narrowest tip pointing downward (Omaggio 1986). The triangle can be divided into horizontal segments depicting levels of proficiency. The lowest portion would indicate the level of language corresponding to a beginning learner. Moving upward, each level marker is indicative of progressive development of proficiency. It represents a linguistic and cognitive threshold that a student who is developing proficiency in English must pass. Characteristics of language produced at each level include aspects of the form, function, and content of the communication. The top of the triangle signifies the level of proficiency of an educated native speaker, a college graduate. At this highest level of proficiency, individuals are able to successfully execute a broad range of language tasks including lengthy intellectual monologues on abstract concepts. Most of the research using the triangle has focused on the language of adult and older teenagers. This research has been pioneered by the American Council of Teachers of Foreign Languages (ACTFL) (Omaggio 1986). Throughout this book differences between the language of children and of adults have been highlighted. The differences between the processes of acquiring English as a new language by adults and by children represent the use of significantly different strategies and learning approaches. Most of the research on English second language acquisition has occurred with adults. Here the emphasis is on the language development of children. It is important to clearly differentiate between these two groups when focusing on the needs of children. Figure 3-3 illustrates a modified version of the triangle of language proficiency designed to describe the development of child language proficiency.

Conceptualizing the language development of young second language learners.

For purposes of discussion, only the lower proficiency levels of the triangle are considered here. Children are not college educated native speakers. Within

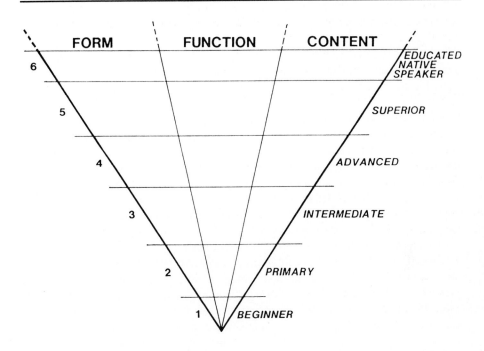

Figure 3-3. The language triangle

the lower range of levels, children's language differs significantly from adult language. Child language is less abstract, less complex and more oriented to the present than the future or the past (Obler 1989). Children also tend to learn different aspects of language better than others and to use different acquisition strategies than adults (Harley 1986; Westby, in press b).

Referring to the example of grabbing a phrase and holding on (Fillmore 1976), children tend to grasp phrases and use them to initiate and maintain communication more readily than adults.

Children seldom develop a large repertoire of language without applying their knowledge in meaningful and creative contexts (Rice 1980; Lindfors 1987). As a result, the amount of language that is learned before the child crosses the first threshold of meaningful communication is much less than it may be for an adult. For babies and toddlers, communicative acts are not memorized; they are generated through the process of conveying meaning. Older children can memorize phrases and sentences, but their repertoire of memorized language is usually substantially less than that of the typical adult learning a second language (Ellis 1985b; Lindfors 1987). For this reason, the triangle of child language has a small starting point or tip. The sides are positioned at wide angles to illustrate the span of concepts, content, and general language that must be mastered before the student crosses the next threshold.

The following represents a brief overview of the development of academic language as illustrated by Figure 3-4, page 137. The first threshold crossed, the movement from beginner to primary level language, represents the distinction between the use of memorized language and the production of creative language to meet personal needs (Chomsky 1972; Lindfors 1987). Achievement of the next threshold, movement from primary to intermediate level language, is much more complex than the achievement of the first threshold. The achievement of the intermediate level reflects the change from expression at the single sentence level to expression in groups of coherent sentences or paragraphs. It represents a significant change in the ways that the learner thinks and conceptualizes, as well as produces language. As discussed within the section on text structures, paragraph development, in either narrative or expository structures, requires an understanding of structure, coherence, and cohesion not observed in early descriptive sentence level language.

Attainment of the next threshold, movement between intermediate and advanced levels, reflects the development of integrative language skills employed in discussing abstract topics. Students who function at the upper intermediate level tend to be able to participate in regular English classrooms with minimal support. Characteristics of language development are not given consideration beyond the upper intermediate level here because students who are able to function at the higher levels do not typically require specialized language assessment or instructional support. A comprehensive description of the characteristics of language at each of the developmental levels is presented in Table 3-9.

Quantity is the first salient feature of production. The space within each area of the triangle symbolically depicts the quantity of language produced at each proficiency level. As students develop greater proficiency, they tend to produce larger quantities of language. This space within the levels can also be depicted as the amount of language that would fill common containers such as a thimble, a cup, a bowl, or a basket. The triangle adapted to illustrate child language acquisition is presented in Figure 3-4.

The passage from one level to another happens slowly. Children may produce some characteristics of more than one level of language development, depending on the tasks, the contexts, and the children's willingness to communicate. In order to avoid giving students tasks which they are unable or reluctant to perform, it is recommended that they be rated at the lowest level of proficiency that they exhibit.

Information on level descriptions can be used in determining students' level of language production. This information is presented as a checklist for eliciting and observing student language (Fradd in press). The list contains mid-level markers as well as indicators of higher and entry level descriptors.

TABLE 3-9. DEVELOPMENTAL CHARACTERISTICS OF STUDENT[2] LANGUAGE

BEGINNER (Level 1):

ENTRY LEVEL: The child is unable to communicate in meaningful words, but may use sounds, gestures, and other forms of non-verbal communication to achieve basic needs and wants.

INDICATORS OF PROGRESS TOWARD THE NEXT LEVEL: The child may be able to recite learned material and produce a list of vocabulary words on demand. Although minimal meaningful communication is produced with words, the child may have an expanded repertory of meaningful gestures and sounds. Imitation of peer and adult behaviors, including words, gestures, intonation, and prosody, may support communication.

PRIMARY (Level 2):

ENTRY LEVEL: Expression is restricted to the phrase or sentence level. Communication generally consists of applications of memorized words and phrases in appropriate and meaningful contexts. Expressions relate generally to personal desires, needs, and observations. An understanding of the grammar and the structure of the language is emerging but is not yet well-developed. Past and future tense may be marked by descriptive words rather than correct verb forms. Question asking and answering is beginning to emerge. The child still requires interactive support to produce sustained meaningful communications. Communication may be difficult to understand by someone unaccustomed to interacting with non-native speakers at this level. Gestures continue to be used to support comprehensible communication.

INDICATORS OF PROGRESS TOWARD THE NEXT LEVEL: Expression is still generally restricted to the sentence level, but there is a clear effort to elaborate on a topic and to create clusters of related phrases and sentences. What, who, where questions are asked and answered. Interactions are beginning to occur on a variety of topics, in different contexts. Grammar is still emerging and not at the level of native-speaker age peers (*according to age appropriate expectations*), in past, present, and future forms. The child continues to need support in sustaining meaningful interactions. An understanding of relationships, characteristics, and sequences emerges here, as the child begins to classify and organize items. Support is required to differentiate important from irrelevant features and characteristics. Coordinating conjunctions and clauses, and frequent use of prepositions appear here. Communication may still be difficult to understand by someone unaccustomed to interacting with non-native speakers. However, the child is beginning to show an awareness of the listener's perspective, and attempts to modify communication and provide listeners with meaning through a variety of forms, including gestures.

(continued on page 134)

[2] For purposes of discussion within this text, the terms "children" and "students" are used interchangeably to refer to individuals within the ages of 5 to 12. Information presented here may be relevant to both older and younger second language learners, but it is not the purpose of this text to make those distinctions.

INTERMEDIATE (Level 3):

ENTRY LEVEL: Communication is characterized by a range of responses from words and sentences to paragraph-like products. Narratives with a beginning, middle, and ending emerge here. Multiple sentences are produced to describe events. What, who, where are asked and answered in more complex question forms. Questioning strategies are applied to ask and answer how, why, and when questions (*within age appropriate expectations*). Consistent use of past, present, and future grammatical structures appear (*within age appropriate expectations*) with 80% to 90% accuracy. The child may need to be requested or prompted to speak in the past or the future tense. Coordinating and subordinating conjunctions appear to mark clausal relationships. Prepositional phrases are used with about 80% accuracy. The child begins to develop elaborate creative fictional stories, to show cause and effect relationships, to infer meanings and intents, and predict outcomes. The ability to categorize and group and to relate items or events in sequence becomes clear. There may still be a need for some support in developing responses involving higher order thinking skills in unfamiliar contexts. The child is usually understood by people unaccustomed to interacting with non-native speakers.

INDICATORS OF PROGRESS TOWARD THE NEXT LEVEL: The child does all of the above with greater elaboration and precision than previously. Comprehension of the difference between figurative and real expressions is in evidence here. The child demonstrates an ability to produce multiple sentences that are well-developed, grammatically correct, and centrally focused on a variety of topics. Appropriate resolution of personal difficulties, and the ability to state and defend personal ideas and preferences emerges (*within age appropriate expectations*). The child demonstrates an understanding of the listener's perspective (*within age appropriate expectations*). While there may be elements of non-native speaker qualities within the communication (such as accented speech and organization of information), the child is generally understood by people unaccustomed to interacting with non-native speakers. At this level, the child is able to participate in academic interactions in a regular classroom setting, but may still require support in mastering concepts involving differences in cultural variations of communications, especially meanings and intents.

ADVANCED (Level 4):

Academic language on abstract topics is coherent and cohesive, and comparable to similar language from age peers. Elementary and middle school students should be evaluated in a manner that is comparable to their age peers.

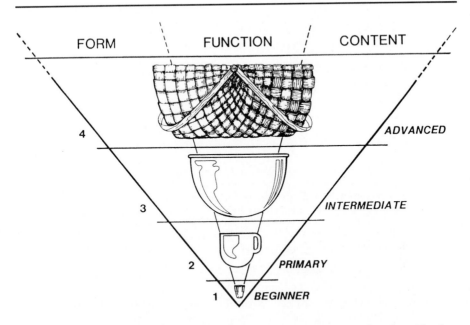

Figure 3-4. The triangle with the illustrations of the thimble, cup, bowl, and basket.

The mid-level descriptors are transitional steps that many students demonstrate in the process of developing higher levels of proficiency. The checklist is presented in Table 3-10.

Sometimes school environments do not provide students with reasons or opportunities for developing higher levels of expressive language that go beyond naming and listing. Tasks can be organized to elicit specific language as well as to promote opportunities for using language meaningfully in increasingly complex exchanges. Unless care is taken to ensure the meaningfulness of this type of language, the elicitation process, as employed by an adult, tends to distort the communicative possibilities students may demonstrate naturally (Labov 1972). There is a great difference between encouraging students to develop language for meaningful exchanges within a variety of purposeful settings and using language to complete the pages in a workbook. An example from *Life* magazine illustrates this reality. Mr. Sweeney taught his intermediate school students to use math to solve problems and develop community spirit. The students conducted surveys and organized campaigns to reduce the amount of graffiti on the walls of their school. By using their math to develop bar graphs, charts, and statistics, the students were able to communicate to civic leaders, businesses and even the state legislature their suggestions for improving community spirit by reducing graffiti (*Life* 1992).

TABLE 3-10. CHECKLIST OF CHARACTERISTICS OF
LANGUAGE PROFICIENCY

BEGINNER LEVEL 1: (Sound to Phrase Level)
Entry Level:
____ Produces sounds related to the fulfillment of wants
____ Uses gestures to communicate

Progression within the Level:
____ Recites memorized words and phrases
____ Begins to combine sounds, words & gestures to express personal intents

PRIMARY LEVEL 2: (Phrase to Sentence Level)
Entry Level:
____ Uses sounds, words, gestures, and short phrases to communicate
____ Demonstrates an awareness that phrases can be segmented into words
and recombined to communicate different intents
____ Combines words & phrases in meaningful ways to express personal intents
____ Asks what and where questions
____ Begins to mark tense with appropriate grammar, but also uses time
markers such as *last night* or *next week* combined with present tense
verb forms
____ Requires less support from others to sustain communication

Progression toward Next Level:
____ Speaks in phrases and sentences with emerging ability to organize
multiple sentences of information around a main topic
____ Asks and answers what, where, and who questions appropriately
____ Requires less support from others to sustain communication, but
not always understood by native speakers
____ Shows emerging developmental but incomplete understanding of
language used to communicate cause-effect relationships, sequences,
and categorization processes
____ Asks why, how & when questions but not necessarily in appropriate
form
____ Demonstrates an emerging awareness of listener's perspective in
communication

INTERMEDIATE (Level 3): (Sentence to Paragraph Level)
Entry Level:
____ Uses a range of responses to communicate, from single words to
sentences and groups of sentences that form paragraph-like speech
____ Produces action narratives with a beginning and ending
____ Asks a range of questions including what, who, where, and how, why,
and when questions, not necessarily with fully developed form

Progression toward Next Level:
____ Consistently uses past, present & future grammatical structures correctly
____ Produces narratives with a beginning, middle, and ending
____ Elaborates creative stories
____ Shows an understanding of cause and effect relationships, sequence,
and temporal order
____ Infers meanings and intents, and predicts outcomes
____ Is usually understood by people unaccustomed to interacting with
non-native speakers
____ Consistently uses past, present & future grammatical structures correctly
____ Uses a range of responses to communicate, from single words and
sentences to coherent paragraphs

In order to determine the range of students' proficiency, elicitation tasks, along with tasks performed as part of the regular school routine, can be utilized to observe and evaluate students. Comparisons can be made between each of the students' performances in using his/her non-English language and in using English. The performances of monolingual and LEP students can be compared by age, grade, and socioeconomic level to determine the developmental aspects of the students' language learning. This information is important in promoting an understanding of the development of academic language skills for students from both mainstream and non-mainstream backgrounds (Ventriglia 1982). It is also important in observing specific differences among learners.

Comparisons can also be made, for example, between LEP students of the same and different language backgrounds in order to understand the developmental process of language learning within an age or grade expectancy range. The process of comparing language development can be extended to include groups of monolingual and LEP students who have been identified as mildly handicapped or as educationally at risk. This information can be helpful in planning proactive school-wide programs that limit the use of special education services to meet students' needs, by promoting collaboration to make regular classroom placements effective in meeting students' needs (Fuchs, Fuchs, Hamlett & Stecher 1991).

Comparative information is also helpful in enabling educators to focus on the similarities rather than the differences in students' language development. Results of comparisons indicate that the language of young students in programs for mild disabilities and young students in regular programs is more similar than different. The developmental process appears to be the same for both handicapped and typical students, whether they are LEP or English proficient (Vázquez-Montilla 1991).

A suggested form for observing a student's performance across time is presented in Table 3-11. This form can be modified to compare the same student in two languages as illustrated in Table 3-12. Table 3-13 illustrates a comparison of the performance of several students on the same task using the same criteria. Students can be classified, for example, as typical LEP students (T/LEP), typical monolingual students (T/MONO), students identified as having specific learning disabilities who are LEP (SLD/LEP), or students identified as having specific learning disabilities who are monolingual in English (SLD/MONO). In Tables 3-12 and 3-13, a small number of criteria are included to illustrate the concept of potential comparisons.

Different language descriptors can be included depending on the features or the aspects of language development under consideration. The form can also be modified to focus on specific aspects of the development of proficiency within one level at a time. For example, information can be collected on a variety of students' performances within the primary or intermediate level. Longitudinal information can be collected on each student across time in order to monitor language development.

TABLE 3-11. LANGUAGE PROFICIENCY OBSERVATION OF A SINGLE STUDENT ACROSS TIME

Descriptors/ Observation Times	1	2	3	4	5	6 etc.
Beginner communicated						
recited learned material						
other						
expressed through single words, formulaic expressions, and gestures						
created new phrases						
other						
Primary expressed using long phrases, sentence level expressions						
controlled syntax						
other						
used past, present, and future verb forms consistently						
gave appropriate responses in different contexts						
answered what, who, and where questions (concrete)						
asked what, who, and where questions (concrete)						
other						
Intermediate answered when, how, and why questions (abstract)						
asked when, how, and why questions (abstract)						
gave accurate descriptions of situations and events						
other						

Descriptors/ Observation Times	1	2	3	4	5	6 etc.
produced well-developed, grammatically correct paragraph responses in a variety of contexts						
narrated with a beginning, middle, and end						
other						

Did All (x); Did Partially (±); Did Not (—)

Adapted with permission from: Vázquez-Montilla, E. (1991). *A comparison of language samples of monolingual and limited English proficient students* (Unpublished doctoral dissertation) University of Florida, Gainesville, Florida.

RESEARCH IN PRACTICE
Defining Language Proficiency

1. Describe the development of language proficiency as depicted by the measurements of the thimble, cup, bowl, and basket. Is this conceptualization helpful in illustrating how language develops?

2. Discuss the characteristics of child language development.

3. Differentiate second language development of children and adults.

4. Tape record a collection of five language samples of students in your school. Try to get samples from students who are considered to be proficient and students who are considered to be limited in English proficiency. Describe your observations of the samples informally and then listen to the tape recording and determine the level of proficiency within the framework. What differences occurred between the informal process and the process of using the framework? What does this information tell you about observing and assessing language? What did you learn from this process?

ASSESSING LANGUAGE FUNCTIONS

Accurate assessment of students' ability to effectively communicate cannot be determined by studying students' utterances in isolation. A framework for assessing speech acts that focuses on the intents of communication or the functional use of language, as well as the contexts in which the communication

TABLE 3-12. USE OF LANGUAGE PROFICIENCY DESCRIPTORS WITH T/LEP AND SLD/LEP GROUPS

| | T/LEP | | | | | | SLD/LEP | | | | | |
| | ENGLISH | | | SPANISH | | | ENGLISH | | | SPANISH | | |
Descriptors	S1	S2	S3	S1	S2	S3	S4	S5	S6	S4	S5	S6
communicated												
recited learned material												
expressed through single words, formulaic expressions, and gestures												
created new phrases												

Adapted with permission from: Vázquez-Montilla, E. (1991). *A comparison of language samples of monolingual and limited English proficient students* (Unpublished doctoral dissertation) University of Florida, Gainesville, Florida.

TABLE 3-13. LANGUAGE PROFICIENCY AND LANGUAGE FUNCTION FOR ALL STUDENTS IN ENGLISH

| | T/LEP | | | T/MONO | | | SLD/LEP | | | SLD/MONO | | |
Descriptors	S1	S2	S3	S1	S2	S3	S4	S5	S6	S4	S5	S6
communicated												
recited learned material												
expressed through single words, formulaic expressions, and gestures												
created new phrases												
used sentences												
controlled grammar												

Adapted with permission from: Vázquez-Montilla, E. (1991). *A comparison of language samples of monolingual and limited English proficient students* (Unpublished doctoral dissertation) University of Florida, Gainesville, Florida.

occurs, is required. The study of the functional use of language is referred to as *pragmatics* (Bloom & Lahey 1978; Mattes & Omark 1984). Researchers have identified children's behavior by action and outcome. The groups of acts that result in specific outcomes are referred to as *functions*. The term refers to specific actions taken to achieve a variety of personal goals and outcomes (Dore 1974; Simon 1979). While the focus of these acts may initially be nonlinguistic behavior, as children develop communicative skills, language begins to play an increasingly important role in the achievement of personal goals. As children develop, language becomes central to their ability to participate and to achieve. The term *language functions* has been applied to the communicative acts children use to convey meaning. Many taxonomies of such functions, or grouped classifications of speech acts and language functions, have been developed for use in observing and assessing children's behavior (Dore 1975; Mattes & Omark 1984). The types of acts considered within these taxonomies vary by the ages and the contexts of the observations.

Two taxonomies are discussed here. The first taxonomy was developed for use with preschool children (Halliday 1975; Simon 1979); and the second for use with school-aged children (Tough 1976). Although there is overlap within the taxonomies, the use of these two taxonomies provides a range of developmental focus to the observation process. It provides a range of actions and activities that can be used in eliciting language and observing children's performance in various activities. This range is important because relatively little research has occurred in the areas of language development with students from NELB backgrounds (Lindfors 1987). If only the functions used by mainstream students in academic contexts are included, the results may indicate that NELB students are deficient in their communicative development. Even with the inclusion of the functions used by younger children, the NELB students may appear deficient (Vázquez-Montilla 1991). However, the limitations may be as much a result of the elicitation and observation process as the lack of linguistic development on the part of the students.

In working with learners from multiple language backgrounds and cultures, the use of a variety of observational procedures and approaches is important. The scarcity of developmental information on NELB students means that the developmental milestones and expectancies based on the development of mainstream children are not necessarily appropriate or accurate for use with students from culturally diverse backgrounds (Lindfors 1987). As research with NELB students increases, new functions as well as innovative ways of observing students are being identified. These innovations may be culture and language specific as well as generalizable to larger groups of students. In the meantime, it is essential that educators remain sensitive to the developmental differences and strive to provide appropriate, supportive instruction that meets students' needs rather than penalizing students for not having skills they have never had the opportunity to learn.

Halliday's functions.

The seven functions contained within the Halliday taxonomy can be grouped into two categories: the first three relating most to social language use, and the last four relating to academic language development as well as social interaction. Suggestions for observation and elicitation can be modified to be made age, gender, and interest appropriate for older learners (Simon 1979). Some school districts have developed sets of activities and suggestions for using the Halliday taxonomy with school-aged students (Florida Department of Education, Division of Public Schools 1988). Specific suggestions for elicitation tasks are offered in the Appendix to this chapter.

When eliciting specific language functions, such as those within the Halliday taxonomy, it is a good idea to keep records of the kinds of activities and materials used. This information has several useful purposes that include providing insight into the types of elicitation procedures that are effective for different age and cultural background groups. The information also promotes standardization of the elicitation process so that other educators can understand how the data were obtained and how the process can be replicated. While standardization is not a primary consideration in the use of informal assessment procedures, it is important in comparing the performance of groups of students across tasks and time. Uniformity and standardization are important considerations in applying similar elicitation procedures with large groups of students.

Language functions can be assessed through observation. A checklist can be developed for noting the functions a student produces and for documenting examples that each child produces. These examples can be useful in observing the kinds of language produced by students within diverse contexts, such as before and after school, in the library, or during the math lesson (Halliday 1973; 1975; Mattes & Omark 1984).

A second, more formal way of observing language functions is through specific elicitation strategies that require a student to produce language while manipulating materials and performing activities. Performance can be quantified through a rating as *attempted, engaged,* or *achieved* (or 1, 2, 3) in combination with an established set of age appropriate performance criteria. A rating of *attempted* would indicate that the student did briefly try the task, but did not persist in its completion. A rating of *engaged* would indicate that while the student did not successfully complete the task, the student did persist in attempting to complete it. Information on how students engage is as useful in developing appropriate instruction as information on their actual achievement. The Halliday taxonomy is presented in Table 3-14.

Performance on these language functions can be documented through the use of an observation checklist. A suggested checklist for observing LEP

TABLE 3-14. HALLIDAY'S TAXONOMY OF LANGUAGE FUNCTIONS

Function: **Instrumental**
Purpose: To satisfy personal needs; *Example:* "I want ... "
Observation: Student requesting something that is not visible

Function: **Interactional**
Purpose: To establish & maintain social interactions; *Example:* "Me and you ... "
Observation: Student interacting with others in social settings, including initiating and responding to others, and maintaining interactions

Function: **Personal**
Purpose: To express self-identity; *Example:* "I like ... "
Observation: Student naturally expressing personal ideas and preferences, or responding to questions about preferences

Function: **Regulatory**
Purpose: To control behavior; *Example:* "Do as I say ... "
Observation: Student in charge of others and interacting to achieve a goal

Function: **Heuristic**
Purpose: To learn about environment and problem-solve; *Example:* "How do you...?"
Observation: Observe student naturally asking questions or pose a problem that can't be solved without asking questions

Function: **Imaginative**
Purpose: To create a new product or an imaginary reality;
Example: "Once upon a time ... " or "Let's pretend ... "
Observation: Observe student interacting with others in free play, or listen to student make up a story using fantasy props

Function: **Informational**
Purpose: To communicate new information to others; *Example:* "I've got something new to tell you."
Observation: Observe student sharing information after a trip or a new experience; or create a situation when student learns something new that must then be presented to peers

students identified as typical (T/LEP) or as having learning disabilities (SLD/ LEP) in English and Spanish is offered in Table 3-15.

Tough's Taxonomy.

Tough's taxonomy focuses on higher order thinking skills as an important aspect of language development with elementary-age and young students. She points out that the language produced by children from educationally advantaged environments tends to be different from the language of educationally disadvantaged learners. For example, students from advantaged environments tend to provide more details, to offer justifications for behaviors, to

TABLE 3-15. SAMPLE OBSERVATION CHECKLIST OF
HALLIDAY'S LANGUAGE FUNCTIONS

| Descriptors | T/LEP | | | | | | SLD/LEP | | | | | |
| | ENGLISH | | | SPANISH | | | ENGLISH | | | SPANISH | | |
	S1	S2	S3	S1	S2	S3	S4	S5	S6	S4	S5	S6
Other language functions												
Regulatory: responded												
attempted task												
gave cohesive response												
gave pragmatically appropriate response												
related coherently												
spoke clearly												
other												
Heuristic: responded												
other												
attempted task												
gave cohesive response												
related coherently												
spoke clearly												
Imaginative: responded												
other												
attempted task												
gave cohesive response												
related coherently												
spoke clearly												
gave pragmatically appropriate response												
Other Functions or Descriptors												

Did All (x); Did Partially (±); Did Not (—)

Adapted with permission from: Vázquez-Montilla, E. (1991). *A comparison of language samples of monolingual and limited English proficient students* (Unpublished doctoral dissertation) University of Florida, Gainesville, Florida.

make comparisons, to sequence events, and to anticipate interactions and consequences. They tend to use present, past, and future tense perspectives. The language of students from educationally disadvantaged environments tends to focus on labeling objects and actions and reporting events in the present tense. In groups of students where the measured intelligence is markedly different, it may be inferred that the disadvantaged learners had not been presented with sufficient language experiences to enable them to acquire the more comprehensive range of language skills demonstrated by the advantaged learners. Since learning is based on analysis and integration of information and skills, students who have not acquired these skills at an early age may be at a particular disadvantage as instruction moves from the concrete toward the abstract tasks (Tough 1976b).

Tough's taxonomy is useful in discerning the uses of children's language and in monitoring development of thinking skills (Tough 1976a). Within each category, Tough provides a set of strategies by which the category of behaviors or language functions may be achieved. These strategies are not necessarily exhibited exclusively within that category alone. Three broad categories of behaviors, *self-maintaining*, *directing*, and *reporting*, appear to emerge first. These categories are similar to Halliday's instrumental, interactional, and personal functions. Later developing functions include: attempts toward logical *reasoning*, *predicting*, *projecting*, and *imagining*. The strategies considered within the categories of directing and reporting may also be used within these later developing language skills. The function of reporting serves the same function as narrative, linking the skills involved in observing, naming, relating, and elaborating with more academic skills such as analyzing, sequencing, and comparing and contrasting. The development of the reporting function is essential, because through it other functions emerge (Tough 1976b).

Although children may use concepts of time and temporal order in their language, they may not fully understand these concepts until much later in their development. Communication that reflects the natural order of events is more easily understood in English by young learners than communication presented with an inverted temporal order. A knowledge of the referents, the content, and the context of the communication influences its comprehensibility (Pease, Gleason & Pan 1987). Older children who have already developed these concepts in one language still need to learn the format and the contexts for asking questions in another language. While the form aspects of language learning are time-consuming, they are not as difficult as the development of the concepts (Lindfors 1987). This is an important distinction differentiating older and younger second language learners. The format for eliciting performance is important, and often sets the stage for what students produce. Within her taxonomy, Tough (1976b) provides examples of the application of the language function strategies within present and past experiences and within imagined contexts.

Synthesizing the process.

Learning to classify language acts enables educators to become effective observers of what students do to achieve meaning. The ability to classify a specific utterance is not as important as the development of the general awareness of children's performance in the process of communicating. Observation of student performance can occur informally through interactions on the way from the cafeteria to the classroom or in more formal classroom settings such as a specifically designated area of the classroom. Each context may produce a different result. For reluctant communicators, a variety of contexts may need to be tried.

The context of the communication also influences performance. For example, when the child is given a set of pictures and asked to tell about them, to tell a story, or to guess what will happen next, each of these requests demands a different response. Each of these requests may produce different types of language. Recording this information can occur on a checklist, through notes recorded by the observer, through the production of a transcription of the language sample, or on audio or video tapes. Before setting out to elicit language, educators need to have a clear understanding of what they want, how the information will be recorded, and how it will be used.

The process of evaluating student performance also provides an opportunity for examining educators' abilities to effectively interact with students. It is a developmental process that may not come easily to some people. In understanding the development of students' language, there are several ways that teachers can focus on performance. If they want to know what students know, they can focus on the content of communication, that is, the ideas and information presented. If they want to know how children perform, they can focus on the functions that the students can achieve and the ways they use language. Both are important sources of information about what children do. Clearly, obtaining an understanding of student competence, rather than the form of the language produced, is the goal of this process. Content and function, however, cannot be separated from form because the form influences the comprehensibility of language. Form can also influence students' attempts to communicate. As students realize that their communicative efforts do not conform to the expectations of the environment, they may desist in communicating (Vázquez-Montilla 1991). As educators become aware of the development of students' language, they become effective facilitators of not only students' attempts to communicate, but also their learning processes. Teachers can assist students in formulating ideas, considering relationships and perspectives, and reflecting on personal experiences. Only when there is a clear process of classifying stu-dents' language is it possible to fully appreciate the complexity of becoming effective communicators and to assist students in becoming successful (Tough 1976b).

RESEARCH IN PRACTICE
Assessing Language Functions

1. Describe Halliday's taxonomy and its uses.

2. How would you develop a taxonomy for observing the imaginative function? What types of activities stimulate children's imagination? How would you observe the development of imagination? Why is an understanding of students' imaginative language important?

3. Why is the ability to accurately observe students' communicative acts important? How would you share this information with colleagues?

4. How does the information on text structures relate to the information on proficiency and performance of language functions?

SUMMARIZING SECTION TWO:
Assessing Oral Language Performance

Students' performances on specific tasks can be used as one way to determine their language proficiency. In order to do this, effective ways to observe and quantify students' language development are needed. Many of the differentiations made in students' performances are artificial and useful only in the mind of those engaged in the assessment process. Language cannot be separated from the context in which it is produced. An understanding of the contexts of language production is helpful in determining the influence of the environment on the language production of students (Ramirez 1987).

To continue the visualization of language proficiency through the use of the triangle, the graphic can be divided into three parts representing *form* (grammar and phonology), *content* (concepts and semantic variables), and *function* (language tasks and communicative acts) observed in the act of communication. Students' language can be monitored using this framework of variables.

The content, or the topic of communication, has the potential for changing proficiency level. If the topic of the communication is not familiar to the student, or if it is too abstract, students will not perform as proficiently as when the content is familiar and less abstract. Similarly, the functions of the students' communication also have the potential to influence perceived proficiency. For example, if students are unaccustomed to asking questions, they will have difficulty completing a *heuristic* (question-asking) task. Variables such as age, sex, ethnicity, and language background must be considered in evaluating the language production of all students. These variables become even more important for culturally and linguistically different students (Fuchs & Fuchs 1989). The content of communication can be considered separately from form and function, but it cannot be isolated from it. In assessing student performance, prior experience with the content being used (the materials, information, and concepts) is an important consideration. If no prior experience has occurred, the students' performance will likely be different from their performance with familiar topics and materials. Form is influenced by familiarity with content.

Decisions must be made about the overall benefits to be obtained through the use of different types of assessment procedures. Trade-offs occur between expediency and benefit, between naturalistic performance and academic focus. Before embarking on an assessment process, these variables need to be considered. Because schooling is an unnatural act for many students, it is not possible to observe and assess students' language at school in ways that would reveal the same information that could be obtained at home. While the focus of the assessment of most students is their performance in academic contexts, care must be taken to provide students with activities and communicative opportunities that reveal what they know as well as what they may not know. Within the constraints of the school environment, dynamic, holistic activities can be organized to promote authentic communication and to engage students in meaningful interactions that reveal their developing skills (Damico 1985). At the same time, these types of activities are more difficult to prepare and more time-consuming to organize than traditional assessment procedures. In developing new assessment procedures, a balance must be attained so that the activities meet the criteria of promoting authentic language without becoming overly difficult to administer or analyze. This balance may be difficult to achieve in classrooms where students are typically sedentary and most activities are paper and pencil based.

In most schools there are performance levels students must achieve for promotion or to meet other criteria included in pupil progression records. These levels are usually stated as numeric information on standardized tests. Little attention has been given to providing assessment information other than standardized test scores to achieve these outcomes. In the discussions presented earlier, examples were provided of alternative ways to assess student performance. Students' academic language is considered in terms of performance assessment type measurement. The development of this type of assessment is based on the requirement that students are expected to demonstrate specific competencies in order to be considered ready for the next grade or the next level. The fact that these levels have not been clearly specified except as numbers on standardized tests does not negate their presence. When student performance is compared to an established achievement criterion, attainment of the specified level is interpreted to mean that the student has demonstrated an ability or achieved a level of mastery (Bloom & Lahey 1978). Academic language performance can be considered within the overall framework of criterion achievement. If the behaviors that successful English proficient students produce are specified, this information can be used to develop similar behaviors with NELB students (Damico 1991). If successful third graders produce coherent oral paragraphs that include a main idea and information with at least three supporting details in different contexts, then we can predict that students who only produce labels and action words may have difficulty in third grade work where they are expected to use more complete language. This is not to suggest that all LEP learners be retained in second grade until they speak in paragraphs or that they should be given drill and practice activities until they develop this skill. It does mean that students with limited academic language development will predictably encounter great learning difficulties unless they are provided with support, effective instruction, and learning activities designed to promote academic language development. Determining students' current levels of performance and developing the support, effective instruction, and learning activities that promote success are what educators are about. Clearly, a great deal remains to be learned.

WHAT CAN YOU DO?

1. What is a taxonomy of language functions? Why is a functions taxonomy useful?

2. How would you use observational information provided by a taxonomy? How would your colleagues feel about the utility of this information?

3. Can you make a taxonomy of the language functions that are prevalent in your school? Would this taxonomy be different for males and females? Would it be different for teachers and students? Are there language functions used by students in your school that have not been included in this list?

4. Discuss the adaptation of these taxonomies to other languages and cultures. What are the limitations of these taxonomies in terms of culture of the language? For example, is question-asking an important function in all cultures? Would other features such as structure, form, and content influence the prevalence of language functions? Why is an awareness of these differences important?

5. Discuss some of the advantages and disadvantages that must be considered in implementing an assessment program that focuses on what students do rather than on the use of standardized tests and placement criteria. Why is a consideration of these advantages and disadvantages important?

6. Why is an understanding of what students do in the process of language learning useful in implementing an effective assessment program?

7. Describe the strategies you believe to be important in implementing a realistic and effective language assessment plan. Prepare to defend your answers in a discussion with colleagues and administrators who may not share your perspective. What would you tell them?

SECTION THREE

CONSIDERING LIMITED LANGUAGE DEVELOPMENT AND LANGUAGE IMPAIRMENT WITHIN THE CONTEXT OF LITERACY

In the mainstream culture of the United States, literacy within a technologically oriented society is central to successful economic and social participation. Schools are a vehicle for socializing students within the mainstream culture and for enabling them to become literate. To many educators, literacy may be interpreted as referring to the ability to read and write. This narrow perception of literacy focuses on the development of reading and writing skills in isolation from the contexts in which these skills are applied. To acquire abstract thinking skills, learners require opportunities that carry meaning and are intrinsically reinforcing. Literacy involves the manipulation of bodies of knowledge, chunks of information including the forms, content, and sociolinguistic structures of language. Literacy develops out of shared, rather than isolated, contexts and events and is closely linked to the communicative interactions arising from participation within these social events. Perceptions and definitions of intelligence influence the ways that learning and language development are conceptualized. These perceptions also influence the ways that learning and language development are measured. Issues of intelligence, learning, and language are central to the development of literacy (Miller 1990). The development of literacy is a sociocognitive activity that enables the learner to become a participant in the discovery of a world of ideas and information not available within the routine passage of daily life.

IDENTIFYING LITERACY TASKS

Before critical decisions can be made about a student's instructional needs, comprehensive data must be collected on the student's performance in various linguistic contexts and environments. These contexts include both social and academic performance. Information from both of these contexts can be integrated to provide a comprehensive and meaningful analysis of what students can do and what they still need to learn to do. A descriptive approach to collecting and organizing data can be helpful in making decisions and in planning for and providing instruction (Damico 1991). The reliability and validity of the data collected must be verified, not only in terms of students' abilities to participate and perform, but also in terms of students' opportunities for participation. In other words, before decisions can be made about the student's limitations, we must verify that the tasks the student is expected to perform meet a set of criteria that ensure the validity and reliability of their use within the decision-making process.

Utilizing observational strategies focusing on what students do within the instructional environment provides information that links and integrates instruction and assessment. This integration can result in effective instructional assessment. Table 3-17 presents suggestions for observing and documenting students' performance on tasks representative of the curriculum in which the student is expected to function.

RESEARCH IN PRACTICE
Identifying Literacy Tasks

1. **How is the language of literacy different from social language?**

2. **How could you combine information on language functions with the information presented in Table 3-17 to develop a plan for assessing students' literacy development?**

ENSURING RELIABILITY AND AUTHENTICITY

The linguistic realism of the communication act is an important aspect of the assessment of meaningful language. For this reason, communicative settings, in which students are producing authentic language to meet personal and group needs, provide a clearer picture of a student's ability to communicate than contrived tasks and settings. Creating environments where students can communicate purposefully is not easy. In most academically oriented school environments, the emphasis is on learning for learning's sake rather than for the production of real world outcomes. However, when students' opinions and suggestions are sought out and implemented, the assessment of comprehension and meaning along with the assessment of grammatical and pragmatic knowledge can be carried out (Damico 1991).

In addition to collecting communication information in authentic environments, it is important to verify that the information collected is representative or typical of the student's actual daily production. The purpose of this information is primarily the development of a comprehensive database on students' social and academic skills. Social skill information forms the foundation of children's academic learning. The reliability and validity of this information is

TABLE 3-17. SUGGESTIONS FOR OBSERVING STUDENTS' PERFORMANCE WITHIN THE CLASSROOM CONTEXT

LANGUAGE PERFORMANCE	OBSERVATION ACTIVITIES
Relating to Others	• Spontaneous interactions with peers • Adults' recorded anecdotal records • Planned elicitation activities recorded on specifically designed observation forms
Expressing Personal Ideas and Interests	• Planned elicitation activities recorded on specifically designed observation forms • Spontaneous interactions with peers • Students' recorded anecdotal records • Adults' recorded anecdotal records • Video and audio recorded responses
Following Directions	• Planned activities that include one, two, three, and four step directions given by adults. • Student executed observation forms • Planned activities that include multiple directions given by peers • Spontaneous performance recorded in anecdotal records
Comprehending Meaning	• Spontaneous performance recorded in anecdotal records • Oral cloze tests • Oral sentence verification tasks • Story retelling
Problem-Solving	• Spontaneous interactions with peers • Planned oral activities recorded on observation forms • Observations in asking relevant questions • Peer-oriented tasks • School-oriented tasks • Social tasks
Developing Proficiency	• Discrete point production • Elicited language samples • Observations in creating new stories • Observations in producing expository language
Perceptions of Self as Learner and Communicator	• Specifically designed records to elicit student's perceptions of self • Interviews • Anecdotal records • Spontaneous interactions and reactions

especially important when students are identified as having learning problems. A set of suggestions for evaluating the authenticity of data collected on students' language performance is provided in Table 3-18. These suggestions can also be used to verify the validity of current data and to ensure that a comprehensive database is organized on which to make educational decisions about the student's placement within the educational system.

TABLE 3-18. SUGGESTIONS FOR EVALUATING AUTHENTICITY OF LANGUAGE DATA

1. Do the data collected include language samples of the students' performance in realistic situations where the goal of communication includes the transmission and comprehension of meaning?

2. Do the data collected include the following observational information on students' performance?
   - target student's interactions with peers in English
   - target student's interactions with peers in non-English language
   - target student's interactions with adults in English
   - target student's interactions with adults in non-English language

Observational information should be summarized in terms of the target student's participation within the social aspects of communicating, including the target student's efforts at initiating interactions, making repairs and maintaining interactions, and accomplishing the transmission of meaning.

3. Do the data include peer and adult reactions toward the target student?

4. Are documented difficulties within normal limits for this language and culture group? Do other students from the same linguistic and cultural background exhibit similar behaviors and linguistic features?

5. Have documented difficulties of the target student been observed in both of his/her languages or only English?

6. Have longitudinal samples been collected to determine if the target student is in the process of losing proficiency in the non-English language?

7. Has the target student participated in a consistent program of instruction that promoted effective participation and language development? *(Check to determine the student's record of school enrollment and attendance. Describe the type(s) of instruction the student received in English and non-English.)*

8. Have the observations of the parents and other family members of the target student been included with regard to language skill development?

9. What information does the target student provide about participating in activities and performing at school and at home?

RESEARCH IN PRACTICE
Ensuring Reliability and Authenticity

---

1. What do the terms *reliability* and *authenticity* mean with respect to the assessment of students who are learning English as a new language?

2. What can you do to ensure reliability in the assessment process?

3. What can you do to ensure authenticity?

ASSESSMENT OF THE LANGUAGE OF LITERACY

The appearance of thoughts and ideas in written form promotes certain ways of thinking; the process of producing written language tends to structure and organize thought in ways that do not occur in oral-only communication (Gee 1986; Scanllon & Scanllon 1981). Persons who have not developed the schema of literacy generally lack the experiences that promote what are considered literate ways of thinking. Diverse thought patterns fostered through orality are usually not congruent with the culture fostered by the development of literacy (Langer 1987; Westby & Rouse 1985).

Communication that is understood and accepted as standard across the nation is dependent on a shared knowledge of literacy within a national cultural context (Toch 1991). Viewing literacy as a broad-based set of competencies shifts the conceptualization of students' instructional needs away from a narrowly defined set of tasks designed to identify and remedy deficits and disorders. The broad focus moves educators toward the consideration of what students need to successfully participate within society, and toward the development of successful performance within both technological and social language contexts. Examining language competence from a macro-social perspective places the emphasis on learning what students can actually do, on an evaluation of their performance that is dependent on engagement in meaningful activities in increasingly abstract, as well as personalized contexts (Miller 1990).

Indicators of communicative competence have been identified and used for evaluating students' oral language within the context of literacy development. An understanding of these indicators is useful in assessing students' language. In the past, information on language errors has been used to identify and certify learning handicaps and disabilities (Simon 1979). Currently there is a trend toward viewing productive errors as indicators of a need for further communicative development (Damico 1991). This approach changes the perception of errors from limitation and lack to potential positive development. Rather than using this information to illustrate a dichotomy of limited or appropriate language, error analysis can be used to identify speech reflecting a less complete developmental form in the process of becoming more like the standard. This change in perception is especially important for students who are learning to use new language. The errors they produce may not necessarily be indicative of a disorder, but of incompletely developed new language system. Rather than needing remediation, these students may require additional time, development models, emotional support, and specific instruction that promotes successful learning. Much of what may be considered language deficits, especially with students who are in the process of learning to function in a new language for most or all of the school day, are related to the acquisition of literacy skills. These skills relate to categorization and sequencing of information. They also represent new ways of thinking (Westby in press a). The ability to demonstrate communicative competence in a new language is also a measure of the individual's fit within that society (Krashen 1987).

Researchers have been examining indicators of language disorders and delays for the past decade (Damico 1985; Damico, Oller & Story 1982). A number of indicators have been identified in bilingual populations. Among the characteristics identified are a lack of specificity in vocabulary selection, lack of clear pronoun referents (anaphora), and unclear sound production (articulation) (Oller 1982). These indicators are not unlike those that have been identified within monolingual English-speaking populations (Simon 1979). There are three general categories of indicators of a need for further language development. These include form, style, and function. Students who display limitations in any of these areas may have real language learning difficulties. However, students who have had inappropriate speech models, limited exposure, opportunity, or stimulation in learning a new language may also display some of the same deficits. The issue is not one of differentiating between students with deficits and those with developmental second language learning needs. It is not in the learners' best interest to label and categorize them. The issue is the provision of effective instruction and opportunities to learn for all students, regardless of their level of language development. Indicators of developmental communicative competence or the acquisition of the language within the culture of literacy are presented in Table 3-19.

RESEARCH IN PRACTICE
Assessment of the Language of Literacy

1. **Discuss the conceptual differences between the perception of errors as behavior patterns that need to be modified and errors as indicative of the developmental process of language learning.**

TABLE 3-19. INDICATORS OF DEVELOPMENTAL[3] COMMUNICATIVE COMPETENCE

FORM

- limited vocabulary -> flexible, precise vocabulary
- syntactic and morphological errors -> mastery of grammar system
- overuse of simple basic syntactic patterns -> complexity and variety of syntax
- incorrect and inconsistent use of tense -> appropriate subject, verb, temporal, and descriptive agreement
- ambiguous use of pronouns -> clear and accurate use of pronoun referents
- slurred and unclear pronunciation -> clear pronunciation
- omission and reversal of syllables -> clear pronunciation, language production

STYLE AND FUNCTION

- presents ideas in an unsystematic fashion -> classification and subordination of ideas
- wanders from topic -> sustains topic of conversation
- makes egocentric comments -> considers listener's informational needs
- states opinions as facts -> supports perspectives with data from a variety of sources
- states the same information repeatedly -> modifies and clarifies messages to meet listeners' comprehension needs
- consistently uses the same register and communication style -> uses stylistic and contextual adaptations of language depending on the setting
- uses incoherent sequencing of details -> plans and expresses main ideas and supporting details clearly
- produces many false starts and mazes -> shows clear organization of ideas
- does not ask questions, or makes requests for information not related to topic -> asks appropriate questions for clarification and for specific information
- does not produce rate and volume of speech appropriate to setting -> produces rate and volume appropriate to setting
- non-selectively uses non-standard language forms and communication styles -> appropriately uses both standard and non-standard language forms and communication styles

---

3 The symbol -> can be read as "moving toward" as in x -> y (x moving toward y).

2. Explain to a colleague how you can use error information to plan a developmental program of language learning.

SUMMARIZING SECTION THREE

Observing and promoting students' development of literacy skills is central to the instructional process. Students from diverse cultures and languages sometimes appear disordered because their development is different from that of other students. Assessment of the language of literacy is different from assessment of basic interpersonal skills. The interpretation of the language of literacy is language specific. The context in which communication in the language of literacy is provided and interpreted is less obvious and less easily accessed than is that of interpersonal communication. In obtaining and interpreting student data, teachers must be aware that the tasks they pose may be inappropriate for their students and that the assessment process, rather than the students, may be limited. Suggestions for enabling teachers to develop skill in correctly identifying students' needs were offered in this section. Whether progressing normally in their language development or appearing different or disordered, all students require instruction.

Information has been presented on the importance of understanding students' prior educational experiences and opportunities for language development, and for using this information to move students from their current performance to more complete and adequate performance levels. Knowing how students may be limited and when students require special corrective or remedial assistance is essential. In collecting information on students' performance, teachers must ensure that opportunities for learning include authentic communication, rather than tasks to be completed for a grade or a homework assignment.

WHAT CAN YOU DO?

1. This chapter has provided specific suggestions for observing and assessing students' language in the process of developing literacy skills. Differentiate between language skills based on the acquisition of literacy and language skills based on an oral tradition of language.

2. Explain why students from an oral tradition may encounter difficulties in learning English as a new language.

3. How can school be proactively organized to meet students' language learning needs? Is this view realistic?

SUMMARY OF CHAPTER THREE
Assessing Oral Language Development

The information on the assessment of students' oral language proficiency and performance on a variety of language functions can be integrated to form an overall picture of students' communicative competence. This information is useful in designing and implementing instructional programs that respond to students' developmental language learning needs. The information can also be used to monitor students' progress toward the development of appropriate social and academic language skills in their new language. Academic language development involves competence in both written and oral literacy forms within expressive and receptive modes. The information presented in this chapter has focused primarily on oral language development that supports thinking and learning within academic contexts. This information is important in identifying students with special learning needs as well as for developing effective programs for typical students. This information is organized in Table 3-20, a summary of the language skills considered within this chapter. Information that can be used for making comparisons about students' language development in two languages is provided within the center column of the Table. Indicators of performance in English can be placed on the left; indicators of performance in the non-English language on the right. In observing students' progress, it can be helpful to note how students perform in both languages. If students are being considered for placement in an exceptional student education program, such comparisons are essential.

The next chapter, Chapter Four, presents case studies of students in the process of developing academic oral language. Each of these learners is representative of large groups of students in the process of learning English as a new language. These cases present opportunities to apply the information presented in Chapter Three in meaningful contexts. Subsequent chapters focus on academic language development in written contexts, and are also accompanied by case studies.

TABLE 3.20. OVERVIEW OF LANGUAGE DEVELOPMENT INFORMATION[4]

ENGLISH LANGUAGE	NON-ENGLISH LANGUAGE
Formal Assessment Information Include the names, administrators, dates, and findings of formal tests. Provide explanations of any discrepant information.	
Language Dominance Information Include information on the assessment of the student's *language dominance*, including dates, assessor, tests or tasks, and results.	
Receptive Language Information Include information on the observation or assessment of the student's *receptive* language skills, including dates, assessor, tests or tasks, and results.	
Question Answering and Asking Provide information on the assessment of student's *performance* in *asking* and *answering* questions, including dates, observer or assessor, tests or tasks, and results.	

Discrete Point Information
Provide information on each of the following areas including dates, observer or assessor, tests or tasks, and results:
    Phonology
    Morphology
    Syntax
    Semantics/Lexicon	

Communicative Competence Provide information on the student's *performance* in each of the following areas including dates, observer or assessor, tests or tasks, and results: **Grammar**	

NON-ENGLISH LANGUAGE

ENGLISH LANGUAGE

Discourse
   Sociolinguistics/Pragmatics

Academic Language Proficiency
   Provide information on the student's *knowledge* in each of the following areas that promotes academic language performance including dates, observer or assessor, tests or tasks, and indicators:
   Sociolinguistic styles
   Text structure
   Content schema
   Metalinguistic performance
   Metacognitive performance

General Language Proficiency
   Provide information on the student's *level of performance* including dates, observer or assessor, tests or tasks, and indicators.

Performance of Language Functions
   Provide information on the student's *performance* in each of the following areas including dates, observer or assessor, and tasks:
   Instrumental/Self-maintaining
   Interactional
   Personal
   Regulatory
   Heuristic
   Imaginative
   Informational/Reporting
   Logical reasoning
   Predicting
   Projecting

4 If interpreters or translators were used, include names, dates, and how they were involved in collecting this information.

Chapter 4

Differentiating Language Disorders from the Effects of Limited Opportunities for Language Learning

One of the most pressing decisions to be made about many NELB students who are experiencing difficulties in mainstream educational settings is whether these students have language learning differences or disorders (Baca & Cervantes 1989; Mattes & Omark 1984; Metz 1991). In the first three chapters, information was presented on the process of assessing students for whom English is not the only language of communication. Within this chapter information is discussed regarding the organization and use of this process in making educational decisions about these students.

Case studies illustrate the data-collection and decision-making process, provide insight into the language development process, and suggest ways that students' educational needs may be met. The cases also offer suggestions regarding the learning requirements of students who may be considered English proficient, but who originate from backgrounds where languages other than English are used. The differences highlighted in the cases illustrate potential difficulties NELB students may encounter in learning English and underscore the importance of effective instruction for these students.

Students who are in the process of learning a new language and culture may also have learning requirements beyond those currently met within typical classrooms. These learning needs may be categorized as *communicative disorders*, *learning disabilities*, or other indicators of learning difficulties within the general category of *mild handicapping conditions*. The differences between these students and their age-peers may result as often from the opportunities these students have had for learning or the perceptions of the educators who teach them as from the needs of the learners. Differences between the opportunities students have for learning and for developing language are often a critical and yet seldom considered factor.

The focus of this chapter is on differentiating developmental language differences and limited instructional opportunities from real language or *communicative disorders* and *learning disabilities*. The cases suggest that new and additional terminology may be required to identify the students' needs. Terms such as *arrested educational development* and *delayed language development* may be more appropriate for some NELB students experiencing learning difficulties in regular classrooms. These terms are offered to suggest differences in learning opportunities which have been available to these students, rather than inherent disabilities manifested by the students themselves. However, regardless of whether students' needs result from intrinsic or extrinsic factors, the need for effective instruction is imperative.

SECTION ONE

LIMITED LEARNING OPPORTUNITIES OR LANGUAGE DISORDER?

Information on students' social skills development, combined with data on students' academic performance from formal and informal sources, provides an integrated foundation for decision-making, planning, and instructing. Performance information is more often available from formal standardized sources and from school tasks that highlight what students cannot do, rather than what they do well. Educators require experience and practice in locating and using a variety of sources of information in order to support or refute the formalized testing process and, most importantly, to determine how to assist the target students. This chapter provides opportunities for observing the collection and analysis of data from formal and informal data sources. The format for the presentation and use of this information is different from the style and procedures used within the first three chapters. Research in Practice sections occur after each case study. The first example to be examined is the case of Yolanda which is presented next.

YOLANDA'S STORY

The case of Yolanda illustrates the difficulties that limited English proficient students sometimes encounter in learning to function in the typical all-English classroom. Yolanda is a prototype of many students who begin the process of learning English by losing proficiency in their other language. The information presented here represents a typical rather than an ideal learning history. As you read through the case, you may want to think of some additional sources of information that could be used to determine and meet Yolanda's instructional needs. Prereferral strategies may also occur to you to try before you would want to refer Yolanda for a psychological evaluation. Yolanda is a real student, who, unfortunately, attended schools that were unprepared to deal with her learning needs. As a result, a great deal of time was spent before her needs were identified and a program was developed to assist her. Fortunately, she was assessed by a competent psychologist who realized that Yolanda had strengths as well as needs, and knew how to communicate and to collaborate with other personnel who were concerned about Yolanda's progress.

As you read, you may want to reflect on what you believe to be Yolanda's instructional needs. Feel free to make notes on how you would develop an effective instructional program for her. At the conclusion of the case, an analysis of information available is presented and suggestions are provided for instructing and monitoring Yolanda's progress.

Background information.

Yolanda had been in the mainland U.S. for a year when her second grade teacher observed that Yolanda was experiencing academic difficulties and referred Yolanda for a psychological evaluation. In Puerto Rico Yolanda had attended her first two years of school, kindergarten and first grade, which were taught in Spanish. According to the records from her school in Puerto Rico, she had performed well. For a brief period after her arrival from Puerto Rico to the mainland, she had been enrolled in a school with a bilingual/ESOL program. When her parents moved to another community later the same year, there was no bilingual program at the new school, so Yolanda was placed in a regular second grade. The second grade teacher noted that Yolanda did not attend to task and did not complete her work. Yolanda was retained in the second grade for another year because of her lack of academic progress. As a result of persistent academic difficulties, Yolanda was referred for a psychological evaluation at the end of the second year in the same grade. The following year, Yolanda was administratively placed in third grade.

A review of her cumulative records indicated that both reading and math achievement performance were below the norm when compared to other youngsters in the same grade. On the Stanford Achievement Test, Yolanda achieved at the second stanine in reading and at the third stanine in mathematics. A review of the comments on her report card over the past three years suggested that she put forth minimal effort in school and that she made below average to failing grades in all subjects. Retention appeared to do no good. Throughout her academic program in the mainland U.S., Yolanda's school performance had been consistent. She had failed. Teacher notes indicate persistent frustration because of Yolanda's behavior, such as talking in class and her considerable difficulty understanding directions and instruction.

Observations during formal assessment.

After three years of instruction in a regular classroom, Yolanda was referred for a psychological evaluation. Prior to assessment, Yolanda was administered the Language Assessment Battery (LAB) in English, on which her performance indicated she was functioning adequately at the 45th percentile. Because Yolanda was able to interact effectively in English, and her performance on the LAB indicated an adequate level of English language proficiency, assessment was conducted primarily in English.

During the assessment sessions Yolanda appeared to be cooperative and to put forth good effort. She conversed freely with the examiner in English and reported that she spoke English most often at school and at home. She also indicated that she occasionally spoke Spanish with her parents.

When asked about her prior elementary school experiences, Yolanda was very vague. She had little knowledge about her school program in Puerto Rico or of her early experiences in the mainland. During the evaluation session itself, Yolanda was quick to respond on nonverbal items. She displayed a keen interest in the tasks and an organized problem-solving approach to completing them. Verbal response items posed much greater difficulties. She appeared to have considerable difficulty understanding what was being asked, and frequently stated that she could not answer.

Results and interpretations.[*]

Yolanda's intellectual functioning, as measured in English by the Full Scale Wechsler Intelligence Scale for Children-Revised (WISC-R) falls within the Low Average range. A 40-point discrepancy was noted between the verbal score of 62 and performance score of 102, with verbal skills being significantly weaker. Performance on the Verbal subtests of the WISC-R suggests considerable difficulties in factual information recall, expressive vocabulary, and classification skills. She was, however, able to respond more effectively on commonsense judgment and reasoning items. A Full Scale score of 80 indicates that at Yolanda's current level of intellectual functioning, she would have difficulties with academic school tasks.

Yolanda's academic achievement was evaluated in the areas of reading, math, and written language using the Woodcock-Johnson Psycho-Educational Battery: Tests of Achievement in English. In reading, her performance was at the beginning second grade level, resulting in a standard score of 81. She was able to sound out some unfamiliar words, but exhibited weak word identification and passage comprehension skills. Her passage comprehension skills appeared to be limited to items in which a visual clue was provided. On the Written Language cluster, Yolanda's performance was at the beginning second grade level and was consistent with her reading skills. She identified two punctuation errors in written sentences, but was unable to identify spelling or word usage errors. In spelling, she was able to spell some simple sight words; however, she displayed weak word attack skills and appeared to have difficulty with word usage.

In mathematics, Yolanda's performance also was limited to a beginning second grade level. She was able to complete items with addition and subtrac-

---

[*] A summary of the formal assessment information appears at the conclusion of each case.

tion facts, but was incorrect on items requiring regrouping. She was unable to complete any items requiring multiplication or division. Her performance on the Applied Problems section was consistent with her rote calculation skills.

Yolanda's performance on academic achievement tests was significantly below her chronological age and more than a year behind her current grade placement. When comparing her performance to her estimated mental abilities, her achievement was consistent with the Full Scale IQ score. This is a relatively strong level of achievement considering the weak verbal skills she exhibited. Results of the psychological evaluation suggest that Yolanda's Full Scale measured intelligence on the WISC-R falls within the Low Average range. Her nonverbal skills, however, fall within the Average range. Taken at face value, the discrepancy between verbal and performance measures, and difficulties completing tasks and following directions, might lead one to suspect a language or learning disability. However, taking into consideration that Yolanda's level of achievement is not discrepant from her measured Full Scale Wechsler IQ, that she had been exposed to English for a limited period of three years, and that she had some previous academic instruction in Spanish, further explanations of her performance were explored. It was believed that the Verbal Score on the English WISC-R might not be an accurate reflection of Yolanda's intellectual functioning. As a further result of this verbal-performance discrepancy, a bilingual psychologist was requested to complete the administration of an intellectual assessment in order to determine more accurately Yolanda's verbal skills and general ability.

Further assessment.

The bilingual psychologist chose to use the Language Assessment Scales (LAS) and the Woodcock Language Proficiency Battery (WLPB) in English and Spanish in assessing Yolanda's language proficiency. The LAS taps such areas as auditory discrimination, articulation, vocabulary, and receptive language, and provides a sample of oral language skills in the form of a story retelling task. The Oral Language cluster of the WLPB taps such areas as receptive and expressive vocabulary, ability to retrieve words to comprehend analogies, skills, memory, and general comprehension of language.

The LAS provides a language classification score based on a 5-point scale with Level 1 indicating a non-speaker and Level 5 indicating a proficient speaker. The results of the LAS indicated that Yolanda scored a 3, a Limited Speaker of Spanish. Although she retains a great deal of Spanish, especially at a receptive level, both grammatical and vocabulary losses were evident. She demonstrated good progress in acquiring English oral language skills by scoring a 4, indicating that she is fluent, but not totally proficient in English. Throughout the assessment process, Yolanda appeared to be a talkative and sociable youngster who enjoyed the individual attention afforded by the testing situation. She was observed to switch easily from English to Spanish during conversation, but clearly separated both languages. Informal observations indicated that she was functioning at a low intermediate level in Spanish and at a slightly higher intermediate level in English. The effects of learning English grammar and structure were observed in her performance in Spanish. Similar influences from Spanish into English were not observed. Her performance in English indicates that she still had limitations in using the English language characteristic of a second language learner.

Further evaluation of Spanish receptive vocabulary with the Hispanic-American adaptation of the Peabody Picture Vocabulary Test, the Test de Vocabulario en Imagenes Peabody, indicated that Yolanda's skills were at the Low Average range when compared with other Puerto Rican students of the same age group. Her obtained age equivalent of 7 years, 4 months, placed her at approximately the age when native language instruction was discontinued and she began a totally new program in English.

Yolanda's limited development of academic Spanish language vocabulary was noted in her performance on the Oral Language cluster of the Woodcock Language Proficiency Battery (WLPB)-Spanish edition, on which she scored at a late first grade, 7 year old level. Judging by her performance on the verbal portions of the WISC-R, her academic vocabulary, when compared with that of monolingual English-speaking students, is low. Academic skills attainment in the areas of reading and written language in Spanish were assessed with the WLPB and compared with those obtained in English. Even though reading instruction had stopped three years earlier in Spanish, Yolanda's reading skills in Spanish were found to be at third grade level, within the average range for her age. She demonstrated excellent word attack and word recognition skills in Spanish that could be used to assist her in developing comparable skills in English. Lack of opportunities to use Spanish reading skills and the limited development of academic vocabulary appeared to affect her comprehension in Spanish. Written language skills in Spanish were at a first grade level and reflected the effect of English, such as the production of the word "catto" for "gato" or "cat."

In reviewing Yolanda's performance in mathematics, it was observed that she scored at a second grade level. The language of mathematics is complex and abstract. It is possible that Yolanda's limited English proficiency has affected continued growth in mathematics as well as reading and language arts. Support in the native language may be required in order to master new concepts and processes.

Summary of testing.

Yolanda is a youngster whose academic language skills reflect the subtractive effect of change in language of instruction and the tremendous gap between the English skills that she was developing and the skills that her monolingual peers already had in place. After three years of attendance in schools in the U.S. mainland, she appeared to remain, for all practical purposes, at the same level of academic performance as when she began school in English. Consideration of Yolanda's academic history prior to the move to the mainland and her initial functioning in a bilingual program in the mainland are important factors to be considered when analyzing her present levels of academic achievement. Her report card from Puerto Rico revealed grades of "A" and "B" during kindergarten and first grade. During the brief period of time that she attended the bilingual/ESOL program in the second grade, her grades continued to be satisfactory. She was doing average second grade work in the native language component and in English oral language development before she was placed in an English-only instructional program. At that time of change to English, it appears that Yolanda was performing overall at a level generally commensurate with her average ability as indicated by the recently obtained Performance score on the WISC-R of 102. A summary of her test results are presented below in Table 4-1.

Parent involvement.

Yolanda's parents were invited for a conference to review the assessment results. They had been concerned about Yolanda's progress in English, her performance at school, and the repeated notes and calls they had received from her teachers. When they realized that Yolanda was having difficulties at school and needed to improve her comprehension in English, they began to communicate more with her in English at home. They were concerned, though, that she should continue to maintain proficiency in Spanish so that she could interact with her cousins and her grandparents in Puerto Rico. Yolanda's parents indicated that they had always observed their daughter as normal, that she had no problems learning to walk or talk as a baby. She had learned and developed at a rate similar to the other children. Her parents observed that at home and with friends, Yolanda was talkative, seemed to have common sense, and showed good problem-solving skills. She enjoyed reading in Spanish and was always looking for books and materials to read at home. They expressed support for the school's efforts to assist their daughter. Yolanda's parents described how they asked family members to bring Yolanda books, games, and puzzle books from Puerto Rico when they came to visit. They strongly agreed to do anything they could to promote her successful achievement in English and her academic success.

Summary and recommendations.

Yolanda is a youngster who is bilingual in English and Spanish. She came to the mainland U.S. from Puerto Rico about three years ago. She was referred

TABLE 4-1. SUMMARY OF YOLANDA'S TESTS

FIRST SERIES OF TESTS

Language Assessment Battery in English: Percentile 45
Wechsler Intelligence Scale for Children-Revised (WISC-R)

Verbal Tests		Performance Tests	
Information	1	Picture Completion	10
Similarities	1	Picture Arrangement	11
Arithmetic	6	Block Design	9
Vocabulary	3	Object Assembly	9
Comprehension	8	Coding	13

IQ Scales	
Verbal IQ	62
Performance IQ	102
Full Scale IQ	80

Woodcock-Johnson Psycho-Educational Battery:
Tests of Achievement (WJA) (in English)

Cluster	Grade Score	Instructional Range	Age Score	Percentile Rank	Standard Score
Reading	2.1	1.8 to 2.4	7-3	10	81
Math	2.0	1.5 to 2.5	7-2	5	75
Written Language	2.0	1.6 to 2.5	7-5	9	80

SECOND SERIES OF TESTS (Conducted one month later)

Language Assessment Scales, Level I, Form A
English: Level 4   Spanish: Level 3

Woodcock Language Proficiency Battery (Spanish Edition)

Subtest	Grade Score	Instructional Range	Age Score	Standard Score
Oral Language	1.7	1.0 to 1.7	7-5	79
Reading	3.0	2.5 to 3.7	8-8	97
Written Language	1.9	1.4 to 2.5	7-0	82

Test de Vocabulario en Imagenes Peabody (TVIP) (in Spanish)
Norms used: Puerto Rican
Standard Score: 82
Percentile Rank: 12
Age Equivalent: 7 years, 4 months

---

for psychological assessment because of her lack of academic performance in English. Initial assessment was conducted in English because language proficiency tests indicated that she was more proficient in English than Spanish. However, because the WISC-R indicated a 40 point discrepancy between verbal and performance scores, with the performance scores indicating normal ability, the school psychologist thought that Yolanda's difficulties might be related to limited English proficiency. Further assessment was conducted in English and Spanish by a bilingual school psychologist.

The present review of available information, individual assessment, post evaluation conferences with Yolanda's parents, and current teacher input reveal a youngster whose early academic foundation was in Spanish. Midway during the second grade, the primary language of instruction was abruptly changed from Spanish to English. At the time of the switch to an all English curriculum, Yolanda had almost no proficiency in English. Within the past three years, she has developed English language proficiency as measured by the LAB and LAS.

The present language and literacy skill assessment reflect the effect of limited language development, within age expectations, in both social and academic skills areas in Spanish. Yolanda is now ten years old. Her present expressive and receptive language skills in Spanish appear to remain at the seven-year-old level, the age at which the Spanish to English change occurred. Yolanda demonstrates a strong phonetic and reading skills foundation in Spanish. Prior to switching to English, she did not exhibit learning problems in Spanish. Her reading comprehension and written language skills do, however, appear to be affected by a lack of continued language development in Spanish. Oral language skills in Spanish manifest the impact of her learning English, such as the finding that many of her grammatical constructions reveal the influence of English language learning. Her vocabulary has not continued to develop, since Spanish has not been the primary medium of communication for more than three years. At first observation, Yolanda appears to be communicatively limited in Spanish, but this limitation appears to originate from external factors rather than internal deficits.

Previous assessment of skills in English reveals serious gaps in vocabulary and mathematical concept development in English in comparison with her U.S. mainland age-mates. In spite of these limitations, the overall picture is that of a youngster who is making progress in the acquisition of oral language and literacy skills in English. This progress may not be immediately evident in the English curriculum because Yolanda appears to be far behind her monolingual, English-speaking peers.

Recommended instruction.

In view of the present results, it was recommended that this youngster be assisted by continued development of social and academic language skills in Spanish as well as in English. Specific support and instruction in ESOL was designed to assist Yolanda in using the already developed literacy skills in Spanish to promote literacy development in English. A direct return to a

Spanish-language curriculum, however, would also present problems for Yolanda at this time because her Spanish-language skills had not kept pace with her overall development. Therefore, instruction built on the reading and comprehension skills developed in both languages included learning strategies, listening skills, and effective support to enable Yolanda to learn to participate successfully in school.

Outcomes.

Yolanda's parents became involved in Yolanda's language development when they realized and fully understood the difficulties that their daughter was experiencing in school. Every night they worked with her in reading, math, and spelling in English. In addition, when Yolanda watched television, she was required to discuss what she saw. From these activities, Yolanda learned to report, to summarize, to infer, and to ask relevant questions. In general, Yolanda learned to become a producer of information and a participant in meaningful discussions. Instead of reinforcing Yolanda's English to the exclusion of her Spanish, Yolanda was encouraged to interact in both languages. Parallel activities were provided in both languages. Suggestions for follow-up activities at home were also provided for her parents.

At first Yolanda was reluctant to use Spanish at school, but when she traveled back to Puerto Rico to visit her cousins, she began to realize the importance of Spanish and of being able to communicate with her family. As Yolanda was provided with instruction and encouragement for learning in both languages, her attention span increased and she began to see herself as a successful and competent learner. In addition to direct instruction in language development, Yolanda was taught to use learning strategies and encouraged to learn ways to participate effectively in school. Within two years of intensive instruction in school and reinforcement at home, Yolanda began to perform at an average level in English. Her on-task behavior increased, and she became a good student.

Yolanda's story in perspective.

Yolanda's story was actually a story of *arrested educational development*. She was making progress in mastering academic language until she abruptly changed from instruction in a language she understood, to instruction with limited meaning. Often it is assumed that students will quickly pick up the language around them, if they are immersed in it. Such was not the case for Yolanda. In considering the needs of students like Yolanda who are experiencing academic difficulties, it is important to ensure that they receive academic and linguistic support in the process for transitioning from the use of one to another.

RESEARCH IN PRACTICE
Yolanda's Story

1. Describe how the assessment information provided by the first and second sessions is similar.

2. How is the information provided in the second session different? What are the salient features of the second set of data?

3. Describe Yolanda's language development.

4. Explain why an understanding of her behavior prior to entry into an English only instructional program is important for defining Yolanda's strengths.

5. Explain how the case of Yolanda may be similar to that of many other students.

6. Are there examples of students with *arrested educational development* in your school? What can be done to meet these students' needs?

SUMMARIZING SECTION ONE:
Limited Learning Opportunities or Language Disorder?

Although Yolanda's case has been presented as a prototype of many LEP students, for many other students the assessment process has been different. Yolanda was enrolled in a school district with access to a trained bilingual school psychologist with the experience and insight to build on the information provided by the monolingual psychologist, and contribute to it by assessing Yolanda's performance in Spanish. The psychologist observed that all indicators of academic performance in Spanish appeared to remain at the level where Yolanda began to learn to function in English. She also noted that Yolanda's performance in English had begun to surpass her performance in Spanish. This information could have erroneously been interpreted to mean that Yolanda had relatively little language proficiency in Spanish and that English was really the more appropriate language of assessment and instruction. The bilingual psychologist, however, saw Yolanda's Spanish as a potential source of support for developing academic skills in English. This interpretation distinguishes Yolanda's case from that of many other students. Yolanda had received literacy instruction in her home language. She had actually learned to read in Spanish. Instruction in Spanish continued for a brief period after she was enrolled in a mainland U.S. school. Her grades, both in Puerto Rico and in her first new school, in which she received bilingual/ESOL instruction, support the observation that she was making satisfactory progress when presented with information in a language she understood. Progress stopped when she failed to comprehend and participate in the instructional process. If Yolanda had not developed literacy skills in her home language, the assessment results might have been much different from those that were presented within this case. The formal assessment process conducted in both languages provided substantial proof that this student did not manifest a disability in her first language, but that she did suffer from the difficulties of a subtractive language learning environment. In other words, the bilingual psychologist used the assessment process to analyze the source of language learning difficulties and to determine that it was an environmental or instructional condition, not an inherent difficulty. Without the literacy skill development that occurred in Spanish, data to support Yolanda's normal development of her home language might not have been available after three years of residence in an English-only environment.

Two facts emerge from the data that could have been chosen to preclude the use of the services of a bilingual school psychologist. First, Yolanda's English language proficiency scores were high enough to qualify her for English-only assessment. Second, her scores in Spanish were lower than her English scores, indicating that she was English dominant. Even though since 1975, P.L. 94-142 has required that students be assessed in their non-English language when being considered for special education services, relatively few school districts have the type of expertise that this bilingual school psychologist provided. The limited availability of skilled bilingual specialists, such as psychologists and speech pathologists, means that the responsibility for the identification of effective and meaningful instructional and assessment procedures sometimes falls strongly upon the educators who provide direct instruction and services.

Teachers trained to use informal observation and instructional procedures can gain a great deal of insight into a student's performance and develop effective strategies for meeting the student's needs without waiting for a formal evaluation that might or might not confirm a student's disability.

WHAT CAN YOU DO?

1. **Are bilingual personnel available in your school?** If not, what can be done to provide appropriate assessment information?

2. **What can you do to obtain information about students' performance in their non-English language?**

3. **What data can be collected on students who do not learn to read in their non-English language? How can these data assist students and teachers?**

SECTION TWO

LIMITED LANGUAGE DEVELOPMENT OR LANGUAGE IMPAIRMENT?

In the previous case, the development of literacy skills was central to an understanding of the story of Yolanda, the young girl with abrupt interruption of language of instruction. The fact that she had developed and was able to demonstrate literacy skills in Spanish, her first language, provided the educators with important clues about her ability to function at an abstract level. This information was especially valuable in considering that she had lost a significant amount of proficiency in Spanish, the language in which she had learned to read.

But what about students who have not learned to read? What happens to students who have no first language because they have learned to function in two languages simultaneously? What if literacy skills exist in neither language? Looking at students' overall language from a developmental, rather than an error analysis perspective, provides insight into the activities and strategies needed to promote effective communication. This issue also emphasizes the importance of professional collaboration in providing students with instruction that will lead toward competency in literacy as well as social interactions. This is the context for analyzing the next case, a case of potential limited language development or disability. This section examines the behaviors of language performance of a young boy who was also in the process of learning English as a new language.

ROBERT'S STORY

Background information.

Robert was seven years old and in first grade for the second time when he was first seen by the school psychologist. Robert's teacher referred him to the child study team because he had been exhibiting a number of learning difficulties. He cried frequently, didn't pay attention, had trouble sitting still in class, and didn't remember what he was taught. Robert was born in the U.S. of Polish parents who had arrived in the United States just before his birth. Most of his early life Robert had spent living in a small one-bedroom apartment, in a section of a large urban center with many other newly arrived Polish people. Because his father and mother had a large group of Polish friends, Robert seldom heard English spoken until he arrived at school. There were many children in his school who spoke languages other than English, but only a few who spoke Polish. Most of these children knew English and were able to participate in the school activities. None of the teachers in the school spoke Polish. Robert's father had a working knowledge of English. His mother had started taking English class when Robert entered kindergarten, but she was unable to continue because of a second pregnancy. She had begun to watch television in English about a year earlier in an effort to learn English at home.

When he was four, Robert had been hit by a car as he crossed the street. He suffered a head injury as a result of the accident and was treated in physical therapy for three months after the injury. His parents were not sure if the accident affected Robert's speech. He seemed to be fine after a few months. Although his injures seemed to be healed by the time he entered school, he had continued to experience some difficulties in expressing himself in English and in Polish.

The parents were invited to attend several conferences at school. Both parents were available to come to school when requested a week in advance. The mother never came alone. When she came, she seldom spoke. She nodded and deferred to the father who spoke in halting English. He consistently affirmed the family's support of the school's efforts to help Robert. He said that he worked two jobs during the week, plus a weekend job, and depended on his wife to assist Robert at home. He said that she reviewed every paper that Robert brought home, but she was not sure what they meant or how to help Robert since she did not read English or understand the U.S. educational system.

Classroom observations.

Robert's classroom teacher noted that Robert required a great deal of individual attention. He was observed to be functioning at a reading readiness level. He did not complete his work and displayed significant difficulty following oral directions. Attempts to assist Robert included modification of his assignments, use of rewards for work completion and appropriate behavior, and individual tutoring by the classroom aide. Robert was sometimes difficult to understand. He often repeated himself when he was trying to express himself. In spite of his efforts, he was often unable to produce the words he wanted or to make people understand him. His speech sounds were described as mushy and unclear. Because he had trouble expressing himself, Robert had difficulty relating to and talking with other children. His teacher said that when Robert first entered the classroom at the beginning of the year, he had tantrums when asked to leave an activity he liked for something he disliked. He still cried when he did not want to do something, and insisted on doing what he wanted to do.

His behavior was erratic. Once, for example, he climbed up a column in the hallway to see a beehive.

As time progressed and he became accustomed to the school routines, Robert's overall behavior improved. He appeared less anxious. His language also began to improve when he was provided with the sounds, words, and meanings. Robert seemed to be aware that he was not being understood and he began to observe the way the other students talked and imitated them. As he observed and imitated, his pronunciation became clearer. In spite of all the progress that Robert made, he was still well behind the other students and appeared to display learning problems beyond the resources of the regular classroom.

After he was referred for observation and assessment, he was seen by the school nurse. He passed the vision and hearing screenings necessary for the current evaluation. There did not appear to be any sensory acuity deficits impeding his learning.

Prior to psychological assessment, Robert was observed in the regular classroom setting during small group reading time. The group was working on readiness level activities. Robert had lost his reading workbook, and instead brought a library book about bees. The teacher indicated that Robert demonstrates a great interest in bees and other insects. During the course of the group reading activity, which involved identifying beginning sounds, Robert at times spoke out without permission. He frequently wanted to be the first to respond and answered for the other students. When he answered, his responses were not always correct. He stood up frequently and had to be admonished to allow other students to respond and to sit still.

As part of the instructional activity, the group played a game. At the conclusion of the game, when another student won, Robert put his head down and whined. When Robert completed his seat-work, he was allowed to use the computer for 15 minutes. He was working with another student on a math drill. A third student came over to the computer. Robert did not want him there and told him to leave. Instead of completing the math activity on the computer, Robert appeared to be having difficulties and began to play with the keyboard. The other student eventually took over the computer and made Robert leave. Robert went to his seat and cried.

Formal assessment.

During the individual testing situation, Robert appeared pleasant and cooperative. He willingly participated in the testing process and expressed himself freely in social interactions. However, when presented with more difficult questions, Robert appeared to have limited comprehension skills in English. These difficulties had been anticipated and an interpreter was available to interact with Robert in Polish. In this school district interpreters were available only through federal funds for special education services. The district had established a bank of trained personnel who served as interpreters and translators as needed by the system.

Results of this interaction revealed that Robert's language skills were more developed in English than Polish. The interpreter noted that his speech patterns were immature and that Robert displayed significant word retrieval difficulties in Polish. As a result of his limited language proficiency in Polish, Robert was tested primarily in English. On the English Language Assessment Battery, Robert scored at the 15th percentile in English when compared to English-speaking grade peers. This test does not exist in Polish.

In order to assess oral language, reading, and written language skills in English, the English form of the Woodcock Language Proficiency Battery was administered. The Oral Language Cluster taps picture vocabulary, antonyms, synonyms, and analogies. The Reading Cluster measures letter-word identification, word attack, and passage comprehension skills. The Written Language Cluster measures dictation and proofing skills. The results indicate Robert to be English dominant by virtue of his expressive vocabulary in English, his preference for English, and his social use of English. His oral language skills appeared severely deficient in both languages and are at approximately a four-year-old level in English, potentially less in Polish.

The Wechsler Intelligence Scale for Children-Revised (WISC-R) was administered in English. A Polish interpreter was present to observe and to note the language used and the information, if any, provided by Robert in Polish. Robert responded primarily in English, but did use Polish at times. He appeared to need to use both languages for expression. Although the information provided in Polish was noted, only the information provided in English was used in calculating the intelligence score. Where additional information was supplied in Polish, these answers were noted and analyzed. Little significant information was provided in Polish that was not expressed in English. Polish appeared to be a language for thinking and for reiteration rather than for direct responses. Robert sometimes stated the question and the answer in Polish, then translated it into English.

Under these circumstances, Robert obtained a Verbal Intelligence Quotient of 65, a Performance Quotient of 91, and a Full Scale of 76. These results place Robert at the 5th percentile when compared with other youngsters his age in the reference group. The present results reflect a significant 26 point discrepancy between Robert's verbal and nonverbal abilities, in favor of nonverbal performance, which was within average limits. Significant difficulties were noted, not only in comprehension and oral expression but also in general informational skills and immediate memory. Interestingly, a relative strength for Robert was found in the area of verbal reasoning. In this area, he was able to establish similarities between objects and concepts presented. It was also in this area that he used Polish the most. He reflected on the similarities first in Polish and then expressed the concepts in English. Within the nonverbal area, Robert displayed significant difficulties in visual-motor dexterity and visual recall when required to copy symbols within a specific time limit. All other performance subtests were within the average range.

The results of the psychological evaluation indicated that significant delays were found in visual-motor, linguistics, and school readiness skills. Adaptive behavior and self-help skills were also found to be below age expectancy.

In addition to the regular psychoeducational evaluation, Robert was seen by a speech/language pathologist for an in-depth language evaluation. This information was collected in order to determine the most appropriate educational programming for Robert. His language problems were at the point where they interfered with academic learning and could be a reason for his frustration and for his disruptive behavior in the classroom. Robert's level of proficiency in Polish was not sufficient to warrant a full assessment, so the assessment was conducted of Robert's English language performance.

During the evaluation, Robert demonstrated a short attention span and restlessness, but appeared sociable and desired to do well on the tests. He was able to add to conversations on topics that were familiar to him. However, even during these exchanges it was necessary to elicit information through questions because Robert did not volunteer information. He did appear to enjoy the hands-on activities used to gather the language samples. Throughout the evaluation, he remained well-mannered and personable, but fidgeted whenever the activities were changed. Four general areas of speech and language were explored: (a) *phonology*, articulation of speech sounds and the rules governing them; (b) *syntax/morphology*, word order and grammar; (c) *semantics*, vocabulary, basic concepts, word meaning; and (d) *pragmatics*, the functional uses of language in social contexts. The scores of objective measures and an analysis of a language sample are included in the report.

Further assessment was accomplished through documented observations during naturalistic tasks set up to elicit language for a variety of functions and social contexts. Overall results indicate a moderate to severe deficit in functioning. Robert experienced difficulty in differentiating between tell and ask orientation, and in the appropriate selection and use of question words. In telling a story he failed to maintain tense reference or to develop a story line with sequential pictures. He was unable to explain the relationship between objects and concepts or to talk about the chores he performed around the house and how to prepare a favorite snack. However, he was adequately able to use language when interacting with the examiner on a social level, and experienced only minor difficulties expressing his opinions about a variety of topics, such as likes and dislikes. Robert was most expressive during role play situations. However, he demonstrated difficulty with explicit and/or precise language. Although she found Robert to be a very personable and social communication partner, the speech/language pathologist judged his academic pragmatic skills to be moderately to severely impaired. Robert demonstrated a severe deficit in language and immediate memory. He presented the characteristics of a language learn-ing disabled youngster.

Results and interpretations.

Robert's intellectual functioning, as measured in English by the Full Scale Wechsler Intelligence Scale for Children-Revised (WISC-R), fell within the Low Average range. A 26-point discrepancy was noted between the verbal score of 65 and performance score of 91, with verbal skills being significantly weaker. Performance on the Verbal subtests of the WISC-R suggest considerable difficulties across verbal subtests with a relative strength in verbal reasoning or abstract concept formation skills. A Full Scale score of 76 suggested that at Robert's current level of intellectual functioning, he would have difficulties with academic school tasks.

Robert's language proficiency in English was evaluated first on the Language Assessment Battery, on which he scored at the 15th percentile. In addition, the Woodcock-Johnson Language Proficiency Battery was used to produce a more in-depth assessment of his academic language skills. On both the Oral Language and Reading subtests, Robert performed at a level lower than the first percentile. However, on measures of Written Language, Robert's performance was higher, with a performance rank at the second percentile, indicating that although Robert was significantly behind his age peers, functioning at the beginning first grade level, he had learned some of the skills measured on this test. Because of the discrepancy between verbal and performance measures, difficulties completing tasks and following directions, and limited language development, Robert could be considered for a Specific Learning Disabilities program. However, there are other factors to take into consideration, such as: (a) Robert had been exposed to English for a limited period of less than two years; (b) It appears that Robert had received no academic instruction in Polish; and (c) Robert manifested significant difficulties in communicative skills using the norms developed on monolingual English-speaking norms. As a result of these intervening considerations, it was recommended that Robert not be placed in a Specific Learning Disabilities program but be placed in a full-time program of speech/language development. This program, it was anticipated, would provide Robert with the cognitive and linguistic input for English language and academic skill development in English without labeling him as disabled.

A summary of Robert's assessment results is provided below in Table 4-2.

Recommended instruction.

The following program was suggested for promoting Robert's language development. In *Phonology*, he needed practice hearing and producing vowels

TABLE 4-2. SUMMARY OF ROBERT'S TESTS

Language Assessment Battery in English: Percentile 15
Wechsler Intelligence Scale for Children-Revised (WISC-R)

Verbal Tests		Performance Tests	
Information	1	Picture Completion	8
Similarities	7	Picture Arrangement	11
Arithmetic	4	Block Design	8
Vocabulary	4	Object Assembly	11
Comprehension	5	Coding	6
Digit Span	1		

IQ Scales	
Verbal IQ	65
Performance IQ	91
Full Scale IQ	76

Woodcock-Johnson Psycho-Educational Battery:
Tests of Cognitive Ability (in English)

Cluster	Grade Score	Age Score	Standard Score
Perceptual Speed	1.3	6-4	77

Woodcock Language Proficiency Battery (English Edition)

Subtest	Grade Score	Instructional Range	Age Score	Percentile Rank	Standard Score
Oral Language	1.0		4-9	<1	49
Reading	1.0	1.0 to 1.0	5-4	<1	46
Written Language	1.3	1.0 to 1.5	6-4	2	69

and consonant clusters in meaningful contexts. Medial and final consonants were modeled clearly. Words and phrases were organized around topics of interest to Robert. Production of multisyllabic words and playful use of language were encouraged so that Robert developed metalinguistic awareness of English. It was recommended that his instructional goals emphasize a variety of opportunities for spontaneous and planned exchanges so that Robert developed conversation skills. In *Syntax/Morphology*, instruction focused on the continuing to increase of language complexity, the variety of verb forms and tenses, referential pronouns, and the inclusion of questioning formats. In *Semantics*, Robert was provided with many experiences that promote description and focus on details, categorization of events and activities, and the development of an understanding of cause and effect relationships. In *Pragmatics*, Robert's instructional goals should emphasize conversation skills with opportunities to engage in spontaneous conversations. Activities should emphasize production of coherent messages, organization and formulation of a variety of responses, perspective-taking, and the use of higher order thinking skills and academically related language.

Outcomes.

Robert was placed in a full-time speech/language development program where he received instruction in English language development. This instruction was supported by the ESOL teacher who provided consultive services to the speech/language development teacher. In addition, the Polish interpreter was hired as an assistant instructor for 10 hours a week. She provided two additional hours a week preparing activities that Robert could accomplish at home, and working with Robert's parents, especially his mother, to assist Robert at home. As the interpreter worked with Robert and his family, she gained many insights that were not only useful in understanding Robert's needs but important in developing an effective program for Robert.

As part of the referral and assessment process, a social worker had visited the home and had spoken with the family about Robert's needs. The interpreter accompanied the social worker on the visit. Because the interpreter was fluent in Polish, she interacted easily with the parents and was welcomed into their home. Interacting with Robert within the home and the school environment enabled her to notice how Robert communicated in both contexts. At home Robert had few opportunities to interact, because the apartment was usually full of newly-arrived Polish adults who discussed politics and the most recent events in Poland. The conversation style was adult focused. Few children ever came to the household, and Robert was not allowed outside to play. When there were no visitors, Robert's mother watched the television. She was determined to learn as much English as possible and enjoyed the afternoon programs, even when she did not understand what was being said. Robert's mother encouraged Robert to watch TV with her, but she seldom interacted with him or talked about the programs. After the second baby was born, Robert's mother had little time to spend with him. Before he entered school, Robert had had few opportunities to acquire or use language, any language, English or Polish.

Combining the suggestions for observations presented in Table 3-17 with the suggestions for evaluating data on students' performance in Table 3-18, the interpreter began to compile data that enabled her to hypothesize about Robert's prior developmental experiences. For example, she realized that one of the reasons that Robert had difficulty expressing himself was that he had never needed to be expressive. When he was little, he was given whatever was available without having to ask for it. As he grew older, there were few opportunities to interact with other children or adults.

At school, because he was limited in English, he tended to avoid situations that required him to express himself, especially when the other students were proficient in English. He was a willing communicator when he had the opportunity to talk with younger children or with other children who were also in the process of learning English. When provided with concrete materials and realistic opportunities to communicate, Robert sought out opportunities for interactions in English. He seldom used Polish and even began denying that he spoke any language but English. In the language development classroom Robert was allowed to select the activities he wanted to perform. He liked the computer and began to ask questions about how to use it. These were authentic questions that enabled him to learn to use the computer correctly. He also chose books about insects, especially bees. He liked to observe insects outside the classroom. When provided with materials, Robert learned to draw bees and other insects he observed. Soon he learned the names of the parts of the insects, the flowers that they liked, and where they lived. He learned to predict where they could be found on the school campus, and when there would be lots of insects and when there would be few.

Robert started using the computer to write stories about the insects he observed at school and at home. He shared his stories with other children and even got them interested in watching for bugs and in observing the environment.

Translating his developing skills to the home environment, the interpreter showed Robert's parents some of the work that he was doing at the school and how he was actually learning to talk and express himself. She told his parents that Robert appeared to be acting as if he were a much younger child because he had never learned to talk and to interact with other human beings. She encouraged the parents to take Robert to parks and other places where he could continue his insect-watching hobby, and to develop other interests with him. She also suggested that some of the children of the adult friends of the family might be invited over to play with Robert. Within a few months, Robert began to develop confidence in himself and in his ability to function in English. He began to become much more outgoing and interactive in the cafeteria and in physical education class. He was invited to come to a regular class and show the children his books on insects and to help the class on a science project. Robert continued to do most of his work in the speech/language class for the next two years, but he stayed in contact with the children who had been with him in first and second grade.

Robert took the achievement tests in reading and math at the end of fourth grade. He scored at the 60th percentile in math computation and problem solving. He had difficulty with the reading passages and scored at the 46th percentile in reading. These scores seemed to indicate that Robert was ready for fifth grade. His teachers decided that he was also ready for full-time placement in the regular program. They made a plan that would enable him to function in the regular classroom with continued support of the speech/language teacher and his friends, and from the interpreter who had become a close friend of the family.

Analysis of Robert's Case

Robert's case is one of *limited opportunities for language development*. This term should be differentiated from the notion of limited language development as a result of innate language learning difficulties. Before he entered school, Robert had been exposed to language as a result of the television and interactions between adults. Neither type of discourse required that Robert respond. Neither provided him with feedback on his efforts to communicate. In effect, until he entered school, the world of communication passed Robert by and left him as a spectator rather than a participant. His language development was delayed because he had limited opportunities to use language meaningfully.

Comparison of Yolanda's and Robert's assessment results.

Yolanda was a child with average nonverbal ability who had learned to read in Spanish, but who was unable to develop comparable academic skills in English. For Yolanda the abrupt change from Spanish to only English instruction placed her in a situation in which she was unable to function successfully. By providing Yolanda with structured language development, the school was able to promote a successful learning outcome for Yolanda. Involving her family in the English language learning process also facilitated the development of academic skills and Yolanda's new language. Because Yolanda had developed literacy skills in Spanish, a formal assessment of her prior knowledge provided a strong indicator of potential to develop literacy skills in English.

Yolanda and Robert were two fortunate students learning English as a new language. They were both enrolled in schools where there were trained educators with insights into the students' learning needs. Once it was discovered that Yolanda could read and that she had no manifested language disorders, it became clear that she did not require the services of any special education program. Robert's needs were not as clearly defined. Robert was a boy who not only lacked literacy skills in his home language, but who lacked language development in general. Limited opportunities to communicate meaningfully left Robert far behind his peers socially and academically when he started school. He wanted to communicate, but he had no real understanding of how to produce meaningful language. As a result, he became easily frustrated. Formal assessment confirmed Robert's limitations but provided little insight into his strengths or the ways that he might be assisted. The observant educator began to understand Robert's needs and to assist in the development of a program that linked the home and the school.

His classroom teacher had indicated that once a structured program was put in place for him, Robert was able to learn. Even his language production improved. However, the teacher was concerned that she was unable to provide all that Robert needed in order to be successful. She thought that he needed a special program. There was evidence that he had a language learning disability. This finding was based on comparisons with English proficient age peers. Robert was a special case. When topics on which he had prior experience were introduced in a social, interactive setting, he could participate. The problem was that there were so few topics on which he had any experience. When topics were introduced on which he had little or no prior experience, he hesitated, repeated himself, and produced low voice quality and hard to understand language. All of this behavior gave the impression that he was communicatively disordered. The fact that he had experienced a brain trauma several years earlier also contributed to the overall picture of a disordered learner.

Little information is available on learners who begin the process of language learning after a significant period of time has lapsed. This type of information is important because there are many students like Robert who are entering school with limited first language development on which to graft their new English language learning experiences. There was evidence that Robert was a boy of normal learning ability. This evidence was found in his performance score on the WISC-R, as well as his interest and persistence in working with insects, and the speed with which he learned new words and sounds once they were made explicit for him.

The speech/language evaluation specialist treated Robert as if he were a monolingual learner because she had no prior experience with students like Robert. The report narrative she wrote did not provide insight into the possibility that Robert was in the process of learning language. Nevertheless, the suggestions she provided were appropriate to his learning need for specificity, structure, opportunities for self-expression, and cognitive development.

Fortunately, the speech/language teacher in whose program Robert was placed understood Robert's needs. Her understanding was enhanced through the information that the interpreter provided. She had a developmental, rather than a remedial, perspective of language instruction. Robert benefited from an intensive structured language development program that allowed him to progress at his own rate while providing him with support and opportunities to learn at his level. If he had not received this type of support, it is questionable whether Robert would have been so successful.

In the cases of both Yolanda and Robert, individuals who were familiar with the language and culture of the students provided direct assistance as well as support. Although the professional role of each of these individuals was different, both served important roles as mediators and cultural informants. Both educators observed what the students were doing and developed instructional programs based on this information. The scores of the formal assessment instruments used to measure these two students' ability and proficiency are included here for further discussion and analysis in Table 4-3.

TABLE 4-3. COMPARISON OF YOLANDA'S AND ROBERT'S ASSESSMENT RESULTS

Percentile Rank on the Language Assessment Battery in English
Yolanda: 45   Robert: 15

Wechsler Intelligence Scale for Children-Revised (WISC-R) in English

Verbal Tests	Y	R	Performance Tests	Y	R
Information	1	1	Picture Completion	10	8
Similarities	1	7	Picture Arrangement	11	1
Arithmetic	6	4	Block Design	9	8
Vocabulary	3	4	Object Assembly	9	11
Comprehension	8	5	Coding	13	6

IQ Scales	Yolanda	Robert
Verbal IQ	62	65
Performance IQ	102	91
Full Scale IQ	80	76
Discrepancy points	40	26

RESEARCH IN PRACTICE
Robert's Story

1. **Summarize Robert's case.** Describe Robert's needs. Do you believe that Robert's needs are typical of many LEP students? Explain your answer.

2. **How is Robert's case different from Yolanda's case?**

3. **Compare the similarities and differences in the assessment results.** How do you account for the similarities? How do you account for the differences?

SECTION THREE

LIMITED LEARNING OPPORTUNITY OR LANGUAGE DISORDER?

PEDRO'S STORY

Pedro was a little over four years old when he arrived in the United States with his father and mother from Costa Rica. His father was a first year medical student at a university near Pedro's home. Although his mother had graduated from a university in Costa Rica with a degree in computers, she stayed at home to take care of Pedro during the period the family lived in the United States. When Pedro was three, his mother took him to a doctor in Costa Rica to have him examined because he had not begun to speak. The doctor confirmed what the family has suspected. Pedro was unusually slow in developing, especially in the area of speech and language. The doctor suggested that there could be many reasons for the slow development. The delay could be related to the fact that Pedro was born four weeks premature. It could also be that Pedro did not walk much or talk at all because he lived for long periods of time on a large farm with his grandparents. Pedro was the only grandson and the apple of his grandparents' eyes. Instead of letting him walk and run, because he was small they picked him up and carried him everywhere he went. They gave him everything he wanted before he asked. He had no needs, and he had no real reason to talk.

Pedro began kindergarten in the United States when he was five. Although the kindergarten was in a public school, almost all of the students in the school were from homes where Spanish was spoken. Most of the kindergarten teachers were fluent in Spanish, or had Spanish-speaking assistants. Pedro's parents were happy to have their son in school and were pleased that he was in an environment where he could easily understand his teachers as well as the students. Pedro had begun to talk. His parents thought that being around other children would encourage language development. When they enrolled Pedro, they didn't say anything to the teachers about their concerns about Pedro's language development.

One afternoon about two months after school had started, the kindergarten teacher called to talk with Pedro's mother about Pedro's development. She said that Pedro was interested in all of the activities of the kindergarten and seemed to like the other children. However, he rarely expressed himself and when he did, his language was difficult to understand. Pedro's mother affirmed that she, too, had found Pedro slow to talk and difficult to understand. Lately, she stated, Pedro had become much more expressive and interested in communicating. She had hoped that he was just a slow developer and that he would learn to communicate in school.

Throughout the year, the teacher and the mother communicated about Pedro's development. He was learning to understand, to comprehend, and to follow directions, but his expressive language development was slow. The teacher gave Pedro's mother suggestions for activities she could do at home with him. She sent home notes and little awards when Pedro performed well at school.

Since Pedro was an only child, his mother had time to spend with him. Her mother had come from Costa Rica that year to live with the family. Both women spent a great deal of time talking to Pedro, taking him on trips, and reading stories to him at home. All of their interactions were in Spanish. They believed that since Spanish was their most proficient language, it should be the language they used with Pedro.

As the year passed, Pedro became more communicative, pointing out different animals when he went for walks, talking about the pictures in his favorite story books, and naming the foods he wanted to eat when he was hungry. While his mother remained concerned about her son's development, she was satisfied that he was learning. Since the teacher continued to share her observations and to encourage the family with new reports of Pedro's progress at school, she felt that Pedro had no real problems.

When Pedro began first grade, his mother was surprised that his teacher spoke no Spanish and there was no assistant in her classroom. Due to budget reductions, all of the newly hired staff and the assistants had not been rehired for the following year. Class size at every grade level had increased. The teachers were encouraged to accept the situation since there were no alternatives. The first grade teacher contacted Pedro's mother the second week of school. She said that she was concerned that Pedro did not speak much English and that he was having a great deal of difficulty learning. He was attending the bilingual class so that he could speak Spanish for 45 minutes a day, but he needed to learn English as soon as possible.

The family was shocked by the strong emphasis that the teacher placed on speaking English and on Pedro's not being able to learn in first grade. They were undecided about what to do. They wanted to help their son, but they did not know how. They tried to contact his kindergarten teacher from the previous year, but she had been transferred to another school. They spoke with the bilingual teacher who was sympathetic but unable to provide any solutions. They spoke to the assistant principal who was also aware of the problem. A Spanish-speaker herself, she began to seek out opportunities to get acquainted with Pedro so that she could determine how to assist him. She enlisted the assistance of the guidance counselor and the speech pathologist. The speech pathologist contacted Pedro's former teacher who described Pedro's progress in kindergarten. Based on this information, the speech pathologist concluded that Pedro's difficulties arose from his need to learn English, rather than any developmental disorder.

The assistant principal disagreed. She found him very difficult to understand in Spanish. She further believed that his efforts at learning English were impacting on the limited Spanish he was able to use. The administrator invited a language specialist to come and interact with Pedro to obtain a clearer idea of his bilingual language development.

Pedro was at the end of first grade when the language specialist interacted with him. She used a number of manipulative activities to elicit language. Although fluent in English and Spanish, she used the services of the bilingual teacher to obtain an idea of how Pedro interacted with familiar adults. Pedro indicated that he preferred to speak English, not Spanish, although he liked his bilingual teacher very much. From that point on, most of the interactions were in English.

School observations and information.

Classroom interactions revealed a shy young boy who was reluctant to interact with other children in English or Spanish. The other children seldom initiated interactions with Pedro. He remained alone and quiet most of the day, except when his teachers made a special effort to engage him in interactions and conversations.

Both the bilingual and the regular classroom teachers reported that they seldom had time to devote specifically to Pedro because of the large size of the classes and the reduced availability of classroom assistants. They expressed concern about Pedro because he was not making academic progress. He was not learning to read and he did not attempt to write. The regular classroom teacher suggested that Pedro might be overprotected by his family and that he needed to become more proficient in English. She said that she believed his father was really trying to help Pedro, but she was not sure about the mother or the grandmother, who spoke to him only in Spanish and who, according to the teacher's observations, appeared to be overprotective for Pedro's own good. She stated that she thought that Pedro himself was trying to learn English, but she was not sure why he hadn't made much progress. She thought part of the lack of progress that she had observed was due to the amount of time that Pedro spent outside her class. She felt that she could provide more instruction if he stayed in the room instead of attending the bilingual program. Observations of the regular classroom interactions with the other students in the classroom revealed that instructional activities required that most students provide single word or short answer responses to pre-established questions. In this classroom, during this observation, there was little time or opportunity to use language in meaningful interactions.

The ESOL teacher said that Pedro was making substantial progress in learning the names of the items in the classroom. She had observed the difficulties he had in expressing himself, such as reversing and omitting syllables, and wondered what she could do to assist him.

The bilingual teacher said that she felt that Pedro liked her and was willing to come to the class, but that she wasn't sure if he felt comfortable expressing himself in Spanish. Often he would give her an English response, or no answer at all, even when they were interacting in small groups or individually. She said that she was sure Pedro's family was very supportive of his school activities, and wanted him to learn to read in Spanish.

Parent input.

Pedro's parents confirmed their concern and commitment. His father talked about the number of times they had made school visits. He stated that he had told the school that Pedro had a speech problem, but they had rejected this idea because he was still in the process of learning English. In spite of the report from the doctor in Costa Rica, the school insisted that they were doing all they could to help Pedro learn English. After this rejection, the father said that he had taken Pedro to a well-known clinic in the community and had an evaluation of Pedro's speech and language and a complete physical evaluation. The doctor stated that Pedro was developmentally delayed and slow in producing language. Even in the face of this new information, the regular classroom teacher assured the father that the family should not be so overprotective and that Pedro was going to develop and learn soon.

Pedro's mother said that she wanted to continue to speak Spanish with Pedro so that he could talk with his grandmother and to interact with all of his family in Costa Rica. She said that he was clearly expressing himself more in English and told her that he did not want to speak Spanish at home any more. He preferred English. He needed English, not Spanish. He had put away all of his Spanish story books and would only look at books in English, even though he appeared not to understand many of the stories. She said that she was concerned about his progress, but had become frustrated since his entry into first grade and the all-English instructional environment. She said she was willing to hire a teacher to work with Pedro at home after school, if necessary, but did not know where to turn next. She had talked with the assistant principal and asked her to help Pedro. She stated that she had a great deal of confidence in the assistant principal who appeared to understand Pedro and to have his interests at heart.

The father said that although he was a student himself, he spent time every night reading with Pedro, reviewing homework, and supporting the instruction he was receiving at school. He was greatly concerned that Pedro was getting older and still not learning to read. He said that he hoped that as Pedro became more mature he would realize that he needed to learn, and he would apply himself.

Developments at school.

The assistant principal expressed continued concern about Pedro. She was certain that he had a learning need beyond the scope of the regular classroom and requested that he receive a full psychological evaluation and a speech evaluation. Results indicated that there was a slight discrepancy between verbal and performance scores on the WISC-R, but not the two standard deviations required for consideration for speech/language services. The speech/language pathologist had used an interpreter in assessing Pedro. She later stated that the results in Spanish were invalid because the interpreter had not been well trained.

An amended report indicated there were no difficulties in language development other than a general need to learn English. Learning difficulties could not be attributed to the process of learning English as a new language. It stated that Pedro had told the examiner that he did not want to speak in Spanish any more. The recommendation of the report, based on the psychological evaluation and the speech/language evaluation, was that Pedro should be removed from the bilingual program and placed in an environment where he would learn English as quickly as possible. The conclusion of the report summarized Pedro's language performance, as well as his general behavior, as indicating that he had limited proficiency in English, but not in general learning ability. The report ended with a paragraph summarizing Pedro's problems as the result of "cultural and linguistic confusion." No data were provided within the report to support this conclusion.

The assistant principal said that Pedro was only one of many children in her school who were experiencing school failure and high levels of frustration because they were not able to participate in English at the level where they were expected to perform. One of the most frustrating outcomes that she observed was the fact that the children were losing their home language faster than they were learning English. In addition, many of the children were made to feel ashamed of their language and their lack of English. It was not unusual for children, even those who were identified as severe disabilities and developmental delays, to deny that they spoke their home languages, even when there was no one at home who spoke English. To counteract the negative outcomes of these experiences, the assistant principal had sought the support of community and business leaders. One of the activities she initiated was a campaign to promote the use of Spanish and Creole, the dominant languages of the school. She started after-school clubs and reading activities to promote the use of both Spanish and Haitian Creole literacy. These activities, she stated, were supported by local business groups since funds were not available through the school district. She also stated that her opinion on what the students needed was not always met with favor by some of the teachers at the school. She had developed a series of workshops and a summer training program to assist the teachers in learning how to work more effectively and positively with the students. Not all of the teachers, she emphasized, were open to learning new skills or changing their ideas about how best to teach students.

Because the administrator was concerned about Pedro's progress, she requested that a bilingual language specialist observe and interact with Pedro to determine his level of language development and to assist the school in developing a program to address these needs. The next section describes some of the activities used to elicit and observe Pedro's language and the findings of this interaction.

Language assessment: performance in Spanish.

Language assessment was carried out in both English and Spanish. The Spanish assessment was conducted first. Pedro selected the farm animal set himself from the many toy collections available. He took the animals out and looked at them with interest. The materials which served as an activity for observing Pedro's language development in Spanish included a set of eight animal-shaped puzzle pieces that fit within a plastic tray. The animals were three-dimensional shapes that could stand alone. The first activity required that Pedro select four animals from the farm set and tell a story about them. This is an activity that is usually executed, at least at the descriptive level, by most English-proficient four year olds. He named the animals when prompted. Although the directions were given in Spanish, most of the names were provided in English. With prompting Pedro said, "the cow and the pig and the cluck," and then he covered his mouth with the back of his hand and looked down. He did not attempt to tell a story. With further prompting, he could provide some descriptive words in Spanish. When asked about the pig he said, "es gordo (is fat)." Further prompting produced no further communication. As the farm collection was about to be put away, Pedro reached out and took hold of the tray saying, "do it." With great care he placed each of the animals back in its respective spot within the tray, then placed the tray in the bottom of the box, and placed the cover on the box. When he finished, he folded his hands and looked around as if to say, "I'm done, now you can take it away." But he actually said nothing. After waiting nearly 30 seconds, the examiner removed the box by saying, "Can we take the box? If we can, you need to tell us." Pedro shook his head in consent and smiled.

For the next activity, the bilingual teacher gave him a set of one step and two step commands for placing two-dimensional plastic forms on the story board. In Spanish, the language Pedro produced consisted of single words and two or three word phrases. This performance indicated that Pedro was performing at a low beginner level during that specific interaction period.

Pedro followed the directions exactly as they were given by watching the board and fixing the locations in his mind. Even though he appeared to understand, he hesitated before executing the action. When he hesitated, the bilingual teacher repeated the command several times. When the activity was completed, Pedro again expressed a desire to put the small flat plastic shapes back on the paper from which they came. The plastic forms were sticky. As his hand touched the board, some of the forms stuck to the side of his hand so that he removed two forms for every one he correctly placed. Carefully, Pedro maneuvered the small forms back into their correct positions. His attention to detail and the care with which he executed the tasks provided insight into his attention span and his interest in correctly completing the tasks.

Analysis of the interactions with the bilingual teacher provided additional insight into Pedro's comprehension and communication strategies. The teacher was not aware that much of her input was beyond Pedro's level of comprehension. She produced long streams of language that appeared to be difficult for him to access and act upon. By observing the interactions, it appeared that Pedro was able to take some of the language the teacher produced and extract at least a word or brief phrase for his own use. Frequently he repeated the same words and phrases the teacher used. When Pedro appeared confused, his communication sounded more garbled than when he was sure of what he was saying. His voice was frequently low and difficult to understand. English was often mixed with Spanish, resulting in many unintelligible expressions. It was not possible, given the environment in which the activities were performed, to determine whether the limited language produced in Spanish was an outcome of reluctance to use Spanish in school, difficulty accessing and understanding the teacher, habits of waiting until being shown what to do, or Pedro's actual level of Spanish proficiency.

Language assessment: performance in English.

Initially, activities were conducted in separate languages, with all of the initial activities in Spanish. Because performance in Spanish appeared to be low, English was used to introduce new tasks and topics. Once a task had been completed, the examiner requested that Pedro perform a similar activity in Spanish. Performance was consistently longer and more complete in a variety of domains, including both the home and the school, in English than in Spanish.

Initial activities in English included story telling and completing directions. When requested to tell a story, Pedro did not engage in any activity. When asked to follow directions, his behavior initially was the same as in Spanish. After he was encouraged to become more active and expressive, he started to move the materials around on his own. In following multiple step directions, Pedro started to move the materials as soon as he heard the first command. He was able to complete one-step commands, but was reluctant to perform more than one step without further input. As he focused on the first step, he excluded the rest of the information. Because his focus on the initial communication resulted in an inability to perform two- or three-step directions, the examiner prevented Pedro from touching the materials until the entire set of commands was given. He was also told that directions would be given only once, so that he must listen carefully. When Pedro would look at the examiner for support, she would smile, look at him and then at the materials, and remain silent. After several tries, Pedro got the idea of listening before acting and completed two two-step commands successfully. Next, a three-step command was given. Pedro executed the three- and then a four-step command carefully and correctly. After the successful execution of the four-step command, Pedro was asked to tell the examiner exactly what he had done. He restated the steps as they were given, pausing after each segment of the command and looking at the board as if to gather information before beginning to express the next segment. While the language Pedro produced in restating this series of commands was somewhat difficult to understand because it was expressed in a soft tone with an indefinite quality, the information was intelligible and accurate. He was able to string sets of phrases together to form a whole. The accurate restating of commands placed Pedro at the mid-beginner level of performance in English. More importantly, this performance in English indicated that Pedro had a great deal more receptive and expressive language than had initially appeared in Spanish.

When asked to respond to the question, "What is this a picture of?" regarding a picture of a family in a kitchen seated around a table, Pedro said it was a picture of "a chicken." The examiner asked, "Is this a chicken or a kitchen?" Pedro responded, "a kitchen." The consonants /tch/ were omitted so that the response sound more like /ki-en/. When asked to tell a story about the family in the kitchen, Pedro produced a low action sequence level story by stating:

A family, a father, a baby.
The father is crazy.
The baby spill milk on floor.

When prompted to tell more about what was happening in the picture, Pedro smiled and said nothing. When asked why the father was crazy, Pedro responded "He is crazy" and pointed to the puddle of milk on the floor by the baby. He failed to mention the other family members or events in the picture.

Throughout the other interactions, Pedro appeared to have an understanding of what was happening even though he was often unable to express ideas in words. He knew what many items were used for, but not their names. When he stated the names, syllables were often missing or their positions were reversed, as in the example of "kitchen/chicken." Other examples include: "casoline" for "gasoline" and "dynamike" for "dynamite" (meaning great or wonderful).

Pedro was administered a word repetition task in Spanish to determine if these reversals, substitutions, and omissions were consistent across languages. Of the 57 words he was requested to repeat, Pedro produced 27 or 47% correctly. An analysis of those correct revealed that they are common, high frequency words. Six of the 27 correct words contained three or more syllables. Of the words repeated incorrectly, more appeared to be lower frequency words that he might not hear on a regular basis. Twelve contained two syllables and 18 contained three or more syllables. The errors in the two syllable words that were produced incorrectly consisted primarily of substitutions and omissions, such as "tarten" for "sarten" (frying pan). The errors in the three or more syllable words were composed of omissions, substitutions, and reversals. In two cases, English words were provided for the Spanish stimulus. The substituted English words were monosyllables where the Spanish words contained three syllables, for example "fish" for "pescado." This type of substitution suggests that Pedro might be aware of the errors that he made and was seeking appropriate alternatives. English might be the easier language for Pedro because it contains fewer multisyllable words than Spanish. The frequency of substitutions and reversals indicated a severe deficit in the ability to repeat meaningful words.

Follow-up.

In spite of the information provided by the language specialist, the child study team was not easily persuaded that Pedro had a language disability or a special learning need. The notion of "cultural and linguistic confusion" contained in the previous assessment report was restated several times during the meeting. It was decided that Pedro should be withdrawn from the bilingual program. At the end of first grade, Pedro remained in the regular program. The amount of time he spent in the ESOL program was increased by an hour.

Because Pedro did not progress in learning to read, in second grade he was placed in an English-only Specific Learning Disabilities program. He continued in the Learning Disabilities program on a part-time resource basis until he entered third grade. At that point Pedro had still not learned to read. He was reluctant to talk in any language. When he did speak, he used single words and short sentences about topics of personal interest. His speech was immature and usually difficult to understand. After school he attended a karate class. He told his parents that he liked karate more than school because he did not have to talk so much. And, he said, he got to do things that he liked to do.

Current status.

Pedro's parents continue to take him on many trips and outings, and to work with him at home. They say that he makes many interesting observations about events that impact on him directly. For example, he selected the colors and the wallpaper for his room. He initiated this selection by telling the painter, who was working in another room in the house, exactly what he wanted his room to look like, red at the bottom, grey on the upper half, with a band of figures in the middle. His parents agreed. Once the room was painted, Pedro asked his parents to take him to the furniture store so he could pick out the bed he wanted, multicolored bunk beds with race cars. Pedro continues to have ideas and interests. With attention and support, he is able to express his ideas and to make his own world.

However, in his current placement in the Learning Disabilities program, Pedro's academic progress indicates that his needs are not being met and that he is not receiving the support or instruction he requires. Because Pedro was not making progress at school, his parents have begun looking for a teacher to work with Pedro at home after school.

Formal assessment results.

The results of the second formal assessment are shown below. There are several significant aspects to this information. There is a significant predictable discrepancy between verbal and performance scores that, taken from a negative perspective, could be indicative of learning disability. The fact that the performance score indicated Pedro demonstrated a normal intelligence is positive. The depressed verbal score and the full scale score indicate that unless Pedro is provided with a program that utilizes his non-verbal skills, he could have difficulty learning and making academic progress in the typical instructional program. This finding is supported by the results of the Wide Range Achievement Test-Revised, Table 4-4, that shows Pedro is performing at the lowest level. This low performance, combined with the information that Pedro is capable of learning at a slow to normal rate, indicates that instruction has not been provided in a way that enables him to be successful.

Conclusion.

Not every story has a happy ending. Pedro was experiencing a real communication difficulty, probably a communication disorder. But the school attributed his learning need to a lack of English language proficiency. They were unable or perhaps unwilling to recognize that he had a language learning difficulty that required specialized attention and therapy.

Notice that Pedro's Performance score on the WISC-R is in the normal range. The Verbal/Performance discrepancy also exists in Pedro's scores. This discrepancy often occurs for students who are learning English as a new language. As a result, it may not necessarily be considered as indicative of any type of special learning need. In Pedro's case, a great deal more information was required in order to determine how he was producing and using language. The

TABLE 4-4. SUMMARY OF PEDRO'S TESTS

Wechsler Intelligence Scale for Children-Revised (WISC-R)

Verbal Tests		**Performance Tests**	
Information	2	Picture Completion	8
Similarities	8	Picture Arrangement	13
Arithmetic	6	Block Design	12
Vocabulary	6	Object Assembly	10
Comprehension	8	Coding	7

IQ Scales

Verbal IQ	75
Performance IQ	100
Full Scale IQ	85

Wide Range Achievement Test-Revised

Subtest	Grade Equivalent	Standard Score	Percentile
Word Recognition	1B	56	.4
Spelling	1B	56	.4
Arithmetic	1E	67	1.0

language difficulties he manifested, such as syllable reversals and omissions, occurred in both languages.

Pedro's case may be similar to the stories of many NELB students because schools are not prepared to assess or instruct students who manifest disabilities while in the process of learning English. There are few trained interpreters, few bilingual speech/language pathologists or school psychologists. Even when such personnel are available, there is no assurance that they have been prepared to accurately assess and assist the students who are learning English. Many bilingual personnel have been trained in professional schools in monolingual environments where their only experience is in working in an English-only context. Even as adults, bilingual personnel in training for careers such as psychologists, speech/language pathologists, special education or regular education teachers find that they must put away their non-English culture and language and try to fit in and sound like their instructors and peers. Instruction in this context means that the learners tend to lose or disregard insights into ways to help the students to whom they might have access.

School administrators also have difficulty developing effective programs in schools where the predominant mind-set is English-only. Fortunately for the administrator in Pedro's school, she had the support of the community. She was also seen by her supervisors as an emerging leader. Had she become an administrator in a school district where there were only a small percentage of students who used languages other than English, she might have had more difficulty organizing effective programs.

RESEARCH IN PRACTICE
Pedro's Story

1. **Summarize and describe Pedro's case.** How is it similar to and different from the first two cases?

2. **What would you do to help Pedro?**

WHAT CAN YOU DO?

1. Describe the type of instructional program that you would develop for each of the three students discussed in this chapter.

2. How would you implement an instructional assessment plan that monitored each of these students' academic and social growth?

3. Explain to colleagues how you would implement this type of program in your school.

SUMMARY OF CHAPTER FOUR
Differentiating Language Disorders from the Effects of Limited Opportunities for Language Learning

A multiplicity of factors influence the instructional process and, by association, the assessment process. One of the most important factors is the conceptualization of students' needs. In the cases of Yolanda and Robert, there were competent educators who observed the students in action and began to develop hypotheses about their needs. They tested hypotheses while trying different approaches and seeking more information. Not all of these effective personnel were bilingual or even experienced in working with linguistically different students. However, they were open to new approaches and to finding ways to enable students to be successful.

Both Robert's and Yolanda's cases were representative of students with limited language learning opportunities. In Yolanda's case, a case of arrested educational development, the limitations occurred as a result of the treatment she received at school and the lack of transition between her two languages of communication. In Robert's case, a case of limited opportunities for language development, he entered school with language learning difficulties that occurred as a result of the environment in which he was raised. Instructional assessment and effective instruction provided opportunities for these students to overcome their learning difficulties and to become successful participants within the mainstream.

In Pedro's case there were competent, willing educators and family members, but they were not able to directly impact on his instructional program, even when they were aware of what he needed. In the schools in the United States today, there are cases like those exemplified by Pedro, Yolanda, and Robert. The challenge is in obtaining the information and insight to identify the unique needs of each learner. Each of us has a responsibility to work toward promoting thoughtful reflection, careful observation, and sound professional judgment in assisting all of our students. We also have the responsibility for sharing our insights with our colleagues.

Chapter 5

Towards an Integrative Academic Performance Assessment

The assessment of academic skills and abilities of NELB students by use of standardized achievement tests has been the subject of debate and research for many years. At times, it has been the impetus for legislation generated in efforts to protect students from unfair practices and inappropriate educational placements. One of the primary underlying issues related to achievement assessment is that of the effects of language difference and language learning on test results. Additionally, biases inherent in the tests, the test-taking process, and the decisions that are made with data obtained from such tests have been brought to light. The outcomes and consequences of assessment, such as overinclusion or underinclusion of youngsters in special programs, or lowered expectations of their achievement potential, have led educators to re-examine evaluation practices. On the two extremes, NELB students may be either overtested or not tested at all in order to attempt to protect the students' or school districts' interests. Increasingly, the use of standardized achievement tests for educational planning purposes is being questioned. When used with NELB students, their validity and utility in determining the students' status or progress in the curriculum is also subject to scrutiny and discussion as described in previous chapters.

The purpose of this chapter is to present an overview of an approach that may be helpful to educators when assessing the academic performance of NELB students. As noted earlier, assessment of academic performance integrates both formal and informal procedures. These methods are presented as congruent with trends in instruction and the increasing body of knowledge in the areas of educational measurement, and language and literacy acquisition theory for monolingual, bilingual, and multilingual students.

SECTION ONE

ACADEMIC ACHIEVEMENT TESTING AND NELB STUDENTS

This section reviews some of the problems associated with the use of standardized achievement tests with NELB students. Educators are challenged to reframe the concept of academic achievement assessment from being primarily test-based to an eclectic, systematic effort to gather information about students' performance in the instructional environment. Examples of innovative reading assessment procedures are provided. The traditional and an integrative approach to academic achievement assessment are compared. The purpose of this section is to lay the foundation for a more integrative approach to the assessment of NELB students' abilities, skills, and behaviors as they relate to academic functioning in the school setting.

PERSPECTIVES ON ACHIEVEMENT TESTING

The insensitivity of traditional, standardized instruments and testing practices to extralinguistic and metalinguistic factors such as culture and problem-solving strategies, and oversensitivity to linguistic factors such as proficiency, has been at the heart of the controversy over the use of standardized tests of academic achievement with culturally and linguistically diverse students. Additionally, the misuse of such instruments for tracking (e.g. ability grouping) and educational placement (e.g. special education) purposes or for grade retention has been identified as a barrier to equitable education services for language minority students (Lam 1988; National Clearinghouse for Bilingual Education 1991a; National Commission on Testing and Public Policy 1990; Ulibarri 1990). Research evidence has led to the conclusion that standardized achievement tests do not assess NELB students fairly and accurately (Figueroa 1990; National Association for Bilingual Education 1991; Ulibarri 1990). While achievement tests demonstrate good internal psychometric properties when administered to NELB students, they predict future achievement poorly (DeGeorge 1988; Figueroa 1990). They may also have low content validity for specific bilingual education programs (Navarrete, Wilde, Nelson, Martinez, & Hargett 1990).

Additionally, there are issues related to test bias, technical problems involved in the development and valid use of the tests, and the effects of language proficiency on the test performance of NELB students (Ulibarri 1990). It has been pointed out, for example, that on state-mandated minimum standards tests and on nationally normed standardized achievement tests, minority students uniformly tend to show a verbal-quantitative discrepancy. They tend to score lower on verbal parts of the tests (Figueroa 1990). Furthermore, standardized achievement tests may be of very limited value in making instructional decisions about LEP students and, therefore, lack instructional validity (Ascher 1990; Cloud 1991; Duran 1989). Research regarding the effects of the presence of an interpreter, if one is used, during assessment is virtually nonexistent (Figueroa 1984). Finally, the use of standardized achievement tests assumes either equivalence or uniformity of curricula both in the United States and across countries, if the tests being used are commercially available native language tests which are normed outside the United States (Figueroa 1990).

There are many factors, including test related issues, that make the evaluation of NELB students a complex process. How can educators/evaluators minimize the negative effects of traditional assessment practices and obtain information that is meaningful and relevant to instruction? At present, there appears to be general agreement within the educational community with the following statement, whether it is applied to minorities as stated or to the majority school population:

"... no single form of assessment can shoulder the unbearable weight of being the sole measure of worth or what passes for worth; and that, to enhance the educational and employment opportunities of minorities, various other forms of assessment must be included in any important decision-making about individuals ... " (National Commission on Testing and Public Policy 1990, p.27).

The manner in which evaluation protocols are expanded to include information beyond that which is provided by standardized tests, the type of information sought and obtained, and the focus of the evaluation may vary. For example, existing models of educational assessment of NELB students (and students in general) may be broadly categorized. Two such categories are environmental and student-centered approaches (Barona & Santos de Barona 1987). Contemporary environmental approaches may include, for example, obtaining information from the home regarding language and cultural mores, family mobility patterns, and educational preparation (Cloud 1991; Collier 1988; Larry P. Task Force 1989). Such procedures may examine the experiential background of students, level of acculturation, and the cognitive learning style of the students by way of the teaching style of the teacher (Cloud 1991; Collier 1988; Garcia & Ortiz 1988). Students may be observed in the home, community, and school in efforts to identify possible points of discord between the students' culture and that of the school (Larry P. Task Force 1989). Criterion-referenced tests, questionnaires, and rating scales are often included (Barona & Santos de Barona 1987; Cloud 1991).

In contrast to the environmental approaches, current student-centered approaches as exemplified by such procedures as Dynamic Assessment

(Feuerstein 1979, in Larry P. Task Force 1989) or Interactive Assessment (Brozo 1990), may evaluate the student in the context of learning new information, attempt to discover the child's learning and cognitive strategies, and use a test-teach-test cycle to analyze the student's competencies and deficiencies in learning. The concept of the examiner/teacher as a mediator of learning rather than as a transmitter of the information required by the student for successful completion of tasks is pivotal to these procedures.

Because the student-centered procedures briefly described are based on theories of cognition and learning, it is helpful to examine how these concepts have been operationalized in the field of reading instruction and assessment. Two such models, Dynamic Reading Assessment Procedure (Kletzien & Bednar 1990) and Interactive Assessment (Brozo 1990), are summarized here.

Dynamic Reading Assessment Procedure.

Dynamic Reading Assessment Procedure (DAP) assesses cognitive and affective variables in the reading process. Reading strategies, where strategies are defined as any action or series of actions that a reader uses to comprehend, are assessed. Additionally, the reader's knowledge of reading strategies, and the reader's adaptability and attitude toward reading instruction are identified. Learning is assessed not only by recognizing those abilities already mastered, but also by identifying those capabilities still in process of maturing. In this model, assessment and instruction are combined. Reading is seen as a strategic problem-solving activity in which the reader's current abilities in reading and the zone of reading potential are examined. The zone of reading potential is the range from readers' independent reading level through that level where readers can be successful working with an adult or a more capable peer. DAP highlights the readers' current level of reading, their level of efficiency, knowledge and use or misuse of reading strategies, and capacity to deal with various reading tasks. Additionally, it examines the capacity for change and potential for reading change given appropriate instruction. It also allows the opportunity for the at-risk reader to examine personal learning abilities and potential.

Implementation of DAP is not limited to one set of materials. A variety of classroom reading materials, including basals, content area books, informal reading inventories (IRIs), and cloze passages can be used. Initial assessment of reading ability is conducted in order to establish a baseline. An analysis of the reading process and strategies applied is then conducted. This process includes examination of the use or misuse of known strategies and targets potentially effective strategies. The examiner/teacher then presents a mediated mini-lesson for the targeted strategy, using such methods as direct instruction, guided practice, and independent practice. The reader's ability to benefit from the presentation of the newly introduced strategy is subsequently analyzed by a post-assessment with an alternate form of the original measure. A comparison of test/retest measures is then used to establish the zone of reading potential.

Interactive assessment.

An interactive approach to reading assessment represents an effort to align assessment practices with recent reading research. This research has revealed that reading comprehension is influenced by motivation, interest, prior knowledge and values, the text, sociocultural factors, and the literacy context. The goal of interactive assessment is to discover the conditions under which students succeed in reading rather than merely describing their current status as readers. Viewing reading as an interaction between readers and texts also suggests that performance on various measures of comprehension varies as a function of the evaluation conditions. From this perspective, ability to comprehend is not seen as being fixed or constant, but as changing across texts, tasks, and settings.

Implementation of an interactive assessment utilizing an informal reading inventory involves the following steps, each with its own activities to gather data about the students in question. First, a diagnostic interview is completed. Information pertinent to students' interests, awareness of the goals and purposes of reading, and their description of their personal reading abilities and strategies, is collected through conversation, questions, or by means of attitude and interest inventories. Placement in a reading passage is determined through administration of word lists. In this process, the evaluator provides assistance with difficult words and teaches word knowledge by presenting various word recognition strategies. Words learned through teaching are counted as correct. Prior to reading the appropriate level passage, motivation for and interest in reading the passage is developed by activating and expanding prior knowledge, setting a purpose for reading, and preteaching vocabulary and concepts that may be necessary. Next, students are encouraged to read the passage silently first in order to work out any miscues, identify unknown words, or indicate confusing parts of the text. They are then asked to read the passage out loud. During this period of time, the evaluator/teacher mediates word learning and comprehension, models comprehension processes through self-questioning and thinking out loud, gathers self-reports from the students regarding their comprehension strategies, and uses reciprocal teaching strategies. Finally, after the students have finished reading they are asked to retell what they have read. Students are allowed to look up information to answer detail and factual questions. Their understanding of the passage is then extended by means of activities that connect prior knowledge and experience with the newly learned content.

The assessment approaches described above differ greatly from the procedures which are used in the administration of standardized tests. For example, standardized tests are administered according to specific instructions provided by the test author for seating, timing, cueing of the examinee, and the response mode expected. Limited, if any, feedback is given to the examinee as to his or her performance on the test. A more holistic view of the factors that form the educational experiences of NELB students and information regarding the limitations of standardized tests when used with such students has led educators to search for more relevant methods to assess achievement and its correlates. Additionally, the view that students must be evaluated in the context of their social, linguistic, and educational environment, as well as in the process of acquiring new skills, challenges educators/evaluators to expand our repertoire of methods, as well as our understanding of the assessment process. This challenge implies that an integrative approach is necessary when directly evaluating the academic achievement of NELB students.

REFRAMING THE CONCEPT OF ACADEMIC ACHIEVEMENT ASSESSMENT

As discussed in Chapter One, there are strengths and weaknesses involved in the use of formal and informal procedures. Whether or not they are used frequently depends more on philosophical approaches and perceptions of their utility in gathering the information necessary to make decisions. Where a traditional approach to assessing achievement relies primarily on the use of standardized tests, an integrative evaluation procedure involves the eclectic use and integration of formal and informal methods of direct assessment of the skills, strategies, abilities, and behaviors related to NELB students' academic functioning in the school setting. In this manner, the parameters of the assessment can be broadened to include information that may not be readily available or obvious on a standardized test. The evaluator is provided with greater freedom to incorporate materials or proven methods that are more culturally and linguistically relevant, or are similar to the curriculum of instruction. Given the many types of ESOL curricula available, the various models of bilingual education and ESOL instruction that exist, and the variety of approaches to instruction in the classroom setting, adaptability is a critical factor in selecting an assessment procedure. While being guided by professional standards of practice and techniques of formal testing to ensure consistency and objectivity, evaluators can use procedures in a flexible manner and adapt them to the learner's culture, style, and language. Assessments and interpretations of the information obtained can be completed by use of trained native language speakers and/or cultural informants. Thus, an integrative approach to assessing achievement allows for adaptation to the learner's particular learning situation and needs.

Educational decisions impact students in both the short and the long term. The reasons for assessing a student may vary but, in general, the educator may want to clarify, specify, and verify possible problems and be sure that learners have actually been presented with real opportunities to learn. Educators may need additional information to plan and make decisions about interventions or placement. Uses of such data obtained include screening, diagnosis, planning instructional strategies, monitoring educational progress, or for the purposes of referral to or possible classification and placement in special programs (Salvia & Ysseldyke 1985). In the case of NELB students, it is important to make educational decisions based on multiple sources of data and information obtained over a period of time, not solely on scores that may be reflections of the students' limitations with the language of the tests. Additionally, NELB students' abilities and skills may be inferred incorrectly, based on a single administration of selected tests when, in fact, later administrations of the same tests may disprove the original conclusions. The case of Maurice exemplifies the previous point further. Although Maurice's case will be discussed more thoroughly in Chapter Six, his case is relevant to the present discussion.

Maurice is a limited English proficient student of Haitian descent who was referred for psychoeducational evaluation due to poor academic achievement. He was 14 years old at the time of referral. As part of the initial evaluation, a standardized test of academic achievement was administered in English. On the initial assessment, Maurice obtained a reading grade equivalent score of 3.0, a written language grade equivalent score of 2.4, and a mathematics grade equivalent score of 2.6. The corresponding standard scores obtained were 67, 58, and less than 65 (the norms did not go lower than 65). As age-appropriate standard scores were used in Maurice's particular school district to determine possible eligibility for special education placement, his obtained scores were interpreted to mean that his achievement was comparable to that of Educable Mentally Retarded (EMR) students, since this is the range in which the standard scores placed his skills. Two years later, Maurice was reevaluated with the same academic test and obtained a reading grade equivalent score of 6.1, a written language grade equivalent score of 5.7, and a mathematics grade equivalent score of 4.5. The corresponding standard scores were then 87, 86, and 65, respectively. These standard scores now placed him in the low average range with respect to reading and written language skills, and, while mathematics skills were still in the EMR range, the increase in grade level equivalent (one per each year of instruction) suggested at least an average learning rate.

The dramatic increases in Maurice's scores over such a relatively short period of time would not have been predicted, nor would his learning potential have been inferred, from the results of the standardized tests administered. Furthermore, the second set of results strongly indicate that, as Maurice's English language proficiency increased, so too did his ability to perform more successfully on the standardized tests. The initial test results might have better been used as baseline measures with which to compare any performance subsequent to additional instructional intervention in the regular classroom.

Maurice's case also underscores one of the major, if not *the* major, problems associated with the use of standardized tests with NELB students: the application of standardized norms as discussed in Chapter One. There are times, however, in the assessment of a student when it is necessary to compare his or her performance with that of other students in order to determine whether or not that performance is significantly below expectancy and if there is a need to explore this further. A comparison of scores obtained by the student with scores obtained by a larger group of same-age youngsters is helpful in determining the need for additional intervention. There are currently available valid and reliable measurement methods that provide quantitative information but allow for comparison with students of the same linguistic and cultural background (Dayan 1992; Shinn 1988). The integration of such methods within the educational assessment of NELB students will provide more valid indices of their abilities and skills.

In sum, traditional approaches to the educational achievement assessment of NELB students provide a partial view of the learners' skills, abilities, strategies, and behaviors related to academic performance. The information derived from the exclusive application of standardized tests may lead evaluators to make erroneous, far-reaching inferences about NELB students' abilities. A comparison of traditional and integrative academic assessment procedures that builds on the information presented in earlier chapters is expanded here in Table 5.1.

While it is very important to collect data relative to the child's social and familial background in order to complete a multifactored assessment, the approach presented here draws directly from the curriculum and the instructional environment in which the student is either succeeding, failing, or perceived to be failing. Traditional measures make decisions about a student's academic skills without adequate consideration of the instructional environment in which these have been taught. Quite frequently, students' failure to master academic skills resides in the instructional environment rather than in the students (Shapiro 1989). In this case, the instructional methodologies used and the environment in which these are implemented must be examined, as well as the students' actual performance (Shapiro 1989; Ysseldyke 1987).

The framework for academic performance assessment presented in this chapter assumes that assessment must reflect an evaluation of school-related behaviors in the environment in which they occur. It is based on the belief that what is taught and expected to be learned is what should be tested, and that the results should be strongly related to planning instruction (Shapiro 1989). This approach implies that assessment methods that facilitate monitoring student progress need to be sensitive to changes in students' performance, and are brief, repeatable, and usable by a variety of educators. These measures must be based on research, have demonstrated validity and reliability, and be useful in the process of making educational decisions (Lentz & Shapiro 1985).

When adopting a holistic approach to evaluation there may, however, be a conflict with measurement-based approaches due to the need to satisfy criteria for validity, reliability, and objectivity. Methods based on naturalistic observation must be trustworthy and dependable (Cambourne & Turbill 1990). This

TABLE 5.1. COMPARISON OF TRADITIONAL AND INTEGRATIVE ACADEMIC ASSESSMENT PROCEDURES

TRADITIONAL	INTEGRATIVE
Relies primarily on the use of standardized tests, restricting the parameters of assessment.	Limitations of test are attenuated, and parameters of assessment broadened by supplementing with informal or other alternative assessment strategies.
Test items are selected scientifically but may be culturally biased.	Incorporates non-norm-referenced materials, empirically proven methods or professional standards of practice, which may be culturally and linguistically relevant.
Explicit, unambiguous directions for use are provided with the tests.	Draws from the techniques of clinical practice and formal testing to ensure consistency and objectivity, but allows for flexibility and adaption to the examinee's culture, style, language.
Test scores are quantitative and comparisons are made based on national norms.	Measurement methods may be chosen that provide quantitative information but allow for comparison with peers.
Educational placement decisions may be made based on scores that reflect the LEP student's limitations in the language of the test.	Decision-making process is enhanced by use of multiple sources of data and information.
Abilities and skills of the child may be inferred based on a single administration of selected tests.	Abilities and skills measured initially may be used as a baseline; supplemented with other more valid indices of progress, skills, abilities.
Tests require formal training for proper administration and interpretation.	Proper training is essential for the professional or para-professional gathering data. Interpretations are best made with a cultural informant.
Broad scope of academic skills sampled and assumed to have been taught or learned.	Draws from curriculum and instructional environment to which child is actually exposed.
Limited range of learned behaviors assessed.	Broad scope of learning behaviors can be tapped.

involves ensuring that, in some manner, data gathered under naturalistic conditions also fulfill the scientific requirements associated with validity, reliability, and objectivity. Differing approaches to this dilemma can be identified. Some may be based on a natural theory of assessment while others propose expanding the framework of validity concepts as established for the development of traditional standardized tests (Cambourne & Turbill 1990; Linn, Baker & Dunbar 1991). For example, a natural theory of assessment proposes analogs to the concepts of internal validity, external validity, reliability, and objectivity: credibility, transferability, dependability, and confirmability. These can be accomplished by such procedures as persistent observation, using uninvolved persons to provide feedback, gathering numerous and varied samples of student products and performance to extend the range of information collected, or using additional materials, test interpretations, and hypotheses made from other data sources. Detailed contextual information and data are documented so that another person can trace back from the interpretation to original data (Guba & Lincoln 1981 and Lincoln & Guba 1986, cited in Cambourne & Turbill 1990). While a detailed description of the specific procedures used to ensure the trustworthiness and dependability of data obtained in this manner is beyond the scope of this chapter, the need to maintain scientific integrity when using methods that are not standardized is highlighted. While the jury is out, so to speak, on the technical adequacy of performance assessment, an integrative approach to academic assessment must incorporate the best practices in the selection or development of methods, and meet the highest measurement standards possible in order to be defensible and useful in the evaluation of NELB students.

RESEARCH IN PRACTICE
Reframing the Concept of Academic Achievement Assessment

Mini-Case Study: Julia

Consider the following sets of information regarding the same student (Data Sets 1 and 2). Julia was referred for psychoeducational evaluation at the end of second grade with teacher concerns related to "difficulty in understanding oral directions and using inappropriate labels or responses such as 'I broke my paper' for 'I ripped my paper.'" She was also noted to exhibit poor grammar and spelling in her written work.

Data Set 1: Julia is an Hispanic, beginning third grade student. On the *Language Assessment Scales,* a test of language dominance and proficiency, the results showed her to be at a Level 2, or Non-Speaker classification, in Spanish, and at a Level 5, or Fluent Speaker classification, in English. Using the Checklist of Characteristics of Language Proficiency presented in Chapter Three, Julia was

Validity in performance assessment.

found to demonstrate characteristics of a beginning Primary Level speaker of Spanish and of an Intermediate Level speaker in English. In English she demonstrated emerging higher level language skills at the Intermediate Level.

Julia was unable to complete any items presented on the *Woodcock Psychoeducational Battery: Tests of Achievement,* Spanish edition. On an achievement test administered in English, Julia scored at a 2.8 grade level on the reading cluster. This placed her in the low average range when age appropriate standard scores were derived. Julia scored at a 1.9 grade level on the written language cluster, which placed her in the deficient range in this area. Furthermore, Julia scored at a 2.7 grade level on the mathematics cluster. This placed her in the low average range when compared with chronological age peers.

Data Set 2: Julia's primary home language is Spanish. Julia entered school as a Spanish-dominant kindergarten student. She received English for Speakers of Other Languages (ESOL) services for a brief period of time before returning to the Dominican Republic, where she completed kindergarten with grades of A and B. She was placed back in kindergarten upon her return to the United States. She again received ESOL services for an undetermined length of time. At the time of referral she was completing second grade and was not receiving ESOL. Julia has been promoted to subsequent grades following her second year in kindergarten.

A whole language, literature based approach to reading instruction is being used in her third grade classroom, as well as a process approach to writing. Work samples obtained are depicted in Figures 5.1 through 5.4 as follows. A reading probe administered using classroom literature revealed that Julia was

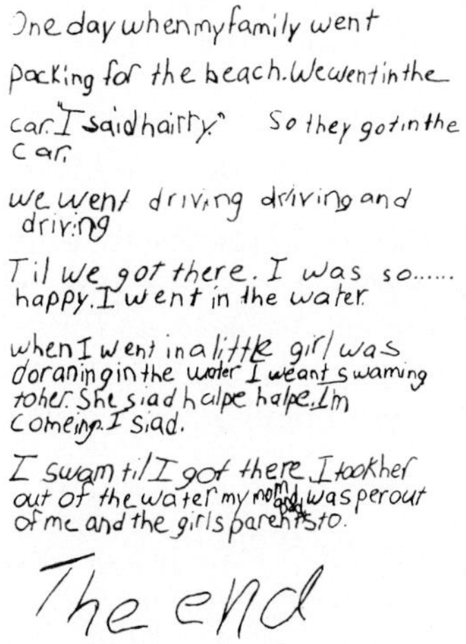

One day when my family went
packing for the beach. We went in the
car. I said hairly." So they got in the
car.

we went driving driving and
driving

Til we got there. I was so......
happy. I went in the water

when I went in a little girl was
doraning in the water I weant swaming
to her. She siad halpe halpe. Im
comeing. I siad.

I swam til I got there I took her
out of the water my mom was perout
of me and the girls parent sto.

The end

Figure 5.1

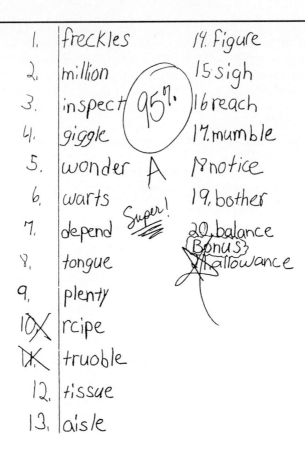

1. freckles
2. million
3. inspect
4. giggle
5. wonder
6. warts
7. depend
8. tongue
9. plenty
10. rcipe
11. truoble
12. tissue
13. aisle

14. figure
15. sigh
16. reach
17. mumble
18. notice
19. bother
20. balance
Bonus: allowance

95% A Super!

Figure 5.2

able to read 100 words correctly per minute with 91% accuracy. Comprehension was compromised by unfamiliarity with word meanings (e.g. "staircase").

1. **Review Data Set 2 for Julia. Examine the work samples provided by Julia's current teacher.** These include a story written during writing as a process time, the results of a spelling test, her work on a language arts lesson, and a math assignment. Comment on these. How do the data obtained in Set 2 contrast with the standardized test information reported in Data Set 1 for Julia?

2. **In reviewing Julia's case, what other assessments would you conduct that would provide information pertinent to the referral concerns?** Give reasons for your selection(s).

3. **Compare both Data Sets provided on Julia. Each Data Set provides a perspective of Julia's language and academic skills.** Which do you perceive as

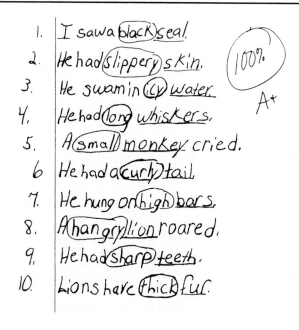

1. I saw a (black) seal.
2. He had (slippery) skin. (100%)
3. He swam in (icy) water. A+
4. He had (long) whiskers.
5. A (small) monkey cried.
6. He had a (curly) tail.
7. He hung on (high) bars.
8. A (hangry) lion roared.
9. He had (sharp) teeth.
10. Lions have (thick) fur.

Figure 5.3

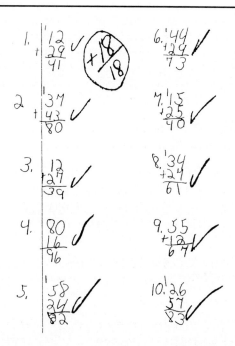

Figure 5.4

being most helpful? Why? What information of value can be found in either or both sets? Does one set appear to be in discord with the other? How?

4. Consider the events in Julia's educational history. How might these affect her achievement and language skills?

5. Develop a hypothesis as to why Julia was referred for psychoeducational evaluation.

6. Develop a hypothesis as to reasons for Julia's language "errors" as described in the reason for referral. How would you test your hypothesis?

SUMMARIZING SECTION ONE
Academic Achievement Testing and NELB Students

This section reviewed some of the problems associated with the use of standardized achievement tests with NELB students. Examples of contemporary approaches to reading assessment were provided as representative of alternative approaches to traditional assessment. The foundation for an integrative approach to assessing NELB students was further developed from previous chapters by comparing the characteristics of traditional assessment with those of an integrative approach. The need to maintain scientific integrity when using alternative procedures was underscored. Trustworthiness and dependability of the information obtained through informal methods are necessary if these are to be defensible and useful for instructional assessment of NELB students.

WHAT CAN YOU DO?

1. Investigate academic achievement assessment practices in your district. Are these the same for all students? Are alternative measures taken to assess NELB students?

2. How might assessment practices become obstacles to educational and employment opportunities for NELB students?

3. How can an integrative approach to assessment improve decision-making within the educational setting?

SECTION TWO

DEVELOPING AN ACADEMIC EVALUATION FRAMEWORK

Underlying any effort to assess the academic performance of students are the questions "How," "Who," "What," "When," "Where," and "Why." These questions are expanded by asking both who is the student to be assessed and who is the educator who will perform this service. What role will the educator assume in the process? What is to be evaluated and why? When or how will evaluation occur? Where and under what conditions will the evaluation take place? How will the evaluation be completed? How will progress be measured? These questions will guide those who are seeking information about students' learning in developing strategies or procedures to be used in evaluation. The strategies chosen must be responsive to the complex dynamics of individual children, programs, and learning contexts. They also imply that evaluators bring to the process their understanding of the learning process, philosophy, training orientation, and personal style or preferences when developing an evaluation plan.

With the many procedures available for evaluation purposes and the ever-changing body of knowledge in education, it is usually helpful to develop a framework based on theory, practice, and research to serve as a guide for assessment. This section presents suggestions regarding the development of an academic assessment framework. Such a framework might clarify the roles of the adult evaluator and the person(s) evaluated and identify what is to be evaluated, the methods to be used, how acquisition and mastery of skills or evidence of learning will be measured, the frequency of evaluation, and the circumstances or conditions under which evaluation will take place.

HOW? DIMENSIONS OF AN INTEGRATIVE ACADEMIC PERFORMANCE ASSESSMENT

In recent years, evaluation systems have been developed that take into account the ecology, or environment, of the classroom, instructional variables, and student behaviors as they occur in the classroom or as a result of instruction. Such systems may define classroom processes by describing the dynamics of instruction and subsequent student responses. Some descriptions may make statements about such variables as the percentage of the day spent in specific language acquisition activities, the instructional model used, or grouping and language usage, while other descriptions focus on the specific behaviors in which teacher(s) and students are engaged. For example, a typical question that might be asked is what types of behavior and language usage students are most likely to be engaged in, given a specific teacher behavior and language of instruction. These evaluation systems, using what is known as *process-product analysis,* codify and quantify the components of the instructional processes and correlate them with specific outcome measures (products), such as scores on language dominance tests or measures of academic achievement. They may focus primarily on discrete instructional skills found, through research, to be effective in producing specific student outcomes (Willig & Ortiz 1991).

Within an integrative perspective to evaluation, the term *process* is broadened to include observations of and interactions with children in the act of learning. These observations are carried out in a systematic and purposeful manner, and are based primarily on either evolving or established theories of how children learn to read, write, or acquire mathematical skills. The descriptions of process become anecdotal and may take on a narrative format, reflecting the dynamic nature of learning. Processes may or may not result in a product. They are difficult to assess due to their complexity; however, they can be evaluated through observation (Preistly 1982). Observation forms, checklists, or rating scales can be devised to better describe the unique features of the classroom context, students' responses to instruction and to the curriculum, and students' interactions with the teacher and each other. The term *product* is extended from its often used meaning referring to the results of standardized measures of achievement or language to measure specific outcomes, to include student-generated data, collected through a variety of media or materials, and gathered over a period of time. These are then evaluated based on indicators, or markers, of student academic growth and increasing control of the material or language (Cambourne & Turbill 1990).

Observations or qualitative descriptions alone are not, however, sufficient in providing indices of student progress. Quantitative information is needed, for example, to assist in determining the degree of mastery of particular content matter or skill, or to determine a particular student's standing when compared to others in the class, school, or district. In this case, measures that are based on the actual curriculum or that tap a broad range of curricular objectives are used. Scoring procedures are either chosen (for informal measures) or applied (to formal measures) to provide the quantitative information required to make instructional decisions about students. For example, scoring may be analytic or holistic, or it may be predetermined, based on standardization. Furthermore, scoring may be based on systematic, direct measurement of the occurrence of a specific response, such as when measuring reading fluency and accuracy. A more common scoring method is that of determining the percentage of correct responses. In any event, the collection of quantitative information to measure student achievement is also necessary if evaluations are going to be meaningful and fulfill their intended purpose.

Figure 5-5 provides a representation of the dimensions of an integrative academic performance evaluation framework for evaluating NELB students (Anthony, Johnson, Mickelson, & Preese 1991). The core of the figure reflects the four components of an integrative assessment: the observation of processes, the examination of student products, and the use of measures representative of the actual academic and language curricula to which students are exposed. These are considered contextualized measures, or measures that provide insight into specific aspects of individual performance. There are also measures that compare the student's performance with the larger population of students and are based on a broader range of academic skills deemed to be representative of either national, state, or local curricular objectives, that is, decontextualized measures. A non-inclusive listing of examples of methods that can be used to gather academic performance data about each student is presented in the quadrants. Information is obtained, to the degree possible, on performance in both the non-English language and also in English. Possible cultural influences on the learning behaviors observed are taken into account. The outer rim of the core indicates how data are to be gathered, analyzed, or interpreted. The figure also denotes the possible roles of the adult evaluator as observer of the ongoing processes and products, or as elicitor and facilitator of student behavior in the learning context.

In sum, within the framework for evaluation presented, the terms *process* and *product* are reframed to include more than discrete components of instructional and learning behaviors. Evaluation of process is extended to include observations of the dynamics of the instructional setting and student learning behaviors. Furthermore, products, and the methods used to demonstrate that learning has occurred or is occurring, include traditional measures of achievement plus a variety of other data. For NELB students, this framework of assessment allows for data to be gathered across time from multiple sources.

WHO? DEFINING EVALUATION ROLES

Within a traditional framework of evaluation, the role of evaluator has been that of an administrator of tests. In such a framework, there is usually a predetermined stimulus to which the person being tested must respond. As noted in the previous section, new awareness of how children learn has prompted efforts to tap those processes more effectively than by the sole administration of tests. This implies that the evaluator is no longer a part of the instrument, to use a descriptive metaphor, but becomes, as it were, the instrument for evaluating behaviors. In this sense, the evaluator is responsive rather than reactive when evaluating students (Cambourne & Turbill 1990). The evaluator becomes involved in and experiences the programs the students are

EVALUATOR AS OBSERVER

Anecdotal records
Observation forms/checklists
Observation rating scales
Documentation of task-related behaviors
(e.g. reading or writing)
Conferences/Interviews
Attitudes inventories
Interactional analysis
(e.g. cooperative learning group)
Responses to reading
(e.g. retelling, reconstruction)

Portfolios
Notebooks/journals
Audio/Videotapes
Self-evaluation reports
Collection of written products
Interest inventories
Logs

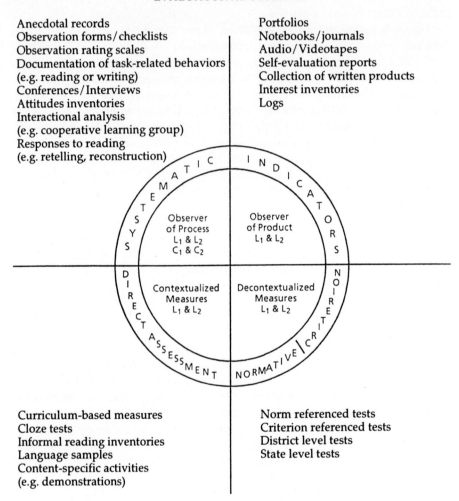

SYSTEMATIC INDICATORS

Observer
of Process
L_1 & L_2
C_1 & C_2

Observer
of Product
L_1 & L_2

DIRECT ASSESSMENT

Contextualized
Measures
L_1 & L_2

Decontextualized
Measures
L_1 & L_2

NORMATIVE CRITERION

Curriculum-based measures
Cloze tests
Informal reading inventories
Language samples
Content-specific activities
(e.g. demonstrations)

Norm referenced tests
Criterion referenced tests
District level tests
State level tests

EVALUATOR AS ELICITOR

Figure 5.5. The Dimensions of an Integrative Evaluation of Academic Performance

Adapted from: Anthony, R., Johnson, T. and Preece, A. (1988) *A Data Gathering Profile*. Pre-convention Institute, International Reading Association, Gold Coast, Australia. Subsequently published in Anthony, R., Johnson, T., Mickelson, N., and Preece, A. (1991) *Evaluating Literacy: A Perspective for Change*. Portsmouth: Heinemann. Reprinted with permission.

participating in by talking to them, observing them in action, and collecting artifacts or outcomes from the various situations observed (Cambourne & Turbill 1990). In effect, the evaluator is an observer, facilitator, and elicitor of behaviors in the context in which learning is occurring.

On occasions, the students in the classroom may become the evaluators by providing peer reports or group evaluation results (Gilbert & Burger 1990). The student(s) in question may do self-assessments or self-reports (Gilbert & Burger, 1990). Students become participants in their own evaluation through reflection and documentation of their growing awareness of their progress by such means as journals, self-reports, or inventories. In this sense, the role of the "evaluator" is flexible and interchangeable among the members of the classroom community.

WHAT?   ESTABLISHING EVALUATION OBJECTIVES

The decision about what will be evaluated will depend largely on the curriculum and instructional objectives established at the classroom and school levels. These, in turn, are influenced by district and state objectives established by local and state education agencies. For the purposes of the present discussion, only curricular and instructional objectives as interpreted and implemented in the classroom setting are of interest.

The decision about what to evaluate in the classroom is one that may be value-laden and differ among educators. It may also be guided by the audience for which the evaluation is intended or by the intended use of the information (Cambourne & Turbill 1990). For example, information gathered to report student progress to parents is different from that gathered to determine a student's understanding of a topic or how he or she arrived at a particular answer. Evaluation to determine student error patterns is different from that used to measure growth and progress. The timelines for and frequency of such evaluations differ depending on whether short or long term growth is being measured (Fuchs & Deno 1991).

Within an integrative model of assessment, the answer to what is to be assessed is anchored in the students' current learning environment. The choices made as to which learning behaviors to assess may be made at the individual or classroom level or in the context of departmental or school-wide objectives. It is necessary to decide whether to evaluate the process students go through, the product students produce, or both (Lange & Cook 1986). For example, language arts assessments based on real-world opportunities to draft, revise, edit, and receive comments prior to preparing a final version of an expository piece, are replacing assessments that focus on isolated skills such as spelling words or writing sentences or paragraphs out of context (Arter 1990). In this case, the final essay, the product, may be the aim of assessment. The drafts, the activities, and other enabling activities the students use to produce the final outcome are also valuable products that reveal the students' learning processes.

Intended learning outcomes, such as flexibility in problem-solving and application of higher order thinking skills, may be targeted for evaluation. The processes the student uses may be the object of assessment. For example, the student may demonstrate how to design and complete an experiment, record observations, and draw conclusions. The processes used to design the experiment, to collect and report the data, and to develop conclusions, become the focus of the evaluation. The student can demonstrate the experiment under real or simulated conditions, such as the use of microcomputers and CD ROM activities. Simulations are valuable if use of realia would be too costly or dangerous. They also provide flexibility in terms of the language used since the programs can include a number of languages.

In some instances, both the processes and the products are of equal interest to the evaluator, such as when assessing the skills and strategies used by emergent readers. In this case, the beginning reader's knowledge of the functions of written language, emergent storybook reading abilities, attempts at writing, and knowledge of letter-sound correspondences, are all the focus of assessment (Teale 1988).

In sum, what is to be evaluated and when will be guided primarily by the instructional objectives established at the classroom and school levels. The intended use of the evaluation information and whether the information is needed to determine short or long term progress will also be factors in establishing the content and frequency of assessment.

WHY? ESTABLISHING A PURPOSE FOR EVALUATION

The evaluation of academic skills attainment is an integral part of the education process. In order to be useful, however, data must be gathered in a carefully planned manner and with specific purposes in mind. The definition of purpose assists in the collection of information pertinent and relevant to the educator's objectives. Major purposes of student assessment are: (a) to measure student progress in attaining knowledge and skills in content areas; and (b) to respond to the need for accountability. Additional reasons include: (c) reporting student progress to parents; (d) assigning grades; (e) providing feedback for students; and (f) assisting students in knowing what is important to learn (Navarrete et al. 1990; Orange County Public Schools 1990). Educators may also be interested in comparing the achievement levels of students or groups of students in their classes. The information collected may also be used to make instructional decisions of a more immediate nature or to determine the effectiveness of particular interventions. Data may be gathered to compare schools and school districts (Orange County Public Schools 1990).

When children are experiencing academic difficulties, evaluations become more focused on such areas as their understanding of the content being taught, error patterns, learning strategies, and ability to generalize what has been learned. In general, the methods selected to evaluate students are determined by the reasons for the evaluation. Specific areas of concern are defined objectively to clarify purposes. For example, there is a difference between stating that a child is "reading below grade level" and stating that the child "demonstrates dysfluencies in reading grade level texts and has particular difficulty with medial vowel sounds." The purpose of evaluation in the second instance becomes one of determining the nature and source of dysfluencies, particular patterns of error or success, in order to determine appropriate instruction. In the first instance, the educator may wish to determine how far below grade level the student is reading by comparing scores on a group administered reading test with the scores obtained by other students in the class. Establishing a clear purpose for assessment of academic skills helps in determining the most efficient manner to accomplish the assessment.

RESEARCH IN PRACTICE
Developing an Academic Evaluation Framework

1. **Reflect upon your role as evaluator.** What activities do you engage in when evaluating students? Categorize these activities. For example, would they fall under "administration," "observation," or "facilitation/elicitation"?

2. **How do you establish evaluation objectives?** Why is it necessary to do so?

3. **Why do you evaluate students?** What constitutes a reasonable amount of evaluation for you?

4. **Research has demonstrated that NELB students are frequently overtested or undertested.** Discuss how establishing objectives and a purpose for evaluation can address this concern.

5. **Develop your own evaluation framework.** Try it out on a single case. Share it with a colleague.

WHERE? IDENTIFYING INSTRUCTIONAL ENVIRONMENTS FOR NELB STUDENTS

If a group of educators were asked to define the terms "Bilingual Education" and "English for Speakers of Other Languages" (ESOL, a term often used interchangeably with "English as a Second Language" or ESL), more than likely a variety of responses would be evoked, and all would probably be equally valid. This diversity of definitions exists because there are varying approaches to the instruction of NELB students (Fradd 1987b). Furthermore, the environments in which these approaches are used may vary across school districts. For example, some districts may choose to implement a program wherein both native language and ESOL strategies are used for instructional purposes, or they may choose to implement a program where English is the only linguistic medium for instruction. Additionally, students may be served in various settings. For example, they may receive services in a resource room, a self-contained class, or in the mainstream with support or consultative services. Table 5-2 presents a description of some of the common programs for instructing NELB students, their salient features, and implications for assessment.

Of critical importance to the success of any approach is the presence or absence of an empowering environment in which cultural pluralism, parent participation, and shared governance are fostered (Ortiz 1988). The student's talents, abilities, and motivation to learn are fostered in a climate of acceptance of diversity (Fletcher & Cardona-Morales 1990). It is an environment in which academically rich programs are provided and in which teachers are trained to work with language minority students. Personal attention is given to the students and these, in turn, are responsible for their own activities (Ortiz 1988). Additionally, instructional approaches that provide contextual support, are comprehensible to the student, provide for mutual and meaningful interaction between student and teacher, and focus less on drill and teaching skills in isolation or in their component parts (rather than as related to a whole), are deemed to be more appropriate for new language learners (Ortiz et al. 1991; Willig & Ortiz 1991).

In a holistic, empowering instruction paradigm, both teacher and learner needs, abilities, and characteristics are acknowledged (Fletcher & Cardona-Morales 1990; Fradd 1987b). The teacher's ability to evaluate and change the learning environment is emphasized, and the curriculum is developed so that it is meaningful to the student (Fletcher & Cardona-Morales 1990). The teacher's evaluative activities and modifications in this paradigm do not, however, take on a directive or prescriptive quality. Instead, they evolve from an attitude of guidance and facilitation, rather than from one of controlling students' learning (Cummins 1984; Cummins 1989). Instructional methods that emphasize reciprocal interaction between teachers and students rather than the transmission of

TABLE 5.2. INSTRUCTIONAL PROGRAMS COMMONLY USED FOR LEP STUDENTS

PROGRAM TYPE	LANGUAGE(S) USED	SALIENT FEATURES	IMPLICATIONS FOR ASSESSMENT
Resource	English	One or two periods of English; student is removed from classroom where English is used.	May focus only on evaluating English skills, losing valuable native language information; lower level skills only may be developing.
Structured Immersion	Teacher uses English; students may use native language.	All subjects taught in English; vocabulary and grammar are simplified.	Provides opportunity for observation of students' understanding and use of both languages, but native language literacy information is unavailable to the observer.
Transitional Bilingual	Native language and English	Use of both languages to teach content until student can benefit from English as the only language of instruction.	Students' understanding, use and literacy in both languages can be observed and assessed, however, results affected by possible native language loss as English is acquired.
Two-Way Bilingual	Native language and English	Serves both minority language and majority language students in a cooperative exchange model to promote native and second language literacy.	Provides opportunity for observation and assessment in an environment which is more naturalistic; social, cultural, linguistic, and biliteracy factors can be examined, compared, and contrasted between and among language groups; native language materials available.
Maintenance Bilingual	Native language and English	Goal is to develop proficiency and literacy in both languages; students' culture is important part of curriculum.	Progress in both languages can be assessed and monitored throughout the student's academic career; integrity of student's cultural identity is maintained; native language materials available.

information by means of direct instruction, are more effective for the target students (Ortiz et al. 1991).

The distinction between instructional environments and methodologies that may be more apt to promote academic achievement and successful new language learning for NELB students and those that may be less apt to do so is relevant to the assessment of academic performance. That native language development and English language acquisition are inextricably linked to academic performance has been discussed in the preceding chapters. In general, as oral language performance increases in English, so too does reading competence, suggesting a positive correlation between oral language proficiency and reading (Lindholm 1991; Peregoy & Boyle 1991). However, reading achievement in English as a second language also appears to be dependent on reading achievement in the native language, possibly more so than on relative oral proficiency in English (Cloud 1991; Lindholm 1991; Saville-Troike 1991). Furthermore, high levels of proficiency in two languages not only facilitate academic achievement but also allow for transfer of content material across languages once sufficient language skills have been acquired. Studies of academic skills in bilingual students' two languages typically show high relationships. For example, a bilingual who performs well in math in one language will more than likely perform well in the same subject in the second language, once the student has acquired the language proficiency necessary to demonstrate that knowledge (Lindholm 1991). Additionally, language learning strategies involve behaviors that may not necessarily be language specific, such as the steps a student uses to acquire, store, and retrieve new information (Oxford 1989).

Contemporary research has demonstrated that reading, particularly reading that is student directed and voluntary, provides for language and literacy development and broadens the student's knowledge base. Reading in the primary language not only develops overall language abilities, but also provides a foundation for the common underlying proficiency that helps English language development. Furthermore, the habit of reading also transfers to the second language, further contributing to the academic success (Krashen 1991). That is, assuming that the student is from a literate, print-oriented society and has had the opportunity to experience and participate in the print environment (Clay 1989; Goodman, Goodman & Flores 1984).

Readers who are learning to function in a new language bring with them their knowledge of the reading process and the cognitive problem-solving strategies they use for comprehension, and then apply these to the language features of the text written in English. The ways readers conceive a particular reading task, what textual cues they attend to, how they make sense of what they read, and what they do when they do not understand informative text, are strategies that are not dependent on the specific language features but are transferred to the process of reading in the second language (Block 1986).

Second language readers may be able to understand more about what they are reading than they are able to express or produce (Goodman, Goodman & Flores 1984). Furthermore, comprehension and the ability to respond to the multiple dimensions of text, as evidenced by the ability to provide expanded, detailed, or specific information to questions, appear to be influenced by general cognitive and academic maturity (Peregoy & Boyle 1991).

For children who are not raised in a literate, print-rich environment, and have little or no opportunity to read outside of school, the acquisition of literacy-related behaviors may be slower. In some instances, even the understanding of the basic concepts of what constitutes a letter or a word may take much longer to develop, extending beyond the primary grade levels (Clay, 1989). For these students, instruction must include engagement and expansion of personal and cultural experiences to provide the link between language and literacy. That background knowledge is necessary for interpretation of meaning has been demonstrated in studies where significant improvement in reading comprehension skills of ESL students has occurred when supplementary background information is provided with written text (Saville-Troike 1991).

Attitude and motivation toward learning the language, as well as the student's individual learning style, have also been found to affect language and literacy development (Cloud 1991; Lewelling 1991; Oxford 1989; Pierce 1987; Saville-Troike 1991). The importance of the instructional environment in fostering achievement and positive self-appraisals among linguistically diverse students has been noted throughout the literature (Castaneda 1991; Ortiz, Wilkinson, Robertson-Courtney & Kushner 1991; Ruiz & Figueroa 1989; Tikunoff & Ward 1991; Willig & Ortiz 1991). Likewise, the systematic and consistent involvement of parents (such as by providing specific information about how they can help their children), even though literacy may not have a prominent role in the home, is a factor in improving achievement (Goldenberg & Gallimore 1991). Variables as correlates to high achievement, such as native language use, linguistic competence, and a facilitative environment which promotes learning, have been demonstrated in studies examining factors related to academic invulnerability.

Academically invulnerable students are "those who sustain high levels of achievement motivation and performance, despite the presence of stressful events and conditions that place them at risk of doing poorly in school and, ultimately, dropping out of school" (Alva 1991, p. 19). These students have been found to have a positive view of their intellectual ability, a strong sense of responsibility and sense of control for their academic future, and high levels of educational support from their teachers, friends, and parents. These students also express positive subjective appraisals of their social environment and of potentially stressful school-related events. It has been found, for example, that stress involving language issues is a powerful discriminator of high and low performance on group achievement tests (Alva 1991). Those students who perceive greater stress with regard to language, such as feeling pressured to speak only English at school, being made fun of by peers about the way they speak English, and not understanding when things are explained in English, are more likely to be correctly classified as vulnerable. That is, these students tend to perform poorly on group achievement tests.

Academic achievement in the new language also depends on previous knowledge and experiences with the general social experience of school and school-type activities. Preexisting knowledge about such things as school routines, what happens in a school setting, teacher-student relationships, and so on, allows students to make inferences and predictions about the meaning of events that will occur in a new school setting. These scripts for school are founded on cultural knowledge and may differ due to social experiences; however, they provide the student the means with which to understand and interpret events and actions in the classroom and school setting (Saville-Troike 1991). An instructional environment that facilitates the transfer of these scripts and of background knowledge to new learning situations contributes to success. For those students who have had no or limited exposure to an educational environment as represented by a school, these experiences will have to be provided and the foundation laid for future learning.

Success in acquiring or transferring those academic skills and learning strategies needed for achievement comparable to that of monolingual peers in the all-English medium classroom is dependent upon, among other factors, the degree to which the instructional environment and methods used facilitate these processes. Table 5-3 summarizes some of the characteristics of instructional environments and methods that are more or less conducive to the acquisition and transfer of skills, knowledge, and cognitive strategies. While the placement on the table implies a strict dichotomy, in reality existing approaches to the instruction of NELB students may be placed on a continuum reflecting the various degrees to which programs or methodologies provide for comprehensible input and allow for meaningful participation on the part of the students. Table 5-3 also serves as a framework for classroom observation when examining the context in which academic performance occurs. Classroom organization, as well as general instructional and linguistic strategies, combine to produce a learning environment that fosters reciprocal interaction and language learning (Cummins 1984; Fradd, 1987b).

The previous discussion and the features of facilitative learning environments identified suggest that there are extralinguistic, as well as linguistic variables, that must be considered in the academic assessment of non-English background students. In spite of the powerful influence these factors have on academic achievement, these factors are not readily identified by the administration of currently available standardized tests. Implications for instruction are frequently difficult to quantify in order to determine the effectiveness of alternative approaches. For example, how does one measure previous knowledge, motivation, or reading habits on standardized reading tests? How can one

TABLE 5-3. CHARACTERISTICS OF FACILITATIVE ENVIRONMENTS AND METHODS FOR INSTRUCTING NELB/LEP STUDENTS

DIMENSION	MORE FACILITATIVE	LESS FACILITATIVE
CLASSROOM ORGANIZATION	Mix of large-group, small group, individual activities.	Large group instruction; extended periods of free interaction among students.
	Quality printed materials are easily accessible in both the native and new language.	Limited or no access to printed materials in the environment.
	A variety of materials for self-expression and experiential activities are available.	Self-expression and learning activities restricted to "paper and pencil" tasks or context-reduced lessons.
	Physical space is allocated and designed to maximize use of materials and foster cooperative interaction.	Physical space is not conducive to cooperative interaction and reflects limitations in materials and areas for independent learning.
INSTRUCTIONAL STRATEGIES (GENERAL)	Material to be taught is organized in a predictable manner, but allows for meaningful exchange and interaction.	Material is presented in a highly structured, drill and repetitive practice format.
	Balance between teacher-directed and individual or small, cooperative group activities.	Teacher directs and controls all or most activities.
	Strategies that develop comprehension and higher order thinking skills are used; any necessary lower level skill is taught in context.	Strategies that emphasize memorization, imitation, chain drill, etc., and teach skills in isolation are used.
	Students' culture is integrated with content and language.	Culture is not recognized or is minimized in the instructional process.
	Students' personal experiences are acknowledged and, if necessary, expanded to provide a link between prior and current learning.	Personal experiences are not taken into account; the provision of new information to be learned is the focus.

(continued on page 228)

DIMENSION	MORE FACILITATIVE	LESS FACILITATIVE
INSTRUCTIONAL STRATEGIES (LANGUAGE)	Teacher uses language that reflects real-world communication, that is, is interactive, purposeful, and meaningful (See also Table 2-1 for Characteristics of Context Embedded and Context Reduced Language).	Language instruction is fragmented when taught as separate subjects (e.g., reading, language mechanics, grammar, spelling).
	Instructional language is modified through such strategies as confirmation and comprehension checks, clarification requests, repetitions, and expansions to accommodate for comprehension.	No accommodations are made to ensure comprehension, or language is so simplified that content, context, meaning, and purpose are lost.
	Language and literacy are linked through teacher modeling literacy behaviors or through planned activities that provide for opportunities to independently practice and re-enact literacy behaviors. Such methods as narratives, story grammars, and provision of an audience with which to share language, are used to enhance learning.	Language and literacy are linked primarily through the use of basal readers or other texts with limited, if any, supportive supplemental strategies.
	Students' native language is valued and seen as the foundation for acquiring the new language. Its use is encouraged to enhance meaning and positive self-identity.	Students' native language is considered an interference to learning the new language; its use is prohibited in the classroom.

gauge the degree of stress or discomfort felt by non-native English speaking students when they are reading or completing a mathematics, group administered, achievement test? How does one know whether a particular instructional strategy has had a positive outcome for the student if the measure used to assess that outcome is based on national norms?

In sum, while methods exist for the purpose of examining instructional environments, these have focused primarily on the presence or absence of specific practices deemed necessary for effective teaching (Tikunoff 1985; Ysseldyke 1987). They have evolved from research in which discrete components of instructional processes, present and observed in classrooms, are quantified and correlated with the end product, student achievement (Willig & Ortiz 1991). Concerns have been expressed regarding the assumption that some of the instructional features identified may not be the most effective for use with students given current theory and research on language and literacy acquisition (Willig & Ortiz 1991). Key elements of facilitative approaches for instructing NELB students include, but are not limited to, integrating reading, writing, thinking, and language activities in a holistic manner rather than teaching hierarchies of subskills, organizing classroom activities and space to promote both shared and individual learning experiences, providing a variety of quality native language and new language materials, and use of language that reflects real-world communication, is meaningful, interactive, and is modified to meet the learners' needs. Such approaches foster literacy and self-expression, and view cultural self-identity in a positive light.

The growing body of research regarding the development of language and literacy skills for monolingual, bilingual, or multilingual youngsters, and the availability of valid and reliable educational measurement methods, holds the key to discovering academic assessment practices that are more congruent with trends in instruction and with the increasing knowledge of the way children learn best. Data collection methods that can be applied to information obtained directly from the classroom, curriculum, or from the student satisfy the need for continued monitoring of student progress and accountability in the instruction process.

RESEARCH IN PRACTICE
Identifying Instructional Environments for NELB/LEP Students

---

1. **Pretend that you are eight years old again.** Your parents have informed you that you are moving to a new country. You have no knowledge of that country's language or customs. You will have to attend a local school, as there are no schools nearby where English is the language of instruction. As a student, what personal and educational resources would you need that would contribute to

your academic achievement in this setting? What resources or experiences would the school have to provide in order to facilitate your achievement if you have no literacy skills? If you have literacy skills? Examine your personal feelings about the move.

2. Consider the concept of academic invulnerability. Think of any students or other persons you have met who have been successful, academically or otherwise, despite seemingly unsurmountable obstacles? What qualities did they possess that made achievement possible? How do you think they developed those attributes? How can academically vulnerable students be assisted in attaining those same qualities?

SUMMARIZING SECTION TWO
Developing an Academic Evaluation Framework

This section presented the dimensions of an integrative academic performance assessment. When developing an evaluation framework, the questions "Who, What, When, Where, Why" and "How" are used to guide the evaluator seeking information about student performance. An integrative assessment recasts the role of the evaluator from one of administrator to that of observer or elicitor of student behaviors. Student behaviors in the process of learning or producing in response to instruction are documented through a variety of methods. These methods are systematic, provide indicators of student progress, and include both contextualized and decontextualized measures. Instructional programs commonly used to instruct NELB students were presented. The impact of a facilitative, empowering instructional environment on academic achievement was discussed. The characteristics of such an environment were identified because of their powerful influence on academic achievement. Identification of the presence or absence of a facilitative classroom environment and instructional strategies is also a critical component in the assessment of the academic performance of NELB students.

WHAT CAN YOU DO?

1. Why is it important to establish a framework for evaluation of student performance? What dimensions would you include in your own framework, based on your current setting?

2. How can the facilitative instructional features described in this section be incorporated into your current setting? Can you observe or document changes in student achievement as a result of implementing some or all of the features?

3. Why is the examination of the instructional environment important in the evaluation of academic performance?

SECTION THREE

LEARNING READING, WRITING, AND MATHEMATICS IN ENGLISH AS A NEW LANGUAGE

While much has been written about the development of reading, written language, and mathematics abilities and skills of native speakers of English, less information is available about how students who are learning English as a new language accomplish these processes. This section first examines some of the basic theoretical foundations regarding the reading process in general. The application of a psycholinguistic theory of reading to reading in English as a new language highlights the importance of ensuring that NELB students possess the necessary background knowledge to understand both the content and structure of texts. The interactive relationship between the reader and the text is underscored. Additionally, accuracy and fluency in reading text are viewed as necessary components to effective reading by NELB students. The developmental nature of written language development is explored, dispelling the myth that writing to convey meaning can only be taught after oral English has been mastered. Finally, the notion that mathematics is the logical content area into which NELB students should be mainstreamed first is examined in light of the complex nature of mathematical language. For many, if not all, NELB students, learning the language of mathematics in English becomes a task of learning a third (or fourth, or fifth) language.

READING IN ENGLISH AS A NEW LANGUAGE

Contemporary researchers and theorists in the field of reading in ESOL have generally come to accept the conceptualization of reading as an interactive process between the reader and the text. Reading is not just a process of extracting information from text. Reading activates a range of knowledge in the readers' minds. This knowledge is used, refined, and extended by the new information supplied by the text. In this view, reading is like a dialogue between the reader and the text (Grabe 1988). This view of the reading process, known as a *psycholinguistic theory* of reading, has evolved primarily from the research conducted with native speakers of English and schema theory as discussed in previous chapters (Goodman 1969, 1970; see Anderson & Pearson 1988; Carrell & Eisterhold 1988, for summaries of the schema theory model). An interactive view of reading in a new language also takes into account the automatic identification, or decoding, of lexical units and syntactic structures encountered in written text (Eskey 1988).

According to the psycholinguistic theory, reading is a process that starts with the printed representation of a word. This representation is created by a writer and results in meaning that is constructed by the reader. Thought and language interact as the writer encodes thoughts into language and the reader decodes the language to thoughts. Proficient readers are able to construct meaning from what they read at a level that is in accord with the original meaning of the author. They are able to do this with minimal effort. Proficient and efficient readers maintain a constant focus on constructing meaning as they read. They are always using strategies to increase comprehension, are selective about the use of cues available for comprehension, and draw from prior conceptual knowledge and linguistic competence. Proficient and efficient readers minimize dependence on the visual aspects of text. According to this theory, readers' proficiency will vary as a result of the semantic background brought to the reading task (Goodman 1988).

This definition of reading has been called the psycholinguistic guessing game, and is frequently referred to as a *top-down*, or *knowledge-based*, approach to reading (Grabe 1988; Carrell 1988). The reading process is viewed as a sequence of cycles, inputs, and outputs wherein cognitive processes are employed to derive meaning from text (Goodman 1988). Top-down processing is said to occur when readers make predictions about the text based on prior experience or background knowledge, and then check the text for confirmation or refutation of those predictions (Carrell 1988b). Along with prediction, confirmation of predictions, or correction of inconsistencies or predictions, the brain must also recognize graphic representations of written language and initiate reading. According to this view, reading is terminated when the reading task is completed, either because it is unproductive, little meaning is being constructed, or the meaning is already known. Additionally, reading may be terminated if the material is not interesting or is inappropriate for the reader's purpose. If reading does not end in meaning, then a short circuit is said to occur, and the reader resorts to inadequate strategies to attempt to reconstruct meaning (Goodman 1988).

Oral *miscue analysis* allows the evaluator to compare actual with expected responses of students as they read a text orally (Goodman 1973). In this manner, the teacher is able to determine which of three cuing systems, graphophonic, syntactic, or semantic, the reader uses to identify words and derive meaning. For example, a reader may rely on decoding letter-sound relationships (graphophonic cues), sentence structure (syntactic cues), or use contextual or pictorial cues (semantic) during the reading process. Further analysis of reading behaviors such as sounding errors (e.g. "fan" for "van"), self-corrections, hesitations, repetitions, substitutions (based on context or visual form), tracking errors, requesting that a word be supplied, or omissions, provides insight into the strategies the reader uses, and whether or not these lead to successful prediction and confirmation, that is, successful reading.

When the psycholinguistic model exclusively is applied to new language readers, several problems are encountered (Grabe 1988). These are related either to lack of information regarding reading processes in other languages and cultures or to preconceived assumptions about new language readers. For example, NELB students are a very heterogeneous group who may or may not read in their non-English language. Very little is known about how, why, and what these youngsters read in their respective cultures and languages. If these youngsters do read, little is known about the purposes for which they read, that is, for academic, professional, entertainment, or other purposes. Additionally, reading is affected by orthographic conventions if the student comes from a culture with different orthographic traditions. Finally, new language readers do not begin reading English with same level of English language knowledge as that of native English speaking youngsters. New readers cannot be assumed to have the extensive vocabulary and control of basic syntactic structures characteristic of native English readers (Grabe 1988). In fact, limitations in vocabulary and syntax impose a language ceiling, or threshold, which NELB students must overcome in order to become fluent, proficient readers (Clarke 1988; Devine 1988; Grabe 1988; Saville-Troike 1991). For new readers of English, including those who are good readers in their native language, limited control over the English language can adversely impact the reader's system for deriving meaning from text. It is also possible that two students with comparable proficiency in the English language may produce similar reading behaviors in English for different reasons: one student may be a poor reader to begin with, while the other may not be able to transfer reading skills to English because of linguistic constraints (Clarke 1988). A top-down approach to reading may fail to take into account or sufficiently emphasize the role and importance of culture-specific background knowledge in the reading processes of non-native English speakers (Carrell & Eisterhold 1988).

Several important facts relevant to instructional assessment and interpretation of the information obtained emerge when miscue analysis is used with new readers of English (see Rigg 1988, for in-depth discussion of the use of miscue analysis with Arabic, Navajo, Samoan, and Spanish-speaking youngsters). First, new readers of English may exhibit phonological, grammatical, and lexical miscues based on their linguistic background. Second, new readers of English may use and sample from the three cuing systems for prediction and confirmation, although there may be wide variability among readers as to how effectively and efficiently these cues are used. Third, the reading abilities of new readers of English can be underestimated: they may be accurate readers and when they do deviate from text, they can produce miscues that make sense in the text. Fourth, when miscues do not make sense, new readers often regress and

why psycho-linguistic might not be true.

attempt to correct their errors. Finally, new readers can demonstrate increasing control of English syntax by producing syntactically acceptable miscues.

While new readers of English may demonstrate reading behaviors that suggest that some aspects of reading may be universal, and may be better readers than expected, they may, however, encounter several stumbling blocks to comprehension. These include the sociocultural aspects of the text or plot presented in the text, level of difficulty of syntactic structures, and the unpredictability of the meanings of words. For example, a story about a typical child in the United States who lives in a large city may present difficulties for a child who has lived in a rural village in Pakistan: the Pakistani reader may not be able to predict what will happen in the text because the way of life presented in the text is foreign. Additionally, words presented in the text may have different meanings, some of which may be unavailable to the reader.

In conclusion, while a psycholinguistic approach to reading provides a theoretical framework and a strategy for understanding and studying the reading process, it may not be sufficient to accurately interpret the performance of students learning to read in English as a new language. Other aspects of interaction with text must be examined.

In contrast to a top-down approach to reading, there is the view that reading is a *bottom-up*, or *text-based*, process. In this view, individual linguistic units, such as phonemes, graphemes, and words are decoded. Textual meaning is constructed from the smallest units to the largest: graphemes are perceived as forming words, words as forming sentences, sentences as forming paragraphs, and so on (Eskey & Grabe 1988). Preexisting background knowledge and current predictions are modified based on the information encountered in the text, such as the decoding of the individual words and their lexical meanings, and decoding the syntactic structures of each sentence and their grammatical-functional meanings as subjects, direct objects, etc. (Carrell 1988b). In this view, the rapid and accurate decoding of language, or automaticity, is essential in the development of fluent reading. Automaticity provides fluent readers with the freedom to think about and interpret what they are reading (Eskey 1988).

Exclusive use of a text-based approach by new readers of English may adversely affect comprehension, if these readers are using graphophonic cues only as the way to comprehend text. The reader may be overly concerned about maintaining correct letter-sound correspondences, preserving grammar and syntax, or maintaining word integrity in order to reproduce the text accurately and faithfully. Examples of a text-bound approach may be observed among new readers of English who struggle with syllable by syllable or word by word reading of English text and who, once the reading is completed, have no idea what they have read, or may interpret what has been read literally because they are unable, do not know how, or are afraid to use context clues.

Research establishing the importance of prior or background knowledge in the comprehension of language has been formalized as *schema theory* (Carrell &

Eisterhold 1988). Schema theory holds that text, whether spoken or written, does not by itself carry meaning: a text only provides directions for listeners or readers as to how they should retrieve or construct meaning from their own, previously acquired knowledge, that is the reader's *background knowledge*. The previously acquired knowledge structures are called *schemata* (review the discussion of components of academic language proficiency in Chapter 3 of this book; see also Carrell & Eisterhold 1988, for additional references and discussion of concepts). Comprehension of the text is thus an interactive process between the text and the reader's background knowledge, with the reader effectively relating the material in the text to his or her knowledge. Furthermore, schema theory holds that both bottom-up and top-down processing occur during reading and should do so simultaneously. What the reader understands from a text is largely dependent on the particular schema that is activated at the time he or she is processing, or reading, the text.

Within schema theory, a distinction is made between *formal* schemata and *content* schemata (Carrell & Eisterhold 1988). *Formal schemata* refers to background knowledge of the formal, rhetorical organizational structures of different types of texts. Examples of formal schemata include the reader's knowledge about differences in genre, the structure of poetry, math or science texts, etc. A literary text that includes a simple story would require the reader to know that stories possess a setting, a beginning, a development, and an ending. On the other hand, content area texts may be structured in outline form, the information may be arranged sequentially in time or in parallel form to compare and contrast, or may present a problem and a proposed solution (Abrams, Herrity, & LaBrot 1991).

In contrast, *content schemata* refers to the reader's background knowledge of the content area of the text. If the reader is unable to activate the appropriate schema, either formal or content, during reading, comprehension is affected. With regard to new readers of English, specific content schema may not exist because the schema is specific to the mainstream culture and not to that of the reader. Furthermore, it has been found that text whose content is based on the reader's own culture is easier to read and understand than text that is syntactically and rhetorically equivalent, but is based on a less familiar culture (Rigg 1986). Additionally, rhetorical patterns and organization have been found to differ according to language and cultural background.

In conclusion, the existence of and the ability to access both formal and content schemata are critical in the reading process. For new readers of English, these schemata may be culture-bound and require that educators who teach reading explicitly activate, expand, or introduce content and formal schemata to enhance reading comprehension.

Attempts to incorporate the basic principles of a psycholinguistic view of reading, the findings of research examining automaticity in reading, and schema theory have resulted in the proposal of an *interactive* model of reading in English as a new language. This model holds that reading skills at all levels are interactively available to process and interpret text. The reader uses both top-down and bottom-up strategies. The reader brings and uses background knowledge, expectations about the text, and context to the process of reading. At the same time, rapid and accurate recognition of letters, words, and lexical forms is viewed as important in an interactive model of reading. That is, automaticity in processing lexical forms and linguistic units without dependence on the context of the text is also a critical component for effective reading (Eskey & Grabe 1988).

An interactive model for teaching reading to non-native speakers of English implies that both top-down and bottom-up skills and strategies must be developed conjointly. Reading programs for NELB students should include such bottom-up skills as rapid and accurate identification of lexical and grammatical forms. Instructional time must also be dedicated to top-down concerns such as reading for global meaning, developing in new readers a willingness to make educated guesses about meaning, and developing appropriate schemata for accurate interpretation of texts (Eskey & Grabe 1988). Unfortunately, many existing reading programs, including those developed in readers' native languages, may be based on a bottom-up approach to reading (Freeman 1988).

The application of an interactive model to teaching reading to students whose native language is not English suggests that instruction include several components. First, readers' background knowledge must be developed. Background knowledge can be activated by means of established methods, such as text-mapping, teaching predicting strategies, communicative pre-reading activities, and other Language Experience Approach type activities. Second, attention must be given to the content and quantity of materials used in order to sustain student interest in reading. Access to relevant reading materials must be provided. Third, NELB students' grammatical skills and vocabulary must be developed through discussion and practical applications. Fourth, students must be taught to identify words, phrases, and meaningful groups of words, rapidly and accurately. Finally, overall reading rate must be developed so that the reader can read as fast as knowledge of the language will allow and according to the purpose for reading (Eskey & Grabe 1988).

Viewing reading as an interactive process and adopting an interactive model for teaching reading to non-native English speaking students have significant implications for the development of an academic assessment framework. They suggest that where reading of text is concerned, background knowledge, especially content schema, be probed in both the non-English language, if possible, and English. Related to this is the assessment of the students' ability to recognize and understand critical vocabulary presented in the text. Furthermore, the students' level of grammatical and syntactic development must be considered and might, as has been suggested by some, be analyzed by comparing it to that of the actual text the student is expected to read

(Gonzales 1981). Additionally, the direct assessment of word and phrase identification skills, of accuracy and fluency in reading, and of reading rate in general, through such methods as miscue analysis and timed reading probes, utilizing the curricular materials to which the students are exposed, becomes a part of the evaluation process. The student is observed in the act of reading, and these behaviors are documented to assist in determining instructional strategies. For students who are non-readers or who are experiencing significant reading comprehension problems, assessment of listening comprehension is indicated. Finally, the student's understanding of the structure of the text, or formal schema, is evaluated, as unfamiliarity with the same may be a stumbling block to comprehension.

In sum, continuing research in the complex dynamics of the reading process has led those who are interested in the acquisition of English reading skills by non-native speakers to further test the resulting theories. No single theory or model of reading presented is sufficient to include all presently known aspects of reading, and, therefore, a more comprehensive view of reading as an interaction between and among processes used by a reader to derive meaning from text has been proposed. Specific activities are necessary, at both the instructional and assessment levels, in order to develop both sound instructional programs and an assessment framework for non-English speaking students. Review the case of Ahmed in the following activity, keeping in mind some of the principles proposed by an interactive model of reading.

RESEARCH IN PRACTICE
Reading in English as a New Language

Mini-Case Study: Ahmed

Ahmed is a 15-year-old, seventh grade student of Palestinian descent who was referred for evaluation due to continuing academic difficulties. He was reportedly working below grade level; a review of work samples revealed grades of C through failing, as did previous report cards. Arabic is the primary home language. Ahmed has been participating in the ESOL program at his school for two and one-half years. According to his father, Ahmed's early schooling was very erratic due to the strife between Palestinians and Israelis. Ahmed recounts that there were many occasions when he had to return home before arriving at school, or was kept home from school due to fighting on the streets. Ahmed's family are devout Muslims. He has memorized many verses of the Holy Koran.

An oral language sample was obtained in Arabic through the assistance of an Arabic educator who served as interpreter and translator. The interpreter reported that Ahmed presented many characteristics of a lower level, intermediate speaker of Arabic. Ahmed became frustrated with some of the more difficult questions posed in his native language, particularly when required to determine cause and effect relationships or infer meaning. Informal assessment of Arabic reading skills reveals that he knows some of the Arabic alphabet and can read at about a first to second grade level. Figure 5.6 illustrates Ahmed's paragraph about his native country. It also illustrates a segment of his writing from a dictated passage.

According to the interpreter, Ahmed's Arabic penmanship is very poor. The content of the passage in Arabic is ambiguous, and, with great difficulty, six words can be distinguished: "I love America" and "I love Palestine." The upper left hand corner contains the date, while the words in the center are from the Holy Koran. The interpreter concluded that, while Ahmed is able to reproduce some of the Arabic alphabet, he is unable to effectively communicate his thoughts in writing. His knowledge of cursive Arabic places him between a first and third grade level with respect to written expression.

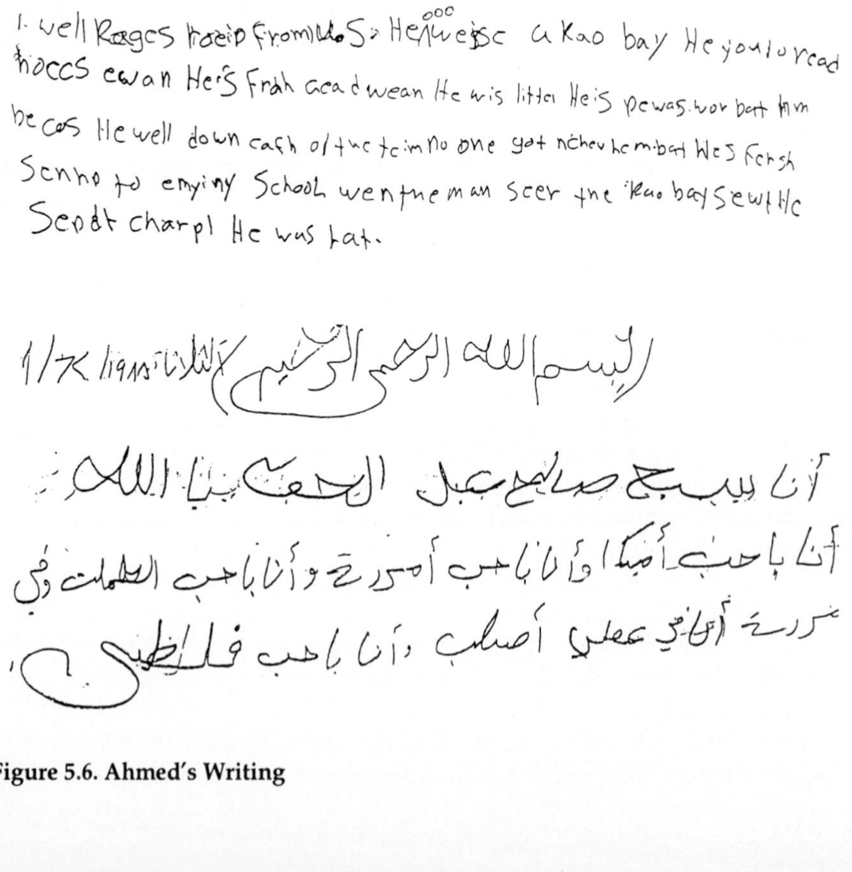

Figure 5.6. Ahmed's Writing

Direct assessment of English word recognition skills was made using curricular materials. Reading was sampled from three 200 word passages in his literature text. Analysis revealed that Ahmed was able to read 80 words correctly per minute (WCM), while an average reader of English in his classroom was able to read over 150 words per minute. Ahmed read the words with 50% accuracy, while the average reader read them with 97% accuracy. Ahmed's reading strengths included self-corrections, but with contextually incorrect substitutions, and sustained effort to read. He displayed letter confusions, word substitutions based on visual cues, repetitions, and tracking or scanning problems. On several occasions, he began reading from right to left. Reading comprehension problems were related to: (1) not knowing the meaning of key vocabulary; (2) not being able to make predictions about the text; (3) remembering only parts of the text, which resulted in his providing incomplete answers to questions; and (4) not knowing where to look in the text for information to respond to questions. He had difficulty attending to the text and presented a somewhat disorganized, haphazard approach to reading, but persisted in his efforts.

1. **Consider the interactive model of reading in English as a new language.** How would you explain some of Ahmed's reading behaviors based on this model?

2. **What role might cultural, content, and formal schemata play in Ahmed's learning to read in English?** What role might cultural and religious values play in the process? How can these be addressed and utilized when teaching him to read in English?

3. **Based on the summary of Ahmed's reading behaviors, would you say that he appears to be using primarily "bottom-up" skills or "top-down" skills to attempt to read?** What clues do you have to support your conclusion?

4. **Develop some instructional strategies to assist Ahmed in becoming a more successful reader.**

WRITING IN ENGLISH AS A NEW LANGUAGE

Although there is extensive research in the development of writing among native English speakers, the study of this process as it relates to non-native English speakers has been quite limited until recently (Johnson & Roen 1989). New information about how monolingual and NELB students create their own texts and about the interrelationships between oral language, reading, and composing written texts has challenged theories about when and how writing activities should be initiated. For example, in some methods of ESOL instruction, writing (and reading) activities are not introduced until the students have acquired what is considered to be sufficient English oral language proficiency. In this view, language abilities involving speaking, reading, and writing, are seen as discrete skills that develop sequentially. Contemporary knowledge of how new learners of English develop as writers, and application of holistic, natural approaches to literacy suggest that writing (and reading) activities be introduced at the very early stages of English language development (Bermudez & Prater 1988; Hudelson 1989a). Having a language other than English is not a barrier to NELB students' ability to display written language competence, nor is it necessarily a source of confusion in writing (Edelsky 1989). Within the context of a holistic ESOL curriculum, writing activities become a part of the entire language experience: the focus is on communication and expression of meaning rather than on the form of language, writing is integrated with content area instruction to develop higher-order thinking skills, and writing is undertaken to develop students' creativity (Freeman & Freeman 1989; Hamayan 1989).

A distinction is frequently made between the terms *writing* and *composition*. While the former is defined as the act of putting a pencil to a paper (or by use of other materials, as appropriate), the latter involves writing to convey meaningful ideas in a logical manner (Barrett 1987). A more comprehensive definition of writing views it as an act of the mind by which a writer creates meaning (Berthoff 1981, as cited by Hudelson 1989a). Writing involves more than application of linguistic processes; it simultaneously involves social and psychological processes as well (Edelsky 1989). Further distinctions are also frequently made between *controlled* and *free* writing activities. Examples of controlled activities include the practice of handwriting, copying texts that are written by others, structured written exercises such as answering questions in workbooks or in response to textbook questions, and writing sentences or stories with predetermined words. In contrast, free, or creative writing, denotes the process of generating original text (Cadiz 1987; Hudelson 1986; Hudelson 1988; Hudelson 1989a). Scholars in the area of writing in English as a new language suggest that in classrooms where writing is limited to controlled activities, new learners may fail to develop as effective writers who are willing to take risks to construct meaning (Hudelson 1989b). Furthermore, such activities become simulations of writing because they are not self-initiated nor are they carried out for social or pragmatic purposes (Edelsky 1989). Thus, it has been suggested that new learners of English need to be provided the opportunity to write on a regular basis and to write for varied purposes and audiences. The development of writing fluency and a willingness to write for purposes other than to fulfill the requirements of assignments become valid instructional goals for new writers of English (Hudelson 1989b).

Within the context of this section, the term *writing* is inclusive of both the physical act and the creative and linguistic efforts of students as they compose text. This is because certain aspects of writing, such as penmanship, as well as composition, are frequently evaluated by teachers, especially in the early elementary grades. For students with non- or pre-literate backgrounds, knowledge of writing as an act by which symbols are inscribed on a surface in order to communicate thoughts, is a critical precursor to composing. Furthermore, literate NELB students may be exposed to an orthography different from the graphemic system of representing speech sounds with letters of an alphabet to make whole words. For example, writing behaviors associated with character writing (where characters represent whole ideas), such as used in Chinese, may be different from those associated with manuscript or cursive writing as taught in U.S. schools (see also Chang & Watson 1988, for discussion of Chinese orthography). The handwriting of students who have never had the opportunity to write or who have learned to write using a different script may, at first glance, appear quite immature when compared with that of their U.S. peers. For example, in Figure 5.6, qualitative differences can be seen in Ahmed's writing in English and Arabic. While Ahmed was noted by the interpreter/translator to display written language deficits in his native language, observation of the relative ease with which he was able to write from right to left, space, and maintain uniformity was in sharp contrast to his labored writing in English manuscript. Perhaps Ahmed would have less difficulty learning to write in cursive in English since he already possesses knowledge of cursive in Arabic.

Observation of writing behaviors and inclusion of written products in the non-English language and English provide valuable information with regard to areas of potential differences that may be interpreted as problem areas. Because written language is a permanent record of a message, the evaluator is able to re-examine concepts, ideas, and language structures (Norris 1991), as well as script, over a period of time. Assessment of the act of writing, as well as the message conveyed in a written piece, provides a more global view of students' strengths and needs in the development of their writing.

As indicated earlier, current information about how NELB students acquire English has led to changes in ESOL instruction approaches. The shift in methodology and focus in ESOL writing instruction has come about due to findings that indicate that the process of writing in English as a new language is similar to the development of writing in a first language (Hudelson 1986; Hudelson 1988; Hudelson 1989a; Hudelson 1989b; see also Edelsky 1986; Edelsky 1989; and Urzua 1987). New learners of English are able to compose in this language while they are learning it and even before they demonstrate full control of the various aspects of the language. They use their existing knowledge of English to develop hypotheses about how to write the language. The influence of the non-English language may also be found when analyzing samples of their writing. If new learners encounter difficulties in expressing meaning, they may use drawings or graphic forms to represent their thoughts. If the educator is evaluating an older NELB student, this strategy may appear immature and unconventional, and may be interpreted as a disorder in written language abilities. The fact may be that the student is attempting to overcome a barrier in communication but may not yet possess the necessary repertoire of graphic or graphophonic forms. For NELB students, drawings constitute an integral part of composition. Even if the resulting text is unintelligible to a reader, the descriptions and narratives that can be elicited from the drawings may be used to assess oral, as well as written, communication.

In general, NELB students' compositions will reflect their increasing control of English. This suggests that pieces created by NELB students will also contain evidence of the various functions of oral language, as discussed in earlier chapters. A student may demonstrate the representational function of language by labeling a drawing or graphic form. For example, Eva, the Hispanic student of the mini-case sample in the Research in Practice following this section, indicates that the graphic forms "AllanBy Eva" represent the words "Illustrated by" as they appear in a book. Because NELB students are able to compose pieces before they are fully proficient in English, assessment of writing can be conducted at the early stages of English language learning. The evaluator can expect, however, evidence of developmental stages in written expression and language acquisition. For example, studies of the early writing of young children exposed to print-rich environments (both English and non-English languages) have illustrated that the children's concepts of writing and their attempts to create their own texts evolve through stages (Hudelson 1989a). These stages are recursive in that, as children mature as writers, they may move back and forth between stages as revisions are made (Bermudez & Prater 1988).

Young children, or beginning writers, may resort to various strategies to construct their written pieces (Sulzby 1986; Teale 1988). At the early stage of writing development, children may distinguish the difference between writing and drawing. They may use different types of strokes or different size forms for what they perceive as writing rather than drawing. Even at this early stage, they display intent and are able to interpret what they have produced. Scribbling in imitation of writing follows the use of drawing as representative of writing. Forms that resemble conventional letters replace scribbles. As children learn letters, they write using those that are familiar to them, such as those that appear in their names. These letters are reordered as children attempt to spell other words. New writers may also attempt to copy environmental print as they progress from this level to that of using invented spelling. This spelling reflects writers' perceptions and predictions of how words should be spelled. The use of syllables or letters as representative of syllables may prevail, as does the writers' understanding of the phonemes of the language. For example, "KRZ" may represent "cars" or "U" represent "you." At this level, the evolving writer demonstrates some knowledge of the English alphabet, uses letter-sound correspondences, and is aware that letters are used to represent sounds in words.

As writers progress, increased use of phonetic spelling is reflected in their pieces. Invention is more systematic and words are more recognizable, though not yet spelled in what is considered to be a conventional manner. The entire sound structure of the word being spelled is evident, as for example, in "elifunt" for "elephant." At the transitional stage in writing development, conventional alternatives are used to represent sounds in words. Spelling also reflects how the words look, as when "eightee" represents "ate" (Abrams, Herrity & LaBrot 1991, p.98). At the final stage of development, writing reflects conventional forms and consistently correct spelling.

Examination of the pieces produced by new learners of English reveals many of the characteristics evident in pieces written by young native speakers of English. The pieces written by non-native speakers of English may reflect unconventional spelling, segmentation of words, and punctuation. Drawings or unconventional graphic forms may be used in conjunction with writing to convey a message. Spelling of words may reflect the influence of the writers' native language orthography, language usage in the native language community, or the writers' interpretation of phonetic cues. Furthermore, the writers' current level of knowledge of English syntax, lexicon, and phonology will be manifested in the written pieces (Hudelson 1989a). This suggests that writing samples obtained in both the non-English and English languages are important for analysis of written language development. Writing samples collected over time are the best indicators of NELB students' progress and growth in English.

New learners of English are also capable of creating a variety of texts for different purposes. They may engage in writing narrative texts to express their feelings. They may also create literary texts, such as poetry, fables, or short stories. New learners may write to present information and a message through transactional writing, as when writing reports or summarizing the results of an experiment. A comprehensive assessment of the writing abilities of NELB students would thus include evaluation of both controlled and free writing products. While educators commonly evaluate students on their responses in workbooks, text-related questions, etc., creative pieces may not be considered. Additionally, evaluation of a variety of pieces, written for different purposes, provides insight into the scope of NELB writers' abilities. In order to accommodate differences in genre, text structure, and purpose, various methods can be used or devised to observe and document writing progress. Such methods include observation, anecdotal records, and checklists developed for specific pieces and according to purpose.

The conceptualization of writing as a sociological, psychological, as well as linguistic process, implies that there must be interaction between the writer and the reader of the written piece. New learners of English are frequently reluctant to express themselves, either orally or in writing, for fear of ridicule or failure, or because they are uncertain of the correct way to express themselves. They may not be willing to share their written pieces with others or to expand their repertoire of writing activities beyond those assigned in class. One method which has been found to be successful in helping NELB students overcome these fears, as well as make the transition to other types of text, is that of *dialogue*, or *interactive*, journal writing. In this method, students and the teacher carry on a written conversation. Dialogue journals provide an opportunity for genuine communication about topics of interest and concern to students as the teacher responds to their writing (Hudelson 1989a). This interactive writing promotes the students' ability to use English and also reflects written language growth. As NELB students become comfortable sharing their thoughts and writing with the teacher, they may feel more at ease sharing other pieces. They are capable of responding to other students' work. As others read their work and react to it, NELB students are able to revise and edit their own pieces. As revisions are made, NELB students' writing may reflect changes, not only at the surface level (e.g. spelling, grammar), but also at a deeper, qualitative level (e.g. sentence, paragraph, or text changes). When assessing NELB students' writing, variations in the quality and quantity of text can be expected. Evaluation of message quality and meaning should be foremost in the assessment process, followed by assessment of language forms, such as spelling, grammar, and punctuation. Because NELB students are able to profit from interactions with readers of their writing, the exclusive use of standardized tests in assessing writing development provides a limited view of their capabilities as writers. Standardized tests of written language are static measures, reflecting current rather than potential writing abilities. To supplement these tests, holistic assessments of writing competence should be included to provide a comprehensive view of the NELB students development as a writer.

The rate of writing development of NELB students is subject to individual differences, home values, and cultural traditions. NELB students develop as writers at their own pace, just as native English speakers do. Their understanding of the functions or purposes for writing, and their perceptions of themselves as writers are influenced by their experiences with writing in their home and community. Community language norms and language usage will affect written language in English. New learners may produce texts that are organized differently and contain culture-specific themes. Understanding that NELB students progress at different rates helps the evaluator avoid thinking that, because students have received instruction in English for X number of years, they should be at a specific level of competence. Furthermore, the evaluator can expect writing in English that is phonologically, syntactically, and lexically different from standard English. Subsequent revisions and editing are necessary for production of effective texts in English. Involvement of NELB students in the evaluation of their own progress as writers promotes learning as well as risk-taking in writing. Finally, the evaluator can gain insights into the students' cultures, values, and traditions through their creations.

Perhaps one of the most important findings of research regarding the development of writing in new learners of English is the fact that classroom environment and teacher beliefs about writing have a significant impact on what and how students write. In general, NELB students will produce what they perceive their teachers want. For example, if students are accustomed to writing in response to textbook or workbook exercises, dittoed worksheets or lists, or to developing sentences or paragraphs with known words or information, they will produce similar types of writing even when encouraged to create their own pieces. Furthermore, NELB students' writing will reflect instructional emphases. If the emphasis is on accuracy and correct spelling and grammar in writing, that is, on the surface-level aspects of written language, NELB students may be reluctant to undertake writing other than as assigned. If, on the other hand, emphasis is on creating meaning, writing for a real audience, and developing writing over a period of time, NELB students are likely to view themselves as capable, effective writers. They are more likely to view writing as a craft rather than a chore. For this reason, when assessing the writing of NELB students, facilitative classroom features and instructional methods used to teach writing must also be identified. Only within this context can an evaluator develop hypotheses or draw conclusions about students' writing.

Table 5-4 summarizes some of the major findings of studies relative to the development of writing in English as a new language as discussed previously. Implications for assessment of the writing abilities of new learners of English are indicated as well.

In conclusion, current understanding of how new learners of English develop as writers provides additional support for the implementation of assessment and instructional methods that reflect the interplay between language and literacy acquisition. Instruction that is based on genuine, facilitative interaction between teacher and student, whether in oral or written form, promotes self-expression in NELB students. Supportive strategies that encourage student-to-student communication, emphasize meaningful language use rather than accuracy and correctness of surface forms of language, and self-selection of topics and occasions for writing, provide NELB students with a greater sense of control of the task and of their learning (Bermudez & Prater 1988; Cummins 1989). Finally, facilitative methods that integrate higher-level thinking skills with reading and writing within the context of the curriculum and the students' everyday, life experiences, help NELB students become critical, creative participants rather than passive recipients in the instructional process.

TABLE 5.4. WRITING IN ENGLISH AS A NEW LANGUAGE

RESEARCH FINDINGS	IMPLICATIONS FOR ASSESSMENT
New learners are able to compose in English as they are learning it and before they demonstrate control over it.	Writing samples obtained in the non-English and English languages are important for analysis of written language development.
• Existing knowledge of English is used to develop hypotheses about how to write in this language.	Assessment can be conducted at early stages of English language learning but expect:
• Compositions reflect increases in language control.	1. evidence of developmental stages in written expression and language acquisition;
• Knowledge of the non-English language is applied to English.	2. non-English language(s) influences; and
• Drawings of graphic forms may be used by beginning writers to overcome expression difficulties.	3. what may appear to be immature and unconventional forms, especially if the student is older.
	Drawings are integral to composition: the descriptions and narratives resulting from them may be used to assess oral, as well as written, communication.
New learners can create a variety of texts for different purposes: they may write to express feelings, to create literary works, or to present information and a message.	Comprehensive assessment of writing abilities includes evaluation of both controlled and free writing products.
New learners can develop texts across content areas.	Assessment of writing abilities should include evaluation of a variety of pieces written for different purposes.
	Various methods for observing and documenting writing progress can be used, including observation, anecdotal records, and checklists, to accommodate for differences in texts.

(continued on page 247)

New learners can respond to others' work and can revise and edit their own pieces based on the reactions of others to their work. • Interactive writing promotes ability to use English and reflects language growth. • Interaction with readers of their writing promotes willingness to revise: qualitative changes at sentence, paragraph, or text levels may be evident.	Realize that standardized tests of written language are static measures, reflecting current rather than potential writing abilities. Holistic assessments of writing competence should be considered. • Expect variations in quality and quantity of writing. Assess message quality and meaning foremost, then assess language forms, such as spelling and grammar. Involve learners in evaluating their own progress as writers.
Individual differences, home values, and cultural traditions affect rate of writing development, understanding of the functions or purposes of writing, and perceptions of self as writer. • Students develop as writers at their own pace. • Community language norms and usage affect written language.	Expect writing in English to reflect language that is phonologically, syntactically, and lexically different from standard English. Subsequent revisions and editing are necessary for production of effective texts in English. Writing samples collected over time are the best indicators of progress and growth.
New learners may produce texts that are organized differently and contain culture-specific themes.	Dialogue regarding structure and themes can promote learning and provide insight regarding cultural issues.
Classroom environment and teacher beliefs about writing significantly impact new learners' development as writers. • Students produce what they perceive their teachers want. • Students' writing reflects instructional emphasis: emphasis may be on accuracy and correctness of surface-level features or on conveying meaning.	Facilitative classroom features and instructional methods used to promote writing must be identified in order to develop hypotheses or draw conclusions about students' writing.

RESEARCH IN PRACTICE
Writing in English as a New Language

Mini-Case Study: Elena

Elena is a six-year-old student of Hispanic descent who was referred for evaluation at the end of kindergarten due to observed difficulties in acquiring letter recognition skills. She was reportedly having difficulty in learning to write her name. Spanish is the primary home language. Although Elena's father speaks English fluently and is literate in this language, her mother speaks very little English and does not read it. When Elena entered the school system she was evaluated by personnel from the ESOL program and found to be English dominant. She did not qualify for native language instruction or ESOL services.

Elena was observed and evaluated two months into the academic year as a beginning first grade student. Observation of the classroom environment revealed the presence of print (e.g. classroom objects were labeled), many and varied printed materials in English (e.g. books, magazines), and a variety of materials for self-expression (e.g. writer's corner, art center). Desks were arranged for cooperative learning groups of four children per group. Many of the other facilitative environment features were evident to some degree; in fact, the environment reflected the teacher's belief in and use of a whole language approach to instruction. The teacher used books with predictable patterns and rhymes for more formal reading instruction.

During one observation period, Elena was noted to contribute to group discussion of the text and to point out that they had learned specific words in another book. She participated in choral reading of the text. She was also noted to follow directions to take out her poem folder and to follow along by pointing to the text, from left to right, as the teacher read the poem. She orally offered a suggestion for an illustration for the poem.

Utilizing the same poem for direct assessment of Elena's literacy and pre-writing skills, it was noted that Elena was able to correctly recognize and name letters selected randomly. She also pointed to and read selected sight words. Another classmate, whose primary home language was English and was considered by the teacher to be performing at an average level, was requested to do the same for comparison purposes. Elena was noted to independently identify 27 letters and words, while the peer identified 25. Elena also knew the difference between upper and lower case letters, and was able to identify a period and a "surprise mark" (exclamation mark), and their functions. When given a library book positioned upside down, she immediately turned it right side up. She recognized cursive writing in the text. She predicted the theme of the book correctly by identifying the most important objects and event depicted in the illustration on the cover.

Elena was also observed to use classroom print effectively to fulfill her writing needs. She knew exactly where to look to find the words or letters she needed to convey her thoughts or satisfy her intent. For example, when creating a heart to give to the evaluator, she looked at her teacher's name to spell "Miss," asked how to spell the evaluator's last name, and proceeded to do so correctly when it was dictated. She also spelled her own name correctly and named the letters accurately. Samples of Elena's writing (and oral interpretations of her writing) as it appeared in her dialogue journal include the following:

Teacher's (T) writing: I will miss you today!
Elena's (E) response: I W M u t. (I will miss you too.)

T: What did you do during the holiday?
E.   Susie Want t M hs. (Susie went to my house.)
     I Wt t the M. (I went to the mall.)
T: Did Susie stay at your house for three days?
E.   No But She D S F A W. (No, but she did stay for a while.)

T: What did you do this weekend?
E.   I w t the Pool. (I went to the pool.)

T: What do you like best about school?
E.   I lIKe A R t.

1. Consider the kindergarten teacher's report that Elena had not mastered letter recognition and name-writing skills by the end of kindergarten. Contrast this with the description of her behavior and writing samples. What factors may have contributed to the perceived delay in reading and writing development?

2. Review the various stages of writing development. Compare Elena's samples with those stages. How do you account for the discrepancy in Eva's reported and current status as a writer and emergent reader?

3. The dialogue journal was one source of information regarding Elena's writing. What are some other sources of information that can provide a broader view of her writing abilities?

MATHEMATICS: THE THIRD (OR FOURTH OR FIFTH) LANGUAGE

A commonly held view is that mathematics is a universal language, taught and learned in the same manner by all peoples around the world. For this reason, mathematics is frequently selected as the first content area into which NELB students who are still in the process of acquiring English may be mainstreamed (Fradd 1987b). A comparison of various number systems reveals that such a view may be erroneous in its assumption of universality of all aspects of mathematics. For example, children in the Oksapmin area of Papua New Guinea learn a number system that is very different from that of Western cultures. The system consists of naming 27 human body parts and has no base structure. When counting, the Oksapmin begin with the thumb on one hand and recite body part names as they count around the upper periphery of the body. While such a system is used to count objects, it is not used for arithmetical computations (Saxe 1988). Cultural and linguistic factors significantly impact the problem-solving strategies NELB students use to resolve word problems and mathematics achievement in general (Cocking & Chipman 1988; Leap 1988). Cultural perceptions of the utility of mathematics, culture-bound learning styles, and technical language development in the non-English language influence the development of mathematical concepts (Schindler & Davison 1985).

Mathematics requires knowledge of language that is specific and specialized to the subject matter. The language of mathematics is technical and has its own register. That is, mathematics draws from natural language words, phrases, or styles of discourse with meanings that serve a particular function (for further discussion of the mathematics register, see Cuevas 1984; Dale & Cuevas 1987; Fradd 1987b; and Spanos, Rhodes, Dale & Crandall 1988). Mathematical language may also be represented by symbols. Mathematics imposes the need for knowledge and use of cognitively demanding academic language that may hinder successful achievement by NELB students (Spanos & Crandall 1990). Even bilingual students who possess the same level of mathematical and computational knowledge as monolingual students may solve word problems incorrectly due to misinterpretations (Mestre 1988). Aspects of language such as syntax, semantics, and pragmatics, affect NELB students' performance in mathematics and their comprehension of math problem statements and of complex mathematical premises (Mestre 1988; Mestre & Gerace 1986). If NELB students do not understand word problems, they may rely on the surface word order to determine which mathematical processes or formulae are required to solve them. For example, students may process a word problem in sequence from left to right although the resulting equation may not match the mathematical meaning of the word problem (Mestre, 1988). They may have difficulty understanding vocabulary and associating symbols with their word referents as they appear in word problems. For native speakers of English, solving math problems at times requires converting English statements into math statements. Non-native speakers of English may then have to engage in a third (or fourth, depending on how many languages they speak) translation, increasing the probability of errors (Cocking & Chipman 1988). Although NELB students may perform as well as their native English speaking peers in mechanical computations, they lag behind in solving word problems. The deficiencies in problem-solving are quite apparent when NELB students are instructed in their weaker language (Mestre 1988).

On a pragmatic level, NELB students may have difficulties due to restricted or different knowledge and experiences with mathematics (Spanos & Crandall 1987). The language and style of mathematics textbooks may lead to their ineffective use by NELB students. Because NELB students may have difficulty interpreting the mathematics text, they may use the textbook only to find assigned problems rather than as supplementary reading or expansion on the material covered in class (Mestre 1988). Some of the situations and vocabulary presented in word problems require prior knowledge or draw from mainstream culture experiences not accessible to some NELB students. For example, secondary level NELB students may be unfamiliar with the U.S. economic system and terms such as "discount," "wholesale," "retail," "stock," "share," "revolving charge account," and "interest" when used in math word problems (Mestre 1988; Spanos, Rhodes, Dale & Crandall 1988). Some students may be accustomed to using the metric system of weights and measures in their daily lives or have knowledge of a different monetary system. Mathematics instruction that is decontextualized, exclusively skills oriented, and lacks relevance for NELB students impacts their achievement in this content area (Secada, Carey & Schlicher 1989; Spanos & Crandall 1987).

Language proficiency is a critical mediator of mathematics problem solving ability among NELB students (Mestre 1988). Four different forms of language proficiency have been identified as influencing mathematical problem solving. In order to be successful problem solvers in mathematics, NELB students must be proficient with language in general, proficient in the technical language of math, proficient with the syntax and usage of language in math, and proficient with the symbolic language used in mathematics. NELB students must be able to read and understand written text effectively. Quite often, NELB students may have difficulty completing timed word problem-solving tasks because they read more slowly and therefore complete fewer problems (Mestre 1986, as cited in Mestre 1988). NELB students must be able to make the transition from the vocabulary found in natural discourse to the precise, semantically different use of words or phrases. As an example, the word "product" in natural discourse refers to an item sold in a store. In its mathematical sense, the word "product" is used to designate the result of the operation of multiplication (Mestre 1988). NELB students must also be able to distinguish the differences between language structures and form as they appear in natural language and as they appear in mathematics. When attempting to use word order only to translate text to symbolic language, errors in interpretation can occur. Finally, NELB students must understand the symbols and grammar peculiar to mathematics. Mathematical symbols may be a source of confusion for NELB students as, for example, the use of the "comma decimal" by Hispanic or European students, instead of a decimal point (e.g. 10,50 instead of 10.50) to indicate a separation between whole numbers and parts in the decimal system.

Given the complexity of the relationship between the various forms of language proficiency and mathematics achievement, it has been proposed that students must attain and cross a technical threshold before becoming fully proficient in the domain (Mestre 1988). Students must attain proficiency in both technical language and symbolic language. For NELB students, this task becomes more arduous as they attempt to also become proficient in English. Prior to initiating mathematics instruction for older NELB students, information regarding their current math abilities, previous experiences and educational opportunities for learning mathematics, as well as their language proficiency and literacy levels in both English and the non-English languages, should be obtained (Cuevas 1984; Hernandez 1983; Mestre & Gerace 1986; Secada, Carey & Schlicher 1989). This information will assist in determining the focus of and methods to be used for instruction. The extent of prior knowledge of mathematical concepts and vocabulary, and the ways the students apply these must be determined. Mathematics instruction for students who are not literate in their native language, have no or limited experiences with mathematics as applied to daily living, and are in the process of acquiring English, will be different from instruction for non-English speaking students who have received formal education in their native language.

For all NELB students, the development and use of interactive activities and teaching strategies that allow students to discuss math problems, how to begin solving them, and how to use language to solve them, allows students to listen to and become comfortable with mathematics language (Spanos et al. 1988). NELB students should be given the opportunity to work together in a systematic way to develop competence in listening to and using mathematical language. Guided practice in writing or translating mathematics into familiar terms by means of concrete objects, pictures, and experiences helps reduce the language barrier often encountered (Dunlap & Tinajero 1985). NELB students need to be taught strategies to deal with difficulties in word problems: they may be taught to focus on what is known (or unknown) and what is asked for, to use diagrams or realia, or to watch for key words that have been pre-taught, among other strategies (Spanos et al. 1988). Integrating language instruction, or a language strand, with mathematics instruction provides support for the teaching of content (Cuevas 1984; Fradd 1987b). It also provides many opportunities for NELB students to develop listening, speaking, reading, and writing skills in English as they are acquiring mathematical language and skills (Spanos et al. 1988). Allowing students to create their own word problems may prompt them to incorporate culturally relevant and meaningful features that enhance learning. Essay-type questions on exams foster use of mathematical language and higher level reasoning; however, NELB students must be thoroughly prepared for these by contextualized practice. The use of dialogue journals in mathematics provides NELB students with the opportunity to reflect and write about math problems, ask questions they may feel uncomfortable asking in front of their peers, and write about their progress in mathematics, predictions about what they are going to learn, and their perceptions of themselves as mathematicians (Orange County Public Schools 1990; Spanos et al. 1988). Finally, the use of student portfolios in evaluation of mathematics progress provides educators with evidence of performance beyond factual knowledge and allows teachers to respond to different learning styles. In this manner, assessment becomes less dependent on cultural influences and less biased (Carl 1992; Orange County Public Schools 1990). Information can be collected in the students' native language(s) and English (O'Malley & Valdez Pierce 1991; Valdez Pierce & O'Malley 1992). The educator must, however, be aware of possible obstacles in mathematics learning for NELB students when evaluating student products or observing student behaviors as they are in the process of learning mathematics.

In conclusion, the mathematics achievement of NELB students in mainstream schools is as dependent on language learning as are reading and writing. Understanding that the language of mathematics in English represents a third (or fourth, or fifth) language for many NELB students can be helpful in assisting educators to develop effective instructional strategies. When evaluating the mathematical abilities and skills of NELB students, consideration must be given to their understanding of mathematical vocabulary and concepts, the structure of the language of mathematics (which may be different from the natural English they are learning), their knowledge of symbols, and their previous experiences with and daily applications of mathematics. These are areas that may not always be tapped by standardized mathematics tests; however, alternative forms of assessment utilizing curricular materials provide the supplementary information needed to design an instructional plan suited to students' individual needs.

RESEARCH IN PRACTICE
Mathematics: The Third (or Fourth or Fifth) Language

---

1. How important is language in the process of learning mathematics? Examine a mathematics textbook. Identify vocabulary, concepts, structural aspects of mathematical equations, symbols, and situations in word problems that are difficult for you to understand. What role does language play in the process of understanding or not understanding mathematics?

2. Examine your beliefs about mainstreaming NELB students into this academic area first. Do you perceive the language of mathematics to be the easiest for these students to understand? What alternatives would you consider to facilitate mathematics learning among NELB students?

3. Investigate how mathematics is taught in different countries. Ask the parents of NELB students at your school, confer with teachers of mathematics from other countries, or read about it in professional journals.

SUMMARIZING SECTION THREE:
Learning Reading, Writing, and Mathematics in English as a New Language

This section reviewed information regarding the acquisition of reading, writing, and mathematical concepts and skills by non-native English speakers. Theories and the results of research in the three major academic domains were discussed in light of the effects of language, culture, and educational experiences of NELB students on achievement. The purpose of this section is to provide an overview of current knowledge regarding the acquisition of academic skills and concepts in English as a new language and to identify those areas within the three domains that need to be included in a comprehensive assessment of NELB students.

WHAT CAN YOU DO?

1. Collect oral reading, writing, and mathematics work samples from NELB students in your setting. Compare and contrast these with those of native English speaking children in the same grade.

2. Consider the instructional strategies commonly used to teach reading, writing, and mathematics to NELB students in your educational setting. Do these strategies take into account the possible effects of learning in English as a new language? If not, what can be done to change or modify the strategies?

SECTION FOUR

PUTTING IT ALL TOGETHER

This final, brief section presents a curriculum-based model for assessing the academic skills and abilities of NELB students. The foundation of the model rests on the premise that student language, culture, and educational background impact academic performance; however, a facilitative instructional environment provides the context within which academics and language either flourish or flounder. In essence, the model is a synthesis of procedures to follow for conducting an integrative academic performance assessment. The dimensions of an integrative academic performance assessment, as presented in Section Two of this chapter, are implicit in this curriculum-based model of assessment. Current knowledge regarding the acquisition of reading, writing, and mathematics skills and concepts by NELB students is taken into account. Areas to be assessed within these domains are identified. This model provides a general framework to guide assessment so that it can be linked to effective instruction of NELB students.

A CURRICULUM-BASED MODEL FOR ASSESSING THE ACADEMIC PERFORMANCE OF NELB STUDENTS

Throughout this chapter and this book, it has been emphasized that meaningful academic performance assessment of NELB students is best undertaken within the context of their language and learning environments. As stated in Section Two of this chapter, it is helpful to develop an evaluation framework to guide academic performance assessment so that it can be linked to effective instruction of NELB students. The framework which the authors of this book propose is one that is anchored in the curriculum and can, therefore, be called a curriculum-based model for evaluating the skills, strategies, abilities, and behaviors related to NELB students' academic functioning in the school setting.

A curriculum-based model for assessing NELB students' academic performance includes five major components: identification and clarification of current academic and language levels and student learning patterns, analysis of the learning environment and observation of the student in the instructional environment, observation or direct assessment of student language and academic performance in the three major academic areas, development of instructional strategies, and, finally, measurement or documentation of progress over time. Table 5.5 summarizes the components of this model. It draws from current information regarding NELB students' acquisition of reading, writing, and mathematics skills and concepts, as was presented in Section Three of this chapter and in previous chapters related to academic language development.

While the sequential format of the table may suggest a step-lock system for assessment, the bold double arrows indicate that the process is dynamic. For example, if measurement or observation of student progress over time reveals poor progress or difficulties in specific areas, instructional strategies may have to be modified based on the results of direct measurement or observation in the target areas. This dynamism is also characteristic of the choice of assessment methods. Numerous methods for assessing NELB students have been provided throughout this book. Others will be presented in Chapter Six. Many more exist or will be created. With assessment that is less dependent on standardized test administration, methods or strategies can be chosen that best fit the individual learner and learning environment.

As stated in Section Two, underlying any effort to assess the academic performance of students are the questions "How," "Who," "What," "When," "Where," and "Why." Through initial identification and clarification of concerns and students' presenting academic levels, decisions are made regarding the purpose, need, and possible areas for evaluation. Collaboration among all educators involved with the target students enhances the problem-solving process. Because learning does not occur in a vacuum, the instructional environment, strategies, programs, curriculum, and language usage in the classroom are observed to determine facilitative qualities. At this level of evaluation, modifications can be made if necessary and student responses to these changes are documented. Student responses are observed or assessed directly, as needed, in both English and the non-English language. Chapter Nine provides additional suggestions for organizing assessment information and collecting data on student performance after instructional interventions and modifications have been made.

In order to obtain a global view of NELB students' academic abilities and skills, a comprehensive assessment includes specific areas in reading, writing, and mathematics that present special problems. As discussed in Section Three and throughout this book, learning academics in a language other than the home language is a complex task; however, the growing body of knowledge regarding how NELB students learn English provides clues as to those areas that are critical for successful achievement. The model presented in this section summarizes sub-areas in the academic domains that are included in a thorough assessment. How these areas can be assessed has been the subject of this book. The source of what is to be evaluated and the measures to be developed lie in the curriculum, linguistic or academic, used to instruct NELB students.

Finally, systematic observation and measurement of students' progress on short and long term objectives established through observation and assessment

TABLE 5.5. A CURRICULUM-BASED MODEL FOR ASSESSING ACADEMIC PERFORMANCE OF NELB STUDENTS

IDENTIFICATION AND CLARIFICATION OF PRESENTING ACADEMIC LEVELS

• Observation   • Interview   • Student Products   • Performance Samples   • Language Status/History   • Educational History

---

OBSERVATION/ANALYSIS OF INSTRUCTIONAL ENVIRONMENT

• Student Behaviors   • Facilitative Instructional Behaviors
• Program(s)   • Curricular Characteristics
• Instructional Strategies   • Language Use/Strategies

OBSERVATION/DIRECT ASSESSMENT OF STUDENT ABILITIES AND SKILLS

• Non-English Language   • English

READING	WRITING	MATHEMATICS

• Prior knowledge
  • Content Schema
  • Formal Schema
• Vocabulary knowledge
• Level of grammar and syntax development
• Word/phrase identification skills
  • Accuracy
  • Fluency
  • Overall rate
• Strategies/Comprehension
	• Composition
	• Samples of Writing
	  • Controlled
	  • Narrative
	  • Literary
	  • Transactional
	  • Across content areas
	• Language forms
	• Fluency
		• Concepts and vocabulary
		• Language structure
		• Knowledge of symbols
		  • Applications
		  • Operations
		  • Computation

DEVELOPMENT OF INSTRUCTIONAL STRATEGIES

• Initial strategies   • Modified strategies as needed

OBSERVATION/MEASUREMENT OF PROGRESS OVER TIME

• Short term objectives   • Long term objectives

provide necessary feedback for instruction. Instructional strategies are initiated, modified, or discarded based on their effectiveness in enhancing student academic achievement.

In conclusion, a curriculum-based model incorporates the dimensions of an integrative assessment while addressing the unique needs of NELB students. This model provides a systematic approach to instructional assessment while taking into account the dynamic, interactive nature of instruction and instructional environments.

RESEARCH IN PRACTICE
Putting It All Together

---

1. What components would you include in a curriculum-based model for assessing students in your setting? Why?

2. Compare a curriculum-based model of assessment with traditional assessment. What are some advantages and disadvantages of a curriculum-based model?

SUMMARIZING SECTION FIVE
Putting It All Together

This brief section provided a graphic representation of an assessment model that synthesizes the ideas presented in previous sections of this chapter. The purpose of this section was to provide a systematic approach to instructional assessment of NELB students. Information regarding specific areas in the reading, writing, and mathematics domains that need to be addressed when assessing NELB students is presented. The relationship between instructional environment, language, student achievement, and instructional strategies is considered. Repeated and continued observation and measurement of student progress over time are viewed as critical to successful instruction and academic achievement.

SUMMARY OF CHAPTER FIVE
Towards an Integrative Academic Performance Assessment

This chapter presented an overview of an integrative approach to the assessment of the academic performance of NELB students. This approach suggests that both formal and informal procedures be used for evaluation.

While there are problems associated with the use of standardized tests with NELB students, the possible negative effects of these can be reduced by responsible use of alternative, supplementary assessment methods. Furthermore, the increasing body of knowledge in the areas of educational measurement, language, and literacy acquisition among monolingual, bilingual, and multilingual students provides new methods and information with which to guide assessment. It was suggested that assessment of the academic performance of NELB students is best undertaken within the context of the instructional environment. The existence of facilitative features in the instructional environment is critical to the linguistic and academic progress of NELB students. Contemporary knowledge of how NELB students learn to read, write, and perform mathematical operations in a new language was reviewed. This chapter presents the theoretical underpinnings for the development of a curriculum-based model for assessing NELB students' academic skills, abilities, and learning behaviors. A schematic representation of a curriculum-based evaluation system was offered.

In the chapter that follows, Chapter Six, a variety of evaluation methods found to be useful for assessing NELB students will be examined. These methods either draw from or can be applied to the curriculum or the learning and instructional processes as they occur in the context of the classroom. They fulfill the requirement that assessment instruments measure what is taught in the classroom, that is, that they be contextualized.

Chapter 6

Assessing Academic Performance Through Contextualized Measures

Throughout the previous chapters, examples of various types of methods to measure linguistic and academic performance have been provided. In some instances, the methods may be applied to both the linguistic and academic areas, as is the case with cloze tests, sentence verification techniques, and story retelling procedures when these are used to measure reading comprehension. These measures were discussed at length in Chapter Three. Due to the variety of evaluation methods available and possible multiple uses, setting objectives and clarifying the purpose of the evaluation are necessary steps in developing an academic evaluation protocol as discussed in Chapter Five. In this manner, appropriate instruments or methods may be chosen or devised.

While a comprehensive listing of techniques is beyond the scope of this chapter, several types of performance, process, and alternative assessment procedures are presented and defined. Descriptions and mini-case studies exemplify some methods that have been found to be useful with NELB students. The procedures and methods include: interviews, observation and anecdotal record keeping, teacher designed rating scales and checklists, informal reading inventories, curriculum-based assessment (CBA), and curriculum-based measurement (CBM). They are presented as congruent with trends in instruction and relevant to the identification of learning problems or opportunities for learning and instruction. These methods and procedures are considered to be contextualized measures in that they draw directly from the curriculum to which students are exposed (and are therefore more meaningful and relevant) or they are applied in the natural instructional environment in which NELB students are being taught.

SECTION ONE

DOCUMENTING ACADEMIC PROCESSES

Recall from Chapter Five that within an integrative perspective to evaluation, the term *process assessment* is understood to include behaviors of both learners and educators/evaluators as they interact in the learning environment. The effects of instructional strategies, use of particular materials, or classroom atmosphere on students can be observed or elicited. This section focuses on selected methods that lend themselves to a more dynamic assessment of student academic and language learning processes.

Assessment within the context of the learning environment implies that ready-made instruments may not be available to the evaluator. Performance measures must be constructed to reflect the specific evaluation and curricular objectives, and are, therefore, embedded in the curriculum to which students are exposed. Rating scales and checklists are frequently used to record either student performance or as aids to structure observations of students in the process of learning. Assessment measures can be constructed using the content of the curriculum. Careful planning is necessary when devising performance tests, rating scales, checklists, and curriculum-based measures. The following subsections review selected structured and unstructured methods of assessment. Some of the major considerations with regards to the development and use of these methods are highlighted.

TYPES OF INFORMAL METHODS

In general, methods for documenting academic processes fall under two broad categories: structured and unstructured (Navarrete, Wilde, Nelson, Martinez & Hargett 1990). Examples of the structured techniques include such activities as completing checklists or rating scales, filling out self-report questionnaires, or responding to structured interviews. Narrative interviews, writing samples, homework, logs or journals, games related to content, student debates, brainstorming activities, and records of student interactions in the classroom are examples of unstructured evaluation methods and materials.

Structured interviews.

One way to understand the differences between structured and unstructured methods is to describe their salient features. For example, in distinguishing between structured and unstructured (or narrative) interviews, the former are found to have codified questions and specific response options. Responses may be forced-choice or open-ended. In this case, the interviewer exerts greater control over the response. Additionally, quantitative scoring methods may be applied. Structured interviews or assessment methods generally outline the targeted behaviors or events to be covered. For example, when interviewing NELB children to determine how they perceive the reading process and what they think they must do to read, one can develop structured questions such as those presented in Table 6-1 (adapted from Burke 1978) in either English or the non-English language. Questions such as these can also assist in determining whether the new reader of English primarily uses a text-bound, or bottom-up approach to reading or a context-based, or top-down, approach.

Structured interviews such as the one presented here provide more predictable and quantifiable responses. Criteria for more effective and less effective

TABLE 6-1. PERSONAL READING PROCESS INTERVIEW

1. What is reading?

2. Why do you read?

3. Do you know how to read in more than one language? Do you read more in one language than another? Which one? How did you learn to read in that language?

4. What did the teachers do to help you learn to read?

5. Do you know how to read well? How do you know, or what makes you think so?

6. What do you think makes the difference between reading well and reading poorly?

7. Is there something that you would like to improve about the way you read?

8. When you are reading and there is a word, a phrase or a sentence you do not know or understand, what do you do? *(Pause for a response.)* Is there anything else you can do?

9. Do you know someone who reads well? How do you know this person is a good reader?

10. What do people do when they come to something they don't know?

11. Do you think your teacher is a good reader? What makes him or her a good reader?

12. What do you think teachers do when they come to something they do not know?

13. Pretend that someone you know is having a hard time reading a school assignment. What would you do to help that person? How would your teacher help this person?

responses can be established, and points can be awarded for the responses that indicate a more effective understanding of the reading process.

Narrative interviews.

In contrast to structured interviews, narrative interviews attempt to elicit a description through less specific prompts (e.g. "Tell me how you did that"). The student has control over the order and manner in which events are described, and qualitative insights are obtained about the student's experiences (Garbarino, Stott & Faculty of the Erikson Institute 1989). The following verbatim excerpts from an interview between an evaluator and Celeste, a student whose dominant language is a Caribbean Creole, demonstrates the variety of school and learning-related attitudes and issues that can surface and be explored through an unstructured interview. Additionally, Celeste's English language abilities can be analyzed for intervention.

> Teacher (T): Tell me about the school you were in before you came here.
> Celeste (C): I forget all my teacher name but I hate school.
> T: You hated the school?
> C: People fight too much.
> T: They did?
> C: Uh huh. I feel sorry for the others.
> T: How about this school? Do you think people fight too much in this school?
> C: No. But they bother me.
> T: How do they bother you?
> C: I don't know.
> T: What do they do that makes you feel that they are bothering you?
> C: They be calling me ugly. They be pointing at me. They be talking about me. They call me all kind of bad words. But my classrooms do tease you like that only in my reading class.
> T: Why do you think it's just in your reading class?
> C: I only have one—um—friend at reading class. I don't how to talk in English so good, that's why. Can't spell it. Can't read so good. They always do that all the time because they see the clothes to be your friend. I wish I had some good clothes, like you know, short clothes like that and shoes, um, I don't have any and I just want some. I, but, I want a little, I want my dreams to come true but always be thinking. I'll always be thinking I got good clothes and I got friends. They say because if you know you from the island, so you have to stay in your own home. You have to stay where you were. They'll kill you if you talk in Creole.

When interviewing NELB students, it is important to remember that the interview situation may be stressful. During the interview reproduced above, it was important to observe the student's nonverbal cues, such as intonation and affect. Cultural differences in interaction styles between children and adults must be considered. For example, in some cultures the dialogue that occurred might not have taken on such a personal tone because of differing parenting styles and established communication patterns between adults and children. Additionally, communicative competence and the student's level of language proficiency will influence how much and how effectively he or she will be able to respond.

Students' responses may be influenced by the preceding questions, what they think the questions mean, what they feel are acceptable answers, and what they believe to be the consequences of the response. Students may feel that adults already know the answers to the questions. As a result, they may either shorten the response or not answer at all. If narrative interview is the method being used, the questions and comments made by the evaluator must be adjusted to the vocabulary and grammatical complexity of the statements made by the student (Garbarino et al. 1989). Successful interviewing of NELB students, and students in general, involves demonstration of empathy and appreciation of the students' feelings and perceptions. Additionally, an effort must be made to understand the world the way the student does (Garbarino et al. 1989).

If conferences and interviews are going to be used as part of the educational assessment of NELB students, the record of interview speech must be complete and accurate. During formal assessment, the student's responses are recorded verbatim. Use of a tape recorder and subsequent transcription of the interview allows for the interview to become part of the official documentation of evaluation. Chapter Three contains additional suggestions relevant to interviewing NELB students.

Anecdotal records.

For teachers, observation of children's behavior in the learning environment is a daily occurrence. When observations are focused on particular student behaviors, insights and information can be gained regarding such areas as interpersonal behaviors, learning style, adjustment, work habits, and functioning in the classroom or other settings. Individual students or groups or students may be observed and their behaviors recorded. The information obtained can be used to develop instructional interventions.

One method of documenting student behaviors that is easily incorporated into an integrative assessment is that of narrative, or anecdotal, recording. Such recording can occur in a systematic or a scientific manner (see, for example, Sattler 1988, for an in-depth treatment of recording methods using scientific principles. See also Grace & Shores 1991 for further discussion of systematic observation and anecdotal record keeping as applied to young children under the age of six.). By means of anecdotal recording, educators can develop a composite picture of a student and gain new insights that may support, refute, or explain other evaluation results (Gilbert & Burger 1990). Other trained observers, parents, relatives, or the students themselves may also maintain anecdotal records, such as journals. These recordings may include any occurrence that seems noteworthy to the observer; specific time frames, codes, or categories are not needed, nor is there any quantitative recording (Sattler 1988).

Some suggestions for documenting student behaviors by means of anecdotal records are summarized in Table 6-2 (Sattler 1988). When recording the behaviors of NELB students, it is recommended that the behaviors of one or two students of similar background, whenever possible, be simultaneously observed and recorded. This assists the educator to determine whether the behaviors observed are typical of the culture and language background of the student. Additionally, the educator may observe whether the instructional or linguistic strategies being used are producing the desired results among all children of the same background.

TABLE 6-2. SUGGESTIONS FOR ANECDOTAL RECORDING OF BEHAVIOR

• Indicate the date, time, and setting of the observation.

• Specify the behavior(s) of the student and relevant others.

• Include factors that appear to affect the behavior(s).

• Document both verbal and nonverbal behaviors of the student and relevant others.

• Record behaviors as soon as possible after they occur.

• Record what the child or relevant others say as precisely as possible. Record only important verbalizations.

• Maintain the sequence of behaviors as they occur.

• Maintain objectivity, accuracy, and thoroughness.

• Remember that the purpose is description, not interpretation of the behaviors while they are occurring.

• Remember that your impressions may change throughout the observation period.

• Monitor your own reactions and feelings.

• During post-observation interpretation of behaviors, try to view these from the perspective of the student.

• To develop a composite, unified picture of the student, integrate all sources of information.

Given the constraints imposed by standardized test use with NELB students, anecdotal recordings take on particular importance when one is attempting to determine the students' educational needs. Following are excerpts from anecdotal records maintained on Lhani, a first grade student and a native of a rural village of India. When reading the excerpts, make notes of your reactions and impressions. Be prepared to complete the activity that follows.

RESEARCH IN PRACTICE:
Types of Informal Methods

Mini-Case Study: Lhani

9/10/91; 7:45 a.m. : I have found out from the front office that my new student, Lhani, is from a rural agricultural village in India. They speak a Hindi dialect which is not the official language of the region. Lhani apparently attended school sporadically as she frequently had to help her parents with the crops. Lhani began kindergarten in January of this year at another school. She is scheduled to receive ESOL services 45 minutes daily. Lhani has not spoken to anyone since her arrival three days ago. Although Lhani has three siblings in this school, there are no other children of her background enrolled.

9/25/91; 10:30 a.m.; Independent seat work: Lhani is sitting at her desk looking around the room. She has not completed the workbook pages assigned. In fact, she has done nothing for the last 10 minutes.

9/27/91; 9:30 a.m.; Reading skills review: I reviewed beginning consonant sounds with Lhani and three other children who are having difficulties retaining the information. I had flash cards with the letters on them; out of five letters, Lhani could identify one, the letter "c" with a picture of a cow. When I asked her to write the letter in the space provided under the picture of the cow in her workbook, Lhani just looked at me and did not write. I had to demonstrate and point to where she needed to write. She is left-handed and has a very awkward pencil grasp. I had to guide her hand to write the letter. During choral recitation, Lhani appears to be verbalizing but what she says does not match the letters I present. Lhani copied from another child in the group; the other child complained to me.

9/29/91; 10:00 a.m.; Reading instruction: Lhani is receiving small group instruction with the same three children observed 9/27/91. On this occasion, the letter "d" is being introduced. Lhani attempted to respond to questions asked while following along in the reading-readiness workbook. She called a "desk" a "table." When the group was told to return to their seats, Lhani did so. They were told to complete the rest of the workbook page on their own. Lhani began to color her worksheet. She leafed through the pictures of her book. She again colored the pictures on the page. She looked around the room frequently but was not disruptive. She remained in her seat. By the end of the work period, Lhani had not written the letters under the pictures. The product is not correct with regards to the required task.

10/07/91; 1:00 p.m. ; Interaction between Lhani and an interpreter: Because of Lhani's continuing difficulties, I have requested the services of a trained language bank volunteer who speaks Lhani's dialect. At this time they are conversing freely.The interpreter tells me that Lhani speaks in simple complete sentences, lacks an extensive vocabulary, does not speak the language clearly nor in its more acceptable form. She repeats herself and there are stuttering-like utterances. Lhani did not know how to write in her native script when re-quested.

Lhani was provided with several picture books, was given time to look at them and was asked to develop her own story in her native language. Lhani chose a book about animals. According to the interpreter, Lhani's responses consisted of concrete descriptions of the actions or events depicted in the pictures. When asked a general classification question, the response to which should have been the "animals" category, Lhani proceeded to name, in her native language, the pictures of the animals individually. She had difficulty elaborating on the story and in creating a story line. The interpreter states that she (the interpreter) had to rephrase comprehension questions at least four times on one particular item. Since we are audio-taping this session, we will review the questions and responses later.

In English, Lhani presents with limitations but she is able to produce fairly complete sentences. While looking at a picture book, Lhani said such things as "They gonna take a shower. Little baby gonna take a shower. That little boy brush his teeth. All of 'em sleeping. That little boy read a story." The story was read to her and, when requested to retell the story, Lhani was able to remember the general sequence of events without looking at the pictures. When asked to suggest a title for the story, Lhani said "They sleeping."

---

1. Write down your overall impressions and conclusions about Lhani's academic difficulties. What behaviors did she exhibit that lead you to your conclusions?

2. How did focused observation and recording of Lhani's behavior help you gain insight into her current problems in acquiring reading readiness skills?

3. What insights did you have regarding the method being used to teach her how to read? Based on the anecdotal record, what reading readiness behaviors does Lhani exhibit that can be developed?

4. **Based on the anecdotal record, write your ideas as to what the next step(s) should be to address Lhani's needs.**

5. **How can the educational environment and methods used with Lhani be made more facilitative?** Review Table 5-3 for this purpose.

6. **Select one or two students on whom to keep anecdotal records.** How can these records help you develop appropriate interventions?

7. **Interview the students on whom you have selected to maintain anecdotal records.** How do the students' perceptions differ from your impressions and observations?

DEVELOPING PERFORMANCE MEASURES

Performance measures can be described as experiences, generally developed by the teacher, that allow students to demonstrate their abilities and skills as determined by specific criteria (Gilbert & Burger 1990; Valdez, Pierce & O'Malley 1992). Students are provided with a task to perform; assessment will involve both observing how the student is completing the task and evaluating the completed product or task.

Performance tests.

Developing performance tests requires several steps (Lange & Cook 1986) which are summarized in Table 6-3. When evaluating NELB students, you can develop performance tests in both the native language, utilizing native language curricula if available, and English. Evaluative criteria are selected from and based on the curriculum to which the student has been exposed, thus providing instructionally relevant information.

Rating scales.

Rating scales are useful when the evaluator wants to have an indication, for example, of how accurately or how well the student performed on the specific task, or how well the product conforms to the standards selected. They may also be developed as guides for holistic scoring or analytic rating of student products, such as writing samples (Hudelson 1989a). The standards for rating are set by the evaluator, based on what is deemed to be important for the learner to know or what is being emphasized in instruction (Hudelson 1989a). For example, a rating scale can be developed based on Tough's Taxonomy of Language Functions as presented in Table 3-14. Such a scale may also be based on developmental indicators of attainment of critical milestones in a certain

TABLE 6-3. GUIDELINES FOR DEVELOPING PERFORMANCE TESTS

• Determine the skill or knowledge to be assessed.

• Determine whether process or product is to be evaluated.

• Based on the instructional objective, such as contained in a unit or a lesson, devise the product or the activity the students must perform.

• Determine the characteristics of acceptable product or performance, that is, the criteria or standards that will be used to evaluate the task.

• Based on the task to be completed, devise a student task sheet that explains the task and the materials required.

• Devise an evaluative rating scale or checklist based on the criteria selected:

>   • Anchored rating scales provide maximum information, especially when a record of progress is needed.
>
>   • Items should be limited to the important aspects or criteria of the process or product.
>
>   • One item, clearly stating the criterion, should be used for each skill assessed.
>
>   • Consistent use of either the past or present tense in the statements is suggested.
>
>   • Review the criteria with a colleague to determine clarity and inclusiveness.
>
>   • Use standardized test conditions to ensure validity and objectivity.
>
>   • Use the scale or checklist with a small number of students first before deciding to use it with a larger group.
>
>   • Modify the scale or checklist based on the results of the trial period.

domain. For example, an evaluator may wish to develop a rating scale that denotes the degree of presence or absence of specific language functions, or the degree of proficiency attained at the various levels of language as presented in Table 3-8. The completion of such a scale would allow the educator to pinpoint areas of mastery and those in need of further intervention.

Rating scales commonly used to assess academic performance may contain three, four, or five points. Points on the scale can be anchored, that is, each point is matched with a description. The points on the scale may also be unanchored, that is, only the two ends of the scale are named (Lange & Cook 1986). Table

6-4 exemplifies a modified anchored rating scale (Malone 1990). In this case, there is little or no ambiguity as to the meaning of each point on the scale. Students' performance in each activity can be observed, scored separately, and documented using the scale. Intra-individual, group, or classwide trends can be examined by collecting information on the rating scale. Student strengths and

TABLE 6-4. SAMPLE ANCHORED PERFORMANCE RATING SCALE

Objective: The student will design and complete an experiment, record observations, and draw conclusions.

Scoring Criteria	Score
A. Designing the Experiment	
• Fails to develop a plan.	0
• Design does not allow comparison of variables to standard.	1
• Design allows comparison of variables but lacks sufficient number of tests to obtain meaningful data.	2
• Design allows comparison of variables and indicates sufficient number of tests to obtain meaningful data.	3
B. Collecting and Reporting Data	
• Fails to collect any data.	0
• Describes observations in rambling discourse.	1
• Makes a data table, but the table lacks meaningful labels.	2
• Makes a meaningful table but fails to record the observations or records them inaccurately.	3
• Makes a meaningful table and records the data accurately.	4
C. Drawing Conclusions	
• Fails to reach a conclusion.	0
• Draws a conclusion that is not supported by the data.	1
• Draws a conclusion that is supported by the data, but fails to show the support for the conclusion.	2
• Draws a conclusion that is supported by the data, and gives supporting evidence for the conclusion.	3

weaknesses may be observed: Using the rating scale on Table 6-4, the information collected may reveal that a student consistently has difficulty designing experiments but does well collecting data. All areas need not be observed and scored, particularly if there is evidence that students are progressing well in given areas.

Rating scales may also be devised to be used as informal observation instruments for purposes other than student evaluation. Figure 6-1, for example, demonstrates a rating scale developed for informal observation of instructional environments in which NELB students may be served. This rating scale is based on Table 5-3 which identified some of the major characteristics of facilitative learning environments. In this case, the points on the scale are unanchored. The development of such a scale allows for systematic data collection; however, scoring of such unanchored scales may be influenced by the rating style and mood of the observer/rater (Lange & Cook 1986). In this case, it is usually helpful to have two or more different observers complete the scale to determine how reliable the findings are, based on interobserver agreement (Sattler 1988). There are also available standardized, commercially distributed scales (see, for example, The Instructional Environment Scale, developed by Ysseldyke & Christensen, 1987). These scales may not, however, take into account the unique needs of NELB students nor the unique features of ESOL instructional environments in which NELB students may be served.

Checklists.

Student performance may also be evaluated on the basis of checklists. Checklists actually list the criteria used to determine whether or not the processes targeted for observation were actually performed. Furthermore, they are designed to indicate whether or not the product completed by the student has the characteristics identified as being acceptable. They specify student behaviors or products expected during progression through the curriculum; items contained in the checklist may be content area objectives (Navarrete et al. 1990). Checklists may include columns to reflect whether or not each desired criterion was accomplished (e.g. YES or NO), or they may simply have space for the evaluator to "check off" whether or not the criterion is demonstrated, as in the Checklist of Characteristics of Language Proficiency presented in Table 3-10.

Checklists, as well as rating scales, can provide for a reliable means with which to document student task-related behaviors or environmental factors. When they are used over a period of time, checklists can be indicators of a student's rate and degree of accomplishment within the curriculum (Navarrete et al. 1990). Checklists can also provide students with a clear and succinct description of the qualities of the performance or product expected of them (Lange & Cook 1986). When devised for use with NELB/LEP students, checklists can be used to monitor developmental gains, such as in native or non-native language acquisition.

FIGURE 6-1. FACILITATIVE ENVIRONMENT OBSERVATION RATING SCALE

Student Name: _____ School: _____

Date of Birth: _____ Grade: _____

Date of Observation: _____ Teacher: _____

Instructional Program(s) Type: _____

Instructional Setting Observed: _____

Language(s) of Instruction: _____

Primary Language of Student: _____

Source of Student Language Data: _____

FACILITATIVE FEATURES:	NOT EVIDENT	EVIDENT	COMMENTS
A. Classroom Organization			
1. Mix of group and individual activities			
2. Presence of printed materials			
a. Easily accessible			
b. In native language			
c. In English			
d. Variety			
e. Quantity			
3. Variety of materials for self-expression			
4. Experiential activities used or available			
5. Physical space allocated			
a. For independent learning activities			
b. For group learning activities			
c. Space designed for learning activities			
B. General Instructional Strategies			
1. Content taught in a predictable manner			
2. Exchange and interaction between instructor and student			

(continued on page 274)

(continued from page 273)

	NOT EVIDENT	EVIDENT	COMMENTS
3. Both teacher and student-directed activities used			
4. Comprehension/thinking skills strategies used during instruction			
5. Lower level skills taught in context			
6. Student's culture integrated in content/language instruction			
7. Student's personal experiences acknowledged			
a. Expression is encouraged			
b. Expansion on student experiences			
8. Student's cultural self-identity is fostered			
C. Instructional Language Strategies			
1. Language used reflects real-world communication			
2. Language is adjusted to the level of cognitive demand			
3. Strategies used to modify language for comprehension			
a. confirmation			
b. comprehension checks			
c. clarification requests			
d. repetitions			
e. expansions			
4. Teacher models literacy behaviors			
5. Activities provide opportunity to practice or reenact literacy behaviors			
6. Activities provide opportunities to share language			
a. peer audience			
b. student narratives			
7. Activities provide opportunity to share literature			
a. story retelling			
b. story grammar			
c. own writing			
8. Native language is valued			

Additional Comments During Observation: _____

RESEARCH IN PRACTICE:
Developing Performance Measures

1. Select an area or objective to evaluate. Develop a performance test, rating scale, or checklist. Jot down some of the difficulties you may encounter. Share it with a colleague for feedback.

2. List some of the advantages and disadvantages of performance tests, rating scales, and checklists.

3. Use the performance test, rating scale, or checklist you developed. What are some of the strengths and weaknesses of the measure you developed?

Informal reading inventories.

Informal reading inventories, commonly referred to as IRIs, are individually administered informal tests of oral reading. Students' reading skills are determined by having them read material that is drawn from basal reading series or other curricular materials, such as content area texts, being used in the classroom (Elliott & Piersel 1982; Gerken 1990). IRIs are generally constructed by selecting words and short passages (of about 60 to 200 words) from graded materials that increase in level of difficulty (Elliott & Piersel 1982; Redmond 1990). Students are then asked to read from the prepared word lists and passages. In order to facilitate accurate scoring, students' oral responses can be tape recorded. Reading strengths, weaknesses, and errors can then be coded or noted based on actual performance. Miscue analysis can be completed and reading behaviors such as requesting assistance, hesitations, omissions, reversals in order, or self-corrections are documented to assist in instructional planning. The students' responses to prepared comprehension questions are noted. Table 6-5 summarizes some guidelines for development and administration of an IRI for secondary level students (Gerken 1990).

By periodically administering IRIs, students' progress can be monitored and students can become aware of their growth as readers. IRIs provide both a diagnostic and learning tool by which interactive reading assessment and mediated instruction in reading can be accomplished as described in Section One of this chapter. While it is recommended that IRIs be used interactively with NELB students rather than to track them into reading groups, IRIs are frequently used to identify students' independent, instructional, and frustration reading levels with respect to given text. Table 6-6 summarizes common definitions and guidelines for each of these levels (Elliott & Piersel 1982; Gerken 1990).

TABLE 6-5. DEVELOPMENT AND ADMINISTRATION OF AN INFORMAL READING INVENTORY

- Obtain the textbooks the students are currently using.
- Randomly select three 100 to 200-word passages. These passages should be from the beginning, middle, and end of the textbooks.
- Determine the readability level of the passages[1].
- Prepare from 6 to 10 comprehension questions which tap various levels of comprehension, such as factual, inferential, etc. for each passage.
- Request the student to read the passages silently.
- Request the student to read orally. Record reading errors.
- Read passages to the student to assess listening comprehension.
- After the passages have been read, ask the questions. Note whether the student or the evaluator read the passage.
- Record the student's responses to the questions.
- Analyze oral reading and comprehension responses.

TABLE 6-6. DEFINITIONS AND GUIDELINES FOR READING LEVELS

LEVEL:	DEFINITION:	DEMONSTRATED BY:
Independent	That reading level at which students are able to read on their own and have no to minimal difficulty with word identification, comprehension, and memory for the contents of a passage.	A score of 98% or above on word recognition; and a score of 90% or above on passage comprehension.
Instructional	That reading level at which students have some difficulty with word identification, comprehension, and memory for the contents of a passage. Difficulties can be overcome with further instruction.	A score of 90-97% on word recognition; and a score of 70-89% on passage comprehension.
Frustration	That reading level at which students are unable to identify words or comprehend passages. The demands of the text exceed the skills of the reader.	A score of 89% or lower on word recognition; and a score of 50% or lower on passage comprehension.

---

[1]Gerken suggests the use of a computerized program, *School Utilities, 1982,* published by Educational Computing Consortium, St. Paul, Minnesota, to obtain an estimate of the level of difficulty of the reading material.

When used as screening devices with NELB students, IRIs provide information that is useful in determining the degree to which a student is able to cope with reading material assigned or used in the classroom. The comprehension questions that are developed can assist in determining NELB students' ability to select the main idea, recall details, make inferences, and understand the vocabulary and concepts presented in reading material (Redmond 1990). When using content area IRIs to assess reading skills of NELB students, it is also necessary to evaluate students' knowledge of the structure of the text as well, as indicated in Section Two of this chapter. Information from such an evaluation, combined with an IRI, can help distinguish whether reading comprehension problems are due to poor reading or to lack of familiarity with text structure. Some studies have demonstrated that NELB students may possess functional reading levels, that is, levels at which they can function adequately in the classroom, that are higher than the students' performance on standardized reading tests indicate (Argulewicz & Sanchez 1982). IRIs can provide information regarding functional reading competencies.

The usefulness of IRIs lies in the ease with which they can be constructed, the source of their content (material taken directly from the curriculum), the opportunity they provide to assess reading in a context that is identical to that of the classroom task, and the information they provide regarding students' reading behaviors (Elliott & Piersel 1982). IRIs can be constructed in both English and non-English languages. They can be used to assess NELB students' ability to comprehend discourse by listening as passages are read to them or by directly reading the passages and then answering questions (Carlisle 1991).

Although the advantages of IRIs are immediately apparent, their limitations must also be considered. Because IRI's are not constructed using rigorous psychometric criteria as required for standardized reading tests, they may be subject to greater errors in administration, scoring, and interpretation (Elliott & Piersel 1982). Reliability of test scores is thus compromised. The examiner must be knowledgeable of scoring procedures. Materials must be suitable for the intended purpose, and variability of passage level difficulty within the same text must be accounted for or controlled in some manner.

While IRIs are promising as an alternative method for assessing NELB students' reading abilities and skills, there are two factors which must be considered when they are developed for use with these students. These considerations relate to content of the inventories and the curriculum from which the content is drawn (Argulewicz & Sanchez 1982). First, as discussed in Section 3, NELB students are better able to interact with text that has culturally familiar content and reflects their unique interests. Second, it is important to determine whether the curricular materials used to develop the IRIs are culturally relevant and linguistically appropriate. The students' level of proficiency in English and non-English language characteristics may contribute to less than adequate performance on IRIs that are developed from materials that are not particularly suitable.

In conclusion, informal reading inventories present a viable method for gathering instructionally relevant information about NELB students' reading abilities. When administered in an interactive manner, using reciprocal teaching strategies, IRIs become powerful tools through which reading processes are integrated and made meaningful for NELB students.

RESEARCH IN PRACTICE:
Informal Reading Inventories

1. **Consult with an ESOL teacher and a reading specialist in your school or district.** Discuss ways in which IRIs might be developed using the curricular materials used for instructing ESOL students.

2. **Develop your own IRI.** Use it with your students, noting the advantages and disadvantages of the method.

3. **Review several commercially developed reading inventories.** Compare the commercial inventories with those that may be developed from classroom materials. List some strengths and weaknesses of each.

SUMMARIZING SECTION ONE
Documenting Academic Processes

This section described and exemplified selected informal assessment techniques, and methods to develop performance measures that have been found to be useful for documenting the academic and learning processes of NELB students. These techniques and methods are used and are constructed to reflect specific evaluation and curricular objectives. Objectivity, accuracy, and careful planning are required to devise performance tests and to interpret data obtained through informal techniques of assessment. This section suggests that these procedures form part of a body of assessment methods that draw directly from the curriculum or are applied in the natural learning environment. The section that follows elaborates further on the use of curricular materials in the assessment process and on the development of contextualized measures of academic achievement.

WHAT CAN YOU DO?

1. **Select several students from your setting, including two or three NELB students, if available.** Plan an assessment framework that includes the use of at

least three of the methods described in this section. Develop instructional strategies for those students based on the information obtained. Document the students' progress by repeated measurement and graphing of results. Share your findings with a colleague.

2. Find curricular materials written in a language other than English. Determine how you would go about assessing a student who speaks the language represented in the text. What steps would you take? Where would you search for resources to assist you? Determine the information you would need to gather.

SECTION TWO

USING CURRICULAR MATERIALS FOR ASSESSMENT AND CONSTRUCTION OF ACADEMIC MEASURES

Throughout this book and this chapter, emphasis has been placed on using curricular materials, content, and the dynamics of the instructional environment as sources of information on the linguistic and academic progress of NELB students. Cloze tests, IRIs, and use of Sentence Verification Technique in assessment protocols exemplify ways in which curricular materials and content are used to assess student performance. By using curricular materials as the basis for evaluation, skills and content that are taught can be assessed. Modifications in instructional strategies can be made and effective instructional practices can be documented. Students' individual or collective progress can be monitored. Furthermore, by applying specific methods for which technical adequacy has been established, educators can ensure that assessment information is obtained in a consistent, therefore more reliable, manner. Additionally, school districts can develop local norms that reflect their students' performance on the local curricula (Shinn 1988; Shinn & Tindal 1988). A frequent criticism of standardized tests when used with NELB students is that language, educational background, and opportunities for learning English are not taken into account. Use of measures based on culturally and linguistically appropriate curricular materials, or other materials to which NELB students are exposed, for assessment and documentation of performance permits educators to control as much as possible for these variables. NELB students' performance may be compared to that of other students who find themselves in similar circumstances. This enhances the validity of assessment results. The purpose of this section is to describe and exemplify through mini-case studies evaluation and measurement procedures that directly use curricular materials for assessment and for the development of academic tests.

CURRICULUM-BASED ASSESSMENT

Within the field of educational assessment, significant attention has been given to systematic collection of information on student performance in the curriculum. The terms curriculum-based assessment (CBA) and curriculum-based measurement (CBM) are used to represent two related, but not necessarily equal, methods for assessing student progress or status within the local or classroom curriculum. Curriculum-based assessment, in particular, is being examined as a a way to reduce bias in the assessment of NELB students, to validate the results of norm-referenced tests, and to guide instructional planning and decision-making (Ortiz et al. 1991; Tucker 1990). For this reason, some basic principles and characteristics of CBA and CBM will be discussed further in this subsection (for an introductory survey of curriculum-based assessment see the special issue of *Exceptional Children, 52* (3), 1985). It must be noted, however, that because of the interrelationship between CBA and CBM, a more inclusive definition of curriculum-based assessment has been proposed: Curriculum-based assessment is any set of measurement procedures that use direct observation and recording of a student's performance in the local curriculum as a basis for gathering information to make instructional decisions (Deno 1987).

Curriculum-based assessment (CBA).

Using curricular materials as the basis for assessing students is a practice that is not foreign to the educational setting; however, for many years educators have come to rely heavily on standardized tests to measure students' academic achievement. The low correlation between standardized, norm-referenced tests and the content of the curricular materials being used with students raises questions regarding the usefulness of tests for instructional planning. While standardized achievement tests provide information regarding students' academic skills relative to those of a larger normative group, they provide less information regarding what students have already learned in the classroom and what they must learn in order to be successful. Standardized academic achievement tests may not be helpful in determining how students should be taught, nor how fast or how much students can learn given specific instructional strategies.

The last 10 to 20 years have seen the growth of a movement to return to assessment that is guided by instructional practices and curricular content. Similarly, it has been proposed that instruction be guided by the results of assessment of students' status in the curriculum. Curriculum-based assessment, or CBA, has come to represent the integration of data-based instruction with assessment techniques in order to determine students' instructional needs (Gickling 1981; Tucker 1990). The data obtained from the assessment are directly used to develop instructional strategies. Repeated, frequent (daily or several times during the week) measurements of the students' ongoing performance in the curriculum to which they are currently exposed form part of a CBA procedure (Gickling 1981; Tucker 1990). The measurement methods are time efficient, easy to use, and reflect the content, skills, or behaviors students must learn (Council for Exceptional Children [CEC] 1988). The term CBA does not, however, represent a set of universally agreed upon assessment methods; rather, it embodies a wide variety of techniques that use curricular materials as the basis for testing (Knutson & Shinn 1991; Shinn, Rosenfield & Knutson 1989). Assessment methods may be designed by the educator or may be selected from those that have been developed through research (CEC 1988). Educator designed CBA methods may, for example, be incorporated into holistic evaluations of students (Abrams, Herrity & LaBrot 1991). Several different models of CBA have been identified in the research literature (Knutson & Shinn 1991; Shinn, Rosenfield & Knutson 1989). The selection of a specific method depends upon the information sought and the types of decisions to be made about students (Shinn, Rosenfield & Knutson 1989; see, for example, Gickling 1981, and Gickling & Havertape 1981, for in-depth description of the use of CBA for instructional design).

By conducting a curriculum-based assessment, the educator is, in effect, sampling student achievement (Shinn & Knutson 1992; Shinn, Tindal & Stein 1988). Students' performance is recorded, frequently on a graph, or may be reported as the percentage of known items to unknown items (Gickling 1981; Shapiro 1992). The information obtained may be used to determine student mastery of specific skills. Students' instructional, independent, and frustration levels on classroom curricular materials is determined. The data obtained assist in the placement of students in the appropriate level of the curriculum. The scope and sequence charts that accompany many commercially produced textbooks may be used to determine what skills the student has mastered, what must be retaught, and what the student has yet to learn. In this manner, instruction can be tailored specifically for students, according to their identified needs. CBA is then used to evaluate the outcome of instructional interventions in the areas identified as requiring additional teaching or practice (Gickling, Shane & Croskery 1989). Repeated measurement of ongoing performance is used to refine instruction and to monitor student progress (Shinn, Tindal & Stein 1988). Additionally, curriculum-based techniques can be used to assess NELB students' ability to handle the language demands of the classroom (see Nelson 1989 for application of CBA to language assessment). When combined with an evaluation of the degree to which the instructional environment is supportive and facilitative of academic success, CBA methods can be very important sources of information regarding the effects of instructional modifications on student achievement and language development (Nelson 1989; Shapiro 1990). In this manner, CBA is used to improve instructional programs (Shinn, Rosenfield & Knutson 1989).

As indicated above, there are various models and methods of conducting CBA. The evaluator may select any one of these depending on the information desired from the assessment. On the other hand, the evaluator may wish to adapt CBA methods to more closely match the content, instructional style, and philosophy of instruction of a particular classroom, school setting, or district (Abrams, Herrity & LaBrot 1991). For example, if a whole language approach to reading is used in the classroom, a curriculum-based approach might include evaluation of students' general knowledge about the topic or content of the text.

One method of CBA.

One method of CBA requires the construction and administration of a series of probes that consist of material taken directly from the curriculum being used with students (Shapiro 1989). Probes are developed to measure oral reading (either sight word vocabulary or passages, or both, if necessary), mathematics computation skills, written expression, and spelling. Once constructed, the probes take from one to three minutes each to administer. The probes are then scored to determine the rate (or fluency) and accuracy with which students are able to respond to the probe tasks. Table 6-7 summarizes one method of constructing, administering, and scoring word list probes to assess sight vocabulary, while Table 6-8 summarizes the processes applied to reading passage probes (see Shapiro 1989 for in-depth treatment of probe development, scoring, and application of information obtained). These examples are for probes developed from basal reading series; however, the general methods can be adapted to literature or content area texts.

TABLE 6-7. CONSTRUCTION, ADMINISTRATION, AND SCORING OF WORD LIST PROBES

- Find the list of words that are introduced in the students' readers. This list is in the teacher's guide to the reading series.

- Randomly select three lists of 100 words from the main list.

- Construct word lists for each level of the reader.

- Type or print the randomized words in five columns of 20 words each.

- Make two copies of each list, one for the student and one for scoring. Laminating the student lists makes them reusable.

- Have the student read the word list out loud for one minute. Score the second copy as the student reads.

- Count the words read correctly per minute (WCM) and the words read incorrectly, or errors (E).

- Administer all three lists at each level of the reading series.

- The median, or middle score, is used as the estimate of reading fluency.

- Decisions about students' reading level are best made when local, grade, classroom, or peer group norms are used for comparison purposes.[2]

- Administer word lists if students have difficulty reading whole passages.

[2] See Shinn 1988, for discussion of the development of curriculum-based local norms.

TABLE 6-8. CONSTRUCTION, ADMINISTRATION, AND SCORING OF ORAL READING PROBES (PASSAGES)

- From each book in the reading series, select 3 passages: one from the beginning, one from the middle, and one from the end.[3]

  - Passages of 50- to 100-words are recommended for first through third grade.
  - Passages of 150- to 200-words are recommended for fourth grade and beyond.
  - Type or print the passages on separate sheets, allowing space for scoring. Laminate them for reuse.

- Make two copies of the passages, one for the student to read from, one to use for scoring.

- If comprehension is to be assessed, develop five to eight questions for each probe. These questions should include both literal and inferential questions.

- Beginning with the book in which the student is currently placed, administer each of the three probes, in the order in which the passages appear in the book.

- Have the student read each probe orally for one minute. Allow the student to finish a sentence if necessary, but indicate where the student was at the end of the minute.

- As the student is reading, score as errors:
  a. omission of entire words;
  b. substitution of words;
     1. mispronunciation of a proper noun is counted as an error only once;
     2. deleted suffixes are *not* counted as errors;
     3. pronounce the word correctly and ask the student to proceed;
  c. addition of word(s) not in the passage;
  d. a pause of 5 seconds. After the pause, read the word for the student.

- Repetition of words and self-corrections are not counted as errors.

- Count the words correct per minute (WCM) and the number incorrect. The number of words read (correct or incorrect) is the overall reading rate per minute. If comprehension questions are administered, the percentage of questions answered correctly is the comprehension score for the probe.

- Score each probe, then find the median correct, median incorrect, and median comprehension score for the passages administered. Remember that the median score is the middle of the three scores on the probes administered for each book.

- Determine whether the student is at frustration, instructional, or independent (mastery) level. One set of recommended guidelines for identifying the instructional reading level follows:

Grade Levels	Frustration Level	Instructional Level	Mastery Level
1-3	<29wcm, > 8e	30-49wcm, 3-7e	50+wcm. <2e
4 or higher	<49wcm, > 8e	50-99wcm, 3-7e	100+wcm, <2e

- Using the guidelines, move up or down in the series, administering probes until the median scores for at least two sets of scores are instructional *and* the one above is frustration.

- Place the student in the book at the highest instructional level obtained.

---

[3]Shinn & Knutson 1992 recommend random selection of passages for measurement purposes.

This method of CBA, when combined with other informal, holistic assessment procedures, may be helpful for screening NELB students' academic skills. The summary of Guadalupe's case in the *Research in Practice* that follows exemplifies how this method of CBA may be integrated with other assessment data for screening purposes.

RESEARCH IN PRACTICE:
Curriculum-Based Assessment (CBA)

Mini-Case Study: Guadalupe

Guadalupe is a seven-year-old youngster of Mexican descent who was referred for screening by her second grade teacher. Guadalupe had participated in a native language (Spanish) and ESOL program since kindergarten. Because she was making slow progress in acquisition of reading skills, Guadalupe's parents requested that she be dismissed from the native language and ESOL program. They believed that such a placement was detrimental to her learning to read. She was dismissed from the program at the end of first grade. After several months in second grade, Guadalupe was referred for academic screening as she was failing in all areas except mathematics computations.

The Facilitative Environment Observation Rating Scale was used to identify those facilitative features that were or were not present. In general, it was determined that the classroom organization and instructional strategies used were more typical of an instructional style that emphasized the transmission of information rather than reciprocal interaction among classroom community members. Guadalupe herself was observed to be working quietly at her desk on a spelling assignment. Work samples revealed poor performance on assignments drawn from texts (e.g. workbooks, dittoes, responses to end of unit questions, etc.). These were the primary source for grades in reading and language arts. The second grade reader of the basal reading series was used for reading instruction.

Screening with Spanish and English standardized tests of oral language (primarily expressive and receptive vocabulary), revealed that Guadalupe possessed age appropriate vocabulary in Spanish. She scored as well as an average five-year-old English speaking student when her vocabulary was assessed in this language. When Spanish reading skills were assessed with a standardized test, she was able to identify three letters of the alphabet and one monosyllabic word. She was unable to complete any of the reading comprehension items presented on the standardized test. Her responses to the written language portions of the test revealed that she was able to write a few letters from dictation and selected monosyllabic words in Spanish. Guadalupe was able to complete selected alphabet recognition items on the English reading test. Her responses to the written language test used consisted of writing selected letters of the alphabet from dictation. One of the major drawbacks encountered with the standardized test was that there were too few items to which Guadalupe could respond. In essence, based on the standardized testing results, one might conclude that Guadalupe was a non-reader or writer in either language; however, Guadalupe's stronger language appeared to be Spanish.

Supplementary assessment methods were then used with Guadalupe. It was determined that, while in the native language classroom, Guadalupe had received reading instruction by use of basal readers. Basal reader word lists and cloze passages were developed for both the Spanish readers previously used and English readers currently used to instruct Guadalupe. Guadalupe was provided with writing materials and primary level storybooks in both languages. These were selected from lists of recommended children's literature. Oral responses and conversation were tape recorded.

Guadalupe's interaction with the storybooks was either observed or elicited for such behaviors as knowledge of the differences between words and letters, of the directionality of print, and of the beginning and ending of sentences. Her attempts to read the texts were noted, as well as the predictions she formulated based on her understanding of what she had read or predicted from the illustrations. Since Guadalupe's word recognition skills were weak, she was asked to select two stories, one in Spanish, and one in English, which were subsequently read to her. Her responses to listening comprehension questions were noted.

Additionally, Guadalupe was administered the basal reader probes. Figure 6-2A and Figure 6-2B are graphic representations of Guadalupe's performance on selected Spanish and English probes. The probes were developed using not only the sight word vocabulary noted in the teacher's guide of the texts, but also randomized letters of the alphabet in each language. This knowledge was deemed important by the teacher. Additionally, the scope and sequence charts of the texts were used to identify possible prerequisite skills needed. For example, the one syllable column on Figure 6-2A, reflects Guadalupe's knowledge of randomized monosyllables which are introduced prior to two syllable words in the Spanish text (e.g. "ma," then "mama").

Figure 6-2B demonstrates Guadalupe's performance on selected probes in English, including alphabet recognition, reading readiness words, and words from the pre-primer.

Guadalupe was provided with writing materials. Her immediate response was to draw a picture, represented in Figure 6.3. Figure 6.4 demonstrates the writing that accompanied her story.

Guadalupe then provided oral narratives of her drawing in Spanish and English. In Spanish, Guadalupe stated:

"Una vez habia una tortuguita. La tortuguita estaba paseando. Habia unos arboles. Las manzanas se iban cayendo. Habia unos pajaritos. Estaban volando! Las nubes estaban volando. Estaba muy bonito el dia que fue. Ya."

FIGURE 6-2A. GUADALUPE'S RESPONSES ON
SPANISH READING PROBES

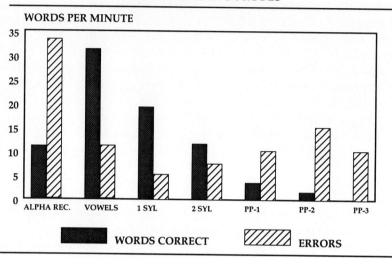

FIGURE 6-2B. GUADALUPE'S RESPONSES ON
ENGLISH READING PROBES

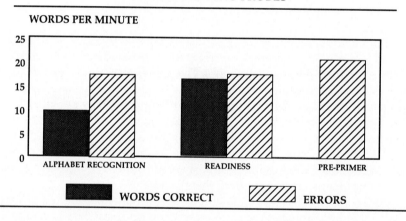

("One time there was a little turtle. The little turtle was out for a walk. There were some trees. The apples were falling. There were some little birds. They were flying! The clouds were flying. It was very pretty the day it went. That's it.")

In English, Guadalupe's story went as follows:

"There is a leetle turnle? See are looking in the park. There are cutiful bird and sun. The cutiful day. I'ember the day I go over there. I'ember to see the stars.

I 'ember I see the apples. And sol is my mother. She really love this part. And I will be happy with me."

Guadalupe's performance on the reading probes and informal assessments provided insight into her language and literacy status. The initial information provided by the standardized tests was expanded by use of the probes. She

Figure 6-3. Guadalupe's Writing (Pictorial Form)

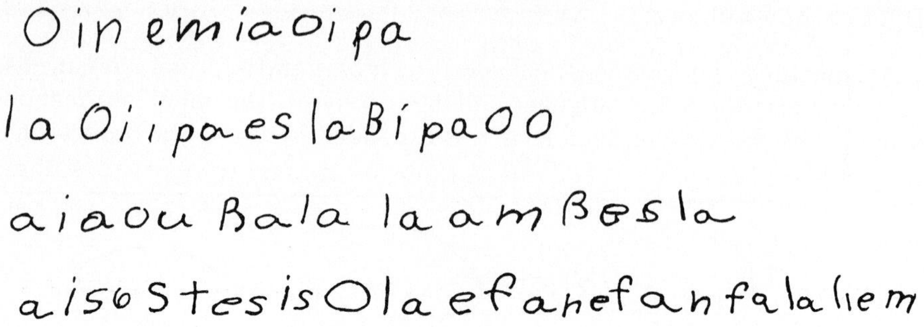

Oin emiaOipA

la Oiipaesla Bipa00

aiaOu Bala laamBesla

also Stesis Ola efahefahfalaliem

Figure 6-4. Guadalupe's Writing (Graphic Form)

could no longer be considered a non-reader. There were indications that she might be able to interact with a higher level of text in Spanish than in English (PP-2 in Spanish versus reading readiness in English), though further instruction was needed. In general, she read more in this language, although her error rate was relatively high once the pre-primer words were introduced. There were indications that, if the parents continued to refuse native language services for Guadalupe, the youngster possessed some emerging word recognition skills in English that could be further developed. Either way, Guadalupe would certainly be working at frustration level with grade level materials.

Guadalupe's spontaneous writing, while consisting of letter strings and drawing, reflected an attempt to convey a message. She demonstrated awareness of writing for a purpose and for an audience, and of the relationship between reading and writing as she used the letters she knew to attempt to write words. The stories she provided for her drawing were more coherent, grammatically, and syntactically correct in Spanish. The information obtained through screening with curriculum-based probes provided preliminary data and a foundation for more in-depth exploration of Guadalupe's academic strengths.

1. **Consider your own curriculum and philosophical approach to instruction.** How might you go about using curricular materials to measure students skills or progress?

2. **Develop your own probes for your reading curriculum.** Select two or three students on whom to practice. Remember, determine (a) words correct per minute (WCM) and (b) errors per minute on a one (1) minute timing per probe. Remember that the median WCM represents the students' final score. What information can be gained from administering probes? How would you use the information to guide instruction?

3. Current recommended approaches to the instruction of NELB students emphasize a holistic rather than discrete skills approach to instruction. What arguments can be made for including CBA methods in an integrative assessment when academic skills are being developed through a holistic instructional approach?

4. Consider Guadalupe's case. What other information would you want to obtain and how? What instructional strategies would you initiate? Some of these strategies should involve the home.

Curriculum-based measurement (CBM).

While CBA methods such as the one described may be prescriptive in attempts to match student needs with course content and instructional strategies, curriculum-based measurement, or CBM, is used to measure the effects of interventions (Shinn, Rosenfield & Knutson 1989). CBM represents a systematic set of assessment procedures which have been subject to extensive investigation (Deno 1989; Shinn 1989; Shinn, Tindall & Stein 1988). These procedures are standardized and are used to quantify student performance in the basic skill areas of reading fluency, math, spelling, and written expression (Knutson & Shinn 1991). Research in the development of curriculum-based reading comprehension measures continues (Fuchs & Fuchs 1992). There is empirical evidence of the reliability and validity of the procedures used in CBM, unlike those that may be used in other CBA or informal assessments ((Deno 1989; Fuchs & Fuchs 1992; Marston 1989). The measures used in CBM are of short duration (from one to three minutes). They are primarily fluency tasks that require students to produce a response (Knutson & Shinn 1991; Shinn & Knutson 1992). By applying a standardized set of procedures to the curriculum, multiple, alternate forms of the measures are obtained (Shinn, Tindall & Stein 1988). This makes CBM cost effective: new or alternate forms of tests do not have to be purchased. Furthermore, repeated samples of student performance can be obtained over time using the same procedures but using different content taken from the curriculum. Measures used for CBM by academic area, task requirement, administration time, and scoring are depicted in Table 6-9 (Knutson & Shinn 1991; Marston 1989; Shinn & Knutson 1992).

CBM measures are curriculum-, norm-, and individually-referenced procedures (Knutson & Shinn 1991; Shinn, Tindal & Stein 1988). The materials used for assessment are obtained from the actual curriculum being used with the students, thus the term curriculum-referenced. The students' performance on the CBM measures will provide an indication of their level of competence in the classroom or local school curricula. CBM measures are also norm-referenced in that local norms can be developed so that students' performance in the curricu-

**TABLE 6-9. CBM MEASURES USED TO ASSESS
ACADEMIC PERFORMANCE**

Academic area	Task	Time	Scoring
Reading[4]	Read aloud from basal reader	1 minute	Number of words read correctly
Spelling	Write dictated words	2 minutes	Number of correct letter sequences
Math	Answer computational problems	2 minutes	Number of digits correct
Written Expression	Write a story from a topic sentence or story starter	3 minutes	Number of words written, words spelled correctly, letters written, and/or correct word sequences

lum can be compared to that of their grade-level peers. Finally, CBM measures provide information regarding an individual student's rate of progress and improvement in the curriculum. The student's current rate of progress is compared to previous progress to determine if he or she is improving relative to an expected rate of growth (Knutson & Shinn 1991). In this manner, CBM measures are individually-referenced and provide information regarding the effectiveness of instructional strategies being used with the student.

Alberto's case demonstrates the use of modified CBM procedures to chart an individual student's progress in a Spanish basal reading series text. This case also exemplifies an educator's willingness to experiment, as it were, with an assessment method that was alien to her. She chose to become acquainted with one aspect of a method and apply it until she felt comfortable with it. Through her own experiences, the classroom teacher gained insight and expressed interest in learning more about alternative assessment. Briefly, Alberto was a fourth grade student who was failing in the native language (Spanish) curriculum. He was beginning to present behavior problems in the classroom. Curriculum-based assessments indicated that he was at a reading readiness (or emergent reader) level in Spanish. The severity of his reading problem prompted the teacher to focus on increasing Alberto's accuracy and fluency in reading. Alberto's teacher determined that it was important for him to master basic sight word vocabulary in order to increase fluency for comprehension. She wanted to document his progress in acquiring basic sight words as they were presented in each unit of the basal reader. In this manner, she could also monitor possible

---

[4] Oral reading fluency is measured in this manner. Reading comprehension is measured through administration of three-minute reading mazes wherein students are scored for words correct. Reading mazes are similar to cloze tests in that students must supply the words omitted in the reading passage, however, several response options are provided (Shinn & Knutson 1992).

difficulties he might encounter. She wanted to determine the general trend of Alberto's progress in reading in each unit. To check Alberto's comprehension, the teacher developed cloze tests based on passages in the readers. She also questioned Alberto orally about what he had read. Alberto reportedly became very interested in charting his own progress and other students soon wanted to do the same. This motivated Alberto even more and he became more willing to read frequently. Figures 6-5A and 6-5B reflect the reading probe results for Alberto.

By developing an error monitor form for her own use, the teacher identified specific areas that presented difficulties for Alberto. Although Alberto's progress was generally on an upward trend, the teacher realized that she might have been introducing new words prematurely, as he did not appear, on the whole, to be making gains rapidly. She also concluded that she must devise a way to ensure that Alberto would not lose any previously learned skills and that he would be able to apply them later when reading less familiar text. This would involve further study of how to develop probes that incorporated a wider range of reading skills, to use the data to set goals and evaluate graph results, and how to adjust both goals and instructional strategies based on the data collected (Fuchs & Fuchs 1991; Fuchs & Deno 1991). This case also highlights the importance of collaboration of educators across disciplines in the school setting.

USING CBA AND CBM WITH NELB STUDENTS

Basic considerations.

Several considerations must be taken into account when CBA and CBM procedures are used for the assessment of NELB students. These relate to

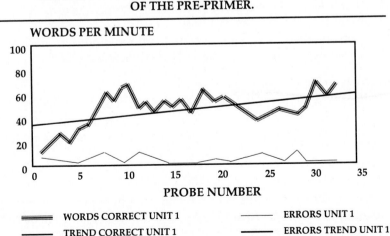

FIGURE 6-5A. ALBERTO'S RESPONSES ON UNIT ONE
OF THE PRE-PRIMER.

FIGURE 6-5B. ALBERTO'S RESPONSES ON UNIT TWO
OF THE PRE-PRIMER.

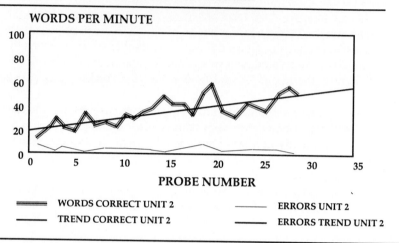

student, curricular, instructional, and assessment characteristics that are unique for NELB students. Table 6-10 summarizes some basic considerations when CBA and CBM are chosen as methods to assess NELB students (Larrinaga McGee 1991).

When using CBA and CBM with NELB students, questions must be asked prior to assessment regarding language background and current language status. The instructional approaches, materials, and programs used with the students must be identified. Consultation and collaboration among educators are necessary in order to define areas to be assessed. The appropriate native language and English language materials must be identified for development of probes. If inter-individual or group performance comparisons are to be made, NELB students' must be matched with peers of the same origin and background. Finally, student progress needs to be monitored through repeated assessment using the curricular materials previously identified.

Advantages of CBA and CBM.

Evaluating NELB students through CBA and CBM methods has several attractive features. First, there are various established procedures from which to select, depending on the purpose of the evaluation. Once the measures or procedures have been selected or developed, they can be administered easily and quickly, thus proving time efficient for the educator. Additionally, students may react positively in that they are able to observe and discuss their progress (Bean & Lane 1990). Students become interested in their own learning, thus increasing motivation and, consequently, achievement (Bean & Lane 1990; Z. De Jesus, personal communication, January, 1991).

TABLE 6-10. BASIC CONSIDERATIONS FOR THE USE OF CBA AND CBM WITH NON-ENGLISH LANGUAGE BACKGROUND STUDENTS

I. Student Characteristics

A. Language Background

What is the student's primary home language?

Does the student speak a dialect or the more standard form of the language?

Does this language have an oral or written tradition?

Did the student learn the language in an urban or rural setting?

Did the student have educational experiences in this language? How long?

B. Current Language Status

Has language dominance been established?

Has language proficiency been evaluated?

Is the student participating in ESOL only?

Is the student receiving native language instruction?

II. Curricular/Instructional Characteristics

Which ESOL approach is used? Which materials?

Are native language materials used? Which?

How are reading, writing, and mathematics taught?

Is a literature-based, basal reader, or combination of both, approach used for reading instruction? Which materials?

What is the student's schedule of classes? Curricular opportunities?

What are the teacher's expectations for performance?

What is the teacher's instructional style?

III. Assessment Characteristics

Consultation among or with the ESOL, native language, and mainstream teachers.

Definition of areas to be assessed.

Selection of appropriate native language and/or English language materials.

Matching of targeted student with a peer or peers of SIMILAR:

-Age and gender (if possible)

-Years in school

-Country of origin

-Language background and current language status

-Participation and years in ESOL

-Educational or curricular experiences

Application of the CBA method selected. This may be to an individual student, or if comparisons are being made, to comparison or control peer(s).

Monitoring of progress through repeated assessment using curricular materials.

Second, CBM methods are adaptable to the content being assessed. There is flexibility with regard to the methods that can be used to assess students. They can be used with traditional basal readers, literature-based approaches to reading instruction, and content area materials. Reading rate measures as used in CBM can be compatible with developmental models of reading (Potter & Wamre 1990). Recall comments made in Chapter Five regarding the need for NELB students to be able to decode words and phrases accurately and quickly in order to free attention for the task of comprehension. When evaluating NELB students, CBA fills in the information gaps left by standardized tests with regard to academic or language performance in the actual curriculum. The techniques used can be applied to curricula written in other languages. In the absence of educators who speak the students' language(s), paraprofessionals who do speak the students' language(s) can be trained to use the techniques to gather data. Table 6-11 demonstrates a sight vocabulary word list probe developed in Haitian Creole from a primary level reader in this language (Jean-Jacques 1982).

Third, by careful recording of student responses and collection of group data, much-needed information regarding learning patterns and academic growth of NELB students can be documented over time. Data obtained through CBA and CBM can be used for screening purposes, to obtain diagnostic information, and to make decisions regarding instructional strategies. In some instances, data may be used to determine special education eligibility; however,

TABLE 6-11. HAITIAN CREOLE SIGHT VOCABULARY READING PROBE

Yon ti pa sou chemen an
creole

dousman	bon	uit	bezwen	lapenn	mwa	byen	(7)
floup	mwen	kwen	bon	floup	bven	lapenn	(14)
mwen	uit	dousman	bezwen	mwa	kwen	kwen	(21)
floup	bon	mwa	dousman	mwen	bezwen	byen	(28)
uit	lapenn	bezwen	mwen	byen	mwa	kwen	(35)
lapenn	floup	dousman	bon	uit	byen	floup	(42)
lapenn	mwa	mwen	uit	kwen	bon	bezwen	(49)
dousman	mwa	bezwen	byen	mwen	kwen	floup	(56)
bon	dousman	lapenn	uit	kwen	bezwen	lapenn	(63)
byen	uit	floup	mwen	bon	dousman	mwa	(70)
kwen	bezwen	uit	bon	floup	lapenn	mwa	(77)
mwen	dousman	byen	dousman	floup	mwa	kwen	(84)
uit	lapenn	bon	bezwen	mwen	byen	kwen	(91)
bezwen	floup	byen	uit	mwa	mwen	dousman	(98)
bon	lapenn	mwen	bon	mwa	uit	byen	kwen	(106)
floup	dousman	bezwen	lapenn	byen	uit		(112)
bezwen	bon	floup	mwa	dousman	kwen	mwen	(119)
lapenn	dousman	bezwen	byen	kwen	mwa	floup	(126)
mwen	uit	lapenn	bon	uit	dousman	bezwen	(133)

there are indications that use of CBM procedures for eligibility purposes may also lead to overidentification of minority students as handicapped (Braden 1991; Lombard 1988). In this case, it is necessary to obtain information regarding the performance of comparable students. That is, a student's performance should be compared to other students of the same racial and ethnic background. In the case of NELB students, these should be compared with other students who have had the same opportunities to learn English and similar educational experiences in general (Shinn & Tindal 1988). One of the authors has had occasion to compare siblings' performance as, for example, in the case of twins or that of siblings who may be placed in the same grade level because parents waited to send an older child to school until the younger child was old enough to attend as well. In one case, both students, one year apart in age, were placed in the same grade.

The case of Alberto, the fourth grader encountered in the previous discussion, and Ricardo demonstrates the usefulness of comparison between youngsters of the same background. This case also reveals how a modified CBM procedure can be used to identify areas for change in instructional practices, in this case to develop more effective writing abilities in NELB students. Recall that Alberto was in fourth grade and failing. It was necessary to first obtain an idea as to the degree of Alberto's problems as compared to his peers. In this modified CBM technique, the teacher identified a comparison student. This comparison student was deemed by the teacher to be performing at an average level in the classroom and across content areas. The comparison student was of similar linguistic and cultural background, had been in the native language and ESOL program for the same length of time, and when school records were compared, appeared to have, on the whole, a similar educational background. Probes were prepared in the areas of reading and math computations. On this occasion, the students were encouraged to write about their personal interests to obtain a measure of written expression. Reading and writing probes were in Spanish, since both youngsters were monolingual in this language. Table 6-12 contains the results of the probes.

The results of the reading and computations probes suggested that Alberto was, in fact, performing significantly below Ricardo in these two areas. Ricardo's score represents the rate of performance expected by the classroom teacher because she had identified him as performing at an average level in her class. Ricardo's score was divided by Alberto's score to obtain a measure of the extent of the discrepancy between expected performance and Alberto's actual performance (this discrepancy formula has been suggested by Shinn & Tindal 1988; however, they suggest using the performance of a group of similar peers on the probes as the expectancy standard. A minimum of seven to ten students should be used to develop classroom level norms according to Shinn & Knutson 1992.). When using CBM in this manner, differences of two or more times discrepant are considered significant (Shinn & Tindal 1988). Alberto's rates were far below

TABLE 6-12. PROBE RESULTS FOR ALBERTO AND RICARDO

ACADEMIC PROBE	SOURCE	ALBERTO'S RATE	RICARDO'S RATE	DISCREPANT
Reading passages	Spanish 4th grade basal reader	15 WCM 32 E	153 WCM 2 E	10.2 x
Math computations (mixed facts)	Grade level text	20 digits corr/min	70 digits corr/min	3.5 x
Written expression	Spontaneous	No words	6 "words"	No difference

what was considered to be average performance in this classroom. The results of the written expression probe were more surprising. Figure 6-6 and Figure 6-7 illustrate Alberto's and Ricardo's written expression responses.

As can be seen, Alberto was unable to develop a written narrative but resorted to drawing a picture and providing some form of graphic explanation. Alberto then provided an oral narrative in Spanish, saying "The horse is my favorite horse and I like to ride it and bathe it and take care of it. That is what I love the most—the horse." On the other hand, Ricardo resorted to a brief listing of activities, which he stated were "play four-square, play soccer, run." He also wrote an unintelligible word that represented his understanding of the pronunciation of a game played during physical education, "igar." These responses revealed not only significant differences between the boys' approach to the task, but also pointed to the possibility that writing in the classroom was limited to answering questions in textbooks or similar formats. In fact, follow-up discussion with the teacher revealed that creative writing was not a part of the curriculum because of the belief that the students needed to be prepared as quickly as possible to handle English textbooks. Furthermore, she believed that the students' tight schedule did not permit time for free writing. Screening of two students with a CBM technique provided opportunity for further discussion regarding the possible implementation of a writing program, including free writing, across content areas.

In some instances, educators may wish to compare an individual or group of NELB students' performance with that of their native English speaking peers in the classroom or in the same grade across the school setting. In this case, a contrastive approach to assessment is undertaken, that is, the NELB students' performance is contrasted with that of native English speakers to determine the extent of the differences in performance. This can be helpful in determining the level(s) at which NELB students must be able to perform in a particular area in

Elapoedio
Aimeuloro'
Emiahea fopro
Malasamila

" El caballo es mi caballo favorito y a mi me gusta
correrlo y bañarlo y cuidarlo. Eso es lo que yo más
quiero — el caballo." (Oral rendition of message intended)

Figure 6-6. Alberto's Story

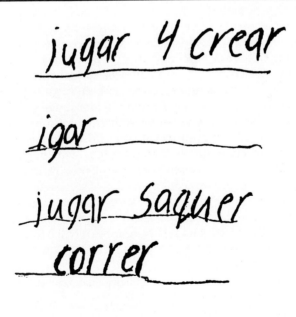

Figure 6-7. Ricardo's Story

order to successfully compete with their native English speaking peers. The degree to which NELB students' performance is different from or equal to that of native English speaking peers is analyzed. Academic goals are established and instruction geared towards NELB students' attainment of these goals for successful performance. By developing norms through CBM procedures, information can be gathered to assist in making decisions about transitioning LEP students into an all English curriculum or into English reading if they are in bilingual classrooms. Furthermore, CBM norms can help evaluate the effectiveness of programs based on language of instruction (Dayan 1992). If district level curriculum-based norms are available, NELB students' standing in relation to that of the larger population can be examined. Table 6-13 summarizes the utility of CBA and CBM procedures when used with NELB students (Larrinaga-McGee 1988).

When gathering curriculum-based data for comparative or contrastive purposes, it is helpful to develop a systematic method of record keeping. Figures 6-8, 6-9A, and 6-9B illustrate data collection forms that can become part of the body of academic performance data being gathered on students instructed through holistic approaches (Abrams, Herrity, LaBrot 1991). These data collection forms pertain to the assessment of reading fluency and emerging literacy behaviors of students.

Among NELB students there may be those who have never had the opportunity to learn or whose educational experiences have been limited by events beyond their control. Students such as these may be judged to be "untestable" or be singled out as candidates for special education programs because they do so poorly on standardized tests. Within an integrative, curriculum-based model, an evaluator can tap into a wider range of behaviors and abilities. For example, pre-literacy, emergent literacy, and literacy behaviors can be observed or elicited. If students are literate, IRIs, cloze passages, Sentence Verification, or text structure maps can be completed with native language or ESOL texts and materials. If students are pre-literate, a curriculum-based listening assessment can be conducted by means of story retell with literature or text commonly used in the classroom. Elements of story grammars can be

TABLE 6-13. UTILITY OF CBA AND CBM WITH NELB STUDENTS

Application	Purpose
Single Case Study	Longitudinal Analysis
Matched Cohorts or Siblings	Comparative Analysis
Peer Group (classroom or across grade level)	Comparative: Group of Origin or Contrastive: Native English Group
District Group	Normative Analysis

FIGURE 6-8. SUMMARY OF CURRICULUM-BASED ASSESSMENT
(CBA) CONVENTIONAL READING, NON-ENGLISH LANGUAGE
BACKGROUND STUDENTS

Student: Teacher:
School: Evaluator:
Grade: Date(s):

Sight Vocabulary: _____ Literature Words List in Native Language and/
                          or English
                  _____ Content Areas Words List in Native Language
                          and/or English

Accuracy on sight vocabulary is assessed by having the student attempt to
read each word as it is presented. The number of words read correctly
indicates the student's accuracy with these words. When a student can
read 85 percent of the words, fluency (rate) is also assessed. The student
reads the words from three randomized lists for one minute each. The
number of words correct per minute (wcm) and number of errors (e) are
determined for each timing. The median or middle score is felt to be the
most valid estimate of the student's fluency (or automatic recognition).
Similar procedures are used to assess the performance of a comparison
student.

WORDS LIST FROM TEXT _____
                                        (Name)

TOTAL NUMBER OF WORDS READ CORRECTLY

	NATIVE LANGUAGE			ENGLISH		
ACCURACY	WCM	E	% Correct	WCM	E	% Correct
Referred Student	____	____	____	____	____	____
Comparison Student	____	____	____	____	____	____
FLUENCY						
Referred Student	____	____	____	____	____	____
Comparison Student	____	____	____	____	____	____

COMMENTS:

From: Abrams, P., Herrity, M.S. & LaBrot, P. (1991). *Curriculum-Based Assessment (CBA) Handbook.* Orlando, FL:
Orange County Public Schools. Reprinted with permission.

analyzed or emerging literacy behaviors checklists completed. Direct assessment of literate students includes assessment of word or phrase identification
skills to determine rates of reading fluency and accuracy. Comprehension and
metalinguistic reading strategies can also be documented by use of CBA and
CBM type techniques. For example, Figure 6-10 demonstrates a data collection
form that can be used to document students' understanding of the language of
textbooks (see Chapter Three section on expository text organization; see also
Howie 1984). Students' responses are compared to those of peers of similar
background.

FIGURE 6-9A. SUMMARY OF CURRICULUM-BASED ASSESSMENT (CBA) EMERGENT LITERACY

Student:	Teacher:
School:	Evaluator:
Grade:	Date(s):

Concepts About Print (Reading):

Concepts about print (reading) are assessed by asking the student to read a familiar storybook aloud, observing reading behavior, and questioning for specific concepts. Storybook reading is categorized by whether the student attends to pictures, formulates a story from pictures, or attempts to read the print.

Check if demonstrated		
Referred	Comparison	
		Book Handling Knowledge Holds the book right side up
		Begins at/identifies front of book
		Opens book correctly/turns pages (front-to-back, one-by-one)
		Print Contains Message Knows where to start
		Points to print
		Knows which way to go
		Knowledge of Terminology/Conventions Word
		Letter
		Space
		First/last letter in a word
		Period/question mark
		Capital letter
		Storybook Reading* Attending to Pictures, Not Forming Stories
		Attending to Pictures, Reading and Story Telling Mixed
		Attending to Pictures, Forming Written Stories (sounds like reading a story)
		Attending to Print

*Categories from Simplified Version of E. Sulzby's Classification Scheme for Children's Emergent Reading of Favorite Storybooks

Source: Abrams, P., Herrity, M.S. & LaBrot, P. (1991). *Curriculum-Based Assessment (CBA) Handbook.* Orlando, FL: Orange County Public Schools. Reprinted with permission.

In conclusion, CBA and CBM methods have much to offer the evaluator. These methods provide systematic guidance for the development of contextualized measures for NELB students and for direct assessment of

FIGURE 6-9B. CONTINUATION CBA, EMERGENT LITERACY

Name/Date

Concepts About Print (Writing):

Concepts about print (writing) are assessed by having the student write a story and reread his or her writing. Three aspects of writing are evaluated: written language level, message quality, and directional principles.

Check if demonstrated		
Referred	Comparison	
		Written Language Level** Drawing
		Scribble
		Nonphonetic letter strings
		Copying
		Invented Spelling
		Conventional
		Message Quality Comprehends that a message is conveyed
		Copies a message
		Uses repetitive sentence patterns
		Attempts to record own ideas
		Shows successful composition
		Directional Principles No evidence of directional knowledge
		Part of directional pattern is known
		Directional pattern is reversed
		Correct patterns are employed consistently

**Categories from: E. Sulzby's Forms of Writing

Source: Abrams, P., Herrity, M.S. & LaBrot, P. (1991). *Curriculum-Based Assessment (CBA) Handbook.* Orlando, FL: Orange County Public Schools. Reprinted with permission.

FIGURE 6-10. CURRICULUM-BASED ASSESSMENT (CBA): UNDERSTANDING TEXTBOOK LANGUAGE

Student understanding of the language used in classroom textbooks is assessed by selecting three passages from the text. Passages are chosen randomly from the text. The student is asked to read orally from each passage for one minute each. Reading accuracy and rate are determined to ensure that the student is able to read the passages fluently. The student may reread the passages after reading rate is determined. Through oral or written response format, the student is asked to answer questions at the passage, sentence, words, and concepts levels. The student also provides personal commentary about the passages. For example, the evaluator can model, through a self-talk technique, how to identify text organization. The evaluator can say "I will read this passage to find signal words that will help me know how the information is presented." If the text has words that signal comparison and contrast, the evaluator states or writes down the words. The evaluator then identifies and states the concepts that are compared and contrasted. Similarities and differences between concepts can be identified and presented as evidence of the organization of the passage.

STUDENT NAME: _____   GRADE: _____

TEXTBOOK: _____ ENGLISH _____   NON-ENGLISH _____

PASSAGES SELECTED: 1. _____
                         2. _____
                         3. _____

PASSAGE NUMBER/ SAMPLE RESPONSE	STUDENT		COMPARISON PEER	
	E*	NE	E	NE
PASSAGES				
Identifies the organization of each passage: a) descriptive b) enumerative c) sequence d) cause/effect e) comparison/contrast f) problem/solution g) no structure identified 1. _____ 2 _____ 3. _____				
Identifies the purpose of each passage: a) to tell what something is like b) to provide information about a main topic c) to provide directions for doing something 1. _____ 2 _____ 3. _____				

*E = Evident   NE = Not Evident

PASSAGE NUMBER/ SAMPLE RESPONSE	STUDENT		COMPARISON PEER	
	E*	NE	E	NE
PASSAGES				
d) to tell why something happens e) to show similarities/differences f) to persuade the reader g) no purpose identified 1. _____ 2. _____ 3. _____				
Identifies where the topic is presented in each passage 1. _____ 2. _____ 3. _____				
Identifies how the topic is presented in each passage 1. _____ 2. _____ 3. _____				
States what prior knowledge the reader requires to understand the passage 1. _____ 2. _____ 3. _____				
SENTENCES				
Identifies variety in sentences 1. _____ 2. _____ 3. _____				
Understands the syntax and grammar of sentences (a) or Perceives the sentences to be too complex (b) 1. _____ 2. _____ 3. _____				

(continued on page 306)

*E = Evident   NE = Not Evident

PASSAGE NUMBER/ SAMPLE RESPONSE	STUDENT		COMPARISON PEER	
	E*	NE	E	NE
SENTENCES				
Identifies whether sentences present several concepts (a) or one idea (b) 1. ___ 2. ___ 3. ___				
Identifies referents (e.g. pronouns) and their antecedents in and across sentences 1. ___ 2. ___ 3. ___				
Identifies sentence structure as relevant to the meaning of the passage: a) sequences combined with examples b) sequences presented in an established order with numbers c) topic sentence and supporting detail d) sentence includes likeness or differences e) topic sentence with a description of problem and solutions following f) no specific structure identified 1. ___ 2. ___ 3. ___				
WORDS				
Identifies transition words that show logical relationships: a) enumerative (first, next, finally) b) sequence (then, before, after, finally) c) cause/effect (so, so that, because, since, in order to) d) problem/solution (a problem is, the answer) e) no transition words identified 1. ___ 2. ___ 3. ___				
Identifies words with multiple meanings 1. ___ 2. ___ 3. ___				

*E = Evident   NE = Not Evident

PASSAGE NUMBER/ SAMPLE RESPONSE	STUDENT		COMPARISON PEER	
	E*	NE	E	NE
CONCEPTS				
Provides simple synonyms for difficult words identified 1. _____ 2. _____ 3. _____				
Describes how new vocabulary words are presented (e.g. highlighting, italics, underlining) 1. _____ 2. _____ 3. _____				
Predicts main ideas from titles 1. _____ 2. _____ 3. _____				
Predicts subordinate ideas from subheadings 1. _____ 2. _____ 3. _____				
Identifies the topic sentence and the main idea 1. _____ 2. _____ 3. _____				
Identifies points that clarify and restrict the main idea in the topic sentence 1. _____ 2. _____ 3. _____				
Identifies details, examples, or reasons that support the main idea 1. _____ 2. _____ 3. _____				

*E = Evident   NE = Not Evident

(continued on page 308)

PERSONAL COMMENTARY

Perceives the language of the text as (a) easy, or (b) difficult.

Reasons: _____

_____

EVALUATOR COMMENTS: _____

_____

_____ EVALUATOR

academic skills and abilities. NELB students' performance is examined in the context of the instructional environment and the actual curriculum. In this manner, what is being taught is evaluated and student progress is monitored.

Disadvantages of CBA and CBM.

While CBA and CBM procedures hold promise in the academic assessment of NELB students, several factors must be considered before deciding to use these methods. First, for several of the methods that fall under the umbrella term of CBA, excluding CBM, there are issues related to the properties of reliability and validity of the procedures. Although CBM measures have been investigated thoroughly and found to be reliable and valid for native English speaking students, the same information is not available for NELB students. The information that is available suggests that CBM procedures retain their reliability and validity when applied to Spanish curricula (Dayan 1992). In addition, there are no guidelines with respect to what constitutes optimal reading rates for NELB students. There is no information regarding what differences in rates of performance might be expected, given students' linguistic and cultural backgrounds. Some students may be unaccustomed to timed tasks. The argument has been made that CBM ignores cultural factors (Braden 1991). Indeed, academic skills instruction varies across languages, cultures, and countries. Although attempts may be made to compare NELB students performance with that of others of the same origin and with similar educational opportunities, educators may find such a group to be heterogeneous in its composition. For example, one group of Mexican American students may be migratory, while others with the same ethnic background may be stable residents of a particular area. In this case, it would be difficult to control for curricular experiences.

Second, when CBA and CBM methods such as those described previously are used with NELB students, there is the danger of falling into assessment of discrete skills rather than of whole processes. There are concerns regarding the appropriateness of the possible use of drills, based on such assessment, to intervene in weak areas identified. In this case, assessment is geared towards determining whether or not specific subskills have been mastered. While this information is needed to guide instruction and to develop short-term instructional objectives, it is not sufficient to measure progress towards long-term curricular goals (Fuchs & Deno 1991; Fuchs & Fuchs 1991). Although there are CBM procedures to measure progress toward long-term goals, to be effective in the evaluation of NELB students, both CBA and CBM must become part of the greater whole in an integrative, interactive evaluation and instruction framework.

Third, the preparation of curriculum-based probes requires careful planning and construction. This may be considered time consuming, given the many other responsibilities of educators. Additionally, formal training is necessary if CBA and CBM are to be implemented. Once implemented, on-going discussion and consultation among educators would be helpful and necessary (Alberto's case is an example). However, such factors as optimal size and composition of discussion groups, the frequency of meetings, and possible ways to facilitate interaction have not been determined (Wesson 1991).

Finally, an integrative approach to assessment suggests that NELB students be evaluated, ideally, in the non-English, as well as English, languages. Curricular materials in the non-English language(s) may not be readily available. Furthermore, NELB students' curricula may be fragmented. For example, students may be taught English with one set of materials devised for ESOL students, may then receive reading instruction in another set of materials, and may use yet another set of materials for a language arts component. They may be instructed by several teachers with differing instructional styles and philosophical approaches to instruction. In this case, information obtained through CBA or CBM will be very specific to the particular materials and methods used and may not be useful in providing a global view of students' progress in acquiring English. In a case such as this, it is important that the curriculum and program be examined carefully to determine the extent to which it is contributing to student failure or success. Involvement of NELB students' families in the educational process and participation of diverse linguistic and cultural groups in the selection of the curriculum are steps in the process of achieving greater effectiveness with CBA and CBM methods when these are used for evaluation (Braden 1991).

In conclusion, CBA and CBM are evaluation and measurement methods that can be adapted and applied to existing instructional practices, that is, to traditional (where, for example, the primary text used for reading instruction is the basal reader) or holistic instruction. CBA procedures can be used to determine students' language needs and progress by identifying activities and skills that can help NELB students become more effective communicators (Nelson 1989). Whether in ESOL or native language instruction, or in the mainstream, CBA and CBM can be used to provide data on student academic performance and progress. The key to their usefulness with NELB students lies in the degree to which the information obtained through their use is validated by other sources of information. CBA and CBM are most meaningful when used in the context of culturally and linguistically appropriate curricula, instructional methods, and of a holistic approach to instruction in general. The strongest argument that can be made in favor of the use of CBA and CBM with NELB students lies in the availability of additional relevant data and subsequent, enhanced decision-making power which these methods can provide. Additionally, the link between the curriculum, instruction, and assessment proposed by CBA and CBM make them appealing alternatives for use with NELB students. The underlying premise that valid instructional assessment occurs when curricular materials are used as the "tests," provides a theoretical foundation to develop an assessment framework.

RESEARCH IN PRACTICE:
CBA and CBM with NELB Students

1. Read additional information on curriculum-based assessment and curriculum-based measurement. The references provided in this section can be initial resources for further study.

2. Select an academic area in which you would apply CBA or CBM. Since detailed information regarding the development of all types of probes is not contained in this section, it is suggested that further reading be completed first. Construct probes for the area chosen. Administer the probes. How can the information obtained be used to determine instructional strategies for the student(s) evaluated? Share and discuss your findings with colleagues.

SUMMARIZING SECTION TWO
Using curricular materials for assessment and construction of academic measures

This section focussed on two related, but not necessarily equal, methods of systematic data collection which fall under the umbrella term of *curriculum-based assessment*. Curriculum-based assessment (CBA) and curriculum-based measurement (CBM) are defined. Their use with NELB students is exemplified. The purpose of this section is to provide information and demonstrate the application of alternative, systematic methods for assessing academic and language performance. There is a dearth of information regarding the use of CBA and CBM with NELB students; however, these methods hold promise for reducing bias in assessment.

WHAT CAN YOU DO?

1. When using new or alternative methods of assessment, it is usually helpful to begin using them with individual or small groups of students first. Additionally, it is helpful to discuss any difficulties or successes with colleagues. Introduce the topic of CBA and CBM to colleagues. Form a study group which will serve as a means of sharing experiences and information. Document those factors that contribute to the success of the study group.

2. How can CBA or CBM methods be applied in your particular setting? Consider some of the advantages and disadvantages of using CBA and CBM in your setting.

SUMMARY OF CHAPTER SIX
Assessing academic performance through contextualized measures

This chapter examined various methods that can be used to evaluate NELB students' academic behaviors and performance within the context of the educational setting. Several types of performance, process, and alternative assessment procedures were presented. The procedures and methods include: interviews, observation and anecdotal record keeping, teacher designed performance tests, rating scales, and checklists, informal reading inventories, curriculum-based assessment (CBA) and curriculum-based measurement (CBM). They were presented as congruent with trends in instruction and relevant to the identification of learning problems or opportunities for learning and instruction.

Further focus on CBA and CBM described them as evaluation and measurement procedures that can be adapted and applied to existing instructional practices. They provide quantitative, as well as qualitative, data on student performance and progress within the curriculum. These data are then used to make instructional decisions. Furthermore, data can be used to measure students' short or long term progress or to compare and contrast students' performance with that of other NELB students or native English speaking students. This chapter suggests that CBA and CBM are most meaningful when used with culturally and linguistically relevant curricular materials to assess NELB students. CBA and CBM can be useful tools with which to identify NELB students' academic strengths or problem areas. To be useful with NELB students, however, CBA and CBM must be part of the larger whole that is an integrative and interactive approach to assessment and instruction.

The chapter that follows, Chapter Seven, discusses the importance of advocacy in promoting effective assessment procedures. The chapter presents historical developments in the assessment of NELB and LEP students. Traditional psychoeducational assessment practices are examined and the role of evaluation specialists within the paradigm of an integrative approach to assessment is discussed. It provides a foundation for Chapter Eight which focuses on the use of both formal and informal performance-based measures to identify special needs NELB students.

Chapter 7

Advocacy in the Assessment Process

This chapter discusses the importance of advocacy in the assessment process with limited English proficient (LEP) and non-English language background (NELB) students. The chapter is designed to assist monolingual as well as bilingual evaluation specialists and consumers of assessment information to better meet the special needs of culturally and linguistically diverse students. It prepares practitioners to think in new directions, to develop additional expertise, and to use multiple sources of information in addition to standard testing practices when making assessment decisions for individual students.

The chapter first examines how historical developments in the field of assessment have evolved to promote more equitable assessment practices with LEP and NELB populations. The chapter then presents basic differences in the assessment of LEP and monolingual English proficient speakers and some of the practical difficulties involved in accurately assessing LEP populations. This information lays a foundation for the discussions of the advocate's role in the assessment process and the advocate's role in promoting effective systems that follow. Concrete examples and positive guidelines are offered to assist educators, school psychologists, speech-language pathologists, school social workers and others in incorporating the material presented into daily practices.

SECTION ONE

HISTORICAL PERSPECTIVE OF ASSESSMENT OF LEP AND NELB POPULATIONS

Scholars have addressed the controversies surrounding the assessment of LEP and NELB populations for a large part of the twentieth century. Over the past two to three decades, testing practices with culturally and linguistically different students have come under particular scrutiny (Figueroa 1990; Oakland 1973; Olmedo 1981). Researchers and policy makers have called for equitable assessment practices appropriate for the populations to be served. The overrepresentation and underrepresentation of NELB students in the exceptional student education programs of our nation's schools have been identified but not remedied (Cummins 1989; Fradd & Vega 1987).

As early as 1973, two large scale conferences were held to initiate a concerted effort aimed at improving tests and their use with minority populations. These were the First Annual International Multilingual Multicultural Conference held in San Diego and the National Conference on Testing in Education and Employment held in Hampton, Virginia (Oakland 1973). Since that time, a multitude of national, state and local psychological and educational meetings and conferences have addressed assessment issues and concerns related to NELB clients.

In addition, testing companies begin to examine, review, and renorm major cognitive assessment instruments, considering their appropriateness for minority group children (Oakland 1973). For the first time, the 1972 Norms Edition of the Stanford-Binet Intelligence Scale, Form L-M (Terman & Merrill 1973) included black and Spanish surnamed individuals in the instrument's normative sample. Likewise, the 1974 revision of the Wechsler Intelligence Scale for Children included non-whites for the first time in the test's standardization sample, and an attempt was made to modify or eliminate items felt to be biased to certain groups of youngsters (Wechsler 1974).

Attempts have also been made to create culture-fair and culture-free tests to assess ethnic minorities, but to date these have not been successful (Sattler 1988). Practitioners pointed out that all tests are culturally loaded. Tests that eliminate prior learning and cultural experiences do not exist (Sattler 1988; Westby 1990). Even if a true culture-free test of intelligence were developed, it would not be relevant to the production of intelligent behavior within a specific culture or across cultural settings (Reynolds 1982).

Since there were no non-biased assessment tools, attempts were made to limit bias. Much of what has been developed during the past two decades has been based on adaptations of traditional standardized tests for use with ethnic and linguistic minorities. For example, the System of Multicultural Pluralistic Assessment (SOMPA) (Mercer & Lewis 1978) used a pluralistic model to interpret the scores of culturally different youngsters on the Wechsler Intelligence Scale for Children-Revised (WISC-R). Corrected WISC-R scores, called Estimated Learning Potentials (ELPs), are obtained, based on the child's socio-cultural background. These corrected scores are a way of augmenting scores for culturally different examinees. The appropriateness of these ELPs has not been established. Using ELPs instead of IQs to predict academic achievement has not been supported by research. One clear limitation for NELB students who are limited in English proficiency is that the ELPs are based on WISC-Rs administered in English (Wilen & Sweeting 1986).

In addition, innovations in minimizing bias, such as the developmental and dynamic approaches, have been suggested for use with the minority and NELB populations (Chamberlain 1987; Holtzman & Wilkinson 1991; Larry P. Task Force 1989). However, although these theoretical approaches have been available for a number of years, their practical application to individual diagnostic assessment in the school setting remains questionable. These approaches are briefly discussed next.

Developmental assessment is based on the theory and developmental stages of Jean Piaget. Cognitive development is seen as an adaptation and reorganization of psychological structures based on interactions of the individual with the environment. Assimilation, accommodation, and equilibration are key factors (see Hergenhan 1982 and Swenson 1980 for a more thorough discussion of these concepts). The presence of cognitive structure is assessed and evaluated in terms of the level of conceptual development within the examinee. This process places conceptual development at one of several stages depending on whether: (a) a concept is emerging; (b) a concept is in the early developmental stages still necessitating cues; or (c) a concept is at the level of a generalized and functional concept in daily life (Larry P. Task Force 1989).

The Cartoon Conservation Scales (CCS) (De Avilla 1980) is a test of intellectual development in cartoon format based on Piagetian developmental theory. It is intended for use with children of diverse linguistic and ethnic backgrounds. The relationship between scores on this test and school functioning has not been established, and at this time it appears inappropriate to use the CCS as a diagnostic tool to identify handicaps in youngsters (Holtzman & Wilkinson 1991).

Dynamic assessment is a non-standardized approach which includes teaching, learning, and mediation during testing. The examiner tries to help the examinee learn how to learn new information successfully (Larry P. Task Force 1989). The Learning Potential Assessment Device (LPAD) (Feurstein 1979) developed in Israel is an example of a dynamic assessment instrument allowing flexibility in test situations including the use of a student's home language or a combination of English and the home language. Difficulties include limited training opportunities for examiners, lengthy administration time, inconsistent results affected by the administration of different tasks to the same examinee if assessed by different examiners, and a lack of evidence that the test predicts scholastic achievement (Caterino 1990; Holtzman & Wilkinson 1991). Though dynamic assessment might provide valuable information for individualized intervention, it is not recommended for diagnostic use at this time (Larry P. Task Force 1989).

To date, there is no instrument or test battery that provides an easy answer to the difficulties involved in the assessment of LEP and NELB students with varying degrees of linguistic proficiency in English and their home languages (Wilen & Sweeting 1986). As a result of the lack of readily available alternatives, assessment personnel continue to rely primarily on standardized testing practices developed for use with mainstream learners in making diagnostic decisions about these students.

Litigation and legislation relative to the assessment of NELB students have resulted from the inappropriate use of assessment instruments and the inappropriate application of the information generated from these practices. In terms of their impact on assessment practices, *Diana v. State Board of Education* (1970) and P.L. 94-142, The Education for All Handicapped Children Act (1975) are the most notable. *Diana* found that Mexican American students in California were misdiagnosed as mentally retarded based on biased testing practices. These practices included the administration of intelligence tests in English to predominantly Spanish-speaking students and a failure of tests to account for the effects of cultural background factors. California agreed to an out-of-court settlement which included proposed remedies to inequitable assessment and special education placement for NELB students (Figueroa 1990). When Congress passed P.L. 94-142, it established that test materials be selected and administered without racial or cultural bias and that tests be administered in a student's native language unless it is clearly not feasible. This federal legislation underscores the need to use non-English languages in the assessment process (Fradd & Vega 1987).

Years later school psychologists, speech-language pathologists, and educational diagnosticians continue to wrestle with the question of how to conduct appropriate assessments of NELB populations. Even in the aftermath of stipulations and mandates, appropriately normed tests for NELB students residing in the United States are lacking, and most practitioners still do not have the training, knowledge, and experience to meet the unique needs of the growing and diverse NELB school population.

Efforts are being made to address the need for improved training and practices. For example, *Standards for Educational and Psychological Testing* (American Educational Research Association, American Psychological Association & National Council on Measurement in Education 1985), a widely used reference on assessment, includes a chapter on testing linguistic minorities. The *Standards* indicate that tests administered in English to non-native speakers of English may become tests of English language or literacy rather than measures of the skills for which the tests are intended. The chapter offers suggestions for improvement that move beyond traditional practices in addressing the unique needs of culturally and linguistically diverse students.

New guidelines and federal legislation requiring expertise regarding the effects of culture and ethnicity on service provision appear to be emerging. The *Guidelines for Psychological Practice with Ethnic and Culturally Diverse Populations* from the American Psychological Association and the revision of the Education for All Handicapped Children Act, renamed the Individuals with Disabilities Education Act, P.L. 101-476, are examples. The effective implementation of these recent directives and others requires enhanced knowledge bases and training to better meet the needs of culturally and linguistically diverse populations (Perry & Rothlisberg 1991).

SUMMARIZING SECTION ONE:
Historical Perspective of Assessment of LEP and NELB Populations

---

This section presented efforts made over the last twenty to thirty years to implement more equitable assessment practices with LEP and NELB populations. The creation of culture-fair and culture-free tests, adaptations of traditional tests, and the use of developmental and dynamic approaches have been attempted, but to date no test instrument or battery provides a solution to the problems involved in assessing NELB students with varying degrees of proficiency in their first language and in English. Even in the aftermath of litigation and legislation mandating appropriate assessment practices, tests normed on LEP students residing in the United States are lacking. Most practitioners do not have the training and expertise required to meet the special assessment needs of our rapidly growing NELB population and continue to rely primarily on traditional standardized tests. The need for improved assessment practices and assessment personnel training continues to be addressed by practitioners, researchers, and policy makers.

WHAT CAN YOU DO?

1. Describe efforts to limit bias in the psychoeducational assessment of LEP and NELB students. What efforts have been made in your school district? Describe the results of these efforts. What is still needed?

2. Describe stipulations and mandates that have emerged from the legal system relative to the provision of equitable assessments to LEP and NELB students. Are there any regulations, stipulations, and mandates particular to your state or school district? Are you thoroughly familiar with them?

3. Does your school district employ enough bilingual evaluation specialists to meet the demands for bilingual assessment services? What provisions have been made for the recruitment of additional bilingual evaluation specialists and the training of existing assessment personnel to meet the diverse needs of NELB populations? How can you facilitate this?

4. What are the professional guidelines or standards of your profession relative to the assessment of NELB populations? Are these adequate? If not, suggest additional changes that might be made and how these changes could be implemented. How can you become involved in developing and improving such standards?

SECTION TWO

ADVOCACY IN THE CURRENT ASSESSMENT PROCESS

The current assessment process reflects a movement toward an inclusive or integrative approach to the assessment of NELB students who are limited in English proficiency. By obtaining information from the student, home, school, and community, the paradigm provides a system of checks and balances for assessing the reliability and validity of the data generated. The goals are comprehensive and more global than the traditional role of testing to determine whether a student does or does not qualify for exceptional student education placement. Methods for attaining information are more specific than the use of standardized measures. As the assessment paradigm changes, so too do the roles and activities of the persons who conduct the assessment.

This section first highlights difficulties in accurately assessing NELB students, as a framework for the discussion of the role of the evaluation specialist as child advocate. The advocate's role in planning interventions, conducting the assessment, and presenting and sharing data follows.

HIGHLIGHTS OF DIFFICULTIES IN ACCURATELY ASSESSING NELB STUDENTS

A host of factors make the assessment of NELB students with limited English proficiency a difficult process that is very different from the assessment of monolingual English-speaking students. These include factors related to the tests themselves, assessment personnel preparation, the traditional assessment process, parent participation, the involvement of interpreters and translators, and school and district plans and procedures. The aforementioned factors are summarized in Table 7-1.

This subsection discusses the highlights of these difficulties and paves the way for school personnel to think more comprehensively about what can be done to improve the assessment process.

Available test instruments.

Tests for monolingual English proficient speakers are readily available; tests for NELB and LEP populations are not. Cognitive, academic, and psychological processing tests traditionally used in our schools have been standardized

Summary of this section.

TABLE 7-1. FACTORS RELATED TO THE DIFFICULTIES INVOLVED IN THE PSYCHOEDUCATIONAL ASSESSMENT OF NELB STUDENTS WITH LIMITED ENGLISH PROFICIENCY

- Available Test Instruments
- Assessment Personnel Preparation
- Traditional Assessment Process
- Parent Participation
- Involvement of Interpreters and Translators
- School and District Plans and Procedures

and normed on English proficient populations. Bilingual students are included in the normative samples of some tests only if they speak English, and, in many instances, are not systematically included at all. Tests standardized on NELB students in the process of learning English are not commercially available (Figueroa 1989). Given the diversity of language and cultural backgrounds served by our nation's schools, and our NELB students' varying and dynamic skill levels in both their home language and in English, specific tests are difficult to develop.

Translating English tests into other languages poses problems as well. These include both commercially available translations and translations done on a local level (Fradd & Wilen 1990). Test translations available from publishers often are not separately normed but rather contain only the norms for the English version of the instrument. Comparability between the psychometric properties of the original test and the translated version cannot be assumed (American Educational Research Association, American Psychological Association, & National Council on Measurement in Education 1985). For example, it cannot be assumed that the original and translated versions have the same reliability and validity. The level of difficulty of items may change by virtue of translation. A concept that is basic in one language may be advanced in another language.

Furthermore, test items may not be translatable because equivalent concepts may not exist across language and cultural groups. For example, in a project undertaken in a school district to translate the Peabody Picture Vocabulary Test-Revised (Dunn & Dunn 1981) with the authors' permission for use with local Haitian Creole speakers, certain English vocabulary items such as *walrus, wooly, bovine* and *sibling* had no comparable Haitian Creole equivalents. These items had to be omitted from the translation. A translation such as this can provide screening information about a student but should be interpreted with extreme caution. The English norms for the test should not be used in scoring such a translation. The appropriate permissions should be obtained when translations of copyrighted material are conducted.

Assessment personnel preparation.

The limited availability of trained professional bilingual assessment personnel in our nation's schools already has been noted. While the demand for bilingual assessment services is great, the numbers of bilingual evaluation specialists in fields such as school psychology and speech-language pathology are quite small. Even when bilingual practitioners are available, they are generally not fluent in all the languages their school district serves or may not have pertinent training and competencies in bilingual/multicultural assessment (American Speech-Language-Hearing Association Committee on the Status of Racial Minorities 1987; Barona, Santos de Barona, Flores & Gutierrez 1990; Fradd & Wilen 1990; Wilen 1989). For example, only a few universities have bilingual and multicultural issues as a major focus of their school psychology training programs (Martinez, Co-Chairman NASP Multicultural Affairs, personal communication, May 17, 1990). In addition, surveys of both school psychologists and speech-language pathologists reflect a professed need for more skills, guidelines, and knowledge related to bilingual-bicultural clients (American Speech-Language-Hearing Association Committee on the Status of Racial Minorities 1987; Figueroa 1989).

School systems and personnel are accustomed to evaluating English-speaking examinees. The monolingual English-speaking examinee is fluent in the language of the test, the language of the school, and the language of the evaluation specialist; the NELB examinee with limited English proficiency is not. Furthermore, the LEP student is more likely to have experienced interrupted and limited schooling, traumatic life events, separation from family and support systems, and cultural experiences and expectations that differ from those of the mainstream (Westby 1990; Wilen 1990). In addition, the LEP examinee is less likely to have had exposure to the information the tests measure and to required test-taking skills than is his or her monolingual English-speaking counterpart. The evaluation specialist must be prepared to take all of these factors into account when assessing LEP students. However, the examiner or evaluation specialist may have limited or no experience in the home language or culture of the NELB examinee and family or in the specialized area of bilingual assessment.

Assessment process.

Administrators, teachers, psychologists, speech-language pathologists, and guidance counselors have a better understanding of the evaluation process for monolingual English speakers and what they are expected to do. They have been trained to work with English proficient students. This is less likely the case with NELB students. The assessment of NELB students requires personnel with diverse skills, requires new resources and procedures, and demands a greater time commitment on the part of school systems than does the assessment of monolingual English speakers (Fradd & Wilen 1990; Wilen & Sweeting 1986). For example, just the basic task of developing consent forms for formal individual evaluation for parents or guardians to read and sign in their home languages is a major task for many school systems. Few school systems have allocated the resources necessary to accomplish this task. The concept of informed consent for psychoeducational assessment may be totally foreign to NELB families, and the terminology used in consent forms may have no direct translation in their language. As a result, the families require a great deal more information on the benefits, limitations, and potential consequences of the assessment than mainstream families may require.

Though traditional psychometric testing has not been a solution to the problems involved in assessing NELB students who are limited in English proficiency, standardized tests, nevertheless, do provide useful information and should not be abandoned (Caterino 1990; De Leon 1990; Rechsley 1981; Sattler 1988). Rather, we need to augment and adapt traditional testing practices with alternative techniques that are more culturally and linguistically appropriate. We need to avoid the common perception of the assessment process as a collection of discrete data sets by various personnel. Assessment needs to be viewed as a total comprehensive process in which multiple strategies are utilized in an interactive, integrated fashion.

Parent participation.

Encouraging the participation of parents in the assessment process with their NELB children is an ethical, legal, and best practice professional mandate for school personnel (Silverstein 1991). Parents can provide valuable information about their children's history and current functioning which can be useful in assessment, intervention, and educational planning. However, a number of factors make active involvement a difficult process for NELB parents. NELB parents who are limited in English proficiency may have difficulty understanding notes and other information sent home in English and may feel uncomfortable attending meetings and interacting with school personnel. (Wilen 1990). They may come from cultures where it is considered embarrassing or shameful to openly discuss difficulties that their children may have, or where it is not customary to actively participate in the educational decision-making process with reference to their children (Wilen 1989). Parents may be unfamiliar with the standards and cultural expectations of the school milieu. They may work long hours and be unable to take time off work to attend conferences during school hours. They may be unable to communicate with monolingual English-speaking school personnel.

Involvement of interpreters and translators.

Because of the lack of bilingual school personnel, interpreters and translators are sometimes utilized in the assessment process with limited English proficient students and families. Interpreters translate information orally for student and parent interviews and conferences, instruction, testing sessions, and exceptional student education staffings and other meetings. Translators, on the other hand, change written material from one language to another for notes, letters, formal documents, and tests (Fradd & Wilen 1990).

Using second language service providers in the assessment process requires specialized rules and is costly and time-consuming. Users of interpreter/translator services need to know how to adapt the assessment process to work effectively with interpreters and translators to obtain the best possible evaluative data. Providers of interpreter/translator services need to understand the expectations of the educational setting and the protocol of the assessment situation, in addition to being skilled in English, the U.S. culture, the target language, and the target culture. Yet few school systems employ professional interpreters and translators, have standards regulating interpreter/translator services, or provide training programs for users or providers of such services. Rather, schools often call on whoever happens to be accessible—be it a bilingual clerk, classroom aide, student, parent, or teacher—with little regard for training or experience or the effects on the interaction. Additionally, school districts do not usually build in time for briefings and debriefings between users and providers of interpreter/translator services before and after the actual interpretive sessions. Nor do they generally allocate the financial resources to professionalize the role of interpreters and translators by providing appropriate compensation (Fradd & Wilen 1990; Wilen & Fradd 1991). The difficulties involved in using interpreters and translators do not exist in the assessment of English proficient students in U.S. schools because the need for a conduit to communicate in English is not an issue.

School and district plans and procedures.

School and district plans and procedures are generally geared to English proficient students and families. Though specific plans related to bilingual and English for Speakers of Other Languages (ESOL) programs do exist, comprehensive plans for providing psychological, social work, speech/language, and exceptional student education services to LEP populations are still uncommon.

Relative to assessment, plans that may work for English proficient students, such as using verbally loaded tests to screen students prior to formal referral for psychological evaluation and using English forms, documents, and parent manuals, can be inappropriate for LEP populations. Districts may have to implement more innovative, collaborative approaches on a system-wide basis. These include new and modified plans, the training of existing personnel, the recruitment of additional bilingual personnel, and the establishment of cooperative relationships within the school district and with local universities and trainers. However, change is often a slow and arduous process in educational systems. Maintaining the status quo is usually more comfortable to those in charge, particularly when new competencies and knowledge bases are required to implement change.

RESEARCH IN PRACTICE:
Highlights of Difficulties in Accurately Assessing NELB Students

---

1. Discuss the differences in the availability of tests for LEP and monolingual English speakers. Are there differences in the instruments used for these populations in your district?

2. Discuss the skills evaluation specialists need to assess LEP students that differ from those needed to assess monolingual English speakers. Are bilingual evaluation specialists available for all the languages represented in your district? If not, what provisions are made to conduct psychoeducational assessments of LEP students?

3. Why is active involvement in the assessment process difficult for NELB parents? What provisions are made to encourage such parental involvement in your district?

4. Describe some of the skills needed by users and providers of interpreter/ translator services in the psychoeducational assessment process. What are the standards regulating the provision of interpreter and translator services in your district?

5. Describe some of the difficulties in using school and district plans and procedures designed for English proficient students with limited English proficient students. How have your school and district modified assessment-related plans and procedures to address the needs of LEP students?

ROLE OF EVALUATION SPECIALIST AS CHILD ADVOCATE

In the psychoeducational assessment of NELB and LEP students, the role of the evaluation specialist is critical. That specialist has a particular responsibility to act as advocate for each individual student referred for services because of the unique challenges involved in the assessment process with this population. The school psychologist, speech-language pathologist or other evaluation specialist must actively solicit parental participation and assist the school in breaking down any existing cultural, linguistic, or other barriers to the involvement of NELB parents in the assessment process (see Correa 1989 and Edwards 1990 for an in depth discussion of potential barriers and strategies to overcome them).

Additionally, referral to an evaluation specialist is often viewed by school personnel as the primary route to accessing educational services for at-risk students. Often a referral for psychoeducational evaluation means a referral to determine if a student qualifies for entry into special education. Special education may be seen as the primary or only available treatment for an NELB student who is floundering academically. Thus, evaluation specialists may feel intense pressure from administrators, teachers, and from within themselves to recommend special education in order to get help for a student. As an advocate for the NELB student, the evaluation specialist must make every effort to avoid this practice. Diagnosing a student as having a specific learning disability or as being mildly mentally retarded goes beyond accessing services. It is calling the student handicapped, and that diagnosis should only be made when the student has a real disability.

Many times with NELB students, we can easily tell that a student is functioning poorly in school, but we do not know why. Causal factors are more covert, yet very important (Damico 1991; Kretschmer 1991). We know that the student is achieving two years below grade level in reading, but is it because of the normal process of second language acquisition? Is it part of the acculturation process? Is it because of a different learning style? Is it motivational? Is it because the current school program is not meeting the student's needs? Is it because the student's prior schooling has been minimal? Is it because of an intrinsic learning problem? Is there another reason? Or is there an interaction among two or more of these variables? If unsure of the diagnosis, the best approach is to recommend interventions, to monitor the student's progress and to review and/or re-evaluate the case at a later date. Decisions should not be based on expediency, particularly with the complexities involved in NELB cases.

Moreover, evaluation specialists should make a plea for early involvement in NELB cases on a consultative basis. By collaborating with teachers and administrators early on, involvement of a school psychologist or other evaluation specialist is not equated with testing to determine placement, but can be viewed as a means of understanding and gaining information about students and their home and school environments, planning suitable interventions, and facilitating learning and adjustment opportunities. Interventions prior to referral for formal evaluation are discussed next.

RESEARCH IN PRACTICE:
Role of Evaluation Specialist as Child Advocate

Describe the role of the evaluation specialist as child advocate in the assessment of NELB students. Ask two school psychologists and two speech-language pathologists to tell you what being a child advocate when assessing

NELB students means to them. What are the similarities and differences in their perspectives?

THE ADVOCATE'S ROLE IN PLANNING INTERVENTIONS PRIOR TO FORMAL REFERRAL FOR PSYCHOEDUCATIONAL ASSESSMENT: COLLECTING BACKGROUND INFORMATION

When an NELB student manifests learning or adjustment difficulties in school and the classroom teacher feels frustrated in meeting that student's needs, the teacher often seeks assistance. The request for assistance may really be a request for removal of that student from the teacher's classroom. Potentially, it is a genuine call for collaboration, consultation, and the development of a plan of action to enhance the student's performance. In either case, it is an opportunity to develop and implement new strategies.

In some schools a multidisciplinary team consisting of personnel such as teachers, an administrator, a guidance counselor, a school psychologist, a school social worker, a speech-language pathologist, an exceptional student education specialist, and a school nurse meet on a regular basis to discuss cases, do pre-referral screening, meet with parents, plan pre-referral interventions, and make recommendations for further evaluation. In other schools within the same school district, such committees may not be operational or may not exist. These committees have different names in different places: child study team, teacher assistance team, interdisciplinary team, multidisciplinary team, and pre-referral team are examples. In addition, many are under the jurisdiction of special education, though a more effective practice would be to place them under the rubric of regular education, with accepted standards and procedures being followed routinely by all personnel within a school or district (Garcia & Ortiz 1988).

Though pre-referral multidisciplinary teams are recommended, in schools where they do not operate, the first step may be for a teacher or administrator to immediately contact an evaluation specialist. In any case, parent conferences should be held and interventions should be implemented prior to formal referral of NELB students for psychoeducational assessment. Rare exceptions to the implementation of pre-referral interventions may include cases of new students with a documented history of significant psychoeducational problems from a previous school system (Wilen & Sweeting 1986).

In order to plan effective interventions, data collection is essential. Background information should be obtained from multiple sources. Record reviews, information from parents, and teacher reports are discussed next.

Record reviews.

A review of existing records is a logical approach with mainstream students and is appropriate for NELB populations as well. However, school records of the NELB students may be more difficult to access. The information may be less complete and may not be up to date and accurate for many reasons (Caterino 1990). Efforts should be made to obtain records from any previous school the student has attended. Though at times this is difficult when students come from schools outside of the United States, requests submitted to a specific person at a sending school in the language of that school accompanied by releases of information signed by parents or guardians often produce effective responses. Pertinent medical, psychological, psychosocial, audiological, and speech and language reports and records should also be requested and reviewed.

Use cumulative folders and other records to try to answer specific questions about NELB students or to determine information available on the students. Personal and family data, educational information, and medical information can often be easily obtained from school record reviews. Examples of questions that may be answered from a review of records appear in Table 7-2. The Table is divided into subsets 7-2A to 7-2C in order to facilitate discussion. The questions suggested in Table 7-2 are particularly relevant to NELB students.

Records of NELB students are more likely to contain multiple sets of information. In many countries personal statistics such as birthdates may be kept in different ways than they are in the United States. Obvious differences in the student's reported chronological age and physical development should be

TABLE 7-2A. SUGGESTED QUESTIONS TO ASK WHEN REVIEWING SCHOOL RECORDS OF NELB STUDENTS: PERSONAL AND FAMILY DATA

- What is the student's date of birth?

- If there are multiple birthdates in the records, can the correct birthdate be verified?

- Where was the student born?

- With whom does the student live?

- What language or languages are spoken in the home?

- What is the student's language dominance classification?

- When did the family come to the United States?

- When did the student come to the United States?

- How long has the student resided in your school district?

- Where did the student live prior to entering your district?

- What is the occupation and educational history of the parent(s) or guardian?

TABLE 7-2B. SUGGESTED QUESTIONS TO ASK WHEN REVIEWING SCHOOL RECORDS OF NELB STUDENTS: EDUCATIONAL INFORMATION

- How long has the student attended school in the United States?
- How long has the student attended school in your district?
- How many different schools has the student attended?
- How old was the student when he or she started school?
- Does the student attend school on a regular basis?
- Is there evidence that the student received consistent schooling prior to moving to the United States?
- How is the type of school program the student is enrolled in now similar to and different from the type of school program the student previously attended?
- Is there evidence that the student was previously in special education or receiving special services?
- Is there a history of retention?
- Have cognitive, academic or behavioral strengths and/or weaknesses been previously noted?

noted. Additionally, dates are written in the sequence month-date-year in the United States, but in many other countries are written day-month-year. School personnel reviewing records should be aware of those differences (Wilen & Sweeting 1986). Other personal and family data such as the origin of the child, the language of the home, and the length of time in the U.S. are also specific to the unique needs of NELB students. Suggested questions related to educational history come next (Table 7-2B).

Educational history obtained from a review of records can help school personnel develop interventions and make better diagnostic decisions. Take the case of a boy from rural Haiti who enters your school at age nine with no previous formal education or the case of an eleven-year-old Mexican girl who was in the third grade prior to entering your school district, where she was immediately placed in fifth grade because of her chronological age. Knowledge of school history, including attendance patterns, type of school program attended, and previously noted strengths and weaknesses enhances understanding of students' current functioning and facilitates planning. Suggested questions related to medical history are next (Table 7-2C).

Medical information is important because students may have had inconsistent medical care, even for known conditions such as diabetes and epilepsy. Treatment and therapeutic intervention may have been too costly or unavailable. There may be vision and hearing problems that are interfering with school performance, but that could be easily corrected.

TABLE 7-2C. SUGGESTED QUESTIONS TO ASK WHEN REVIEWING SCHOOL RECORDS OF NELB STUDENTS: MEDICAL INFORMATION

- What is the student's present health status?
- Is the student taking medication or under a physician's care for a medical condition?
- What was the date of the last physical exam in the records?
- Were recommendations for additional examinations or referrals to specialists made? If so, has follow-up been completed?
- Is there a history of neurological, psychiatric, physical, or other medical problems?
- What are the results of current vision and hearing screenings?

Information from parents.

In addition to reviewing records, school personnel may need to initiate direct contact with NELB families to clarify and obtain further background data. Though parent information forms are often sent home to mainstream parents for completion, more reliable information is obtained from NELB families through personal interviews or home visits by bilingual personnel such as a school social worker (Wilen & Sweeting 1986). These meetings help to answer questions generated from the records and are a valuable step in establishing rapport and encouraging parental participation in the entire assessment process. Regular parent information forms used in your school district can be adapted for NELB families. An example of an adapted intake interview form is presented in Figure 7-1. This table is divided into subsets 7-1A to 7-1H for discussion purposes. The various parts of the table can be used together as one integrated form and can be further modified based on local district needs.

The Personal Information section of the NELB Parent Intake Interview Form includes basic identifying information that might be requested about any student. The inclusion of the student's language classification and the date of that classification, however, is specifically geared toward the special needs of NELB students. Information on language classification of students is generally obtained directly from school records, but is included in this first section of the intake form to quickly identify whether or not the student is classified by a district as limited English proficient. The Family History section is next (Figure 7-1B).

A Family History section of a general parent intake form can easily be augmented to include information about the length of time the student has resided in the United States and in the present school district, and the circumstances that brought the student to this school district. Did the student's family migrate to the United States for reasons of political asylum, for economic

FIGURE 7-1A. NELB PARENT INTAKE INTERVIEW FORM: PERSONAL INFORMATION

Date: _____

Name of Student: _____
             (Last)   (First)   (MI)

Address: _____
     (Street)

_____
     (City)   (State)   (Zip)

Telephone: _____
        (Home)   (Work)

Date of Birth: _____   Grade: _____

Place of Birth: _____   Sex: _____

Language Classification: _____

Date of Classification: _____

Reason for Referral: _____

advancement, or to escape from a war-torn country? (Wilen & Sweeting 1986). Has the student ever lived apart from one or both parents? For example, did the student's parents send the student to the United States to live with a relative? Or did the parent(s) immigrate to the United States first and send for the child at a later date? All of these details are important in understanding the student's current functioning. Other information requested in this section that does not generally appear in the typical school parent intake form relates to the nationality of the student and parents. The Developmental and Language History section comes next (Figure 7-1C).

Obtaining a developmental and language history including information about birth history and developmental milestones is important in understanding current functioning. Are factors such as prematurity, low birth weight, and complications of childbirth involved? Were language milestones such as the age of onset of speaking in words and sentences accomplished within normal limits in the native language or were these milestones delayed? What language is the child most comfortable speaking? Does the child have difficulty communicating in the home environment? Were there difficulties in the native language prior to the introduction of English? Is there a family history of speech and language problems? Such data are important to evaluation specialists in making a differential diagnosis. The Medical History section follows. (Figure 7-1D)

The medical history requested here is thorough but is not really different from the history that should be obtained on all youngsters referred for psychoeducational assessment. However, information reported in this section sometimes reveals that a student has medical problems that are undiagnosed or that are not being treated (Wilen & Sweeting 1986). The Behavioral History section is next. (Figure 7-1E)

When collecting the behavioral history from the parent, it is important to obtain data about the age of onset, duration, and intensity of reported problems. Could behavioral problems be a result of situational stressors related to uprooting or the process of acculturation? Are the reported self-help skills age-appropriate in the student's culture? The Educational History section follows (Figure 7-1F).

FIGURE 7-1B. NELB PARENT INTAKE INTERVIEW FORM: FAMILY HISTORY

How long has the student lived in the United States? _____

Arrival date: _____

How long has the student lived in this school district? _____

What are the circumstances that brought the student to this school district?

_____

_____

With whom is the student living? _____

Has the child lived with individuals or relatives other than parent(s)? Y( )N( )

Whom: _____ How long: _____

	MOTHER	FATHER	GUARDIAN/OTHER
Name:			
Address:			
Telephone:			
Age:			
Education:			
Occupation:			
Marital History:			

Is the child adopted? Y( ) N( )

If yes, what were the circumstances? _____

BROTHER(S)/SISTER(S)

Name:	Sex:	Age:	Living at Home	School/Occupation

NAMES OF OTHER PERSON(S)

IN THE HOME	RELATIONSHIP	AGE

Birth Order of Child: _____

Nationality: _____

| (Parent/Guardian) | (Student) |

FIGURE 7-1C. NELB PARENT INTAKE INTERVIEW FORM: DEVELOPMENTAL AND LANGUAGE HISTORY

Pregnancy: Complications ( ) No complications ( )
Duration: _____
Explanation: _____
_____

Birth weight: _____
Delivery: Normal ( ) Caesarean ( )

<table>
<tr><td></td><td>MOTHER</td><td>CHILD</td></tr>
<tr><td>Complications: </td><td>_____</td><td>_____</td></tr>
<tr><td>Hospitalization: </td><td>_____</td><td>_____</td></tr>
<tr><td>Explanation: </td><td>_____</td><td>_____</td></tr>
</table>

Developmental Milestones and Language Background:
Age sat up: _____ Age walked: _____
Age of first spoken words and in what language: _____
Age of first sentences and in what language: _____
Age toilet trained: _____
What language is the child most comfortable speaking? _____
Do friends and family find it difficult to understand the
child's speech? _____
When talking to friends and family members does the child sound
age-appropriate? _____
Is there a family history of communication problems? _____

Information about prior schooling is an integral part of the psychoeducational assessment process with NELB students. Present school performance should be interpreted in light of the student's educational history. Did the student attend school sequentially and consistently? What were the expectations of the student in the previous school setting? Did the student begin formal schooling at an earlier or later age than is customary in your district? Did the student have prior difficulties with academics, behavior or truancy? Or is this the first time such problems have been noted? Has the student previously received bilingual/ESOL, special education or related services? Is there a history of learning problems in the student's family? Answers to these questions help assessment personnel make better decisions about NELB students. The Social and Family Relationships section follows (Figure 7-1G).

This section is important because it provides data on the student's functioning outside of school and includes information on family relationships. Stressors such as family difficulties and other significant life events that could affect the student are requested. Also, the student's interests, hobbies, and strengths

FIGURE 7-1D. NELB PARENT INTAKE INTERVIEW FORM: MEDICAL HISTORY

HEALTH: Has the child had problems in the following areas?

	Y	N	Age(s)	Explanation
Seizures	( )	( )	_____	_____
Epilepsy	( )	( )	_____	_____
High Fevers	( )	( )	_____	_____
Ear Infections	( )	( )	_____	_____
Headaches	( )	( )	_____	_____
Asthma	( )	( )	_____	_____
Diabetes	( )	( )	_____	_____
Head Injury	( )	( )	_____	_____
Accidents	( )	( )	_____	_____
Surgery	( )	( )	_____	_____
Allergies	( )	( )	_____	_____
Meningitis	( )	( )	_____	_____
Hearing	( )	( )	_____	_____
Vision	( )	( )	_____	_____
Coordination	( )	( )	_____	_____
Physical	( )	( )	_____	_____
Other	( )	( )	_____	_____

Current Health Status: _____

Hospitalization (Where)	Age	Reason	Duration

Is child presently on medication? Y( )   N( )
If so, name: _____
Reason: _____
Frequency: _____
Child's Physician: _____
Address: _____
Telephone: _____
Date of Last Examination: _____
Parents' significant medical history:_____
_____

Family's significant psychiatric history: _____
_____

are requested so that the focus is on what the student can do and not just on problematic areas. The Current Functioning section comes next (Figure 7-1H).

This final section summarizes the clinician's observations and also includes specific data on the family's involvement with outside agencies. Requests for releases to obtain further information are documented here and signatures of all the parties involved in the intake interview are obtained.

FIGURE 7-1E. NELB PARENT INTAKE INTERVIEW FORM:
BEHAVIORAL HISTORY

Does the child have problems in the following areas?

	Y	N	Explanation
Eating	( )	( )	_____
Sleeping	( )	( )	_____
Toileting	( )	( )	_____
Nail biting	( )	( )	_____
Thumb sucking	( )	( )	_____
Overactivity	( )	( )	_____
Aggressiveness	( )	( )	_____
Withdrawal	( )	( )	_____
Self-concept	( )	( )	_____
Nightmares	( )	( )	_____
Unusual fear(s)	( )	( )	_____
Argumentativeness	( )	( )	_____
Temper tantrums	( )	( )	_____
Impulsivity	( )	( )	_____
Daydreaming	( )	( )	_____
Nervousness	( )	( )	_____
Other	( )	( )	_____

Describe self-help skills: _____

_____

Has the student ever had or participated in any of the following?

	Y	N	Explanation
Psychological examination	( )	( )	_____
Psychiatric examination	( )	( )	_____
Neurological examination	( )	( )	_____
Counseling	( )	( )	_____

Teacher reports.

In addition to collecting background information from existing records, parent conferences and intake forms, background data should also be collected directly from the NELB student's teacher(s). Teachers instructing the student should be asked to complete a teacher report form describing the student's current functioning in academic, language, and behavioral and social/emotional areas. Not only is such information valuable in planning interventions, but it is also an important aspect of assessment. The teacher's observations of a student's daily functioning in class can be compared to findings from formal and informal tests and work samples to provide a more comprehensive picture of the student's needs.

The use of general teacher report forms as part of the psychoeducational process is not uncommon in school systems. However, adapting such report forms to the special needs of NELB populations is a relatively new practice.

Suggested items related to general information, academics, learning modalities, language, and behavioral/social/emotional functioning are discussed next.

General information requested on a teacher report form for NELB students should include items such as the following:

- student's name
- student's language(s)
- grade in school

FIGURE 7-1F. NELB PARENT INTAKE INTERVIEW FORM: EDUCATIONAL HISTORY

List schools attended (Nursery - 12th grade):

Name   **Location**   **Grade(s)**

_____

_____

_____

_____

Age started school (Kindergarten): _____

1. Has student been in an exceptional education program? Y( )   N( )
If yes, type and/or title of program? _____
Location: _____
Dates of enrollment: _____

Has student repeated a grade? Y( ) N( ) If so, what grade(s)? _____

Summary of school performance: _____
_____

Description of previous school setting(s): _____
_____

Child's attitude toward school: _____
_____

Problematic Areas in School
Academics: _____
Behavior: _____
Truancy: _____
Other: _____
When and how did problem(s) begin? _____
_____

Has the student received speech, physical, or occupational therapy?
Y( )   N( )
If yes, type: _____
Location: _____
Dates: _____

Has student attended a bilingual/ESOL program Y( )   N( )
If yes, location: _____
Dates of enrollment: _____
Is there a family history of learning problems? Y( )   N( )

FIGURE 7-1G. NELB PARENT INTAKE INTERVIEW FORM: SOCIAL AND FAMILY RELATIONSHIPS

Relationship with parent(s)/guardian:
Mother: _____
Father: _____
Guardian: _____
Other: _____
Description of child by parent(s)/guardian/other: _____

_____

Relationship with siblings and others:
Brother(s): _____
Sister(s): _____
Peer(s): _____
Other(s): _____

Interests, Hobbies: _____
Strengths/Weaknesses: _____
Problematic areas at home: _____
Significant events: _____
To whom is the child closest in the family? _____
Disciplinarian: _____ How? _____
For what reason? _____
Do parents differ on discipline? _____

FIGURE 7-1H. NELB PARENT INTAKE INTERVIEW FORM: CURRENT FUNCTIONING

Observations:

Area(s) of Concern: _____

Area(s) of Strength: _____

Involvement with other agency(ies): _____

Recommendations: _____

Summary: _____

Release for further	Sent	Date	Location
information	Y( ) N( )	_____	_____

Signatures:
Mother   _____
Father   _____
Guardian   _____
Interpreter   _____
Social Worker   _____
Other   _____

                     (Relationship or Title)

Date: _____

Figures 7-1A-7-1H adapted from Godsted, G. (1990). *School social work services intake interview.* Fort Lauderdale, FL: Multicultural Education Department, School Board of Broward County.

- teacher's name
- teacher's language(s)
- language(s) in which instruction is provided
- type of school program (e.g., ESOL, bilingual, regular)
- length of time teacher has known the student
- reason for referral
- interventions attempted to make the school program more sensitive to the student's language and cultural needs.

These items provide information on the match between the student's language, the teacher's language, and the school program; the reason for referral; and the type of interventions implemented.

Relative to academics, ask the teacher to complete questions such as the following:

- In (reading, language, spelling, math), at approximately what level is the student currently functioning?
- In (reading, language, spelling, math), at what level are you currently instructing the student?

Many times a student's current skills may be below the instructional level provided, making learning difficult.

The teacher should also be asked questions about learning modalities. Examples of such questions suitable for use with NELB populations include:

- Does the student have difficulty understanding and retaining information presented orally? If yes, describe and state what you have done to accommodate this.
- Does the student have difficulty understanding and retaining information presented visually? If yes, describe and state what you have done to accommodate this.
- Does the student have difficulty with gross or fine motor tasks? If yes, describe and state what you have done to accommodate this.

Relative to language, the teacher can be asked to compare the NELB student's communication patterns to cohorts from the student's language and cultural group. Examples of items on a teacher report form addressing this area appear below:

- Does the student communicate his or her needs easily in the native language?
- Does the student communicate his or her needs easily in English?
- Does the student communicate easily with peers in class? (Pomerantz, 1991a)

In the area of behavioral, social, and emotional functioning, the teacher report form can include items such as:

- Describe the student's school behavior. If problems exist, are these behaviors unusual in comparison to peers from the student's cultural group?
- Describe any changes you have noticed in the student's behavior over time.
- How does the student get along with other students? Other teachers?

Integrate background information obtained from teacher reports with data from school records and parent interviews to better understand the total student. The main point of the entire background collection process is to gather information that will provide insight into the needs, history and prior learning opportunities of students so that schools can build on what students know and can do.

Clarifying the reason for the referral.

At this stage, the referral problem should be better defined (see the school-based consultation literature including Curtis & Meyers 1988 and Zins & Ponti 1990 for information relative to problem clarification). Is the problem student-related, teacher- or instructional setting-related, or at the level of the school organization (Curtis & Meyers 1988)? All too often we have focused on the student as the primary reason for academic failure without carefully considering other sources. We have both over-referred NELB students who may be experiencing normal second language acquisition problems or whose teachers may be unqualified to meet their needs and under-referred other students by attributing all their school problems to their NELB status. We must make every effort to clarify the presenting problem through specific steps addressing issues at the level of the teacher or classroom and school or school system in addition to the level of the individual student and his family. That is, are the teacher's instructional and behavioral management styles or knowledge, experience, and expectations with NELB students affecting the student's progress? Is the school's curriculum appropriate for NELB students who have had limited prior schooling (Garcia & Ortiz 1988)? Are programs and support services available to facilitate the adjustment of NELB students and families? Examples of specific interventions are discussed next.

Development of resources and support to implement, evaluate, and document interventions should be an integral part of the pre-referral and assessment process for all students. Multidisciplinary teams of school professionals and parents should work collaboratively in this regard. Interventions are especially important with culturally and linguistically diverse students as a deterrent to premature labeling and potential misplacement and as a means of assessing the effectiveness of instruction and the need for in depth assessment.

The interventions we are recommending must be systematically applied and monitored for a reasonable time to evaluate their success. We want to design interventions that will ameliorate the student's problem prior to referral. If they work, the referral process stops. If they do not, the interventions should be altered and other options tried. Sometimes teachers, administrators, and other members of the multidisciplinary team see requirements for interventions prior to referral as one more hoop to jump through before testing can be done. They may call retention in first grade or changing a seat assignment in class an intervention. Though these may indeed be interventions, they are not the type and scope of pre-referral interventions we are suggesting for NELB students.

Interventions such as ongoing inservice programs to train entire faculties in the unique needs of culturally and linguistically diverse populations, multilingual parent education programs, supportive counseling groups to facilitate student adjustment, pairing of a new immigrant student with a model student from that same country or with a mainstream student, and alternative teaching techniques and ESOL strategies are recommended. Cooperative learning techniques, discovery learning, language experience approaches, dialogue journal writing, reteaching techniques, multisensory approaches, contextualized learning, teaching pre-requisite skills, and providing native language instruction are a few examples of potential strategies (Fletcher & Cardona-Morales 1980; Garcia & Ortiz 1988; Wilen & Sweeting 1986). Interventions may also include obtaining glasses for a student with a visual acuity problem, obtaining medical treatment for a student with a neurological disorder, implementing a study skills program in partnership with a student's parents, and accessing social services and financial aid for a needy family. If interventions implemented at the pre-referral stage are not successful in meeting the student's needs, and the multidisciplinary team feels that further evaluation is needed, individual psychoeducational assessment is often the next step.

RESEARCH IN PRACTICE:
Advocate's Role in Planning Interventions

PRIOR TO FORMAL REFERRAL FOR PSYCHOEDUCATIONAL ASSESSMENT: COLLECTING INFORMATION

1. Does your school have a process for pre-referral intervention? What steps are involved? How can it be improved?

2. Discuss the importance of collecting background information from multiple sources in the pre-referral process. Give an example of how knowledge of pertinent background information has facilitated the educational planning process for two specific students with whom you have worked.

3. Discuss the need to clarify the referral problem at the pre-referral intervention stage. Think of a particular NELB student for whom you have been involved in pre-referral consultations. Did identifying whether the problem was student-related, teacher- or instructional setting-related, or school system-related facilitate planning? How?

4. Describe the design and application of one successful and one unsuccessful intervention utilized with NELB students in your school. In what ways was the successful intervention different from the unsuccessful one?

ADVOCATE'S ROLE IN CONDUCTING THE ASSESSMENT

Psychoeducational assessment should be thorough with a variety of data used to corroborate findings. The presenting referral problems of LEP students are often intertwined with language and cultural factors. This makes diagnostic decisions difficult, especially in differentiating between at-risk students and those who are mildly handicapped. Diagnosis of profound and severe handicaps are often easier because of the more obvious nature of these problems in any population (Esquivel 1988).

Prior to beginning the psychoeducational assessment, the school psychologist should verify that recent vision and hearing screenings have been passed or that the use of glasses, hearing aids, or other recommended corrective measures that may affect the student's ability to perform during the evaluation have been implemented. Language dominance and proficiency testing, and speech and language screenings should also be completed prior to assessment. Informed parental consent should be documented.

In approaching the assessment, the psychologist should allow extra time to establish rapport, and to orient the student to the setting and to the achievement aspect of the testing. That is, the students should be told to try their hardest and do their best. The psychologist should provide frequent encouragement and should closely monitor motivational factors and other test-taking skills that may be influencing a student's performance (Cloud 1991; Sattler 1988). The presence or absence of prerequisite skills like knowing how to hold a pencil should also be noted and assessment techniques should be adjusted accordingly. Students should be asked what name they would like to be called. Names are written in a different order in some countries than they are in the United States which often causes confusion. For example, school personnel may mistakenly call Vietnamese students by their family name instead of their first name because Vietnamese names are written in the order of last name, middle name, first name without the use of commas (Wilen 1990). Special considerations in assessing the cognitive, academic, adaptive behavioral, and behavioral/emotional functioning of NELB students are discussed next.

Cognitive assessment.

Intellectual assessments of NELB students who are limited in English proficiency are an index of current measured cognitive functioning rather than of intellectual potential. Intelligence tests provide information about a student's strengths and weaknesses, can measure change and growth, and can reveal the need for interventions or special services (Sattler 1988).

Students who have recently arrived in the United States and who speak little or no English can be given foreign-normed intelligence tests in their native language (Caterino 1990). However, the availability of intelligence tests in non-English languages other than Spanish is limited. Even in Spanish there are few published intelligence tests normed on Spanish-speaking populations.

As previously noted, test translations are sometimes used but are often fraught with difficulties. For example, the translation may not be measuring what the test was originally designed to measure. The level of difficulty of the language in a translated item may vary greatly from that of the original item (American Educational Research Association, American Psychological Association & National Council on Measurement in Education 1985; Fradd & Wilen 1990). Direct test translations may contain culturally biased items with content inappropriate for the population being assessed (e.g., items referring to historical events, foods, articles of clothing, professionals, and household objects) (Cheng 1991). Lastly, spontaneous translations done during a testing session are frequently error-ridden and are not recommended (Caterino 1990; Figueroa 1990; Wilen & Sweeting 1986).

Intelligence tests in English may not be valid unless an NELB student is fluent in English or sufficiently bilingual to demonstrate cognitive academic language proficiency in English. Developing such proficiency takes an average of five to seven years. Do not mistake a student who has basic interpersonal communication skills in English, which are usually acquired after one and one-half to two years, as English proficient enough to take an English intelligence test. (Caterino 1990; Cummins 1982)

Some English intelligence tests have been adapted to include directions and responses in another language, while the test items remain in English. Adaptations such as these may be helpful for bilingual students but are not sufficient for LEP students who would have difficulty with English test items.

Whether full scale cognitive test batteries are administered in English or in a student's native language, large discrepancies between scores on verbal and performance components are common in NELB populations. Higher scores have been reported for NELB populations on performance as opposed to verbal measures (Gerkin 1978; Kaufman 1979). Such discrepancies should not be interpreted as an indicator of a possible learning or language disability as they often are in mainstream populations, but as an indicator of a language difference that merits further investigation. Exercise caution in using a global score to measure general cognitive functioning in an NELB student if the global score is depressed by a combined lower verbal scale-higher performance scale profile.

Take the case of an Hispanic student born in the United States who obtained a measured Verbal IQ of 62, a measured Performance IQ of 80, and a measured Full Scale IQ of 69 on the Wechsler Intelligence Test for Children-Revised (WISC-R). The test protocol reflected significant scatter of Verbal subtest scaled scores ranging from 1 on the Information subtest to 9 on the Arithmetic subtest. Scores on Performance subtests were relatively consistent. The Performance IQ is within the low average range. Even though the Full Scale IQ is within the mildly mentally handicapped range, it was lowered by the deficient Verbal score. A diagnosis of mildly mentally retarded intellectual functioning based on the Full Scale score would be suspect with this NELB student. Even though the WISC-R has recently been revised and there is now a third edition of the Wechsler Intelligence Scale for Children (WISC-III), the above scenario depicting a verbal-performance discrepancy resulting in a lowered Full Scale score would still apply.

Non-verbal tests of intelligence are a viable alternative in the assessment of NELB students who are limited in English proficiency and who may have varying degrees of proficiency in their native language as well (Esquivel 1988; Kaufman 1979; Wilen & Sweeting 1986). Though verbal mediation is certainly involved, non-verbal tests reduce the effects of language on test performance. Non-verbal cognitive measures include separate non-verbal tests and performance or non-verbal scales of full scale intelligence tests. Some of those non-verbal instruments have instructions that can be pantomimed while others require short verbal directions. Some are timed while others are not. The responses required of the examinee are generally motoric. Many allow demonstration or contain sample or teaching items that are useful with NELB students. Non-verbal intelligence tests can be helpful in ruling out suspected problems in NELB students such as low cognitive functioning. For example, the verbal functioning of a seven-year-old Greek NELB student who has resided in the United States for two years appeared depressed in both English and the native language and the student's academic skills were minimal. When assessed, the student scored in the average range on a non-verbal test of intelligence, enabling the psychologist to rule out low cognitive functioning and explore alternative explanations. It is a good practice to administer a second intelligence test to an NELB student if results of the initial assessment appear questionable. It may be appropriate to supplement a non-verbal measure with a full scale instrument or verbal measure for comparison purposes or to supplement one non-verbal measure with a second non-verbal measure. Testing the limits on standardized intelligence tests is a useful diagnostic strategy with some NELB students. It allows the psychologist to observe the student's performance under altered and more flexible conditions and is a source of clinical insight (Holtzman & Wilkinson 1991). Examples include allowing an examinee to work beyond an allowed time limit, questioning the examinee to solicit a response more than is allowable, and permitting the examinee to respond bilingually to verbal items on either an English or non-English intelligence test. However, any time that limits are tested, standardization is altered. Tests should be scored according to standard procedures, but the insight gained from testing the limits should be clearly reported.

Academic achievement assessment.

Academic skills of NELB students who are LEP should be assessed in both English and their native language. Students who come to the United States with a strong educational background in their native language and/or in English have an obvious advantage over students who have had limited prior schooling in any language. Such factors must be considered in interpreting current academic functioning.

Standardized achievement tests are becoming increasingly available in Spanish-English versions. The availability of published instruments in other languages, however, is extremely limited. The judicious analysis and interpretation of test results from these instruments in both English and the native language can provide more than scores for exceptional student education eligibility decisions. Results can be used to facilitate appropriate educational planning. For example, if an LEP student achieves in the deficient range on a reading test in English and in the average range on a Spanish version of that reading test, the student probably does not have a reading problem but rather is in the process of acquiring English language and academic skills. The psychologist should not just report scores but should analyze the protocol for strengths and weaknesses. Furthermore, an error analysis of responses can reveal diagnostic information such as difficulty with initial and medial vowel sounds, for example.

Another assessment alternative is the use of locally developed informal instruments. These instruments can be produced in the languages a school district serves with the assistance of cultural and linguistic informants. Readiness items such as knowledge of colors, numbers, and copying tasks along with reading, written language, and arithmetic items can be included.

Work products, classroom observations of student performance, criterion-referenced tests, teacher reports and interviews (Wilen & Sweeting 1986), mastery of district pupil progression plan skills, and the use of curriculum based assessment (Esquivel 1988) can also provide important data. Supplementing standardized tests with a variety of informal techniques is a recommended practice. Findings should be corroborated by multiple sources of information.

Adaptive behavior assessment.

If mental retardation is suspected, adaptive behavior assessment should be an integral part of the psychoeducational evaluation. Adaptive behavior reflects the degree to which the student is able to comply with the cultural expectations and demands of daily living and to function independently. Adaptive behavior assessment reflects current performance as opposed to potential (Levine 1989).

One adaptive behavior measure should be obtained with the teacher serving as informant and another measure should be obtained with the parent or primary caretaker serving as informant. This enables assessment personnel to make comparisons across settings. It is a good practice for a bilingual school social worker to make a home visit to conduct the adaptive behavior assessment with the parent. Observations gained in that setting can provide further clinical insight.

The assessor must be aware of sociocultural and linguistic factors that may affect scores on adaptive behavior instruments. For example, scores on the communication domain of an adaptive behavior measure could be influenced by an NELB student's lack of schooling or limited English proficiency. Scores on items measuring economic activity could be affected by the student's lack of experience with U.S. currency. Scores on self-help items could be affected by child-rearing practices such as a tendency for some cultural groups to discourage independent functioning in their children (Wilen & Sweeting 1986). Some skills assessed on these tests are not part of a culturally and linguistically diverse student's normal repertoire, such as bedmaking for a Vietnamese youngster who sleeps on a mat.

Emotional/behavioral functioning assessment.

School behaviors such as withdrawal, crying, anxiety, and acting out have been reported among newly arrived LEP students. LEP students and families are frequently confronted with tremendous stressors such as separation from family, financial problems, political unrest in their homeland, multiple moves, fear of deportation if illegal, and difficulties adjusting to a new culture (Esquivel 1988; Wilen 1990; Wilen & Sweeting 1986). Some students may have lived in conditions where social skills acceptable in the mainstream school environment were not learned. They may have had to steal to survive or may have never been asked to sit at a desk and attend to task or wear shoes before entering the U.S. school. Sociocultural differences and situational adjustment problems should be differentiated from behavior disorders and emotional disturbances.

A variety of techniques can be utilized. Parents, teachers, and the referred student should be interviewed to try to ascertain whether the presenting problems are atypical for the student's sociocultural background. The use of cultural informants can be helpful in this regard (Caterino 1990).

Norm-referenced behavior observation (Alessi & Kaye 1983) can be used to compare the referred student's behavior to that of an adjusted comparison student of similar background or to a group of newly arrived LEP students. The comparisons can be made across typical school settings such as the playground, the regular classroom, and the ESOL classroom (Wilen & Sweeting 1986). Behavioral improvement can be monitored using these techniques as well.

Other methods often used to assess behavioral/emotional functioning in LEP students include anecdotal records, behavior rating scales administered to parents and teachers, and projective testing such as human figure drawings, incomplete sentence forms, and story-telling techniques. Projective techniques are often interpreted using clinical judgment; more research needs to be done on the use of these instruments with NELB populations and cautious interpretation is advised (Barona & Hernandez 1990).

RESEARCH IN PRACTICE:
Advocate's Role in Conducting the Assessment

---

1. Discuss the importance of using multiple sources of data in conducting psychoeducational assessments with LEP students. In addition to standardized testing, what types of techniques are used with LEP students in your school district?

2. Discuss the use of tests in English, tests in other languages, and non-verbal tests in assessing the cognitive functioning of NELB students. What useful information can cognitive assessment measures provide? What types of cognitive assessment measures are used in your school?

3. Discuss the use of test translations. Can they be assumed to have the same psychometric properties as the original version of the test? Why or why not?

4. Describe the advantages of obtaining measures of an NELB student's academic achievement in English and the native language. How can this be accomplished?

5. Discuss the use of adaptive behavior instruments in the psychoeducational assessment of NELB students. How might sociocultural and linguistic factors affect such measures?

6. What are three techniques used to assess emotional/behavioral functioning in NELB students? Is an effort made to differentiate sociocultural differences and situational adjustment problems from behavioral disorders and emotional disturbance in your school?

ADVOCATE'S ROLE IN DEVELOPING AND USING REPORTS

Written psychoeducational reports are an important component of the assessment process. The report summarizes the assessment; provides information on the student's history and current functioning; makes recommendations for remediation, individual educational planning, and services to enhance the student's progress; and is a permanent record with enduring influence on a child's life. Not only is the report used within the school system, but it may also become a legal document or a document used by social service and community agencies, physicians, and outside consultants (Ross-Reynolds 1990; Sattler 1988).

The purpose of this section is not to discuss report writing in general. Extensive overviews of that topic are available elsewhere (see for example Ownby 1987; Ross-Reynolds 1990; Sattler 1988; Shellenberger 1982). The goal is to present information specific to the needs of practitioners and educators interpreting and writing reports on NELB and LEP students. Reports can be written to include the standard identifying data, reason for referral, background information, instruments employed, assessment results, observations and interpretations, and summary and recommendations. However, certain additional guidelines apply. These are summarized in Table 7-3.

Reports on NELB and LEP students are likely to be longer than those written on English proficient students just by virtue of the involvement of two languages in the assessment process. Reports should be clearly written so they are understandable to school personnel receiving and referring to them. Evaluation specialists should write reports and share data in such a way as to encourage educators to look beyond the numbers or scores obtained on tests by the NELB students. The report should synthesize data from a variety of sources, describe and interpret the student's functioning in the areas assessed considering the effects of cultural and language background factors, and recommend further interventions based on the evaluation results.

RESEARCH IN PRACTICE:
Advocate's Role in Developing and Using Reports.

Discuss five guidelines that should be followed in writing psychoeducational reports on NELB and LEP students. Are reports written differently for NELB and LEP students than they are for monolingual English speakers in your school district? How?

TABLE 7-3. GUIDELINES FOR PSYCHOEDUCATIONAL REPORTS ON NELB AND LEP STUDENTS

- State the home language and country of origin of the student.

- State the length of time the student has resided in the United States.

- State the language or languages in which the student's schooling has been conducted.

- State the results of language dominance and proficiency testing.

- State the language or languages used during assessment.

- State the full name, date of service, and type of service of any interpreter used in the assessment.

- Document pre-referral interventions implemented and results.

- Avoid statistically based statements that may not apply to the student.

- State exactly what you did if limits were tested during standardized testing.

- Discuss effects of cultural, educational, language, and other experiential background factors on performance.

- Include a precautionary statement that test results should be interpreted in light of cultural and language background.

- Integrate and interpret assessment results, placing less emphasis on specific test scores.

- Recommend close monitoring of the student's progress to assess the continued appropriateness of suggested interventions.

- Recommend early re-evaluation of students if appropriate.

ADVOCATE'S ROLE IN CONDUCTING INTERPRETIVE CONFERENCES

The importance of advocating parental involvement and multidisciplinary team participation in the assessment process has been noted throughout this chapter. Conferences between parents and school personnel need to occur at the pre-referral stage, at the referral stage and during and after psychoeducational assessment. This involvement expands the ability of school personnel to understand the student as an individual within the context of the home, school, and community. The evaluation specialist's role in conducting post-assessment interpretative conferences with both NELB parents and school personnel are discussed next.

After assessment is completed, it is a good practice for the evaluation specialist to hold a parent conference to discuss findings and recommendations (Holtzman & Wilkinson 1991; Wilen 1989). In actuality, separate conferences between parents and evaluation specialists to discuss assessment results are rarely held prior to staffings. More likely, assessment results are initially reported to parents at the required eligibility and placement/individual educational plan (IEP) meeting where a number of professionals meet with parents in a group. Since such meetings can be intimidating, confusing, and emotionally charged for an English-speaking mainstream parent (Silverstein 1991), they are particularly likely to pose difficulties for an NELB parent who does not speak the language of the school and who is unfamiliar with the educational system of the United States. Communication and parental input at eligibility and placement/IEP meetings can be enhanced by prior contact with an NELB family.

Interactive communication should be a goal of any parent conference. Too often communications by school personnel to culturally and linguistically diverse parents at these meetings are one-sided, with the professionals doing the talking and the parents playing a passive, accepting role. In many countries, school personnel are recognized authority figures who are completely in charge of the student's education (Correa 1989). Parents are contacted only when a serious problem arises. Care must be exercised in this regard. Take the case of ten-year-old Pierre from Haiti whose mother received a note that she should come to school for a conference with the psychologist about her son. Pierre's mother immediately punished her son because of an assumption that he must be blameworthy since she was contacted to come to school. When inviting parents from some cultures to a meeting, in addition to the purpose of the meeting, it is important to emphasize that their child is not in trouble or at fault. Make every effort to encourage parental participation. If parents seem unresponsive, call them in the evening when they are likely to be home from work or arrange for a bilingual visiting teacher or school social worker to make a home visit and explain the importance of their presence at the meeting.

Be flexible about the meeting time to accommodate work schedules and the need for parents to sometimes bring younger children with them because of their lack of childcare. Also, in some cultures, when you invite parents, they may bring other relatives or friends. Make these other parties feel welcome as long as the parent is comfortable with their presence.

If you do not speak the home language of the parent, arrange for an interpreter, and communicate this to the parent in advance of the meeting. LEP parents often breathe a sigh of relief when they hear that someone who speaks their language will be present at the conference.

Encourage the father, as well as the mother, to attend the conference. This practice is especially important in working with families from cultures where the father is the primary authority-figure or decision-maker in the family (Correa 1989).

At the time of the meeting, set the stage for productive interaction. Reinforce the parents for coming. Make the parents feel comfortable and communicate your role as a child advocate. Tell the parents it is normal to have questions at these meetings and that they should ask you to explain anything you have said that they do not understand and that you will do the same. Begin with something positive about the child. Communicate the student's strengths as well as his weaknesses. Speak to them at their level when describing assessment results and recommendations, avoiding the use of technical jargon whenever possible. If technical terms such as a specific exceptionality need to be used, prepare advance descriptions of the terms in words the parent can understand. Some languages do not have direct translations for special education or psychological terminology (Fradd & Wilen 1990). Cultural and linguistic informants may need to be consulted.

Solicit parental input and feedback. Ask the parents to explain to you their concerns and perceptions and their understanding of your recommendations. Throughout the conference, be aware of cultural differences that may affect the sharing of information with parents including behavior toward authority figures, educational expectations, perceptions of handicapping conditions, feelings about their own ethnicity, and spiritual beliefs. (Jensen & Potter 1990). For example, do the members of the parents' culture usually deal with issues in direct or indirect ways? Are members of the parents' culture generally receptive to help from outside agencies such as community mental health centers? Do they value independence or dependence in their children? Is the family more important than the individual in the family's culture? (Nuttall, De Leon & Valle 1990). Observe the parents' verbal and non-verbal responses and revise communications as necessary (Fradd & Wilen 1990).

At the end of the meeting, give the parents your card and tell them to call you if they have any questions. Tell them what will happen next. For example, inform them that they will be invited to a staffing and explain the protocol and format of such a meeting. Invite the parents to visit new programs that may be recommended. Make parents feel an important part of the educational process for their children and solicit their assistance in enhancing their children's success in school.

Services to students and families can be further enhanced by sharing insight and information generated through the assessment process with teachers, administrators, and others who may work with the family or become advocates for the students. The multidisciplinary team involvement recommended earlier in this chapter should continue here. Assessment results empower team members and other school personnel with increased awareness of the student as learner and facilitate planning to accommodate individual needs. For example, by sharing diagnostic data that a student does not have a learning disability, but could benefit from a cooperative learning situation and a language sensitive curriculum while in the process of acquiring English, the evaluation specialist encourages teachers and administrators to provide effective instruction to meet the student's needs.

RESEARCH IN PRACTICE:
Advocate's Role in Conducting Interpretive Conferences

1. **Discuss the advantages of evaluation specialists holding interpretive conferences with NELB parents prior to formal staffings.** How are interpretive conferences conducted in your school?

2. **By sharing assessment information with teachers, administrators and others working with NELB students, the assessor can empower these individuals to function as advocates for the students and families.** Give an example of such a situation from your school district.

SUMMARIZING SECTION TWO:
Advocacy in the Current Assessment Process

This section began with a discussion of difficulties involved in the psychoeducational assessment process with NELB students with limited English proficiency. Such difficulties include factors related to available test instruments, preparation of assessment personnel, the traditional assessment process, parent involvement, the use of interpreters and translators, and school and district plans and procedures. An understanding of these issues lays the groundwork for a more inclusive or integrated approach to assessment wherein data are collected from multiple sources including the parent, teacher, and student. The evaluation specialist takes the role of an advocate for the student and family and encourages advocacy throughout the process of planning interventions, conducting the assessment, developing and using reports, and holding interpretive conferences with parents and school personnel.

WHAT CAN YOU DO?

1. **As child advocates, evaluation specialists may make diagnostic recommendations which they feel are in the best interest of an NELB student but which are unpopular with administrators, teachers and other school personnel.** Give an example of such a case. What can you do if faced with this situation in your school district?

2. **Why is it advantageous to involve a multidisciplinary team in the pre-referral process with LEP students?** Do such teams operate in your school on a regular basis? Are there bilingual and multicultural experienced members on this team? Is this team approach successful? How can you improve it?

3. **Describe the psychoeducational assessment process with LEP students in general.** How thorough is this process in your school? Are a variety of data used to corroborate findings and recommendations? How can the psychoeducational process be improved for the LEP students in your school or district?

4. **Are there differences in the way psychoeducational reports should be written for monolingual English speakers as opposed to NELB and LEP students?** How can reports on NELB and LEP students be improved in your district?

5. **What are the main components of positive and interactive post-assessment interpretative conferences with NELB parents?** How can such conferences better meet the needs of NELB families in your school or district?

SECTION THREE

ADVOCACY IN PROMOTING EFFECTIVE SYSTEMS

In addition to acting as advocates for LEP students and families on a case by case basis, assessment personnel should assume a leadership role in promoting school and district-wide change to better meet the needs of LEP students. The implementation of productive systemic modifications will facilitate the learning process for all students, and will reduce inappropriate referrals for in depth individual assessment services for students having difficulties because of the normal process of acculturation or second language acquisition. This section calls for advocacy in improving interpreter/translator service provision and advocacy in linking the school and district to the language and culture of the home.

ADVOCATE'S ROLE IN IMPROVING INTERPRETER/ TRANSLATOR SERVICES

To enhance second language service provision during the assessment process, assessment personnel need to make a strong case for the development of district-wide programs and procedures relative to the use of interpreters and translators. These include the development of training programs for providers and users of interpreter/translator services and the development of guidelines for using interpreters and translators in the assessment process. These are discussed next.

Development of training programs for providers and users of interpreter/translator services.

Second language service providers are often selected based on expediency and availability with little regard for task demands and the need for specific skills and training. Programs to train second language service providers to assist psychologists, social workers, speech-language pathologists, and educators in the assessment of LEP students are a rarity in U.S. schools (Fradd & Wilen 1990; Wilen & Fradd 1991). Assessment personnel must build support for such training so that interpreters and translators can provide meaningful assistance in assessment. Advocacy begins with documenting the need for training in your district. Collect data such as:

- the number of LEP students in the district and any projected increase in that number by language and cultural groups;

- the number of bilingual assessment personnel employed by the district by language, professional assignment, and location;

- any gaps between LEP students referred for assessment services and availability of bilingual assessment personnel proficient in their home languages;

- the names of individuals currently providing interpreter/translator services by home language, job assignment, and location;

- the perceptions of users and providers of interpreter/translator services as to the need for formal training programs in the district;

- the types of training programs users and providers see as necessary.

Such information can be obtained through available statistics and brief surveys.

Once the need is established, develop the training content, delivery system, and evaluation strategies. Adapt training to local needs including the language and cultural groups served by the district and the types of services, procedures, and techniques required in the assessment process with LEP students and families (see, for example, American Speech-Language-Hearing Association 1985; Fradd & Wilen 1990; Langdon 1988; and Wilen & Fradd 1991 for information pertinent to interpreter/translator training). Build in evaluative components such as pre-tests and post-tests and participant rating forms. Analysis of such evaluative data facilitates the effective planning and delivery of future training. Give participants who successfully complete the inservice certificates or some other form of recognition and verification of professional development.

Similarly, school personnel must demand training programs for assessment personnel who use second language services. Such professionals often find themselves in the position of directing the second language service provider without adequate preparation for so doing. Programs geared to the specific needs of psychologists, social workers, speech-language pathologists, and educators should be developed. Such programs could include role-playing activities and simulations of assessment situations, home visits, parent conferences, staffings, and other instances in which these professionals commonly use interpreter/translator services (Wilen & Fradd 1991).

Development of guidelines for using interpreters/translators in the assessment process.

In addition to implementing training programs, school systems need to develop guidelines and procedures for the use of interpreter/translator services in their district, including whom to contact when services are needed and how much notice is required. Plans should also be developed for recruiting and compensating consultants to the school district. This is often necessary when bilingual personnel from a particular language group are unavailable within the school system. Time should be allocated for briefing and debriefing between users and providers of second language services before and after the interpretation/translation session (Fradd & Wilen 1990).

Even when users and providers are experienced, it is advantageous to use written checklists to promote consistency, and as a reminder of steps to follow when using interpreters in assessment. Separate lists can be developed for users and providers. An example of such a checklist for users of interpreters appears in Table 7-5.

The suggestions in Table 7-4 highlight areas psychologists, social workers, speech-language pathologists, and educators should address when using interpreters. Such professionals can use the suggestions as a checklist to facilitate quality service provision to LEP students and families. Suggestions for interpreters appear in Table 7-6.

TABLE 7-4. SUGGESTIONS FOR USERS OF INTERPRETERS

- Meet with the interpreter prior to the session and discuss the assignment.
- Ask the interpreter if he/she has the skills and knowledge to complete the assignment.
- Discuss the importance of maintaining confidentiality.
- Remind the interpreter that he/she **must not alter, omit** or **add to** the communication.
- Make sure the interpreter has a dual language dictionary.
- Review key concepts, phrases, and words.
- Review evaluation instruments and special forms with the interpreter.
- Inform the interpreter of unusual circumstances.
- Remind the interpreter to inform you if specific concepts/words are not translatable during the session.
- Remain in control of the session. Do not allow the interpreter to take charge.
- Meet with the interpreter after the session.
- Discuss behaviors, outcomes, questions, and problems observed during the sessions.
- Ask the interpreter about cultural considerations (e.g. child rearing practices, non-verbal language, dialectal differences).

Source: From Pomerantz, J. (1991c). *Suggestions for users of interpreters.* Ft. Lauderdale, FL: Multicultural Education Department, School Board of Broward County.

TABLE 7-5. SUGGESTIONS FOR INTERPRETERS

- Meet with the professional you are assisting before the interpretation session.

- Do not be afraid to tell the professional if you feel that an assignment is beyond your capabilities.

- Ask the professional questions if you are unsure about an assignment.

- Do not talk about information obtained from students, families, or school personnel to anyone other than professionals involved in the interpretation session.

- Review key concepts, phrases, and vocabulary words with the professional.

- Review with the professional any tests or special forms to be used.

- Make sure that you have a dual language dictionary.

- Report all information obtained from the student or family to the professional.

- **Do not alter, omit** or **add to** any communication that you are interpreting.

- Do not give the student any hints when he/she is trying to answer a test question.

- Inform the professional you are assisting if any words or concepts are not translatable.

- Write down important information that you will need to share with the professional after the session.

- Remember to share any important cultural information with the professional. This will help him/her make better educational decisions about the student.

Source: From Pomerantz, J. (1991b). *Suggestions for interpreters.* Ft. Lauderdale, FL: Multicultural Education Department, School Board of Broward County.

Giving interpreters a written list of suggestions such as these helps professionalize their role and provides them with some specific and uniform direction. Such guidelines encourage open communication between interpreters and professionals using their services and empower interpreters to perform more effectively (Fradd & Wilen 1990).

RESEARCH IN PRACTICE:
Advocate's Role in Improving Interpreter/Translator Services

1. Discuss three ways to establish the need for interpreter/translator training programs in school districts. How can the need for such training best be established in your school system?

2. **Discuss five practices that both users of interpreters and interpreters could follow to enhance second language service provision during the assessment process.** What steps could be taken in your district to professionalize interpreter services for LEP students and families?

ADVOCATE'S ROLE IN LINKING THE SCHOOL DISTRICT WITH THE LANGUAGE AND CULTURE OF THE HOME

Educators must assume the role of change agents to develop the capacity of schools and districts to promote effective services for NELB students and families. They must call for examination of existing plans and modification or development of new processes and procedures for this population where appropriate. In an effort to improve the whole package of services for NELB populations, educators must encourage recruitment of bilingual personnel, write grants, develop pilot programs, conduct research, involve parents, and develop training for paraprofessionals, teachers, administrators, and support personnel. They should conduct needs assessments, foster interdisciplinary collaboration, and adapt instruction. They may need to revise documents and translate them into other languages. They may have to include sections on multicultural awareness in manuals and handbooks used by personnel. They may have to develop new forms such as forms to request language dominance classifications prior to psychological and speech and language assessments and forms to request interpreter/translator services. Schools may have to establish bilingual child study teams and bilingual assessment teams. Districts may have to modify procedures to allow for informal assessment techniques and different approaches for involving parents. They may need to augment exceptional student education procedures to include a requirement for addressing language proficiency development in individual educational plans for LEP exceptional students.

One effective mechanism for analyzing existing services and advocating change that was implemented in a local school system is a district-level task force on referral, assessment, and programming for LEP students. Members of this task force include representatives from areas such as school psychology, social work, guidance, speech and language, exceptional student education, bilingual/ESOL education, vocational education, pre-school education, and school-level and district-level administration. Among the outcomes of the task force have been:

- identifying inservice needs of each discipline and formulating plans;
- identifying problems in service provision within and across disciplines and formulating plans;
- reviewing and recommending revisions of current procedures, documents, and forms (i.e., LEP exceptional student education procedures);

- increased understanding of the complexities involved in providing appropriate assessment services to LEP populations;
- increased understanding of the importance of interdisciplinary collaboration in problem-solving with LEP populations;
- identifying and augmenting resources within the school district.

A task force such as this can be easily adapted to the needs and requirements of individual school districts.

RESEARCH IN PRACTICE:
Advocate's Role in Linking the School and District with the Language and Culture of the Home

---

1. Describe four ways school districts can improve the whole package of services for LEP students. What efforts have been made to link your school district to the home language and culture of the LEP students it serves?

2. Discuss the concept of a district-level task force on referral, assessment and programming for LEP students as a mechanism for enhanced services to LEP populations. What types of individuals could be on this task force? What types of activities could the task force perform?

SUMMARIZING SECTION THREE:
Advocacy in Promoting Effective Systems

This section called for school-level and district-wide change to improve assessment and instructional services to LEP populations. The discussion encompassed the development of interpreter/translator training programs for users and providers, district guidelines for second language service provision, and other comprehensive plans to link the school and school system with the language and culture of the home. This section cast assessment personnel in new roles as advocates for more effective systems to meet the needs of all LEP students and families.

WHAT CAN YOU DO?

1. Plan a district wide interpreter/translator training program that addresses the needs of both users and providers of second language services. How does this program differ from any such training currently being done in your district?

2. **Assessment personnel should assume leadership roles in promoting more effective school and district-level services for LEP populations.** Give examples of changes that could be implemented in your district to better meet the needs of LEP populations. How can you become involved in this system?

SUMMARY OF CHAPTER SEVEN
Advocacy in the Assessment Process

This chapter discusses the importance of advocacy in promoting a more effective assessment process with NELB and LEP students. It presents historical developments and the call for more equitable assessment practices with this population over the last two to three decades. It suggests a movement toward a more comprehensive integrated approach to assessment with data collection from multiple sources. Assessment personnel are cast in the role of advocates for LEP students and families on a case by case as well as on a system-wide basis.

Chapter 8

Identifying Special Needs

Previous chapters have presented case studies of NELB students who may have learning requirements that can be met within typical classrooms with effective instructional practices. Additionally, cases of students who may require more specialized intervention have been presented. Chapter Four, for example, focused on differentiating language differences and the effects of limited instructional opportunities from language disorders. This chapter extends the discussion to the identification of students who may have learning needs commonly associated with placement in special, or exceptional, education programs. Although procedures for identification of special needs students may vary at state and district levels, these procedures are guided by federal definitions and requirements that specify what constitutes an exceptionality. More often than not, the process of identifying special needs students involves the administration of standardized psychological and educational tests, and inventories of behavioral or social development. Educational specialists such as school psychologists, speech-language pathologists, school social workers, or special education teachers are typically called upon to assess students in a multidisciplinary approach to determine the existence of special needs. Chapter Seven provided an overview of this process as it relates to NELB students and suggested ways in which the process can be made more effective.

Given the problems associated with the exclusive use of standardized tests with NELB populations, alternative assessment practices are useful tools to examine student learning processes and performance. By using alternative methods, either prior to use of, or supplementary to standardized procedures, additional data are gathered which are relevant to developing hypotheses regarding students' presenting problems. These procedures can assist in determining the appropriateness of the referral of an NELB student for further evaluation by specialists. This chapter challenges a "deficit hypothesis" approach when addressing NELB students' poor school and standardized test performances. This hypothesis assumes that NELB students are displaying inherent cognitive, academic, and behavioral deficits, evidenced by school failure, low test scores, and behavior problems, that require specialized instruction. Such an hypothesis assumes a pre-existing disability in students: the hypothesis may be proven true or false by psychological and educational testing. Whether or not special education placement follows as a result of evaluation, the burden of proof as to whether or not the disability exists may lie directly with the students. Low test scores, school failure, or behavioral adjustment problems accepted at face value, without further analysis of the many variables affecting NELB students' performance, serve to perpetuate inappropriate special education placements and treatments.

This chapter provides additional case studies to exemplify some of the problems related to the use of standardized tests for identifying special needs NELB students. The use of supplementary assessment methods is recommended to enhance decision-making when referral or eligibility for special education is in question. The first section of the chapter examines the status of NELB students in special education. The scope of discussion is limited to students with milder or higher prevalence disabilities, specifically those commonly falling under the categories of Specific Learning Disabilities (SLD), Mild Mental Retardation (MMR), and Emotional/Behavioral Disorders (E/BD).

The chapter expands the notion of performance assessment for special education accountability purposes. It links the assessment process to the ninth and final chapter of the book which focuses on the use of assessment information to promote instructional effectiveness.

SPECIAL EDUCATION AND THE NELB STUDENT

There are eight special education categories commonly recognized by public school systems. These categories include: visually impaired, hearing impaired, communication disordered, physically handicapped, gifted, learning disabled, emotionally disturbed/behavior disordered, and mentally retarded. Of these, certain categories are overrepresented with students of lower socioeconomic status (SES) who are from minority and linguistically different backgrounds (Kretschmer 1991). Certain minority and linguistically different students are underrepresented in other categories and are generally misdiagnosed (Kretschmer 1991). Categorical programs with typically disproportionate numbers of minority group students include learning disabilities, mental retardation at the educable level, communication disorders, and emotionally disturbed/behavior disordered (Kretschmer 1991). For example, it has been found that Hispanics in Texas have been overrepresented by 300% in the learning disabilities category (Ortiz & Yates 1983). With unusually large numbers of NELB students in certain programs, special education laws and related litigation appear to have limited, rather than expanded, the range of educational program options, including those in regular education, that are considered for culturally diverse students (Macmillan, Hendrick & Watkins 1988).

As a result of both over- and under-representation of minorities in special education, the referral, assessment, identification, and placement processes have come under close scrutiny and review (Cegelka, Lewis & Rodriguez 1987; Garcia & Ortiz 1988; Jones 1988; Olson 1991). Placement in special education programs may not be the most effective way to serve some NELB students. When such placements do not result in gains in achievement test scores and may, in fact, result in lower scores on tests used to measure intelligence, it is difficult to justify special education placement (Ortiz & Yates 1988; Wilkinson & Ortiz 1986). Although intelligence test scores obtained by native English speaking students are generally stable over time, that is, scores upon re-evaluation tend to approximate those obtained upon initial testing, this may not hold true for NELB students. There is not necessarily a direct causal relationship between special education placement and subsequent lowered test scores; however, the evidence suggests that, in the case of NELB students, careful consideration of the whole process is warranted. It cannot be assumed either that all NELB students who are placed in special education will score lower on tests administered at re-evaluation. In fact, some NELB students, such as Maurice who was presented in Chapter Five, may score higher, making the initial identification of a disability suspect.

The issue of lower test scores implies that even if best practices and procedures for evaluation and placement of NELB students are followed, these efforts may be futile if the environments in which the students are placed do not provide for their unique linguistic and academic needs. Special education placement must include meaningful instruction, including perhaps the use of the native language, and other facilitative strategies, if growth is to occur. Additionally, special education programs must be integrated within the main-stream programs and curriculum to be effective. The case of Estela, discussed next, poignantly illustrates the need for a special education identification and placement process that is sensitive and responsive to the linguistic, as well as academic requirements of NELB students.

The Case of Estela.

Estela is an eleven-year-old youngster from Guatemala who began her school career in a transitional bilingual education program with ESOL services. Spanish is the primary home language. During kindergarten and first grades, Estela learned oral English rapidly, so that by second grade she was starting to be mainstreamed in the all English medium classroom. During the second semester of second grade, however, Estela was noted to be reading below grade level in both her native language and English. Her writing skills were noted to be poor, and she was experiencing difficulty acquiring math concepts. Estela was referred for evaluation for possible special education services. The initial intellectual evaluation was conducted with the WISC-R, while the academic evaluation was conducted with both formal and informal measures. The examiner, who was bilingual, reported Estela was dominant in English and fluent in Spanish. The youngster scored at Level 5, or Fluent Speaker, in English, and at Level 4, also Fluent Speaker, in Spanish on the Language Assessment Scales (LAS). The WISC-R was administered in English and resulted in a Verbal IQ of 94, a Performance IQ of 123, and a Full Scale IQ of 107. The results indicated Average verbal abilities, Superior nonverbal abilities, and an overall functioning level in the Average range for age. The academic measures revealed pre-primer level reading skills and deficient writing skills in English, while mathematics skills were at a late first grade level. Spanish literacy skills were at a primer level. Because there was a significant discrepancy between Estela's average full scale score on the intelligence measure and her reading and written language scores on the academic measures, the special education committee determined that she was eligible for placement in a self-contained classroom for Specific Learning Disabled (SLD) students. As Estela was deemed to be English dominant, her instructional program was implemented in this language. The focus of Estela's Individual Educational Plan (IEP) was to develop her reading and written language skills, as well as her understanding of mathematical concepts.

Estela was still in a self-contained SLD classroom in fifth grade at the time of the mandatory three-year re-evaluation. By this time the family had relocated to a new school district. The teacher reported that Estela was progressing; however, the youngster experienced comprehension difficulties both in reading and when oral directions or concepts were presented. Additionally, Estela occasionally wrote words in Spanish when she couldn't think of them in English. As part of the re-evaluation process, a screening of language dominance was requested. On the Language Assessment Battery utilized by the school district, Estela was found to score at the 36th percentile rank in Spanish and at the 20th percentile rank in English. Due to her low scores in both languages, Estela was recommended for native language and ESOL services through the regular education program; however, the final decision as to how and where Estela should be served was left to the multidisciplinary team developing her IEP.

Estela was also re-evaluated with the WISC-R in English. Although the language dominance test had indicated somewhat higher Spanish language skills, during individual testing Estela demonstrated significant difficulties expressing her thoughts in Spanish. She preferred and was more fluent in English. This was the same situation reported three years earlier. On the second administration of the WISC-R Estela obtained a Verbal IQ of 77, a Performance IQ of 117, and a Full Scale IQ of 94. This placed her verbal abilities in the Borderline range (sometimes called slow learner range), her nonverbal abilities in the High Average range, and her overall functioning level in the Average range for age. Academically, while Estela was able to decode words at a beginning third grade level, her reading comprehension was at a second grade level, while written language skills were at a late first grade level as measured by a standardized test. Estela's mathematics skills were at a fourth grade level in the area of computations, and at a second grade level in math concepts.

The most striking outcome of Estela's re-evaluation was the realization that after three years of what was assumed to be intensive academic intervention, not only were there very limited gains, there were also significant losses, particularly in language related areas. Although Estela might have appeared to be English dominant at initial evaluation, any advantage she might have demonstrated as a second grader in a linguistically and culturally supportive instructional environment appeared to have been lost in spite of three years of special education assistance. Not only was Estela less proficient in her native language, she was also less competent in the academic English needed for continued successful performance on a standardized test of intelligence and academics. Her test scores dropped, and Estela appeared, on the whole, to be no better off than when she was first placed in special education three years earlier.

Cases such as Estela's typify the dilemma associated with the differentiation of normal second language acquisition processes and learning handicaps, possible inappropriate special education placements, and overidentification of NELB students for special services. This may lead to an unwillingness on the part of educators to refer these students for special education consideration (Cegelka, Lewis & Rodriguez 1987). It is estimated, however, that about 12% of the linguistically different population in the United States may require special education services (Olson 1991). These students need to be identified and be provided equal access to any services for which they may be eligible, including special education (*Education of the Handicapped,* 1991, referring to the Individuals with Disabilities Education Act (IDEA) of 1990). For this reason, many aspects of the special education process as it relates to NELB students are the object of ongoing inquiry among interested special and regular educators. Specific areas under consideration include pre-referral intervention, teacher training, curriculum and materials development, parent education and involvement, and administrative practices, as well as assessment. There appear to be more questions than there are answers regarding the most effective methods for meeting students' needs at this time. Every effort must be aimed at providing relevant, proven, and responsive education services for all NELB students. On this, educators in all areas agree.

RESEARCH IN PRACTICE:
Special Education and the NELB Student

1. Are there any NELB students in your school who are receiving special education services? Survey the special education staff to determine the numbers of NELB students, the types and amount of services they are receiving (remember, do not ask for names of students, in order to maintain their anonymity and respect confidentiality). Are any patterns evident in the data? For example, are there greater or fewer numbers of NELB students in programs for the learning disabled given the total NELB student population at your school? Are there greater or fewer numbers of NELB students in programs for the mildly mentally retarded? Given the total number of NELB students at your school, does this population appear to be over- or under-represented in special education at your school? School personnel are sometimes not aware that students may have a language other than English. What steps can be taken to rectify over- or under-representation? What steps can be taken to identify student language background? Discuss your findings and ideas with colleagues.

2. What are the procedures established at your school for referring students for special education? Are there any procedures that are specific to the referral of NELB students? If not, identify areas where such procedures may be needed. Discuss your ideas with colleagues. What do they think? Referral procedures may often be determined at the district rather than school level. You may want to involve the school administration and district personnel in the discussion.

3. Consider Estela's case.

a. List hypotheses regarding the reasons for initial referral for special education. Include hypotheses regarding the reasons for her low academic achievement at the time of referral. What other information would you want to obtain?

b. List hypotheses regarding the reasons for the drop in Estela's IQ test scores, especially the Verbal IQ. Include hypotheses regarding what appear to be limited academic gains.

c. How would you develop an educational plan to address Estela's needs? Would you include more, or less, special education services? What services should be increased or decreased?

d. How would you develop a plan for both short and long term monitoring of Estela's progress?

THE CONCEPT OF LEARNING DISABILITIES AND THE NELB STUDENT

Perhaps one of the greatest challenges facing assessment personnel, particularly those whose data may ultimately result in student placement in a special education program, is the identification of youngsters who present academic and learning difficulties commonly categorized as Specific Learning Disabilities, or SLD. This challenge is made more complex if the student being evaluated is of a non-English or culturally diverse background or has limited English proficiency (Barona & Santos de Barona 1987).

Defining the concept of learning disabilities.

In order to better understand the dilemma of misclassification, over-identification, or under-identification, of NELB students in programs for learning disabled students, it is helpful to examine the definition and practices that generally guide school districts in the identification process. The definition provided in the *Federal Register* (Aug. 1982), and included in the Handicapped Children's Act (P.L. 94-142, Section 300.4, 1974), states:

> "Specific learning disability" means a disorder in one or more of the basic psychological processes involved in understanding or in using language, spoken or written, which may manifest itself in an imperfect ability to listen, think, speak, read, write, spell, or to do mathematical calculations. The term includes such conditions as a perceptual handicap, brain injury, minimal brain dysfunction, dyslexia, and developmental aphasia. The term does not include a learning problem which is primarily the result of a visual, hearing, or motor handicap, of mental retardation, or of environmental, cultural, or economic disadvantage." (*Federal Register* 1982, p. 33845)

Application of this definition of a learning disability in the school setting generally includes the determination of a discrepancy between students' learning potential and their actual school achievement. Within the school setting a learning disability is identified when student achievement does not occur at a level commensurate with chronological age and ability level even though suitable learning experiences have been provided. A student may be diagnosed as having a learning disability in one or more of the following areas: oral expression, listening comprehension, written expression, basic reading skill, reading comprehension, mathematics calculation, or mathematics reasoning (Barona & Santos de Barona 1987). Assessment to determine the possible existence of a learning disability usually requires the administration of a measure of intelligence, a measure of achievement, and a measure of basic psychological processing (sometimes called information processing) abilities. Examples of measures of basic psychological processing may include tests of listening abilities or tests of visual-motor development as would be needed for writing.

The concept of what constitutes a learning disability has been the object of much discussion and debate in the fields of special education and assessment, due to the difficulties in clearly defining it (Barona & Santos de Barona 1987; Rewilak & Janzen 1982; Reynolds 1990; Rueda 1989). There is a tendency to call every type of school problem a "learning disability," because the term is less stigmatizing than other special education terms. The vagueness of the definition has resulted in a wide variation in the numbers of children identified as learning disabled in the general population. There is not a common trait shared by all youngsters who are so identified (Cummins 1984; Whitworth 1988). This is not to say that among the larger group of NELB students there are none who may experience difficulty learning due to problems independent of linguistic and cultural differences. In this case, it is the educators' responsibility to evaluate all possible sources of problems through the use of both formal and informal methods (Thonis 1983). Although some students enrolled in classes for the learning disabled may display linguistic and perceptual problems of neurological origin, a great majority of children categorized as learning disabled do not. This latter group exhibits slower progress in the acquisition of academic skills (Cummins 1984). Additionally, the proportion of students identified as learning disabled depends on the instruments and procedures used by school systems (Cummins 1984; Reynolds 1990). Because the construct of a learning disability is poorly defined, assessment instruments designed to identify learning disabilities have significant validity problems (Cummins 1984). There are also difficulties related to measuring ability among linguistically diverse students using the current achievement below ability, or ability-achievement discrepancy model to determine learning disabilities (Shinn & Knutson 1992). These problems have been addressed throughout this book.

LD or language learner?

The problems associated with the identification of a learning disability in monolingual youngsters are magnified when the students involved are culturally and linguistically different from the mainstream. No definition can be applied unilaterally to youngsters of diverse cultural and racial backgrounds (Barona & Santos de Barona 1987). The lack of demonstrated validity of tests used to identify learning disabilities in monolingual contexts suggests that extreme caution is needed when relying on these tests in bilingual contexts (Cummins 1984; Rueda 1989). Furthermore, learning patterns commonly associated with a learning disability may also be characteristic of normal second language learning, making it very difficult to distinguish between what might be a learning handicap from limitations in language proficiency (Ainsa 1984; Garcia 1985; Ortiz & Yates 1988). Common learning and behavior characteristics that may be shared by learning disabled native English speakers and second language learners are presented in Table 8-1.

Language proficiency has been found to be the single most critical factor in predicting non-English language background students' performance on academic achievement tests (Ulibarri 1990). Both prior knowledge or familiarity with the content, and cultural factors affect the achievement test performance of

TABLE 8-1. LEARNING AND BEHAVIOR CHARACTERISTICS SHARED BY LD NATIVE ENGLISH SPEAKERS AND SECOND LANGUAGE LEARNERS

Domain	Characteristics

LANGUAGE (Receptive and Expressive)

Delayed acquisition
Difficulties in expression (including articulation)
Low vocabulary
Problems understanding what is said (comprehension)
Difficulty following oral directions
Poor immediate auditory memory
Poor retention of information
Unable to rhyme words

READING

Poor reading progress
Reads below grade level
Confusion in sound/symbol associations
Poor eye tracking: loses place during reading
Unable to remember what has been read
Poor progress in content areas

WRITTEN LANGUAGE

Spelling is below grade level
Words or letters may be reversed
Inconsistent spelling
"Bizarre" spelling
Poor recall of sequences of syllables
Poor visual memory
Difficulty expressing ideas in writing
Poor grammar and syntax

MATHEMATICS

Mathematics skills below grade level
Difficulty in remembering processes apparently known
Uses fingers or counting aids

BEHAVIORS

Limited attention span and poor concentration
Work may be "unpresentable"
Low frustration tolerance
Anxious or cries easily
Poor peer relationships
Poor eye contact

NELB students. Additionally, language is a factor in the content and the context of the items presented, in the administration of the tests, the responses to the tests, and in the interpretation of the test results from norms that assume a particular standard of English proficiency (Ulibarri 1990). As in the case of Estela, low test scores are often interpreted as evidence of deficits or even disorders (Ascher 1990; Ulibarri 1990). For NELB students, some tests normed on and administered to native English speakers to determine the possible existence of a learning disability become tests of language proficiency and literacy in English, rather than of abilities and competencies. Differences in scores obtained by NELB students and native English speaking students on tests commonly used to identify learning disabilities suggest that language and sociocultural factors, rather than true learning disabilities, may account for misclassification of NELB students (Whitworth 1988). Even youngsters deemed to be proficient in English may encounter problems with tests presented in this language. Central information processing variables necessary for successful completion of tests require knowledge of linguistic rules in English. Students learning English as a new language may not possess knowledge of these rules (Ulibarri 1990). Furthermore, nonverbal items on tests may also present difficulties for NELB students, if they are presented in an unfamiliar context. This increases the amount of information that needs to be processed and results in greater item difficulty (Ulibarri 1990). Despite the impact of language on test performance, the language status and proficiency of NELB students who are being considered for special education placement may not be assessed (Bozinou-Doukas 1983; Garcia 1985). Because NELB students' academic performance may be below the norm in the classroom, the tendency may be to assume that this underachievement is due to a specific learning disability, a learning problem intrinsic to the student. An examination of factors that affect NELB students' academic performance must include an analysis of opportunities for learning, both past and present, within the current educational setting (New York City Board of Education 1990). NELB students' unique educational and life experiences, when placed in the mainstream U.S. classroom context, may make them appear more, or less, academically and socially competent. Evaluation of present opportunities for learning in the context of daily instruction and instructional strategies is as necessary as examining students' current life experiences and personal development. Accepting low test scores and poor school performance at face value as evidence of learning disabilities in NELB students will only result in continued inappropriate placements in special education. At best, premature referrals for evaluation for special education can occur. Interpretation of standardized test scores can be confusing if scores are analyzed only in light of special education criteria. The difficulties inherent in the exclusive use of standardized tests for purposes of identification of learning disabilities among NELB students is exemplified by the cases of Souriya and Phon, Cambodian siblings.

THE CASES OF SOURIYA AND PHON

Both Souriya, fifth grade female student, and Phon, her brother, also placed in the fifth grade, were referred for evaluation for special education placement due to continued failure in the classroom. Both students were failing fifth grade; they were not in the same classroom. Phon demonstrated behavior problems: he was frequently off task, played with objects and school materials, talked to other students, and displayed poor eye contact when addressed by the teacher. Samples of mathematics, language arts, and reading assignment responses revealed failing grades: the students did not know how to divide, spell words, nor comprehend the fifth grade level reading assignment represented in the work samples. They were noted to have difficulty drawing conclusions, determining main ideas, understanding multi-meaning words, recognizing vowel sounds, reading vowel pairs, and vowel + R words. Both students had participated in ESOL instruction for three years and spoke English fluently, with no trace of an accent. Because the students' achievement levels were very low, school personnel were concerned that these youngsters might have a learning problem that could be better addressed through special education. The teacher had had a difficult time communicating with the parents, who worked in a local hotel in the housekeeping department. Both parents spoke Khmer and were limited English speaking. There were no other Cambodian children in the school, siblings or peers.

According to available school records, the students had attended five different schools prior to entering the present one. The first record of school attendance indicated second grade placement in summer school, followed by continued placement in that grade for the following academic year. They were currently attending school regularly for the first time since their arrival in the United States.

Formal assessment results.

The students were evaluated by the visiting nurse, the speech and language clinician, and the school psychologist. The children had normal visual and hearing acuity. They did not appear to have any significant health problems. The speech and language clinician indicated that the youngsters had done well on tests of pragmatic use of language and syntax but were having difficulty pronouncing the "r" sound. While both youngsters conversed well in English, they scored poorly on expressive and receptive vocabulary tests. They had difficulty responding to "why" questions and following multi-step directions. It was recommended that the students participate in speech and language therapy.

Due to speech and language concerns, a largely nonverbal measure of cognitive abilities was used as part of the psychoeducational assessment. The school psychologist administered the Kaufman Assessment Battery for Children, or K-ABC (Kaufman & Kaufman 1983). The Woodcock-Johnson Psychoeducational Battery: Tests of Achievement (WJPB:TOA) was used to assess reading and mathematics skills. Table 8-2 summarizes the students' scores on these measures.

After scoring the tests, the school psychologist encountered the dilemma of interpreting the scores. On the one hand, the Mental Processing Composite (MPC) scores for both students indicated that they were functioning in the low average range of ability. On the other hand, if NELB students' scores on nonverbal tests may be better indicators of intellectual potential, then Souriya could be considered as functioning in the borderline range of slow learner to Mildly Mentally Retarded (MMR). If the nonverbal score was used as the indicator of intellectual potential, she might be considered for placement in a class for MMR students. Her academic scores could support a classification of

TABLE 8-2. STANDARDIZED TEST SCORES FOR SOURIYA AND PHON

MEASURE	SOURIYA	PHON
K-ABC Mental Processing Composite	Standard score 83	Standard Score 87
K-ABC Nonverbal	Standard Score 73	Standard Score 84
WJPB Reading	Grade Equivalent 1.8 Standard Score 72	Grade Equivalent 2.8 Standard Score 69
WJPB Math	Grade Equivalent 2.2 Standard Score 69	Grade Equivalent 2.8 Standard Score 69

MMR in some districts. On the other hand, use of the MPC as the indicator of intelligence would then place Souriya in the category of learning disabled since there is a discrepancy between her ability and her scores on the academic achievement tests, especially math.

An interpretation of Phon's scores was more straightforward. There is a discrepancy between the cognitive abilities scores obtained on the K-ABC and the academic scores obtained on the WJPB. Because Phon also did poorly on language-related tests, it might easily be concluded that a language learning disability was contributing to poor achievement.

In effect, both students presented as viable candidates for special education placement. Were they REALLY handicapped students? Additional information is critical for decision-making in cases such as these. In fact, many pieces of information were missing, beginning with a thorough account of the students' linguistic, educational, and sociocultural background and including an assessment of Souriya and Phon's actual skills levels within the school and classroom curriculum. All that was known was that they were failing in the classroom and that the standardized test scores could predict such failure.

A clearer picture of the students' instructional needs was obtained by means of informal and alternative assessments. A detailed account of all steps taken is not possible here, however the following are highlighted to demonstrate the use of some methods described in previous chapters.

Informal assessment results: parent interview.

The services of a trained interpreter were obtained through a local church refugee relocation program. For the first time in the educational and referral process, contact was made in the parents' native language. Through the interpreter it was learned that Souriya had briefly attended school in a refugee camp at about the age of 5. Although Phon was one year older, his schooling had been delayed until both children could attend together. School attendance was discontinued due to relocation. When the family finally arrived in the United States, the children did not attend school for an entire year. When they were finally registered in school, Souriya was 7 years old and Phon was 8. They were placed in summer school as second graders. They continued in that grade for the upcoming academic year; however, attendance was interrupted because the parents were in search of suitable employment.

The parents reported experiencing considerable hardships during the children's early years as they fled their country. The children were frequently ill but were generally well-nourished. Furthermore, the parents were not literate in their home language. The parents indicated that they taught their children about the customs and traditions of their country through narratives and story-telling. The children were expected to do their homework by helping each other.

As the parents were just learning English themselves, they attempted to help as much as possible.

Observation of the learning environment: curriculum-based and informal measures.

Observation revealed that, in both students' classrooms, instruction was aimed at the larger group, with small group instruction for skills development. Both students were removed from the class for individual assistance four times a week for thirty minutes from a compensatory education teacher. In Phon's class, the students were expected to complete their seatwork independently, while some cooperative interaction was allowed in Souriya's class. Souriya's teacher was also beginning to implement a writing process approach in the classroom, while Phon's writing was related to the language arts assignment book, basal text, and paragraph writing. In both cases, no modifications were made in instructional language. Since the students were in different classes, with different instructional treatments, they were often unable to assist each other at home, or even explain what had happened in class.

Reading probes developed from the basal reading series being used at the school were administered. Additionally, arithmetic computations probes that tapped skills beginning with basic addition and subtraction and on through division (where the students were expected to function given their grade placement) were also administered. Creative writing samples were gathered. Through the interpreter, three native language folktales were transcribed. The stories were read by the interpreter. The students were asked to retell the stories in both Khmer and English. As the principal of the school was concerned about the students' ability to pass the state mandated minimum skills competency test for fifth grade, probes that contained vocabulary from the third and fifth grade level test were administered. Souriya's and Phon's performance and reading trends on the basal reader probes are presented in Figures 8-1 and 8-2. The probes were used to identify the students' actual reading skills given current reading curricula. They helped determine where in the reading curriculum they might be placed to allow for success. Additionally, goals for future instruction could be established.

Briefly, the results suggest that, for instructional purposes, both students were reading at an independent level significantly below the fifth grade level. Reading fluency with the greatest number of correct responses was at a reading readiness level, followed by pre-primer, and primer/first reader levels. Phon was able to perform slightly better than Souriya, including successes at a beginning third grade level but was less successful at the readiness level. Qualitative analysis revealed that both youngsters demonstrated similar error patterns. The performance trends suggest that the students would experience significant frustration with third grade reading materials: fifth grade level performance was an unrealistic expectation. A formal plan of intervention geared toward strengthening independent reading skills was developed, along with a plan for using repeated measurement of progress in order to obtain better indicators of learning rates for both students.

Other informal measures provided more insight into the students' native language abilities, reading and mathematics skills, and writing development. Figure 8-3 depicts Souriya and Phon's performance on various different measures.

Their ability to recall a story with 60% to 80% accuracy (median score) indicated that both students retained more native language than was expected. Souriya was more competent in retelling the story in English while Phon demonstrated almost equal facility in both languages. In response to the principal's question regarding the competency tests, it was not surprising to find that the students would be less successful at reading the fifth grade level test than the third grade level one. The principal decided to request a waiver based on the students' limited English language. In effect, there was increasing evidence that Souriya and Phon were not yet as proficient in English as had been thought. With regard to math skills, both youngsters understood addition and subtraction (Math 1 on the graph), but needed to develop speed and accuracy in solving basic math facts. They both possessed a beginning knowledge of basic multiplication facts, but neither knew how to divide (Math 2 on the graph). Informal review of mathematical language and concepts development with math series books revealed that the students required further instruction at a second grade level. With regard to writing, Souriya provided a full page story about a friend but Phon indicated that he couldn't think of anything to write about. His behavior suggests that he may have had limited experience in writing about personal ideas.

Developing an intervention plan.

An intervention plan, such as the one presented in Figure 8-4, with the students' scores represented on a graph, can be used to document student progress. It can also be helpful in determining the success of the classroom strategies used. The data sheet and plan could provide a written record that would be readily available for special education pre-referral decision-making purposes, if needed.

In fact, for Souriya and Phon, both standardized tests and informal measures suggested that, given their background, educational experience, and language proficiency, the students were making progress. Coordination of regular education and ESOL services, with more clearly defined instructional goals could enhance progress. Both students demonstrated similar patterns of skills and abilities: Was Souriya learning disabled or was she mentally retarded? Can Phon's low academic scores be attributed, without a doubt, to a "language

FIGURE 8-1. READING PROBES PERFORMANCE FOR
SOURIYA AND PHON

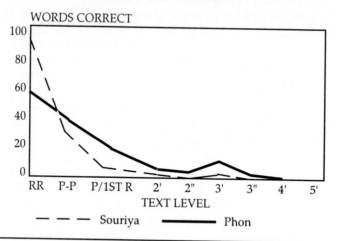

FIGURE 8-2. READING PROBES PERFORMANCE TRENDS
FOR SOURIYA AND PHON

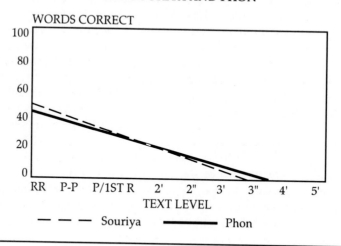

learning disability"? Before referral for special education, students require effective instruction and realistic expectations in the regular classroom setting.

Recalling Alberto.

Remember Alberto and Ricardo in Chapter Six? Alberto is the fourth grader who was experiencing school failure. Curriculum-based assessment and

FIGURE 8-3. PERFORMANCE ON INFORMAL MEASURES
FOR SOURIYA AND PHON

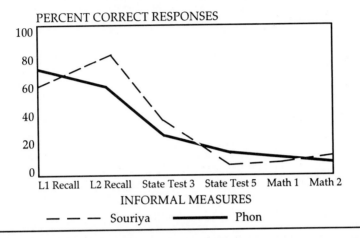

modified measurement methods were used in Alberto's case. The present discussion again focuses on Alberto to illustrate the use of alternative, supplemental achievement assessment strategies to enhance identification of learning problems and to increase the validity of referral made for possible special education placement.

Recall that, for screening purposes, Ricardo, another fourth grader in Alberto's class, was selected by the teacher as being representative of an "average" mainstream peer. At the time of screening, Alberto's median score on grade level passages was 10.2 times discrepant from Ricardo's median score; his basic computations median score was 3.5 times discrepant; and there was no quantitative difference between their writing samples (review Chapter Five section on curriculum-based measurement). Following this initial screening, it was decided to provide Alberto with additional resource room (regular education) remedial assistance in reading. The resource room teacher and her aide provided Alberto with both individual and small group instruction. In order to determine progress, she developed reading probes to assess word recognition skills and cloze tests, also based on the Spanish reading series, to monitor comprehension. Alberto and five other Spanish speaking, fourth grade at risk readers were included in the intervention and monitoring process.

Figure 8-5 reflects the weekly median scores obtained by Alberto and his five resource room peers for a period of thirteen weeks. Throughout the period of time, Alberto's scores were consistently lower than those of his peers, although the trend for weeks 1 through 8 for Alberto indicated progress. When the median score for the group for the thirteen weeks was determined, Alberto's median score for the same period of time was 2.2 times discrepant from that of

FIGURE 8-4. DATA SHEET AND INTERVENTION PLAN

Data Sheet and Intervention Plan for _____

School: _____ Grade: _____

Teacher: _____ Starting Date: _____

Primary Home Language: _____

Language Dominance Evaluation Results: _____
_____

Academic Program(s): _____
_____

Transition Initiated/Area(s): _____

ACADEMIC AREA ASSESSED: Reading   Math   (Circle one)

Classroom Level Text: _____

Probe: _____ Correct/min _____ Error/min _____

Suggested Level Text: _____

Probe: _____ Correct/min _____ Error/min _____

Goal Level Text: _____

Probe: _____ Correct/min _____ Error/min _____

Reading Comprehension Assessment:
   Method: _____
   Results: _____

If non-text based approach to instruction is used, indicate area and method(s) of assessment: _____
_____
_____

Intervention: _____

What: _____ will receive instruction in _____

_____ to increase _____

Comments: _____

How: Materials used: _____
   Strategies used: _____
   Language(s) used: _____

When: _____

Where: _____

Self-Management Strategies to be taught: _____

Study Skills to be taught: _____

Additional Comments: _____

Documentation of Progress: Attached is a graph indicating student scores.

FIGURE 8-5. WEEKLY MEDIAN SCORES OF READING GROUP
AND ALBERTO

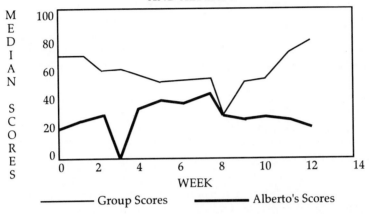

the group, fluctuating between no discrepancy at week 8 to a high of 4.1 times discrepant.

The graphic representation of the students' progress was revealing in several ways. It helped the teacher see the outcome of her efforts to assist Alberto and develop several hypotheses regarding her instruction methods and the behavior of the group. For the first several weeks, as Alberto was progressing, the rest of the group was either maintaining or "losing" skills as their performance dropped. The teacher hypothesized that she was teaching to Alberto's skills levels and not challenging the others enough. At week 8 she decided to change the level of difficulty of the material and instructional methods to meet the needs of the larger group. From that point, while the group progressed quickly for the next few weeks, Alberto struggled, maintaining low reading skills. As the teacher began to consider the students' needs, she concluded that a different intervention plan designed for Alberto alone was needed. Furthermore, the teacher began to consider referral for special education evaluation. The teacher made the decision to refer Alberto for further evaluation by specialists because there was some evidence that he continued to require modifications for success, even in a small regular education, remedial group. Alberto's performance was being compared to other students learning to read in their native language, yet he trailed behind them.

Alberto's case demonstrates the usefulness of informal methods for documenting student performance for decision-making and accountability purposes. As the teacher implemented a more systematic data-gathering procedure in her classroom, she was able to examine the outcomes of her instruction for other students as well. She also realized that she needed to refine her skills in systematic data collection to improve instruction in order to obtain more immediate feedback. She recognized the importance of monitoring the progress of the group, rather than allowing precious time go by without making adjustments. Generally, 4 to 6 weeks of data collection can provide sufficient information for instructional planning (Shinn & Knutson 1992). In Alberto's case, it was possible to gather additional data to substantiate the need for further special education assessment. Alberto proved capable of acquiring academic skills; however the intensity of his needs, compared to those of his native language classroom and small group peers, suggested that special education instruction might be necessary. Alberto was eventually evaluated in Spanish and found to be eligible for the specific learning disabilities program.

In sum, the identification of learning disabilities among native speakers of English is plagued by controversy related to the application and implementation of a definition that has been charged with being too ambiguous or poorly conceived. The identification of learning disabled NELB students is complicated not only by problems of definition, but by the effects of language and many other variables, such as background and classroom environment. Application of informal and student performance assessment methods prior to special education referral help prevent inappropriate or premature referrals, as was the case with Souriya and Phon, or can provide additional data needed to support a referral, as with Alberto. These methods also allow for teacher self-monitoring to determine effective instructional practices.

RESEARCH IN PRACTICE:
The Concept of Learning Disabilities and the NELB Student

1. **Investigate how learning disabled students are identified in your school district.** Are any provisions made for linguistic diversity? What are these provisions? Discuss these provisions with the people who use them to determine how useful they are.

2. **Why is an understanding of NELB students' language abilities, background, and academic skills status in the curriculum important for special education referral purposes?** Are educators in your school provided with this information? What specifically do you think educators should know?

3. **Discuss the concept of learning disabilities with a colleague.** What, in your mind, constitutes a learning disability? What characteristics in learners would prompt the thought that a student might be learning disabled? How might the instruction of a student be different if the student were determined to be SLD, or learning English as a new language?

4. Consider the processes of new language learning, new language literacy development, and the acquisition of math concepts in a new language. Describe how characteristics unique to these processes might be confused with a learning disability as defined in the Federal Register. Have these similarities and differences been a topic of discussion at your school?

5. **Review the cases of Souriya, Phon, and Alberto.** Contrast and compare them. Explain how informal methods of assessing student performance can help reduce inappropriate referrals for special education.

MENTALLY RETARDED, MISIDENTIFIED, OR THE EFFECTS OF LANGUAGE, CULTURE, AND OPPORTUNITY?

One of the most stigmatizing labels that students can carry in the school setting, specifically at a social and peer level, is that of mental retardation. If a student is culturally or linguistically different from the mainstream students, the chances of being identified as mentally retarded, perhaps erroneously, may be great. As indicated in Chapter Seven, litigation and legislation relative to the assessment of NELB students resulted from the inappropriate use and application of information obtained from assessment. In general, the students represented in the courts, in both early and more recent litigation, have been culturally and/or linguistically diverse in their backgrounds but have had the commonality of having been placed in programs for the mentally retarded. In some cases, the use of standardized IQ tests has been the focus of argument; in other cases, adaptive behavior assessment has come under scrutiny (Reschly 1980; Reschly 1985; Reschly, Kicklighter & McKee 1988a). As a result, efforts to address and rectify the predicament in which special education found itself have included anything from bans or moratoria on testing students, to overtesting. Increasingly, however, the courts are examining educational outcomes as a result of special education placement (Reschly 1985; Reschly, Kicklighter & McKee 1988b).

To place the blame for the inappropriate identification of NELB or other culturally different students entirely on the results of formal psychoeducational assessment alone is a rather simplistic, easy way out of a much more complex problem. Awareness, sensitivity to, and a sense of advocacy for students, at all levels of personnel in a school building or district, also play a significant part in whether or not students are perceived as being handicapped, regardless of test results. If, as has been discussed in Chapter Six and in previous chapters, the assessment of NELB students is to be a collaborative, on-going, well-documented effort among all members of the school team, then the ultimate burden of identification lies in the combined efforts and decisions of all involved. The case of Lhani, presented in Chapter Five to illustrate anecdotal record keeping, also exemplifies the importance of advocacy at the classroom and school building level in the process of identification of possible mental retardation.

Recalling Lhani.

Lhani had arrived mid-year from a rural agricultural village in India. Her family had been sponsored by relatives living in the United States. Lhani was seven years old and was placed in kindergarten due to her very limited school experiences. By March, Lhani's kindergarten teacher had referred her to the child study team at the school. The teacher was concerned about Lhani's low skills and feared the child would be further frustrated by first grade level work. The teacher reported that Lhani still spoke little English and, although she was seven years old, still could not "color within the lines, trace, cut, or even identify the eight basic colors, much less recognize letters or numbers. She has trouble staying on task for more than five minutes." The team decided to refer her for further evaluation for possible special education placement.

The evaluating psychologist reported that an interpreter was used to assist in evaluating Lhani over two sessions. Lhani was initially shy but quickly warmed up to the interpreter. The first session was reported to be more intrusive in order to obtain an idea of Lhani's language and conceptual abilities. This session was characterized by interviewing, questioning, and obtaining language samples in the native language. During the second session, attempts were made to evaluate Lhani using several nonverbal measures of intelligence, including the Performance Scale of the WISC-R. The evaluator reported that it became immediately obvious that Lhani did not understand the testing requirements despite directions in the native language. Faced with unfamiliar testing materials, Lhani did not know what to do with them. The evaluator indicated that inexperience with the demands of the individual testing situation was instrumental in depressing Lhani's performance. Lhani had not developed the types of problem-solving skills necessary to work with the manipulatives presented. The evaluator then opted to conduct the evaluation in a teach-reteach and testing-of-limits format. No IQ scores were reported. An analysis of cognitive and academic strengths and weaknesses was reported. Figure 8-6 depicts Lhani's rendition of herself. The script on the top of the page indicates her name, while the vertical lines and circles, according to Lhani, are numbers. It was evident that Lhani was beginning to acquire a sense of the act of writing and of symbols as representative of letters or numbers. She was using graphic forms to convey her message. Observation of Lhani handling storybooks revealed emergent literacy behaviors.

The school social worker had, in the meantime, obtained additional information regarding Lhani's developmental history and adaptive skills. The social

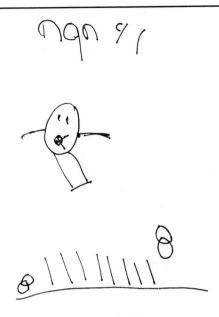

Figure 8-6

worker's report indicated that Lhani's adaptive behavior scores on a standard-ized scale, were in the Moderately Mentally Retarded range. The social worker was concerned, however, that Lhani did not have many opportunities to learn the behaviors mentioned in the scale, and some of the items were culturally inappropriate.

The information was presented to the child study team, along with recom-mendations for interventions. Several members of the team suggested that the results were indicators of mental retardation and that additional tests should be administered. In the end, but not without heated discussion, it was decided to leave Lhani in the regular kindergarten setting with modifications in the instructional strategies and materials used. Lhani completed the remainder of kindergarten and was promoted to first grade.

Her new teacher was less inclined to focus on Lhani's weaknesses. Figures 8-7, 8-8, and 8-9, are work samples collected at various intervals over a period of weeks during the first semester of school. Figure 8-10 demonstrates Lhani's writing (in December) with the teacher's corrections superimposed to assist Lhani with spacing. Lhani's unfinished paper, written in May without teacher assistance, is demonstrated in Figure 8-11. By May, Lhani was also completing math problems involving basic addition and subtraction, and was reading at a pre-primer level.

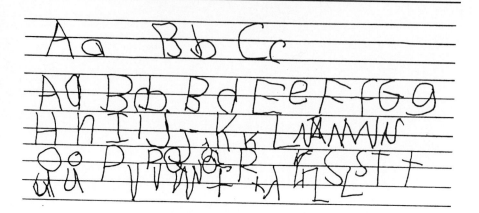

Figure 8-7

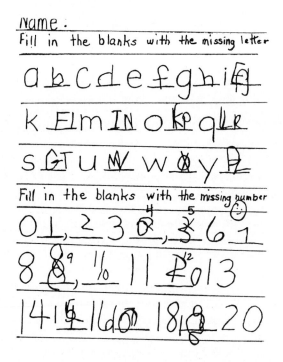

Figure 8-8

Figure 8-9

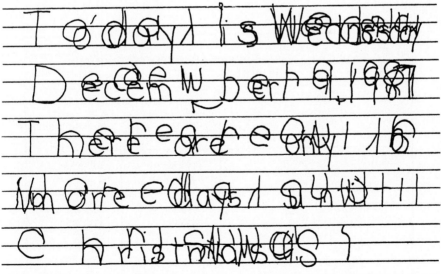

Figure 8-10

Lhani's family moved at the end of the school year, only to return to the same school two years later. Lhani was nine and in third grade. The third grade teacher was concerned about the youngster's inability to complete grade level work. Lhani was referred for re-evaluation, this time with a different evaluation team. Lhani was evaluated with the WISC-R, the Woodcock-Johnson Tests of Achievement, and the Vineland Adaptive Behavior Scale (VABS) (Sparrow,

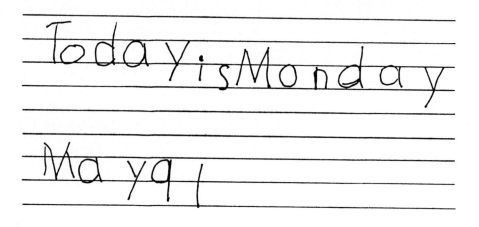

Figure 8-11

TABLE 8-3. LHANI'S STANDARDIZED TEST SCORES UPON RE-EVALUATION

MEASURES	STANDARD SCORES	
	Initial Evaluation	Re-evaluation
Intellectual	Not Reported: diagnostic	Full Scale: 64
Academic	Not Reported: diagnostic	Reading: 55 Math: 69 Written Language: 69
Adaptive Behavior	Composite: 46	Composite: 62

Balla & Cichetti 1984). Her obtained standard scores on these tests are found on Table 8-3: they are compared with the results of initial testing. At the time of re-evaluation, Lhani was reading at a beginning first grade level, with written language skills at a mid-first grade level, and mathematics skills at a second grade level, according to the results of the Woodcock-Johnson. Assessment of language abilities was not conducted.

Based on these results, the school team decided to place Lhani in special education. Her scores fell within the range for placement in the Mildly Mentally Retarded range. Little consideration was given to the fact that Lhani had progressed from the point of not being able to complete any standardized testing at all to being able to score as high as she did only two years later. Furthermore, her increased acculturation to the mainstream was evident in an adaptive behavior score increase of slightly over one standard deviation. Yet Lhani was placed in a self-contained program for mildly mentally retarded students. Evidence used to support her placement included her inability to perform on grade level in the regular classroom, the interpretation that the scores obtained on the standardized intelligence, academic, and adaptive behavior measures used were in the mentally retarded range, and the belief that regular education could not provide Lhani the instruction she needed.

RESEARCH IN PRACTICE:
Mentally Retarded, Misidentified, or the Effects of Language, Culture and Opportunity?

---

1. **Review Lhani's case with colleagues.** The fact that Lhani was ultimately placed in special education has far-reaching ramifications, legal, as well as educational, for the student as well as the school district. Discuss possible legal and educational consequences of the case.

2. **Why is an understanding of the school climate and perceptions of what constitutes a disability important in the referral and assessment process?**

3. **What does mental retardation mean to you?** What characteristics do you commonly associate with mental retardation? How might these be different from "six hour" retardation, that is, delays that are evident only while students are in school?

4. **Discuss the following statement with colleagues whose primary role is to assess students for possible special education placement:** "The fundamental problem is the outcome of test use, not the test per se." (Reschly 1980, p. 24). What role did "test use" play in Lhani's case? What role did the perceptions of a disability play in the decision to place Lhani in special education?

5. Discuss the role of cultural expectations on the identification of a handicapping condition.

DETECTING MENTAL RETARDATION

The definition of mental retardation is less fraught with controversy than that of learning disabilities. Although the definition of mental retardation has changed over the years, it has been guided primarily by the definitions and classification criteria set forth by the American Association on Mental Deficiency (AAMD) (Reschly 1980). State education agencies may, however, establish their own criteria for educational programming purposes. Definitions may therefore vary from state to state. Within public school settings, definitions and criteria set by the state are used to determine eligibility for services from programs for the mentally retarded.

Mental retardation is diagnosed when a person exhibits deficits in both intellectual functioning and adaptive behaviors. School districts frequently assess academic skills to determine academic deficits as well. Intellectual and adaptive behavior deficits must surface during the developmental period, that is, between birth and age 18. With regards to intellectual functioning, the degree or severity of mental retardation is classified on a continuum that ranges from mild to profound, as indicated on Table 8-4 (Grossman 1983).

TABLE 8-4. LEVELS OF MENTAL RETARDATION

LEVEL	IQ RANGES	STANDARD DEVIATION
Mild	50-55 to Approximately 70	-2 to -3 SD (55-70)
Moderate	35-40 to 50-55	-3 to -5 SD (25-55) (Includes Severe)
Severe	20-25 to 35-40	
Profound	Below 20-25	Below -5 SD (Below 25)

The most commonly accepted definition of adaptive behavior is that provided by the AAMD: adaptive behavior refers to the "effectiveness with which the individual meets the standards of personal independence and social responsibility" (Grossman 1983, p.1). As indicated in Chapter Seven, adaptive behavior reflects the degree to which a student is able to comply with the cultural expectations and demands of daily living. Adaptive behavior is viewed as being developmental, that is, the person must accomplish different tasks at different ages and is, therefore, age-specific. For example, during infancy and the preschool period, children are expected to demonstrate increasing mastery over sensory and motor skills, manifest beginning communication skills, initiate self-help skills, and develop primary socialization abilities. Failure to accomplish these may be indicators of future adaptive behavior deficits. School age children, including early adolescents, are expected to continue developing self-care and communication skills, but are required to demonstrate the ability to acquire basic academic skills. They are expected to demonstrate reasoning abilities and increasing mastery of their environment. The quality of their interpersonal relationships changes, and they are expected to participate in group activities. Finally, by late adolescence and into adulthood, individuals are expected to perform in a vocation of choice, be gainfully employed, and maintain independence in the community. They are expected to be socially responsible and adhere to community norms (Grossman 1983; DeStefano & Thompson 1990). What may be a developmentally appropriate task in one culture may not, however, be appropriate in another. For example, in mainstream U.S. families, young children are expected to give up drinking from a bottle at an earlier age than is expected among Hispanic families. It is not unusual to find kindergarten age Hispanic children still drinking out of a bottle or using a pacifier. Furthermore, economic independence may be achieved at a later time among Hispanic adolescents, as they may not be encouraged to leave home when they turn 18 or get jobs at age 16. Many Hispanic young adults do not leave home until they marry.

Additionally, adaptive behaviors must be viewed within the context of the person's culture and are, therefore, culture-specific. The measurement of adaptive behaviors with scales that are representative of behaviors expected by the mainstream U.S. culture may have serious validity problems when used to diagnose mental retardation among NELB or culturally diverse students (Reschly 1985). Even when mental retardation is suspected, as in the case of Lucia, cultural influences may provide a distorted view of students' capabilities.

The case of Lucia.

Lucia is a 12 year 6 month old Portuguese student who was initially registered as a second grade student by her parents. When they were told that she must be promoted to a higher grade due to her age, the parents were very concerned because Lucia had never been promoted beyond second grade in her native country. As an infant, Lucia had been in an automobile accident and had suffered significant brain injuries. The family had moved to various Portuguese speaking countries, but Lucia was always placed in second grade. Lucia's parents recognized that their child did not function educationally or socially like a normal 12-year-old; however, they also recognized their tendency to overprotect her. The parents were interviewed by the school social worker through an interpreter. The social worker, utilizing the Vineland Adaptive Behavior Scales (VABS), highlighted the following facts. Within the Communication domain of the VABS, Lucia was noted to have difficulty expressing herself in her native language. She was unable to tell a story or the sequence of events. She did not read in Portuguese nor could she print more than a few words from memory. Lucia had no concept of time or money. Within the Daily Living skills domain, it was noted that Lucia lived all her life in countries where she was not exposed to the many conveniences typical in the United States, such as electrical appliances, telephone, and vacuum cleaner. She was able to use a broom. Lucia's mother still cut her meat for her. Although Lucia helped her mother set the table, household tasks were not routinely expected of her. Within the Socialization domain, Lucia was noted to have good manners, apologize for mistakes, and respond appropriately when introduced to strangers. Lucia's association with peers had been very restricted. She did not have a best friend and seemed uncomfortable with other children. She preferred the company of her mother. She did not like to share her possessions and toys with other children for fear they would be broken. Lucia's adaptive behaviors, as measured by the VABS and if interpreted solely by mainstream standards, were comparable to moderately to severely mentally retarded (or trainable) students. On the other hand, assessment of intellectual abilities suggested higher abilities in the mildly (or educable) retarded range. Within the classroom, Lucia had demonstrated increasing self-assurance, had several friends with whom she had frequent contact and who apparently served as role models for her. She had been noted to become more motivated toward school work, attempt more activities, and interact more frequently with the teacher at a non-verbal level. At home, Lucia had rebelled against her mother's efforts to comb her hair and assist her with dressing. Lucia had begun to manifest greater social competence by virtue of her current experiences, to the great surprise of her parents.

Adaptive behaviors depend on the demands of the situations in which the person is functioning and are situation-specific (Burns 1990; DeStefano & Thompson 1990). For example, an NELB student's adaptive behaviors at school may be different from those observed at home or in the community, as was the case with Lucia. Observation of student behaviors across settings and the importance of cultural informants and trained interpreters in the process of identifying mental retardation has been highlighted previously due to the need to distinguish adaptive behaviors that are appropriate for age and cultural expectations. Adaptive behavior measures that take into account personalities, motivational factors, and unique linguistic, physical, and social environments provide information relevant to educational planning (Scott & Fisher 1988).

While more severe forms of mental retardation are diagnosed fairly easily, identification of milder mental retardation is more problematic. This is due to various factors: first, the majority of persons identified as mildly retarded do not exhibit distinct physical traits such as might be evident among severely retarded individuals. Second, mild mental retardation is generally identified later in life, usually when the child has been in school for a period of time. Third, evidence of mild retardation may be limited to the school setting. The student may be perceived by others outside the school setting as performing normally. Fourth, both socioeconomic status and ethnicity are related to the probability of being identified as mildly retarded. Finally, many people who are diagnosed as mildly retarded are able to care for themselves as adults (Reschly 1980).

For NELB students who may be failing academically or have low scores on intelligence and academic achievement tests and other measures used to identify mental retardation, the dilemma is confounded by new language acquisition and related issues. Studies have shown that on non-norm-referenced measures of cognitive abilities (e.g. Piagetian-based Cartoon Conservation Scales) and of metalinguistic awareness, bilingual mildly retarded NELB youngsters outperformed monolingual students on the metalinguistic tasks. Access to two linguistic codes may yield greater cognitive flexibility than is generally attributed to mildly retarded students (Rueda 1983). In effect, mildly mentally retarded bilingual students may possess the same cognitive advantages that are present in normal, language proficient bilingual students (Rueda 1984). An appropriate education is provided for these students when instruction is in the native language and when they participate in a structured program for learning English that is adapted to their level of understanding and need. Furthermore, instruction takes into account and is accommodated to the handicap(s) and to the students' sociocultural background (Padilla 1989).

In many school districts, an intelligence test and a measure of adaptive behavior, usually a standardized scale, are administered when mental retardation is suspected. Low scores on both the test and the scale may be viewed as supporting evidence of mental retardation. Even though low cognitive abilities may be related to lower adaptive functioning, this relationship does not always hold true with NELB students. If NELB students have been evaluated in their non-dominant language, artificially depressed scores will be obtained. There is the danger, then, of falsely identifying mental retardation. Furthermore, intelligence tests and adaptive behavior measures do not necessarily assess the same aspects of an individual's capabilities (Reschly 1980). NELB students may, for example, demonstrate high adaptive behavior abilities but score poorly on an intelligence test.

On the other hand, reliance on measures of adaptive behavior alone to identify mental retardation among NELB students would not provide a solution to the problem. In general, on measures of adaptive behavior, the greater the number of items that pertain to learning and academic skills, the higher the correlation with tests of intelligence (DeStefano & Thompson 1990). NELB students with limited or varied educational opportunities or poor proficiency in English may also be falsely identified as mentally retarded by means of adaptive behavior measures. Other indicators and methods must be used to confirm or refute the existence of mental retardation among such students. Observation of functional behaviors in the classroom and in the natural environments of home and community, observation of peer play or social interactions, collection of permanent products over time, video-taping, and structured role-play activities are a few of the many methods that can be used to evaluate adaptive behavior skills development and cognitive problem-solving abilities (Burns 1990). For NELB students, it is important that such methods tap native language and culture, and that students' behavior be compared to that of other similar background students.

Recalling Maurice: classroom teacher advocacy in action.

Maurice was introduced in Chapter Five. Recall that he is a student of Haitian descent who was 14 years old at the time of initial evaluation. His initial evaluation, conducted in English, included a measure of academic achievement. His obtained scores placed him in the mildly mentally retarded range. Upon re-evaluation two years later, Maurice's scores demonstrated significant gains, suggesting that a diagnosis of mental retardation would have been inappropriate. Here is the rest of Maurice's story.

Maurice was noted by his sixth grade teacher to spend a great deal of time daydreaming, unable to complete most classroom assignments. Although Maurice was not a major disruption in the classroom, he did engage in some off-task behaviors, such as whispering to others around him, drawing, or playing with objects on his desk. A strength area noted was his word calling ability when reading. He frequently volunteered to read out loud and did well; however, he understood very little of what he read when questioned. It was noted that Maurice attended ESOL classes three times per week for approximately 30 minutes per session. Maurice was noted to speak Haitian Creole at home. The rest of the time was spent in the mainstream classroom. He demonstrated many skill deficits and was therefore referred for psychoeducational evaluation.

Maurice was evaluated with the WISC-R, in English, and the WJPB achievement test. The examiner noted that Maurice had been exposed to the English language and American culture for about eighteen months and that his limited language development had a negative effect on his ability to perform on the verbal items on the test. However, Maurice had also done poorly on the performance scale, which is non-verbal, and on an additional perceptual-motor development test. Because of these scores and those on the academic tests, the examiner concluded that Maurice's low scores were not due solely to his cultural and language background. His profile suggested that Maurice's overall level of intellectual functioning was far below average as he scored in the Moderately Mentally Retarded to Mildly Mentally Retarded range. All his deficits were attributed to low cognitive functioning. The results of the adaptive behavior measure also placed Maurice in the moderately retarded range; however, the school social worker noted that there were cultural and language barriers during the interview. The caregiver interviewed was a legal guardian who knew little about Maurice's early history and spent little time with him. Maurice was placed in a program for mildly mentally handicapped students. He was also socially promoted to a higher, more age-appropriate grade.

Two years later, Maurice was in the ninth grade, participating in special education. He was also taking French as an elective in high school. It was the French teacher who alerted evaluation personnel to Maurice's case. Maurice was making progress in French and the teacher could not understand why he was in a program for the mentally retarded and requested a re-evaluation.

On the second occasion, Maurice was evaluated over a period of several days with the assistance of a trained educator from Haiti serving as interpreter/translator. The French teacher also participated in assessment, by obtaining oral language and literacy samples in standard French, which were then scored by both the teacher and the Haitian assistant. The vernacular Haitian Creole was also used throughout the evaluation. The following are highlights from the evaluation.

Maurice appeared as well-groomed, polite, and sociable. He displayed humor in his conversation and expressed a desire to be dismissed from the mildly mentally retarded program, indicating that he knew his legal rights. He expressed a desire to pursue a career in law enforcement and to finish school. He had attended school in his native country, but admitted to not being as studious as he should have been.

Assessment of language abilities conducted in Haitian Creole and French revealed the effects of language loss due to discontinuance of formal instruction in standard French. On the other hand, Maurice was rated by both evaluators as possessing language abilities at an intermediate-high to advanced level in both English and French in some areas (review Chapter Three for characteristics of language proficiency). Although his ideas were concrete, his train of thought was logical. He was able to perceive a picture as part of a larger story and to indicate time, place, sequence, and cause and effect. He inferred meaning and intent, but had some difficulty predicting outcomes. He used a range of responses to communicate. He talked freely in English, expressing concerns for his country, family, and other personal issues. He expressed his opinion of right and wrong, and voiced fears and frustration in situations he had no power to change. As far as writing was concerned, Maurice's main problem was spelling and grammar in French. He attempted to spell phonetically.

Utilizing a French secondary-level text, Maurice was requested to read and answer comprehension questions. The Haitian assistant indicated that Maurice displayed good phonics and word attack skills in this language, evidence of a more than adequate foundation in reading. He had greater difficulty completing comprehension questions, providing descriptions of the information read rather than establishing relationships among concepts or ideas; however, previous instructional methods may contribute to his not using reading strategies for comprehension. He was more adept at providing facts than interpreting. He was estimated to possess skills comparable to a sixth grade to beginning secondary level student in Haiti, skills that would be appropriate for his age and more advanced than the general school-age population of the country would obtain. Maurice's weakest area proved to be mathematics; however, gains in skills were evident, based on a comparison of previous and current test results. Maurice would have to learn math vocabulary and concepts in English, although the French teacher was willing to provide assistance in this area as well.

Finally, because Maurice could not be dismissed from special education without an indication that he no longer qualified for the program, intellectual assessment was conducted. This time, the Leiter International Performance Scale (LIPS) was administered, as well as the WISC-R, with the assistance of the Haitian interpreter. Maurice's initial and re-evaluation scores are presented in Table 8-5, where G.E. stands for grade equivalent and SS represents standard score.

Because the WISC-R was the primary test used to determine eligibility in the district and it was informally translated to meet the requirements of testing, those results were interpreted with caution. The results do, however, indicate significant gains in scores, even on the Performance Scale. The Leiter results confirmed the suspicion that Maurice possessed significantly higher abilities

TABLE 8-5. MAURICE'S TEST SCORES UPON INITIAL AND RE-EVALUATION

TEST	INITIAL SCORES	RE-EVALUATION SCORES
LIPS WISC-R	Not administered Verbal IQ 51 Performance IQ 60 Full Scale IQ 51	IQ 90 Verbal IQ 75 Performance IQ 77 Full Scale IQ 74
WJPB: Achievement Reading Mathematics Written Language	G.E. 3.0; SS 67 G.E. 2.6; Below 65 G.E. 2.4; SS 58	G.E. 6.1; SS 87 G.E. 4.5; SS 65 G.E. 5.7; SS 86

than the initial evaluation results reflected. Maurice was dismissed from the special education program and placed under the guidance and mentorship of his French teacher.

Lhani and Maurice: two sides of the same coin.

The stories of Lhani and Maurice represent two possible outcomes of performance evaluation for NELB students who may be considered for special education: in Lhani's case, formal testing was used to place her in special education without regard for classroom performance indicators. In Maurice's case, performance indicators were used to support the conclusion that he was not a special education student. Maurice's French teacher was an active participant in the evaluation and in the decision-making process. Collaboration across disciplines and advocacy for Maurice were evident. In both cases, the initial diagnosis of mild mental retardation is suspect. Ethical questions regarding assessment and decision-making practices are present. How then can accurate diagnosis of mild mental retardation among NELB students be accomplished?

The answer is obviously not a simple one. It may just take longer to attain, and even then, mistakes can be made. However, through collaborative efforts and student advocacy as guide, the numbers of inappropriate placements can be reduced. The issue is only in part the assessment process, and remains in much larger part, the educational process. So Lhani was placed in special education. What does that indicate about instruction? How will instruction be different for her now? What assurances are there that her needs will actually be met? What about Maurice? Is the French teacher adequately prepared to assist a student with the learning difficulties Maurice has demonstrated? Neither of these two students' difficulties are reduced by the assignment or removal of a label. This seems like a straightforward observation, that students require effective instruction geared to their particular needs. Yet it is an outcome that sometimes appears to escape the attention of those who continue to use outdated and inappropriate formulae and categorical descriptions for placing students in programs. We are beginning to evolve the technology for really addressing students' educational needs. Now we must also develop the will and determination to apply it.

A comparative method: the story of Jacques and Rose.

Like Maurice, Jacques and Rose are students from Haiti. Siblings, Jacques, age 13, and Rose, age 14, were placed in seventh grade. They participated in ESOL instruction on a daily basis for fifty minutes per day. Both had attended the same school in Haiti, and both were learning English as a third language since they spoke Haitian Creole but had been formally instructed in French at school. Both attended the equivalent of first through fifth grades in their native country prior to moving to the U.S. Their father still resided in Haiti. Both students currently lived with their mother and step-father. Here the resemblance ends.

Jacques was failing all his courses. Rose was making grades of C and D. While Rose demonstrated good study habits and completed her work, Jacques' work was incomplete to nonexistent, he was unable to stay on task, and he displayed poor conduct. He would try to play with other students during class and, when bored, would put his head on the desk top and suck his thumb. He was impulsive and playful, had a difficult time changing classes, was often late because he could not tell time, and required adult supervision in the lunch room, on the bus, and at school assemblies. While Rose could provide, in her native language, detailed information about her past history, Jacques did not remember much about his native country or his previous school. He did not know his birthdate, current address, or telephone number.

School personnel were concerned about both Jacques' and Rose's academic progress, but realized their problems were different. The assistance of the curriculum specialist, the ESOL teacher, the school social worker, and a trained interpreter was used to evaluate both students. In the absence of other similar peers at the school, the strategy of comparative assessment was used with the siblings. Initial assessment of skills in the school curriculum was conducted by the curriculum specialist. The results of the informal reading inventory used with Rose and Jacques are presented in Table 8-6.

The specialist reported that Rose was well on her way toward acquiring English reading skills. Jacques, on the other hand, recognized a few letters of the alphabet, displayed no knowledge of sound-symbol relationships, and did not appear to realize that words are formed from a series of sounds. Additionally, while Rose was able to write simple sentences in English, Jacques scribbled on the page. In mathematics, Rose was able to complete problems involving addition, subtraction, and multiplication. She demonstrated emerging concepts of division in computations. She had difficulty understanding word problems. Jacques, on the other hand, was able to complete simple addition and numeration problems, using manipulatives only.

The ESOL teacher indicated that, although both students were still limited in English, Rose was progressing faster than Jacques. Jacques was still using words and simple phrases to express personal intents (Beginner, Higher Level), while Rose was speaking in complete sentences, was able to narrate a sequence in a simple story, and was increasingly able to organize multiple sentences around a main topic (Primary, Higher Level). While Jacques was still drawing pictures for stories, Rose was developing simple stories when writing in English. Both students still required ESOL assistance.

According to the interpreter, Rose was able to complete a reading comprehension test in Haitian Creole with 100% accuracy at the sixth grade level, the highest level on the test, indicating that the results probably underestimate her

TABLE 8-6. ROSE'S AND JACQUES' PERFORMANCE ON AN EN-
GLISH INFORMAL READING INVENTORY

LEVELS MEASURED	GRADE SCORES OBTAINED	
	Rose	Jacques
Independent Word Recognition	2nd	Readiness
Instructional Word Recognition	3rd	Readiness
Frustration Word Recognition	4th	Readiness
Independent Comprehension	Primer	Readiness
Instructional Comprehension	1st	Readiness
Frustration Comprehension	2nd	Readiness

comprehension abilities. On the other hand, Jacques was unable to read in
Haitian Creole. When the passages and questions were read to him, Jacques
obtained a total of 40% correct responses at a primer level. Rose and Jacques
were also provided a secondary level text in standard French. Rose was able to
read a passage with only occasional errors and at 93% accuracy. She answered
all comprehension questions correctly. Jacques was unable to read in French at
all. Rose completed French grammar items with 90% accuracy, and wrote a
passage from dictation with 60% accuracy, with errors noted only in spelling.
Jacques was only able to write "Mama" and "Papa," as well as his name.

From the parent, through the interpreter, and through the social worker, it
was learned that Jacques had never been promoted beyond the first grade in
Haiti. The teachers had told the parent that Jacques was not progressing like
other children in his class. Rose, on the other hand, had had no difficulties in
school and, in fact, frequently had to help her brother. Jacques had demonstrated delays in the onset of speech and language in his native language, was
difficult to train in self-help skills, and preferred to play with younger children.
Students his age frequently made fun of him or took advantage of him. Jacques
also had difficulty maintaining appropriate behavior at the grocery store and at
church. He required supervision in other community settings, as well as at
home. His current favorite activity was watching cartoons on T.V.

Based on the combined efforts of school personnel, and after review of the
information obtained, the team decided to refer Jacques for further evaluation
for possible special education placement. Rose, on the other hand, demonstrated low academic levels due to limited proficiency in English and probable
differences in exposure to information, such as in mathematics. Interventions

for Rose could more appropriately be carried out in the regular education setting. Jacques appeared significantly delayed in all areas, even when compared to other youngsters his age in his native country, as reported by his mother and when compared to his natural sibling who is only one year older.

Jacques was evaluated, using nonverbal measures and the assistance of the interpreter. He was found eligible for a program for the moderately mentally retarded (or trainable); however, the placement committee agreed that placement in a classroom for the mildly retarded would be less restrictive and would allow for further observation of his progress. Jacques would continue receiving ESOL services. A re-evaluation prior to the mandatory three years was recommended.

RESEARCH IN PRACTICE:
Detecting Mental Retardation

1. Visit a classroom for mildly mentally retarded students in your district. Review the curriculum, the student products, and the student behaviors. Discuss your observations with the special educator. What behaviors or characteristics of NELB students might be perceived to be similar to those of mildly retarded students? How might they be different? Consider how a student who might be limited in English proficiency would be assisted to become English proficient in this learning environment. What modifications might be needed to meet this student's requirements?

2. Contrast and compare the cases of Lhani, Maurice, Jacques, and Rose. Contrast and compare conceptions of testing, the use of tests, possible attitudes towards perceived handicaps, degree of collaboration among school personnel, and the usefulness of informal methods of evaluation. Share your insights with a colleague. Do you agree? Do you differ? How?

3. How can measures of adaptive behavior be useful? How can they be detrimental to NELB students? Consider your school, community, and environment. What behaviors are expected of people residing in that area? What would constitute "adaptive behavior" in that area? How might cultural differences be addressed through observations of adaptive behavior?

EXAMINING EMOTIONAL AND BEHAVIORAL DIFFICULTIES

Research indicates that approximately seven percent of all children and adolescents in the United States may have emotional disorders that require treatment (Brandenburg, Friedman, & Silver 1990). About one third to one half of these youngsters may exhibit academic or related problems that require intervention provided through special education. At least two to three percent of the total of school-aged children may need to be served in programs that address their emotional and behavioral difficulties; however, public schools identify fewer than one percent of all children enrolled in schools as receiving special services allocated for emotional disturbance (Forness & Knitzer 1992). Of all children served in programs for severe emotional disturbance, culturally and linguistically diverse students are among the most poorly served. They may receive services in highly restrictive settings, or they may receive no services at all (Bazron 1989). The parents of these students receive less culturally relevant social support services than do mainstream parents (Cross, Bazron, Dennis, & Isaacs 1989). The definition of what constitutes emotional disturbance, and the ways in which emotional disturbance is different from a behavioral adjustment or a conduct disorder are related difficulties. Problems of definition of characteristics of emotional or behavioral disorders lead to differences in how school districts apply definitions to assess and identify students for special programs. In some areas of the United States, some groups of culturally diverse students are over-represented in classes for students with behavior problems, while other cultural groups are under-represented (Sugai, Gibbs & Huang 1989). Issues of cultural bias in tests used to assess personality and of interpretation of cross-culturally administered personality tests have yet to be resolved (Diaz-Guerrero & Diaz-Loving 1990; Moran 1990). Few studies have addressed the possible effects of culture on the causes and consequences of emotional disturbance (Garrido 1989).

For the purpose of simplifying discussion in this section, the terms *emotional and behavioral difficulties* will be used generically to indicate individual psychological and social adjustment problems that NELB students may manifest and that affect their performance in the school setting. In general, school districts must abide by the definition of serious emotional disturbance found in the IDEA (formerly known as Education of the Handicapped Act, see Chapter Six for review), that is, "a condition exhibiting one or more of the following characteristics over a long period of time and to a marked degree which adversely affects school performance:

(a) an inability to learn which cannot be explained by intellectual, sensory, or health factors;

(b) an inability to build or maintain satisfactory relationships with peers and teachers;

(c) inappropriate types of behavior or feelings under normal circumstances;

(d) a general pervasive mood of unhappiness or depression; or

(e) a tendency to develop physical symptoms or fears associated with personal or school problems" (*Federal Register, 47,* p.474, 1977).

Arguments have been presented against continued use of this definition in school settings in general for various reasons (Forness & Knitzer 1992). A new definition is being proposed that is more relevant to the identification of emotional/behavioral disturbance among all students. The section of the proposed definition that has significant implications for the assessment of NELB students holds that "The term emotional or behavioral disorder means a disability characterized by behavioral or emotional responses in school different from appropriate age, cultural, or ethnic norms such that they affect educational performance. Educational performance includes academic, social, vocational, and personal skills. Such a disability:

(a) is more than a temporary, expected response to stressful events in the environment;

(b) is consistently exhibited in two different settings, at least one of which is school-related; and,

(c) is unresponsive to direct intervention in general education or the child's condition is such that general education interventions would be insufficient" (Forness & Knitzer 1992, p.13).

The proponents of the new definition stress the use of developmental and ethnic or cultural standards for judgment of what constitutes contrasting, or "different" behavior; however, because normative standards or rating scales have not been well developed, there is a potential for abuse. In the absence of standards for judging behaviors, the proponents suggest that school personnel consult educational or mental health professionals, community leaders, or other informants from the students' ethnic or cultural background. These informants serve as culture brokers and assist in determining the appropriateness of students' behavioral or emotional responses and the extent to which the students manifest differences from the standards or norms of the local community (Forness & Knitzer 1992). This effort encourages the differentiation of student behaviors resulting from stresses related to migration, war, or evacuation from their home countries, and severe psychopathology due to a more permanently disabling condition. While stress related disorders might be effectively treated in school settings through collaborative efforts between community and school resources (Messer & Rasmussen 1985), severe psychopathy may require hospitalization or a more restrictive therapeutic setting. The new definition would also advocate what others have proposed as best evaluation practices for culturally different students:

- observation of student behaviors in both the natural context of the home and the community, as well as the learning environment;

- direct and on-going academic and social skills assessment; and
- on-going monitoring of the effects of instructional practices (Council for Children with Behavior Disorders 1989).

Assessment methods such as those described throughout this book can be readily incorporated into the identification process, allowing for the active participation of school instructional and support personnel, as well as parents and relevant community members. In this manner, evaluations to determine the possible existence of an emotional or behavioral disorder become socially and ethnically valid.

In sum, the identification of NELB students who may be experiencing severe emotional or behavioral problems that warrant special education services is complicated by the same or similar issues related to other special education categories discussed. Increasing awareness of the inadequacies and ambiguities of current identification practices has led to proposals for changes that reflect a pragmatic and sensitive attitude and the realization that student emotions and behaviors evolve in the context of culture and community, not just school.

RESEARCH IN PRACTICE:
Examining Emotional and Behavioral Difficulties: The Case of Tran

---

The case of Tran reveals many of the complexities of assessment of emotional and behavioral difficulties among NELB students. As you read Tran's case, make notes or write questions, then complete the activity that follows.

Tran was an 11-year-old Vietnamese student referred for psychoeducational evaluation due to both behavioral and academic achievement concerns. Tran reportedly displayed lack of interest in school work and appeared to crave peer attention. He was reported to be disruptive in class and was failing sixth grade. Tran was receiving ESOL services on an itinerant basis: he was in the regular curriculum for the greater part of the day. Figure 8-12 shows a drawing Tran had made during class. This drawing alarmed his teacher, who then consulted with support personnel.

The school social worker was sent to the home to obtain additional information regarding Tran. It was discovered that Tran was the youngest of five children. All his siblings were adults. Tran's relationships with his brothers were described as very close. Tran was more obedient with his mother. He reportedly did not present severe behavior problems at home, although he did like to play roughly with the others. Tran enjoyed computer games and, although he had a bike, he was not allowed to ride it because of the heavy traffic in his neighborhood. Because of parental restriction, Tran did not have any friends in the neighborhood. Tran reportedly enjoyed cartoons, but also liked movies with violent themes. Tran frequently crept into his parent's bed at night because of nightmares. The parent reported that Tran had been in a refugee camp and had developed an unspecified lung problem. Because the social worker had difficulty communicating with the parents, he suggested that the services of an interpreter be obtained, not only to assist in communication but to provide input regarding Vietnamese lifestyle. It was anticipated that this information could be useful in addressing Tran's case.

Figure 8-12. Tran's Drawing

The services of a Vietnamese interpreter/informant were obtained through a local refugee resettlement program. What information became available about Tran was pieced together through an interview of previous teachers, one of whom was Vietnamese. Additional interviews were held with present teachers, parents, the informant, and a local Vietnamese clergyman. Through these sources it was learned that Tran had been born in Saigon subsequent to the Vietnam War, when the country was under Communist regime, but Tran never attended school there. The father had been opposed to the Communists and was imprisoned and tortured for his beliefs. The children were not sent to school for fear of reprisals against them for their father's beliefs. The family had been divided as the older children had been sent out of the country to live with strangers, while the rest of the family lived in several refugee camps in Thailand. When Tran's father was finally released from prison, the family made their way to the United States. Tran entered school for the first time at the age of nine. He was placed in a bilingual education program where he was taught in Vietnamese and received ESOL services as well. Tran was placed in first grade, repeated second grade, and was then promoted to sixth grade due to his age and maturity.

Within the bilingual classroom setting, Tran was noted by his former teacher to display a general lack of interest in school work, and a lack of motivation and discipline unlike the other children. He was restless and showed a short attention span. Tran was becoming literate in his native language, but he did not finish his classwork or school work. Tran's former teacher indicated that he was very different from other students in her class, even those who started school as late as he did. She indicated that Vietnamese children have been exposed to very inhumane conditions in the refugee camps and while escaping from their country. She reported that the families frequently underwent humiliation and blackmail by people from the countries through which they traveled. This was confirmed by the clergyman, who also reported many other stressors encountered by children in those conditions.

The native language teacher also reported that, while in her classroom, Tran disrupted others and talked out inappropriately. The other Vietnamese children tended to ignore him or isolate him despite his attempts to get their attention. She indicated that Tran enjoyed math over all other subjects presented and would frequently just sit and draw. Tran's previous teachers were concerned about his obsession with violence and death. He frequently displayed mood swings and bouts of anger. Additionally, he was frequently absent from school.

Within the current academic setting, Tran displayed an uncommon fear of alarms and bells. He at times appeared tired and listless, and was sometimes in trouble for making "wise" remarks to teachers. The dean of students reported discipline referrals due to classroom disruption, use of profanity, insubordination, and conflict with another student. Tran had received both in-and out-of-school suspension and detention. Tran's father, when told of the boy's problems, was upset and angry at the boy for dishonoring the family. Tran received corporal punishment at home: he was hit on the hands with a bamboo stick.

Tran was interviewed through the interpreter who, although trained and briefed prior to interview, appeared primarily concerned with providing Tran with guidance regarding his responsibilities to his parents and school. The interpreter also indicated that Tran's writing in the native language reflected a low level of literacy; however, he was fluent in the native oral language at a Primary, Higher Level to an emerging Intermediate, Lower Level (review Chapter Three). Tran's conversation in English was disjointed and at a Primary, Mid-Level. His verbalizations related to evil and death or to Ninja heroes.

Tran's spontaneous drawings were generally very detailed pictures of a negative and violent orientation. On the other hand, he drew cartoons reflective of prevailing American culture and of high creativity.

Tran's performance on a nonverbal ability measure estimated his functioning to be comparable to that of average monolingual, English speaking students. His reading and written language skills were comparable to those of first grade English-speaking students, while his math skills were at a late third grade level.

1. Review both the current federal definition and the proposed revised definition of serious emotional disturbance. Reflect upon the ease or difficulty with which they can be applied to Tran's case. For example, what data are needed and how can those data be collected in order to comply with the requirements of the two definitions? Once data are collected, how can they be used to plan for Tran's education?

2. Describe what appear to be cultural, linguistic, and social influences in Tran's life. How do these appear to be affecting his current behavior? How does understanding these influences affect the way in which educational services will be planned for him? How did the use of an interpreter and cultural informants help in understanding Tran's background? What were some of the drawbacks?

3. Plan for additional assessment of Tran. What information is lacking or what would you like to explore further? How will this information be relevant to educational planning?

4. Develop an intervention plan for Tran. What areas would you target? What resources would you request? How would you monitor his progress?

5. Consider the importance of sensitivity to cultural differences. What would you do to learn more about your students' cultures and traditions? How might your own established patterns of behavior appear to be "different" to others?

SUMMARIZING CHAPTER EIGHT
SPECIAL EDUCATION AND THE NELB STUDENT

This chapter examined the status of NELB students in special education. The scope of discussion was limited to students with milder or higher prevalence disabilities, particularly those identified under the categories of Specific Learning Disabilities (SLD), Mild Mental Retardation (MMR), and Emotional/ Behavioral Disorders (E/BD). The section reviewed contemporary conceptualizations of learning disabilities, mental retardation, and emotional/ behavioral disorders and the ways in which these are operationalized in the school setting. Students from culturally and linguistically diverse backgrounds may be over- or under-represented in special education categorical programs. Because of this, the referrral, assessment, identification, and placement processes mandated for special education placement consideration have been subjected to scrutiny and review. This section provided case studies that exemplified a more intergrative approach to the assessment of NELB students who are being considered for special programs. Data collected through an integrative approach to assessment can be used to develop hypotheses regarding students' presenting problems, to develop pre-referral intervention plans, and assist in determining the appropriateness of referrals for further evaluation by specialits. Once NELB students are identified as having special needs that cannot be met in the mainstream classroom, special education must include meaningful instruction that is sensitive and responsive to students' cultural and linguistic, as well as academic requirements.

WHAT CAN YOU DO?

1. Request and review special education procedures in your school or district. Are there procedures in place that serve as "checks and balances" to ensure that linguistic, sociocultural, and educational opportunity factors are considered prior to referral, assessment, and placement of NELB students? If not, what procedures would you recommend to ensure that these factors are considered? How would those procedures assist in reducing bias in evaluation and decision-making in the special education student identification and placement process? Write a proposal to your district special education administrator that includes your recommendations and rationale.

2. Consider the "deficit hypothesis" approach presented in the introductory remarks of this chapter. This hypothesis assumes that students display inherent cognitive, academic, and behavioral deficits that are made evident by school failure. Review the definitions of selected special education categories. How helpful are "deficit" model approaches to the identification of students' learning requirements? How can instructional, integrative assessment be a catalyst for change in how special education NELB students are identified, perceived, and served? What role does teacher advocacy play in overcoming perceptions of deficiencies in students being considered for or placed in special education?

Chapter 9

Using Assessment Information to Promote Instructional Effectiveness

E ffective instructional assessment is a complex, long-term process that impacts on all aspects of school. The process of determining students' needs and designing instructional programs is ongoing. Data must be collected, summarized, and reported in a meaningful manner. If students are experiencing learning difficulties, hypotheses about their performance must be developed and tested and the results reported to personnel involved in making modifications. Strategies must be developed and implemented to respond to identified needs. Personnel must be prepared to provide diverse, sometimes new, services.

The long-term benefit of effective instructional assessment is the implementation of a process for moving schools from a remedial toward a developmental approach to teaching and learning. The instructional approach to assessment is especially important for students who have traditionally been at risk of educational failure. Within this approach, schools can be conceptualized as wellness centers that move students toward goals of social and academic language learning and achievement (Fradd & Weismantel 1989).

The process of instructional assessment integrates the content and overall educational procedures of the school with students' specific needs and abilities to participate within the system. Within this approach, it is accepted that not only the behavior of the students may have to be changed to promote successful achievement, but the learning opportunities provided by the school may also require modification to meet students' needs.

Throughout this book, information has been provided for assessing students' growth in terms of performance and achievement. Cases have been provided that exemplify the concepts discussed. This chapter summarizes this information and offers suggestions for developing a comprehensive approach to assessment for ongoing planning and instruction as well as for monitoring students' progress.

Educators who are developing expertise in the assessment process may find it tempting to focus only on final outcomes as a means for assessing NELB students. To do so circumvents the learning process. An understanding of the learning process for students who use English as a new language combined with an understanding of the process of collecting and using performance data is central within the instructional assessment paradigm.

The chapter is organized into five sections. Section One presents a set of guidelines for collecting and using student data. The guidelines are divided into two parts. Table 9-1a provides a series of tasks for collecting and summarizing descriptive information regarding a student's current performance. Table 9-1b provides a process for refining and using the information to generate and test hypotheses about the student's instructional needs. Following the guidelines are Section Two to Section Five, which present four case studies to which the process can be applied.

SECTION ONE

COLLECTING AND ORGANIZING INFORMATION

In the cases presented throughout this book, the initial focus of the assessment information has been on the use of formal assessment data. This emphasis on the use of formal assessment information has occurred because schools typically rely on norm-referenced tests in making placement decisions. Because this type of information is often readily available, it provides a basis from which decisions can be made about the additional or alternative data to be collected. Many child advocates have strong concerns about the use of standardized assessment in placing students in special education programs (Figueroa 1989; Rueda 1989). Yet standardized information can also be used as a positive source of information for ensuring that students receive appropriate instruction. For example, in the cases of language development presented in Chapter Four, several of the students appeared to be communicatively disordered or to manifest a language-oriented disability because they lacked the skills needed to express the language used in their academic environment. The formal assessment information revealed these students to be of normal intelligence and ability. Formal assessment procedures, in these cases, were useful in ruling out specific types of difficulties. Formal tests are not so helpful in indicating how to address students' learning needs.

While it can be accurately argued that the use of informal assessment strategies during the period when students are being identified as having learning difficulties can prevent the need for formal assessment, few schools have personnel who have been trained to use and interpret informal measures (Langdon 1989). The use of informal assessment strategies during pre-referral interventions has the potential to provide educators with insight into these students' needs. In current practice, educational systems at the national, state, and district level are not prepared to accept feelings or insights as the basis for legal decisions about students. And, unfortunately, the legal process for determining what is appropriate for students is an aspect of the educational system that must be acknowledged. Because schools are becoming arenas of litigation and legal interpretation, formal assessment information continues to be used as the basis for decision-making (Fradd & Vega 1987). As expertise in the use of informal assessment increases, and the recognition of the limitations of formal assessment procedures becomes widely acknowledged, the use of formal procedures may be minimized and reserved for only the most difficult cases (Baca & Cervantes 1989).

For some students, formal assessment procedures can provide a safety net that mitigates unfair or biased assessment of their performance and of their ability to learn. However, standardized procedures can also promote bias and lead to misidentification of students' potential. If students have never been exposed to literacy experiences, never been provided with the academic information schools expect them to know, and never been taught the skills they are expected to be able to perform, then these students may appear to be developmentally delayed or disabled on every type of formal measure currently available (Duran 1989).

The purpose of this book is to promote the development of instructional assessment procedures that meet the needs of students in the process of learning English as a new language. The needs of these students vary and include a range of abilities and prior experiences with literacy. Educators are increasingly expected to meet the educational needs of all of these students (Baca & Cervantes 1989). Some students require minimal additional instructional support to function in a regular instructional program. Other students manifest learning difficulties that can, with assistance, be overcome. Still others have substantial disabilities that will not be completely overcome, but that also require effective instruction to enable these learners to develop to their full potential linguistically, socially, and academically.

There is no simple process for collecting and using information on students' learning progress. The process must be done on an individual, case by case basis. Because the process is lengthy and time consuming, concerted efforts have been made by researchers as well as school districts and individual educators to streamline it. These efforts have further confirmed the reality that, while the process can be organized, it still remains labor-intensive and time-consuming (Baca & Cervantes 1989; Moscoso 1989).

Throughout the book, information has been presented that emphasizes both the short and long-term outcomes of effective assessment and instruction. This section provides specific steps for collecting information and hypothesizing students' needs. The process presented here is designed to promote the development of long-term planning as well as of assessment skills that assist educators in gathering information, developing hypotheses, and providing effective short-term educational responses to students' needs (Hudson & Fradd 1990). This data-collection and decision-making process is presented in the Guidelines for Instructional Assessment, Part I and Part II.

Part I of the Guidelines consists of a series of questions designed to summarize students' performance data. The process is intended to encourage educators to think deeply and reflectively about the types of instruction and support being provided to the student as well as to make them aware of the student's current level of performance. Completion of Part I often provides insights into immediate ways to meet students' needs. Part I also provides a synthesis of information that can be used in Part II to develop and test hypotheses about students' performance. Through the testing of the hypotheses developed in Part II of the Guidelines, decisions can be made at the formal level about students' specific needs and the instructional objectives that could be implemented to meet these needs. Together, Parts I and II promote collaboration in observing, collecting, and using the information in making decisions and in developing specific approaches for instructing students. The major headings of the Guidelines are presented below as an overview in anticipation of their review in the detailed format that follows.

Overview of Guidelines for Instructional Assessment

Part I

- Literacy Development and Performance within Instructional Contexts

- The Influence of Social, Personal, and Family Factors

- Contextual Availability of Information and Cognitive Demand of Tasks

Part II

- Overall Summary of Information on Student Performance to date

- Hypothesis Development and Testing

- Development and Monitoring of Instructional Objectives

These categories are presented in Table 9-1 in their entirety, along with an explanation of how this information can be used. The case studies following this first section provide practice in selecting and organizing data on students' performance. Sample responses presented in the appendices suggest possible responses.

Not all information is readily available. Most information can be obtained only after careful observation of target students in a variety of settings over a period of time. While every effort should be made to meet students' instructional needs during this observation period, it is recommended that instruction for these students continue until school personnel have collected sufficient information on which to make accurate decisions. At the same time, educators are encouraged to act as quickly as possible to avoid the legal as well as the pedagogical consequences of inappropriate placement and instruction.

To expedite the data-collection process, the Guidelines can be organized electronically on a computer and input and monitored as needed. While any or all components of the guidelines may be used in collecting student information, it is recommended that modifications not be made until the Guidelines have been used in their entirety several times. A complete set of the Guidelines, without commentary, is located in the Appendix to this chapter.

TABLE 9-1a. GUIDELINES FOR INSTRUCTIONAL ASSESSMENT, PART I

I. DESCRIPTION OF LITERACY SKILL DEVELOPMENT AND PERFORMANCE WITHIN INSTRUCTIONAL CONTEXTS

1. Literacy instruction used with this student (Chapters 3, 5)

✓ Describe learning outcomes produced through the use of the instruction programs listed below. Provide additional information, if the type of instructional program(s) used with this student is not listed. *The information requested is designed to determine which instructional programs have been used with the student and, of these, which have produced the most successful outcomes.*

- whole language and language experience reading instruction
- literature based reading
- basal readers
- phonics
- instructional reading games
- computer assisted instruction for drill and practice reading activities
- computer assisted instruction for word processing, self-generated texts
- other

✓ Describe student's performance in self-generated oral or written responses. *Is the production of language painful or pleasant? Are written responses preferred to oral communication?*

✓ Describe student's interest and interactions with animals. *Sometimes students relate to animals in ways that are different from the ways they interact with humans. Animals may be seen as less potentially threatening and more responsive than humans. Suggestions for eliciting information include observations of students' behavior with pets or other animals in school, discussions that include students' ideas and reactions to pictures of animals, discussions about family pets, and similar activities where students can express their perspectives.*

✓ Describe student's performance on teacher directed tasks.

✓ Describe student's performance in other instructional alternatives.

✓ Describe student's observations of performance and preferences. *Again, it is important to know what this student thinks about school, learning, and instruction.*

- **Summarize performance in terms of instructional opportunities and outcomes to date.** *Some students are provided with very few instructional alternatives. Before beginning any program modifications, it is important to understand what has already occurred and the results produced.*

2. Language as a factor in instruction and performance (Chapters 3, 4, 5)

✓ Is there a time during the day when the student's non-English language is used? *This question looks at two types of data: (a) academic instruction provided that uses the students non-English language as a vehicle for instruction; (b) opportunities during which the student can interact in meaningful ways with others who share the same language background. Both types of opportunities can be important. As the case studies indicated, some learning difficulties appear to be related to the abrupt switch from non-English to all English instruction.*

If yes, describe how the language is used. *Descriptive information is requested here because there are many different ways that the information can be organized and presented. Use of description here has two goals: (a) it promotes analysis and synthesis of information; and (b) it avoids long lists of questions that would be potentially irrelevant to some learners.*

If yes, describe how the student responds in diverse language settings, especially when the non-English language is used. *Students often respond differently to adults and to peers. They also may respond differently to different languages. For example, some students will claim that they have no knowledge of a non-English language, even when it is the only language that their parents use when communicating at home. Some students appear shy in one language, outgoing in another. The environment where the language is used and the perceptions of adults and peers often influences the ways that students use language and as a result, perceive themselves as users of those languages.*

✓ Describe student's personal description of prior experiences. *It is important to involve the student in the information collection process. The student can often provide insight into prior experience that is not available through records, family members, and other sources of information.*

- **Summarize performance in terms of availability and use of English and non-English for instructional purposes.**

3. Exposure to languages as a factor in learning

✓ Describe student's prior schooling and educational experiences, including length of residence in English-use environment. *This question asks how long a student has been living in an environment in which English was the primary language of communication. The question could be interpreted as meaning how long has the student been in the United States, but sometimes answers are more complex than just the number of years of living in the United States. Many students travel back and forth between two different language environments. Their exposure to English is quite different from students who have moved directly to the United States and remained there permanently. Many students also come from other English-speaking environments, such as the Caribbean, Africa, Europe, Australia, Canada, or New Zealand. Again, the language features as well as the culture in which English is used varies by geographical region. It is helpful to be aware of all of this information.*

✓ Length of time of exposure to English. *This question asks how long the student has been exposed to English. This refers to several possibilities, such as a family member or other caregiver who may use English even though another language is used in the larger community. It also considers that the student may have formally studied English prior to arriving in the United States Information on informal exposure should be differentiated from information on academic instruction.*

- **Summarize prior school experiences including exposure to English and other languages.**

4. Awareness of metalinguistic and metacognitive organization (Chapters 3,5)

This subsection looks at what the student knows and understands about books, written language, and general literacy skills. Aspects of metalinguistics, metacognition, and text structures are considered here. Students from preliterate language backgrounds and from environments where few literacy experiences are available have different orientations to learning than students who enter school from environments in which literacy skills are already highly developed. Students who enter school with limited literacy skills should not be penalized for their lack of experience. They do require specific assistance and motivation to develop both the skills and the understanding of language required for academic success.

✓ Describe student's orientation to use of books and writing materials. *How does the student use books and writing materials?*

✓ Describe student's awareness, motivation, and interest in literacy as vehicle for learning.

✓ Describe student's use of self-talk and reflection on performance in completing a task. *Students who have developed strategies for executing and monitoring their own performance often demonstrate what they are thinking through their behavior. They may use expressions like, "I wonder how this would work," "Slow down, you're rushing," "No, don't you see, you still haven't got it," and "Well, it seems to me…" when they are working alone to complete a task.*

✓ Describe student's awareness of sound/symbol relationships (consider both English and non-English language, if possible). *This item is looking for information on the student's ability to understand and*

✓ Describe student's ability to play with language. *This item is looking for information on the student's ability to understand and produce rhyme, to organize words by beginning or ending sounds, and to see language as a system of patterns.*

✓ Describe student's awareness of graphics and text in interpreting information. *This is a more subtle observation. Pictures can both support and distract from the meaning of written text. Sometimes students interpret the pictures in ways that differ from the text. This type of interpretation can result from the diverse experiences that students have had or as a result of misleading graphics. In either case, it is important to enable students to accurately read text and interpret graphics. In order to assist the students, an understanding of both the student's skill in graphic and text interpretation is required.*

✓ Describe student's understanding of idioms, factual and figurative expressions, and humor. *One of the most difficult skills for some students to develop is the ability to distinguish between literal and idiomatic or figurative expressions. Both intellectual maturity and experience with the language are required to effectively differentiate between literal and implicit meanings.*

✓ Describe student's awareness of the meaning provided through organizing, sequencing and organization and spacing of graphics and words. *As language becomes more abstract, the organization of information plays an increasingly important role. Students who don't understand the subtleties of written language often can produce the words but fail to understand the meaning conveyed.*

✓ Describe student's awareness of syntactical and semantic relationships in communicating meaning. *This item is looking for information on the student's awareness of information provided through specific aspects of language. The question here is how the student comprehends the subtleties of meaning that are communicated through word order as well as word choice.*

• **Summarize student's awareness of form, organization, and content in applying literacy skills.**

5. Performance as measured by formal and informal tests (Chapters 3, 5, 8)

✓ Describe student's performance in reading, language arts, and math as measured by standardized tests.

✓ Compare information on student's academic performance as measured by standardized tests with standardized tests of ability or intelligence.

✓ Describe student's performance as measured by informal procedures. *Frequently only formal assessment information is used in determining students' needs. Here is an opportunity to compare and contrast information gathered through both data sources and determine where there are major discrepancies or not. Sometimes information from one source can lead to a clearer understanding of a student's needs than data from another. But often together these sources corroborate what is known about a student.*

• **Summarize information gained from formal and informal measures.**

6. Language proficiency as a factor in communicating and performing (Chapters 3,5)

✓ Describe student's level of demonstrated proficiency in English-language social activities. *The emphasis here is on oral rather than written language. Terms such as spontaneous, shy, highly verbal, eagerly engaged, easy to motivate are all potential descriptors that might be used here. Descriptions should be based on at least three different observations of the student. Some students are inclined to be very verbal, others prefer to write their responses.*

✓ Describe student's level of demonstrated proficiency in non-English-language social activities (as assessed with the assistance of trained interpreters). *Similar types of activities can be used to assess and observe students' performance in using their non-English language in social settings.*

✓ Describe student's level of demonstrated proficiency in English in the academic tasks.

✓ Describe student's level of demonstrated proficiency in non-English language development in the academic tasks (as assessed with the assistance of trained interpreters).

✓ What are the student's perceptions of personal performance in English?

✓ What are the student's perceptions of personal performance in non-English?

✓ What are the teachers' perceptions of the student's performance?

This section looks at several pieces of information: (a) what the student does in social and academic settings in English; (b) what the student does in parallel academic activities in non-English; (c) what the student thinks of his or her performance in both social and academic settings; and (d) what the teacher thinks about the student's performance. It might be helpful to create a chart something like the one below to summarize this information.

PERFORMANCE IN ENGLISH

	Social	Academic

PERCEPTIONS OF PERFORMANCE IN ENGLISH

	Social	Academic

PERFORMANCE IN NON-ENGLISH

	Social	Academic

PERCEPTIONS OF PERFORMANCE IN NON-ENGLISH

	Social	Academic

Student

Teachers

• **Summarize proficiency observed and perceptions of language performance.**

7. Language as a vehicle for achieving goals (Chapter 3)

✓ Describe student's performance using a variety of language functions in English. *Refer to the last section of Chapter Three on elicitation and analysis of language functions. Include information on both social and academic functions at an age appropriate level.*

✓ Describe student's performance using a variety of language functions in non-English.

✓ Describe the student's perceptions of the use of language for achieving goals, in English and in non-English.

✓ Contrast the student's use and performance on language functions in English and non-English.

• **Summarize language performance to achieve a variety of purposes.**

8. Mathematics as a vehicle for learning (Chapter 5)

✓ Describe student's performance in math computation. *Mathematics has a specific register of language. Sometimes students learn this aspect of language more easily or with greater difficulty than other academic aspects. Descriptive information is important here.*

✓ Is there a discrepancy between the student's level of math computation and overall performance in math? If yes, describe the discrepancy. *Often test information doesn't differentiate between computation and problem-solving skills, yet information on both is important.*

✓ Is the level of math performance similar to or different from general literacy performance? Describe discrepancies, if they exist. *Again, an understanding of the discrepancies and commonalities is important.*

• **Summarize math performance as it relates to overall language performance.**

9. Movement toward success

Sometimes the tasks and skills that a student has not mastered are well documented, but little attention is given to the areas in which the student is able to achieve. This section is designed to promote a focus, perhaps a refocusing, on what a student can do and use that information to promote further success and learning.

✓ Describe the tasks in which the student excels.

✓ Describe the motivating and energizing activities or aspects of the school day.

✓ Describe the instructional approaches that provide success. *Include information on how success is defined and determined. Sometimes the definition of success influences its measurement.*

✓ Describe the student's perceptions of school success. *Include the student's perceptions of personal success at school.*

• **Summarize the movement toward academic success.**

•• *Section Summary:* **Summarize information in terms of opportunities for learning, instruction, and performance.** *Summarize information from diverse sources in terms of student's learning opportunities, exposure to English, and in terms of language proficiency and performance. How does the information available from language samples and observations fit with the information available from teachers and formal assessment procedures? Is there significant mismatch or agreement? Be sure that reasons for the beliefs expressed and the data sources are included within each subsection. This information is not necessarily within the summary. Reduce data to a brief synthesis here.*

II. THE INFLUENCE OF CULTURE, HEALTH, SOCIAL, AND FAMILY FACTORS ON INSTRUCTION AND LEARNING

10. Culture as a factor influencing participation and learning (Chapters 5, 8)

✓ Describe efforts to identify and use information on similarities between student's prior educational experiences and the current setting. *Often the differences are identified and the similarities are not observed. Usually there are more similarities than differences. Observing similarities builds on strengths.*

✓ Describe efforts to identify and address differences between student's prior educational experiences and the current setting.

✓ Describe efforts to address similarities and differences between student's cultural background and the culture of the current setting. *Being aware of similarities and differences is the first step in assisting students. How this information is used is very important. Sometimes well-meaning educators use this information to excuse poor performance or to avoid sensitive topics that the student needs to understand in order to perform appropriately.*

✓ Describe the student's thoughts about cultural differences and similarities between current and previous schools and learning environments. *The student may not be able to give information in terms of specific cultural similarities and differences, but he or she can describe preferences and observe similarities and differences between current and former educational settings.*

• **Summarize similarities and differences between student's prior educational experiences and cultural background and the current setting and expectations.**

11. Health, school attendance and other physical and environmental factors (Chapter 8)

✓ Describe the student's current general health. *Include information here on vision and hearing, if possible.*

✓ Describe the student's previous health including any factors that might have influenced attendance and learning.

✓ Describe school attendance in current and previous settings. If there is a history of absence or irregular attendance, please explain. *A summary of previous school attendance is important here.*

• **Summarize school attendance and performance as influenced by health or other factors.**

12. Family background as a factor influencing participation and learning (Chapter 8)

✓ Describe family background including siblings' and other family members' achievements. *Discretion should be used in collecting this type of information. Sometimes when socioeconomic information is obtained, it is used to explain why a student is not achieving or as a means for justifying current performance. If this information is insightful in assisting the school to develop an effective program, then it should be included. If the information does not provide insight into ways to assist the student, then it may not be very important. In any case, care must be taken to use the information to assist, not to stereotype or bias the assessment process.*

✓ Describe efforts to involve family in the educational process. *There are many ways that family members, including parents, siblings, and others can be involved. It would be helpful to describe ways that the school has used to involve family members.*

✓ Describe student records from prior settings. *Be sure that there is someone available within the school or school district who can accurately translate and interpret educational records and reports from other countries.*

✓ Include other useful information about the student and family available from other sources. *It is important to include other* sources of information, if these sources can be used to assist educators to understand the student. For example, the student may be a Girl Scout and have achieved a number of awards for good conduct and sportsmanship, but when at school the student may have discipline problems.

- **Summarize information on family background as it influences this student's learning.**

13. Environmental and other factors as an influence on participation and learning (Chapters 2, 3, 5, 8)

✔ Describe and summarize any environmental factors that may influence this student's school attendance, participation, and learning. This item was included because there may be other influencing factors that have not been covered elsewhere. Consider this an optional question.

•• *Section Summary:* **Summarize the influence of culture, health, social, and family factors on participation, instruction and learning.**

III. CONTEXTUAL AVAILABILITY OF INFORMATION AND COGNITIVE DEMAND OF TASKS

The information requested within this section is not typically collected by schools, yet this can be some of the most important and useful information available to teachers. It is especially valuable in developing instructional interventions, because it provides insight into what students can do, what they find difficult, and how instructional support may be provided. By understanding the type of contextual information and support available to the student, and combining this with information on the cognitive demands of the tasks the student is being expected to perform, teachers can adjust instruction and make support available to meet students' needs.

14. Familiarity with content and persons as variables (Chapters 2, 3)

✔ Compare and contrast the student's performance with familiar and unfamiliar content or materials. *Sometimes students perform differently with materials or topics with which they are familiar than with materials and topics with which they are not familiar. These two questions examine these differences.*

✔ Compare and contrast the student's performance with familiar and unfamiliar persons (include information on both peers and adults). *This subsection considers information presented on communication within natural and academic settings. Here influences that promote and inhibit participation and communication are being considered.*

✔ Describe, where appropriate, the student's performance on cooperatively structured classroom tasks. *Has the student participated in learning activities that were cooperatively structured and has the student been taught how to participate effectively?*

✔ Describe the student's performance using familiar and new subject matter.

✔ Describe the student's perceptions about learning and working with others.

- **Summarize familiarity with persons, materials or context, and content as variables that influence performance.**

15. Cognitive demand as a variable in performance (Chapters 2, 3)

✔ Describe the student's performance on concrete and abstract tasks. *Here consideration is given to the level of abstraction as a factor influencing performance.*

✔ Describe the student's performance as the cognitive demand of tasks increases or decreases. *It is not always possible to* determine the cognitive demand of a specific task. However, it is possible to observe student performance differences as tasks become more abstract or less abstract. Describe the performance changes. When faced with abstract tasks, does the student withdraw, become angry, try to disturb others? Observing the ways that students react to difficulties is important in being able to assist them.

✓ Describe the student's performance when performing similar tasks alone and with peers. Some students do better when they can provide their own support and structure. Others require support and structure from others. What does this student do?

✓ Describe the student's perceptions of his or her performance and reactions on tasks of increasing difficulty. Which tasks are seen as difficult or easy? There may be a discrepancy between the student's perception and the teachers'.

✓ Describe efforts to modify the level of difficulty of the tasks in meeting this student's needs and discuss the resulting outcomes.

• **Summarize information on cognitive demand and contextual support as variables affecting performance.**

•• *Section Summary:* **Summarize information on the effect of familiarity, interpersonal interactions, and reduced cognitive demand as influences affecting performance.** *Summarize information on previous efforts to provide the student with instructional support. What is instructional support? It could be the student's proximity to the teacher, it could be the availability of peer tutors, it could be the use of the non-English language for comprehension checks or for social interactions. This section considers how instructional support has been defined by the school or by the educators working with this student.*

TABLE 9-1b. GUIDELINES FOR INSTRUCTIONAL ASSESSMENT, PART II

OVERALL SUMMARY OF STUDENT PERFORMANCE

1. Summary of known information (list specific known information)

- . . . .
- *and potentially more*

2. Specific information to be obtained (list specific information that is not known)

- . . . .
- *and potentially more*

Once the information still unknown has been listed, determine which specific information is required to make decisions and to assist the student, as opposed to information that might be interesting or helpful but not really essential.

Prioritize the specific information to be obtained, then indicate the persons responsible and the timeline for obtaining information. This information can be helpful in developing hypotheses.

Information	Person responsible	Date for obtaining
.	•	•
.	•	•
.	•	•

and potentially more

HYPOTHESIS DEVELOPMENT AND TESTING

3. Hypotheses about student's instructional needs
Hypothesize what may be interfering with the student's learning process and what can be done to promote success. Hypotheses are guesses about what the factors or forces are that influence what students do.

(a)

(b)

(c)

(d) *and potentially more*

4. Prioritize hypotheses and establish procedures for testing them.
First, all of the guesses or hypotheses about the causes of the student's behavior are written down. Once the hypotheses have been listed, they can be prioritized. Next, the persons responsible for testing them and the date by which the information is to be obtained can be specified.

List the highest priority hypothesis first.

(a) Hypothesis	Person(s) responsible	Date for obtaining

Summary of outcomes
Reserve this space for recording the information obtained by testing the first hypothesis.

(b) Hypothesis	Person(s) responsible	Date for obtaining

Summary of outcomes
Reserve this space for recording the information obtained by testing the second hypothesis. Continue until all hypotheses determined to be important have been tested.

5. Summarize information on student gained from observation and from hypothesis testing.

Hypothesis a:

Hypothesis b:
Continue list as needed.

6. Develop instructional objectives based on hypothesis information, and continue to monitor.

The next step is dependent on the information obtained from the process of hypothesis testing. Continued hypothesis testing and monitoring will be needed to ensure that appropriate instruction and support are provided.

7. Develop specific instructional objectives for the student and determine how these objectives will be assessed and monitored.

The Guidelines for Instructional Assessment have been developed to assist educators in collecting and using student performance information effectively and efficiently. Following this section, four case studies have been developed to provide practice in applying the Guidelines. Although fictional, each case is based on real life stories and student records. You can reproduce the Guidelines from the Appendix and use them to organize and record information about these four students. You are encouraged to develop and share your own ideas. As you work with colleagues, you will find many alternate ways to assist students and to meet their needs through instructional assessment.

WHAT WOULD YOU DO?

1. Review the information requested for each component of Part I of the Guidelines for Instructional Assessment. Bring to mind a student who you believe needs assistance in becoming successful. How would you use the Guidelines to determine how best to assist this student? Collect information necessary to meet this student's needs. Discuss Part I of the Guidelines with a colleague. Consider ways that you would use the Guidelines in your school.

2. Review the way that student data are organized in Part II of the Guidelines for Instructional Assessment. Next, use the process outlines in Part II. Involve at least one colleague with you in this process. Together plan specific ways to organize a collaborative environment for problem-solving to assist the students with whom you work.

SECTION TWO

BEN'S STORY

Ben had been in the United States for five years when his fourth grade teacher referred him to the Child Study Team because of his poor grades and failure to make academic progress. Although he was born in Mexico, all of Ben's educational experience had occurred in the United States. Ben lives with his mother and younger brother in a modest home near the school. Ben's mother is a seamstress in a small clothing factory. Ben has always attended this same school. His attendance records show that he seldom missed a day of school.

Ben's instructional program.

The instruction Ben received in kindergarten included the use of both English and Spanish. But from first grade on, Ben's instruction was only in English. When Ben had not learned to read at the end of first grade, he was referred to the Chapter I program. He received tutorial and compensatory instruction through Chapter I beginning in second grade. Reading instruction consisted primarily of exercises to reinforce phonic skills and grammar. Because the time available for Ben to attend Chapter I conflicted with the reading time in his second grade classroom, he received all of his reading instruction in Chapter I. In spite of the intensive instruction, Ben continued to have difficulty with long and short vowels and consonant blends. In addition to Chapter I instruction, in the third grade Ben was given tutorial assistance in language arts, reading, and math so that he could pass the state minimum skills tests. He did pass the minimum competency test and was promoted to fourth grade. Although he was referred for special assistance in fourth grade, Ben continued in the regular fourth grade placement throughout the year. During the fourth grade whole language activities were introduced into Ben's program, although his instruction continued to emphasize phonics drills, and reading in a basal reader. Ben appeared to like the basal instruction more than the whole language activities because he consistently participated in and completed more of the assigned basal work. Ben had difficulty developing sentences on his own and seldom completed the whole language activities. Eventually, whole language activities were discontinued, and language instruction was emphasized through the basal reader and phonics workbook. Ben was also encouraged to check out books from the library. He often looked at and checked out books on cats. He especially liked Garfield, the cat.

At the end of fourth grade, when Ben was 10 years and 2 months old, his performance on the Comprehensive Test of Basic Skills indicated that he was functioning at the 12th percentile, stanine 3, in Reading; at the 10th percentile, stanine 2, in Language Arts; at the 16th percentile, stanine 3, in Mathematics. These results suggest achievement well below average for grade placement. In terms of his current academic functioning, Ben was functioning at a second grade level.

Ben's classroom performance.

During a classroom observation by the educational assessment specialist, Ben was observed reading a cartoon book about Garfield during the morning announcements. Though he participated in the opening exercises, he appeared to be engrossed in the book and continued to look at it until he was called to participate in an instructional group. Ben sat throughout the group instruction. He smiled occasionally, but most of the time he looked down or away from the other children. The behavior observed during the first part of the day continued throughout the observation. Ben was passive; he waited to be called upon rather than anticipating or initiating opportunities for participation. When he did respond, his responses were brief and infrequent. Many times he only shook his head, nodded, and uttered single hard-to-hear words.

Ben seldom looked directly at the teacher or the other students. Since he did not initiate interactions with other students, and tended to withdraw to the sidelines whenever possible rather than joining in with small activities, it was difficult to determine Ben's level of language proficiency within the classroom setting. Because of the lack of opportunities to see Ben in action, it was also difficult to determine whether standardized test results were an accurate estimation of Ben's academic performance.

Individual performance.

On a one-to-one basis, Ben participated in a social conversation about his Garfield book. Although he appeared to enjoy the books, he was observed to hold one of the books upside down and turn the pages from front to back. When asked to talk about the book, Ben told a brief story about Garfield. When asked to read a specific page out loud, Ben responded by reciting two sentences that appeared several pages earlier. After some probing on the part of the assessor, Ben stated that he didn't actually read the book, he just liked to look at the pictures. He had several Garfield books and he had memorized the captions from several of the pictures in each book. He did show the assessor the cartoons that he liked and then revealed that his mother liked some of these cartoons, too. He read several of the captions from his favorite cartoons. Through his conversation about the Garfield books, Ben indicated that he was able to use language for personal and social functions. He was aware of personal preferences and even included information about his mother.

From the discussion about Garfield, the regulatory language function (see Chapter 3, Section Two) was introduced. Ben successfully completed the regulatory function using small wooden blocks to build a design and then to explain how the assessor could also build one. When a barrier was placed between Ben and the assessor, he initially resisted telling the assessor how to build the figure on the other side of the barrier. He did not know the names of the blocks and became frustrated when he could not tell the assessor where to put the blocks. However, when he was encouraged, he regained his composure and described the blocks by color, shape, and size.

Ben was unable to complete the heuristic language function by asking appropriate questions about an imaginary party to be held on Saturday. When shown a set of sequence cards, Ben was unable to order the cards or predict what the final card might be. In eliciting the heuristic function, Ben was told the examiner had a bicycle for sale and that she would like him to ask questions about the bike, Ben asked only three questions, "Can I see?" "What color are the tires?" and "Does it have covers?" When prompted to ask more questions, such as information about the location and price, Ben looked down. When given three items and the request to "Guess which thing I am thinking of by asking me questions," Ben said, "Is this one (touching one of the items, the shell)?" He appeared to be unwilling to guess at outcomes. With Ben, the notion of obtaining information through the process of questioning and drawing conclusions appeared not to be well developed, perhaps nonexistent.

In retelling a short story about a boy and his dog, Ben replied with a story of five sentences, one introductory, one descriptive, and an action sequence. The story was as follows:

1. It about a dog.
2. The dog black and white.
3. He play with the boy.
4. He go to the boy.
5. They go home.

Even with probing, Ben was unable to provide information on the actions or main idea of the story. He displayed similar behavior when given a set of five sequence cards about a boy getting ready for school. He was able to generate a brief story about a boy who tore his pants, based on a set of three cards. Based on this information, Ben appeared to be functioning at the mid-primary level of language development. He had not developed control over the syntax indicating past and future tense. When probed about activities that happened in the past, he tended to speak in the present tense. He also tended not to use third person present tense, indicating a limited awareness of the grammatical structures of language. For example, he stated, "I go movies last night." and, "My mother work hard so I go to school."

Because Ben was born outside the United States and had participated in a bilingual program, it was suggested that he might still be limited in English proficiency, even though he had actually been in an all English instructional program for nearly four years. He was administered the Language Assessment Battery in English and Spanish in order to determine language dominance and proficiency. He scored at the 18th percentile in English and at the 7th percentile level in Spanish. He was able to read in English, but not in Spanish. These results revealed Ben to be limited in both languages, but English dominant and ineligible for further participation in bilingual instruction, according to state guidelines.

Formal assessment information.

The Woodcock Language Proficiency Battery was administered in English and Spanish in order to provide further information on Ben's academic language development. This instrument tapped both receptive and expressive vocabulary, through ability to retrieve words to resolve analogies, and provided information on his listening skills, memory, and general comprehension. The results of this assessment supported the findings of the Language Assessment Battery, that though English dominant, Ben's language skills appeared to be undeveloped in comparison with his age peers. On the Woodcock, he was found to be functioning at a first grade level in the use of oral English. In Spanish his language skills were found to be at a kindergarten level, resulting in severe deficits in both languages.

Intellectual assessment was completed in English using the Wechsler Intelligence Scale for Children-Revised (WISC-R). Although Ben appeared to prefer to respond in English, he also responded to some of the questions in Spanish. Results were calculated first using only the English data, then to test performance limits, the results were recalculated using both English and Spanish responses. This recalculation did not significantly change the outcomes by adding the Spanish responses, therefore, results are reported only in English. Ben received a Verbal Intelligence Quotient of 59, a Performance Quotient of 88, and a Full Scale Intelligence Quotient of 72. These results reflect intellectual functioning in the Slow Learner educational classification. A significant discrepancy was noted between Ben's verbal and performance results suggesting that the non-verbal abilities were in the Low Average range while the verbal abilities were deficient. These results are in line with the Woodcock assessment results. Ben displayed significant problems in the areas of verbal reasoning, vocabulary, and comprehension. Additional assessment of non-verbal abilities was completed by administration of the Hiskey-Nebraska Test of Learning Aptitude, a non-verbal intelligence measure commonly used with hearing impaired or language disordered youngsters. Six subtests of the Hiskey-Nebraska were administered. These subtests tapped such areas as visual attention, memory, and reasoning by association. Ben obtained a mental age of 8 years, 6 months using norms for hearing youngsters, and a deviation Intelligence Quotient of 79. These results indicate overall ability in the Slow Learner range.

Academic skills attainment was assessed with the Woodcock-Johnson Psycho-Educational Battery, Tests of Achievement. The Reading, Written Language, and Mathematics clusters tap areas such as word decoding, reading comprehension, and application of grammar and spelling, as well as math computation and numerical reasoning skills. These results indicate that Ben's reading skills in Spanish were at the beginning first grade level. He retained some basic sight vocabulary skills, but could not read for comprehension. Ben's written language skills in Spanish were at a mid-first grade level; he was only able to write selected letters of the alphabet and simple words. His overall skills in Spanish were severely limited or virtually nonexistent. Assessment of English literacy skills revealed that Ben was reading at a beginning second grade level. When standard scores were considered, however, Ben's skills were commensurate with his ability in the Slow Learner range. His written language skills were also at the second grade level and appeared to be commensurate with ability. Mathematics skills were at a beginning third grade level and also appeared to be commensurate with his ability as measured by other tests. The Bender Visual-Motor Gestalt Test, a test of skills necessary for copying and for written tasks, was also administered. Ben scored at the 8 year to 8 year 5 months level, with a standard score of 82, commensurate with other measures of ability. The overall picture was of a youngster who was acquiring academic skills at a rate comparable with his developmental ability.

Teacher's perceptions.

Ben's teacher expressed concern both for his academic progress and for his reluctance to participate in learning activities. She reported that she tried to talk to him several times about his work, but he just looked down and did not respond. The teacher further stated that she had tried to contact the mother, but had been unsuccessful. In talking to Ben about the possibility of having his mother come to school, he responded, "Mother work hard, no come to school." Cumulative record information indicated that the mother spoke only Spanish. No bilingual social worker was available to visit the home or to locate the mother at work.

Summary of current performance.

Ben was a student from a Spanish-language background who was referred for psychoeducational evaluation because of continued academic difficulties.

His evaluation results reflect a youngster displaying severe limitations in academic language, limited verbal abstract reasoning, and a lack of comprehension skills in both English and Spanish. While his poor linguistic development in both languages appears to hamper his progress in school, it is also commensurate with his general mental development. Though more dominant in English, Ben retained Spanish language skills at a receptive level, but was not fully proficient in either English or Spanish, and had limited literacy skills in both languages. In English he was working at a second to third grade level in the three major academic areas measured, reading, written language, and mathematics. His rate of learning, as measured by standardized tests, was commensurate with a Slow Learner educational classification. Ben will require continued adjustments in his curriculum and level of instruction if he is to function successfully in upper elementary, middle, and high school academic instruction.

WHAT WOULD YOU DO?

1. Use Part I of the Guidelines for Instructional Assessment to organize the information presented on Ben. When you have finished, you may want to compare your results with those of one or more colleagues.

2. Consider alternatives to the explanation of Ben's performance provided here. Ben has been in school for five years. He hasn't developed the language skills that he needs to be academically successful. He appears to have given up on learning and is highly frustrated by the demands of the fourth grade curriculum. There is evidence that part of his frustration in learning may grow out of the difficulties he encountered in first grade when he was switched from bilingual to English only instruction, but there is not any substantial data base to support that position. More importantly, an effective instructional program must be developed for Ben now. He has limited communicative ability in Spanish, so a bilingual program at the fourth grade level might prove to be more demanding and frustrating than an English-only program. Use Part II of the Guidelines for Instructional Assessment to organize available data and to develop a plan for gathering additional informal assessment information that would provide more insight into Ben's needs.

3. How would you communicate the currently available information, including additional explanations of Ben's performance, to administrators, instructional and support personnel, and other staff? How would you build support for providing innovations that will meet Ben's needs?

4. How would you involve Ben's family in assisting Ben?

SECTION THREE

MARINA'S STORY

Marina was referred for assessment because she was experiencing learning difficulties and because she was establishing a pattern of truancy and school refusal. Marina had moved with her family to the United States from Colombia two years earlier, when she was thirteen. When her parents enrolled Marina in the middle school she was to attend, they brought her school records with them from Bogotá where Marina had attended a private school. This private school, according to the records, was designed to give students individual attention and to promote learning in small groups. Marina's mother reported that Marina consistently had problems with math and with written language skills. She had received medical and psychological treatment as a result of febrile convulsions which she experienced at the age of six. Subsequent to these convulsions, the mother observed that Marina's behavior had changed. She seemed reluctant to try new things, to take risks, or to even express herself openly. It was shortly after the convulsions and the subsequent behavior changes that Marina seemed to show signs of learning difficulties, according to her mother. In spite of these difficulties, Marina's mother insisted that Marina learn English, like her older brothers and sisters who had already moved to the United States. When she was seven Marina began private English lessons at home. When she entered the special private school at the age of nine, Marina received English instruction as a regular part of the school day.

When Marina entered school in the United States, she was initially placed in a regular English program because she appeared to be proficient in both written and spoken English. After a review of Marina's records, she was placed in a self-contained learning disabilities program. Time passed and Marina failed to make academic progress. She appeared, according to her teachers, to be uninterested in learning. Her parents stated that she was not accustomed to being with students like the ones in her school in the United States and that they wanted her placed in a different class.

Shortly after the parents began to express concern about the current placement, the family moved and Marina began attending a new school. Soon after the move, Marina began complaining of being sick and unable to go to school. On days when Marina did attend, the school would call the home and inform the mother that Marina was ill. Her mother would then come and take Marina back home.

Her parents took Marina to several doctors but found nothing wrong. After several months, Marina refused to attend school altogether. Marina's illnesses and her refusal to attend school appeared to be sources of great concern to her parents who reported that she never refused to go to school before coming to the United States Interventions, such as behavior contracting, were used unsuccessfully in assisting Marina. The present evaluation was requested to determine Marina's learning needs. Since the problem had become difficult, and Marina was already in a full day exceptional education program, the formal assessment process began at once.

Formal assessment.

Marina came to the first assessment session accompanied by her father. Throughout the session she appeared very reserved and shy. She demonstrated discomfort with oral questions by placing her hand over her mouth. She tended to say that she didn't know, instead of attempting to answer any questions. A great deal of positive reinforcement was needed in order to obtain an answer longer than a single word. When single words and brief answers were sufficient, Marina appeared more willing to respond than when she was required to give longer explanations. Attempts to engage Marina in informal conversations also produced brief answers and little conversation or interactions.

Although an agreement had been made between Marina and the psychologist to meet at school for the second appointment, Marina failed to appear. A phone call to her home resulted in Marina arriving at school with her mother. No explanation was given regarding the absence. Marina agreed to continue with the evaluation, but again appeared to be filled with anxiety when required to perform. She stated, however, that she was willing to continue the evaluation, which was completed during the second session.

Because Marina came from a home in which English was not the only language, she was given the Language Assessment Battery to help determine her language dominance and proficiency. Both English and Spanish forms were administered. She scored at the 27th percentile in English, in comparison to other English-speaking peers, and at the 74th percentile on the Spanish version in comparison with other Spanish-speaking peers. Additionally, due to Marina's observed reticence to participate in oral tasks, the Hispanic American adaptation of the Peabody Picture Vocabulary Test-Revised was administered. This test taps areas such as receptive vocabulary. Marina's results on the Peabody in Spanish were at the 95th percentile and reflect receptive language skills in the superior range. These results indicate that because Marina continued to be Spanish-dominant, she might have difficulties within the English language curriculum.

Intellectual evaluation was completed by a trained bilingual psychologist in Spanish using the WISC-R, Spanish Translation. The Wechsler Scale taps such areas as verbal comprehension, and ability to apply language concepts and information, as well as perceptual organization and non-verbal reasoning abilities. On this administration Marina obtained a Verbal Intelligence Quotient of 101, a Performance Intelligence Quotient of 114, and a Full Scale of 108. These results reflected intellectual functioning in the upper end of the average range of ability and placed Marina at the 70th percentile when compared with other youngsters her age in the normative reference group. The present results reflect strengths in non-verbal reasoning. Additionally, a relative strength was noted in verbal abstract reasoning and general information as measured on the verbal scale. A significant weakness was evident in numerical reasoning.

Academic skills attainment was assessed with the Woodcock-Johnson Psycho-Educational Battery Test of Achievement and the Arithmetic subtest of the Wide Range Achievement Test-Revised, Level II. The Reading, Written Language, and Mathematics clusters of the Woodcock tap such areas as word decoding, reading comprehension, and application of grammar and spelling, as well as math computation and numerical reasoning.

Marina's reading and written language skills in Spanish were found to be in the Average to Above Average range and generally commensurate with measured ability. Her skills in these same literacy areas in English are at a mid-fifth to early sixth grade level, when compared with monolingual, English-speaking students her age. Thus, while Marina exhibited well developed skills in Spanish, she was at a disadvantage when required to participate with peers in an English curriculum.

Mathematics was the area of greatest concern. The results of the Woodcock Psycho-Educational Battery and the Wide Range Achievement Test-Revised, Level II reflect achievement in this area significantly below expectancy for ability. Though she appeared to have an understanding of arithmetical processes involved in addition, multiplication, and division, errors were evident in the computations when regrouping was required. She had yet to master division completely and appeared confused when faced with it. This confusion could result from the fact that the format for writing and solving multiplication and division problems is different in Latin America from the format used in the United States.

Information processing functions were assessed with the Visual Aural Digit Span test and the Perceptual Speed cluster of the Woodcock Psycho-Educational Battery. The former is a test of immediate memory for digits in sequence, using both visual and auditory modes. Marina was requested to repeat orally and in written form the digits that were presented to her. Her performance placed her in the mid eight-to-nine-year-old age range and reflected significant difficulties in sequential memory. Her performance was not enhanced by either visual or auditory mode of presentation. She exhibited the greatest difficulties when she had to listen for the digits and then immediately write them down. These results indicate that Marina might be expected to experience difficulties with a dictation format in the classroom setting.

On the Perceptual Speed cluster, which taps ability to determine part-whole relationships between the component parts of abstract designs and ability to recognize identical pairs of digits in a sequence, Marina scored in the average range for age. There did not appear to be any significant difficulties in visual-perceptual processing, although she did exhibit some confusion and organization problems when working with printed text.

Social and emotional concerns were explored with the student rating scales of the Perfil de Evaluacion del Comportamiento, a Spanish adaptation of the Behavior Rating Profiles. This scale taps possible areas of difficulty in the home, school, and peer relationships domain. Marina's self-reported difficulties appeared to lie primarily in the area of establishing new friendships. She indicated that she did not tell others her feelings and did not have any friends. Additionally, she reported that she was not interested in school work. Although she conceded that she had disobeyed her parents, the total score in the Home domain reflected a youngster who regarded her family highly and who was comfortable within the home setting. Overall, despite the critical situation in which Marina wanted to avoid attending school and failed to make academic progress, test results indicated that her perceptions of herself and her family were not significantly deviant from the norm for students her age.

Parent involvement.

After the second session, Marina's parents met with the school psychologist. They brought copies of Marina's academic record in Colombia with them. These records included a copy of the psychological assessment that was conducted with Marina when she was nine years old and enrolled in the special school. The report indicated that Marina did not have learning disabilities as the term is understood in the United States, but that she had specific areas of deficiency that could be impeding her overall learning progress. The information contained in this report confirmed the information in the most recent evaluation, in that both batteries of tests identified deficiencies that impeded learning, but found Marina to be of average to above average general intelligence.

Marina's parents were shocked to learn that the school had understood the information to mean that Marina was mentally handicapped or learning disabled. All of the children in Marina's family were professionals with high levels of scholarly achievement. While the parents were concerned when they observed that Marina was not following the same pattern as her siblings, they had enrolled her in a special school so that she could develop normally, not because she was disabled.

WHAT WOULD YOU DO?

1. Use the Guidelines for Instructional Assessment, Part I to organize the available information on Marina. Compare results with one or more colleagues.

2. Use the Guidelines for Instructional Assessment, Part II to organize the available information on Marina. Discuss your results with colleagues.

3. Describe what you would do to establish and maintain clear communication with Marina's parents about her current level of functioning, her needs, and the school's on-going efforts to meet her needs, both socially and academically.

SECTION FOUR

MARC'S STORY

arc recently transferred from a school district in another state where he had been placed in the Educable Mentally Handicapped Program. He was referred for psychological evaluation in order to determine appropriate programming.

At the time that he entered the new school district he was 14 years old. Marc came to the United States two years earlier with his father from Haiti. His mother continues to reside in Haiti. On the day that Marc enrolled in the new school, his father came with him to school. The father stated that he had brought Marc to the United States because of political difficulties in Haiti and because he wanted Marc to receive a good education. It had not been possible for Marc to attend school on a consistent basis in Haiti, the father stated. Both Haitian Creole and English were used to communicate at home now that father and son were living in the United States. In his previous school district, Marc was experiencing learning problems at school. Documents on Marc's attendance and enrollment at the previous school were included in the packet presented to the guidance counselor. This documentation included a psychoeducational evaluation that the school district had conducted seven months earlier. Although the father appeared to understand that Marc was experiencing academic difficulties in his former school in the United States, since it was he who brought up the subject, the father appeared to be unaware of the seriousness of the problems in terms of Marc's placement in a special education program. No records were available on Marc's attendance or performance in schools in Haiti. The following is a summary of Marc's psychological report as prepared by the educators in Marc's present school district.

Intellectual functioning.

On the Leiter International Performance Scale, a non-verbal test of measured intellectual functioning, Marc obtained a measured intelligence quotient of 82, calculated on the basis of a measured mental age of 10 months, 8 months and a maximum chronological age of 13. This information indicates that Marc is functioning at a Below Average level in comparison with other students on whom the test was normed. The Leiter was chosen over more traditional measures of intellectual functioning, such as the Wechsler Scale, in an effort to minimize the effects of language and cultural background differences.

Academic functioning.

Marc's academic skills in English were assessed with the Woodcock Language Proficiency Battery and the Arithmetic section of the Wide Range Achievement Test-Revised. Table 9-2 shows Marc's results from the Woodcock Battery.

TABLE 9-2. WOODCOCK LANGUAGE PROFICIENCY BATTERY:
MARC'S RESULTS

Subtest	Score	Grade Range	Age	Standard Score
Oral Language	2.2	1.3 to 3.3	7-8	58
Reading	2.4	1.9 to 2.6	7-4	50
Written Language	1.3	1.0 to 1.5	6-4	59
Broad Language	2.6	2.1 to 3.1	7-9	53

On the Arithmetic subtest of the Wide Range Achievement Tests-Revised, Level II, Marc obtained a Standard Score of 73, and a Grade Equivalent of beginning sixth grade. Marc's academic skills in the areas of Reading and Written Language are below chronological age expectations and discrepant from measured intelligence.

Visual-perceptual functioning.

Marc's visual-perceptual motor skills were assessed with the Bender Gestalt and the Developmental Test of Visual-Motor Integration and were found to be commensurate with measured intelligence.

Adaptive behavioral functioning.

Marc's father had been interviewed eight months earlier by the school social worker, using the Vineland Adaptive Behavior Scale. Based on the father's responses, Marc obtained scores within the average range in the areas of Daily Living Skills and Socialization. The father noted that Marc had been going to night school to receive special instruction in U.S. history. He had attended several basketball games and other events with friends. He appeared capable of independently weighing the consequences of his actions, and he had performed routine household chores, made repairs and done maintenance tasks in the apartment complex where he resided without being asked. Marc was able to use the telephone for many different kinds of calls, including calling his mother in Haiti. He used both the home and the pay telephone without difficulty. In general, Marc appeared to have age-appropriate social and self-help skills.

Summary.

Marc is a 14-year-old boy who recently transferred from a school district in another state where he was placed in the Educable Mentally Handicapped Program. Currently, he was placed in the regular program within the current school district, but was referred for psychological evaluation in order to determine appropriate programming.

WHAT WOULD YOU DO?

Think about how you would use the Guidelines for Instructional Assessment to organize the information on Marc. Compare your thoughts with those of others.

SECTION FIVE

RAHDA'S STORY

Rahda's story is about the progress she made during her year in second grade. It is also about her prior language learning experiences, and about district policies that influenced the ways that teachers worked with Rahda. Her story begins much earlier.

Rahda was born in India. About a year after her birth, her mother and father migrated with Rahda to Trinidad where they lived with her mother's brother. She grew up in an environment where Tamil, English, and Spanish were the languages of communication. During her early years, Rahda's most proficient languages were English and Tamil. When Rahda was five, her mother died and her father moved to Panama to live with his brother's family. In Panama, most of Rahda's daily care was given over to the maid, who spoke only Spanish. Within a short time Rahda began speaking almost exclusively in Spanish. When Rahda was almost eight, her father remarried and moved with Rahda and his new wife to the United States.

The school where Rahda was enrolled was friendly and open. The teachers greeted Rahda and made her feel welcome. There were many students who spoke Spanish. The students also welcomed Rahda.

Language development.

Rahda was placed in an ESOL program where she received English language instruction for two hours a day. The rest of the school day was spent in the second grade. Although Rahda had not spoken English for nearly three years, she started speaking English so quickly that she surprised her teacher. Because Rahda had entered from Panama, no one had realized that Rahda had an English language background. In spite of her prior oral experience in English, Rahda had never learned to read in English, and she found the letters and sounds confusing. She told her teacher that she didn't like to read in English because the words weren't like Spanish where everything was so easy.

By the end of second grade, Rahda's teacher was concerned about Rahda's progress in learning to read and write when her oral skills were progressing so well. "Rahda almost sounds like she was born here. She speaks English just like the other children," she told the guidance counselor as she requested the referral papers to have Rahda tested for reading disabilities.

Rahda had the appearance of many other children who came from Central America. Closer observation revealed many differences between Rahda and other Spanish-speakers in the school. As a result of the changing circumstances in her life, Rahda had lost command of English and had become a proficient user of Spanish when she left Trinidad and moved to Panama. Spanish, in effect, became her native language. Even though she was able to communicate in Spanish, because Rahda had moved several times, she did not have a strong foundation of oral skills in any language. Rahda's language development revealed that, although she had mastered the sounds of English and Spanish, she had not mastered age appropriate development. She was even less fluent in Tamil.

Rahda was aware that she sometimes sounded different from the other students, and she felt unsure of herself. Although she had an outgoing personality, she sometimes remained quiet and shy because she did not want to call attention to her differences. Rahda was a keen observer who was aware that she needed to develop proficiency in English. Often, rather than creating new information, she added to conversations by imitating or repeating what the other students said. Because she was tuned in to watching what other children did and to imitating their behavior, she was accepted into their play. Although she was shy at school, Rahda was sought out by several children who liked to play with her. Sometimes the children would work together. Rahda was reluctant to let anyone see her work.

Rahda was good in math computation. She knew all of her multiplication tables from the twos through the twelves, could add and subtract three digit problems with regrouping, and could do simple division. Because she did not read well in English, she did not do well in problem solving. No instructional materials were available in Spanish for math problem solving, so no one was able to find out how she performed on problem-solving tasks in Spanish.

Rahda's Spanish skills were more developed than her English skills. She had more control over the tense, talking easily and correctly about the events that happened in the past and in the future. She still lacked control over some of the sounds such as the double r /rr/ and some grammatical structures such as the use of the conditional. In comparison with English, her sentences were longer and more complex in Spanish. Although her knowledge of the names of many items was limited in both languages, she knew many more names for zoo animals, books, and items found in the kitchen, for example, in Spanish than in English.

Informal assessment information.

The guidance counselor had been observing Rahda since her first day at school. She too was concerned about Rahda's academic progress. She had begun the informal assessment process by talking to Rahda the day after she had enrolled in school. She had also administered to her the Language Assessment Scales (LAS), Form A in English and in Spanish, in order to determine where she should be placed. She had determined that Rahda should be in the ESOL program, but in doing so, she realized that Rahda was different from the other children she had tested. She was surprised when Rahda did not perform as a proficient native speaker of Spanish. At the same time, the counselor had not expected Rahda to perform well in English and was surprised that she could name some objects. On a scale from 1 to 5, in English Rahda was a Level II, but in Spanish she was a low Level IV. Rahda's greatest limitations on the LAS were in repeating phrases correctly and in matching the correct sentences with the pictures. Rahda was, however, found to be capable of listening to short stories in Spanish and repeating them in correct order. She showed that she understood what was being communicated to her, even when she was unsure of some of the specific names for the items. She never fully retold a story in Spanish and reduced the grammar to a less complex level in order to retell the stories. Because the guidance counselor was puzzled, she decided that she would observe Rahda more closely. When she heard the second grade teacher say, after Rahda had been in school several months, that she thought that Rahda had a potential learning problem, the counselor was surprised and dismayed. To be sure that there were no physical problems, the counselor referred Rahda to the school nurse for a visual and auditory screening. She passed both tests without difficulties. No obvious health problems were observed. Attendance was regular.

The counselor suggested that Rahda receive both whole language and phonics instruction in English since she had a strong language base in Spanish. She believed that whole language instruction would be beneficial because Rahda already had a strong sense of oral literacy in Spanish. Rahda was able to retell a story including a beginning, a set of actions and outcomes, and a conclusion. Rahda liked literature and wanted to take new storybooks out of the library whenever she had a chance. She was able to read in Spanish and liked to write stories, illustrate them, and share them with other students. One day about five months after she had enrolled in school, Rahda told a story in Spanish to a group of students in her class. The teacher recorded the story with the video camera so that she could show it back to Rahda and let her see how well she was able to communicate. She shared the video with the ESOL teacher who translated the story into English. Rahda had not made up an original story, she had retold a folk tale from one of the library books. The tale consisted of a well developed paragraph with an introduction and a conclusion, a total of 8 fully developed sentences. The teachers decided that it would be a good idea to continue to videotape Rahda from time to time and to use these tapes to monitor Rahda's progress in developing and using language.

The ESOL teacher expressed the concern that because Rahda was not receiving instruction in Spanish, she might lose the proficiency she had already developed. The teacher emphasized her concern by relating that Rahda did not have age-appropriate language skills in either language. If Rahda did not make substantial progress in English, she could lose proficiency faster in Spanish than she would gain equivalent proficiency in English. As a result of this subtractive process of language learning, Rahda could become comparably limited in both languages.

Progress in English Language Development

Rahda appeared to become aware that her teachers were watching her. She began talking less. When provided with opportunities for academic expression in English, Rahda seldom spoke and rarely made more than a few squiggly lines on a sheet of paper. Some of the squiggles Rahda drew looked like letters; other were more like shapes, like birds, houses, or people. None of the shapes were well defined or clearly meaningful. Rahda never read her writing or provided an explanation of what she did. Sometimes she would show a friend her work, and occasionally she appeared to talk with her friends about her papers, but she never talked about her work out loud. She was not interested in having the teachers look at her work. Whenever a teacher came near, Rahda would cover her paper. The teachers did not insist, but they did encourage Rahda to show and to talk about what she was doing. They gave Rahda language arts work sheets and work from a basal reading series used at the school. Although she always wrote her name at the top, she never completed any of the sheets. Most of the time she kept them neatly in a folder in her desk. When asked why she did not complete the work, Rahda would reply, "I keep it for later."

In terms of phonics and word attack skills, learning sounds and their corresponding symbols proved to be difficult for Rahda. Although in Spanish she could do rhymes and songs, and could sort words by their initial and final consonants, she could not perform the same tasks in English. One day when she was presented with a set of words and pictures that began with the /m/ sound, she said, "mama, ...m, ma, ma. This is the ma sound. This is the mother sound Mamá. Mamá." At the point she seemed to realize that the same letter made the same sound in English and Spanish. She appeared to be very happy with herself as she began to write the letter m all over her paper. When she completed writing small ms and capital Ms, all over her paper, she began to look for words that began with /m/. Her teacher had been watching and heard what Rahda was saying. She was surprised and hopeful that this would be the breakthrough that Rahda needed to begin reading. The following day the teacher included Rahda in instructional games related to beginning and ending sounds, activities she had rejected a few months earlier. The teacher also encouraged Rahda to use the computer to do some drills on beginning and ending sounds. Rahda's favorite sound seemed to be /m/. She wrote the following sentence with the help of one of her friends,

"Mi mama mueve conmigo [My mother moves with me].
Mi mama muere [My mother dies]. My mother moves with me.
My mother muere [dies]."

It was hard to tell from the look on her face what Rahda was thinking. She seemed happy to be producing writing. She also seemed troubled by the message she had just written. The teacher was encouraged by the production of this amount of written language, but troubled by the meaning of the writing.

The teacher showed the guidance counselor what Rahda had written and told her about the experience with the letter m. They had been planning to invite Rahda's parents to school for a visit. They were concerned because they had not been able to get the interpreter that they liked to work with and had been reluctant to have the parents come without being able to communicate effectively. Although the guidance counselor was able to carry out basic communication and simple informal assessment tasks in Spanish, she was unable to communicate effectively with adults. When they read the message Rahda wrote, they decided to invite the parents for a conference as soon as possible.

Parental input.

The educators were present when Rahda's parents arrived at school. While the mother spoke only Spanish, the father spoke English with a British accent. He was quick to inform the educators of Rahda's prior experiences and the fact that English was one of her several languages. He explained the current family situation. When the family moved from Panama, he had brought along the maid who had always taken care of Rahda. The maid continued to care for Rahda while the father and Rahda's new mother worked. Outside of school, Rahda actually received little exposure or opportunity to use English. He admitted that he was really unaware of what Rahda was doing at school, but he was very supportive of her learning and wanted her to do well. He said that he would look for ways to encourage Rahda to use English more, and suggested buying her some English language books to use at home. But, he explained, communicating in English at home could present some difficulties since his new wife was still getting used to Rahda and spoke only Spanish.

Program changes.

After the meeting with Rahda's parents, the educators agreed that it was important to provide Rahda with as much support as they could. At the same time, they were limited about what they could do to assist Rahda as an individual learner. If they could obtain a bilingual aide to assist the ESOL teacher, they could provide her, and other students with similar needs, with additional instructional support. They met and spoke with the principal about hiring a bilingual assistant to work with Rahda and other students who were in the process of learning English. The ESOL teacher thought it would be a good idea because she had over 50 students with whom she worked on a daily basis. She thought that the additional assistance could be very beneficial for the students and could provide them with more adult input and guidance in communicating.

When the principal agreed, the educators elicited input from all the regular classroom teachers about how the assistant should be used. The ESOL teacher worked with the new assistant to develop instructional and assessment activities for the targeted students. She encouraged the assistant to learn to promote the students' use of language as a tool for achieving personal and academic goals, as well as for learning to read and write.

Collecting language samples of the students oral and written language production became a regular part of the assistant's activities with the students. The assistant obtained several interesting language samples from Rahda. She learned that Rahda was able to talk about personal preferences and her likes and dislikes in Spanish and in English. In Spanish, Rahda was also able to ask and answer who, what, where, why, and how questions. She asked questions in ways that were appropriate for problem solving and for gaining meaningful information. As a result of her question asking skills, she was able to successfully play several guessing games. Although Rahda did not have the same level of question asking skills in English, she showed interest in developing similar skills in both languages. With the additional attention and support the bilingual assistant provided, Rahda began to make steady progress and to overcome her reluctance to read and write in English. However, she still did not make substantial progress in English literacy skills.

End of the year decisions.

As the end of the academic year grew near, the educators met again to discuss students' progress. All of the educators involved indicated a strong belief that Rahda would become successful in English because of the good progress she had already made in Spanish. At the same time, they realized that if Rahda, and other students like her, had not learned to read and write, they could become frustrated as they moved into the more difficult material of third and fourth grade. They were concerned that the ESOL students could give up on learning altogether, unless there was some way to ensure a smooth transition between grades and instructional levels. In addition, there was the continued concern that Rahda might have a reading disability, since she had not made progress in learning to read. Perhaps she did qualify for special education and her instructional needs could be met there.

The group decided to promote Rahda to third grade because of her oral proficiency in English, her math ability, and her recent progress in mastering phonics skills. At the same time, they all expressed concern about the instructional program that Rahda would receive in third grade. Because of her oral English proficiency, she would be expected to pass the third grade minimum standards test and the national achievement tests in reading, language arts, and math. To make matters more difficult, the district had recently issued a directive that all students in ESOL classes who were orally proficient in English should be mainstreamed into full-time regular grade placement. An exception could not be made for Rahda because English was her native language. The educators decided to refer Rahda to the school committee for further consideration.

WHAT WOULD YOU DO?

1. Use the Guidelines for Instructional Assessment, Part I to organize the available information on Rahda. Compare results with one or more collegues.

2. Use the Guidelines for Instructional Assessment, Part II to plan a program for Rahda. Compare your program with those of others, and discuss similarities and differences.

SUMMARY OF CHAPTER NINE

This chapter has provided a framework for addressing the needs of students and educators engaged in the process of promoting and using English as a language of communication and academic skill development. This framework, the Guidelines for Instructional Assessment, has been designed to promote the collection and use of student data on individual students. Four case studies have been prepared to provide opportunities for practice in using the Guidelines. If you worked through the cases and compared your results with those of others who did the same thing, you found that there were multiple hypotheses about the students' performance. Following through on the development of each of these hypotheses required the involvement of a variety of school personnel who typically do not interact with each other on an ongoing basis. Promoting the involvement of diverse personalities and personnel with divergent professional training and expertise requires tact, leadership, and a commitment to educational change. A variety of formats were used for presenting the case studies to emphasize the diverse ways in which information is currently collected and presented. None of the cases contained all the information requested. Data were purposely omitted to emphasize that the search for relevant data is ongoing. However, Part I of the Guidelines can serve as a guiding format for collecting and organizing information. The emphasis is on the process of making educational decisions and the continuing need to review and revise the decisions that have already been made. Performance assessment leads to effective instruction. Assessment of instructional processes leads to the development of effective instructional programs. Its success depends on the commitment and capacity of educators and educational systems that are willing to meet the real needs of all their students.

Appendix

GUIDELINES FOR INSTRUCTIONAL ASSESSMENT, PART I

I. DESCRIPTION OF LITERACY SKILL DEVELOPMENT AND PERFORMANCE WITHIN INSTRUCTIONAL CONTEXTS

1. Literacy instruction used with this student

✓ Describe learning outcomes produced through the use of the instruction programs listed below. Provide additional information, if the type of instructional program(s) used with this student is not listed.
- whole language and language experience reading instruction
- literature based reading
- basal readers
- phonics
- instructional reading games
- computer assisted instruction for drill and practice reading activities
- computer assisted instruction for word processing, self-generated texts
- other

✓ Describe student's performance in self-generated oral or written responses.

✓ Describe student's interest and interactions with animals.

✓ Describe student's performance on teacher directed tasks.

✓ Describe student's performance in other instructional alternatives.

✓ Describe student's observations of performance and preferences.

• **Summarize performance in terms of instructional opportunities and outcomes to date.**

2. Language as a factor in instruction and performance

✓ Is there a time during the day when the student's non-English language is used? If yes, describe how the language is used. If yes, describe how the student responds in diverse language settings, especially when the non-English language is used.

✓ Describe student's personal description of prior experiences.
• **Summarize performance in terms of availability and use of English and non-English for instructional purposes.**

3. Exposure to languages as a factor in learning
   ✓ Describe student's prior schooling and educational experiences including length of residence in English-use environment.
   ✓ Length of time of exposure to English.
• **Summarize prior school experiences including exposure to English and other languages.**

4. Awareness of metalinguistic and metacognitive organization
   ✓ Describe student's orientation to use of books and writing materials.
   ✓ Describe student's awareness, motivation, and interest in literacy as a vehicle for learning.
   ✓ Describe student's use of self-talk and reflection on performance in completing a task.
   ✓ Describe student's awareness of sound/symbol relationships (consider both English and non-English language, if possible).
   ✓ Describe student's ability to play with language.
   ✓ Describe student's awareness of graphics and text in interpreting information.
   ✓ Describe student's understanding of idioms, factual, and figurative expressions and humor.
   ✓ Describe student's awareness of the meaning provided through organizing, sequencing, and organization and spacing of graphics and words.
   ✓ Describe student's awareness of syntactical and semantic relationships in communicating meaning.
• **Summarize student's awareness of form, organization, and content in applying literacy skills.**

5. Performance as measured by formal and informal tests
   ✓ Describe student's performance in reading, language arts, and math as measured by standardized tests.
   ✓ Compare information on student's academic performance as measured by standardized tests with standardized tests of ability or intelligence.
   ✓ Describe student's performance as measured by informal procedures.
   ✓ Compare information on student's performance using standardized and informal measures.
   • **Summarize information gained from formal and informal measures.**

6. Language proficiency as a factor in communicating and performing
   ✓ Describe student's level of demonstrated proficiency in English-language social activities.

✓ Describe student's level of demonstrated proficiency in non-English-language social activities (as assessed by trained interpreters).

✓ Describe student's level of demonstrated proficiency in English in the academic tasks.

✓ Describe student's level of demonstrated proficiency in non-English language development in the academic tasks (as assessed by trained interpreters).

✓ What are the student's perceptions of personal performance in English?

✓ What are the student's perceptions of personal performance in non-English?

✓ What are the teachers' perceptions of the student's performance?

PERFORMANCE IN ENGLISH		PERFORMANCE IN NON-ENGLISH	
Social	*Academic*	*Social*	*Academic*

PERCEPTIONS OF PERFORMANCE IN ENGLISH		PERCEPTIONS OF PERFORMANCE IN NON-ENGLISH	
Social	*Academic*	*Social*	*Academic*
Student			
Teachers			

• **Summarize proficiency observed and perceptions of performance.**

7. Language as a vehicle for achieving goals.

✓ Describe student's performance using a variety of language functions in English.

✓ Describe student's performance using a variety of language functions in non-English.

✓ Describe the student's perceptions of the use of language for achieving goals, in English and in non-English.

✓ Contrast the student's use and performance of language functions in English and non-English.

• **Summarize language performance to achieve a variety of purposes.**

8. Mathematics as a vehicle for learning

✓ Describe student's performance in math computation.

✓ Is there a discrepancy between the student's level of math computation and overall performance in math? If yes, describe the discrepancy.

✓ Is the level of math performance similar to or different from general literacy performance? Describe discrepancies, if they exist.

• Summarize math performance as it relates to overall language performance.

9. Movement toward success
✓ Describe the tasks in which the student excels.
✓ Describe the motivating and energizing activities or aspects of the school day.
✓ Describe the instructional approaches that provide success.
✓ Describe this student's perceptions of school success.
• **Summarize the movement toward academic success.**
• • *Section Summary*: **Summarize information in terms of opportunities for learning, instruction, and performance.**

II. THE INFLUENCE OF CULTURE, HEALTH, SOCIAL, AND FAMILY FACTORS ON INSTRUCTION AND LEARNING

10. Culture as a factor influencing participation and learning
✓ Describe efforts to identify and use information on similarities between student's prior educational experiences and the current setting.
✓ Describe efforts to identify and address differences between student's prior educational experiences and the current setting.
✓ Describe efforts to address similarities and differences between student's cultural background and the culture of the current setting.
✓ Describe the student's thoughts about cultural differences and similarities between current and previous schools and learning environments.
• **Summarize similarities and differences between student's prior educational experiences and cultural background and the current setting and expectations.**

11. Health, school attendance, and other physical and environmental factors
✓ Describe the student's current general health.
✓ Describe the student's previous health including any factors that might have influenced attendance and learning.
✓ Describe school attendance in current and previous settings. If there is a history of absence or irregular attendance, please explain.
• **Summarize school attendance and performance as influenced by health or other factors.**

12. Family background as a factor influencing participation and learning
✓ Describe family background including siblings' and other family members' achievements.
✓ Describe efforts to involve family in the educational process.
✓ Describe student records from prior settings.

✓ Include other useful information about the student and family available from other sources.

• **Summarize information on family background as it influences this student's learning.**

13. Environmental and other factors as an influence on participation and learning

✓ Describe and summarize any environmental factors that may influence this student's school attendance, participation, and learning.

• • *Section Summary*: **Summarize the influence of culture, health, social, and family factors on participation, instruction, and learning.**

III. CONTEXTUAL AVAILABILITY OF INFORMATION AND COGNITIVE DEMAND OF TASKS

14. Familiarity with content and persons as variables

✓ Compare and contrast the student's performance with familiar and unfamiliar content or materials.

✓ Compare and contrast the student's performance with familiar and unfamiliar persons (include information on both peers and adults).

✓ Describe, where appropriate, the student's performance on cooperatively structured classroom tasks.

✓ Describe the student's performance using familiar and new subject matter.

✓ Describe the student's perceptions about learning and working with others.

• **Summarize familiarity with persons, materials or context, and content as variables that influence performance.**

15. Cognitive demand as a variable in performance

✓ Describe the student's performance on concrete and abstract tasks.

✓ Describe the student's performance as the cognitive demand of tasks increases or decreases.

✓ Describe the student's performance when performing similar tasks alone and with peers.

✓ Describe the student's perceptions of his or her performance and reactions to tasks of increasing difficulty.

✓ Describe efforts to modify the level of difficulty of the tasks in meeting this student's needs and discuss the resulting outcomes.

• **Summarize information on cognitive demand and contextual support as variable affecting performance.**

• • *Section Summary* : **Summarize information on the effect of familiarity, interpersonal interactions, and reduced cognitive demand as influences affecting performance.**

GUIDELINES FOR INSTRUCTIONAL ASSESSMENT, PART II

Overall Summary of Student Performance

1. Summary of known information
-             •
-             •

2. Specific information to be obtained
-             •
-             •

Information	Person Responsible	Date for Obtaining
•	•	•
•	•	•
•	•	•

HYPOTHESIS DEVELOPMENT AND TESTING

3. Hypotheses about student's instructional needs
(a)

(b)

(c)

(d)

4. Prioritize hypotheses and establish procedures for testing them.
(a) Hypothesis   Person(s) Responsible   Date for Obtaining

Summary of Outcomes

(b) Hypothesis   Person(s) Responsible   Date for Obtaining

Summary of Outcomes

5. Summarize information on student gained from observation and from hypothesis testing.
Hypothesis a:
Hypothesis b:

6. Develop instructional objectives based on hypothesis information, and continue to monitor.

7. Develop specific instructional objectives for the student and determine how these objectives will be assessed and monitored.

References

Aaron, P. G. (1991). Can reading disabilities be diagnosed without using intelligence tests? *Journal of Learning Disabilities, 24,* 178-187, 191.

Abbeduto, L. & Nuccio, J. (1989). Evaluating the pragmatic aspects of communication in school-age children and adolescents: Insights from research on atypical development. *School Psychology Review, 18,* 502-512.

Abel, R. R. & Kulhavy, R. W. (1986). Maps, mode of text presentation and children's prose learning. *American Educational Research Journal, 23,* 265-274.

Abrams, P., Herrity, M. S. & LaBrot, P. (1991). *Curriculum-based assessment (CBA) handbook.* Orlando, FL: Orange County Public Schools.

Adelman, C. (1989). The context of children's learning: An historical perspective. In G. Barrett (Ed.). *Disaffection from school? The early years.* (pp. 59-76). Bristol, PA: Falmer Press.

Adler, L. (1982). Cross-cultural research and theory. In B. Wolman (Ed.). *Handbook of developmental psychology.* (pp. 76-90). Englewood Cliffs, NJ: Prentice-Hall.

Ainsa, T. (1984). The LD label and the Spanish-dominant secondary student. *NASSP Bulletin, 68 ,* 105-109.

Airasian, P. W. (1987). State mandated testing and educational reform: Context and consequences. *American Journal of Education, 95,* 393-412.

Alessi, G. J., & Kaye, J. H. (1983). *Behavior assessment for school psychologists.* Kent, OH: National Association of School Psychologists.

Alexander, S. K. (1985). *School law.* St. Paul, MN: West Publishing.

Algozzine, B., Christenson, S., & Ysseldyke, J. (1982). Probabilities associated with the referral to placement process. *Teacher Education and Special Education, 5* 19-23.

Allen, P., Swain, M., Harley, B., & Cummins, J. (1990). Aspects of classroom treatment: Toward a more comprehensive view of second language education. In B. Harley, P. Allen, J. Cummins, & M. Swain (Eds.). *The development of second language proficiency.* (pp. 57-81). New York: Cambridge University Press.

Allender, J. S. (1986). Educational research: A personal and social process. *Review of Educational Research, 56,* 173-193.

Alva, S. A. (1991). Academic *invulnerability* among Mexican-American Students: The importance of protective resources and appraisals. *Hispanic Journal of Behavioral Sciences, 13,* 18-34.

Ambert, A. N. (1982, fall). The identification of LEP children with special needs. *The Bilingual Journal, 7,* 17-22.

American Educational Research Association, American Psychological Association, & National Council on Measurement in Education (1985). *Standards for educational and psychological testing.* Washington, D.C.: American Psychological Association.

American Speech-Language-Hearing Association (1985). Clinical management of communicatively handicapped minority language populations. *ASHA, 27,* 29-32.

449

American Speech-Language-Hearing Association Committee on the Status of Racial Minorities (1987). *Multicultural professional education in communication disorders: Curriculum approaches.* Rockville, MD: American Speech-Language-Hearing Association.

Anderson, R. C. & Pearson, P. D. (Eds.) (1988). *Interactive approaches to second language reading.* New York: Cambridge University Press.

Andrews, R. L. & Morefield, J. (1991). Effective leadership for effective urban schools. *Education and Urban Society, 23,* 270-278.

Anson, A. R., Cook, T. D., Habib, R., Grady, M. K., Haynes, N., & Comer, J. P. (1991). The Comer school development program: a theoretical analysis. *Urban Education, 26,* 56-82.

Anthony, R., Johnson, T., Mickelson, N., & Preese, A. (1991). *Evaluating literacy: A perspective for change.* Toronto, Canada: Irwin Publishing.

Apple, M. W. (1991). Conservative agendas and progressive possibilities: Understanding the wider politics of curriculum and teaching. *Education and Urban Society, 23,* 279-291.

Applebee, A. (1978). *The child's concept of story.* Chicago: University of Chicago Press.

Argulewicz, E. N. & Sanchez, D. T. (1982). Considerations in the assessment of reading difficulties in bilingual children. *School Psychology Review, 11,* 281-289.

Armstrong, L. S. (1991, March 20). Census confirms remarkable shifts in ethnic makeup: Cultural diversity called challenge for educators. *Education Week,* pp. 1, 16.

Arter, J. A. (1990). *Using portfolios in instruction and assessment.* Portland, OR: Northwest Regional Educational Laboratory.

Ascher, C. (1990a). *Testing students in urban schools: Current problems and new directions,* (ERIC Clearinghouse on Urban Education, Urban Diversity Series No. 100) New York: Institute for Urban and Minority Education Teachers College, Columbia University.

Ascher, C. (1990b). Assessing bilingual students for placement and instruction *Digest, 65,* (ERIC Clearinghouse on Urban Education, EDO-ED-90-5).

Au, K. H. (1980). Participation structures in a reading lesson with Hawaiian children: Analysis of a culturally appropriate instructional event. *Anthropology and Education, 11,* 91-115.

Ayers, W. (1991). *Perestroika* in Chicago's schools. *Educational Leadership, 48,* 69-71.

Baca, L. M. & Cervantes, H. T. (1989). *The bilingual special education interface* (2nd ed.). Columbus, OH: Merrill.

Baca, L. M. & Cervantes, H. T. (1991). *Bilingual special education,* ERIC Digest E496, ERIC Clearinghouse on Handicapped and Gifted Children, Reston, VA.

Baca, L., Collier, C., Jacobs, C. & Hill, R. (1990). *BUENO modules for special education.* Boulder, CO: BUENO Center for Multicultural Education, School of Education, University of Colorado.

Baca, L., Fradd, S. H., & Collier, C. (1990). Progress in preparing personnel to meet the needs of handicapped limited English proficient students: Results of a survey in three highly impacted states. *Journal of Educational Issues of Language Minority Students, 7* (Special Issue), 5-20.

Bachman, L. F. (1990). Constructing measures and measuring constructs. In B. Harley, P. Allen, J. Cummins, & M. Swain (Eds.). *The development of second language proficiency.* (pp. 26-38). New York: Cambridge University Press.

Baez, T., Fernandez. R. R., Navarro, R. A., & Rice, R. L. (1985). Litigation strategies for educational equity: Bilingual education and research. *Issues in Education, 3,* 198-214.

Baker, K. (1991). Yes, throw money at schools. *Phi Delta Kappan, 72,* 628-630.

Barona, A. & Garcia, E. E. (1990). *Children at risk: Poverty, minority status, and other issues in educational equity.* Washington, D. C.: National Association of School Psychologists.

Barona, A. & Santos de Barona, M. (1987). A model for the assessment of limited English proficient students referred for special education services. In S. Fradd & W. J. Tikunoff (Eds.). *Bilingual education and bilingual special education: A guide for administrators* (pp. 183-209). Boston: Little, Brown.

Barona, A. (1991). Assessment of multicultural preschool children. In B. A. Bracken (Ed.). *The psychoeducational assessment of preschool children* (2nd ed.) (pp. 379-391). Needham Heights, MA: Allyn & Bacon.

Barona, A., & Hernandez, A. E. (1990). Use of projective techniques in the assessment of Hispanic school children. In A. Barona & E. Garcia (Eds.). *Children at Risk: Poverty minority status and other issues in educational equity* (pp. 297-304). Washington, D.C.: National Association of School Psychologists.

Barona, A., Santos de Barona, M., Flores, A., & Gutierrez, M. H. (1990). Critical issues in training school psychologists to serve minority group children. In A. Barona & E. Garcia (Eds.). *Children at risk: Poverty, minority status, and other issues in educational equity* (pp. 187-200). Washington, D.C.: National Association of School Psychologists.

Barrett, M. E. (1987). Two critical elements in teaching composition. In TESOL, *A TESOL professional anthology.* Lincolnwood, IL: National Textbook Company.

Bates, E. *Language and context: The acquisition of pragmatics.* New York: Academic Press.

Bazron, B. J. (1989). *The minority severely emotionally disturbed child: Considerations for special education and mental health services.* Washington, D.C.: CASSP Technical Assistance Center, Georgetown University Child Development Center.

Bean, R. M. & Lane, S. (1990). Implementing curriculum-based measures of reading in an adult literacy program. *Remedial and Special Education (RASE), 11 ,* 39-46.

Beebe, V. N. & Mackey, W. F. (1990). *Bilingual school and the Miami experience.* Coral Gables, FL: Institute of Interamerican Studies, University of Miami.

Benderson, A. (1984). Critical thinking. *Focus, 15.* (A publication of the Educational Testing Service, Princeton, NJ.)

Berdine, W. H. & Blackhurst, A. E. (1985). *An introduction to special education.* Boston: Little, Brown.

Bergenske, M. D. (1987). The missing link in narrative story mapping. *The Reading Teacher, 41,* 333-335.

Berko-Gleason, J. (1985). The development of language. Columbus, OH: Merrill.

Bermudez, A. B. & Prater, D. L. (1988). Developing writing skills for the exceptional LEP and at-risk students: Differentiating developmental from learning problems. Workshop presented at University of Florida, Gainesville, FL, Project INFUSION.

Bernal, M. E., Saenz, D. S. & Knight, G. P. (1991). Ethnic identity and adaptation of Mexican American youths in school settings. *Hispanic Journal of Behavioral Sciences, 13,* 135-154.

Bernstein, D. K. (1989). Assessing children with limited English proficiency: Current perspectives. *Topics in Language Disorders, 9,* 15-20.

Berry, R. (1991). *Performance assessment and TIMSS: An issues paper.* Washington, D.C. National Science Foundation.

Blank, M. & White, S. J. (1986). Questions: A powerful form of classroom exchange. *Topics in Language Disorders, 6,* 1-12.

Block, E. (1986). The comprehension strategies of second language readers. *TESOL Quarterly, 20 ,* 463-494.

Bloom, L. & Lahey, M. (1978). *Language development and language disorders.* New York: Wiley.

Bouvier, L. & Gardner, R. (1986). Immigration to the U.S.: The unfinished story. *Population Bulletin, 41,* 3-50.

Bouvier, L. F. & Davis, C. B. (1982). *The future racial composition of the United States.* Washington, D.C.: Demographic Information Services Center of the Population Reference Bureau.

Boyan, C. (1985). California's new eligibility criteria: Legal and program implications. *Exceptional Children, 52,* 131-141.

Bozinou-Doukas, E. (1983). Learning disability: The case of the bilingual child. In D. R. Omark and J. G. Erickson (Eds.). *The Bilingual Exceptional Child* (pp. 213-232). San Diego, CA: College-Hill Press.

Bracey, G. W. (1989). Educational disadvantage: A threat from within. *Phi Delta Kappan, 71,* 76-79.

Braden, J. (1991, March). *Curriculum-based measurement and human diversity: Friends or foes?* Paper presented at the Annual Convention of the National Association of School Psychologists, Dallas, TX

Braden, J. P. (1989). Organizing and monitoring data bases. In S. H. Fradd & M. J. Weismantel (Eds.). *Meeting the needs of culturally and linguistically different students: A handbook for educators* (pp. 14-33). Austin, TX: Pro-Ed.

Braden, J. P. & Fradd, S. H. (1987). Proactive school organization: Identifying and meeting special population needs. In S. H. Fradd & W. J. Tikunoff (Eds.). *Bilingual education and bilingual special education: A guide for administrators* (pp. 211-230). Austin, TX: Pro-Ed.

Bradley, A. (1991, May 15). Newly diverse suburbs facing city-style woes. *Education Week,* pp. 1, 15-17.

Brandenburg, N. A., Friedman, R. M., & Silver, S. E. (1990). The epidemiology of childhood psychiatric disorders: Recent prevalence findings and methodologic issues. *Journal of the American Academy of Child and Adolescent Psychiatry, 29,* 76-83.

Brandt, R. (1990). On restructuring schools: A conversation with Al Shanker. *Educational leadership, 47,* 11-16.

Brandt, R. (1991). Does "less is more" apply to funding? *Educational Leadership, 48,* 3.

Brice Heath, S. (1986). Taking a cross-cultural look at narratives. *Topics in Language Disorders, 7,* 84-95.

Brown, J. D. (1989). Language program evaluation: A synthesis of existing possibilities. In R. K. Johnson (Ed.), *The second language curriculum* (pp. 222-241). New York: Cambridge University Press.

Brown, L. L. & Hammill, D. D. (1982). *Perfil de Evaluacion del Comportamiento,* Austin, TX: Pro-Ed.

Brozo, W. G. (1990). Learning how at-risk readers learn best: A case for interactive assessment. *Journal of Reading, 33,* 522-527.

Bruner, J. (1983). *Child's talk: Learning to use language.* New York: W. W. Norton.

Burke, C. (1978). *The reading interview.* Unpublished guide. The Reading Program, Indiana University.

Burns, C. W. (1990). Assessing the psychological and educational needs of the moderately and severely retarded. In C. R. Reynolds and R. W. Kamphaus (Eds.). *Handbook of psychological and educational assessment of children: Intelligence and achievement* (pp. 789-802). New York: Guilford Press.

Butler, A. (1988). *The elements of the whole language program.* Crystal Lake, IL: Rigby Education.

Cadiz, Y. (1987). Teaching intermediate composition to the adult learning English as a second language. In TESOL, *A TESOL professional anthology.* Lincolnwood, IL: National Textbook Company.

Cage, M. C. (1991, June 26). 30 states cut higher-education budgets by an average of 3.9% in fiscal 1990-91. *The Chronicle of Higher Education,* pp. A1, A17.

California Department of Education. (1990). *California: The state of assessment.* Sacramento: Author.

Cambourne, B. & Turbill, J. (1990). Assessment in whole-language classrooms: Theory into practice. *The Elementary School Journal, 90 ,* 337-349.

Canale, M., & Swain, M. (1980). Theoretical bases of communicative approaches to second language teaching and testing. *Applied Linguistics, 1,* 1-47.

Cardenas, J. & Cortez, A. (1986). The impact of *Plyler v. Doe* upon Texas public schools. *Journal of Law & Education, 15,* 1-17.

Carey, L. (1989). On alienation and the ESL students. *Phi Delta Kappan, 71,* 74-75.

Carl, K. L. (1992, May). *Using alternative assessment with potentially English proficient (PEP) students.* Paper presented at the Annual GULF TESOL Conference, St. Petersburg, FL.

Carlisle, J. F. (1991). Planning an assessment of listening and reading comprehension. *Topics in Language Disorders, 12,* 17-30.

Carnegie Foundation for the Advancement of Teaching. (1988). *Report card on school reform.* Princeton, NJ: Author.

Carrasco, R. L. (1979). *Expanded awareness of student performance: A case study in applied ethnographic monitoring in a bilingual classroom.* Austin, TX: Southwest Educational Development Laboratory.

Carrell, P. L. (1988a). Interactive text processing: implications for ESL/second language reading classrooms. In R. C. Anderson & P. D. Pearson (Eds.). *Interactive approaches to second language reading* (pp. 239-255). New York: Cambridge University Press.

Carrell, P. L. (1988b). Some causes of text-boundedness and schema interference in ESL reading. In R. C. Anderson & P. D. Pearson (Eds.). *Interactive approaches to second language reading* (pp. 101-112). New York: Cambridge University Press.

Carrell, P. L. & Eisterhold, J. C. (1988). Schema theory and ESL reading pedagogy. In R. C. Anderson & P. D. Pearson (Eds.). *Interactive approaches to second language reading* (pp. 73-89). New York: Cambridge University Press.

Carter, J. & Sugai, G. (1989). Survey on prereferral practices: Responses from state departments of education. *Exceptional Children, 55 ,* 298-302.

Castaneda, L. V. (1991, April). *Social organization of communication and interaction in exemplary SAIP classrooms and the nature of competent membership.* Paper presented at the Annual Meeting of the American Educational Research Association, Chicago.

Caterino, L. C. (1990). Step-by-step procedure for the assessment of language minority children. In A. Barona & E. Garcia (Eds.). *Children at risk: Poverty, minority status and other issues in educational equity* (pp. 269-282). Washington, D.C.: National Association of School Psychologists.

Cazden, C. (1986). ESL teachers as language advocates for children. In P. Rigg & D. S. Enright (Eds.). *Children and ESL: Integrating perspectives* (pp. 7-22). Washington, D.C.: Teachers of English to Speakers of Other Languages.

Cazden, C. (1988). *Classroom discourse: The language of teaching and learning.* Portsmouth, NH: Heinemann.

Cegelka, P. T. Lewis, R. & Rodriguez, A. M. (1987). Status of educational services to handicapped students with limited English proficiency: Report of a statewide study in California. *Exceptional Children, 54,* 220-227.

Chamberlain, P., (1987). The role of the psychologist in the evaluation of language minority students. *Linguathon, 3,* 1-4.

Chamberlain, P., & Medinos-Landurand, P. (1991). Practical considerations for the assessment of LEP students with special needs. In E. V. Hamayan & J. S. Damico

(Eds.). *Limiting bias in the assessment of bilingual students* (pp. 111-156). Austin, TX: Pro-Ed.

Chamot, A. U. & O'Malley, J. M. (1984). Using learning strategies to develop skills in English as a second language. *Focus, 16,* 1-7.

Chamot, A. U. & O'Malley, J. M. (1986). *Cognitive academic language learning approach: An ESL content-based curriculum.* Rosslyn, VA: National Clearinghouse for Bilingual Education.

Chaney, C. (1990). Evaluating the whole language approach to language arts: The pros and cons. *Language, Speech, and Hearing Services in Schools, 21,* 244-249.

Chang, Y. L. & Watson, D. J. (1988). Adaptation of prediction strategies and materials in a Chinese/English bilingual classroom. *The Reading Teacher, 42 ,* 36-43.

Chaudron, C. (1985). A method for examining the input/intake distinction. In S. M. Gass & Madden C. G. (Eds.). *Input in second language acquistion* (pp. 285-302). Cambridge, MA: Newbury House.

Cheng, L. L. (1991). *Assessing Asian language performance: Guidelines for evaluating limited-English-proficient students.* Oceanside, CA: Academic Communication Associates.

Cheng, L. R. L. (1989). Service delivery to Asian/Pacific LEP children: A cross-cultural framework. *Topics in Language Disorders, 9,* 1-14.

Chilcott, J. H. (1987). Where are you coming from and where are you going? The reporting of ethnographic research. *American Educational Research Journal, 24,* 199-218.

Chomsky, N. (1972). *Language and mind.* New York: Harcourt Brace Jovanovich.

Clarke, M. A. (1988). The short circuit hypothesis of ESL reading—or when language competence interferes with reading performance. In R.C. Anderson & P. D. Pearson (Eds.). *Interactive approaches to second language reading* (pp. 114-123). New York: Cambridge University Press.

Clay, M. M. (1989). Concepts about print in English and other languages. *The Reading Teacher, 42 ,* 268-276.

Cloud, N. (1991). Educational Assessment. In E. V. Hamayan & J. S. Damico, (Eds.), *Limiting bias in the assessment of bilingual students* (pp. 220-245). Austin, TX: Pro-Ed.

Cocking, R. R. & Chipman, S. (1988). Conceptual issues related to mathematics achievement of language minority children. In R. R. Cocking & J. P. Mestre (Eds.) *Linguistic and cultural influences on learning mathematics* (pp. 17-46). Hillsdale, NJ: Lawrence Erlbaum Associates.

Collier, C. (1988). *Assessing minority students with learning and behavior problems.* Lindale, TX: Hamilton Publications.

Collier, V. P. & Thomas, W. P. (1989). How quickly can immigrants become proficient in school English? *The Journal of Educational Issues of Language Minority Students, 5,* 26-38.

Collier, V. P. (1987). Age and rate of acquisition of second language for academic purposes. *TESOL Quarterly, 21,* 617-641.

Collier, V. P. (1988). The effect of age on acquisition of a second language for school. *New Focus, 2.* Wheaton, MD: National Clearinghouse for Bilingual Education.

Collier, V. P. (1989). How long? A synthesis of research on academic achievement in a second language. *TESOL Quarterly, 23,* 309-331.

Connolly, J. & Doyle, A. (1984). Relation of social fantasy play to social competence in preschoolers. *Developmental Psychology, 20 ,* 797-806.

Connor, U. & Kaplan, R. (1987). *Writing across languages: Analysis of L2 text.* Reading, MA: Addison-Wesley.

Correa, V. I. (1989). Involving culturally diverse families in the educational process. In S. H. Fradd & M. J. Weismantel (Eds.). *Meeting the needs of culturally and linguistically different students: A handbook for educators* (pp. 130-144). Austin, TX: Pro-Ed.

Council for Children with Behavior Disorders (1989). Best assessment practices for students with behavioral disorders: Accommodation to cultural diversity and individual differences. *Behavioral Disorders, 14* , 263-278.

Council for Exceptional Children. (1988, December). *Curriculum-based assessment.* (Research Brief for Teachers, T2) Reston, VA: ERIC Clearinghouse on Handicapped and Gifted Children.

Cross, T. R., Bazron, B. J., Dennis, K. W., & Isaacs, M. R. (1989). *Towards a culturally competent system of care: A monograph on effective services for minority children who are severely emotionally disturbed.* Washington, D.C.: CASSP Technical Assistance Center, Georgetown University Child Development Center.

Cuban, L. (1990). Reforming again, again, and again. *Educational Researcher, 19,* 3-13.

Cuevas, G. J. (1984). Mathematics learning in English as a second language. *Journal for Research in Mathematics Education, 15* , 134-144.

Cummins, J. (1979). Cognitive/academic language proficiency, linguistic interdependence, the optimal age question, and some other matters. *Working Papers on Bilingualism, 19,* 197-205.

Cummins, J. (1981a). *Bilingualism and minority language children.* Toronto, Canada: Ontario Institute for Studies in Education.

Cummins, J. (1981b). Four misconceptions about language proficiency in bilingual education. *Journal of the National Association for Bilingual Education, 5,* 31-46.

Cummins, J. (1982). Tests, achievement and bilingual students. National Clearinghouse for Bilingual Education, *Focus, 9,* 1-7.

Cummins, J. (1984). *Bilingualism and special education: Issues in assessment and pedagogy.* San Diego, CA: College Hill Press.

Cummins, J. (1989). A theoretical framework for bilingual special education. *Exceptional Children 56* (2), 111-120.

Cummins, J. (1989). The sanitized curriculum: Educational disempowerment in a nation at risk. In D. M. Johnson & D. H. Roen, (Eds.). *Richness in writing: Empowering ESL students* (pp. 19-38). White Plains, NY: Longman.

Cummins, J., Harley, B., Swain, M. & Allen, P. (1990). Social and individual factors in the development of bilingual proficiency. In B. Harley, P. Allen, J. Cummins, & M. Swain (Eds.). *The development of second language proficiency.* (pp. 119-133). New York: Cambridge University Press.

Cummins, J. & McNeely, S. N. (1987). Language development, academic learning and empowering minority students. In S. H. Fradd & W. J. Tikunoff (Eds.). *Bilingual education and bilingual special education: A guide for administrators* (pp. 75-98). Austin, TX: Pro-Ed.

Cummins, J. & Swain, M. (1986). *Bilingualism in education: Aspects of theory, research and practice.* New York: Longman.

Cummins, J., Swain, M., Nakajima, K., Handscombe, J., Green, D., & Tran, C. (1984). Linguistic interdependence among Japanese and Vietnamese immigrant students. In C. Rivera, (Ed.). *Communicative competences approaches to language proficiency assessment: Research and application* (pp. 60-81). Clevedon, Avon, England: Multilingual Matters.

Curtis, M. J., & Meyers, J. (1988). Best practices in school-based consultation: Guidelines for effective practice. In A. Thomas & J. Grimes (Eds.). *Best practices in school psychology* (pp. 79-94). Washington, D.C.: National Association of School Psychologists.

d'Anglejan, A. (1990). The role of context and age in the development of bilingual proficiency. In B. Harley, P. Allen, J. Cummins, & M. Swain (Eds.). *The development of second language proficiency.* (pp. 146-157). New York: Cambridge University Press.

Dade County Public Schools, Management Information. (1989). Active students born in other countries. Miami, FL: Author.

Dale, T. C. & Cuevas, G. J. (1987). Integrating language and mathematics learning. In J. Crandall (Ed.), *ESL through content area instruction: Mathematics, science, social studies.* West Nyack, NY: Prentice-Hall.

Damen, L. (1986). *Culture learning: The fifth dimension in the language classroom.* Reading, MA: Addison-Wesley.

Damico, J. (1991, September). *Performance assessment of language minority students.* Paper presented at the Second National Research Symposium on Limited English Proficient Student Issues sponsored by the U. S. Department of Education, Office of Bilingual Education and Minority Languages affairs in collaboration with the Office of Educational Research and Improvement, Washington, D.C.

Damico, J. S. (1985). *The effectiveness of direct observation as a language assessment technique.* (Doctoral Dissertation). Albuquerque, NM: University of New Mexico.

Damico, J. S. (1991). Descriptive assessment of communicative ability in limited English proficient students. In E. V. Hamayan & J. S. Damico (Eds.). *Limiting bias in the assessment of bilingual students* (pp. 157-217). Austin, TX: Pro-Ed.

Damico, S. B., Roth, J., Fradd, S. H., & Hankins, A. D. (1990). *The route to graduation: Perceptions of general curriculum students.* (Final Report, STAR Grant 89-041 funded by the Florida Institute of Government for the Office of Policy Research and Improvement. Tallahassee, FL: Department of Education.

David, J. L. (1991). What it takes to restructure education. *Educational Leadership, 48,* 11-15.

Dayan, J. (1992). Spanish curriculum based measurement: A solution to the problem of bias in the academic assessment of limited English proficient students. *Communique, 21 ,* 3-4.

De Avila, E. (1991, April 23). *Defining limited English proficiency makes national test premature.* Testimony before House Subcommittee on Select Education.

De Avila, E. A. (1980). The Cartoon Conservation Scales. Corte Madera, CA: Linguametric Group.

de Castell, S. & Luke, A. (1987). Literacy instruction: Technology and technique, *American Journal of Education, 95,* 413-440.

DeGeorge, G. (1988). Assessment and placement of language minority students: Procedures for mainstreaming. *FOCUS, 3.* National Clearinghouse for Bilingual Education.

De Leon, J. (1990). A model for an advocacy-oriented assessment process in the psycho-educational evaluation of culturally and linguistically different students. *The Journal of Educational Issues of Language Minority Students, 7,* 53-67.

Deno, S. L. (1987). Curriculum-based measurement. *Teaching Exceptional Children, 20,* 41.

Deno, S. L. (1989). Curriculum-based measurement and special education services: A fundamental and direct relationship. In M. R. Shinn (Ed.). *Curriculum-based measurement: assessing special children* (pp. 1-17). New York: Guilford Press.

Deno, S. L. & Mirkin, P. K. (1977). *Data-based program modification: A manual.* Reston, VA: Council for Exceptional Children.

Deshler, D. D., & Schumaker, J. B. (1986). Learning strategies: An instructional alternative for low-achieving adolescents. *Exceptional Children, 52,* 583-590.

Deshler, D. D., Schumaker, J. B., & Lenz, K. B. (1984). Academic and cognitive interventions for LD adolescents: Part I. *Annual Review of Learning Disabilities, 2,* 57-66.

DeStefano, L. & Thompson, D. S. (1990). Adaptive behavior: The construct and its measurement. In C. R. Reynolds and R. W. Kamphaus (Eds.). *Handbook of psycho-*

logical and educational assessment of children: Personality, behavior, and context (pp. 445-469). New York: Guilford Press.

Development Associates and Research Triangle Institute. (1984). *The national longitudinal evaluation of the effectiveness of services for language-minority limited-English-proficient students.* Rosslyn, VA: National Clearinghouse for Bilingual Education.

Devine, J. (1988). Relationship between general language competence and second language reading proficiency: Implications for teaching. In R. C. Anderson & P. D. Pearson (Eds.). *Interactive approaches to second language reading* (pp. 260-277). New York: Cambridge University Press.

Diana v. State Board of Education. C-70 37RFP; District Court for Northern District of California (1970).

Diaz Soto, L. (1991). Understanding bilingual/bicultural young children. *Young Children, 46,* 30-36.

Diaz, S., Moll, L. C., & Mehan, H. (1986). Sociocultural resources in instruction: A context-specific approach. In Bilingual Education Office, California State Department of Education (Ed.). *Beyond language: Social and cultural factors in school language minority students.* (pp. 187-230). Los Angeles: Evaluation, Dissemination and Assessment Center, California State University.

Diaz-Guerrero, R. & Diaz-Loving, R. (1990). Interpretation in cross-cultural personality assessment. In C. R. Reynolds & R. W. Kamphaus (Eds.). *Handbook of psychological and educational assessment of children: Personality, behavior, and context* (pp. 491-523). New York: Guilford Press.

Dollaghan, C. A. (1987). Comprehension monitoring in normal and language-impaired children. *Topics in Language Disorders, 7,* 45-60.

Dollaghan, C. & Miller, J. (1986). Observational methods in the study of communicative competence. Schiefelbusch, R. L. (Ed.). *Language competence assessment and intervention* (pp. 99-130). San Diego, CA: College-Hill Press.

Dolson, D. P. (1985a). Bilingualism and scholastic performance: The literature revisited. *The Journal of the National Association for Bilingual Education, 10,* 1-35.

Dolson, D. P. (1985b). The effects of Spanish home language use on the scholastic performance of Hispanic pupils, *Journal of Multilingual Multicultural Development, 6,* 135-155.

Donaldson, M. (1978). *Children's minds.* New York: W. W. Norton.

Dore, J. (1975). Holophrases, speech acts and language universals. *Journals of Child Language, 2,* 21-40.

Dore, J. (1986). The development of conversational competence. In R. L. Schiefelbusch. (Ed.). *Language competence assessment and intervention* (pp. 3-60). San Diego, CA: College-Hill Press.

Duchan, J. F. (1986). Language intervention through sensemakiing and fine tuning. Schiefelbusch, R. L. (Ed.). *Language competence assessment and intervention* (pp. 187-212). San Diego, CA: College-Hill Press.

Duncan, S. E. & DeAvila, E. A. (1984). *Language Assessment Scales.* Monterey, CA: CTB/McGraw-Hill.

Dunlap, W. P. & Tinajero, J. V. (1985). Reading activities for solving story problems for the limited English proficient student. *Reading Improvement, 22,* 162-167.

Dunn, L. M., & Dunn, L. M. (1981). Peabody Picture Vocabulary Test-Revised. Circle Pines, MN: American Guidance Service.

Duran, R. P. (1989). Assessment and instruction of at-risk Hispanic students. *Exceptional Children, 56,* 154-158.

Edelsky, C. (1986). *Writing in a bilingual program: Habia una vez.* Norwood, NJ: Ablex Publishing Company.

Edelsky, C. (1989). Bilingual children's writing: Fact and fiction. In D. M. Johnson & D. H. Roen (Eds.). *Richness in writing: Empowering ESL students* (pp. 165-176). White Plains, NY: Longman.

Edmonds, R. (1979). Some schools work and more can. *Social Policy, 9,* 26-31.

Education for All Handicapped Children Act of 1975. 34 C. F. R. 300 1975.

Education of the Handicapped. (1991). Special supplement. The new Individuals with Disabilities Act. Alexandria, VA: Capitol Publications.

Edwards, P. A. (1990). Strategies and techniques for establishing home-school partnerships with minority parents. In A. Barona & E. Garcia (Eds.) *Children at risk: Poverty, minority status and other issues in educational equity* (pp. 217-236). Washington, D.C.: National Association of School Psychologists.

Elliott, S. N. & Busse, R. T. (1991). Social skills assessment and intervention with children and adolescents. *School Psychology International, 12,* 63-83.

Elliott, S. N. & Piersel, W. C. (1982). Direct assessment of reading skills: An approach which links assessment to intervention. *School Psychology Review, 11 ,* 267-280.

Ellis, R. (1985a). Teacher-pupil interaction in second language development. In S. M. Gass & Madden C. G. (Eds.). *Input in second language acquisition* (pp. 69-85). Cambridge, MA: Newbury House.

Ellis, R. (1985b). *Understanding second language acquisition.* New York: Oxford University Press.

Englert, C. S. & Hiebert, E. (1984). Children's developing awareness of text structures in expository materials. *Journal of Educational Psychology, 76,* 65-74.

Enright, D. S. & McCloskey, M. L. (1988). *Integrating English: Developing English language and literacy in the multilingual classroom.* Reading, MA: Addison-Wesley.

Enright, D. S. & Rigg, P. (1986). Introduction: Children and ESL. In P. Rigg & D. S. Enright (Eds.). *Children and ESL: Integrating perspectives* (pp. 1-6). Washington, D. C.: Teachers of English to Speakers of Other Languages.

Epstein, J. L. (1991). Paths to partnership: What we can learn from federal, state, district, and school initiatives. *Phi Delta Kappan, 72,* 344-349.

Erickson, J. G. (1985). How many languages do you speak? An overview of bilingual education. *Topics in Language Disorders, 5,* 1-14.

Ervin-Tripp, S. & Gordon, D. (1986). The development of requests. Schiefelbusch, R. L. (Ed.). *Language competence: Assessment and intervention* (pp. ix-xvii). San Diego, CA: College-Hill Press.

Escovar, P. & Lazarus, P. (1982). Cross-cultural child-rearing practices: Implications for school psychologists. *School Psychology International, 3 ,* 143-148.

Eskey, D. E. & Grabe, W. (1988). Interactive models for second language reading: perspectives on instruction. In R. C. Anderson & P. D. Pearson (Eds.) *Interactive ap-proaches to second language reading* (pp. 223-238). New York: Cambridge University Press.

Eskey, D. E. (1988). Holding in the bottom: an interactive approach to the language problems of second language readers. In R. C. Anderson & P. D. Pearson (Eds.). *Interactive approaches to second language reading* (pp. 93-99). New York: Cambridge University Press.

Esquivel, G. B. (1988). Best practices in the assessment of limited English proficient and bilingual children. In A. Thomas & J. Grimes (Eds.). *Best practices in school psychology* (pp. 113-123). Washington, D.C.: National Association of School Psychologists.

Farrell, E., Peguero, G., Lindsey, R., & White, R. (1988). Giving voice to high school students: Pressure and boredom, 'ya know what I'm sayin'? *American Educational Research Journal, 25,* 489-502.

Federal Register, 45 Fed. Reg. 52, 052 (1980).

Federal Register (Part II), No. 150, p. 33845, Washington, D.C.: Dept. of Health, Education and Welfare, August 1982.

Feldman, M. J. (1985). Evaluating pre-primer basal readers using story grammar. *American Education Research Journal, 22,* 527-547.

Feuerstein, R. (1979). *The dynamic assessment of retarded performers: The learning potential assessment device, theory, instruments, and techniques.* Baltimore, MD: University Park Press.

Figueroa, R. A. (1989). Psychological testing of linguistic-minority students: Knowledge gaps and regulations. *Exceptional Children, 56 ,* 145-152.

Figueroa, R. A. (1990). Assessment of linguistic minority group children. In C. R. Reynolds & R. W. Kamphaus (Eds.). *Handbook of psychological and educational assessment of children: Intelligence and achievement* (pp. 671-696). New York: Guilford Press.

Figueroa, R. A. (1990). Best practices in the assessment of bilingual children. In A. Thomas and J. Grimes (Eds.). *Best practices in school psychology-II* (93-106). Washington, D.C.: National Association of School Psychologists.

Fishman, J. (1976). *Bilingual education: An international sociological perspective.* Rowley, MA: Newbury House.

Fishman, J. (1980). Language maintenance. *Harvard encyclopedia of American ethnic groups* (pp. 189-195). Cambridge, MA: Harvard University Press.

Fitzgerald, J. & Miramontes, O. (1987). Language assessment barriers in perspective. *Academic Therapy, 23,* 135-141.

Fletcher, T. V. & Cardona-Morales, C. (1980). Implementing effective instructional interventions for minority students. In A. Barona & E. Garcia (Eds.). *Children at risk: Poverty, minority status, and other issues in educational equity* (pp. 151-170). Washington, D.C.: National Association of School Psychologists.

Flores, D. J. (1981). *An Investigation of the long-term effects of bilingual education upon achievement, language maintenance and attitudes.* Unpublished doctoral dissertation, University of Florida.

Florida Department of Education, Division of Public Schools. (1988). *A resource manual for the development and evaluation of special programs for exceptional students,* (Volume IV-I: A training and resource manual for the implementation of state eligibility criteria for the speech and language impaired). Tallahassee, FL: Bureau of Education for exceptional Students.

Forness, S. R. & Knitzer, J. (1992). A new proposed definition and terminology to replace "Serious emotional disturbance" in Individuals with Disabilities Education Act. *School Psychology Review, 21,* 12-20.

Foster, H. & Iannaccone, C. (1991, April). *A study of indicators of multicultural content in special education introductory level education tests.* Paper presented at the 11th Annual Symposium for Research in Bilingual Multicultural Education, Buffalo, NY.

Fradd, S. (1982). Bilingualism, cognitive growth, and divergent thinking skills. *The Educational Forum, 46,* 469-474.

Fradd, S. H. (1984). Language acquisition of 1980 Cuban immigrant junior high school students. Doctoral Dissertation, University of Florida, Gainesville, *Dissertation Abstracts International, 44* (7), DA8324961, p. 20274.

Fradd, S. H. (1985). Governmental policy and second language learning. *Educational Forum, 49,* 431-443.

Fradd, S. H. (1987a). The changing focus of bilingual education. In S. H. Fradd & W. E. Tikunoff (Eds.). *Bilingual education and bilingual special education: A guide for administrators* (pp. 1-44). Austin, TX: Pro-Ed.

Fradd, S. H. (1987b). Accommodating the needs of limited English proficient students in regular classrooms. In S. H. Fradd & W. J. Tikunoff, (Eds.). *Bilingual education and bilingual special education: A guide for administrators* (pp. 133-181). Austin, TX: Pro-Ed.

Fradd, S. H. (1991). *Collaborative instructional practices.* Paper presented at the Special Education and the Language Minority Student Pre-Conference Training, Illinois State Board of Education, Oakbrook, IL, February 5.

Fradd, S. H. (in press). *Educating limited English proficient special needs students: An overview of current practices.* Washington, D.C.: Center for Applied Linguistics in collaboration with Prentice-Hall.

Fradd, S. H., Barona, A. & Santos de Barona, M. (1989). Implementing change and monitoring progress. In S. H. Fradd & M. J. Weismantel (Eds.). *Meeting the needs of culturally and linguistically different students: A handbook for educators* (pp. 63-104). Austin, TX: Pro-Ed.

Fradd, S. H., Gard, B., & Weismantel, M. J. (1988, September). *Meeting the Needs of Handicapped Limited English Proficient Students in ESOL Classrooms: A Review of State Certification Requirements.* A paper presented at the Southeast Regional TESOL Conference, Orlando, FL.

Fradd, S. H., & Vega, J. E. (1987). Legal considerations. In S. H. Fradd & W. J. Tikunoff (Eds.). *Bilingual education and bilingual special education: A guide for administrators* (pp. 45-74). Austin, TX: Pro-Ed.

Fradd, S. H., Weismantel, M. J. & Braden, J. P. (1987). Aiming for student success: A model of proactive school organization. *Planning and Changing, 18* , 238-245 (ERIC, CIJE/ RIE Reference Nos. EJ376194 EA522438).

Fradd, S. H., Weismantel, M. J., Correa, V. I., & Algozzine, B. (1988). Developing a personnel training model for meeting the needs of handicapped and at risk minority students. *Teacher Education and Special Education, 11* , 30-38 (ERIC, CIJE/ RIE Reference Nos. EJ373462 EC210017.

Fradd, S. H., Weismantel, M. J., Correa, V. I., & Algozzine, B. (1990). Ensuring equity in education: Preparing school personnel for culturally and linguistically divergent at-risk handicapped students. In A. Barona & E. E. Garcia (Eds.). *Children at risk: Poverty, minority status, and other issues in educational equity* (pp. 237-257). Washington, D.C.: National Association of School Psychologists.

Fradd, S. H., & Wilen, D. K. (1990). *Using interpreters and translators to meet the needs of handicapped language minority students and their families.* Washington, D. C.: National Clearinghouse for Bilingual Education.

Freeman, Y. S. (1988). Do Spanish methods and materials reflect current understanding of the reading process? *The Reading Teacher, 41* , 654-662.

Freeman, Y. S. & Freeman, D. E. (1989). Whole language approaches to writing with secondary students of English as a second language. In D. M. Johnson & D. H. Roen (Eds.). *Richness in writing: Empowering ESL students* (pp. 177-192). White Plains, NY: Longman.

Fuchs, D. & Fuchs, L. (1991, March). *Linking assessment to intervention in the regular education setting.* Advanced professional training workshop presented at the Annual Convention of the National Association of School Psychologists, Dallas, TX.

Fuchs, D. & Fuchs, L. S. (1989). Effect of examiner familiarity on black, caucasian, and Hispanic children: A meta-analysis. *Exceptional Children, 55,* 303-308.

Fuchs, D. & Fuchs, L. S. (1990). Making educational research more important. *Exceptional Children, 57,* 102-108.

Fuchs, L. & Fuchs, D. (1992). Identifying a measure of monitoring student reading progress. *School Psychology Review, 21* , 45-58.

Fuchs, L. S., Fuchs, D., Hamlett, C. L. & Stecher, P. M. (1991). Effects of curriculum-based measurement and consultation on teacher planning and student achievement in mathematics operations. *American Educational Research Journal, 28,* 617-642.

Fuchs, L. S. & Deno, S. L. (1991). Paradigmatic distinction between instructionally relevant measurement models. *Exceptional Children, 57 ,* 488-500.

Futrell, M. H. (1989). Mission not accomplished: Education reform in retrospect. *Phi Delta Kappan, 71,* 8-15.

Gallas, K. (1991). Arts as epistemology: Enabling children to know what they know. *Harvard Educational Review, 61,* 40-50.

Garbarino, J., Stott, F. M. and Faculty of the Erikson Institute. (1989). *What children can tell us.* San Francisco: Jossey-Bass.

Garcia, E. (1991). *Evaluating credentialing programs for teachers of LEP students.* Paper presented at the Second National Research Symposium on Limited English Proficient (LEP) Student Issues with a Focus on Evaluation and Measurement, September, Washington, D.C.

Garcia, S. B. (1985). Characteristics of limited english proficient Hispanic students served in programs for the learning disabled: Implications for policy, practice and research (Part I). *Bilingual Special Education Newsletter, 4,* pp. 1, 3-6.

Garcia, S. B. & Ortiz, A. A. (1988). Preventing inappropriate referrals of language minority students to special education. *Focus, 5.* National Clearinghouse for Bilingual Education. Occasional Papers in Bilingual Education.

Garnett, K. (1986). Telling tales: Narratives and learning-disabled children. *Topics in Language Disorders, 6,* 44-56.

Garrido, L. (1989). The culturally diverse student in the ED classroom. *Perceptions, 25 ,* 14-15.

Gartner, A. & Lipksy, D. K. (1987). Beyond special education: Toward a quality system for all students. *Harvard Educational Review, 57,* 367-395.

Geertz, C. (1973). *The interpretation of cultures.* New York: Basic Books.

Gelb, S. A. & Mizokawa, D. T. (1986). Special education and social structure: The commonality of "exceptionality." *American Educational Research Journal, 23,* 543-557.

Genesee, F. (1978). Is there an optimal age for starting second language instruction? *McGill Journal of Education, 13,* 145-154.

Genesee, F. (1985). Second language learning through immersion: A review of U.S. programs. *Review of Educational Research, 55,* 541-562.

Genishi, C. (1979). *Code-switching: A review of the literature and comments on future research* (Report of the National Institute of Education, U. S. Department of Education). Austin, TX: The University of Texas.

Gerken, K. (1990). Best practices in the academic assessment of secondary-age students. In A. Thomas & J. Grimes (Eds.). *Best practices in school psychology - II* (pp. 13-28). Washington, D.C.: National Association of School Psychologists.

Gerken, K. C. (1978). Performance of Mexican American children on intelligence tests. *Exceptional Children, 44,* 438-443.

Gibbs, J. T. & Huang, L. N. (1989). A conceptual framework for assessing and treating minority youth. In J. T. Gibbs, L. N. Huang, and Associates (Eds.). *Children of color: Psychological interventions with minority youth* (pp. 1-29). San Francisco: Jossey-Bass.

Gibbs, J. T. & Huang, L. N. (Eds.) (1989). *Children of color.* San Francisco: Jossey-Bass.

Gickling, E. E. (1981). Curriculum-based assessment. In J. R. Tucker (Ed.). *Non-test-based assessment: A training module.* Minneapolis, MN: University of Minnesota, National School Psychology Inservice Training Network.

Gickling, E. E., & Havertape, J. (1981). *Curriculum-based assessment (CBA).* Minneapolis, MN: National School Psychology Inservice Training Network.

Gickling, E. E., Shane, R. L., & Croskery, K. M. (1989). Developing mathematics skills in low-achieving high school students through curriculum-based assessment. *School Psychology Review, 18,* 344-355.

Gickling, E. E. & Thompson, V. P. (1992). *Curriculum-based assessment: A naturalistic guide to reading and mathematics instruction.* Workshop presented at the 70th Annual Convention of the Council for Exceptional Children, Baltimore, MD.

Gilbert, J. C. & Burger, P. (1990). *Performance based assessment resource guide.* Denver, CO: Colorado State Dept. of Education.

Gilhooly, K. J. & Green, A. J. K. (1989). Learning problem-solving skills. In A. M. Colley & J. R. Beech (Eds.) *Acquisition and performance of cognitive skills* (pp. 85-112). New York: Wiley.

Gilmore, P. & Glatthorn, A. A. (Eds.). (1982). *Children in and out of school: Ethnography and education.* Washington, D.C.: Center for Applied Linguistics.

Gitlin, A. D. (1990). Educative research, voice, and school change. *Harvard Educational Review, 60,* 442-466.

Glickman, C. D. (1990). Open accountability for the '90s: Between the pillars. *Educational Leadership, 47,* 38-41.

Glickman, C. D. (1991). Pretending not to know what we know. *Educational Leadership, 48,* 4-10.

Godsted, G. (1990). *School social work services intake interview.* Ft. Lauderdale, FL: Multicultural Education Department, School Board of Broward County.

Goldenberg, C. & Gallimore, R. (1991). Local Knowledge, research knowledge, and educational change: A case study of early Spanish reading improvement. *Educational Researcher, 20,* 2-14.

Gonzales, P. C. (1981). Beginning English Reading for ESL students. *The Reading Teacher, 35,* 154-161.

Gonzales, P. C. & Hansen-Krening, N. (1981). Assessing the language learning environment in classrooms, *Educational Leadership, 39,* 450-450.

Goodenough, W. H. (1981). *Culture, language and society.* Menlo Park, CA: Benjamin/ Cummings.

Goodman, K. (1973). Analysis of oral reading miscues: Applied psycholinguistics. In F. Smith (Ed.). *Psycholinguistics and reading.* New York, NY: Holt, Rinehart and Winston.

Goodman, K. (1988). The reading process. In R. C. Anderson & P. D. Pearson (Eds.). *Interactive approaches to second language reading* (pp. 11-21). New York: Cambridge University Press.

Goodman, K. S. (1969). Analysis of oral reading miscues: Applied psycholinguistics. *Reading Research Quarterly, 5,* 9-30.

Goodman, K. S. (1970). Behind the eye: What happens in reading. In K. Goodman, & O. Miles (Eds.). *Reading: Process and program.* Urbana, IL: National Council of Teachers of English.

Goodman, K. S. (1986). Basal readers: A call for action. *Language Arts, 63,* 358-363.

Goodman, K., Goodman, Y. & Flores, B. (1984). *Reading in the bilingual classroom: Literacy and biliteracy.* Rosslyn, VA: National Clearinghouse for Bilingual Education.

Goodman, K. Goodman, Y, & Hood, W. (1989). *The whole language evaluation book.* Portsmouth, NH: Heinemann.

Goswami, D. & Stillman, P. R. (Eds.). (1987). *Reclaiming the classroom: Teacher research as an agency for change.* Portsmouth, NH: Heinemann.

Grabe, W. (1988). Reassessing the term "interactive." In R. C. Anderson & P. D. Pearson (Eds.). *Interactive approaches to second language reading* (pp. 56-67). New York: Cambridge University Press.

Grace, C. & Shores, E. F. (1991). *The portfolio and its use: Developmentally appropriate assessment of young children.* Little Rock, AR: Southern Association on Children Under Six.

Green, M. (1991). Texts and margins. *Harvard Educational Review, 61,* 27-39.

Greenburg, D. (1989). The *Tenth Annual Report to Congress:* One more ride on the merry-go-round? *Exceptional Children, 56,* 10-13.

Greenfield, P. M. (1984). *Mind and media: The effects of television, video games, and computers.* Cambridge, MA: Harvard University Press.

Greer, J. V. (1991). The tyranny of words. *Exceptional Children, 57,* 486-487.

Grossman, H. J. (Ed.). (1983). *Classification in mental retardation.* Washington, D.C.: American Association of Mental Deficiency.

Guralnick, M. & Weinhouse, E. (1984). Peer-related social interactions of developmentally delayed young children; Development and characteristics. *Developmental Psychology, 20,* 815-827.

Hakuta, K. (1986). *Mirror of language.* New York: Basic Books.

Hakuta, K. & Diaz, R. M. (1983). The relationship between degree of bilingualism and cognitive ability: A critical discussion and some new longitudinal data. In K. E. Nelson (Ed.). *Children's language.* Hillsdale, NJ: Lawrence Erlbaum Associates.

Hall, E. T. (1973). *The silent language.* New York: Anchor Books.

Hall, E. T. (1977). *Beyond culture.* New York: Anchor Books.

Halliday, M. (1973). *Explorations in the functions of language.* New York: Elsevier Nort Holland.

Halliday, M. (1975). *Learning how to mean: Explorations in the development of language.* London: Edward Arnold.

Halsall, S. W. (1985). An ethnographic account of the composing behaviors of five young bilingual children. (Doctoral dissertation, University of Florida). *Dissertation Abstracts International, 48/09-A,* DA 85-23835.

Hamayan, E. (1989). *Teaching writing to potentially English proficient students using whole language approaches.* Washington, D.C.: National Clearinghouse for Bilingual Education.

Hamayan, E. V. & Damico, J. S. (1991). Developing and using a second language. In E. V. Hamayan & J. D. Damico (Eds.). *Limiting bias in the assessment of bilingual students* (pp. 39-76). Austin, TX: Pro-Ed.

Handscombe, J. (1990). The complementary roles of researchers and practitioners in second language education. In B. Harley, P. Allen, J. Cummins, & M. Swain (Eds.). *The development of second language proficiency* (pp. 181-186). New York: Cambridge University Press.

Harley, B. (1986). *Age in second language acquisition.* San Diego, CA: College-Hill Press.

Harley, B., Cummins, J., Swain, M., & Allen, P. (1990). The nature of language proficiency. In B. Harley, P. Allen, J. Cummins, & M. Swain (Eds.). *The development of second language proficiency* (pp. 7-25). New York: Cambridge University Press.

Harp, L. (1991, June 19). States slashing reform programs as funding basics becomes harder. *Education Week,* pp. 1, 26.

Hart, B. & Risley, T. (1986). Incidental strategies. Schiefelbusch, R. L. (Ed.). *Language competence assessment and intervention.* (pp. 213-226). San Diego, CA: College-Hill Press.

Harter, S. (1975). Developmental differences in the manifestation of mastery behavior on problem-solving tasks. *Child Development, 46,* 370-378.

Hayes, E. (1989). Hispanic adults and ESL programs: Barriers to participation. *TESOL Quarterly, 23,* 47-63.

Heckhausen, H. (1983). Concern with one's competence: Developmental shifts in person-environment interaction. In D. Magnusson & V. Allen (Eds.). *Human development: An interactional perspective* (pp. 167-185). New York, NY: Academic Press.

Hedburg, N. L. & Stoel-Gammon, C. (1986). Narrative analysis: Clinical procedures. *Topics in Language Disorders, 7,* 58-70.

Herbst, J. (1989). *And sadly teach: Teacher education and professionalization in American culture.* Madison, WI: University of Wisconsin Press.

Hergenhan, B. R. (1982). *An introduction to theories of learning* (2nd ed.). Englewood Cliffs, NJ: Prentice-Hall, Inc.

Hernandez, N. G. (1983). Diagnosing and remediating bilingual students in arithmetic. *Focus on Learning Problems in Math, 5,* 15-22.

Heron, T. E. & Harris, K. C. (1987). *The educational consultant: Helping professionals, parents and mainstreamed students.* Austin, TX: Pro-Ed.

Hiebert, E. H. (1989). Beyond Lake Wobegon: Increasing the role of teacher-based assessment. *The Colorado Communicator, 12,* 10-11.

Hiskey, M. S. (1966). *Hiskey-Nebraska Test of Learning Aptitude.* Lincoln, NB: Union College Press.

Ho, M. (1987). *Family therapy with ethnic minorities.* Newbury Park, CA: Sage Publications.

Holtzman, W. H., Jr., & Wilkinson, C. Y. (1991). Assessment of cognitive ability. In E. V. Hamayan & J. S. Damico (Eds.). *Limiting bias in the assessment of bilingual students* (pp. 247-280). Austin, TX: Pro-Ed.

Honig, A., Lally, J., & Mathieson, D. (1982). Personal-social adjustment of school children after five years in a family enrichment program. *Child Care Quarterly, 11,* 138-146.

Hord, S. M., Rutherford, W. L., Huling-Austin, L. & Hall, G. E. (1987). *Taking charge of change.* Alexandria, VA: Association for Supervision and Curriculum Development.

Hoskins, B. (1990). Language and literacy: Participating in the conversation. *Topics in Language Disorders, 10,* 46-62.

Howie, S. H. (1984). *A guidebook for teaching writing in content areas.* Boston: Allyn and Bacon.

Hudelson, S. (1986). ESL children's writing: What we've learned, what we're learning. In P. Rigg & D. Scott Enright (Eds.). *Children and ESL: Integrating perspectives* (pp. 25-54). Washington, D.C.: Teachers of English to Speakers of Other Languages.

Hudelson, S. (1988). Children's writing in ESL. *ERIC DIGEST.* Washington, D.C.: Center for Applied Linguistics.

Hudelson, S. (1989a). *WRITE ON: Children writing in ESL.* Englewood Cliffs, NJ: Center for Applied Linguistics and Prentice-Hall Regents.

Hudelson, S. (1989b). A tale of two children: Individual differences in ESL children's writing. In D. M. Johnson & D. H. Roen (Eds.). *Richness in writing: Empowering ESL students* (pp. 84-99). White Plains, NY: Longman.

Hudson, P. J. (1989). Instructional collaboration: Creating the learning environment. In S. H. Fradd & M. J. Weismantel (Eds.). *Meeting the needs of culturally and linguistically different students: A handbook for educators* (pp. 106-129). Austin, TX: Pro-Ed.

Hudson, P. J. & Fradd, S. H. (1987). Learning strategy instruction: Modifications to meet educational needs of limited English proficient learning disabled students. *Journal of Reading, Writing and Learning Disabilities International, 3,* 195-212.

Hughes, J. (1990). Assessment of social skills: Sociometric and behavioral approaches. In C. R. Reynolds & R. W. Kamphaus (Eds.). *Handbook of psychological and educational assessment of children: Personality, behavior, and context* (pp. 423-444). New York: Guilford Press.

Iglesias, A. (1985). Communication in the home and classroom: Match or mismatch? *Topics in Language Disorders, 5,* 29-41.

Jastak, S. & Wilkinson G. (1984). *Wide Range Achievement Test-Revised*. Wilmington, DE: Jastak Associates.

Jean-Jacques, N. (1982). *Yon ti pa sou chemen an*. Miami, FL: Dade County Public Schools, Southeast Curricula Development Center.

Jenkins, J. R. & Pious, C. G. (1991). Full inclusion and the REI: A reply to Thousand and Villa, *Exceptional Children, 57*, 562-564.

Jensen, B. F., & Potter, M. L. (1990). Best practices in communicating with parents. In A. Thomas & J. Grimes (Eds.). *Best practices in school psychology - II* (pp. 183-193). Washington, D.C.: National Association of School Psychologists.

Johnson, D. M. & Roen, D. H. (Eds.). (1989). *Richness in writing: Empowering ESL students*. White Plains, NY: Longman.

Jorge, A., Lipner, J. K., Moncarz, R., Salazar-Carrillo, J. (1983). *The economic impact of bilingualism* (Discussion papers in economics and banking, Paper No. 9). Miami: Department of Economics, Florida International University.

Joyce, B. R. (1991). The doors to school improvement. *Educational Leadership, 48*, 59-62.

Kamhi, A. G. (1987). Metalinguistic abilities in language-impaired children. *Topics in Language Disorders, 7*, 1-12.

Kaufman, A. S. (1979). *Intelligent testing with the WISC-R*. New York: Wiley.

Kaufman, A. S. & Kaufman, N. L. (1983). *Kaufman Assessment Battery for Children*. Circle Pines, MN: American Guidance Service.

Kawakami, A. J. & Au, K. H. (1986). Encouraging reading and language development in cultural minority children. *Topics in Language Disorders, 6*, 71-80.

Kean, T. H. (1991, April 24). Do we need a national achievement exam? Yes: To measure progress toward national goals. *Education Week* (pp. 28, 36).

Kelley, M. F. & Surbeck, E. (1991). History of preschool assessment. In B. A. Bracken (Ed.). *The psychoeducational assessment of preschool children* (2nd ed.) (pp. 1-17). Needham Heights, MA: Allyn & Bacon.

Kemper, S. & Edwards, L. (1986). Children's expressions of causality and their construction of narratives. *Topics in Language Disorders, 7*, 11-20.

King, D. F. & Goodman, K. S. (1990). Whole language: Cherishing learners and their language. *Language, Speech, and Hearing Services in Schools, 21*, 221-227.

Kirst, M. W. (1991). Improving children's services: Overcoming barriers, creating new opportunities. *Phi Delta Kappan, 72*, 615-618.

Kleifgen, J. A. (1985). Skilled variation in a kindergarten teacher's use of foreigner talk. In S. M. Gass & Madden C. G. (Eds.). *Input in second language acquisition* (pp. 59-68). Cambridge, MA: Newbury House.

Kletzien, S. B. & Bednar, M. R. (1990). Dynamic assessment for at-risk readers. *Journal of Reading, 33*, 528-533.

Knutson, N., & Shinn, M. R. (1991). Curriculum-based measurement: Conceptual underpinnings and integration into problem-solving assessment. *The Journal of School Psychology, 29*, 371-393.

Kopp, C. (1982). Antecedents of self-regulation: A developmental perspective. *Developmental Psychology, 18*, 199-214.

Koppitz, E. (1977). *Visual Aural Digit Span Test*. San Antonio, TX: The Psychological Corp.

Koshinen, P. S., Gambrell, L. B., Kapinus, B. A., & Heathington, B. S. (1988). Retelling: A strategy for enhancing students' reading comprehension. *The Reading Teacher, 41*, 892-896.

Kramer, C. J. (1990). Documenting reading and writing growth in the primary grades using informal methods of evaluation. *The Reading Teacher, 44*, 356-357.

Krashen, S. D. (1987). *Principles and practice in second language acquisition*. Englewood Cliffs, NJ: Prentice-Hall International.

Krashen, S. D. (1991). Bilingual education: A focus on current research. *Focus, 3.* Washington, D.C.: National Clearinghouse for Bilingual Education.

Kretschmer, R. E. (1991). Exceptionality and the limited English proficient student: Historical and practical contexts. In E. V. Hamayan & J. S. Damico (Eds.). *Limiting bias in the assessment of bilingual students* (pp. 1-38). Austin, TX: Pro-Ed.

Labov, W. (1972). *Language in the inner city: Studies in the Black English vernacular.* Philadelphia: University of Pennsylvania Press.

Lam, T. C. M. (1988). *Testing, opportunity allocation, and Asian and Pacific Americans.* The Proceedings of a Hearing Co-Sponsored by the National Association for Asian and Pacific American Education; Eric Document Reproduction Service No. (ED297058).

Lambert, W. E. (1990). Persistent issues in bilingualism. In B. Harley, P. Allen, J. Cummins, & M. Swain (Eds.). *The development of second language proficiency.* (pp. 201-220). New York: Cambridge University Press.

Lambert, W. E. & Tucker, G. R. (1973). *Bilingual education of children.* Rowley, MA: Newbury House.

Langdon, H. (1989). Language disorder or difference: Assessing the language skills of Hispanic students. *Exceptional Children, 56,* 160-167.

Langdon, H. W. (1988). *Interpreter/translator in the school setting module.* Sacramento: California State Department of Education.

Lange, R. R., & Cook, D. (1986). *Florida teacher performance development program learning package 17: Constructing tests.* Tallahassee, FL, Florida Dept. of Education.

Langer, J. A. (1987). *Language, literacy, and culture: Issues of society and schooling.* Norwood, NJ: Ablex.

Larrinaga McGee, P. M. (1988, November). *The LEP Haitian student in Florida: Challenges in service delivery and assessment.* Paper presented at the annual convention of the Florida Association of School Psychologists, Tampa, FL.

Larrinaga McGee, P. M. (1991, February). *Curriculum-based assessment: Applications for linguistically diverse children (LDC).* Workshop presented at the Fourteenth Annual Statewide Conference for Teachers of Linguistically and Culturally Diverse Students, Chicago.

Larry P. Task Force. (1989). *Larry P. task force report: Policy and alternative assessment guideline recommendations.* Sacramento: Resources in Special Education.

Leap, W. L. (1988). Assumptions and strategies guiding mathematics problem solving by Ute Indian students. In R. R. Cocking & J. P. Mestre (Eds.). *Linguistic and cultural influences on learning mathematics* (pp. 161-186). Hillsdale, NJ: Lawrence Erlbaum Associates.

Lee, A. (1989). A socio-cultural framework for the assessment of Chinese children with special needs. *Topics in Language Disorders, 9,* 38-44.

Lentz, F. E., Jr. & Shapiro, E. S. (1985). Behavioral school psychology: A conceptual model for the delivery of psychological service. In T. R. Kratochwill (Ed.). *Advances in school psychology,* (Vol. 4, pp. 192-232). Hillsdale, NJ: Lawrence Erlbaum Associates.

Lentz, F. E., Jr. & Shapiro, E. S. (1986). Functional assessment of the academic environment. *School Psychology Review, 15,* 336-345.

Lerner, R. (1983). A "goodness of fit" model of person-context interaction. In D. Magnusson & V. Allen (Eds.). *Human development: An interactional perspective* (pp. 279-294). New York: Academic Press.

LeTendre, M. J. (1991). Improving Chapter 1 programs: We can do better. *Phi Delta Kappan, 72,* 577-580.

Levin, H. M. (1989). Financing the education of at risk students. *Educational Evaluation and Policy Analysis, 11,* 47-60.

Levine, M. N. (1989). *Mental retardation handbook.* Los Angeles: Western Psychological Services.

Lewelling, V. W. (1991). Academic achievement in a second language. *ERIC Digest* (EDO-FL-91-01). Washington, D.C.: Center for Applied Linguistics.

Lewis, A. C. (1991). America 2000: What kind of nation? *Phi Delta Kappan, 72,* 734-735.

Li, A. K. F. (1992). Peer relations and social skills training: Implications for the multicultural classroom. *The Journal of Educational Issues of Langauge Minority Students, 10,* 67-78.

Liceras, J. (1985). The role of intake in the determination of learners' competence. In S. M. Gass & Madden C. G. (Eds.). *Input in second language acquisition* (pp. 354-373). Cambridge, MA: Newbury House.

Lieberman, A. (1986). Collaborative work. *Educational Leadership, 43,* 4-8.

Lieven, E. V. M. (1984). Interaction style and children's language learning. *Topics in Language Disorders, 4,* 15-23.

Life. (1992, March). Mr. Sweeney has an off-the-wall approach to teaching math, p. 6.

Linder, T. (1990). *Transdisciplinary play-based assessment: A functional approach to working with young children.* Baltimore: Paul H. Brooks Publishing.

Lindfors, J. W. (1987). *Children's language and learning,* (2nd ed.) Englewood Cliffs, NJ: Prentice-Hall.

Lindholm, K. J. (1991). Theoretical assumptions and empirical evidence for academic achievement in two languages. *Hispanic Journal of Behavioral Sciences, 13,* 3-17.

Linn, R. L., Baker, E. L., & Dunbar, S. B. (1991). Complex, performance-based assessment: Expectations and validation criteria. *Educational Researcher, 20,* 15-21.

Lombard, T. J. (1988, March). *Curriculum-based measurement: Megatesting or McTesting?* A position paper (revised) submitted to the Minnesota School Psychologists' Association. Available from the author at the Minnesota Dept. of Education, St. Paul, MN, 55101.

Lovitt, T. C. & Horton, S. V. (1987). How to develop study guides. *Journal of Reading, Writing and Learning Disabilities International, 4,* 333-344.

Loyola, J. L., McBride, D. F., & Loyola, L. J. (1991). Cognitive and linguistic abilities of Puerto Rican bilingual children: Implications for assessment. *The Journal of Educational Issues of Language Minority students, 8,* 31-50.

Lucas, T. & Katz, A. (1991). *The roles of students' native languages in exemplary SAIPs.* Paper presented at the Annual Meeting of the American Educational Research Association, Chicago, April.

Lurie, J. (1982). America...globally blind, deaf and dumb. *Foreign Language Annals, 15,* 413-420.

Maccoby, L. (1968). Early learning and personality. In R. Hess & R. Bear (Eds.). *Early education: Current theory, research, and action.* Chicago: Aldine Publishing Company.

Mace-Matluck, B. J. & Koike, D. A. (1991). Story recall in the language assessment of bilingual and monolingual children. *Journal of the New York State Association for Bilingual Education, 7,* 40-54.

Macmillan, D. L., Hendrick, I. G. & Watkins, A. V. (1988). Impact of Diana, Larry P., and P. L. 94-142 on minority students. *Exceptional Children, 54,* 426-532.

Malone, V. (1990). *Promising practices.* Unpublished paper presented at the annual conference of the National Science Teachers Association.

Malone, V. (1991). *Promising practices.* A workshop presented at the National Convention of the National Science Teachers Association, Houston, TX. (Paper available from Psychological Corporation, San Antonio, TX).

Marston, D. B. (1989). A curriculum-based approach to assessing academic performance: What it is and why do it. In M. R. Shinn (Ed.). *Curriculum-based measurement: Assessing special children* (pp. 18-78). New York: Guilford Press.

Martin, N. (1987). On the move: Teacher-researchers. In D. Gaswami & P. R. Stillman (Eds.). *Reclaiming the classroom: Teacher research as an agency for change* (pp. 20-27). Portsmouth, NH: Heinemann.

Matsumoto, D. (1989). Cultural influences on the perception of emotion. *Journal of Cross-Cultural Psychology, 20*, 92-105.

Mattes, L. J. & Omark, D. R. (1984). *Speech and language assessment for the bilingual handicapped.* San Diego, CA: College-Hill Press.

McDill, E. L., Natriello, G. & Pallas, A. (1985). Raising standards and retaining students: The impact of the reform recommendations on potential dropouts. *Review of Educational Research, 55*, 415-434.

McGuire, C. K. (1982). *State and federal programs for special student populations.* (Education Commission on the States, Denver, CO. Report No. ECS-F82-2) (ERIC Reproduction No. ED 220179).

McLaughlin, B. (1984). *Second-language acquisition in childhood: Volume 1. Preschool children* (2nd ed.). Hillsdale, NJ: Lawrence Erlbaum Associates.

McLaughlin, B. (1990). The relationship between first and second languages: Language proficiency and language aptitude. In B. Harley, P. Allen, J. Cummins, & M. Swain (Eds.). *The development of second language proficiency* (pp. 158-174). New York: Cambridge University Press.

McLoughlin, J. A. & Lewis, R. B. (1986). *Assessing special students* (2nd ed.). Columbus, OH: Merrill.

McNeely, S. N. (1986). *Informal oral language proficiency assessment: (Teaching Training Monograph No. 3).* Gainesville, FL: College of Education, University of Florida.

Mercer, J. R., & Lewis, J. F. (1978). *System of Multicultural Pluralistic Assessment.* New York: Psychological Corporation.

Merrill, K. W., Johnson, E. R., Merz, J. M., & Ring, E. N. (1992). Social competence of students with mild handicaps and low achievement: A comparative study. *School Psychology Review, 21*, 125-137.

Messer, M. M. & Rasmussen, N. H. (1985). Southeast Asian children in America: The impact of change. *Pediatrics, 78*, 323-329.

Mestre, J. P. (1988). The role of language comprehension in mathematics and problem solving. In R. R. Cocking & J. P. Mestre (Eds.). *Linguistics and cultural influences on learning mathematics* (pp. 201-220). Hillsdale, NJ: Lawrence Erlbaum Associates.

Mestre, J. P. & Gerace, W. (1986). Interplay of linguistic factors in mathematical translation tasks. *Focus on Learning Problems in Mathematics, 8*, 59-72.

Mestre, J. P. & Royer, J. M. (1988). *Cultural and linguistic influences in Latino testing.* (ERIC Reproduction Number ED 307 814).

Metz, I. B. (1991). Limited language proficiency and language disorders: Issues and concerns regarding the language screening of preschool linguistically diverse children. *Journal of the New York State Association for Bilingual Education, 7*, 81-93.

Miller, J. A. (1991, May 22). Chapter 1: An educational revolution. *Educational Week*, pp. 1, special section 1 C1-C20.

Miller, L. (1990). The roles of language and learning in the development of literacy. *Topics in Language Disorders, 10*, 1-24.

Mischel, W. (1983). Delay of gratification as process and as person variable in development. In D. Magnusson & V. Allen (Eds.). *Human development: An interactional perspective* (pp. 279-294). New York: Academic Press.

Mishler, E. G. (1990). Validation in inquiry-guided research: The role of exemplars in narrative studies. *Harvard Educational Review, 60,* 415-442.

Moll, L. C. & Diaz, S. (1987). Change as the goal of educational research. *Anthropology & Education, 18,* 300-311.

Montalvo, F. (1984). Making good schools from bad. In National Commission on Secondary Schooling for Hispanics. (Ed). (1984). *"Make something happen": Hispanics and urban high school reform.* Vol. 2. (pp. 71-74). Washington, D.C.: Hispanic Policy Development Project.

Moran, M. (1990). The problem of cultural bias in personality assessment. In C. R. Reynolds & R. W. Kamphaus (Eds.). *Handbook of psychological and educational assessment of children: Personality, behavior, and context* (pp. 524-545). New York: Guilford Press.

Murphy, C. U. (1991). Lessons from a journey into change. *Educational Leadership, 48,* 63-67.

Murphy, J. (1989). Is there equity in educational reform? *Educational Leadership, 46,* 32-33.

Narremore, R. C. (1985). Explorations of language use: Pragmatic mapping in L1 and L2. *Topics in Language Disorders, 5,* 66-79.

National Association for Bilingual Education. (1991). Bilingual Education Expert Testifies Against National Achievement Test. *NABE News, 15,* pp. 1, 12.

National Association of School Psychologists. (1990). NASP Position Statement on Advocacy for Appropriate Educational Services for all Children. In A. Barona & E. E. Garcia (Eds.). *Children at risk: Poverty, minority status, and other issues in educational equity* (pp. xix-xxi). Washington, D.C.: National Association of School Psychologists.

National Center for Education Statistics. (1990). *A profile of the American eighth grader.* Washington, D.C.: U.S. Department of Education, Office of Educational Research and Improvement.

National Center on Education and the Economy. (1990). *America's choice: High skills or low wages.* Rochester, New York: Author.

National Clearinghouse for Bilingual Education. (1991). Equity in education and the language minority student. *Forum, 14,* pp. 1-3.

National Coalition of Advocates for Students. (1988). *New voices: Immigrant students in U. S. public schools.* Boston: Author.

National Commission on Excellence in Education. (1983). *A nation at risk: The imperative for educational reform.* Washington, D.C.: U. S. Government Printing Office (ERIC Reproduction No. 226006).

National Commission on Testing and Public Policy. (1990). *From gatekeeper to gateway: Transforming testing in America.* Boston College, Chestnut Hill, MA: National Commission on Testing and Public Policy.

National Science Foundation (1991). *Assessing student learning: Science, mathematics and related technology instruction in the precollege level in formal and informal settings. Program solicitation and guidelines.* Washington, D.C.: Author.

Navarette, C., Wilde, J., Nelson, C., Martinex, R. & Hargett, G. (1990). *Informal assessment in educational evaluation: Implications for bilingual education programs.* George Washington University, Washington, D.C.: Center for Applied Linguistics and National Clearinghouse for Bilingual Education.

Neill, M. (April 24, 1991). Do we need a national achievement exam? No: it would damage, not improve, education. *Education Week,* pp. 36, 28.

Nelson, N. W. (1986). Individual processing in classroom settings. *Topics in Language Disorders, 6,* 13-27.

Nelson, N. W. (1989). Curriculum-based language assessment and intervention. *Language, Speech, and Hearing Services in Schools, 20,* 170-184.

New York City Board of Education. (1990). *Linking assessment to instruction: A handbook for assessing linguistically and culturally diverse students.* Brooklyn, NY: Division of Special Education.

Nolan, T. E. (1991). Self-questioning and prediction: Combining metacognitive strategies. *Journal of Reading, 35,* 132-138.

Norris, J. A. (1991). From frog to prince: Using written language as a context for language learning. *Topics in Language Disorders, 12,* 66-81.

Norris, J. A. & Damico, J. S. (1990). Whole language in theory and practice; implications for language intervention. *Language, Speech, and Hearing Services in Schools, 21,* 212-220.

Nuttall, E. V., De Leon, B., & Valle, M. (1990). Best practices in considering cultural factors. In A. Thomas & J. Grimes (Eds.). *Best practices in school psychology - II* (pp. 219-233). Washington, DC: National Association of School Psychologists.

O'Malley, J. M. & Valdez Pierce, L. (1991). Portfolio assessment: Using portfolio and alternative assessment with LEP students. *Forum, 15,* 1-2.

O'Neil, J. (1990). Piecing together the restructuring puzzle, *Educational Leadership, 47,* 4-10.

O'Neil, J. (1991, June). Transforming the curriculum for students 'at risk'. *ASCD Curriculum Update,* pp. 1-3, 6-8.

Oakland, T. (1973). Assessing minority group children: Challenges for school psychologists. *Journal of School Psychology, 11,* 294-303.

Obler, L. K. (1989). Language beyond childhood. In J. B. Gleason (Ed.) *The development of language* (2nd ed.) (pp. 275-301). Columbus, OH: Merrill.

Office of Bilingual Education and Minority Languages Affairs. (1990). *Staffing the multilingually impacted schools of the 1990s* (A publication developed from the National Forum on Personnel Needs for Districts with Changing Demographics, Washington, D.C., January 1990). Washington, D.C.: Author, U. S. Department of Education.

Oller, J. W. Jr. (1979). *Language tests at school: A pragmatic approach.* London: Longman.

Oller, J. W. Jr. (Ed). (1983). *Issues in language testing research.* Rowley, MA: Newbury House.

Olmedo, E. L. (1981). Testing linguistic minorities. *American Psychologist 36,* 1078-1085.

Olshtain, E. & Blum-Kulka, S. (1985). Crosscultural pragmatics and the testing of communicative competence. *Language Testing, 2,* 16-29.

Omaggio, A. C. (1986). *Teaching language in context,* Boston: Heinle & Heinle.

Orange County Public Schools (1990, July). *Alternative assessment: Ideas to build on.* A session designed by the Elementary Mathematics Team especially for Principals and Assistant Principals for the Principal's Curriculum Institute. Orlando, FL: Orange County Public Schools.

Orfield, G. (1986). Hispanic education: Challenges, research, and policies. *American Journal of Education, 95,* 1-25.

Ortiz, A. A. (1987, Spring). Communication disorders among limited English proficient Hispanic students. *Bilingual Special Education Newsletter, 5,* pp. 1, 3-5, 7-8 (A publication of the University of Texas at Austin).

Ortiz, A. A. (1988). Evaluating educational contexts in which language minority students are served. *Bilingual Special Education Newsletter, 7,* pp. 1-4, 7.

Ortiz, A. & Maldonado-Colon, E. (1986). Reducing inappropriate referrals of language minority students to special education. *Journal of Reading, Writing and Learning Disabilities International, 2,* 43-56.

Ortiz, A. A. & Ramirez, B. A. (Eds.) (1986). *Schools and the culturally diverse exceptional student: Promising practices and future directions.* Reston, VA: Council for Exceptional Children.

Ortiz, A. A. & Yates, J. R. (1988). Characteristics of learning disabled, mentally retarded, and speech-language handicapped hispanic students at initial evaluation and re-evaluation. In A. A. Ortiz & B. A. Ramirez (Eds.). *Schools and the Culturally Diverse Exceptional Student: Promising Practices and Future Directions* (pp. 51-62). Reston, VA: Council for Exceptional Children.

Ortiz, A. A. & Yates, J. R. (1988). Incidence of exceptionality among Hispanics: Implications for manpower planning. *National Association for Bilingual Education Journal, 7,* 41-54.

Ortiz, A. A., Wilkinson, C. Y., Robertson-Courtney, P., & Kushner, M. I. (1991). *AIM for the BEST: Assessment and intervention model for the bilingual exceptional student.* Handbook for teachers and planners. Arlington, VA: Development Associates.

Ownby, R. L. (1987). *Psychological reports.* Brandon, VT: Clinical Psychology Publishing Co.

Oxford, R. (1989). *The role of styles and strategies in second language learning.* ERIC DIGEST. ERIC Clearinghouse on Languages and Linguistics. Center for Applied Linguistics, Washington, D.C.

Padilla, E. (1989, May). *Program development for Hispanic LEP handicapped students.* Paper presented at the annual conference of the National Association for Bilingual Education, Miami, FL.

Pallas, A. M., Natriello, G. & McDill, E. L. (1989). The changing nature of the disadvantaged population: Current dimensions and future trends. *Educational Researcher, 18,* 16-22.

Paris, S. & Lindauer, B. (1982). The development of cognitive skills during childhood. In B. Wolman (Ed.). *Handbook of developmental psychology.* (pp. 76-90). Englewood Cliffs, NJ: Prentice-Hall.

Passow, A. H. (1991). Urban schools a second (?) or third (?) time around: Priorities for curricular and instructional reform. *Education and Urban Society, 23,* 243-255.

Paulston, C. B. (1980). *Bilingual education: Theories and issues.* Rowley, MA: Newbury House.

Paulston, C. B. (1986). Linguistic consequences of ethnicity and nationalism in multilingual settings. In B. Spolsky (Ed.). *Language and education in multilingual settings* (pp. 117-152). Clevedon, Avon, England: Multilingual Matters.

Pease, D. M. & Gleason, J. B. & Pan, B. A. (1987). Gaining meaning: Semantic development. In J. B. Gleason, (Ed.). *The development of language* (pp. 101-133). Columbus, OH: Merrill.

Pehrsson, R. S. & Denner, P. R. (1988). Semantic organizers: Implications for reading and writing. *Topics in Language Disorders, 8,* 24-32.

Penfield, J. (1987). ESL: The regular classroom teacher's perspective. *TESOL Quarterly, 21,* 21-39.

Peregoy, S. F. & Boyle, O. F. (1991). Second language oral proficiency characteristics of low, intermediate, and high second language readers. *Hispanic Journal of Behavioral Sciences, 13,* 35-47.

Pérez, B. & Torres-Guzmán, M. E. (1992). *Learning in two worlds.* White Plains, NY: Longman.

Perez, C. (1991). *Clarifying issues and concerns related to Florida's ESOL Agreement.* Paper presented at the 15th Annual Gulf Area TESOL Conference, West Palm Beach, FL, May 15.

Perry, J. D., & Rothlisberg, B. A. (1991). New challenges and practice guidelines. *The school psychologist, 45,* 4.

Pettit, G., Dodge, K., & Brown, M. (1988). Early family experience, social problem-solving patterns, and children's social competence. *Child Development, 59,* 107-120.

Phinney, J. S. & Rotheram, M. J. (Eds.). *Children's ethnic socialization.* Newbury Park, CA: Sage.

Piccolo, J. A. (1987). Expository text structure: Teaching and learning strategies. *The Reading Teacher, 40,* 838-847.

Pierce, L. V. (1991, October). *Portfolio assessment for limited English proficient students, grades k-12.* Paper presented at the Southeast Regional TESOL Conference, Atlanta.

Plisko, J. W. (Ed.) (1984). *The condition of education.* Washington, D.C.: National Center for Education Statistics, U. S. Department of Education.

Polonio, N. A. & Williams, R. A. (1991). The politics of funding at-risk programs in the 1990s. *Urban Education, 26,* 43-55.

Pomerantz, J. (1991). *Preferral screening form: Identifying the communicatively impaired/ potentially English proficient student.* Ft. Lauderdale, FL: Multicultural Education Department, School Board of Broward County.

Pomerantz, J. (1991). *Suggestions for interpreters.* Ft. Lauderdale, FL: Multicultural Education Department, School Board of Broward County.

Pomerantz, J. (1991). *Suggestions for users of interpreters.* Ft. Lauderdale, FL: Multicultural Education Department, School Board of Broward County.

Porter, R. P. (1990). *Forked tongue: The politics of bilingual education.* New York: Basic Books.

Potter, M. L. & Wamre, H. M. (1990). Curriculum-based measurement and developmental reading models: Opportunities for cross-validation. *Exceptional Children, 57,* 16-25.

Priestley, M. (1982). *Performance assessment in education and training: Alternative techniques.* Englewood Cliffs, NJ: Educational Technology Publications.

Purkey, S. C. & Smith, M. S. (1983). Effective schools: A review. *The Elementary School Journal, 83,* 427-452.

Ramirez, J. D. Comparing structured English immersion and bilingual education: First-year results of a national study. *American Journal of Education, 95,* 122-148.

Ramsey, R. S. & Algozzine, B. (1991). Teacher competency testing: What are special education teachers expected to know? *Exceptional Children, 57,* 339-352.

Redmond, D. (1990). Use of informal reading inventories. In N. Cloud, P. Medeiros-Landurand & S. Wu, (Eds.). *Multisystem: Systematic Instructional planning for exceptional bilingual students* (pp. 95-98). New York, NY: Institute for Urban and Minority Education at Teachers College, Columbia University.

Reissman, F. (1991, June 5). Plotting a 'thematic' third stage of reform. *Education Week,* p. 27.

Reschly, D. J. (1980). *Nonbiased assessment.* Ames, IA: Iowa State University.

Reschley, D. J. (1981). Psychological testing in educational classification and placement. *American Psychologist, 36,* 1094-1102.

Reschly, D. J. (1985). Best practices: Adaptive behavior. In A. Thomas & J. Grimes (Eds.). *Best practices in school psychology* (pp. 353-368). Kent, OH: The National Association of School Psychologists.

Reschly, D. J., Kicklighter, R. & McKee, P. (1988a). Recent placement litigation: Part II minority EMR overrepresentation: Comparison of Larry P. (1979, 1984, 1986) with Marshall (1984, 1985) and S-1 (1986). *School Psychology Review, 17,* 22-38.

Reschly, D. J., Kicklighter, R. & McKee, P. (1988b). Recent placement litigation part III: Analysis of differences in Larry P., Marshall and S-1 and implications for future practices. *School Psychology Review, 17,* 39-50.

Rewilak, D. & Jenzen, H. L. (1982). Learning disabilities: A futile attempt at definition? *School Psychology International, 3,* 85-90.

Reyes, M. d. l. L. & Molner, L. A. (1991). Instructional strategies for second-language learners in the content areas. *Journal of Reading, 35,* 96-103.

Reynolds, C. R. (1982). The problem of bias in psychological assessment. In C. R. Reynolds & T. B. Gutkin (Eds.). *The handbook of school psychology* (pp. 178-208). New York: Wiley.

Rice, M. (1983). Contemporary accounts of the cognition/language relationship: Implications for speech-language clinicians. *Journal of Speech and Hearing Disorders, 48,* 347-359.

Rice, M. L. (1980). *Cognition to language.* Baltimore: University Park Press.

Rice, M. L. (1986). Mismatched premise of the communicative competence model and language intervention. In R. L. Schiefelbusch (Ed.). *Language competence assessment and intervention* (pp. 261-280). San Diego, CA: College-Hill Press.

Riche, M. F. (1991). We're all minorities. *American Demographics,* 26-34.

Rigg, P. (1986). Reading in ESL: Learning from kids. In P. Rigg and D. Scott Enright (Eds.). *Children and ESL: Integrating perspectives* (pp. 57-91). Washington, D.C.: Teachers of English to Speakers of Other Languages.

Rigg, P. (1988). The miscue-ESL project. In R. C. Anderson & P. D. Pearson (Eds.), *Interactive approaches to second language reading* (pp. 206-217). New York, NY: Cambridge University Press.

Robey, B. (1989). Two hundred years and counting: The 1990 census. *Population Bulletin, 44,* 1-7.

Rodriguez, R. (1982). *Hunger of memory: The education of Richard Rodriquez.* Boston: David R. Godine.

Roos, P. D. (1984). Equity and excellence. In National Commission on Secondary Schooling for Hispanics. (Ed). *"Make something happen": Hispanics and urban high school reform,* Vol 2. (pp. 75-78). Washington, D.C.: Hispanic Policy Development Project.

Ross-Reynolds, G. (1990). Best practices in report writing. In A. Thomas & J. Grimes (Eds.). *Best practices in school psychology - II* (pp. 621-633). Washington, D.C.: National Association of School Psychologists.

Roth, F. P. (1986). Oral narrative abilities of learning-disabled students. *Topics in Language Disorders, 7,* 21-30.

Rothman, R. (1991, October 30). Schools stress speeding up, not slowing down. *Education Week,* pp. 1, 15.

Royer, J. M. & Carlo, M. S. (1991). Transfer of comprehension skills from native to second language. *Journal of Reading, 34,* 450-455.

Rueda, R. (1983). Metalinguistic awareness in monolingual and bilingual mentally retarded children. *NABE Journal, 8,* 55-67.

Rueda, R. (1984). Cognitive development and learning in mildly handicapped bilingual students. In P. C. Chinn (Ed.). *Education of Culturally and Linguistically Different Exceptional Children.* Reston, VA: The Council for Exceptional Children.

Rueda, R. (1989). Defining mild disabilities with language-minority students. *Exceptional Children, 56,* 121-129.

Ruiz, N. & Figueroa, R. (1989). Optimum learning environment for Hispanic RSP students (OLE). *The Special Edge, 4,* 3.

Russell, N. L. & Ortiz, A. A. (1988, fall). Assessment and instruction within a dialogue model of communication, Part I. *Bilingual Special Education Newsletter, 8,* pp. 1, 3, 4 (A publication of the University of Texas at Austin).

Salomon, G. (1991). Transcending the qualitative-quantitative debate: The analytic and systemic approaches to educational research. *Educational Researcher, 20,* 10-18.

Salvia, J. & Ysseldyke, J. E. (1988). *Assessment in special and remedial education* (4th ed.). Boston: Houghton Mifflin.

Salvia, J. A., & Ysseldyke, J. E. (1985). *Assessment in special and remedial education,* (3rd edition). Boston: Houghton Mifflin.

Sansone, J. & Zigmond, N. (1986). Evaluating mainstreaming through an analysis of student' schedules. *Exceptional Children, 52,* 452-458.

Sattler, J. M. (1988). *Assessment of children.* (3rd edition). San Diego, CA: Jerome M. Sattler.

Sattler, J. M. (1988). *Assessment of children.* San Diego, CA: Jerome M. Sattler.

Savignon, S. J. (1983). *Communicative competence: Theory and classroom practice.* Reading, MA: Addison-Wesley.

Saville-Troike, M. (1985). Cultural input in second language learning. In S. M. Gass & Madden C. G. (Eds.). *Input in second language acquisition* (pp. 51-58). Cambridge, MA: Newbury House.

Saville-Troike, M. (1988). Private speech: Evidence of second language learning strategies during the 'silent' period. *Journal of Child Language, 15,* 567-590.

Saville-Troike, M. (1991). Teaching and testing for academic achievement: The role of language development. *Focus, 4.* Washington, D.C.: National Clearinghouse for Bilingual Education.

Sawyer, D. J. (1991). Whole language in context: Insights into the current great debate. *Topics in Language Disorders, 11,* 1-13.

Saxe, G. B. (1988). Linking language with mathematics achievement: Problems and prospects. In R. R. Cocking and J. P. Mestre (Eds.). *Linguistic and cultural influences on learning mathematics* (pp. 47-62). Hillsdale, NJ: Lawrence Erlbaum Associates.

Saxon, B. (1991). *Tally's Corner* revisited, *Harvard Educational Review, 61,* 88-95.

Schindler, D. E. & Davison, D. M. (1985). Language, culture, and the mathematics concepts of American Indian learners. *Journal of American Indian Education, 24,* 27-34.

Schmidt, P. (1991, February 20). Three types of bilingual education effective, E. D. study concludes. *Education Week,* pp. 1, 23.

Schory, M. E. (1990). Whole language and the speech-language pathologist. *Language, Speech, and Hearing Services in Schools, 21,* 206-211.

Schuele, C. M. & van Kleeck, A. (1987). Precursors to literacy: Assessment and intervention. *Topics in Language Disorders, 7,* 32-44.

Schuster, B., Forsterling, F. & Weiner, B. (1989). Perceiving the causes of success and failure: A cross-cultural examination of attributional concepts. *Journal of Cross-Cultural Psychology, 20,* 191-213.

Scollon, R. & Scollon, S. B. K. (1981). *Narrative, literacy and face in interethnic communication.* (Vol. 7 in the series Advances in Discourse Process). Norwood, NJ: Ablex.

Scott, L. S. & Fisher, A. T. (1988). The Texas environmental adaptation measure: Test development and standardization, and a case study. In R. L. Jones (Ed.). *Psychoeducational Assessment of Minority Group Children: A Casebook* (pp. 109-189). Berkeley, CA: Cobb & Henry.

Scully, M. J. (1991). The use of an educational therapy model with an illiterate adult. *Journal of Reading, 35,* 126-131.

Secada, W. G., Carey, D. A., & Schlicher, R. (1989). *Innovative strategies for teaching mathematics to limited English proficient students.* Program Information Guide Series, No. 10. Washington, D.C.: National Clearinghouse for Bilingual Education.

Seidenberg, P. L. (1988). Cognitive and academic instructional intervention for learning-disabled adolescents. *Topics in Language Disorders, 8,* 56-71.

Semmel, M. I., Abernathy, T. V., Butera, G. & Lesar, S. (1991). Teacher perceptions of the regular education initiative. *Exceptional Children, 5,* 9-26.

Shanklin, N. L. (1991). Whole language and writing process: One movement or two? *Topics in Language Disorders, 11,* 45-57.

Shannon, S. M. (1990). English in the barrio: The quality of contact among immigrant children. *Hispanic Journal of Behavioral Sciences, 12,* 256-276.

Shapiro, E. S. (1989). *Academic skills problems: Direct assessment and intervention.* New York, NY: The Guilford Press.

Shapiro, E. S. (1990). An integrated model for curriculum-based assessment. *School Psychology Review, 19,* 331-349.

Shapiro, E. S. (1992). Use of Gickling's model of curriculum-based assessment to improve reading in elementary age students. *School Psychology Review, 21,* 168-176.

Shapiro, E. S. & Skinner, C. H. (1990). Best practices in observation and ecological assessment. In A. Thomas and J. Grimes (Eds.). *Best Practices in School Psychology II* (pp. 507-518). Washington, D.C.: National Association of School Psychologists.

Shellenberger, S. (1982). Presentation and interpretation of psychological data in educational settings. In C. R. Reynolds & T. B. Gutkin (Eds.). *The handbook of school psychology* (pp. 51-81). New York: Wiley.

Shepard, L., & Smith, M. L. (1983). An evaluation of the identification of learning disabled students in Colorado. *Learning Disability Quarterly, 6,* 115-127.

Shinn, M. R. (1988). Development of curriculum-based local norms to use in special education decision-making. *School Psychology Review, 17,* 61-81.

Shinn, M. R. (Ed.). (1989). *Curriculum-based measurement: Assessing special children.* New York: Guilford Press.

Shinn, M. R. & Knutson, N. M. (1992, July). *Curriculum-based measurement and problem-solving assessment.* Workshop presented at the Summer Institute of the Florida Association of School Psychologists, Palm Beach Shores, FL.

Shinn, M. R., Rosenfield, S., & Knutson, N. (1989). Curriculum-based assessment: A comparison of models. *School Psychology Review, 18,* 299-316.

Shinn, M. R. & Tindal, G. A. (1988). Using student performance data in academics: A pragmatic and defensible approach to non-discriminatory assessment. In R. L. Jones (Ed.). *Psychoeducational assessment of minority group children: A casebook* (pp. 383-407). Berkeley, CA: Cobb and Henry.

Shinn, M. R., Tindal, G. A., & Stein, S. (1988). Curriculum-based measurement and the identification of mildly handicapped students: A research review. *Professional School Psychology, 3,* 69-85.

Shuy, R. W. (1981). Conditions affecting language learning and maintenance among Hispanics in the United States. *The Journal of the National Association for Bilingual Education, 6,* 1-18.

Silliman, E. R. & Lamanna, M. L. (1986). Interactional dynamics of turn disruption: Group and individual effects. *Topics in Language Disorders, 6,* 28-43.

Silliman, E. R. & Wilkinson, L. C. (1991). *Communicating for learning: Classroom observation and collaboration.* Gaithersburg, MD: Aspen Publication.

Silverstein, J. (1991). *IEP meetings often confusing for parents.* National Association of School Psychologists *Communique, 19,* 6.

Simon, C. (1979). *Communicative competence: A functional-pragmatic approach to language therapy.* Tucson, AZ: Communication Skill Builders.

Sizer, T. R. (1991). No pain, no gain. *Educational Leadership, 48,* 32-34.

Skrtic, T. M. (1991). The special education paradox: Equity as the way to excellence. *Harvard Educational Review, 61,* 148-206.

Slavin, R. E. (1989). PET and the pendulum: Faddism in education and how to stop it. *Phi Delta Kappan, 70,* 752-758.

Slavin, R. E. & Madden, N. A. (1989). What works for students at risk: A research synthesis. *Education Leadership, 46,* 4-13.

Sleeter, C. E. & Grant, C. A. (1987). An analysis of multicultural education in the United States. *Harvard Educational Review, 57,* 421-444.

Smith-Burke, M. T., Deegan, D. & Jaggar, A. M. (1991). Whole language: A viable alternative for special and remedial education? *Topics in Language Disorders, 11,* 58-68.

Snow, C., Midkiff-Borunda, S., Small, A., & Proctor, A. (1984). Therapy as social interaction: Analyzing the contexts for language remediation. *Topics in Language Disorders, 4,* 72-85.

Snowdon, S. (1986). *The global edge.* New York: Simon and Schuster.

Spanos, G. & Crandall, J. (1987, May). *Integrating language and content: Improving academic achievement for LEP children.* Paper in the proceedings of the Statewide Conference on the Education of Children of Limited English Proficiency, Dover, DE.

Spanos, G., Rhodes, N., Dale, T. C. & Crandall, J. (1988). Linguistic features of mathematical problem-solving: Insights and applications. In R. R. Cocking and J. P. Mestre (Eds.). *Linguistic and cultural influences on learning mathematics* (pp. 221-240). Hillsdale, NJ: Lawrence Erlbaum Associates.

Sparrow, S. S., Balla, D. A. & Cichetti, D. V. (1984). *Vineland Adaptive Behavior Scales.* Circle Pines, MN: American Guidance Service.

Spolsky, B. (1986). Overcoming language barriers to education in a multilingual world. In B. Spolsky (Ed.). *Language and education in multilingual settings* (pp. 182-191). Clevedon, Avon, England: Multilingual Matters.

Staff. (1986, November). When children speak little English: How effective is bilingual education? *Harvard Education Letter, 2,* 1-4.

Staff. (1991, Spring). Individuals with Disabilities Education Act challenges educators to improve the education of minority students with disabilities. *The Bilingual Special Education Perspective, 1,* 3-6.

Stainback, W. & Stainback, S. (1984). A rationale for the merger of special and regular education. *Exceptional Children, 51,* 102-111.

Stanovich, K. E. (1991). Discrepancy definitions of reading disability: Has intelligence led us astray? *Reading Research Journal, 26,* 7-29.

Stedman, L. C. (1987). It's time we changed the effective schools formula. *Phi Delta Kappan, 69,* 215-224.

Stern, J. D. & Chandler, M. O. (1987). *The condition of education.* Washington, D.C.: National Center for Educational Statistics, U. S. Department of Education.

Sternberg, R. J. & Lubart, T. I. (1991). Creating creative minds, *Phi Delta Kappan, 72,* 608-614.

Sugai, G. (1988). Educational assessment of the culturally diverse and behavior disordered student: An examination of critical effect. In A. A. Ortiz & R. A. Ramirez (Eds.). *Schools and the Culturally Diverse Exceptional Student: Promising Practices and Future Directions* (pp. 63-75). Reston, VA: The Council for Exceptional Children.

Sulzby, E. (1985). Children's emergent reading of favorite storybooks: A developmental study. *Reading Research Quarterly, 20,* 458-481.

Sulzby, E. (1986). Writing and reading: Signs of oral and written language organization in the young child. In W. Teale and E. Sulzby (Eds.). *Emergent literacy: Writing and reading.* Norwood, NJ: Ablex. (ERIC Document Reproduction Service No. 280 004.)

Sulzby, E. (1989). *Emergent literacy: Kindergartners write and read.* Ann Arbor, MI: University of Michigan and North Central Regional Educational Laboratory.

Sutton-Smith, B. (1986). The development of functional narrative performances. *Topics in Language Disorders, 7,* 1-10.

Swain, M. (1985). Communicative competence: Some roles of comprehensible input and comprehensible output in its development. In S. M. Gass & Madden C. G. (Eds.). *Input in second language acquisition* (pp. 235-253). Cambridge, MA: Newbury House.

Swanson, H. L. & Watson, B. L. (1989). *Educational and psychological assessment of exceptional children.* (2nd ed.) Columbus, OH: Merrill.

Swenson, L. C. (1980). *Theories of learning: Traditional perspectives/contemporary developments.* Belmont, CA: Wadsworth.

Szapocznik, J., Kurtines, W., & Fernandez, T. (1980). Bicultural involvement and adjustment in Hispanic-American youth. *International Journal of Intercultural Relations, 4,* 353-365.

Teale, W. H. (1988). Developmentally appropriate assessment of reading and writing in the early childhood classroom. *Elementary School Journal, 89,* 173-183.

Telzrow, C. F., Fuller, A., & Siegel, C. (1989). Collaboration in the treatment of children's communication disorders: A five-year case study. *School Psychology Review, 18,* 463-474.

Terman, L. M., & Merrill, M. A. (1973). *Stanford-Binet Intelligence Scale: Manual for the third revision form L-M.* Boston: Houghton Mifflin.

Thousand, J. S. (1991). A futuristic view of the REI: A response to Jenkins, Pious, and Jewell, *Exceptional Children, 57,* 556-562.

Tikunoff, W. J. (1983). *An emerging description of successful bilingual instruction: Executive summary of part I of the SBIF study.* San Francisco: Far West Lab. for Educational Research and Development.

Tikunoff, W. J. (1983). *Utility of the SBIF features for the instruction of LEP students.* San Francisco, CA: Far West Lab. for Educational Research and Development.

Tikunoff, W. J. (1984). *Applying significant bilingual instructional features in the classroom.* Rosslyn, VA: InterAmerican Research Associates, National Clearinghouse for Bilingual Education.

Tikunoff, W. J. (1987). Mediation of instruction to obtain equality of effectiveness. In S. H. Fradd & W. J. Tikunoff (Eds.). *Bilingual education and bilingual special education: A guide for administrators* (pp. 99-132). Austin, TX: Pro-Ed.

Tikunoff, W. J. & Vazquez, J. A. (1982). Successful instruction for bilingual schooling. *Peabody Journal of Education, 59,* 234-271.

Tikunoff, W. J. & Ward, B. A. (1991, April). *Modifying instructional environments: Overview of findings of the exemplary SAIP descriptive study.* Paper presented at the Annual Meeting of the American Educational Research Association, Chicago.

Timar, T. (1989). The politics of school restructuring. *Phi Delta Kappan, 71,* 265-275.

Toch, T. (1991). *In the name of excellence: The struggle to reform the nation's schools. Why it's failing, and what should be done.* New York: Oxford University Press.

Toohey, K. (1984). Language proficiency assessment for child second-language learners. *The Canadian Modern Language Review, 41,* 388-396.

Tough, J. (1976a). *The development of meaning: A study of children's use of language.* Portsmouth, NH: Heinemann.

Tough, J. (1976b). *Listening to children talking: A guide to the appraisal of children's use of language.* Portsmouth, NH: Heinemann.

Tough, J. (1977). *The development of meaning.* New York: Wiley.

Tucker, G. R. (1990). The project in perspective. In B. Harley, P. Allen, J. Cummins, & M. Swain (Eds.). *The development of second language proficiency* (pp. 221-226). New York: Cambridge University Press.

Tucker, J. A. (1990, October). *Neutralizing assessment barriers for culturally diverse exceptional students through curriculum-based assessment.* Workshop presented at the Council for Exceptional Children Symposium on Culturally Diverse Exceptional Children, Albuquerque, NM.

U. S. Department of Commerce, Bureau of the Census. (1987a). *Statistical abstract of the United States* (108th edition). Washington, D.C.: U. S. Government Printing Office.

U. S. Department of Commerce, Bureau of the Census. (1987b). *The Hispanic population in the United States* (March, 1986 and 1987 Advance Report). (Series P-20, No. 416). Washington, D.C.: U. S. Government Printing Office.

U. S. Department of Education (1980). Nondiscrimination under programs receiving federal assistance through the Department of Education, Effectuation of Title VI of the Civil Rights Act of 1964. *Federal Register, 45* (152) (Tuesday, August 8), 52052-52076.

U. S. Department of Education, Office for Civil Rights. (1986). *Directory of elementary and secondary school districts and schools in selected districts: 1976 and 1984 elementary and secondary school civil rights survey.* Washington, D.C.: U. S. Government Printing Office.

U. S. Department of Justice, Immigration and Naturalization Service. (1987). *Statistical Yearbook of the Immigration and Naturalization Service.* Washington, D.C.: U. S. Government Printing Office.

U. S. General Accounting Office. (1986). *School dropouts: The extent and nature of the problem.* (Briefing Report to Congressional Requesters). Washington, D.C.: Author.

U. S. General Accounting Office. (1987). *Bilingual education: Information on limited English proficient students* (Briefing report to the chairman, Committee on Labor and Human Resources, United States Senate, Washington, D.C.: Author.

Ulibarri, D. M. (1990). Use of achievement tests with non-native English-speaking language minority students. In A. Barona & E. E. Garcia (Eds.). *Children at risk: Poverty, minority status, and other issues in educational equity* (pp. 325-351). Washington, D.C.: National Association of School Psychologists.

Ulibarri, D. M., Spencer, M. L. & Rivas, G. A. (1981). Language proficiency and academic achievement: A study of language proficiency tests and their relationship to school ratings as predictors of academic achievement. *Journal of the National Association for Bilingual Education, 5,* 31-46.

Urzua, C. (1986). A children's story. In P. Rigg & D. S. Enright (Eds.). *Children and ESL: Integrating perspectives* (pp. 93-112). Washington, D.C.: Teachers of English to Speakers of Other Languages.

Urzua, C. (1987). "You stopped too soon": Second language children composing and revising. *TESOL Quarterly, 21,* 279-304.

Valdez Pierce, L. & O'Malley, J. M. (1992). *Performance and portfolio assessment for language minority students.* Washington, D.C.: National Clearinghouse for Bilingual Education.

Van Dongen, R. & Westby, C. E. (1986). Building the narrative mode of thought through children's literature. *Topics in Language Disorders, 7,* 70-83.

Van Kleech, A. (1990). Emergent literacy: Learning about print before learning to read. *Topics in Language Disorders, 10,* 25-45.

Van Kleeck, A. & Schuele, C. M. (1987). Precursors to literacy: Normal development. *Topics in Language Disorders, 7,* 13-31.

Vázquez-Montilla, E. (1991). *A comparison of language samples of monolingual and limited English proficient students* (Unpublished doctoral dissertation) University of Florida, Gainesville, FL.

Ventriglia, L. (1982). *Conversations of Miguel and Maria: How children learn a second language.* Reading, MA: Addison-Wesley.

W. T. Grant Foundation (Commission on Work, Family and Citizenship). (1988). *The forgotten half: Pathways to success for America's youth and young families.* Washington, D.C.: Author.

Waggoner, D. (1987). Foreign born children in the United States in the eighties. *National Association for Bilingual Education Journal, 12,* 23-50.

Wallach, G. (1990). Magic buries Celtics: Looking for broader interpretations of language learning and literacy. *Topics in Language Disorders, 10,* 63-80.

Wang, M. C. & Reynolds, M. C. (1985). Avoiding the "Catch 22" in special education reform. *Exceptional Children, 51,* 497-502.

Wang, M. C. & Reynolds, M. C. (1986). "Catch 22 and disability help": A reply to Alan Garner. *Exceptional Children, 53,* 77-79.

Wang, M. C., Reynolds, M. C., & Walberg, H. J. (1988). Integrating children of the second system. *Phi Delta Kappan, 70,* 248-251.

Wang, M. C., Reynolds, M. C. & Walberg, H. J. (1989). Who benefits from segregation and murky water? *Phi Delta Kappan, 71,* 64-67.

Weaver, C. (1991). Whole language and its potential for developing readers. *Topics in Language Disorders, 11,* 28-44.

Wechsler, D. (1976). *Wechsler Intelligence Scale for Children-Revised.* San Antonio, TX: The Psychological Corporation. A subsidiary of Harcourt Brace Jovanovich.

Weinstein-Shr, G. (1990, August). Family and intergenerational literacy in multilingual families. *National Clearinghouse on Literacy Education.* Center for Applied Linguistics.

Wells, G. (1986). *The meaning makers: Children learning language and using language to learn.* Portsmouth, N.H.: Heinemann.

Wesson, C. L. (1991). CBM and 2 models of follow-up consultation. *Exceptional Children, 57,* 246-256.

West, J. F. & Idol, L. (1987). School consultation (Part I): An interdisciplinary perspective on theory, models, and research. *Journal of Learning Disabilities, 20,* 388-407.

Westby, C. (1990). There's no such thing as culture-free testing. *Texas Journal of Audiology and Speech Pathology, 16,* 4-5.

Westby, C. E. (1985). Learning to talk—talking to learn: Oral-literate language differences. In C. Simon (Ed.). *Communication skills and classroom success* (pp. 181-218). San Diego, CA: College-Hill Press.

Westby, C. E. (1990). The role of the speech-language pathologist in whole language. *Language, Speech, and Hearing Services in Schools, 21,* 228-237.

Westby, C. E. (in press a). The effects of culture on genre, structure, and style of oral and written texts. In G. Wallach & K. Butler (Eds.) *Language, learning disabilities in school-age children and adolescents.* Columbus, OH: Merrill.

Westby, C. E. (in press b) Communicative refinement in school age and adolescence. In W. O. Haynes & B. B. Shulman (Eds.) *Communicative development: Foundations, process and clinical applications.* Englewood Cliffs, NJ: Prentice-Hall.

Westby, C. E. & Rouse, G. R. (1985). Culture in education and the instruction of language learning-disabled students. *Topics in Language Disorders, 5,* 15-28.

White, R. W. (1959). Motivation reconsidered: The concept of competence. *Psychological Review, 66,* 297-333.

Wilen, D. K. (1989). Working with language minority students. *Communique, 17,* 20.

Wilen, D. K. (1990). Children and limited English proficiency (Handouts Section). National Association of School Psychologists *Communique, 18* .

Wilen, D. K., & Fradd, S. H. (1991). Training interpreters and translators to assist school psychologists, social workers, and speech-language pathologists. *Idiom, 21,* 1-11.

Wilen, D. K., Fradd, S. H., & Vázquez-Montilla, E. (1992). A comparison of psychological services provided by bilingual and monolingual school psychologists. *SABE Journal, 8,* 60-72.

Wilen, D. K., & Sweeting, C. V. M. (1986). Assessment of limited English proficient Hispanic students. *School Psychology Review 15,* 59-75.

Wilkinson, C. & Ortiz, A. A. (1986). *Characteristics of limited English proficient and English proficient learning disabled Hispanic students at initial assessment and at reevaluation.*

Austin, TX: University of Texas, Handicapped Minority Research Institute on Language Proficiency. (ERIC Document Reproduction Service No. 283 314).

Wilkinson, C. Y. & Ortiz, A. A. (1986, Fall). Reevaluation of learning disabled Hispanic students: Changes over three years. *Bilingual Special Education Newsletter, 5,* pp. 1, 3-6 (A publication of the University of Texas at Austin).

Wilkinson, L. C. & Milosky, L. M. (1987). School-age children's metapragmatic knowledge of requests and responses in the classroom. *Topics in Language Disorders, 7,* 61-70.

Wilkinson, L. C., Milosky, L. M. & Genishi, C. (1986). Second language learners' use of requests and responses in elementary classrooms. *Topics in Language Disorders, 6,* 57-70.

Will, M. (1988). Educating students with learning problems and the changing role of the school psychologist. *School Psychology Review, 17,* 476-478.

Will, M. C. (1986). Educating children with learning problems: A shared responsibility. *Exceptional Children, 52,* 411-415.

Williams, J. P. (1988). Identifying main ideas: A basic aspect of reading comprehension. *Topics in Language Disorders, 8,* 1-13.

Williams, M. L. (1991, September 27). *Policy update on schools' obligations toward national origin minority students with limited-English proficiency (LEP students).* (Memorandum written from the Assistant Secretary for Civil Rights to Office of Civil Rights Senior Staff, U. S. Department of Education, Washington, D.C. and disseminated through the Office of Bilingual Education and Minority Languages Affairs to Project Directors with Title VII Programs).

Willig, A. C. & Ortiz, A. A. (1991). The non-biased individualized educational program: Linking assessment to instruction. In E. V. Hamayan and J. S. Damico (Eds.). *Limiting bias in the assessment of bilingual students* (pp. 282-302). Austin, TX: Pro-Ed.

Willis, S. (1991, September). The complex art of motivating students. *Update, 33* (A newsletter of the Association of Supervision and Curriculum Development, Alexandria, VA) pp. 1, 4-5.

Willshire Carrera, J. (1989). *Immigrant students: Their legal right of access to public schools.* Boston: National Coalition of Advocates for Students.

Wilson, C. L. & Sindelar, P. T. (1991). Direct instruction in math word problems: Students with learning disabilities. *Exceptional Children, 57,* 512-520.

Winograd, P. & Niquette, G. (1988). Assessing learned helplessness in poor readers. *Topics in Language Disorders, 8,* 33-55.

Witrock, M. C., Marks, C., & Doctorow, M. (1975). Reading as a generative process. *Journal of Educational Psychology, 67,* 484-489.

Wong Fillmore, L. (1976). *The second time around: Cognitive and social strategies in second language acquisition.* Doctoral Dissertation, Stanford University.

Wong Fillmore, L. (1982) Instructional language as linguistic input: Second language learning in classrooms. In L. C. Wilkinson (Ed.) *Communicating in the classroom.* New York: Academic Press.

Wong Fillmore, L. (1985). When does teacher talk work as input? In S. M. Gass & Madden C. G. (Eds.) *Input in second language acquisition* (pp. 17-50). Cambridge, MA: Newbury House.

Wong Fillmore, L. (1991). Second-language learning in children: A model of language learning in social context. In E. Bialystok (Ed.). *Language processing in bilingual children* (pp. 49-69). New York: Cambridge University Press.

Wong Fillmore, L. (1991, June 19). A question for early-childhood programs: English first or families first? *Education Week,* pp. 32, 34.

Woodcock, R. E. (1982). *Bateria Woodcock Psico-educativa en Espanol.* Allen, TX: DLM Teaching Resources.

Woodcock, R. W. (1981). *Bateria Woodcock de Proficiencia en el Idioma*. Allen, TX: DLM Teaching Resources.

Woodcock, R. W. (1984). *Woodcock Language Proficiency Battery*. Allen, TX: DLM Teaching Resources.

Woods, K. D. (1988). Guiding students through informational texts. *The Reading Teacher, 41*, 912-920.

Yopp, R. H. (1988). Active comprehension and Spanish reading. *Journal of Educational Issues of Language Minority Students, 3*, 27-32.

Ysseldyke, J. E. & Christenson, S. L. (1987). *TIES: The Instructional Environment Scale*. Austin, TX: Pro-Ed.

Zamel, V. (1985). Responding to student writing. *TESOL Quarterly, 19*, 79-10.

Zigler, E. & Trickett, P. (1978). IQ, social competence, and evaluation of early childhood intervention programs, *American Psychologist*, 789-798.

Zins, J. E., & Ponti, C. R. (1990). Best practices in school-based consultation. In A. Thomas & J. Grimes (Eds.), *Best practices in school psychology - II*. (pp. 673-693). Washington, D.C.: National Association of School Psychologists.

Index